Principles of Economics

AF660977

Dr. Manas Pandey
Professor of Business Economics
Faculty of Management Studies
VBS Purvanchal University
Jaunpur (U.P.)

PHI Learning Private Limited
Delhi-110092
2025

*In fond memory of **Shri Asoke K. Ghosh** (October 1942 – February 2024), Founder Chairman and Managing Director of PHI Learning, whose vision endlessly inspires.*

The Legacy Continues....

Published by Pushpita Ghosh, PHI Learning Private Limited, Rimjhim House, 111, Patparganj Industrial Estate, Delhi-110092 and Printed by Syndicate Binders, A-20, Hosiery Complex, Noida, Phase-II Extension, Noida-201305 (N.C.R. Delhi).

₹1050.00

PRINCIPLES OF ECONOMICS
Manas Pandey

© 2025 by PHI Learning Private Limited, Delhi.

All right reserved. This publication is protected by copyright and may not be reproduced, in whole or in part, in any form or by any electronic, mechanical, or other means, now known or hereafter invented, including photocopying, recording, or any information storage and retrieval system, OR to train artificial intelligence systems without permission in writing from the publisher.

ISBN-978-93-5443-774-8 (Print Book)
ISBN-978-93-5443-937-7 (e-Book)

The export rights of the book are vested solely with the publisher.

Dedicated
with
Reverence and Gratitude
to
My Mother, Late Urmila Pandey

Contents

PART-II
MICROECONOMICS

PART-III
MACROECONOMICS

Preface

The economic analysis presented in this book is essentially of conventional static or equilibrium variety, which constitutes the core of economic theory and with which a thorough acquaintance is of utmost importance for imbibing economic analysis and making predictions. It presents a system of thoughts, which offer explanations and predictions of how the individual economic entities, viz. consumers, producers, input buyers and suppliers and output suppliers and buyers interact and attain their equilibrium positions and how macroeconomic variables like national income, national employment, general price level, etc. behave. There has been a significant development in the field of economic analysis, making it more mathematical. Postgraduate and Honours students of commerce and economics with a meagre grounding in mathematics, find it difficult to grasp the various economic concepts drawing heavily upon the mathematical exercises. This volume is oriented to offer a systematic exposition of micro and macroeconomic principles through lucid statements, simple algebraic equations and derivations, arithmetical calculations and graphical presentations.

As a comprehensive book on fundamentals of micro and macroeconomics, it is virtually arranged in three parts. The First part contains an elaborate introduction with chapters on nature and scope of economics, micro and macroeconomics, economic-statics and dynamics, and equilibrium positions. The Second part of this volume comprises the microeconomic analysis, which is further divided into four sub-parts, where the first sub-part is devoted to the analysis of consumption behaviour, which contains elaboration of consumption and demand analysis, elasticity of demand analysis, theories of consumer behaviour through cardinal utility, indifference curve, revealed preference and logical ordering analyses and the analysis of consumer's surplus. The second sub-part examines the production behaviour comprising production, inputs and production functions, analyses production behaviour, through traditional or Marshallian analysis and modern or Hicks-Allen analysis, linear programming and cost of production. The third sub-part deals with exchange consisting of supply and price determination in general, pricing under perfect competition, monopoly, duopoly, oligopoly and monopolistic or imperfect competition. The fourth sub-part is devoted to distribution comprising microeconomic income distribution-general principles and the theories of rent, wages, interest and profit. The last part, i.e., Third part of the book contains six chapters dealing with various aspects of the macroeconomics.

The economic analysis presented in this volume basically represents the conventional doctrines of micro and macroeconomics, which have emerged from neo-classical to neo-Keynesian traditions. Efforts have been made to develop synthesis of related principles of economics to introduce novel elaborations of received theories and to reformulate and develop certain conclusions, which follow from conventional theoretical arguments. Since the present volume is designed primarily as a textbook for students of commerce and economics, no attempt has been made to draw lines between reproduction of received theories and their extensions and elaborations. As far as possible, all recent developments in the field of micro and macroeconomics have been suitably incorporated in the present volume and review questions at the end of each chapter shall enable the readers to test their own understanding of the subject. It has a logical structure from introduction to elaboration of the complete set of micro and macroeconomic concepts, whose appreciation will be possible only through a thorough study. The treatment of the subject to be well acceptable to the Postgraduate and Honours students of commerce and economics. The use of micro and macroeconomic concepts, principles, diagrams and mathematical derivations at places are likely to make the text more readable, facilitating the understanding and retention of the micro and macroeconomic concepts quite conveniently.

In preparation of the present volume the author owes a great deal to his teachers and students, who created interest in and inspired him for writing on the subject. The author sincerely expresses his gratefulness to the various authors whose works have been consulted and accessed in the course of preparation of this volume. The author is also thankful to those colleagues and friends, who inspired him for this publication and Ms. Babita Misra and her team of PHI Learning for bringing out the book expeditiously.

The author will gratefully acknowledge the constructive suggestions from the readers for improvement of the text in subsequent editions.

Manas Pandey

PART-I

INTRODUCTION

1

Nature and Scope of Economics

Economics is the study of principles, which govern the functioning of an economy and its various components. Initially it has been named as economicus or oeconomicus (i.e., the science of household management) by the ancient Greek Philosophers, but subsequently it has been named as Catallactics (i.e., the science of exchange), Plutology (i.e., the science of wealth), *Chremalistics* (i.e., the science of money making), etc. During 18th century, it has been named as 'Political Economy' by Adam Smith, through his famous book titled 'An Inquiry into the Nature and Causes of Wealth of Nations'. The name 'Political Economy' signified the manner in which a particular society (or state) organised its resources for the maximum production of desired goods and services. It carried this name till the close of 19th century, when it has been named as Economics. This term is applied to a frugal use of one's limited resources and has two distinct advantages: (i) the termination 'ics' indicates that our study is or at least it aspires to be a science, like mathematics, physics, etc. and (ii) by dropping out the word 'Political' it emphasises that our ultimate concern is with individuals and not with states.

There is no single all acceptable definition of economics on account of the two basic requirements of a good definition. Firstly, it must clearly bring out the central problem or the common denominator of all the multiplicity of problems to be taken up in the subject; and secondly, it must clearly determine the boundaries between the subject defined and the neighboring subjects. These requirements are quite demanding and therefore, the various definitions have been found wanting in one respect or the other.

The plethora of definitions of economics are placed into four broad categories: (i) Wealth; (ii) Welfare; (iii) Scarcity; and (iv) Modern.

WEALTH DEFINITIONS

At the early stages of the development of economics it was regarded as the science of wealth. Adam Smith considered economics **'as a science that studies the process of production and consumption of wealth'.** J.S. Mill in his famous book 'Essays on Some Unsettled Questions of Political Economy' has defined it as **'the science, which traces the laws of such phenomena of society, as arise from the combined operations of mankind for production**

of wealth', and regarded economics as **'the practical science of production and distribution of wealth'**. J.B. Say in his famous book titled 'A Treatise on Political Economy' defined economics a **'the study of the laws that govern wealth'**. Similarly, J.R. McCulloch has defined that **'economics is a science that regulates production, accumulation, distribution and consumption of those products that are necessary, useful or agreeable to people and which, at the same time, possess exchangeable value'.**

These economists believed that individuals' self-interest was a ruling motive in society and that the greatest social good was a mere sum of maximum individual happiness. Thus, they believed in harmony between individual and social interest, i.e., whatever was most profitable to produce from the point of view of the individual entrepreneur, the same was in the best interest of the society, because it was considered to be the most conducive to increase the welfare of the community.

In case the term 'wealth' is considered to mean scarce goods and services used to satisfy wants, there could not be much opposition to these definitions of economics. However, for these definitions the 'wealth' was interpreted in a narrow sense to mean riches or abundance of money and economics has been expected to suggest ways and means for increasing the wealth of the society. So it has been dubbed as **'bread and butter science', 'gospel of mammon', 'a science that taught selfishness and love for money', 'a dark and dismal science'**, etc. Ruskin in his famous book 'Unto the Last' has stated **'Among the delusions which, at different periods, have possessed themselves the minds of large masses of the human race, perhaps the most curious and certainly the least creditable, is the modern soi-disant science of political economy'.** He characterised economics as **'a bastard science– the science of getting rich'.** Such criticisms were not unjustified in those days, when religious sentiments were supreme and spiritualism held sway over human mind.

The German Historical School of Economics criticised these definitions on the ground that these have narrow individualistic scope of economics as a science of individual wealth. Secondly, the postulates and the laws or generalisations based on them were static in character, but these must be dynamic and based on realistic study of life. Lastly, economics, as per earlier economists, was based on abstract, deductive or **a priori** method of reasoning, while it should be based on realistic or inductive method of reasoning, It should be considered as 'National' economics, as distinct from the 'Universal' economics as 'by national or political economy we mean the science, which has to do with the laws of development of the economy or a nation or with its economic national life'. In words of Roscher 'Political economy treats chiefly the national interest of nations.

It enquires how the various wants of people of a country may be satisfied; how the satisfaction of these wants influences the aggregate national life and how, in turn, they are influenced by the national life'. Thus, because of its association with meaner or baser things of life (i.e., money), the economics remained under cloud for quite a long time. These definitions were considered unsatisfactory and, as such, discarded towards the close of the nineteenth century.

WELFARE DEFINITIONS

By the close of the nineteenth century earlier economic doctrines had been seriously undermined and economics had fallen into disrepute. The weakness of the earlier theory of value, based on the cost alone, was fully exposed. Smith's myth of harmony between individual and social interest was also exposed due to growing mass misery along with increasing production. Moreover, during this period great changes took place in the techniques of production and economic life, like numerous inventions, banking and financial developments, monopolistic cartels and trusts, business cycles, etc., all exposing the hollowness of earlier economic doctrines. There was growing realisation that earlier economists overemphasised the acquisition of wealth and ignored human happiness.

With this background and with a vivid sense of the paradox of 'poverty amidst plenty' Marshall and his contemporaries shifted the emphasis in economics from 'wealth' to 'welfare'. Marshall emphasised that wealth was not the end but only a means to an end, and the end being human welfare. He put great stress on the ethical element and, thus, successfully 'humanised' the otherwise a 'dismal science'. He defined economics as **'a study of mankind in the ordinary business of life; it examines that part of individual and social action, which is most closely connected with the attainment and use of the material requisites of well-being'.**

Marshall, thus, emphasised both mankind and wealth, as according to him economics was, 'on the one hand, a study of wealth and, on the other, a part of the study of man'. Wealth, according to Marshall, constitutes material requisites of well-being, which provides means for existence, comfort and enjoyment.

Thus, economics according to wealth definitions, became a study of mankind or human beings. Secondly, it studied human beings in their ordinary business of life, that is, the business with which human beings were concerned most of the time in their life (i.e., earning and spending of money). Such business or activity had been known as economic activity. Thirdly, the study aimed at promoting the material well-being or human welfare. The emphasis on human welfare placed this definition in the category of 'welfare definitions'.

Besides Marshall, a few other economists also attempted to relate economics with human welfare. According to Edwin Cannon **'the aim of Political Economy is the explanation of the general causes on which the material welfare of human beings depends'**. Similarly, according to A.C. Pigou **'economics is the study of economic welfare which is that part of social welfare that can be brought directly or indirectly into relation**

with the measuring rod of money'. It, thus, extends the scope of economics to cover all goods and services which command money price and whose acquisition involves effort or sacrifice.

These definitions were accepted widely and were thought to have put to an end all controversies regarding the scope of economics, but these too have been criticised severely by Leonel Robbins:

(i) These definitions include within their purview only material things and ignore or exclude non-material things. In real world, the demarcation between the material and non-material things is not as clear-cut as is assumed by the advocates of these definitions. There are several things in our daily life which satisfy our wants and there are several services like that of doctors, advocates, teachers, which are highly conducive to human welfare and yet have nothing 'material' in them.

(ii) These definitions regard economics as being concerned with material welfare and yet take certain non-material products, such as, services of teachers, lawyers, doctors as part and parcel of economics, which is a paradox.

(iii) These definitions seek to establish relationship between 'economics' and 'welfare' but in real world, economics studies several activities which are economic but are hardly conducive to human welfare, e.g., production and sale of intoxicants. Though it will not promote human welfare, even then production and distribution will be studied by economists, as it satisfies human wants. Thus, it is self-contradictory and shaky in extreme.

(iv) Economic welfare is not amenable to quantitative measurements, because it is to some extent subjective. Money is generally regarded as an instrument for the measurement of welfare, but it is a rough and certainly not a satisfactory measure. Two persons paying the same price for a commodity derive an unequal amount of utility or welfare depending on their richness or poverty.

(v) These definitions make economics a purely social science, which studies man as a social being and will not study problems of those individuals who are cut off or isolated from the society. However, these individuals are as much subject of some of the fundamental laws of economics as regular members of the society. Thus, economics should be treated as a human rather than a social science.

(vi) These definitions are classificatory rather than being analytical in character. They classify human activities into two categories–economic and non-economic, the former dealing with activities 'closely connected with attainment and use of material requisites of well-being' whereas the latter with social, political and religious activities. Similarly, according to these definitions the economics concentrates on 'material requisites of well-being' or material welfare only ignoring the non-material welfare. It is a study of 'mankind in the ordinary business of life', leaving aside the 'non-ordinary' businesses of life. Thus, classification of the activities into economic and non-economic; of welfare into material and non-material; and business of life into ordinary and non-ordinary, render such definitions as classificatory ones. An analytical definition, on the other hand, would mention the central problem and not just vaguely delimit the field of study vis-à-vis other related subjects.

(vii) These definitions limit the scope of economics to human action related to material welfare. In other words, it is the study of those activities connected with the production and consumption of goods and services, which aim at increasing material welfare only come under the scope of economics.

(viii) The welfare definitions have an implicit normative character, as we have to pass value judgments in order to know whether a particular activity is helping or hindering in promotion of human welfare. Economics is a positive science and pronouncing value judgments is going into the territory of ethics, which is not a science.

SCARCITY DEFINITIONS

Leonel Robbins not only vehemently criticised 'welfare definitions' of economics but also contributed a new definition through his book 'Nature and Significance of Economic Science'. According to him, economics studies the problems, which arise because of the scarcity of resources. Nature has not gifted mankind sufficient resources to satisfy all its wants and therefore, it has to choose for what purposes the resources are to be utilised, He defines economics as **'a science, which studies human behaviour as a relationship between ends and scarce means, which have alternative uses'**. His contemporary Phillip H. Wicksteed has stated that **"economics may be taken to include the study of the general principles of administration of resources and the examinations of the ways in which waste arises in such administration."**

These definitions lay emphasis on the problem of choice among competing ends (objectives) and allocation of 'scarce' resources, so as to satisfy our ends (objectives) to the maximum possible extent. These are based on the following three facts:

(i) **Unlimited Wants:** Human wants are unlimited. According to Robbins's definition 'ends' implies 'wants' and these wants are unlimited. It is the most important fact of economic life of the people. Had these wants been limited, there would have been no economic problem. However, in real life, there are numerous wants and all are not of equal intensity, which enable people to allocate their resources to satisfy some of their wants.

(ii) **Scarce Means:** The problem of choice arises, because resources are scarce in relation to wants. Had the resources been unlimited, there would have been no problem of choice. It is because of scarcity, people have to decide for the satisfaction of what wants the resources should be used and what wants should be left unsatisfied. Resources or means refer to natural productive resources, man-made capital goods, consumer goods, etc. Since these are limited and are not free goods to be obtained in the desired quantity, we have to pay price for them or to do labour to obtain them.

(iii) **Alternative Uses of Means:** The scarce means or limited resources have the various alternative uses. For example, monetary resources can be utilised for the production of consumer goods, capital goods, employing labour, purchasing things for consumption, giving donations, etc. The men or the society, therefore, have to choose the uses to which resources have to be employed. In case the resources had only one use, there would have been no problem of choice, because the single use resources would be employed in uses for which they are meant.

It is evident that economic problems would not arise unless all these conditions are satisfied simultaneously. In other words, multiplicity of ends, scarcity of means or alternative applicability of scarce means taken alone cannot create an economic problem, as it arises only when these conditions are satisfied simultaneously. Thus, in the face of multiplicity of ends, the time and the material means of achieving these ends being limited, the consumers, consequently, are forced to choose some and give up the other ends. Such 'scarcity, of means to satisfy ends of varying importance is almost ubiquitous condition of human behaviour'. Certain merits of 'scarcity definitions' are as follows:

(i) Economics, as per these definitions, applies as much to an individual as to a nation and transcends all economic systems (from capitalism to communism) alike, because the problems of 'allocation' and 'efficiency' are universal. It has dispelled all misconceptions or haziness about economics and has brought into sharp focus the scope of economics, they have brought it nearer to science. Any problem marked by scarcity of means and multiplicity of ends becomes **ipso facto** an economic problem.

(ii) The distinction between material and non-material, between welfare and non-welfare is done away with these definitions. Economics studies human activities in regard to all goods and services, whether they are material or non-material and whether conducive to human welfare or not, provided they satisfy human wants.

(iii) The concept of 'opportunity cost' which is of great importance in economic analysis is the direct outcome of the scarcity of means in relation to ends. Since all ends cannot be satisfied with the scarce means at our disposal, choice becomes inevitable and the choice of one alternative means that the other alternative is foregone, which is the opportunity cost of the choice of one alternative.

(iv) Similarly, the concept of 'scale of preferences' is also implicit in the scarcity definitions. In economics, individuals are expected to behave rationally, that is, if they have to make a choice, they will always choose the alternative, which yields them the maximum satisfaction to be followed by the alternative yielding lesser satisfaction. Thus, individuals are expected to be in a position to distinguish between their most and the least pressing wants.

(v) Economics has no responsibility regarding the choice of ends. It reveals in what ways the given ends or wants can be achieved with the scarce resources. Economics has no concern with what ends or wants are selected for satisfaction. The ends may be good or bad, noble or ignoble, all these are to be studied in economics, which is neutral between ends. Its task is not to praise or condemn but only to analyse and explain.

Thus, Robbins has made economics a scientific study and has widened the scope of economics, which had been narrowed down even by 'welfare definitions'. These definitions bring to the light the basic economic problems faced by the society. However these definitions have also been criticised by economists on the following grounds:

(i) Robbins declaims too much against the welfare definitions, yet the concept of welfare is implicit even in his own definition. The scarce means are to be applied to the multiple ends in such a manner as to secure the maximum satisfaction, which is nothing but the maximum welfare. Thus, the concept of welfare gets a backdoor entry in economics through his definition, as without considering welfare, the question of allocation of scarce resources does not arise.

(ii) Robbins had made economics quite impersonal, colourless and devoid of any normative element. In his bid to raise economics to the status of a pure or positive science, he has completely lost the sight of the fact that it is also a social study. Barbara Wooten has rightly observed that **'it is very difficult for economists to divest their discussions completely of all normative significance'.**

(iii) Robbins has been criticised also on the ground that he has made economics neutral between ends. If economics is to serve as a means for promoting social welfare and economic growth, it has to give its decision in terms of good or bad to achieve these ends. In other words, if it has to serve as an engine of social betterment, then it would have to abandon the neutrality between ends. In this regard, Professor Thomson has rightly observed that **'the functions**

of economists are not only to explain and explore but also to educate and condemn.'

(iv) It has reduced economics to a mere value theory. It considers how the prices of products and factors of production are determined and, consequently, how the allocation of resources to the production of the various goods is determined. However, economics is more than this and is now concerned with how the national income and employment is determined. The economies, in past, have been subject to great instability due to periodic occurrence of mass unemployment, depression, boom and inflation and the economics is called upon to explain this instability and shorten fluctuations in the levels of income, price, output and employment. Thus, the macroeconomics dealing with above mentioned problems should also come within the purview of economics.

(v) It has also been pointed out that economic problems do not always arise from the scarcity of resources, as these can also arise form abundance as well. The Great Depression was not due to scarcity but due to abundance (over-production) of goods. Similarly, unemployment problem, which arises due to abundance of labour resources in relation to its demand is very much an economic problem, as it is the duty of the economist to study the unemployment problem and suggest ways to solve it to increase social welfare.

(vi) Scarcity definitions also do not cover the theory of economic growth, which deals with increase in national income and per capita income of a country over a long period of time and with factors responsible for such increases. These definitions take **'scarce means'** as given and deal with their allocation only, but the economics should also concern with economic growth, which implies as to how to minimise the scarcity of resources. Modern economists have propounded the various theories regarding initiating and accelerating the economic growth in underdeveloped countries. Such theories have become core of economics both in developed as well as underdeveloped countries but Robbins would ignore such an important aspect in economic study.

(vii) Economics, according to **'scarcity definitions'** is a human science and not a social science. It studies human behaviour, even if they are isolated from the society. For example, a saint in a forest is also faced with the problem of allocation of scarce time to different activities, therefore, his behaviour is under the purview of economics. This unnecessarily widens the scope of economics. For many economists, economics is a social science and it should study the problem of choice only when such choice affects other members of the society. Cairn Cross has rightly observed that **'Economics is a social science studying how people attempt to accommodate scarcity to their**

wants and how these attempts interact through exchange'. Thus, the economics should study the problem of choice only when it has social implications.

(viii) Economics, as per scarcity definitions, is static in content and suffers from inadequacies. According to these definitions, economics deals with the adjustment of given scarce means to given ends or wants. It admits no possibility of a change taking place either in the means or in the ends. This is highly static and rigid view of dynamic problems, as in real world the ends and the means both are subject to change.

Thus, despite the fact that these definitions are accepted as proper, there is growing feeling that they do not indicate adequately the content, scope and subject matter of economics and also do not cover theories of income, employment, economic growth and economic instability and therefore, modern economists have adopted different definitions of economics to cover these under its purview.

MODERN DEFINITIONS

Modern economists, as regards definitions of economics, are classified into two categories: (i) definitionists, and (ii) non-definitionists. Economists of the former category have tried to define economics making it growth, business or wantlessness oriented but, by and large, these definitions resemble to the scarcity definitions. The latter category of economists believe that it is futile to attempt a definition of economics, as it is of little use in explaining what economics is about.

Amongst definitionists Professor Paul A. Samuelson has given a growth oriented definition of economics, which states that **'Economics is the study of how men and society choose, with or without the use of money, to employ scarce productive resources, which could have alternative uses, to produce the various commodities over time and distribute them for consumption now and in the future among various people and groups of society'.**

It is similar to that of Robbins, but Professor Samuelson has made his definition dynamic by including the element of time in it. It is certainly a new edifice on the foundation provided by Robbins. Phrases, **'to produce various commodities over time'** and **'distribute them for consumption now and in the future'** included in his definition, were intended to stress on dynamic nature and to include in its purview the problem of growth. Secondly, it is not only dynamic in content but also wider in scope, as it is applicable even to a barter economy. This definition has made it amply clear that the problem of choice or economising arises not only in money economy but also in barter economy. Lastly, the problem of choice, according to this definition, is dealt with in a dynamic setting, as it relates not only to the present but also to the future. It is obvious that human wants never remain constant or static, but continually change with the lapse of time. Due to change in taste, fashion, etc. wants not only change, but also multiply in course of time, which calls for corresponding changes in resources. Economics, therefore, has no option but to be dynamic in character. It has to concentrate on suggesting ways and means for increasing resources-income, output and employment to cope with increasing and changing wants of society.

Thus, economics is rightly considered as the study of the allocation of scarce resources in relation to unlimited ends and of the determinants of income, output, employment and economic growth. This appears to be the most satisfactory and acceptable definition of economics, as it has a universal appeal and transcends all ideological differences being equally applicable to capitalist, mixed, socialist and communist economies, because the problem of choice in its dynamic setting arises in all types of economies.

Professor J.K. Mehta has defined economics as **"A science that studies human behaviour as an endeavour to gain freedom from wants and reach the state of happiness (wantlessness).** He broadly agrees with Robbins regarding the scope of economics but differs with him as regards the satisfaction of wants. Human behaviour, according to Professor Mehta, is induced by the state of disequilibrium of the mind. Since human mind dislikes disequilibrium, which is painful and, therefore, makes persistent efforts to attain the state of equilibrium, which is pleasuresome.

Professor Mehta visualises two methods for reaching the state of equilibrium or happiness:

(i) External forces, which bring disequilibrium in the mind, should be adjusted, which is the same as allocation of scarce resources, as suggested by Robbins. However, efforts to remove some existing wants may create some new wants, which may again create disequilibrium in the mind. Thus, it is not possible to attain the state of equilibrium of mind by making adjustment with external forces or allocating the resources only.

(ii) This requires that the mind should be trained in such a way that it is not affected by the environment or external forces. This should be done through 'education' and not through 'repression' of mind.

Thus, Professor Mehta has gone ahead of Robbins, when he states that mind cannot attain the state of equilibrium through the satisfaction of wants alone and hence, as an alternative, minimisation of wants should also be attempted. It is only through the minimisation of wants and satisfaction of bare minimum wants by the available resources that the human beings can attain the state of 'happiness' or 'wantlessness'. This state of wantlessess or elimination of all wants or freedom from wants may be achieved by man's control over his body and mind. He relates economics with metaphysics, philosophy and religion, which is not a correct approach. Existence of wants and their recurrence are the basis for all economic activities. Minimisation of wants will result into minimisation of economic activities which, in turn, may hinder the economic progress of the society. Associating economics with attainment of the state of wantlssness or *Nishkam* is a sheer idealism, impossible of attainment for the great majority of thc human racc in the real world situation.

Non-definitionists, however, are opposed to any attempt at defining economics. They think that there is no need of definition for explaining what economics is about, as it can be better understood by knowing the activities, which economists have been concerned with. Professor Jacob Viner, on being asked to define economics has rightly remarked **'Economics is what economists do'** this apt remark serves to highlight the fact that whatever comes under the ken (range of knowledge and experience) of economists is economics. The science of economics is growing and no rigid definition can survive long.

Professor M. Dobb is equally critical of attempting for any precise definition of economics, and he states that **"the search for logically concise definitions of one's subject matter, which is so popular today, must generally be barren, and when pushed to an extreme, must result in emptying ideas of real content and attaining little but an arid and scholastic dogmatism".**

Professor Gumnar Mrydal is positively critical to the idea of defining economics and remarks that **'such definitions are both unnecessary and undesirable'.** It is unnecessary because of the one concept, which an economist need not define precisely is 'economics'. Just as no chemist can draw any scientific conclusion from a definition of 'chemistry', similarly no argument can possibly be affected by any definition of economics.

Modern economists fear that any definition of economics is likely to yield only a misleading picture of the various problems, which economics has to deal with. This is the reason why attempts made in the past to circumscribe the actual field of economic studies have failed. Some of these definitions were too narrow and restricted in nature leaving out several important economic problems from their orbit. Thus, it would be difficult if not impossible, to attempt a clear-cut delimitation of the scope of economics through definitions. Moreover, such delimitation is not going to render any help to individual economist in discovery of economic generalisations. For example, accepting 'scarcity' definition after rejecting 'welfare' definition will not help the analytical economist in formulation of economic laws.

Robbins insisted on delimitation of the field of economics, so as to avoid "the preoccupation with the irrelevant multiplication of activities having little or no connection with the solution of problems **related** to economists' subject". But such delimitation shall tend to **reduce** the economic science to a closed system of thought, because inconvenient arguments shall be dismissed on the ground that these are not relevant. It may also lead to emergence and multiplication of artificial barriers between the various social sciences and will tend to shut out all external influences. Such compartmentalisation is not at all desirable and is even harmful in the larger interest of social and economic research. Since economic study relates to men and their environment, it cannot be rigidly separated from other social sciences like ethics, politics, sociology and psychology. William K. Kapp has rightly remarked that **'the departmentalisation of the social sciences tends to obstruct and defeat the search for truth by restricting the scope and horizon of scholarly enquiries.**

Thus, a really dynamic subject to come to grips with the ever-changing realities, has to admit any help from neighboring disciplines to perfect its tools and to improve its analysis. Modern research has become more and more a team work and economists have to understand and appreciate the point of view of other social scientists. Thus, there is need for not merely collaboration but the closest possible integration and synthesis of the various social sciences and there is need for assimilating latest developments in all social sciences for a proper understanding of economic problems.

SCOPE OF ECONOMICS

A large variety of definitions reveal that there has been a lot of controversy amongst economists about the true scope or content of economics. Majority seems to accept economics as a study of economic aspect of human life. If we look around, we see that the farmers are cultivating their fields, workers are working in the factories, teachers are teaching their students, doctors are attending to their patients, and so on. They are all engaged in what are called as economic activities. Through these activities they earn money to satisfy their wants. It is this part of human life that the economics is concerned with. Human beings want food, clothes, shelter, etc. for which they must have money and for money they must work or make an effort. Thus, wants-efforts-satisfaction sum up the subject matter of economics.

In primitive society, wants-efforts-satisfaction (i.e., production and consumption) are close and direct, but in modern society things are not so simple and straight. Here a man produces what he does not consume and consumes what he does not produce. He sells the surplus produce for money with which he buys the things he needs. This is called exchange, which also forms the subject matter of economics along with consumption, production and exchange.

Most of the things, we need today, are manufactured in factories. To make them workers supply labour, landlords supply land, capitalists supply capital, managers supply organisation and entrepreneurs stand ready to bear the risk arising out of production. In lieu of their co-operation, they get rewards in terms of money, in the forms of wages, rent, interest, salary and profit respectively. In economics, we study how these incomes are determined, which is called distribution. It also forms subject matter of economics along with consumption, production and exchange.

Modern economists divide the subject matter into two parts microeconomics and macroeconomics. Microeconomics deals with the analysis of the behaviour of individual economic units, such as individual consumers, producers, sellers, buyers, workers, capitalists, landlords, managers, entrepreneurs, etc. It seeks to determine the mechanism by which different economic units attain their equilibrium positions. It is generally concerned with pricing of products or factors of production, hence it has also been named as 'Price Theory.'

Macroeconomics, on the other hand, deals not with individual quantities as such but with aggregates of these quantities, not with individual incomes but with the national income, not with individual prices but with the price levels, not with individual outputs but with the national output, etc. Macroeconomics analyses the behaviour of the whole economic system in totality or entirety. In other words, it studies the behaviour of large aggregates, such as total employment, the national product or income, the general price level, etc. in the economy. Thus, it deals with aggregates and averages of the system rather than with particular items in it and attempts to define these aggregates and examine their relationships.

The recent thinking on the subject matter of economics is that it is concerned with the following six basic questions, which arise because of the basic problem of scarcity confronting an economy:

(i) Whether all the available productive resources are being fully utilised by the economy?
(ii) What goods in what quantities are being produced?
(iii) How different goods are being produced?
(iv) How is the total product being distributed?
(v) Whether the productive resources are being used efficiently?
(vi) Whether the productive capacity of the economy is increasing?

All economies including capitalist, socialist and mixed are confronting these problems and must take decisions on them. Economic theory studies how these decisions are arrived at in the various societies. These questions give rise to six basic problems as follows:

1. **Problem of Employment of Productive Resources:** Since resources are scarce, the society will try to use all the available resources to achieve the maximum welfare of the people and, for this it will not consciously allow the resources to remain idle. However, in capitalist economies, at times, resources remain idle. It has been observed during great depression that, on the one hand, workers were unemployed and on the other hand, the factories employing workers remained under worked. Keynes through his famous book 'General Theory of Employment, Interest and Money', has offered an explanation to such a situation, which has widened the scope of economic theory and has improved our understanding of the working of the capitalist economic system, which suffers from huge unemployment of capital and human resources at the time of depression. This branch of economic theory, which deals with the

problem of employment of resources, falls under the purview of macroeconomics.

2. **Problem of Allocation of Resources:** The question of what goods in what quantities should be produced also owes its origin to the scarcity of resources. Resources being scarce, if the society decides to produce one good more, the production of some other good would have to be reduced. Determinants of the allocation of resources and the results of a change of allocation have occupied the attention of economists in all economies. In capitalist economy, the allocation of resources is governed by the price mechanism through the forces of demand and supply. The producers in the capitalist economy being motivated by profit considerations decide what goods in what quantities are to be produced on the basis of relative prices of the various goods. Thus, the relative prices of goods, as determined by the forces of demand and supply, ultimately determine the production of goods and services and the allocation of resources. This branch of economics, which deals with determination of relative prices of goods and services and consequently the allocation of resources, is called 'Price Theory' or 'Microeconomics'.
3. **Problem of Choice of Technique:** The question of how different goods should be produced or what production methods to be employed for production of the various goods and services also commands attention of the economists. There are the various alternative methods of producing goods and services depending upon the use of different quantities of the various resources. There can be labour-intensive technique, where more labour and less capital are used. Similarly, there can be capital-intensive technique, where more capital and less labour are employed. Thus, there is problem of the combination of resources to be used and the technology to be adopted for the production of things. The resources being scarce, it is necessary that the goods should be produced with most efficient methods. The choice among different methods would depend upon the relative scarcity and the prices of the various factors of production or inputs. Thus, it will be in the interest of the society that those methods of production are employed, which make the greatest possible use of the relatively abundant resources and the least possible use of the relatively scarce resources. The choice of the method of production lies under the purview of the theory of production, which deals with the physical relationship between factors of production and production, which is technically called 'production function'. It helps to determine the cost of production, which governs the supply of goods. Supply together with demand for goods determines the prices of goods. Thus, the theory of production becomes a part of Price Theory or Microeconomics.

4. **Problem of Distribution of Total Production:** Economists have always paid attention to the problem of distribution of national production among different social groups, such as workers, landlords, capitalists, entrepreneurs, etc. The distribution of national production depends upon the distribution of money income, as people with larger income would have greater capacity to buy goods and vice-versa. The greater the equality in the distribution of incomes the more the equal distribution of national production. The income can be earned either by doing some work or by providing services of certain property, such as land and/or capital. Land, labour, capital, organisation and entrepreneurship are different 'factors of production or inputs, which contribute to the national production and, in turn, get rewards for their contribution. The determination of rewards of the various factors of production is the subject matter of 'Theory of Distribution' and with introduction of marginal analysis in the economic theory, the theory of distribution has boiled down to the Theory of Factor Pricing, which is an important part of 'Price Theory' or 'Microeconomics'.

   The theory of distribution deals with the functional rather .than the personal distribution of income. In other words, it explains how wages of labour, rent for land interest on capital and profit of entrepreneurs are determined. However, distribution of national production is not explained through such functional distribution, rather it is the personal distribution of income that determines who would get how much from the national production. The personal income depends not only upon the amount of work one does but also upon the extent of property in the form of land and capital, one owns, which is the fundamental to the capitalist system. The distribution of ownership of property greatly affects the distribution of personal incomes. In capitalistic system, because of large inequalities in the ownership of property, there are greater inequalities in the distribution of personal income and, as a result, the distribution of national product is uneven. Such distribution of personal income is the subject matter of macroeconomics.

5. **Problem of Welfare Maximisation:** It is desirable that scarce resources should be used most efficiently so that maximum output is obtained with employment of the minimum resources and the national production is distributed amongst members of the society in such a way that it maximises the welfare of the society in the economy. In other words, the production and distribution should be efficient. The production is efficient, if increase in production without reducing the output of any other good becomes impossible through any reallocation of the productive resources. Similarly, the distribution of national product is efficient, if it becomes impossible

to make any person better off without making any other person worse off through any redistribution of national production. It is generally believed that inefficiencies of production and distribution exist in all types of economies. In case these inefficiencies are removed then national production as well as people's welfare can be increased. The removal of inefficiencies requires certain cost to be incurred, which is weighed against the gains or benefits to be derived from their removal. This branch of economics is 'Welfare Economics' which also forms the part of the 'Microeconomics'.

6. **Problem of Economic Growth:** Economists are also, concerned with whether the productive capacity of the economy is increasing or not. In case the productive capacity is growing, it will be able to produce more, which will enhance the standard of living of people. This increase in capacity to produce goods and services over time is known as economic growth. Economists were primarily interested in determinants and rate of economic growth and they developed numerous growth models, such as Harrod-Domar Model, Neo-Classical Growth Model, Cambridge Growth Model and others, which explain and analyse the problems of growth of developed countries. Similarly, to initiate and accelerate the process of growth in underdeveloped countries, the various growth theories and models have been developed. In recent years there has been remarkable progress both in content and volume of economic growth theory, which forms the part of Macroeconomics. Thus, the various problems falling under the purview of micro and macroeconomics form the subject matter of economics.

NATURE OF ECONOMICS

The controversy over the definition of economics has largely centered on determining the exact nature of economics. Once it is determined, the definition automatically follows. For this we have to indicate whether it is a science or an art or both and if it is a science then whether it is a positive science or a normative science or both.

ECONOMICS AS A SCIENCE

Every subject has two aspects-knowledge and application. Knowledge is science, whereas application is art. Science is generally defined as a systematised body of knowledge, which traces the relationship between cause and effect. Science is not merely a collection of facts, although facts serve as a basis of science. 'Science is built up of facts just as a house is built up of stones'. However, just as a heap of stones is not a house, an accumulation of facts cannot be regarded as science. Thus, the facts should be systematically collected, classified and analysed. Another attribute of science is that its phenomena should be easily amenable to measurement, otherwise, according to Lord Kelvin, 'the knowledge is of a meagre and unsatisfactory kind'.

Judged on the basis of above characteristics, we find that economics is a branch of knowledge, where the various facts relevant to it are systematically collected, classified and analysed Secondly, economic phenomena are also amenable to measurement, as the economists are said to have in their possession the measuring rod of money with which they can easily measure individual and business motives.

Some economists are of the view that economics cannot be given the status of a science, as there is no universal acceptance of economic phenomena. According to Barbara Wootton **'wherever six economists are gathered, there are seven opinions'.** It is undoubtedly true, but this is no reason for denying economics the status of a science, as in a growing and developing science, there is always room for differences of opinion and their existence is a healthy sign of the vigour and vitality of a science. Similarly, another ground on which the economics is denied the status of a science is, its so-called inability to predict the future course of events as accurately as other physical and natural sciences. It is true, but it very often happens that economic predictions are falsified by subsequent events, hence economics is not to be blamed for this.

The only reason for the lack of accurate predictability is that the economics deals with highly complex and variable forces and some of which are not amenable to correct predictions. It deals with men endowed with freedom of will and there is no guarantee that they will behave in a preconceived manner, therefore, the economic forecasts may not be borne out by subsequent events. Thus, the accuracy in forecasts is not sufficient to question the scientific nature of economics. In case accuracy of forecasts is the main basis for any subject to be the science, then meteorology should also not be considered as science, because the meteorological forecasts often prove to be false. Thus, economics rightly deserves the status of a science and those who challenge its scientific character seem to have closed their eyes to the basic realities of the situation.

ECONOMICS AS A POSITIVE SCIENCE

After ascertaining that economics is a science, the question is whether it is a positive science or a normative science. The Classical School of England held that 'economics is purely a positive science' but the Historical School of Germany held just the contrary view and stated that 'economics should not cut itself apart from ethical considerations'. According to J.M. Keynes, 'positive science may be defined as a body of systematised knowledge concerning 'what is'. In other words, it deals with things as they are and explain their causes and effects but remains neutral as regards ends and refuses to pass moral or ethical judgments. Thus, positive science deals with the real situation and performs the following functions:

Positive Science

- Descriptive
  - Formal
    - Definitions
    - Divisions
  - Narrative
    - Historical Evolution
    - Comparative Evaluation
- Constructive
  - Inductive
  - Deductive

Descriptive function of a positive science is to describe the subject matter in a formal way through definitions and divisions and in narrative way through the elaboration of historical evolution and comparison with other sciences. Similarly, constructive function is concerned with formulation of laws, which is done either by following inductive methodology or deductive methodology.

Economics, as a positive science, performs all these functions and establishes relationship between cause and effect. Robbins and his followers believed that **'the role of the economist is more and more conceived of as that of the expert who can say what consequences are likely to follow certain action but who cannot judge the desirability of ends'** and insisted upon treating economics as a pure and positive science only. They argue that:

(i) There shall be a good deal of confusion in the minds of enquirers, if the enquiries as to 'what is' (positive) are linked with enquiries as to 'what ought to be' (normative). The scientific base of the economics would not be safe, if the two types of enquiries are not separated.

(ii) The progress of science of economics would be jeopardised if it is not treated strictly as a positive science. The scope of disagreement would be wider in respect of enquiries regarding, 'what ought to be' than in respect of enquiries regarding 'what is'. Because of their own ideas regarding the desirability of a particular course of action, people generally do not agree on how things ought to be. Thus, inclusion of normative considerations into purely economic matters would multiply and perpetuate areas of disagreement.

(iii) An attempt to combine enquiries of positive and normative nature, shall place the economist in a very awkward position, as he will have to pass on every occasion an ethical judgment on his findings, which will render his task more arduous and difficult.

(iv) The combination of the two may tend to mislead the public at large as—what economists lay down as theorems of pure science may be interpreted by the people as if these were maxims for practical guidance.

Few economists were too much enamoured of the positive character of economics. Senior once remarked that **'an economist is not authorised to add even a single word of advice.'** Similarly, Robbins stated that **'economics**

deals with ascertainable facts, while ethics with valuations and obligations. The two fields of enquiry are not on the same plane of discourse' and has further remarked that **'the function of economists consists in exploring and explaining and not in advocating and condemning'.**

ECONOMICS AS A NORMATIVE SCIENCE

There is now complete agreement on the scientific nature of positive economics but whether it is also a normative science, it has been a controversial issue. Normative science or regulative science is a body of systematised knowledge relating to the criteria of 'what ought to be' and is concerned with the ideal situation as distinguished from the actual situation. The objective of normative science is the determination of ideals. Thus, a normative science deals with things as they ought to be and has no objection to discussing the morally right or wrong of things.

It is generally believed that economics is not only a positive science but also a normative science, because the attempts to restrict the economics to only theoretical tool building is to rob the subject completely of its value. The whole development of economics can be traced back to be the result of logical reasoning to justify one type' of policy or the other. Whatever be the nature of normative economics 'there can be no doubt that the desire to evaluate the performance of economic system has been the great driving force behind the development of economic thoughts and certainly it has been the source of inspiration of almost every great economist'.

An economist can as well guide economic policy, as a botanist can advise on the layout of a garden and by doing so he does not cease to be a scientist. Paul Streeten has observed that **'economists cannot and should not refrain from making value judgments, if their studies are to be more than a purely formal technique of reasoning or an algebra of choice. The technique or the algebra is important and ought to be as scientific as possible, but it is significant only as a means to the study of wealth and welfare and of the ways to improve them'.** In case economics is to become **'an engine of social betterment'**, it has to develop the normative aspect. An economist needs to ask for the important norms and on these bases build up a **'welfare function'**, which he tries to optimise.

Some economists have insisted upon the assignment of normative functions to economics. Hawtrey has stated that **'economics cannot be dissociated from ethics'.** Similarly, Fraser has stated that **'economics is something more than value theory or equilibrium analysis'.** They argue that:

(i) For making the most efficient use of scarce resources of the economy, economics must set certain norms. Economics cannot remain indifferent to end but has to set them.

(ii) Man is not only sensible but also sensitive and his behaviour must be studied in toto. Since the normative aspect is related to sensitivity of human beings, therefore, its study is also a must in economics.
(iii) Separation of 'actual' and 'ideal' aspects of economic study is inappropriate division of labour. It is similar to that where one is allowed to take food only, while the other is allowed to take water only.
(iv) To consider 'equilibrium is equilibrium', is not sufficient, one must judge the appropriateness of the equilibrium. For example a high rate of interest will not be justified simply because it has been determined by the equality of the forces of demand and supply of capital. Here the economist will try for a fair rate of interest.
(v) Economic planning is based on normative economics as·ends are set before the plans for economic development are chalked out.

Thus, economics is not only a positive science but a normative science as well.

ECONOMICS AS AN ART

Art is a system of rules for the attainment of a given end. The objective of art is formulation of precepts immediately applicable to policy. According to Cossa **'a science is any reasoned or theoretical body of knowledge that explains a group of homogeneous phenomena with purely speculative aim of attaining complete knowledge in that field. An art, on the contrary, has to do with what is vaguely called applied knowledge... the function of an art is to supply norms, rules, maxims, and to indicate what means are most appropriate to a given end... art does not explain theorem, it solves general problems.. Its aim is not speculative but operative and it is not concerned with laws, but only with rules that simplify practices...... a science teaches us to know; and art teaches us to do. In a word, science explains and expounds; and art directs; art imposes precepts or proposes rules'.**

On the basis of this definition of art, it appears that economics is an art as well. Professor A.C. Pigou has rightly remarked that **'our impulse is not the philosopher's impulse–knowledge for the sake of knowledge; but rather the physiologists'–knowledge for the healing that knowledge may help to bring'**. There are several branches of economics, which offer us practical guidance in the solution of economic problems. Economics, as an art, is concerned with devising ways and means for achieving the ideal situation by removing the defects in the existing system. The study of present or 'actual' situation and its examination in the light of the 'ideal' situation' may 'point out certain shortcomings which, if removed, will certainly augment economic welfare. Economics has been suggesting some methods, advocating certain remedial measures and opposing others for removal of these shortcomings of the system. Suggestions regarding banking, currency, public finance, planned economy, war economy, minimum wage fixation, discount rate, etc. indicate that economics is an art as well.

Thus economics is both a science and an art simultaneously. The two are complementary, as every science has an art or the practical side and every art has a theoretical or the scientific side. Cossa has rightly remarked **'science requires art; art requires science; each being complementary to the other'**. Therefore, it is sane and balanced attitude to regard economics both a science and an art at the same time.

ECONOMIC LAWS

Economics too, like every other sciences, has drawn its own set of generalisations known as economic laws. These generalisations or laws are helpful in understanding the past and offer trustworthy guidance for the future. Every science uses terms, such as hypothesis, theory and laws. Scientists have tentative hypothesis, which attempts to explain a group of facts. If the hypothesis is not contradicted by new discoveries, it may be promoted to the rank of a theory. If a theory continues to stand the test of time and experience, a law may be formulated. Every science attempts at obtaining laws, as a science progresses by increasing the numbers and exactness of its laws.

A law in the context of any science is a statement of causal relationship between two sets of phenomena, one being the cause and the other being the effect. Every cause has a tendency to produce, some definite result, if nothing happens to prevent it. For example if a thing is left in the space, then due to gravity power it will come down to earth, if nothing prevents it in the midway. Marshall has defined scientific law as **'a general proposition or statement of tendencies, more or less definite'.** Similarly, according to R.G. Tugwell **'a law is a summary of observed relations, a brief resume of experiences, a shorthand symbol, which assists in understanding of a number of phenomena'.** Apart from these scientific laws, there are statutory or government laws, social or customary laws, moral laws, etc.

Economic laws are scientific laws and represent economic tendencies expressing what is likely to happen under a given situation. In other words, economic laws are statement of the course of action, which may be expected under certain given conditions from the member of an industrial group. Consumers, producers, workers, capitalists, landlords, etc. are members of different industrial groups and the course of actions generally adopted by them in a given situation are formulated as economic laws. According to Marshall **'economic laws or statements of economic tendencies are those social laws, which relate to branches of conduct in which the strength of the motives, chiefly concerned, can be measured by a money price.** Similarly, according to Robbins **'Economic laws are statements of uniformities, which govern human behaviour in the allocation of scarce resources between given ends.'**

A few examples of economic laws are:

(i) **Law of Demand:** It states that 'other things being equal, at a high price the quantity purchased is less and purchase increases as price declines'.

(ii) **Law of Supply:** It means that 'other things being equal, at low price the quantity supplied is less and supply increases as price rises'.

(iii) **Law of Diminishing Marginal Utility:** It reveals that 'other things being equal, the marginal utility of successive units of consumption or possession diminishes'.

(iv) **Law of Equi-Marginal Utility:** It indicates that 'consumer with a given money income will obtain maximum satisfaction, when the utility of the marginal unit of income devoted to one commodity or service is equal to the utility of the marginal unit of income devoted to any other'.

(v) **Law of Substitution:** It states that 'other things being equal, the producer with a given outlay can obtain maximum output, when after due substitution, the ratio of marginal productivity and price of one input becomes equal to the ratio of marginal productivities and prices of all other inputs used in the production process'.

As regards the nature of economic laws, they are primarily concerned with the relations of men in their dealings with wealth as economic goods. In other words, they deal with human tendencies observed in the market place as purchasers or sellers. Thus, economic laws are human laws, as they deal with men and not with things. Consumers, producers, employers, employees, borrowers, lenders, etc. are members of the various industrial groups and economic laws study their behaviour under given conditions.

Secondly, economic laws are positive laws, as they establish relationship between the cause and the effect of the economic phenomena. For example, law of demand states that if price rises (cause) then demand contracts (effect) and *vice versa.*

Thirdly, economic laws are hypothetical. According to Marshall economic laws are 'not exact and certain like those of the physical sciences'. They are always stated with a number of qualifications expressed in the phrase ***'ceteris paribus'*** (i.e., **other things remaining the same**). Unlike the precise and universal law of physical sciences, economic laws lack definitivity and exactitude. Economic data are the outcome of a large number of variables, both economic and non-economic, as a result, whatever laws are framed, and they have an element of uncertainty in them and are, as such, hypothetical in nature.

Fourthly, economic laws are relative laws. Classical economists were of the view that economic laws were immutable, eternal, inexorable and universally applicable without any qualification whatsoever. The Historical School held the view that economic laws are relative. Some are historic relative in the sense that they are applicable under certain historical conditions, that is, economic policies have to be different for different countries and at different times for the same country. Others are institutional-relative in the sense that they are applicable under certain institutional set-up. Historical school denied absolute truth for general economic laws. They recognised only national economics holding that every age and every country had its own peculiar problems and hence, according to this school, economic laws were relative to a particular time, place and situation and consequently could have only limited application.

Lastly, economic laws are mere statement of tendencies, they are qualitative rather than being quantitative. They state the direction of change that is expected rather than the amount of change. Marshall has aptly stated that **'economic laws are to be compared with the laws of tides rather than with simple and exact law of gravitation'.** He wanted economists to form some notions of the tendencies of human action and 'for turning to account the experience, that has been reaped by more advanced physical sciences; and for framing, as best as we can, well-thought- out estimates or provisional laws of the tendencies of human action.

Thus, it is true that economic laws are seldom exact and are never final, but economists are trying to make economic laws more exact and comparable to physical laws. Marshall has aptly observed that 'just as the chemist's fine balance has made chemistry more exact than most other physical sciences; so this economist's balance, rough and imperfect, as it is, has made economics more exact than any other branch of the social science.'

METHODOLOGY OF ECONOMIC GENERALISATIONS OR LAWS

Methodology means the logical process of discovering or demonstrating the truth. Every science follows certain methodology for formulation of its laws, principles or theorems, the same is true with economics. There are two methodologies for investigation that an economist can adopt for exploration and they bear two types of generalisations. One is deductive methodology, which means deducing generalisations through a process of reasoning on the basis of some assumptions that are either self-evident or based on observation. In this methodology, the logical reasoning proceeds from the general observations to particular principles. The other is inductive methodology, where the logic mounts from particular to general. As per this methodology, we begin with the observation of particular facts and then mount up with the help of reasoning founded on experience, so as to formulate laws on the basis of observed facts. Thus, the deductive methodology leads to analytical generalisations, while the inductive methodology offers empirical (statistical) generalisations.

DEDUCTIVE METHODOLOGY

The classical and neoclassical economists used the deductive methodology also known as the abstract, hypothetical or *a priori* method of enquiry for the analysis of economic problems. The deductive methodology deduces conclusions from certain fundamental assumptions or axioms established through other methods by logical processes of reasoning. Here we start from a few indisputable facts about human nature and deduce or draw inferences from them about individual problem. We know that the larger the stock of a commodity at one's disposal, the lower shall be the utility of its marginal unit. This general statement can be applied to money. The larger the stock of money with a person, the lower the utility from the marginal unit of money. Thus, rich persons derive less marginal utility than poor persons from marginal unit of their income. On the basis of this inference, we can draw another inference that taxation must not be on a proportional basis, where everybody pays a fixed percentage of the income as tax, otherwise rich persons would go comparatively lightly taxed, while poor persons have to bear a comparatively heavier burden of tax, which is unjust and against the canon of equity for taxation. Thus, the principle of progressive taxation has been directly derived from the law of diminishing marginal utility on the basis of deductive reasoning.

The whole deduction process involves certain steps: (i) the exploration of the problem; (ii) setting up of hypotheses; (iii) theoretical development of hypotheses; and (iv) verification of the theories.

(i) The exploration of the problem is an indispensable preliminary to any investigation. Human mind explores a definite problem. The perception of a problem is by no means an easy job. The problem should be stated in simplest conceivable form and then it should be grappled progressively with less simple forms. The real world problems are very complex and complicated. So we reduce complex problems to its simplest form and gradually introduce more and more complications as we proceed further and, thus, we succeed in treating the reality itself.

(ii) The next step is ascertaining the assumptions as per which the conclusions are to be drawn. It is highly desirable that the assumptions taken are as close to reality as possible. Since, the real world problems are so complicated that we make only broad assumptions, which recognise the major characteristics of a number of situations but ignore variations in individual cases. By ignoring too much of details, we do lose rigour but achieve generality and, thus, economic analysis presents a map of reality rather than a perfect picture of it. K.E. Boulding has aptly remarked that **'Just as we do not expect a map to show every tree, every house and every blade of grass in a landscape, so we should not expect economic analysis to take into account every detail and quirk of real economic behaviour'**. Thus, in deductive methodology, a compromise is necessary 'between the use of assumptions, which resemble to the real conditions and the need for simplification and generality'.

On the basis of these assumptions hypotheses may be formulated. The hypothesis is a conjecture, a hunch of the possible connection between two phenomena. It requires sufficient insight and constructive imagination and states the likely relationship between different factors affecting certain economic phenomenon. Thus, as per this methodology we start from very simple premises to work up gradually to more and more complex hypotheses.

(iii) After developing hypotheses, the nature and implications of the hypotheses have to be analysed to frame a theory or a principle. Since, every hypothesis involves certain assumptions and has certain implications, they have to be analysed to see the existence of contradictions within themselves. It considers logical basis and implications of the hypothesis, as a result, the simplifying assumptions may have to be introduced or the hypothesis suitably modified.

(iv) Lastly, the verification of theories, thus developed, must be attempted. Milton Friedman has observed that **'any adequate scientific theory must be put into the form of a testable hypothesis'**. However, advocates of deductive methodology believe that the economic theory is not amenable to verification or refutation on purely empirical ground and they think that 'economic science is a system of **a priori** truth, a product of pure reason, and a system of pure deduction from a series of postulates'. Thus, staunch advocates of deductive methodology rely upon introspection and logic to develop the whole body of economic principles. Testing and verification of theories is also done through introspection and logic.

The deductive methodology is of two types–mathematical and non-mathematical. Classical and neo-classical economists used the non-mathematical deductive methodology in which they used only verbal expressions and not mathematical symbols. The mathematical deductive methodology was used for the first time by F.Y. Edgeworth for the study of economic problems. Later on, use of diagrams and mathematical symbols became popular with economic discussions and now-a-days more elaborate and higher mathematics is being employed for building economic growth models and linear programming. H. Stackelberg has observed that **'wherever quantitative analysis is necessary, mathematics is employed-all that mathematics can do is to produce precise thinking even about imprecise data.' R.J. Stigler remarked that 'mathematics can exhaust the implications of known quantitative relationships and it can often bring much information from only generally defined relationships'**.

Under mathematical method, every economic problem is reduced to a series of mathematical symbols and algebra and calculus of the most complicated variety are used to derive certain conclusions. Use of mathematical deductive methodology helps in derivation of good economic theory and it has an inherent clarity, which is absent when the problem is treated in a non-mathematical style. In certain type of analysis, such as general equilibrium analysis, microeconomic and dynamic analysis, mathematical method is indispensable. However economics is still a developing discipline as compared to natural sciences and it possesses relatively few tested economic laws. In the absence of many and diverse generalisations, the need for mathematical systematisation did not exist.

Marshall though himself a great mathematician, opposed too frequent and avoidable use of mathematics. He realised that, **'at times, the use of mathematics in economics could prove helpful to economists in understanding a complex economic phenomenon.** He was very clear in his mind that the economist should not be overpowered by the mathematician in him. He knew that most helpful applications of mathematics to economics are short and simple, which employ few symbols and aim at throwing a bright light on some small part of the great economic movement rather than representing its endless complexities. He suggested that mathematical formulae should be used as an abbreviated language and not as a means of research and should be translated into ordinary language as soon as conclusions are derived. Thus, the craze for two much use of mathematics on the part of economists in the analysis of complex economic problems is never free from the risk of misinterpretation for mathematics, dealing, as it does with equality equations, fails to focus sufficient attention on the cause – effect relationship persisting between those economic variables, which constitute the mathematical equations. However, despite the various criticisms and objections, the use of mathematical method has been increasing in importance in modern economic analysis.

MERITS AND DEMERITS OF DEDUCTIVE METHODOLOGY

The deductive methodology for building up generalisations enjoys several advantages, which cannot be ignored in evaluation of economic methodology. Firstly, the use of deduction is exceedingly simple affair, as from a few basic facts of human nature we can derive a large number of inferences in a short time. Secondly, in view of limited scope of experimentation in economics compared with other sciences, the deductive method is the best alternative to be relied upon, which obviates the necessity of experimentation. Thirdly, it brings accuracy and exactness in generalisations because of invariable use of logic and mathematics. The most powerful mathematical tools can be brought to bear in this method and logically consistent theorems can be derived without any tenuous collection and analysis of data.

Despite these merits we should not lose sight of its shortcomings. It requires unusual competence in logic and abstraction. Many experienced economists have been trapped by faulty reasoning. M. Blaug has aptly remarked, **'it is perfectly true that economists have often deceived themselves and their**

readers by engaging in 'implicit theorising' presenting tautologies in the guise of substantive contributions to economic knowledge.' Secondly, the generalisations arrived at as a result of deductive reasoning can be true only if the assumptions upon which they are based hold good. There is every danger in this method of developing elegant models based on so ideal and unrealistic assumptions that the model may have no operational significance. Thirdly, deductive method proves particularly harmful when universal validity is claimed for economic generalisations derived from deductive reasoning from incorrect or partially correct premises or assumptions. It will be more harmful if government's policies are based on the deductive generalisations, which has been illustrated by the harm done to the underdeveloped economies through the application of Keynesian, remedies. Professor A.P. Lerner has rightly remarked that **'the deductive arm-chair analysis should be properly qualified, so as to guard against its failings.**

INDUCTIVE METHODOLOGY

Historical School of Germany has strongly denounced deductive methodology and has advocated for inductive methodology, which is also known as historical, empirical and a ***posteriori*** method. It has a practical approach for formulating generalisations. This school was of the view that the national economy of every country, the nature, the volume, the distribution and the consumption of wealth was the result of a long evolution and would be best studied with reference to the history and the general laws of society and social evolution. They conceived political economy as being based upon the ideas of economic evolution and their ultimate objective was to make economics **'a doctrine of the economic development of nations.'** Therefore, they collected material through the study of history of contemporary events and then proceeded to form generalisations from the study of a number of particular cases.

The inductive methodology takes two forms, i.e., experimentation and statistical. The former is concerned with testing the validity of generalisations derived on the basis of deductive reasoning by resorting to the study of actual facts, while the latter is concerned with framing generalisations on the basis of a large number of facts collected from the various sectors of the economy. The latter (i.e., statistical) form of induction is more popular in economics.

(i) **Experimentation Approach:** It is generally used in natural and physical sciences for testing the theoretical deductions and has only a limited scope in economics. It is due to the fact that the experimentation is very difficult in economics and much easier in physical sciences, because such sciences deal with inanimate aspects of nature or matter, which hardly offers any resistance against being experimented. As against this, economics studies unmanageable material of human beings, who may not put up with the idea of being experimented upon individually or collectively. Professor A.L.

Meyers has aptly remarked that **"human beings have wills of own and resent being treated as guinea pigs for the purpose of social experimentation."**

Secondly, economic phenomena are very complex and complicated. In fact, economic phenomena are so closely inter-mixed and inter-twined that it is almost impossible to segregate them for the purpose of experimentation. An economic event is ordinarily a net result of many causes and the event does not recur in the same manner and with same pattern of causal conditions. There is less uniformity of sequence, less exact repetition and more variability in the flow of economic occurrences than in natural phenomena. Every economic event is in some way unique set against a different background and, therefore, carries different implications.

Lastly, economists deal with phenomena in which the various pressure groups, like employers, trade unions, etc., participate and it is difficult for them to remain objective in experimentation. Some would like them to prove that free trade is the best, others may insist them to prove that protection is the best; employers would press them to prove that high wages cause unemployment, while trade unions would like them to prove that employment is bound to increase, if wages are raised. These pressure groups render experimentation in economics inaccurate and subjective.

These difficulties of experimentation, however, do not imply that there is no scope for experimentation in economics. Experimentation may be resorted to find out the validity of certain laws, like the law of diminishing return. Experiments can also be done in factories to watch the effect of new form of industrial organisation on the efficiency of labour. A monopolist firm, like electricity undertakings or transport corporations may, also carry on experimentation to gauge the effects of changes in their rates on demand for their products and services.

(ii) **Statistical Approach:** In view of the various difficulties in the way of successful experimentation in economics, the economists rely on the use of statistics to test their hypotheses and establish quantitative relationships between economic facts. It has much larger field in economic investigations than the method of experimentation. There has been great improvement in the statistical tools that can be employed to test economic theorems. We have now sufficient literature on econometrics, which is nothing but empirical testing of economic theories and assumptions through appropriate statistical tools. At present there is sufficient data on economic matters and economists relying on inductive methodology have now almost unparalleled opportunities of investigation and research into the fields hither to inaccessible. This method of statistical induction has also become indispensable for the formulation of economic policy, which is essential for the successful and smooth functioning of any economy. Thus, statistical induction gives us empirical generalisations, which can be reformulated into analytical principles by selection of appropriate assumption and determination of logical conclusions that follow.

MERITS AND DEMERITS OF INDUCTIVE METHODOLOGY

Inductive methodology, whether experimental or statistical, possesses certain distinct advantages in economic research. The economic generalisations derived through the process of inductive methodology from a set of carefully collected facts generally lead to precise and measurable conclusions. These generalisations are based on a very sure and realistic foundation and, as such, their validity is not open to challenge. Secondly, some of the important theorems in economics have been discovered from the empirical studies of facts. The development of consumption function, that is, the relation of income and consumption and acceleration principle for building more comprehensive theories of investment, are the result of induction. Lastly, inductive methodology underlines the importance of relativity in economic generalisations. It emphasises the fact that any generalisation will have validity only under certain conditions and circumstances.

Despite these advantages of inductive methodology, there is always a serious risk of hurried conclusions being drawn from insufficient data. Secondly, collection of facts itself is not an easy job. Since, the real world economic problem is complex, the facts bearing on them would necessarily be complex and intermingled. Before using this method, the investigator must be given good grounding in economic theory and statistics. Lastly, inductive methodology alone is not enough, as it will not do the trick unless it is supplemented by the process of deductive reasoning. Durbin has rightly remarked that **'facts do not speak for themselves, it is only by analysis, comparison, hypothesis and prophecy that they can be made to speak at all'.**

AN INTEGRATION OF THE TWO METHODOLOGIES

There has been a lot of controversy over the relative desirability of the two general approaches to the furtherance of economic knowledge. The Classical School of Britain stood solidly for deductive methodology, while the Historical School of Germany stood firm for inductive methodology. However the line of demarcation between the two methodologies is not very clear cut. Malthus, Mill and Senior, though staunch supporters of the deductive methodology also resorted to empirical analysis and they did a lot of factual research to test or verify their theoretical conclusions. Similarly, Von-Thunen and Wagner, though staunch supporters of inductive methodology, did not hesitate to use even highly abstract methods in their treatment. This controversy, barring a few exceptions, continued till Marshall, the great compromising genius, offered a compromise formula by holding that instead of being considered competitors, the two methods should be regarded as complementary to each other. He approved Schmoller's statement that **'induction and deduction are both needed for scientific research, as the right foot and the left foot both are needed for walking'.**

It has been recognised that the furtherance of economic knowledge requires use of both empirical and analytical studies, each being necessary for the successful use of the other. Now the disagreement among the economists is mainly over the relative importance of the two rather than over the desirability or the exclusive use of any. Empirical studies, without an analytical framework to direct the selection of relevant data, are completely futile and analytical studies without any empirical content are mere exercises in logic without usefulness.

Thus, the two methods be blended together for the purpose of economic analysis and investigation. The two methodologies should be considered partners rather than rivals and should be adopted simultaneously as counter-checks or supplements to each other. Samuelson has rightly remarked that **'properly understood, therefore, theory and observation, deduction and induction cannot be in conflict'.**

Review Questions

1. "Economics is the study of mankind in the ordinary business of life" Critically examine this statement.
2. Discuss the scarcity definition of economics and explain how it differs from welfare definitions of economics.
3. 'Whatever economics is concerned with, it is not concerned with the causes of material welfare as such (Robbins).' Explain this statement.
4. What do you mean by welfare economics? Examine the place of value judgment in welfare analysis.
5. Explain the concept of scarcity. How does it give rise to economic problems?
6. Is economics by nature an art or a science?
7. Economists have to work as a pure scientists. They are neither to advise nor to bother about welfare" Discuss this statement.
8. "Economics studies human behaviour, concerned with changes and growth in means in relation to ends" Discuss.
9. "The laws of economics are hypothetical, less exact and therefore, useless". Discuss.

2

Micro and Macro Economics

In recent years the subject matter of economics has been divided into two parts: microeconomics and macroeconomics. The term micro has been derived from Greek word 'mikros', meaning 'small' and the term macro is derived from the word 'makros' meaning 'large'. Thus, microeconomics deals with economic behaviour of individuals or of well-defined groups of individuals, such as consumers, producers, firms, industries, markets, etc. On the other hand, macroeconomics is the study of broad aggregates, such as, total national output and income, total employment, total consumption, total investment, etc. The former originated with Adam Smith, continued with Ricardo, Say and Mill and culminated with Marshall, while the latter originated with mercantilists in 16th century and continued with Malthus, Sismondi, Marx and Keynes, who were concerned with economic system as a whole and not with individual units.

Micro-macro distinction in economics is of recent origin, as formerly these were termed as price theory and income theory respectively. Price plays a major role in microeconomic theory, as its goal is generally the analysis of price determination, which, in turn, determines the allocation of resources to the various uses. Macroeconomic theory, on the other hand, is concerned with the determination of the levels of national income, price level, aggregate resource employment, etc. However, it does not mean that income concepts are altogether ignored in microeconomic analysis and that prices are non-existent in macroeconomic analysis. Actually determination of income of individuals is encompassed within the general pricing process, as individuals earn their incomes by selling inputs they own, whose prices are determined in the same way as prices of all other goods. Similarly, prices are also relevant in macroeconomic theory, although instead of dealing with determination of individual prices and their relations to one another, it deals with price level as determined by the level of aggregate spending. Such aggregation may reveal the position and progress of the whole economy, which would be impossible, if the micro emphasis on individual behaviour and relative prices were maintained.

MICROECONOMICS

Microeconomics is that part of economic analysis, which studies economic behaviour of individual unit, may be a person, a particular household or a particular firm. In microeconomic theory we examine how various units of the economy, such as, consumers, producers or firms, workers and other resource suppliers behave and attain their equilibrium positions. It is a microscopic study of the economy, where we discuss equilibrium of innumerable units and their inter-relationships on a piecemeal basis. Professor A.P. Lerner has rightly remarked that **'Microeconomics consists of looking at the economy through a microscope, as it were, to see how the millions of the cells in the body economic—the individuals or households as consumers and individuals or firms as producers, play their part in the working of the whole economic organism'.**

Thus, microeconomics seeks to determine the mechanism by which different economic units attain the position of equilibrium, proceeding from individual units to narrowly defined groups. Professor Campbell R. McConnel has observed that **'Microeconomics is concerned with specific economic units and a detailed consideration of the behaviour of these individual units.... In microeconomics we examine trees not the forest. Microeconomics is useful in achieving a bird's-eyes view of some very specific component of our economic system'.**

Microeconomic theory is primarily concerned with the flow of goods and services from producers to consumers, the flow of productive services from consumers to producers and with the composition and pricing of the components of these flows. The study of these flows conceives the economic problem, which concerns with allocation of scarce resources among alternative uses. Such allocation is made possible only through the price mechanism in the economy. Therefore, to determine the allocation of resources microeconomics proceeds to analyse the determination of relative prices of products and factors of production. Thus, the theory of product pricing (i.e., the theory of exchange) and the theory of factor pricing (i.e., the theory of distribution) fall in the domain of microeconomics. Prices of products depend upon the forces of demand and supply. Since, the demand for products depends upon the consumer's behaviour pattern and the supply of goods depends upon production and cost, therefore, the consumption theory and production theory also fall within the domain of microeconomics.

Besides, microeconomics also seeks to explain whether the allocation of resources determined is efficient. The efficiency in allocation is attained when the resources are so allocated that the satisfaction of the people is maximised. It involves three types of efficiencies, namely, production efficiency, consumption efficiency and overall economic efficiency. Microeconomics reveals under what conditions these efficiencies are attained and the possible causes for departure, if any, from these efficiencies.

Production efficiency involves producing maximum possible quantity of the various goods and services from the given resources. Consumption efficiency, on the other hand, involves distribution of product among people for consumption in such a way, as to maximise their satisfaction. Similarly, overall economic efficiency involves production of those goods, which are most desired by the people, that is, when the direction of production is such that maximises the satisfaction of the people. These efficiencies when attained, maximise the welfare of people, which is an important part of the microeconomics. A.P. Lerner has remarked that **'Microeconomic theory spells out the conditions of efficiency and suggests how they might be achieved. These conditions can be of the greatest help in raising the standard of living of the population'. Consumption and production efficiencies relate to the individual welfare, whereas overall economic efficiency relates to social welfare.**

The contents of the microeconomics are as follows:

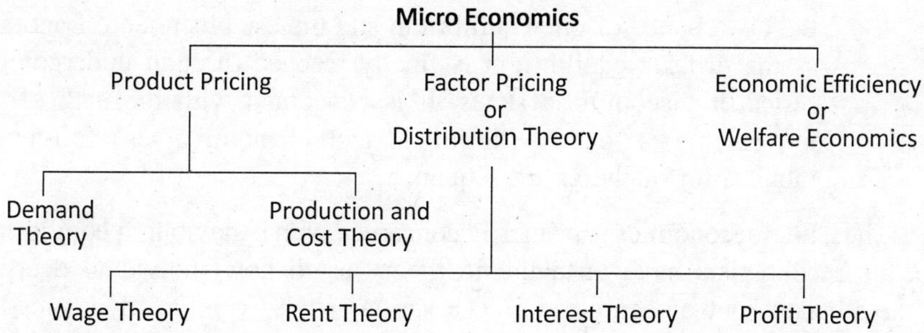

Thus, microeconomics is the study of price theory, the theory of individual and household (i.e., consumption theory), the theory of firm and industry (i.e., production theory) and welfare theory.

Microeconomics which analyses the behaviour of individuals, households, firms, industries, prices, etc. is of three types: (i) Simple Micro Statics, (ii) Comparative Micro Statics, and (iii) Micro Dynamics.

(i) **Simple Micro Statics:** It deals with a set of microeconomic variables and the interrelations between them, when they are in equilibrium at a given point of time. For example, the price of a commodity in a market is determined by the equilibrium of demand and supply at a given time, assuming that the forces of demand and supply do not undergo any change. Simple micro statics does not throw any light on the process through which the forces of demand and supply have reached the position of equilibrium. So long as demand and supply functions remain unchanged, the equilibrium price shall remain unchanged and consequently the market will remain in a state of static equilibrium.

(ii) **Comparative Micro Statics:** In simple micro statics, we assume that demand and supply functions do not change through time, hence the price will remain in the state of static equilibrium. However, when either of the two or both the functions (i.e., demand and/ or supply) change, then after the process of adjustment, there will be a new state of equilibrium, having a new set of price and quantity demanded and supplied. Comparative micro statics studies the relationship between original equilibrium and new equilibrium. Thus, it is a comparative study of different equilibrium positions at different points of time but throws no light on transition, rather it jumps over from one equilibrium position to another.

(iii) **Micro Dynamics:** Due to the change in the demand function, the original equilibrium is disturbed and commodity market faces a lot of disturbance before attaining the new equilibrium. Micro dynamics refers to the process through which we go from one equilibrium to another. It throws full light on the happenings in the transition and involves full study of forces, which come into operation between the disturbance of one equilibrium and the establishment of another, as the *exposte* equilibrium is finally reached through undergoing a series of disequilibria states. It is concerned with the path of the movement from one equilibrium to another and involves a full-length movie film of the entire sequence.

Thus, microeconomics is primarily concerned with behaviour at equilibrium because economists have virtually no theory as to how individual decision makers behave out of equilibrium. The serious study of micro dynamics has barely commenced and the simple micro static model is 'timeless', because the choice over time is not fully integrated into the model.

IMPORTANCE OF MICROECONOMICS

Microeconomics occupies a vital place in economics and has both theoretical and practical importance:

(i) It helps in understanding the working of the economy. It is the microeconomics that tells us how a free market economy with its millions of consumers and producers work to decide about the allocation of productive resources among the thousands of goods and services. It reveals how a decentralised system of a free private enterprise economy functions without any central control. Professor A.P. Lerner has aptly remarked that **'microeconomics teaches us that completely direct running of the economy is impossible and that a modern economy is so complex that no central planning body can obtain all the information and give out all the directives necessary for its efficient operation.'** Thus, microeconomics helps in understanding how decisions regarding how, what and for whom to produce, how to distribute and what to consume, are taken by producers and consumers without any external interference.

(ii) It provides a tool in the form of price mechanism for evaluating economic policies of the states. The prices fixed on no-profit and no-loss basis for public utility (like postal services, railways, water, electricity, etc.) by the respective governments, in turn, influence the prices of other goods and services in the private sector of the economy. Prices of products of public enterprises, which compete with private enterprises, cannot exceed the prices determined through the forces of demand and supply in the market. Thus, microeconomics helps the state in formulating proper price policies and in evaluating them in proper perspective.

(iii) It is helpful in the efficient employment of scarce resources among competing ends. This is the principal problem, faced by every economy and microeconomics helps in this regard for achieving growth with stability.

(iv) The analytical tools of microeconomic theory are quite helpful to business executives in taking decision regarding demand, cost, price, etc.

(v) It is helpful in understanding the problems of taxation and international trade. It is used to explain the factors that determine the distribution of the incidence or burden of a commodity tax between producers or sellers and consumers. It also helps in gauging the damage done to the social welfare or economic efficiency by the imposition of tax. Further, it is applied to show the gain from international trade and to explain the factors that determine the distribution of this gain among the participant countries. It also helps in determining whether the devaluation will succeed in correcting the disequilibrium in the balance of payments through the elasticity of demand and supply of exports and imports. It further helps in determining the foreign exchange rate through the forces of demand and supply of a currency.

(vi) It helps in examining the conditions of economic welfare. The whole structure of welfare economics is built entirely on microeconomic theory of perfect competition, as maximisation of social welfare is possible only under perfect competition. Under monopoly, oligopoly or monopolistic competition, there is generally misallocation of resources leading to considerable wastage of resources, which involves loss of economic efficiencies or welfare. Microeconomics helps in suggesting ways and means of eliminating wastages in order to bring maximum social welfare.

(vii) It serves as basis for making predictions, which is generally put in the form–if something occurs then a certain set of results will follow. Thus, microeconomics helps in making conditional predictions. It reveals the facts to be collected and suggests tools to be applied for interpretation and economic models based on different assumptions are quite helpful in making different conditional predictions.

(viii) It enables construction and use of economic models. It facilitates the understanding of what would be a hopelessly complicated confusion of millions of facts by constructing simplified models of behaviour, which are sufficiently similar to the actual phenomena. These models also enable economists to explain the extent to which the actual phenomena depart from certain ideal constructions that would most completely achieve individual and social objective. Thus, these help not only to describe the actual economic situation, but also to suggest policies that would most successfully and most efficiently bring about desired results and to predict the outcomes to such policies and other events.

Thus, the microeconomic theory is the basic language of economists. Words and phrases have been coined to convey precise meanings and have come to enjoy a fair amount of currency and respectability as the economists' short-hand. Knowledge of fundamental concepts of microeconomics may not out rightly help them in being more precise and clear in their analysis and avoid some errors in logic. According to H.H. Liebhafsky **'there is very practical reason for acquiring a knowledge of price theory, the language and concepts of price theory permeate the whole of economics and in all fields of economic analysis they serve the practical purpose of economy of efforts and constitute generally accepted methods of organising and classifying ideas about economic activities and magnitudes'.**

LIMITATIONS OF MICROECONOMICS

After Great Depression (1929-39) microeconomics has ceased to attract much attention and the best talent has gone in for extension and refinement of macroeconomics. The lack of enthusiasm amongst contemporary economists for the study of microeconomics is partly due to its highly abstract nature and largely due to its being an unsatisfactory guide for policy decisions. The limitations are:

(i) It is based on unrealistic assumption of full employment in the economy. It is highly unrealistic assumption, as full employment is not the rule but an exception in the real world. According to Keynes **'to assume full employment is to assume our difficulties away'**. In fact, Keynes advocated the giving up of the unrealistic assumption of self-interest, full employment, perfect competition, etc.

(ii) It does not give a correct and proper picture of working of the economy because microeconomic analysis is too much pre-occupied with the functioning of the parts of an economy at the cost of the general working of the economy. However what is true in case of individual units may not be true in case of aggregates. For example individual thrift (saving) may be good but social thrift is definitely harmful for the community, as that will reduce effective demand and will ultimately retard employment. Thus, it is not essential that the principles that are true in the case of a particular household, firm or industry may also be correctly applicable to the economy as a whole.

(iii) There are certain economic problems that cannot be analysed through microeconomics. Thus, important problems relating to public finance, monetary and fiscal policies, etc. are beyond the purview of microeconomics.

MACROECONOMICS

Macroeconomics is the study of aggregates or averages covering the entire economy, such as, total employment, national income, national output, total investment, total consumption, total savings, aggregate supply, aggregate demand and general price level, wage level, cost structure, etc. It examines the interrelations among the various aggregates, their determination and causes of fluctuations. According to K.E. Boulding **'macroeconomics deals not with individual quantities as such but with aggregates of these quantities; not with individual incomes but with national income; not with individual prices but with price levels; not with individual outputs but with national output'.** The study of aggregates of the important variables in the economic system–income, consumption, saving, investment, employment, etc. is conducted independently of the behaviour of the economic units that constitute the economic system. It is the study of economic system as a whole and **'studies the characteristics of the forest independent of the trees that compose of it'.** Thus, macroeconomics is that part of the economics that deals with great aggregates and averages of the system rather than with particular items in it and attempts to define these aggregates in a useful manner to examine their relationships. According to Gardner Ackley **'macroeconomics concerns itself with such variables as the aggregate volume of the output of an economy, with the extent to which its resources are employed, with the size of the national income and with the general price level'.**

Macroeconomics is also known as the theory of income and employment, as income occupies the central place in the study of macroeconomics. It is concerned with the problems of unemployment, economic fluctuations, inflation or deflation international trade and economic growth. It studies the various determinants of employment and causes of unemployment. It also studies business cycles, where it concerns with the effect of investment on total output, total income and aggregate employment. In monetary field, it studies the effect of the total quantity of money on the general price level. In the field of international trade, the problems of balance of payments and foreign aid fall within its purview. Macroeconomics also determines the relative shares from the total national income of the various classes, particularly workers and capitalists in the society.

Macroeconomics is also of three types: (*i*) macro statics, (ii) comparative macro statics, and (iii) macro dynamics.

(i) **Macro Statics:** It explains certain aggregate relations in the stationary state, but throws no light on the process by which the final equilibrium is reached. For example,

$$Y = C + I$$

Here macroeconomic variables Y, C and I represent total income, total consumption outlay and total investment outlay respectively. This equation reveals that total national income is equal to the aggregate of the total consumption and total investment outlays. It deals with the final equilibrium of the economy at a particular point of time and is considered as a technique of analysing the relations between macro variables in the final position of equilibrium without dealing with the process of adjustment implicit in that position of equilibrium.

(ii) **Comparative Macro Statics:** Various macro variables in an economy, such as, total consumption, total investment, and total income, keep on changing with the lapse of time. Comparative macro statics involves comparing the different levels of equilibrium income corresponding to or resulting from changes in the above macroeconomic variables. It renders the different equilibrium positions comparable but fails to explain the process of transition from one equilibrium position to another.

The comparative macro static analysis, which makes a comparison between the **ex ante** and the **ex poste** equilibrium positions, itself is the result of change in one or more macroeconomic variables of the model. The change in $Y = C + I$ may take place either through a change in the aggregate consumption outlay (C) or through a change in the aggregate investment outlay (I) or through a change in both.

Similarly, the quantity theory of money states that the price level in an economy is influenced by changes in the quantity of money. If the economy is already in equilibrium at certain price level, any change in the quantity of money will disturb the original equilibrium and after a series of disequilibria, a new equilibrium is established at a changed price level. Under such circumstances, it only compares the new equilibrium with the original one and throws no light on what happens during the transitional period.

(iii) **Macro Dynamics:** It studies how the equilibrium in the economy is reached consequent upon changes in the macro variables and aggregates. It enables us to separate 'the process of trial and error into a series of continuously changing reactions and indicates, step by step, cause and effect.' It analyses the discrete or continuous changes of aggregates, the sequence of cause and effect on events arising from some initial disturbance and the time paths of macro variables and aggregative relationships. It also furnishes guidance relating to the practical problems of short and long period economic stability.

This enables us to see the movie picture of the entire economy as a progressive whole and is considered as the most comprehensive and complete method of economic analysis. In case, the economy is in equilibrium at a particular level of income and at a particular point of time, it will be disturbed by a change in the volume of investment, which will immediately set off a series of adjustments through multiplier and accelerator and will bring the economy to a new point of equilibrium at a changed level of income, output and employment. This will present a full account of all developments taking place in the economy in the transitional period between the breakup of the old equilibrium and the establishment of the new one.

IMPORTANCE OF MACROECONOMICS

By adding, multiplying or averaging the results obtained from the behaviour of the individuals, firms and industries, we cannot obtain the laws governing the macro economic variables, like national income, total employment, general price level, etc. In fact, true to the whole and generalisations based on the microeconomic analysis for the economic system as a whole or macroeconomic aggregate, is incorrect or may lead to misleading conclusions. It is a paradox that the generalisation or laws true of a constituent individual parts but untrue and invalid in case of the whole economy. Professor K.E. Boulding has called these paradoxes as **'macroeconomic paradoxes'** which justify a separate macro analysis of the behaviour of whole economic system. For example, savings are always good for an individual for their old age, for education of children, for purchasing durables, for start or expansion of business, etc., but it is not always good for the whole society. In depression period increase in savings will increase the intensity of depression and unemployment. Similarly, a cut in money wage in depression and unemployment may lead to increase in employment is true for any industry but if wages are cut all round in the economy, the aggregate demand for goods and services in the society will decline, which will ultimately create more unemployment. So a separate and distinct macroeconomic analysis is essential for understanding the true working of the economic system as a whole, which has the following merits:

(i) Macroeconomics helps us to understand the functioning of the complex economic system and gives bird's eye view of the vast panorama of the economic universe. Our main economic problems are related to the behaviour of total income, output, employment and general price level in the economy. These variables are statistically measurable and help in making the elimination process understandable and transparent. Thus, one may not agree on the best method of measuring different prices, but the general price level is helpful in understanding the nature of the economy.

(ii) Macroeconomics is extremely helpful to the government in formulation of appropriate economic policies for tackling the problems of inflation, balance of payment, over-population, and underproduction. Professor J. Tinbergen has aptly remarked that **'working with macroeconomic concepts is a bare necessity in order to contribute to the solutions of great problems of our times.'** Generally governments are concerned with the regulation of aggregates of economic system, the general price level, the general level of production, the general volume of trade, etc., which make them concerned more with the aggregates and averages than with the individual variables. It is possible only through macroeconomic analysis.

(iii) Macroeconomics is indispensable for a proper and accurate knowledge of the behaviour patterns of the aggregative variables. According to Professor Boulding **'the forest is an aggregation of trees, yet it does not exhibit the characteristics and behaviour pattern of individual trees'.** It would be incorrect to say that the behaviour pattern of the forest, as an entity in itself, can be obtained by studying the behaviour patterns of individual trees, because such an attempt would be highly misleading. Thus, the aggregate and its individual components are entirely two different things and characteristics of one do not necessarily pertain to the other.

(iv) It also helps in understanding the behaviour of individual units. For example, demand for individual products depends upon aggregate demand in the economy. Unless the causes of deficiency in aggregate demand are analysed, it is not possible to understand fully the reasons for a fall in the demand of an individual product. Similarly, the reasons for increase in cost of a particular firm or industry cannot be analysed without knowing the cost conditions of the whole economy.

Thus, macroeconomics enriches our knowledge of the functioning of an economy by studying the behaviour of national income, output, investment, saving and consumption and throws much light on solving the problems of unemployment, inflation, economic instability and economic growth.

LIMITATIONS OF MACROECONOMICS

Macroeconomics is gaining popularity and strength in recent years, yet there are certain inherent pit-falls or limitations in it, which are as follows:

(i) Macroeconomics regards the aggregates as homogeneous without caring about their internal composition and structure. The average wage in a country is the average of wages in all occupations, for example, wages of teachers, factory workers, agricultural workers, clerks, doctors, etc. The volume of employment depends on the relative wage structure rather than on the average wage. For example, if the wages of doctors increase but that of teachers decrease, the average wage may remain unchanged, although the employment may increase, if there is slight fall in employment of doctors, while there is greater rise in the employment of teachers.

(ii) The aggregate tendency may not influence all sectors of the economy in the same manner. A rise in price level may not reflect rise in prices of all commodities. Similarly, study of aggregates may lead us to believe that no change has taken place. For example, if agricultural prices fall while industrial prices rise, the general price level may remain unchanged and may not call for any policy for removal of this imbalance.

(iii) The aggregate variables, which form the economic system may not be of much significance, for sample, a rise in national income is not necessarily a healthy sign for the economy, if it is the result of an increase in the income of a few rich persons in the country.

(iv) An indiscriminate and uncritical use of macroeconomics in analysing the problems of the real world can often be misleading. For example, measures aimed at controlling general prices cannot be applied with much advantage for controlling prices of individual products.

(v) Macroeconomics also presents a number of statistical and conceptual difficulties. These problems relate to the aggregation of micro-economic variables. If the individual units are similar, the aggregation does not present any difficulty, but if these units are dissimilar, their aggregation into one macroeconomic variable may be inaccurate and misleading. For example, in measurement of national product, we might be led to over-estimate it as a result of the difficulty of measurement of heterogeneous units of product.

INTER-DEPENDENCE OF MICRO- AND MACROECONOMICS

Micro- and macroeconomics are two seemingly alternative approaches to economic analysis, but at the essence these are complementary to each other. We cannot attain a complete understanding of the functioning of the economic system unless we integrate the two approaches in a judicious manner.

Truly speaking, microeconomics depends upon the macroeconomics. Various costs, like raw material cost, labour cost, etc. of a particular firm are determined not by the demand of that particular firm but by the demand of the entire economy for such raw materials and labour. Similarly, sale of the product of the firm too is determined, not by its own price, but also to a very large extent by the total purchasing power available with the community. Further, when the aggregate demand rises during a period of prosperity, the demand for individual product also rises. This will lead to increase in demand for capital goods, labour, etc. Thus, a macroeconomic change brings about changes in the values of microeconomic variables–in the demand for particular goods, in the wage rates and profits of particular industries and in the employment of a particular category of workers.

Similarly, macroeconomics is also dependent on the microeconomic analysis. The total is made up of parts, for sample, national income is sum of incomes of individuals, households, firms and industries. Macroeconomic variables, like total savings, total investment and total consumption are decisions of individual industries, firms, house-holds and persons. The general price level is the average of all prices of individual goods and services and total output of the economy is the sum of outputs of all the individual producing units.

Thus, micro and macroeconomics are interdependent and both contribute to each other. Though they deal with different subjects, yet there is a good deal of interdependence between them. The two approaches are, therefore, not in any way mutually exclusive and, as such, must be properly integrated to secure fruitful results. Professor Samuelson has aptly remarked that **'there is really no opposition between micro and microeconomics. Both are absolutely vital. You are less than half educated if you understand the one, while being ignorant of the other'.**

All modern developments in macroeconomics are directly or indirectly inspired by some earlier developments in microeconomics. Similarly, recession in structural fabrication, railways, spare parts and consumer durables in India during 1967, would have not been diagnosed properly with macroeconomics alone. It was well explained through micro analysis, as the rise in the prices of food was responsible for less demand for consumer's durables, The rise in price of food stuffs was due to famine conditions prevailing in the country for two years at that time. This reduced the demand for consumer's durables which, in turn, reduced the demand for many engineering goods. Thus, the recession was analysed only through the use of both macro and microeconomic tools.

Thus, we cannot restrict the sphere of the two analyses–they are complementary and not competitive. According to Professor Gardner Ackley **'actually the line between macroeconomics and microeconomics cannot be precisely drawn. A truly general theory of the economics would clearly embrace both... Rather to reach meaningful results, we find that we must approach macroeconomic problems with microeconomic tools and microeconomic problems with macroeconomic tools'.**

MARKET IN MICRO AND MACRO ANALYSIS

Market refers to places, where consumers and producers meet for the purpose of purchase and sale of goods and services and productive resources. It does not refer to any geographic location, as on account of modern means of communication, there is no fixed boundary for the market.

All individuals (i.e., consumers and producers) in the economy are assumed to play a double role, namely that of buyers and sellers. Consumers and producers are buyers and sellers of finished goods and services, but simultaneously they are sellers and buyers of the productive services respectively. Thus, there are two sets of markets in any economy: (a) product or output markets; and (b) factor or input markets.

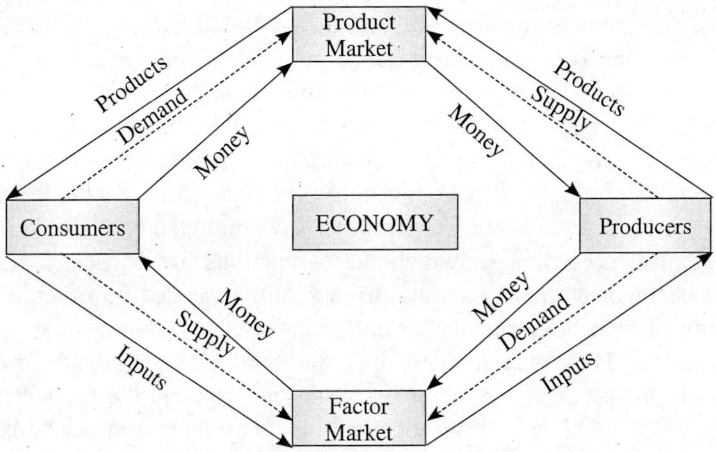

FIGURE 2.1 Role of the Markets in the Economy.

Figure 2.1 reveals the circulation of money in the economy from producers to consumers and from consumers to producers through the product and the factor markets. The consumers purchase goods and services from the product markets with the money they receive from the factor markets in lieu of the inputs they supply. Producers get money in lieu of product supplied to product markets, in return they demand productive services for which they make payments to the suppliers (i.e., individual consumers) in the factor markets. Thus, the receipt of producers from the sale of the output is spent on the purchase of inputs and the receipt of consumers from the supply of inputs is spent on the purchase of final goods and services.

Thus, products flow from producers to consumers and productive services from consumers to producers into eternity and in the opposite direction money flows from consumers to producers and then back again from producers to consumers into eternity. The opposite circular flow of goods and money incorporates both macro- and microeconomic analysis. Considering the overall opposite flows of money and goods, we can view inflation as a situation in which flow of money exceeds the flow of goods. By breaking consumers' income into parts saved (which reduces the flow of money into the product market) and parts spent, we can assess the impact of the central bank's actions of increasing or reducing money supply in the economy. Similarly, we can consider the impact of government's actions as the purchaser of inputs or products or as tax claimant upon the consumers' incomes. Linkewise, we can consider the impact of international trade on the flow of goods and money in the economy. All these are concerns of macroeconomics, which deals with the level of operation of the economic system.

The microeconomic theory, on the other hand, is concerned with determination of prices of the inputs and of the products with factors affecting such price determination and with determination of quantities of inputs and products, the rational producers and consumers would like to buy. Thus, in this case we are concerned with the analysis in detail of the various determinants of and relationships among the parts of the economic system.

Market is expected to perform the functions of determining goods and services to be produced, kinds and quantities of inputs to be employed, the distribution of product and the provision to be made for the maintenance and possibly for the growth of the system. Microeconomic theory seeks to establish the principles, according to which these functions are to be accomplished in the system on certain assumptions regarding the degree of competition, rationality of behaviour and the extent of knowledge possessed by producers and consumers. Thus, the microeconomic theory is devoted to the determination of prices in the product and factor markets. The prices in the product markets are interpreted to be reflections of wants of consumers and serve as guides to producers in their allocation of resources to the production of goods and services and in the factor markets prices are seen as costs to the producers.

The analysis of the process through which consumers' valuations are reflected in the prices, which they pay for goods and services, is known as the Theory of Demand. The products on which the consumers place the highest valuations will command higher prices and changes in such valuations are reflected in their prices. The goods for which there is no demand, will not command a price and the producers will not like to produce such goods. However, consumers' valuations are not independent but can be influenced by the advertising and selling activities of the producers.

Similarly, decisions regarding quantities of inputs used and the proportions of the employment of the various inputs for production are taken by the producers. Assuming the absence of governmental actions and presence of perfect competition with no advertising or selling expense, where given price prevails in the economy, the producers, to maximise their profits, would make the use of the least costly methods of production.

The prices, which producers pay for inputs are costs to firms, but the same are the income of the owners of those inputs. This income, in turn, depends on prices and quantities of inputs owned by the consumers. The rational or functional distribution of income under such circumstances reveals that price for the use of a unit of a given factor of production is exactly equal to the additional value of the product, which results from the use of the same. For maintenance of the system, certain sum sufficient to replace the capital equipments, being used up in the production process, is included in the cost of production of final products.

Thus, markets are expected to perform five major functions. Firstly, these set values, which are measured by the prices. Secondly, these organise production and advocate for the most efficient production method. Thirdly, these distribute the product among persons for whom it has been produced. Fourthly, these ration the current rate of consumption to the available production. And, lastly, these provide for the future, as the saving and investment take place for the maintenance of the economic system and for bringing about economic progress.

Review Questions

1. Bring out the themes of microeconomics and macroeconomics.
2. Discuss the nature of macroeconomics and point out the necessity of macro approach to economic analysis.
3. State the characteristics of simple micro statics and discuss the importance of microeconomics.
4. Distinguish between microeconomics and macroeconomics and bring out their interdependence.
5. "There is really no opposition between micro and macroeconomics. You are only half-educated it you understand the one while being ignorant of the other". Discuss.
6. Bring out the distinctions amongst simple micro statics, comparative micro statics and micro dynamics analyses.
7. Distinguish between microeconomics and macroeconomics. Explain that what is true for an individual unit is not true for the whole society.
8. 'Microeconomics and macroeconomics are interdependent'. Discuss the statement.
9. 'Microeconomics constitute the most fundamental part of the economic theory'. Comment.

3

Economic Statics and Dynamics

It has been well recognised that statics and dynamics are two distinct approaches of vital importance to the study of economics. According to Harrod **'the correct charting of a line of demarcation between them should have beneficial results on the progress of economics and that the absence of recognition of such a line, even of an understanding of the necessity for it, has led to much confusion and fallacy in recent works'.** At earlier stages, static analysis was more popular and the dynamic analysis mainly confined to the exploration of the business cycles, but later on, it has also been extended to income, growth and price theories.

In the static analysis, we concentrate our attention on those things, which seem most important by assuming *ceteris paribus* (i.e., all other things remain constant). On the other hand, in the dynamic analysis there is no question of *ceteris paribus*, as all the relevant factors having some bearing on the problem are to be considered simultaneously without any time gap. The distinction between statics and dynamics owes its origin to August Comte (1798-1857) and J.S. Mill was the first to use these terms in economics, but there has been a lot of controversy about their true meaning and nature, especially about dynamics.

ECONOMIC STATICS

The term is derived from the Greek word '*Statike*', which means bringing to a standstill state. In physics it means a state of rest, where there is no movement, but in economics it is concerned with static state. The static state of an economy does not mean lack of movement or motion in the economy. It is one where there is movement but that movement is constant, regular, smooth and certain. Such an economy is devoid of all sudden jerks and shocks and assumes away uncertainty. The economy continues to churn over with constancy of all quantitative measurements and all qualitative factors, like technology, tastes, etc. Marshall named this active but unchanging process as static economics. J.B. Clark regards it as the state, where five kinds of changes are conspicuous by their absence, viz., size of the population, supply of capital, methods of production, forms of business organisation and wants of people remain constant, but the economy continues to work at a steady pace.

Static economy is a timeless economy, as there is neither past nor future in the static state. According to Samuelson **'Economic statics concerns itself with the simultaneous and instantaneous or timeless determination of economic variables by mutually interdependent relations'.** On account of this, the element of uncertainty is also found absent.

Static analysis refers to that type of analysis, where we establish the functional relationship between two variables, whose values relate to the same point or period of time. It is a state in which there occurs no essential modification of the general conditions under which consumption, production, exchange and distribution are generally carried on. Thus, in static analysis the effects of changes of a specific kind, are considered but the general social and economic conditions are supposed to be fixed. It is assumed that no fundamental changes take place in the general character of social wants, that no invention leads to the introduction of new methods of production on a large-scale, that no sudden diminution of population is caused by war or famine, that there is no progressive exhaustion of sources of supply. Thus, statics simply depicts a 'still' picture of the economy, which catches the economic scene at a moment of time and analyses the interrelationship between variables at that moment of time. Any system that does not involve time functionally (i.e., the variables are not function of time) is an object of study of statics. It does not establish any relationship between the preceding and succeeding events.

Product pricing is a good example of economic statics, where the price of a commodity is to be determined at a particular time by the forces of supply and demand existing at that very moment of time. It will be a static analysis of price determination, because all the variables involved, such as, quantity demanded, quantity supplied and the price determined refer to the same point of time. In case the demand and supply are supposed to be influenced by past prices or expected prices of the future, to secure realistic explanation of price-determination, we may have to refer not only to the present, but also to the past and future. Once we refer to different points of time in establishing relationship of the various elements of the economic system, we then depart from statics and enter the domain of dynamics.

Time element in static analysis is ignored, because its introduction makes the analysis complex and complicated. Real world problems are very complex but ever changing world may be treated statically, each of its changing positions being treated as successive states of static equilibrium. This simplifying procedure applied not only to the time element, but also to the various other elements of economic system. For example, in the analysis of price determination the factors, such as, income of people, their tastes and preferences, prices of related goods, prices of productive resources and production techniques are assumed to remain constant.

According to Marshall **'forces to be dealt with are, however, so numerous, that it is best to take a few at a time and to work out a number of partial solutions as auxiliaries to our main study'.** Thus, we begin by isolating the primary relation of supply, demand and price in regard to a particular commodity, we reduce to inaction all other forces by using the phrase, other things being equal. We do not suppose that they are inert, but for the time being, we ignore their activity. Thus, the economists must isolate the subject of his study form the extraneous influences. This technique of static analysis should be used in a careful or discriminating manner, as it is easily open to abuse. In case an investigator makes certain assumptions at the beginning of his analysis, he must consider them, while finalising his conclusions, as it may require some modification in the light of these assumptions.

Static analysis is the traditional method also known as the method of decreasing abstractions, successive approximations or isolating one-at-a-time procedure. Recently it has also been known as optimistic approach, where the analysis proceeds stage by stage towards the still far distant ideals, is of constructing an analysis, which will be capable of solving the problems of the real world. Thus, this analysis consists of gradually advancing from the more simplified to the more realistic postulates.

The method of static analysis is generally associated with the concept of a stationary state, which is only a methodological fiction, essentially a simplifying device or a tool of analysis and facilitates an approach to the real conditions. It should, however, be remembered that the conception of stationary state does not wholly rule out changes taking place in the economic system. The point is that changes take place at even or uniform rates, so that the economic process merely reproduces itself. According to A.C. Pigou **'stationary state does not mean 'frozen fixity'; individual drops composing the waterfall are continually in movement though the waterfall remains'.** Thus, the economic system as a whole may remain static, though its individual constituents may play an important role in the economic analysis and aid in the explanation of difficult and complex problems, but the concept is highly artificial and unrealistic. It has made some economic theorists stationary state minded, which, in turn, has checked the proper development of economic theory.

Micro and Macro Statics

The static analysis can be explained in terms of micro and macro static equilibrium models. In the micro static model, supply and demand relationships determine the price at a point of time. Similarly, macro static analysis explains the static equilibrium position of say, the national income in the economy. It investigates relations between macro-variables in the final position of equilibrium without reference to the process of adjustment implicit in that final position. The two static equilibria are as follows:

The micro static relationship is explained by Figure 3.1(i) where demand and supply curves intersect at *E* equilibrium position.

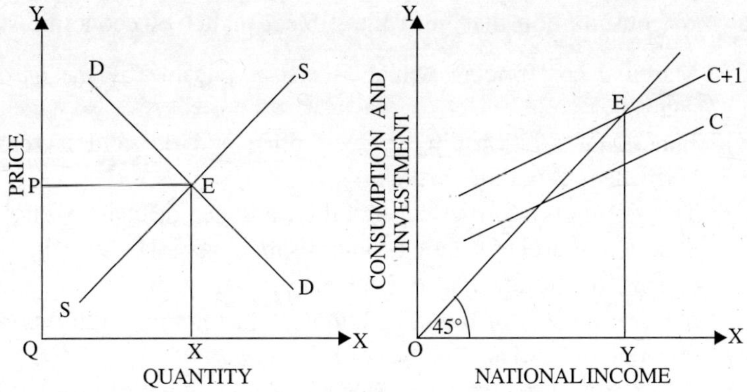

(i) Micro static (ii) Macro static

FIGURE 3.1 Micro and Macro Static Equilibria.

At this equilibrium *OX* is the quantity demanded and supplied and *OP* is the price. In the absence of change in demand and supply conditions, this equilibrium position will apply not only to the present, but also to the future.

Similarly, Figure 3.1(ii) explains macro static or Keynesian model, where the level of national income is determined by the intersection of aggregate supply function and the aggregate demand function. The 45° line represents the equality between aggregate demand and aggregate supply functions (i.e., $Y = C + I$) and $(C + I)$ line represents only the aggregate demand function. Both intersect at *E* equilibrium position, which determines *OY* level of national income. Here total national income (*Y*) is equal to total consumption expenditure (*C*) plus total investment expenditure (*I*). It simply shows a timeless equality equation without any adjusting mechanism. Thus, economic statics refers to a timeless economic analysis. It neither develops nor decays. It is like snap-shot photo from a still camera, which would be the same whether the previous and the subsequent positions of the economy, were subject to change or not.

Scope of Static Analysis

Various assumptions, like perfect knowledge, absence of uncertainty, given consumer tastes, given population, given capital, given techniques of production, given forms of industrial establishment, perfect factor mobility, etc., associated with statics, have narrowed down its application. Certainty and perfect knowledge are inherent in the static economy and, therefore, profits, as a pure surplus arising out of uncertainty, will never arise. We have to study only rent as a surplus, which is expected and certain in static economy. These drastic assumptions have narrowed down the scope of static economics in the study of real world problems. However, in spite of these limitations, it still covers the study of several economic problems specially those connected with equilibrium conditions, that do not involve any variations in the element of time. The static analysis is found relevant for:

Laws of consumption that form the subject matter of economic statics.

(i) Marginal cost pricing, which is also explicable by means of static analysis.
(ii) Functional relationship between price and demand is reasonably permanent economic statics.
(iii) The assumption of perfect mobility, absence of change, etc., though generally present in static economy, are never inherent in it. Thus, the international trade is also a subject of static economics, although the theory flows from the assumption of factor immobility as between different countries.
(iv) Static economics can also study problems arising out of the once-over changes, as such changes are analysed through comparative statics.
(v) Change and roundabout methods of production, which involve uncertainty and an once-over change generates more uncertainty than a continuing change, hence the theory of profits may also be studied under static economics.
(vi) Trade cycle theories lie on the border line. Sometimes these are studied through static analysis while at other times these may lie within the scope of dynamic analysis.

Thus, according to Hicks, **'static economics contains much of the more important part of the traditional economics, the theories of rent, comparative cost and monopolistic exploitation, all of which can be studied without reference to the time element'**. Modern economists have shifted their emphasis from statics to dynamics, but as we know, the traditional economics was almost wholly cast in statical terms and if we are going to discard the method of statics that means the entire body of traditional theory shall be lost to us. It is rather more deplorable to let down statics due to 'a certain tendency to denigrate the works of the earlier economists'. Despite this Professor Harrod remarks, **'static will remain an important part of the whole, because this is the only way to make the treatment of complex problems clearer, simpler and more precise'.**

Merits and Demerits of Static Analysis

Although the static analysis is artificial and unrealistic, as the determining conditions are never constant, yet it is used in economic analysis, because it makes the otherwise complex phenomena simpler and easier to handle. In order to establish important causal relationships between certain variables, it becomes easier, if we assume other forces and factors as constant; not that they are inert but for the time being we ignore their activity. Secondly, in order to understand the working of the dynamic economy, a study of economic statics is essential in the same manner as the study of the laws of rest is necessary to understand the laws of motion. If one wants to study the propeller of an aeroplane, it is useful to examine it thoroughly before it starts moving and the same is true to the study of economy.

The main weakness of the method of statics lies with the fact that it proceeds on the basis of the various unrealistic assumptions, such as, perfect competition, perfect mobility, perfect knowledge, perfect foresight, etc. which are untenable in practice. However, making of these assumptions cannot be helped, because unless these assumptions are made, the matter to be studied cannot be isolated for the purpose. Besides, it assumes as constant what is variable in practice, but the variables are treated as constants only for the purpose of simplifying or facilitating the task of analysis. As the analysis proceeds, these variables, which have hither to been considered as constants, can be gradually introduced into the analysis, one by one, to watch their repercussions on the main body of conclusions. Further economic statics is itself not very appropriate. It may even be misleading because in statics we too frequently engage ourselves in examining the effect of particular changes like changes in demand, cost of production, etc. Moreover it can provide only limited treatment of life's vast economic problems and thus, is like a map without any indication of the various altitudes. In ease we are concerned with a flat region this map will be adequate and satisfactory but if we feel interested in real topography–mountains, plains and plateaus of the region, then the practical utility of the map is nil. Furthermore there are certain problems which cannot be treated through static analysis, because if it is applied to them, it will give altogether misleading conclusion, the problem of stability of equilibrium can be analysed only through dynamic economics. Moreover, there are certain economic phenomena, such as, economics of growth and business cycles, which can be successfully treated only through economic dynamics. Lastly, it also lends rather poorly to econometric verifications. It is hedged about with too many assumptions to take care of empirical econometric studies. Thus, considering all these points, Professor J.R. Hicks has rightly remarked **"Although some notable economists have been content to mould their thought as this, it (statics) leaves out far too much of the real problems to be a secure resting place."**

Comparative Economic Statics

Statics is generally concerned with the stationary or non-evolutionary process, but this can be applied to explain even an evolutionary or a dynamic process by a series of static models. So, when the method of statics is called upon to study a changing process, it is referred to as the method of comparative statics. It is a mid-way between statics and dynamics, where we study the evolutionary process in a series of equilibria, and compare the new position of equilibrium with that of the old. Such comparison of different equilibrium positions corresponding to different sets of data is really of great interest. It does not analyse the whole path, as to how the system grows out from one equilibrium position to another, when the data have changed. It merely explains and compares the initial equilibrium position with the final one reached after the system has adjusted to a change in data.

In order to grasp fully the effects of change in the set of data on the corresponding position of equilibrium, we must allow change in single datum at a particular time. Richard G. Lipsey has observed that comparative statics involves **'a comparison of new equilibrium position with the original equilibrium position...The differences in the two positions of equilibrium must be due to the changes in the data that were introduced'.** It does not deal at all with transitional period from one position of equilibrium to another but simply jumps over the transition development. Here we have only two 'still' pictures to compare and not a movie, as under dynamic analysis.

There can be two types of comparative statics: (i) comparative micro statics; and (ii) comparative macro statics and these can be illustrated with the help of following diagrams:

In Figure 3.2(i) consequent upon an increase in demand, there is an upward shift in the demand function from *DD* to *D'D'* and the old equilibrium at *E* shifts to new equilibrium *E'*, where the price and the quantity demanded and supplied are *OP'* and *OX'*, respectively. It is comparative micro-statics, as it enables comparison of the two successive micro-equilibrium positions. Similarly, in Figure 3.2(ii) since the equilibrium income (*Y*) is determined by consumption (*C*) and investment (*I*), it is obvious that *Y* cannot change without there being a prior change in the income determining variables *C* and *I*. Here original equilibrium is disturbed due to positive change in consumption and investment (*C* + *I*)′ and get settled at *B*, where the equilibrium income has gone up from *OY* to *OY'* level. It, however, does not show the path through which the economy has travelled through time before hitting at new level of equilibrium income *OY'*.

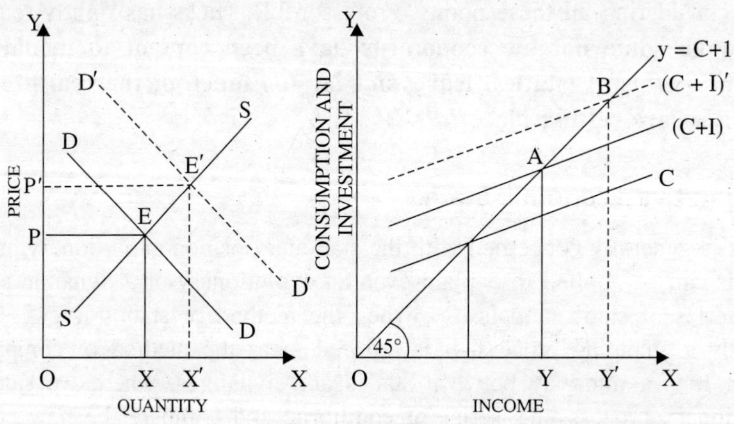

(i) Comparative Micro Statics (ii) Comparative Macro Statics

FIGURE 3.2 Micro and Macro Comparative Equilibria.

Similarly, 'Quantity Theory of Money' may also be taken as an excellent example of comparative statics, where we examine the effect of changes in the supply of money on the price level. Change in supply of money will shift the price level, which will enable a comparison of the two equilibrium positions. Thus, in comparative statics we are not interested in transitional development, but only in the final phenomena, as according to David Recardo **'transitional developments have no effect on the final position of the equilibrium'. However there are economists like Sismondi, who urged that 'the road to it may be so long and lead through upheavals terrible suffering as to make it practically impossible for the analyst to deal cavalierly with the incidental phenomena'.** In other words, he gives so much importance to the transitional or the intervening phenomena that these could not simply be ignored.

The comparative static treatment provides some very important insights into the mechanism of the exchange economy. Traditionally, the comparative statics has been the method, most commonly used, for formal analysis of the economic system. It is the form of analysis for the student, who does not have a knowledge of mathematics and is often used to derive predictions from the theories of monopolies and competition.

Despite their merits, the comparative statics are not so informative, comprehensive and realistic, as the method of economic dynamics. It cannot be used to predict the path, which the market follows, when it shifts from one position of equilibrium to another. It can also not predict whether or not a given equilibrium position can ever be attained. Professor J. McKenna has aptly remarked **'comparative statics gives only a partial glimpse of the movement, as we have only two 'still pictures to compare, whereas true dynamics would give us a movie'.**

ECONOMIC DYNAMICS

The technique of static analysis is exceedingly simple and unrealistic and in the comparative statics we deal with an evolutionary process but only by a series of static models, where the equilibrium so obtained are compared with the initial equilibrium, The method of dynamics, however, deals with the whole evolutionary process in a dynamic manner, which takes into account all the changes, lags, sequences, cumulative magnitudes and even expectations. There is no assumption of *ceteris paribus* (i.e., other this being equal) as in statics and there is also no break up of evolutionary process in a series of static equilibria, as in comparative statics. Economic dynamics is very comprehensive method, as it excludes nothing important from the purview of the study, although in this process, it becomes very complex and complicated method of analysis.

Economic dynamics is the method, which considers the relationship between relevant variables, whose values belong to different points or periods of time. According to professor Schumpeter **'we call a relation dynamic,**

if it connects economic quantities that refer to different points of time, Thus, if the quantity of a commodity that is offered at a point of time (t) is considered as dependent upon the price that prevailed at prior to the point of time (t-1) this is a dynamic relation'.

Thus, the element of time is given due recognition in the economic dynamics for the adjustment of the given variables to each other. According to Ragnar Fissel **'Here we consider not only a set of magnitudes in a given point of time and study the interrelation between them, but we consider the magnitudes of certain variables in different points of time, and we introduce certain equations, which embrace at the same time several of those magnitudes belonging to different instants'. It explains** how one situation grows out of the foregoing situation.

According to Professor J.R. Hicks economic dynamics refers to **'that part of economic theory in which all quantities must be dated.'** Similarly, according to William J. Baumol **'dynamic economics is the study of economic phenomena in relation to preceding and succeeding events'.** Professor Richard G. Lipsey defines dynamic analysis as **'the study of the behaviour of systems, single markets or whole economies, in disequilibrium conditions.'**

According to Professor Kuznets, **'Economic theory, which seeks to explain the phenomenon of economic change, the implications of given change and trace the process of that change and the consequences of succeeding movements, step by step, is called economic dynamics'.**

These definitions, thus, emphasise the 'time element' and consider economic dynamics as **'the analysis of the process of change, which continues through time'.** The change in the economy may be either without changing its pattern or by changing its pattern. Economic dynamics relate to the latter. If there is change in population, capital, techniques of production, forms of business organisations and wants of people in any one or all of them, the economy will assume a different pattern and the economic system will change its direction. In such a case, the values of the economic variables, at a given moment of time, depend partly on their values at the past moments of time. Economic processes are traced over a time path made up of a sequence of periods, with the use of appropriate lags. An economic model is characterised as dynamic, if, at least, one observable variable in the equations, has values taken at different points of time. Complex problems in economics, particularly when they involve movements towards a constantly changing equilibrium, may also be analysed by economic dynamics.

Micro and Macro Dynamics

Dynamic analysis can be explained in terms of micro and macro dynamic equilibrium models. The simplest micro dynamic analysis can be explained through the cobweb model and the macro dynamic analysis can be explained in terms of the process of income propagation through the investment (multiplier), where consumption is a function of the income of the preceding period as follows:

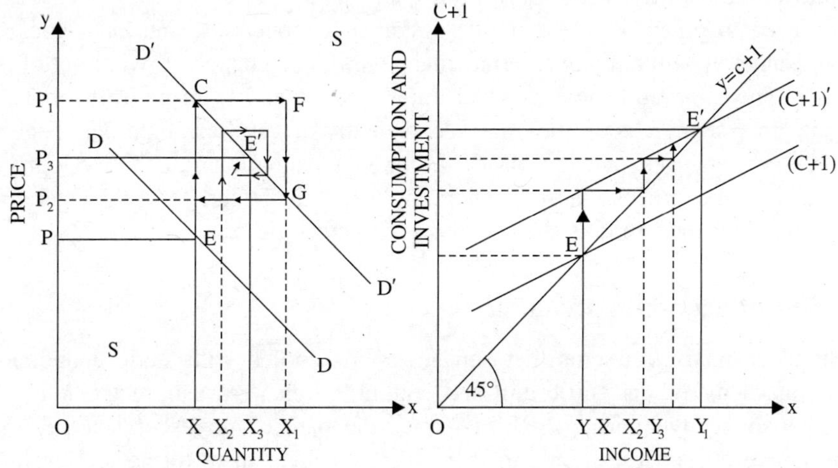

(i) Micro Dynamics (ii) Macro Dynamics

FIGURE 3.3 Micro and Macro Dynamic Equilibria.

In Figure 3.3(i), *E* is the initial equilibrium position, where the original demand curve (*DD*) intersects the original supply curve (*SS*). In case, the demand increases, the demand curve shifts to *D′D′* level and the price, at once, shoots up to $OP_1 = CX$. This increase in price will increase the supply to meet the new demand at point *F* in the period $(t + 1)$. The excess supply over demand at this point will reduce the price to $OP_2 = GX_1$. Excess of demand over supply will induce the price to increase to OP_3 and the quantity demanded and supplied will increase to OX_3. Thus, the equilibrium will be established ultimately at *E′*, which is a dynamic equilibrium with lagged adjustments.

Similarly, macro dynamics treats discrete movements or rates of change of macro-variables. According to Professor Kurihara **this method separates the process of trial and error into a series of, continuously changing reactions and indicates, step by step, what is cause and what is effect...** It analyses the discrete and continuous changes of aggregates, the sequence of cause and effect events arising from some initial disturbance and the time paths of macro-variables and aggregative relationships'. In Figure 3.3(ii), we start from an initial equilibrium of income at *OY* where initial consumption and investment $(C + 1)$ line intersects the 45° angle line at *E* point. In case $C + 1$ line shifts upwards due to rise in investment from $(C + 1)$ level to $(C + 1)'$ level, the income rises by the amount of increased investment in the initial period. This will raise the consumption resulting from increased income. This process of income propagation will continue till the aggregate demand function $(C + 1)'$ interests the aggregate supply function (i.e., 45° angle line representing equality of aggregate demand and aggregate supply functions throughout) at E'. Thus, we reach from E to E', i.e., the new equilibrium through the steps, known as macro dynamic equilibrium path.

The movement in the dynamic system is endogenous, that is, it goes on independently without any external change in it, one change growing out of the other. There may be some external initial change and in response to that the dynamic system goes on moving independently of any fresh external changes, successive changes growing out of the previous situations. Such development of a dynamic process is self-generating and this feature of self-generating development over time is the crux of every dynamic process.

Scope of Economic Dynamics

There are many problems that can never be handled with static economics. The problems of disequilibrium and continuing changes can be tackled only by economic dynamics, which can trace the path of forces of stability that are active during transition and that ultimately help in restoring equilibrium. Similarly, economic problems, which depend upon the psychology of the economic subject can be studied through the economic dynamics. Complex problems like cyclical fluctuations and secular growth can be tackled by economic dynamics, which is flexible and can create infinite number of models to explore all possibilities. It is indispensable for a correct understanding of the nature of business cycle. It has helped in distinguishing between different types of theories of business cycles. Economic dynamics is nearer to reality than economic statics and is superior to latter as a guide to practical economic problems. The macroeconomic problems of determination of income, employment and growth can also be treated dynamically.

Economic dynamics is of recent origin, but some traces of this method can be found in the field of price theory. Modern contributions in the dynamic analysis relate to three fields of economics, viz. trade cycles, price theory and income determination. Theories of interest and profits and the concept of quasi-rent also fall in the domain of dynamic analysis. Dynamic analysis uses two mathematical methods (i) differential equations, where functions are continuous and amenable to calculus techniques of manipulation; and (ii) difference equations, where period analysis and time lags are to be treated. Therefore, the dynamic analyses are not easily within the reach of non-mathematical students. Cobweb model, dynamic stability of multi-market equilibrium, trade cycle models and growth models are interesting exercises in dynamics. Day by day, economists are heading towards more and more sophisticated models to get nearer to reality by using complicated mathematical methods.

Merits and Demerits of Economic Dynamics

Economic dynamics possesses great significance in theory and practice as follows: (i) It is a realistic analysis and is indispensable to correct the unrealistic nature of economic statics. It explains the causes and effects of changing economic phenomena and enables us to see a moving picture of the working of an economy. (ii) It is a study of stability of equilibrium, because it studies the behaviour of the economic system in disequilibrium and traces the path of the forces that bring a new equilibrium position. (iii) It helps in analysing the problems involving time lags, rate of growth and sequence analysis and helps in explaining the connection between certain given conditions and their corresponding developments. (iv) It is imperative for presenting a realistic analysis of secular growth, speculation and cyclical fluctuations, as they all involve elements of time. (v) It helps in developing new techniques of economic analysis. Econometric models of national income, trade cycles and economic growth are being extensively built on macro dynamic analysis. (vi) It possesses considerable amount of elasticity that enables it to investigate all possibilities concerning a particular problem. Thus, it serves as an indispensable tool for the analysis of problems pertaining to real economic life.

Despite this method being useful, informative, comprehensive and realistic, it has its own limitations viz., (i) It is highly delicate and intricate method of investigation, not only because there is no *ceteris paribus*, but also because time element must be taken fully into account. This time element introduces sequences, periodicities and lags in economic process and these, in turn, make the dynamic analysis very complicated and complex, requiring a good deal of mathematical treatment. (ii) On account of lack of favorable conditions, the economic dynamics fails to build theoretical models with empirical contents. A.W. Stonier and D.C. Hague have rightly remarked that **'real world is a very complex place and the creation of a theory of economics, which tries to take account of all or even most of that complexity, would be beyond the capacity of human brain.'** (iii) The trend of economic model building has made economics complex and difficult for an ordinary student of economics, which creates doubts about the practical utility of economic dynamics.

Thus, we can conclude that none of the two types of analysis is free from defects, still the economic science can neither do without dynamics nor without statics. There are certain problems, which can only be tackled with the help of economic dynamics, while many other can be better managed by the relatively simple tools of static analysis. There might be still some more problems, which can be tackled neither by dynamic analysis nor by static analysis alone but require active involvement of both for their solution. Thus, statics and dynamics are both complementary to each other and needed simultaneously for the study of economic problems.

ECONOMIC MODELS

Economic model building is another method of investigation, being used increasingly by modern economists. A model refers to the theoretical environment assumed by an economist, who wishes to work out the relationships between variables in precisely known condition. In economics, we study the relationships among economic variables in the world, which is highly complex and complicated. Innumerable economic forces are at work in the economy and it really becomes a problem for the economists to isolate the economic variables from those economic forces. It is precisely for this purpose that the economists build models. So, a model is nothing but simplification of reality. An economic model is, thus, a method of analysis, which presents an oversimplified picture of the real world and is always clear and exact.

Since human mind has a limited capacity, it cannot take into account all the factors having bearing on the problem under investigation. It enables the economist to concentrate upon those factors in which he is immediately interested and also enables to postpone consideration of those factors, which have only a distant bearing on the problem. Since so many factors are excluded from the model, its conclusions must be accepted with particular set out in equation form, which also requires sufficient working knowledge of the mathematics.

Review Questions

1. Distinguish between micro and macro dynamic processes.
2. Bring out the scope of static analysis in economics and elucidate the features of the economic dynamics.
3. 'Statics is a timeless concept'. Discuss and explain the importance of economic statics.
4. 'Those parts of economic theory, where we do not trouble about dating, are called economic statics and those parts, where every quantity must be dated, are called economic dynamics'. (J.R. Micles). Discuss.
5. Distinguish between economic statics and economic dynamics and explain the importance and demerits of economic statics as a method of economic analysis.
6. Bring out the static analysis and comparative static analysis and illustrate the two concepts.
7. Define the terms 'statics', 'comparative statics' and 'dynamics'. Elucidate their importance in economic analysis?
8. 'Comparative static discusses and compares two or more equilibria positions'. Elucidate the statement.

4

Equilibrium

DEFINITIONS

The concept of equilibrium has been derived from two Latin words '*acqua*', which means equal and '*libra*', which means balance. Thus the term equilibrium means the state of balance between the opposite forces working on a particular entity or body. This term has been borrowed from physics, where it refers to a body at rest, as the opposite forces acting on it cancel each other and sum up to zero.

Marshall has defined equilibrium as the **'simple balancing of forces, which corresponds rather to the mechanical equilibrium of a stone hanging by an elastic string or of a number of balls resting against one another in a balance.'** If we tie a ball with a string and hang it from a nail fixed in the wall, it will oscillate (move to and fro) and after some time come to stand just in the centre, if no further disturbance is caused to it. The central point, where the string with ball tied to it, come to rest finally, is the equilibrium point, where the two opposite forces are exactly equal and balanced against each other. However, it may be an equilibrium for the physical sciences.

In economics, equilibrium does not necessarily mean absence of movement. In fact, the economic system would collapse, if all movements in it come to a standstill. Thus, for equilibrium the idea is not that the movements should cease to exist, rather there should be no change in the rate of movement. According to Professor J.K. Mehta **'equilibrium denotes in economics the absence of change in movement, while in the physical science, it denotes the absence of movement itself.'** The earth, on which we live, is rotating and even then it is in equilibrium. Similarly, in an economy, goods and services are flowing from producers to consumers and productive services (inputs) are flowing from consumers to producers, but so long as the rate of production and consumption does not change, the economy **may be said to be in equilibrium**. Professor T. Scitovosky has further enlarged the concept of equilibrium by stating that **'a person is in equilibrium, when he regards his actual behaviour as the best possible under the circumstances and feels no urge to change his behaviour as long as circumstances remain unchanged.'** The same is true to the equilibrium of a firm. A market or an economy or any other group of persons and firms, is in equilibrium, when none of its members feel impelled to change their behaviour.

Thus, in economics equilibrium means the position reached by the individual, the firm or the industry, from which there is no tendency to move. A consumer is said to be in equilibrium, when he gets the maximum satisfaction from his given expenditure on different goods and services. The firm is in equilibrium, when it attains the maximum profit or incurs the minimum loss from the sale of its product in the market. The industry is in equilibrium when there exists no incentive either for old firms to leave it or for new firms to enter into it. In short, essence of an equilibrium position is that where no participant believe that it can improve its lot by altering its behaviour.

The importance of equilibrium analysis lies with the fact that it enables us to know in advance the change in economic phenomena. Thus, the importance of the study of equilibrium flows not so much from the fact that it is actually reached in life, rather it flows from the fact that it is acting as the goal to which all the economic activities tend to approach. An economic unit, which has run into disequilibrium, strives hard to get out of it by moving towards the equilibrium. In a dynamic economy, where changes in consumer's tastes and preferences, innovations, size of population, techniques of production, etc., which disturb the attained equilibrium position, generally recur and such changes induce the various economic units to move towards the new equilibrium position having a greater economic efficiency as compared to the previous position from which **they have been disturbed.**

The equilibrium serves as economist's compass with which he can indicate the change in economic phenomena. Moreover, it would not be difficult to anticipate the future behaviour of a firm or an industry, if its equilibrium position is indicated beforehand, because all economic phenomena, prices or wages, firms or industries, are tending all the time to move their equilibrium positions. According to Professor KE Boulding **'it is usually more interesting to know where a train is going than to know where it is at any moment.'** Thus, through equilibrium we are more interested in knowing the tendency, rather than the actual position, to explain the economic phenomena. In real world, the equilibrium remains an ideal, as despite ceaseless movements and tendencies towards equilibrium, it is rarely attained.

Kinds of Equilibrium: There are several types of equilibrium, such as, stable, unstable or neutral equilibrium; static or dynamic equilibrium; single or multiple equilibrium; short run or long run equilibrium; and partial or general equilibrium. These are as follows:

Stable, Unstable or Neutral Equilibrium

A position is said to be a stable equilibrium, which the economic unit or the system has a tendency to regain or reproach, no sooner it is disturbed from this position. After the system is disturbed from equilibrium, forces of corrections are set in motion, which take the system back to the original position of equilibrium. According to Professor A.C. Pigou, **'a system is in stable equilibrium if, when any small disturbance takes place, forces come into play to re-establish the initial position.'** Similarly, Professor J.A. Schumpeter defines **'a stable equilibrium value is that if changed by a small amount, calls into action, forces that will tend to reproduce the old value.'**

A system is said to be unstable equilibrium, where an initial disturbance generates further chain of disturbances, so as to take the system further away from the said equilibrium position in a cumulative way. Professor Pigou states that, **'a system is in unstable equilibrium, if a small disturbance calls out further disturbing forces, which act in a cumulative manner to drive the system away from its initial position'**. According to Professor Schumpeter, **'an unstable equilibrium is one, change in which calls forth forces, which tend to move the system farther and farther away from the initial equilibrium value.'**

A position of neutral equilibrium is one, which after being disturbed, does not show any tendency to move back to the original position but instead comes to rest in the new position to which it has moved under the impact of forces of disturbance. Professor Pigou regards a system **'in neutral equilibrium if, when such a disturbance takes place, no re-establishing forces but also no further disturbing forces, are evoked, so that the system remains at rest in the position to which it has moved.'**

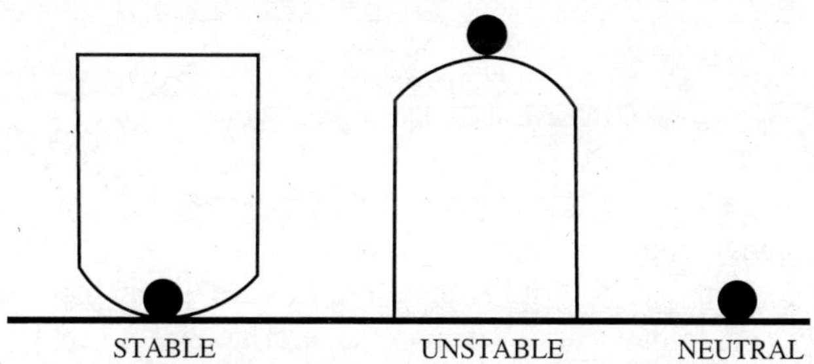

FIGURE 4.1 The Three Kinds of Equilibria.

Professor Pigou has given appropriate analogy to explain the distinction among three equilibrium positions, when he states, **'a ship with a heavy keel is in stable equilibrium; an egg lying on its side is in neutral equilibrium; and an egg poised on one of its ends, is in unstable equilibrium.'** Professor Schumpeter has illustrated the distinction among these equilibria with the help of different placements of balls, as according to him **'a ball that rests at the bottom of a bowl illustrates the stable equilibrium; a ball that rests on a billiard table illustrates the neutral equilibrium; and a ball that is perched on the top of an inverted bowl illustrates the unstable equilibrium.** Thus, a ball resting at the bottom of the bowl is in a stable equilibrium because, if disturbed it will tend to return to the original position. The ball balanced on the top of an inverted bowl is in unstable equilibrium, because even the slightest push will cause it roll down the side of the bowl away from the original position and will never return to the top of the inverted bowl. Lastly, a ball resting on the flat floor is in neutral equilibrium, because when moved away from its initial position it will rest at some new position.

In a competitive market assuming instantaneous adjustment to take place between supply and demand, stable equilibrium exists, if the prevailing market price has a tendency to be maintained, as long as the underlying demand and supply condition remain unchanged. This generally happens, where a negatively sloping demand curve faces a positively sloping supply curve, as shown in Figure 4.2.

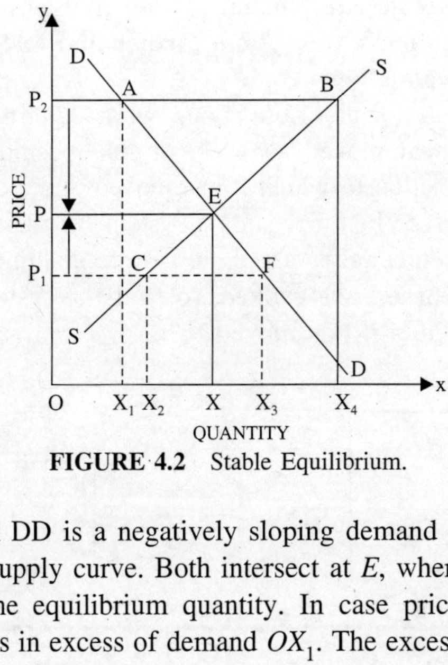

FIGURE 4.2 Stable Equilibrium.

In this diagram DD is a negatively sloping demand curve, while *SS* is a positively sloping supply curve. Both intersect at *E*, where *OP* is equilibrium price and *OX* is the equilibrium quantity. In case price increases to OP_2, where supply OX_4 is in excess of demand OX_1. The excess supply will initiate competition amongst sellers, which will bring down the price to *OP* level. On the contrary, if the price falls to OP_1, the demand OX_3 is in excess of supply OX_2. This will initiate competition amongst buyers, which will cause an increase in the price to OP level. Thus, *OP* is the stable equilibrium price. According to Marshall '**when the demand price is equal to the supply price, the amount produced has no tendency either to be increased or to be diminished; it is in equilibrium. Such an equilibrium is stable, that is, the price, if displaced a little from it, will tend to return, as a pendulum oscillates about its lowest point**'.

In case of unstable equilibrium, the price, once disturbed from the initial equilibrium position, would tend to move further away from the initial equilibrium. This can be illustrated either by taking a normal demand curve and negatively slopping supply curve or by taking a normal supply curve and a positively sloping demand curve as in Figure 4.3.

Figure 4.3(i) reveals that negatively sloping supply curve (which is rare and caused by decreasing cost of increasing production due to the various internal and external economies enjoyed by the producers) intersects negatively sloping demand curve at point *E*, which has fixed the equilibrium price at *OP* and the equilibrium quantity at *OX* level. An increase in price to OP_2 results in excess of demand OX_2 over the supply OX_1, which may cause further increase in price. On the other hand, a decrease in price to OP_1 results in excess of supply OX_4 over the demand OX_3. This excess in supply over demand may cause further reduction in the price. Thus, *E* represents an unstable equilibrium.

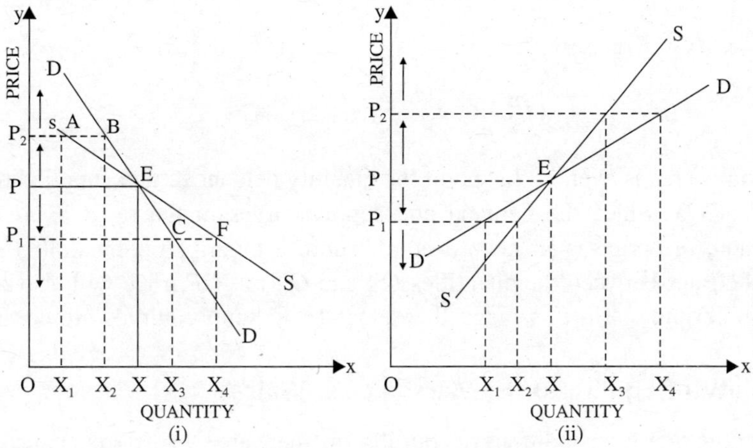

FIGURE 4.3 Unstable Equilibrium.

Similarly as, in Figure 4.3(ii) the demand curve is positively sloping. It is rare and is found in case of 'Giffen Goods' where despite increase in price, the demand continues to increase and *vice-versa.* This exceptional demand curve intersects the normal supply curve at *E*, which determines the equilibrium price at *OP* and the equilibrium quantity at *OX*. An increase in the price will result is excess of demand OX_4 over supply OX_3. This excess of demand over supply will cause a further increase in the price. On the other hand, a decrease in price to OP_1 will result in excess of supply OX_2 over demand OX_1. This will cause a further reduction in the price. Thus, *E* in this diagram is an unstable equilibrium, as the price has no tendency to return back to the original equilibrium position, once it is disturbed.

In case of neutral equilibrium, the price or output may shift from one point to the other and may get settled there. In Figure 4.4(i) demand curve *DD* intersects supply curve *SS* at *E*, where equilibrium price is *OP* and the quality demanded and supplied is *OX*. When the price comes down to OP_1 it

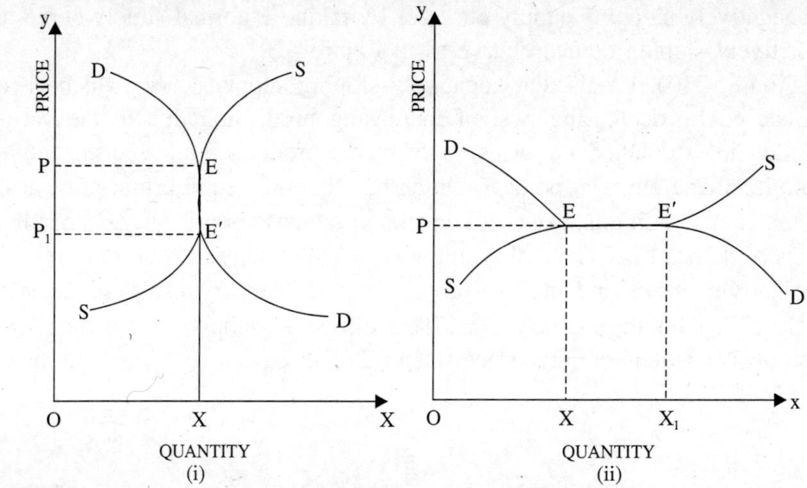

FIGURE 4.4 Neutral Equilibrium.

will stay here, as even at this point the quantity demanded and supplied remain equal at *OX*. Since the demand and supply curves in the range *E* to *E*′ are common, the price is in neutral equilibrium. Similarly, Figure 4.4(ii) shows that the sales between the quantities *OX* and OX_1 at *OP* price will also remain in equilibrium, as in this range the demand and supply curves are common.

Stability of Equilibrium—Marshall Vs. Walras

Regarding stability conditions of equilibrium, there are two different approaches, one by Marshall and the other by Walras. Marshall's approach is the price-dependent approach, where the quantity adjusts as the price changes, while Walras's approach is the quantity-dependent approach, where the price adjusts as the quantity changes.

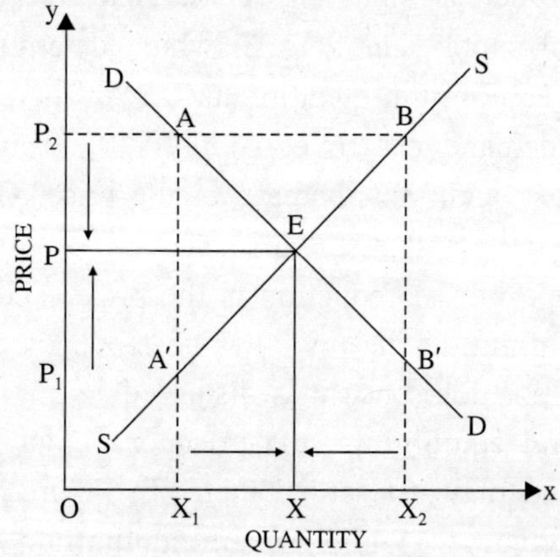

FIGURE 4.5 Stability of Equilibrium as per Marshall and Walras.

Marshall's stability condition states that when the excess demand price is positive, producers will increase the supply of the product, and will reduce it when it is negative. In Figure 4.5, when excess demand price is positive or $AX_1 > A'X_1$, that is, the demand price is greater than supply price, it means that the consumers are offering a higher price than is being planned to be charged by the producers. This will induce the producers to increase the supply from OX_1 to OX to restore the original equilibrium. On the other hand, when the excess demand price is negative, or $B'X_2 < BX_2$, that is the demand price is less than the supply price, it indicates that the buyers are offering a lower price than is being charged by the producers. This will induce producers to reduce the quantity supplied from OX_2 to OX and will, thus, restore the original equilibrium.

On the other hand, the Walrasian stability conditions state that when excess demand is positive, buyers will raise the price and if it is negative, the sellers will reduce the price. In Figure 4.5, when excess demand is positive, or $P_1B' > P_1A'$, that is, the quantity demanded is greater than the quantity supplied, the buyers will bid the price upward and when the price rises, demand falls and supply increases and the original equilibrium is restored at *E*. In case the excess demand is negative or $P_2A < P_2B$, the supply being in excess of demand, will induce the sellers to lower the price of the product form OP_2 to *OP*. It reveals that when price falls supply declines and demand increases till the original equilibrium is attained at E. Thus, both the Marshallian and Walrasian stability conditions are satisfied simultaneously, when demand curve has a negative slope and the supply curve has a positive slope.

In case, the supply curve has a negative slope, the two stability conditions cannot be fulfilled simultaneously, rather both will hold in opposite directions. Whatever is a stable equilibrium according to Marshall, the same is unstable equilibrium according to Walras and *vice-versa*. It can be explained with the help of a zig-zag negatively inclined supply curve along with the normal demand curve at in Figure 4.6.

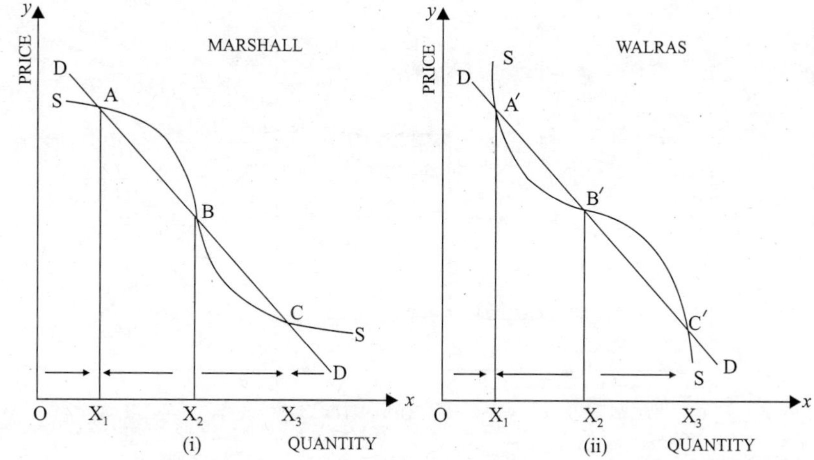

FIGURE 4.6 Comparison of Stability of Equilibrium.

There are three equilibrium positions in each figure, as on these points the demand equals the supply. According to Marshall, if the demand curve lies above the supply curve before intersecting the latter, as on points *A* and *C*, the points of intersection will result in stable equilibria Figure 4.6(i). On the contrary, if the demand curve lies below supply curve before intersecting it (B in the present case) it will be a point of unstable equilibrium.

On the other hand, according to Walras, where the demand curve intersects the supply curve from below, as on *A′* and *C′* points, the equilibria will be stable but when the demand curve intersects the supply curve from above, as on *B′* point, the equilibrium will be unstable Figure 4.6(ii). This also reveals that where the demand and supply curves intersect each other more than once, positions of stable and unstable equilibria alternate. The two approaches are directly opposite to each other, but this contradiction is only apparent. It is because both Marshall and Walras have taken different periods in their analysis. Walras has explained stability and instability, considering short period, during which adjustment takes place through changes in price. Marshall, on the other hand, had long period in his mind in which the adjustment is carried on through changes in the quantity.

Time Lag and Stability of Equilibrium

So far we discussed stable, unstable and neutral equilibrium in cases where the market adjustment to price-output changes takes place instantaneously. There are, however, situations particularly in agriculture, where adjustment takes place after a time lag, i.e., the supply adjusts itself to changes in the price not immediately but after some time has elapsed. The supply of wheat this year is not a dependent function of the price of the wheat this year but of the price that ruled in preceding year. In such case, the stability and instability can be explained through cobweb models as in Figure 4.7.

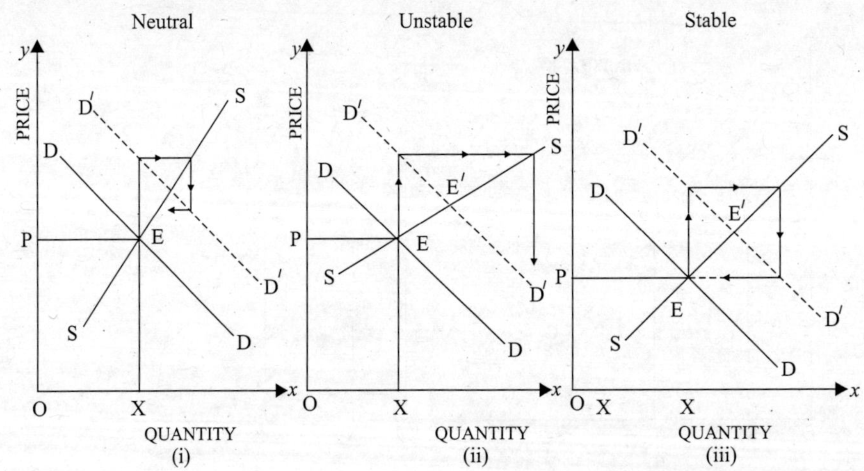

FIGURE 4.7 Time Lag and Stability of Equilibrium.

In case there happens any disequilibrium due to change in demand, then the equilibrium is attained through a series of adjustments. This adjustment process assumes the form of a cobweb woven converging towards [(Figure 4.7(i)] or diverging away [Figure 4.7(ii)] of equilibrium or oscillating along a new path [Figure 4.7(iii) that shows no tendency either towards or away from the original equilibrium. These convergent, divergent and continuous cobwebs illustrate the neutral, unstable and stable equilibrium respectively. This may happen depending upon steep, flat and normal slope of the supply curve visa-vis normal demand curve.

Static or Dynamic Equilibrium

Static equilibrium is the equilibrium in a static or stationary economy. A stationary economy is a sort of closed economy, where there is no incentive for change on the part of any organism. Such equilibrium is based on given and constant prices, quantities, incomes, tastes, technology, population, etc. Static equilibrium is a state of rest, characterised by absence of movement, where opposite forces are counteracting each other. It is a state, which every firm, industry or factor wants to attain and once reached would not like to leave. Under this the various variables are brought to equilibrium independent of time period. According to Professor J.K. Mehta **"static equilibrium is that equilibrium, which maintains itself outside the period of time under consideration"**. Similarly, Professor K.E. Boulding offers a mechanical analogy of **'a static equilibrium in the form of a ball rolling at a constant speed or better still of a forest in equilibrium, where trees sprout, grow or die out, but the composition of the forest, as a whole, remains unchanged'.**

Dynamic equilibrium relates to a progressive economy. An economic system may be said to be in a dynamic equilibrium, if its total stock, including both, things and people, changed at a constant rate and if the rates of production and consumption of all items of the stock increases at the same rate. Thus, for dynamic equilibrium the various organisms like prices, quantities, incomes, tastes, population, capital, technology, etc. must change (increase or decrease) and the change must be at a uniform rate. Such qualifications make this concept, artificial and unrealistic, as the organism do change but not necessarily at the uniform rate. Thus, over a period of time, a state of disequilibrium rather than of equilibrium is to be found. If some market participants disagree with decisions taken, it tends to alter the existing equilibrium position and the state of disequilibrium sets in. Those participants, who are in disequilibrium, in their efforts to attain the equilibrium position, throw others into disequilibrium. Thus, a chain reaction sets in, which ultimately brings the decisions of all the participants in harmony and a new equilibrium position is established. According to Professor J.K. Mehta **'when after a fixed period the equilibrium**

state is disturbed, it is called dynamic equilibrium'. Thus, the time period is of great importance in deciding whether an equilibrium is static or dynamic in nature.

Single or Multiple Equilibrium

Equilibrium is single or unique, when there is only a single set of variables like price and quantity demanded and supplied, which conforms to the conditions of equilibrium. According to George J. Stigler **'a position of unique equilibrium arises, if there is a single set of prices and quantities, which fulfill the conditions of equilibrium'.** Thus, when a demand curve intersects a supply curve at any point to determine the equilibrium, it is a single or unique equilibrium, as it determines only a single set of price and quantity demanded and supplied (Figure 4.8(i)).

Equilibrium is multiple, when there is more than single set of variables, like price and quantity demanded and supplied satisfying the conditions of equilibrium. According to Professor George J. Stigler **'multiple positions of equilibrium exist, when several different sets of prices and quantities will meet the equilibrium conditions'.** There was a widespread impression prevalent that there could be only one position of stable equilibrium, i.e., a single set of price and quantity could bring about an equilibrium. However, according to Marshall, **"under certain conceivable, though rare, conditions, there can be two or more positions of real equilibrium of demand and supply, any one of which equally consistent with the general circumstances of the market and any of which, if reached, would be stable, until some great disturbance occurred".**

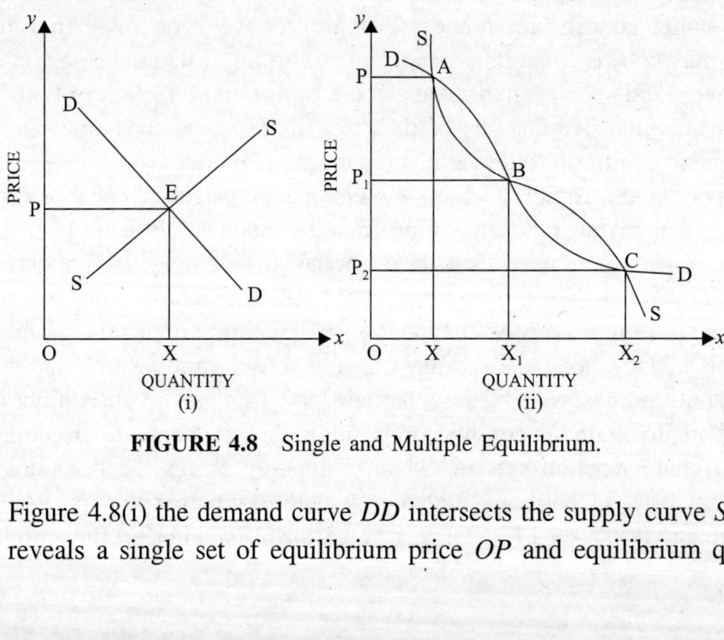

FIGURE 4.8 Single and Multiple Equilibrium.

In Figure 4.8(i) the demand curve *DD* intersects the supply curve *SS* at *E*, which reveals a single set of equilibrium price *OP* and equilibrium quantity

OX. On the other hand, in Figure 4.8(ii) the demand curve changes its slope, which is highly elastic over a portion of its length then becomes relatively inelastic and again it becomes elastic. This so happens when the market is composed of several groups of consumers, each with different income levels. Similarly, the supply curve also follows a zig-zag path and intersects the demand curve at *A*, *B* and *C* points, which represent the multiple equilibria. According to Marshall **'the position in which a small amount is produced and is sold at a higher price would be the first to be reached........ which gave the absolute maximum of aggregate satisfaction. But another position of equilibrium corresponding to a large production and a lower price would be equally satisfactory to the producers and would be much satisfactory to the consumers; the excess consumer's surplus in the second case over the first would represent the increase in aggregate satisfaction.'** The multiple equilibrium is extremely rare and is purely a formal concept, while in the real world, the single equilibrium is common.

Short Run or Long Run Equilibrium

The credit for introducing the concepts of long and short periods in economic analysis goes to Marshall, who introduced the element of time in the theory of value. He visualised four types of values; namely, market value, short period value, long period value and secular value. These values are determined by the forces of demand and supply, but the time available for adjustment to new equilibrium differs. In case of market value and short period value, the time available to adjust supply to the demand is short, hence the supply is adjusted to the changes in demand with the existing means of production. Such equilibrium is named as 'short run equilibrium'. On the other hand, in case of long period value and secular value, there is sufficient time available for adjusting the supply to changes in demand, even by varying the means of production. Such an equilibrium is called 'long run equilibrium'.

The steep positive slope of supply curve *SS* in Figure 4.9(i) reveals that the possibility of adjustment in supply to changes in demand is less. As a result, due to increase in demand, the supply increases only slightly to match the demand. It is a short run equilibrium, where the quantity exchanged is almost constant, while the price has undergone a change sufficiently at the new equilibrium *E'*. On the other hand, a flat positive slope of supply curve *SS* in Figure 4.9(ii) indicates sufficient possibility of adjustment in supply to changes in demand. As a result, due to increase in demand, the supply increases sufficiently. In such a case due to change in demand, there is slight change in price with sufficient change in quantity exchanged at the new equilibrium *E'*. Thus, in short period, the influence of demand is greater, while in long period the influence of supply is more important.

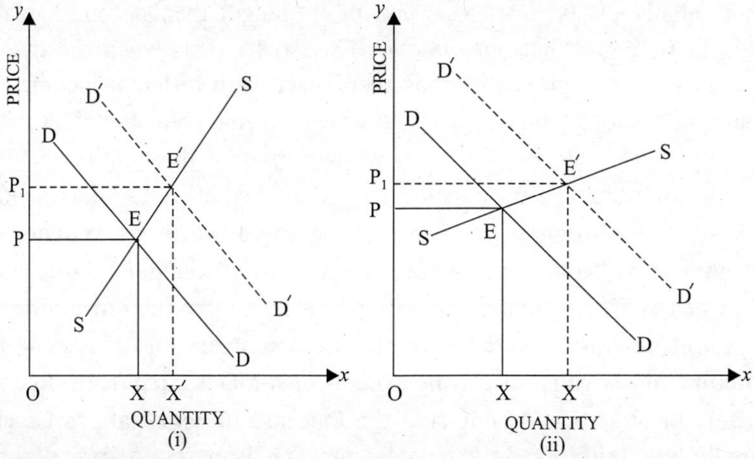

FIGURE 4.9 Short Run and Long Run Equilibrium.

Partial or General Equilibrium

Partial equilibrium analysis is generally applicable in microeconomic analysis. It is preferably called particular-equilibrium analysis, as the word partial speaks of incompleteness of the analysis, although there is nothing incomplete about it. It is a market process for the determination of product prices and factor prices in which one or two variables are discussed, keeping all others as constant. According to G.J. Stigler, **'a partial equilibrium is one, which is based on only a restricted range of data, a standard example is price of a product when prices of all other products are held fixed during the analysis'.**

Partial equilibrium analysis is concerned with two types of economic problems. Firstly, it is concerned with those pertaining to only particular aspects of the economic behaviour of a certain individual, firm or industry. Secondly, it studies only the first order consequences of the economic events. It ignores the effects on the prices of other commodities brought about by the product pricing being analysed.

Thus, it is concerned with the equilibrium determination of particular economic units, like a consumer, a resource owner, a firm, or an industry. A consumer, with given tastes, preference and money income, is in equilibrium, when he spends his money income on different goods and services in accordance with the law of equimarginal utility. A firm, with given demand conditions of its product, technological conditions and resource supplies, is in equilibrium, when it adjusts its production in such a way that it has no tendency to change its output. An industry is in equilibrium, when all its firms are earning only normal profits and there is no tendency for existing firms to leave it or new firms to enter into it. The most important representative of the partial equilibrium analysis is the Cournot-Marshall demand curve, showing price quantity relationship drawn on the *ceteris paribus* assumption. The quantity demanded of any commodity at any given time is treated as function of the price of that commodity alone, all other variables, such as purchasers' income, their tastes, and prices of related goods being assumed as given or fixed.

Partial equilibrium analysis is helpful in analysing the causes of change in the behaviour of a price, a consumer, a firm or an industry. Secondly, it helps in predicting the consequences of change in the behaviour and plans of the market participants. Thirdly, it serves as an indispensable tool of analysis for the solution of practical problems. By concentrating on limited range of economic variables, it makes the economic problems simple and intelligible. Finally, for understanding the general working of the economic system, which involves the analysis of interdependence of several economic variables, it serves as a stepping stone. According to Marshall **'the partial equilibrium analysis is easily comprehensible and more effective; it gives us simple propositions and simple analysis'.**

However, this analysis has certain limitations. It is confined to one particular economic participant, may be an individual, a firm or an industry. It is incompetent to study the inter-relations of all parts of the economy. Marshall was of the view that **'the best we can do is to examine a commodity from the angle of such variables as price, cost and quantities. We cannot easily examine every aspect, every repercussion'.** Secondly, it is based on unrealistic assumptions, which separate the study of a specific market from the rest of the economy and if such assumptions are dropped the partial equilibrium analysis breaks down. Lastly, it is based on the assumption that an economic disturbance in a particular industry has only localised effect, but it generates forces moving from one market to another and, thus initiating second, third and higher order waves of changes in the entire economy.

General equilibrium analysis is an extensive study of a number of economic variables, their inter-relations and interdependence for analysing the working of the economic system as a whole. The whole economic system is a network in which all segments are mutually dependent and interact with one another. Goods and services are either complementary or competitive, therefore, change in demand of any commodity or factor of production sets in motion a chain reaction. General equilibrium analysis considers all relevant variables that may affect a particular problem and offers an all-round analysis of the repercussions of the economic disturbance. In other words, general equilibrium analysis deals with the equilibrium of all organisms in the economy—consumers, producers, resource-owners, firms and industries.

Firms enter in product markets as suppliers of products, but they enter in factor markets as buyers of inputs; individuals or house-holds are buyers in product markets but suppliers in factor markets. General equilibrium prevails, when both the product and factor markets are in equilibrium in relation to each other in the economy. George J. Stigler has aptly remarked that **'the theory of general equilibrium is the theory of inter-relationship among all parts of the economy'.** Thus, the general equilibrium is attained when all consumers, all firms, all industries, and all factor services are in equilibrium simultaneously.

General equilibrium analysis has two variants: the first one is Walrasian model, which explains the interdependence of commodity prices, factor prices, their demands, supplies, costs, etc. in a mathematical way through a system of simultaneous equations. The second one is input-output analysis developed by Professor Leontief, who, with the help of computers and other high speed calculating machines, has made it possible to solve hundreds of equations to find out a solution.

Walrasian Model

According to this model, the economy is in a state of general equilibrium, where the demand for every commodity and service is equal to their supplies. It implies perfect harmony of decisions made by all the market participants. The quantity of each commodity the buyers want to buy is equal to the quantity sellers want to sell. Similarly, the quantity of the various factors, the owners are willing to supply, is equal to the quantity firms or producers are willing to employ.

Such model is based on certain assumptions: (i) There exists a closed economy having households and firms, where the firms sell commodities to the households which, in turn, sell resources to the firms. (ii) There is perfect competition both in the commodity market and factor market. (iii) Incomes and tastes of consumers are given, known and constant. (iv) There is no change in technology and all firms operate under identical cost conditions. (v) All units of a productive service are homogeneous and firms experience constant returns to scale, (vi) There is full employment, as house-holds derive their income solely from the sale of resources and spend the whole of their incomes on consumption.

Under such a situation in the economy, the quantity of each commodity demanded depends not only on its own price but also on the prices of each other commodity. In the model, each consumer is assumed to spend his entire income on consumption. The income depends on the price, the consumer fetches on the productive resources he supplies. Thus, the demand of consumers for the various commodities depends upon their prices and prices of productive resources. For this the product and factor prices are determined simultaneously. Similarly, on the supply side, the price at which the commodities are to be sold depends on its cost of production. The costs depend on the quantities of the various factors employed and the prices paid for them. The supply depends on cost to firms, which, in turn, on the prices and the quantities of the various services used by them.

Thus, the economy will be in the state of general equilibrium, when the commodity prices make each demand equal to its supply and factor prices make the demand of each factor equal to its supply, so that all commodity markets and factor markets are in equilibrium. It also implies that all consumers and producers in the economy are in equilibrium.

Regarding process of adjustment for the equilibrium, Walras suggested a gropping process. Here all buyers and sellers announce the quantities they wish to buy and sell at stated prices. In case there is negative excess demand, sellers offer at lower prices and when there is positive excess demand buyers offer higher prices. All consumers and producers continue to make such announcements till they hit upon a price, which makes excess demand equal to zero and brings equilibrium in the general market.

This general equilibrium analysis presents a picture of economy's equilibrium, where consumers are attuned to a position of maximum satisfaction and the producers to that of maximum profits. It helps in understanding the working of economic system and the complex problems of the market. It enables to understand the working of the pricing process and serves as a basis for modern monetary theory and welfare economics.

It suffers from certain limitations, as it is based on a number of unrealistic assumptions like, perfect competition and others. Secondly, it is a static model, as all consumers and producers in the model consume and produce the same products day in and day out without any time lag and thus, their decisions are in perfect harmony. Lastly, many of the unrealistic assumptions cannot be ignored, as the entire Walrasian model is a set of simultaneous equations, which breaks down in the absence of these assumptions.

Input-Output Analysis: It is a recent and simpler variant of the general equilibrium analysis and is an empirical descendant of the abstract Walrasian approach. In this analysis, the whole economy is divided into a number of sectors or industries. Households and government are considered as sectors or industries of final demand. Each industry is viewed as sellers of its products, which become inputs (factors of production) of purchasing industries. Thus, all industries are interdependent and the interdependence is established in the form of input-output tableau, which consists of duly classified data about the inter-industry flows of goods, services and resources. With this, equations are established relating to outputs of each industry and the industries of final demand. While doing so, it is assumed that the technology will remain unchanged; there are no joint products; and there is no change in the relative quantities of inputs used in various industries.

Under such situation, the output of each industry will depend directly upon the outputs of all industries, which utilise these products. Here, we have one equation for each industry's product relating its output to outputs of other industries. These equations are mathematically soluble. In case available input supplies, consumer's demand and production functions are known, it is possible to calculate the magnitudes of output of all sectors by a system of simultaneous equations.

Theoretical framework of input-output analysis is simple, but it is difficult to fill the necessary statistical data for determining the actual magnitudes in a system of equations. Secondly, there are numerous sectors in the real economy, but due to limited resources, capacities (like, data, computer, etc.) the number of sectors or industries is kept small. As a result, each represents a heterogeneous conglomeration of goods and services. Thirdly, the assumptions of unchanged technology and constant returns to scale are highly unrealistic. Lastly, the fixed input-output relationship between the various sectors precludes the possibility of change in the inventories, which, as a result, ignores the consideration of capital formation. These limitations coupled with lack of adequate data on consumer demand functions and production functions resulted in slow progress of this analysis.

Despite these limitations, the general equilibrium analysis is getting wider applications in the field of international trade, theory of value, welfare economics and monetary theory. Thus, there is hardly any aspect of macroeconomic theory, which has not been benefited from the application of general equilibrium analysis.

Review Questions

1. Explain the term 'equilibrium' in economics and bring out its various kinds.
2. Distinguish between stable and unstable equilibrium and bring out the neutral equilibrium.
3. Elucidate the general equilibrium and bring out the limitations of partial equilibrium analysis.
4. Explain the conditions for Marshallian and Walrasian stable and unstable equilibrium.
5. Distinguish between partial and general equilibrium approach to economic analysis. What are the advantages and limitations of general equilibrium analysis?
6. 'Equilibrium is that model condition that cannot be achieved in the real world.' Discuss and state the conditions under which the equilibrium has utility in the economic analysis.
7. Explain the concept of general equilibrium and bring out the importance of this concept in economic analysis.
8. Elucidate the Walrasian model of general equilibrium analysis.

PART-II

MICROECONOMICS

SUB PART-I
CONSUMPTION

5

Consumption and Demand Analysis

The dictionary meaning of consumption is 'destruction' and therefore, earlier economists defined consumption as 'destruction of matter'. However, matter is never destroyed, it simply changes its form in the process of consumption. Later on, consumption has been considered as 'destruction of utility' but this is the result of consumption, rather than being consumption itself. Moreover, mere destruction of utility is not consumption. For example, when clothes are burnt to ashes and ink is poured on the floor, their utility is destroyed, but by no means can these actions be regarded as consumption.

Thus, the consumption refers to process through which the utility of goods is destroyed for the satisfaction of human wants. According to Albert Julius Meyer, 'consumption is the direct and final use of economic goods or personal services in the satisfaction of human wants.'

Alfred Marshall regards 'consumption as negative production, as both are regarded as acts for removal of wants, where in the process of production it yields unit by unit an increasing satisfaction, while in the process of consumption, it yields unit by unit decreasing satisfaction. American economist Richard T. Ely has defined consumption as, the use of economic goods or personal services in the satisfaction of human wants. Thus, consumption refers to the use of goods or services for satisfaction of human wants. The expectation of satisfaction before actual consumption in economics is called utility.

MEANING OF UTILITY

Utility refers to the power, quality or capacity of a commodity or service that satisfies human wants. It is subjective and relates to inner sentiments and emotions. It has no physical or material existence and is an abstract thing. It simply depends upon the mental frame of the consumer of a commodity or service. It lies with the desire of the consumer and not with the things. Thus, it can be defined as **'the quality of a commodity or service, which makes it an object of the desire to the consumers'.** In other words, utility is the power, quality or capacity that makes **'an object a good and not rubbish, an action a service and not a futile gesture'.** For utility, desiredness is the sole consideration; usefulness, legal or ethical considerations have nothing to do with the determination of utility. Utility is a relative phenomenon, which varies from person to person, from time to time and from place to place and depends to a large extent on culture and civilisation.

The term utility should be differentiated from 'satisfaction', **Utility implies 'expected satisfaction', whereas 'satisfaction stands for realised utility'**. A consumer thinks of 'utility', when he is contemplating the purchase of a commodity, but he secures the satisfaction only after the consumption of the commodity. There may be a glaring gap between utility and satisfaction, for example, while contemplating purchases the consumer may expect high utility but after actual consumption, the 'satisfaction' may not come up to the expectation. Similarly, the utility is measurable indirectly but satisfaction can be measured neither directly nor indirectly. Despite these gaps, in the entire theory of consumer's behaviour, it is assumed that utility and satisfaction are synonymous.

Utility can be measured in terms of either cardinal numbers or ordinal numbers. Classical economists expressed the utility in terms of the cardinal numbers, like 5, 25, 125, etc. which are derived on the basis of the amount the consumer stands ready to pay in order to get the commodity. Neo-classical economists introduced an arbitrary unit of measurement of utility called 'utils' to express utility in terms of the cardinal numbers. Modern economists believe that utility is a psychological phenomenon and is inherently immeasurable, therefore, they advocated for the ordinal measurement in place of the cardinal measurement . According to this measurement, utility is expressed in terms of ranks or orders and this has introduced iso-utility or indifference curves in the economic analysis.

Utility expressed in terms of cardinal numbers is usually the marginal utility, and from this, the total and the average utilities are derived. The total utility reveals the level of total satisfaction expected from the consumption or possession of certain quantity of a commodity or service. It depends on the quantity of expected consumption or possession and increases at decreasing rate till the consumer is fully satisfied. The average utility is equal to the total utility divided by number of units of expected consumption or possession. It decreases as the number of units of expected consumption or possession increases. The marginal utility signifies extra satisfaction to be derived by a consumer from the consumption or possession of an extra unit of commodity. This represents the difference made to the total utility due to unit reduction or addition to the quantity of consumption or possession. In other words, it is the rate of change in total utility, as the consumption or possession of a commodity changes.

The utility is, thus, an important phenomenon in economics. This may be measured in terms of the cardinal numbers like 5, 25, 100 and so on, which may be expressed as total utility, average utility and marginal utility. Alfred Marshall and other contemporary economists analysed the consumer's behaviour as per this measurement of utility. As per cardinal measurement of marginal utility, economists have discovered two fundamental laws related to the marginal utility. These are: (i) law of diminishing marginal utility, and (ii) law of equi-marginal utiliy, where the former reveals the behaviour pattern of the marginal utility on the successive units of consumption or possession, and the latter related expenditure pattern of buyers on different goods of consumption or possession (This has been detailed in the cardinal utility analysis chapter on consumer's behaviour.)

LAW OF DIMINISHING MARGINAL UTILITY

The law has been discovered for the first time by a **Prussian economist Hermann Heinrich Gossen, hence it is also known as the Gossen's first law of consumption, which states that 'the amount of one and the same enjoyment diminishes continuously, as we proceed with that enjoyment without interruption until satiety is reached'. This has been elaborated and refined by Alfred Marshall later on. According to Marshall, "The additional benefit, which a person derives from a given increase of his stock of a thing diminishes with every increase in the stock that he already has."**

This law is based on two important facts. Firstly, while the total wants of a consumer are virtually unlimited, but each want, taken by itself, is capable of being satisfied to the full extent. Thus, a consumer, when he feels the want of a thing, initially expects positive utility, which declines along with every increase in the quantity of that thing and ultimately a point in consumption is reached, when he needs no more of that thing. It is the point of satiety, which means zero marginal utility of that commodity. Secondly different goods are imperfect substitutes for one another in the satisfaction of the various particular wants. Everything consumed by a person has some quantitative relation with other things and if the purchase of only one thing, say shirt, is increased, it cannot substitute other things (say trousers and shoes) and therefore, it will yield diminishing satisfaction.

Thus, the goods are consumed in certain appropriate proportions and by increasing the quantity of a single commodity, the consumer disturbs this proportion and by doing so, he will get only decreasing satisfaction. **This law is derived through the method of introspection, wherein the observer reconstructs event, which go on in the mind of another person with the help of self-observation.** This form of comprehension may be just a guess work or intuition or the result of **'long lasting experience.'**

Thus, the law is based on such a psychological reading of the consumer, where we attribute to another person, what we know of our own mind. We know for ourselves that as we get more of a thing, the less utility we derive from additional units of it, the same is true with other persons. Some economists contend that 'we cannot see inside the heads of other persons' and hence they used an alternative method known as behaviourism for judging the consumer's behaviour. Here we draw conclusions about consumer's behaviour by observing his actual behaviours in a given price income situation and judge the effect of price and income changes on his purchases.

Thus, derived on the basis of introspection or observation, the law of diminishing marginal utility describes a familiar and fundamental tendency of human nature. It further assumes that; (i) the tastes of the consumer remain unchanged during the process of consumption; (ii) all units of the commodity are homogeneous, that is, they are alike in size and quality; (iii) there is no time-gap between the consumption of successive units of the commodity; (iv) units of consumption are of appropriate size; (v) prices of different units remain unchanged; (vi) the commodity should be perfectly divisible; (vii) the consumer exhibits rational behaviour; and (viii) the commodity is one single and not a combination of many goods.

The law of diminishing marginal utility can be explained with the help of a schedule and a figure as follows:

TABLE 5.1 Marginal Utility and Total Utility

Units of Commodity	*Total Utility*	*Marginal Utility*
0	0	0
1	4	4
2	7	3
3	9	2
4	10	1
5	10	0
6	9	–1
7	7	–2

The total utility refers to the total satisfaction to be derived by the consumer from the consumption of a given quantity of goods. The marginal utility, on the other hand, refers to the additional utility to be derived from the consumption of an additional unit of the goods. Symbolically,

$$u_1 = \frac{dU}{dQ}$$

where u_1 means the marginal utility, dU means change in total utility and dQ stands for a change in the quantity.

Thus, the marginal utility is the rate of change in total utility caused by a unit change in the total quantity of the goods. The total utility has increased from 4 to 10 utils, but the marginal utility has declined from 4 to 0. Beyond this level of consumption the marginal utility is negative, as the consumer suffers disutility, while even the total utility, though positive, has started declining.

Figure 5.1 relating to total and marginal utilities show a well-defined relationship between these two utility concepts as follows:

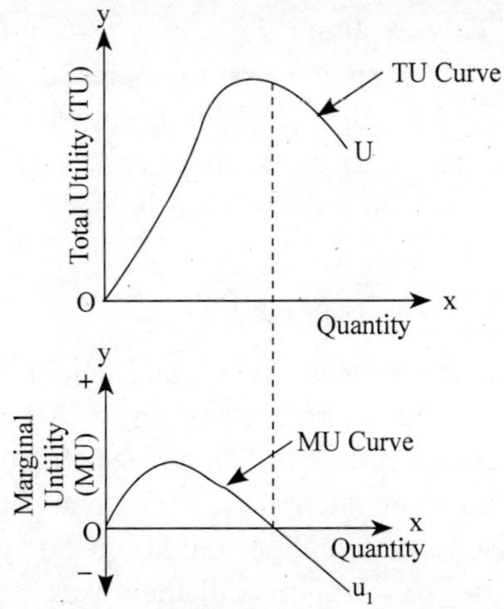

FIGURE 5.1 Total and Marginal Utility Curves.

Thus, while the marginal utility keeps on declining, the total utility continues to increase, as long as the marginal utility is positive. It indicates that the positive slope of the total utility (i.e., marginal utility) curve goes on diminishing until it reaches the zero mark. In terms of the differential calculus it means that while the value of the first derivative or the slope of total utility curve is positive (i.e., $dU/dQ > 0$), the value of the second derivative or the slope of the marginal utility is negative (i.e., $dU/dQ < 0$).

This means that while the slope of the total utility is positive and that of the marginal utility it is negative. The point where the slope of the total utility is zero, the marginal utility is zero and the total utility is maximum. Beyond this, the slope of total utility becomes negative showing that the marginal utility is negative.

There are certain exceptions to this law. Firstly, the consumption of intoxicants is not subject to the law of diminishing marginal utility. Secondly, acquisition of money is also not subject to this law. Thirdly, in case of certain hobbies, such as collection of stamps, coins, rare pictures, etc, the more one collects the more utility he derives. Fourthly, if the commodity is consumed in critical minimum quantities, (e.g., water is consumed drop by drop) the law of diminishing marginal utility will not apply.

Despite these exceptions or limitations of the law, it is one of the basic laws of economics. It provides foundation for the various laws of consumption, such as, law of demand, law of equi-marginal utility, consumer's surplus, etc. Law of demand, which states that the larger quantity of the commodity would be bought at a lower price than at a higher price, is explained largely in terms of the principle of diminishing marginal utility. Thus, if more and more units of a commodity are bought, its marginal utility to the consumer becomes less and less and, as a result, he progressively gives lesser importance to additional units of the commodity. He will, therefore, buy additional units of the commodity only at a lower price. **This explains the famous 'diamond– water paradox' of Adam Smith**, as due to its relative scarcity diamond possesses high marginal utility and so a high price, though its total utility in use is not that high. On the other hand, since the water is abundant, it possesses low marginal utility and hence low price, though its total utility in use is high.

NATURE AND KINDS OF DEMAND

There are three terms namely, desire, want and demand, that are, in general, used interchangeably, but in economics these differ. All individuals may desire goods and services for consumption, but all desires are not wants, as only those desires are wants for whose satisfaction the individuals have means (resources) at their disposal and also have intention, unlike misers, to use those resources for satisfaction of the desire. Similarly all their wants are not demands, but only those wants for goods and services may become their demands, which the consumer stands ready to buy at given price per unit of time, i.e., per day, per week, per month, etc. Thus, favourable price and time considerations for wants may turn them into demands.

The study of demand is of prime importance in the microeconomics or the price theory, as it is one of the two forces that determine the price of any product, the other being the supply. **The demand refers to the various quantities of a commodity or service that consumers would buy in a given period of time at the various prices, at the various income levels or at the various prices of the related goods.** The demand for a product depends upon a number of factors, such as price, buyers' incomes, availability and price of substitutes or competing goods, advertising and sales promotion activities, population, geographic location of buyers, expected future trend in prices, changes in consumer's tastes, needs and preferences, changes in consumer credit facilities, etc. However, it is rather difficult to consider all these factors simultaneously to study the demand for a particular product. A few of the above factors deserve consideration, as they underlie the consumers demand behaviour of almost all products. These factors are: price, income and price of related goods. These factors have greatest influence on demand and represent controllable variables, commonly used in demand studies.

There are, accordingly, three kinds of demand, namely, price demand, income demand and cross demand. The demand of an individual consumer for a product is called individual demand, whereas that of all consumers combined together is known as market demand. An effort is being made here to explain the various kinds of demand as well.

Price Demand

In refers to the various quantities of a commodity or service that consumers would buy in the market at the various hypothetical prices in a given period of time. In other words, **the price demand reveals the relation between the two variables (i.e., price and quantity demanded) assuming all other determinants of the demand, including income of buyers, price of related goods, consumers' temperament and future expectations of price changes to remain unchanged.** Thus, price demand shows the relation of the price change with the quantity demanded in the market. Mathematically,

$$Q = f(P)$$

is read as the quantity demanded (Q) is a function of or depends upon the price (P) of the commodity. When the quantities bought by one buyer at the various prices is dealt with, it is called individual price demand, but when the quantities purchased by all buyers of the commodity at the various price levels are dealt with, it is known as total demand, industry demand or market demand.

Demand Schedules and Curves: The tabular presentation of the relationship between the variation in price and the quantity demanded is known as demand schedule. In case, we put down the various hypothetical prices of the commodity in one column and the corresponding quantities that buyers would purchase in the other, it is individual price demand schedule. Similarly, we may have industry demand schedule representing the purchases of all buyers in the market at the various prices.

TABLE 5.2 Price Demand Schedule

Individual Demand		*Market-Demand*			
Price (P)	*Quantity Demanded (Q)*	*Quantity Demanded (units)* $(Q_1)\ (Q_2)\ (Q_3)$			*Total Quantity (units)*
₹	Units				
10	20	10	15	5	30
9	22	14	20	6	40
8	25	18	25	7	50

The schedule can be extended to any range of the prices, but ordinarily it is for a limited range. The market demand schedule is nothing, but the total sum of a large number of individual demand schedules.

The demand schedule can be plotted on a graph paper with the quantities measured along the horizontal x-axis (or abscissa) and the prices measured along the vertical y-axis (or ordinate) as in Figure 5.2.

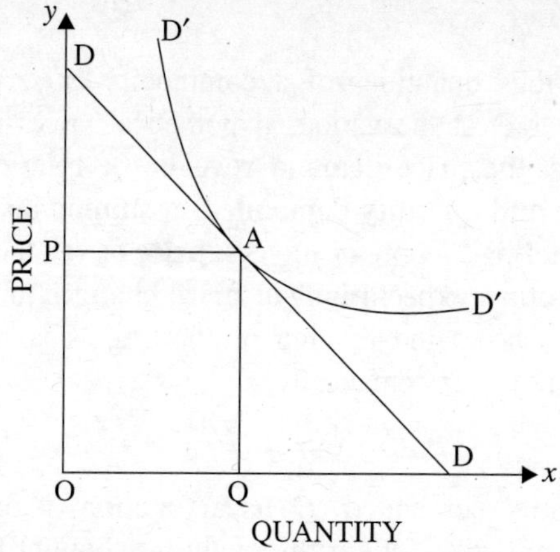

FIGURE 5.2 Demand Line or Curve.

The combination of the various points showing price-quantity relations yields a price demand curve. Sometimes, such relationship is linear and the demand function is shown by a straight line (*DD*), but generally the relationship is more complex and is portrayed by a curve (*D'D'*). In Figure 5.2 at point *A* the price charged is *OP* and the quantity demanded is *OQ*. An increase in price along with the demand curve results into a decrease in quantity demanded also known as a contraction of demand. Similarly, a decrease in price along with the demand curve will result into an increase in the quantity demanded, which is also known as an extension of demand. Price remaining the same, due to a shift in the demand curve upwards or downwards, the quantity demanded may increase or decrease, which is known as change (increase or decrease) in the demand.

Extension and Contraction of Demand

Extension or contraction in quantity demanded is caused by changes in the price of the commodity. It is also known as increase or decrease in quantity demanded, which indicates a movement up or down on the same demand curve. In Figure 5.3(i) at point *A* on *DD* curve, the price is *OP* and the demand is *OQ*. Movement towards point *B* indicates a contraction in the demand, as it has come down to OQ_0 in response to an increase in price from *OP* to OP_1 and movement towards *C* indicates an extension in the demand or increase in quantity demanded, which has increased to OQ_1 in response to a decrease in price from *OP* to OP_0.

Increase and Decrease of Demand

Increase or decrease in demand, on the other hand, involves a shift of the demand curve. An increase in demand is denoted by a shift of entire demand

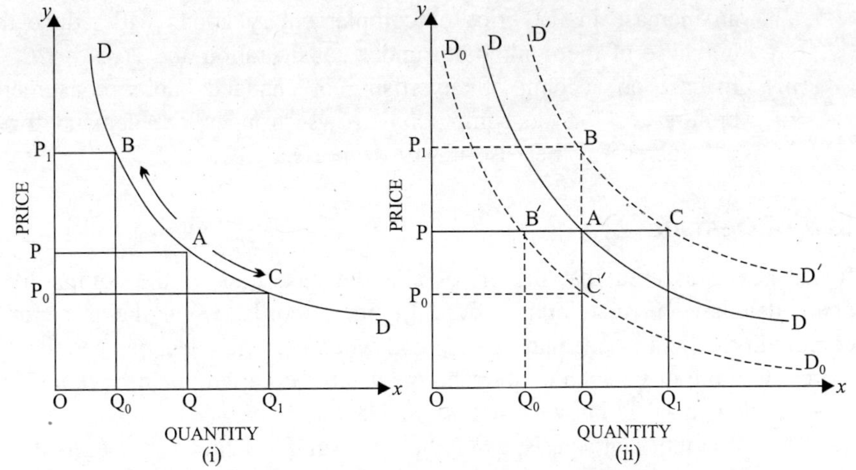

FIGURE 5.3 Kinds of Change in Demand.

curve to the right to *D'D'* level and decrease in the demand is represented by a shift of the demand curve to the left to D_0D_0 level. Figure 5.3(ii) depicts increase and decrease in demand.

At point *A* on the original demand curve *DD*, the price is *OP* and the quantity demanded is *OQ*. Increase in demand involves a shift of the demand curve to the right from *DD* to *D'D'* level, which means a larger quantity may be bought (OQ_1 at point *C*) at the original price *OP*; (ii) the same *OQ* quantity in the absence of its increase may be bought at a higher price (OP_1 at point *B*). Similarly, a decrease in demand involves a shifting of the demand curve to the left from *DD* to D_0D_0, which means a lesser quantity may be bought at the original price *OP* at point *B'* on D_0D_0 demand curve; or (ii) the original quantity *OQ*, in the absence of its reduction, may be bought at a lower price OP_0 at point *C'* on the D_0D_0 demand curve. Such increase or decrease in demand is the result of change in the income of consumers, relatively higher or lower prices of related goods or consumers' temperaments:

(i) A rise in money income will impel people to raise their demand for all kinds of goods. As income goes up, more goods are demanded at existing prices. On the other hand, a decrease in income during a depression compels the consumers to curtail their demand for goods, hence at current prices the consumers would buy less of that commodity.

(ii) A change in the price of related goods will also bring a change in the demand for given commodity. In case the price of substitute commodity increases, the demand for the commodity under consideration increases, because consumers will shift their purchases to this commodity from the costlier substitute goods. Reverse will be the case, if the price of substitute goods declines. Similarly an increase in the price of complementary goods will reduce the purchase of the commodity under consideration and *vice-versa.*

(iii) In case on account of advertising or changed habits, consumers' preferences for the commodity grows stronger, the demand for it will increase, otherwise it will decrease.

Law of Demand

It has been observed that the prices and the quantities of the commodities demanded have inverse relationship. In other words, when the price of a commodity is high the demand is low and when the price declines people buy more and more of it. Such relationship between the variations in price and the quantity demanded is known as 'Law of Demand'.

The important characteristics of the 'Law of Demand' are as follows:

1. There is inverse relationship between the variation in the price and the variation in the quantity demanded. Thus if the price rises, the demand falls and if the price falls, the demand goes up.
2. Under the law of demand, the price is an independent variable and the quantity demanded is a dependent variable. Thus, it is the effect of the variation in price on demand, that is examined and not the effect of the variation in demand on price.
3. Law of demand also assumes other things to remain unchanged. In other words, it assumes that there is no change in the consumer's income, prices of related goods, consumer's tastes and preferences, expected future trend in prices, etc. otherwise despite rise in the price, there may be an increase in the demand and *vice-versa.*
4. The inverse relationship between the price and the quantity demanded as per 'Law of Demand' rests on three considerations:

   (i) **Income Effect:** In the case the price of a commodity falls, after the usual purchase of the lower priced commodity, the buyer will have some money left unspent at his disposal, which may be considered as equivalent to an increase in the money income of the consumer. A part of money, thus saved, may be 'utilised for purchasing some more units of the commodity. Similarly, when the price of a commodity rises, the consumer's income is, in effect, reduced and he has to curtail his expenditure on all commodities, including the commodity, whose price has increased.

   (ii) **Substitution Effect:** When the price of a commodity declines, it becomes cheaper in relation to all other goods purchased. As a result, many consumers will shift their purchases from high-priced substitute goods to the low-priced commodity under consideration, which may result in an increase in its demand. It other words, the consumers will substitute that commodity for other commodities, which have now become relatively costly.

(iii) **Law of Diminishing Marginal Utility:** In order to obtain maximum total utility, the consumers are bound to demand more units of the commodity, whose price has gone down. This statement is based on the 'Law of Diminishing Marginal Utility'. The consumer is supposed to be in equilibrium, when the ratio of marginal utility and price of all commodities, he consumes is equal, mathematically when,

$$\frac{U_1}{P_1} = \frac{U_2}{P_2} = \ldots\ldots\ldots\ldots\ldots = \frac{U_n}{P_n} = d$$

where U_1, U_2 and U_n represent marginal utilities and P_1, P_2 and P_n, represent the prices of Q_1, Q_2 and Q_n commodities respectively. In case P_1 declines, in order to remain in the equilibrium, the consumer will try to reduce U_1, which is possible only when the consumer purchases more units of Q_1 commodity. Thus, all this results into demand for a larger quantity at a lower price and a smaller quantity at a higher price.

(iv) **Entry or Exit of Buyers:** In case, there is a decrease in the price of any commodity, the consumers, who were not purchasing that commodity previously, because of higher price, will now enter into the market to purchase some units of that commodity. Similarly, if there is an increase in the price of any commodity, the marginal consumers will stop purchasing the commodity. This will result into a change in the market demand for the commodity.

The inverse relationship between the price and the quantity demanded is almost universal and, hence, has been named as 'Law of Demand', but it does not hold well in the following cases:

1. 'The Law of Demand' does not apply in case of goods generally meant for conspicuous consumption, where purchases are made not for the direct satisfaction, which these purchases may yield, but for the impression, which they create on other persons. In such cases, along with rise in the price, these goods are purchased in larger quantities, as is the case with demand for diamonds, costly jewelleries, etc.
2. Future expectations also render the 'Law of Demand' inapplicable. In speculative market, a rise in price is frequently followed by larger purchases and *vice-versa.* If the price of shares or securities rises, people expect further rise in its price in future, hence they rush to

buy more of it. Similarly, when price of shares or securities falls, buyers wait for further decrease in price and, hence, they stop buying.

3. Giffen's Paradox is another exception to the 'Law of Demand'. It is based on the survey of people of Ireland conducted by Sir Robert Giffen, hence called Giffen's Paradox. Working class people of Ireland were so poor that they spent a major part of their income on bread (a cheap food stuff) and a small portion on meat. When the price of bread increased they had to economise on meat consumption and to fill the gap caused by a reduction in meat consumption, more bread had to be purchased, because bread were still considered as the cheapest food stuff. Thus, the sale of bread increased along with increase in its price. Such an exception may recur in case, where a considerable part of the total income is spent on inferior commodities.

Despite these exceptions, the law of demand is valid generalisation for most of commodities demanded in the market. Thus, other things remaining unchanged, more units of a commodity are bought at a lower price and *vice-versa*, though some of the buyers may not behave on this generalised pattern under exceptional circumstances.

Income Demand

It refers to the various quantities of a product, which a consumer would be prepared to purchase at various levels of his income. It is assumed that all other things, that is, the price of the product, consumer's preference and price of related (substitute or complementary) goods, will remain unchanged. Thus, the income demand expresses the relationship between the income and quantity of the commodity demanded. Such relationship depends on the nature of the commodity, which may be superior or inferior.

In case of superior commodities there is a positive relationship between variation in income of the consumer and the quantity of the commodity demanded. Such goods are purchased in larger quantities, as consumer's income increases. Empirical studies have also confirmed, that valuable things, like automobiles etc., have brisk sales in the periods during which the national income rises.

Inferior goods are of cheaper quality and are not strongly desired for one reason or the other. Such goods are usually purchased by people belonging to lower income strata. When people reach higher income brackets, they become reluctant, sooner or later, to purchase goods identified with the tastes of the poor, if even more expensive substitute is available.

The relationship between income and quantity demanded can be expressed with the help of an income demand schedule as follows:

TABLE 5.3 Income Demand Schedule

Superior Goods		*Inferior Goods*	
Income ₹	*Quantity (Units)*	*Income ₹*	*Quantity (Units)*
100	10	100	35
250	20	250	15
500	35	500	5

The quantity of the superior commodity is increasing along with increase in the income of the consumer, because quantity purchased by him previously, when his income was at lower level, was insufficient to give him full satisfaction (i.e., zero marginal utility). Hence, along with increase in income, the consumers will add more and more units to his schedule of consumption, which will increase the demand of the commodity. On the other hand, the purchase of inferior goods declines along with increase in the income of the consumer. It is because previously such goods (like, coarse grains) were demanded under compulsion for want of money and when the income goes up, the consumer shifts to the purchase of superior goods (like superior grains), which he can now afford due to increase in his income. This can also be exhibited with the help of income demand curves as shown in Figs. 6.4. Income demand curve for superior goods has a positive slope indicating a rise in purchases of the commodity as income of the consumer increases Figure 5.4(i), whereas the same for inferior goods has exhibited a negative slope indicating a decrease in purchases along with increase in the income of the consumer Figure 5.4(ii).

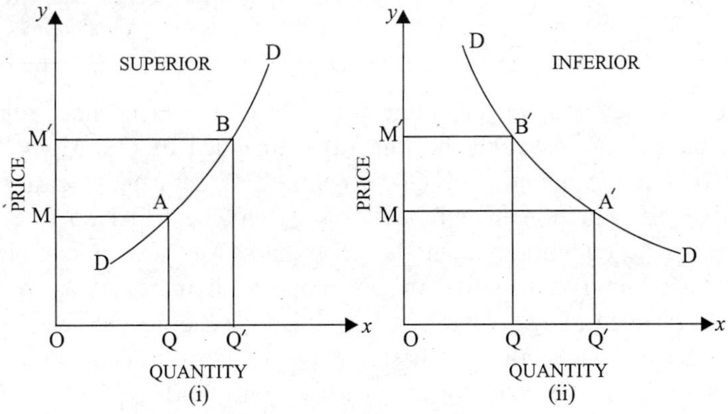

FIGURE 5.4 Kinds of Income Demand.

Cross Demand

It refers to the various quantities of a product, which a consumer would buy at the various prices, not of this product, but of a product closely related to it. We again assume that the other determinants of demand, namely, the price of the product, income of the consumer and consumer preferences should remain unchanged. Generally all goods are interrelated, in the sense that as the price of any good changes, less or more purchasing power is left with which to buy other goods. But for this type of demand, a close relationship of each other is needed. Among closely related goods the relation can be either that of substitute or of complementary to each other.

In case of substitute, competitive or rival product, if the price of one product increases, it induces people to shift their purchases to the other product, whose demand, as result, increases. The basic reason is that they purchase less of the product, whose price has increased and purchase more of the substitute product.

On the other hand, the complementary or jointly demanded products are commonly used together in satisfying a given want. If we acquire less or more of a product, we desire less or more of the other product, such as, pen and ink. In such a case, if the price of one product rises, less of it will be bought and, as a result, less of the complementary product associated with it.

The demand for a particular product in relation to the price of a related product can be explained with the help of cross demand schedule as follows:

TABLE 5.4 Cross Demand Schedule

Substitute products		*Complementary products*	
Price of Q_1	*Quantity of Q_2*	*Price of Q_1*	*Quantity of Q_2*
₹	Units	₹	Units
5	10	5	15
7	12	7	12
9	15	9	10

The cross demand for substitute products reveals a positive relationship between the price of Q_1 and the quantity demanded of Q_2. Along with rise in price of Q_1, the quantity of Q_1 as per law of demand, declines and the gap caused by reduction in purchases of Q_1 will be filled up by additional purchases of Q_2 commodity. On the other hand, in case of complementary goods such relation is negative, where along with increase in price Q_1 the quantity demanded of Q_2 commodity diminishes because increase in price of Q_1 might have reduced the purchases of Q_1, which ultimately have reduced the purchases of Q_2, because Q_2 can be used only with Q_1 and never alone.

Diagrammatic presentation shows a positively sloping cross demand curve for the substitute goods and a negatively slopping one for the complementary goods. Here *DD*, a cross demand curve for substitute goods Q_1, slopes upwards to the right showing an increase in the quantity demanded from OQ_2 to OQ_2' in response to increase in the price of substitute goods from OP_1 to OP'_1

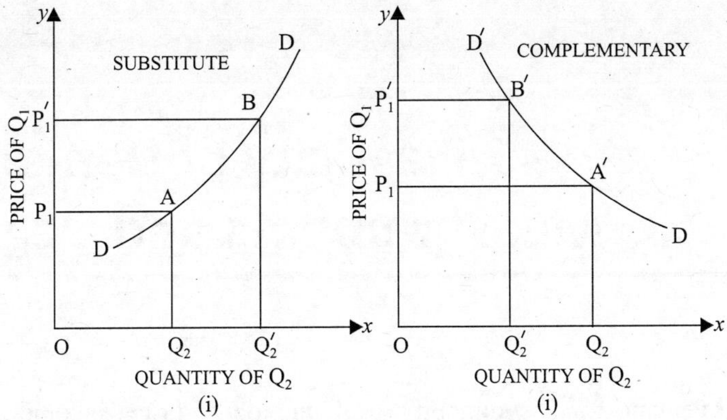

FIGURE 5.5 Kinds of Cross Demand.

Figure 5.5(i). *D'D'*, a cross demand curve for complementary goods, sloping downwards to the right, shows a decrease in the quantity demanded from OQ_2 to OQ'_2 along with increase in the price of complementary goods (Q_1) from OP_1 to OP'_1 and *vice-versa* (Figure 5.5(ii)). Thus, the exact relationship between price of a particular commodity and quantity demanded of a related commodity depends upon the nature of such relationship.

Review Questions

1. Elucidate consumption and explain the term utility and its measurements.
2. Examine the law of diminishing marginal utility and state reasons for its application and exceptions.
3. Examine the factors that determine the demand for a commodity.
4. Discuss the law of demand. What are its assumptions?
5. Substitution effect is the result of change in relative price of the commodity, when the price of other things remain the same. Explain.
6. 'There exists no law for income and cross demand'. Discuss.
7. Bring out the reasons for application of law of demand.
8. Explain the distinction between change in demand and change in quantity demanded.
9. Bring out the exceptions to the law of demand and explain the Giffen's Paradox.
10. 'Income demand patterns reveal the quality of the product bought.' Explain.
11. 'Cross demand patterns indicate the degree of substitutability of the products'. Discuss.

6

Elasticity of Demand—Measurements and Degrees

The demand for a commodity is a function of price, income and price of related goods, as the three are the main determinants of the demand. The nature of dependence of quantities demanded on these determinants, has been explained through price demand, income demand and cross demand analyses in earlier chapter, which reveal that the quantity demanded changes with a change in price, income or price of related goods. It simply reveals the direction of change, but our endeavour is to know the exact relationship between changes in the size of above determinants and changes in the quantity demanded. In other words, it is of vital importance to know the responsiveness of the quantity demanded to changes in the price, income and price of related goods. The measurement of such responsiveness is called elasticity of demand. **The elasticity of demand is a quantitative measurement of the responsiveness of demand for a commodity to some changes in its price, income of the consumer or the prices of related goods.** Just as we have three kinds of demand, correspondingly we consider three types of the elasticities of demand, viz. the price elasticity, the income elasticity and the cross elasticity.

PRICE ELASTICITY OF DEMAND

The law of demand states the direction of relationship between the variation in price and the variation in the quantity demanded, but is does not state by how much the quantity demanded increases or decreases as a result of certain fall or rise in price of the commodity. In other words, the law of demand simply states the direction of change and not the rate of change, as the latter falls within the domain of the price elasticity of demand. The term 'price elasticity' expresses the degree of correlation between the demand and price change and measures the rate at which the quantity demanded varies with a change in price. More exactly, **the price elasticity of demand is a measure of the relative change in amount purchased in response to a relative change in price on a given demand curve. According to P.A. Samuelson 'elasticity of demand is a concept devised to indicate the degree of responsiveness of quantity demanded (*Q*) to change in market price (P). It depends primarily on**

percentage changes and is independent of units used to measure Q and P'. Similarly, according to Marshall 'the elasticity of demand in a market is great or small, according as the quantity demanded increases much or little for a given fall in the price and diminishes much or little for a given rise in price'. Thus, 'the elasticity of demand, at any price or output, is the rate of change in the quantity purchased in response to a small change in price divided by the rate of change in price.'

The change in demand is not always proportionate to the change in price. In case a small change in the price leads to a greater change in the demand, it is said to be an elastic demand. On the other hand, if a big change in price is followed by a smaller change in demand, it is said to be a case of inelastic demand. When certain change in the price is followed by a proportionate change in the demand, it is a case of unitary elastic demand. The above types of the price elasticity of demand can be shown on the different types of the demand curves, having varying slopes, as follows:

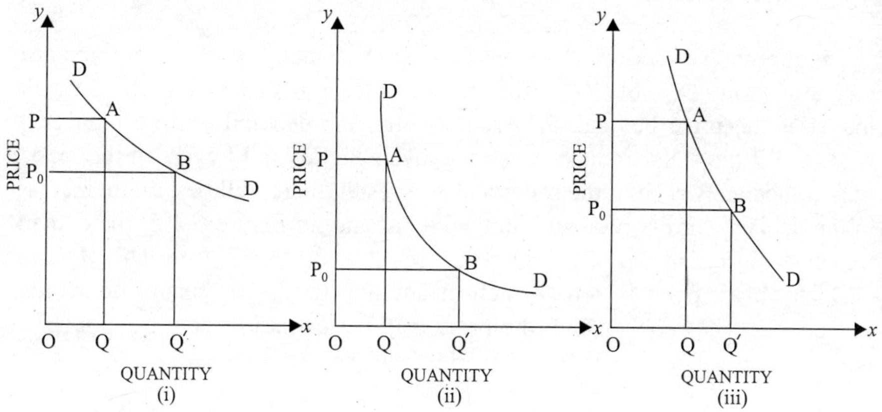

FIGURE 6.1 Price Elasticity on Different Slopes of the Demand Curve.

In Figure 6.1(i) the demand curve is relatively flat, where slight decrease in price (from OP to OP_0) causes increases in quantity demanded (from OQ and OQ') In Figure 6.1(ii) the demand curve is rectangular hyperbola, where decrease in price (from OP to OP_0) brings a proportionate increase in the quantity demanded (from OQ to OQ'). Similarly, in Figure 6.1(iii) the demand curve has a steep slope, where even greater decrease in price (from OP to OP_0) could bring only a smaller increase (from OQ to OQ') in the demand.

Sometimes, even without any change in price, the demand undergoes a change. In other words, the seller may sell any quantity from zero to infinity on that price and a slight increase in price, definitely brings down the demand to zero. It is the case of perfectly elastic demand, which is represented by a horizontal straight demand line. In case, despite change in the price, the demand remains unchanged, it is a case of perfectly inelastic demand, which is represented by a vertical straight demand line. It is also called zero elasticity of demand, indicating that there would be no change in quantity purchased, regardless of the change in price. It is as follows:

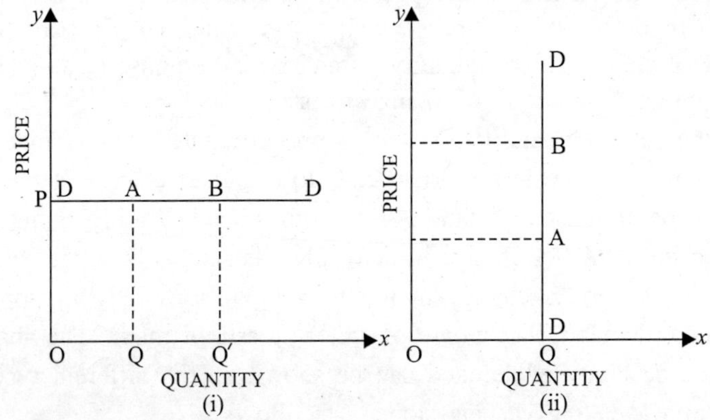

FIGURE 6.2 Extreme Types of the Price Elasticity of Demand.

Figure 6.2(i) shows a perfectly elastic demand line, where quantity increases from *OQ* to *OQ'*, although the price remains at *OP*. If the seller increases the price beyond *OP* even slightly, the demand will be reduced to zero, and if the seller reduces the price, even slightly, all buyers in the market will immediately rush to the seller and as a result, there will be infinite increase in the demand for the product. On the other hand, in Figure 6.2(ii) the demand remains constant at *OQ*, although price has gone up to *OP'* from *OP*. Here the elasticity of demand is zero, which means that the buyer cannot do without this quantity, howsoever high the price may be, or they cannot be induced to buy any more, howsoever low the price may be.

Measurements of the Price Elasticity

Diagrammatic presentation of the elasticity of demand reveals the degree of price elasticity from the very slope of the demand curve, but it is erroneous. The slope of a demand curve shows the ratio between the absolute changes in price and demand, while the elasticity of demand refers to relative (percentage or proportionate) change in price and demand. Later on, it will be seen that a straight line demand curve having the same slope throughout, will have different degrees of price elasticity at different points. No demand curve is elastic or inelastic throughout its length, excepting a rectangular hyperbola demand curve showing a unit elasticity, linear (straight line) demand curve showing infinitely elastic or absolutely inelastic demands of the commodity. It is a point or segment of the demand curve, which reflects varying degrees of price elasticity of demand. Moreover, it is not enough to know whether the demand on a particular point or segment is elastic or inelastic, but we require, for practical purpose, a precise measure of the elasticity of demand. There are three methods for measuring the price elasticity of demand. (i) total outlay measurement; (ii) proportional measurement, and (iii) geometrical measurement.

(i) Total Outlay Measurement: In this method, we compare the total outlay (expenditure) on a particular commodity before and after a change in its price:

(a) In case, the total outlay of the consumer, on a particular commodity after a price decline, is larger than the total outlay before the price decline or if the total expenditure after price increase is less than the same before the price increase, the demand for the commodity is said to be elastic for that range of the price. In other words, **if change in total outlay proceeds in the opposite direction of the price change, the demand is elastic one.**

(b) In case, with a fall in the price of the commodity, the total outlay on that commodity also falls or with a rise in price, the total outlay also rises, the demand for that range of the price is said to be inelastic. Here the total outlay and price move together in the same direction.

(c) In case, even after a change in the price of commodity, the total outlay of consumers on it remains unchanged, the demand is said to be unitary elastic for that range of the price. The three possibilities are as follows:

TABLE 6.1 Price Demand Schedule

Price	*Quantity*	*Total Outlay*	*Elasticity*
₹	Units	₹	
5	50	5×50 = 250	Inelastic
6	45	6×45 = 270	
7	40	7×40 = 280	Unitary Elastic
8	35	8×35 = 280	
9	25	9×25 = 225	Elastic
10	20	10×20 = 200	

This reveals that as the price increase, the quantity demanded declines, but the total outlay derived by multiplying the price with the quantity increases initially, it becomes constant later on and declines ultimately. At initial stages, due to increase in price, the quantity demanded declines, but only to a relatively smaller extent and, as a result, the total outlay increases. Thus in this range of price, there is inelastic demand. Subsequently, along with increase in the price of the commodity, the quantity demanded has decreased in such a way that the total outlay on the commodity has remained unchanged. In this range of price, the demand is said to be unitary elastic. Lastly, along with increase in the price, the quantity demanded declines to a greater extent and, as a result, the total outlay declines, the change in price of the commodity is associated with a still greater change in the quantity bought, therefore, in this range of the price the demand is elastic one.

By reversing the process, we can also analyse the different degrees of elasticity of demand, if there is a decrease in the price. When the price declines from ₹ 10 to ₹ 9 the total outlay increases, therefore, in this range the demand is elastic, because increase in quantity demanded is greater than the decrease in the price of the commodity. In the price ranges from ₹ 8 to ₹ 7, due to decrease in the price, the quantity demanded has increased in such a way that the total outlay remained unchanged, therefore, the demand is unitary elastic. Further decrease in price from ₹ 6 to ₹ 5 causes relatively lesser increase in the quantity demanded and, as a result, the total outlay diminishes. In this range of price, the demand is inelastic.

Thus, in case the change in total outlay corresponds the change in price, the demand will be inelastic and if it is in the opposite direction, the demand is said to be elastic. The demand will be unitary elastic, if the total outlay remains unchanged despite change in the price. The table also reveals that the demand is elastic at higher price level, it is inelastic at lower price level and in unitary elastic in between the two price levels.

The price-outlay relationship can also be exhibited in Figure 6.3, where the total outlay in relation to price has been shown by lines connecting *ABCD* points, where from *A* to *B* the total outlay is rising along with increase in price from *OP* to OP_1. It is constant between *B* to C despite increase is price from OP_1 to OP_2 and it declines between *C* to *D* along with increase in price from OP_2 to OP_3. Thus, the demand is inelastic on *AB* segment of the total outlay line beyond this, on BC segment of the line, the demand is unitary elastic and on CD segment, it is elastic. This is a simple measurement of the price elasticity of demand but it fails to separate highly elastic with slightly elastic in the elastic demands or highly inelastic with slightly inelastic in inelastic demands, therefore more accurate measurements are used for measuring the price elasticity of demand.

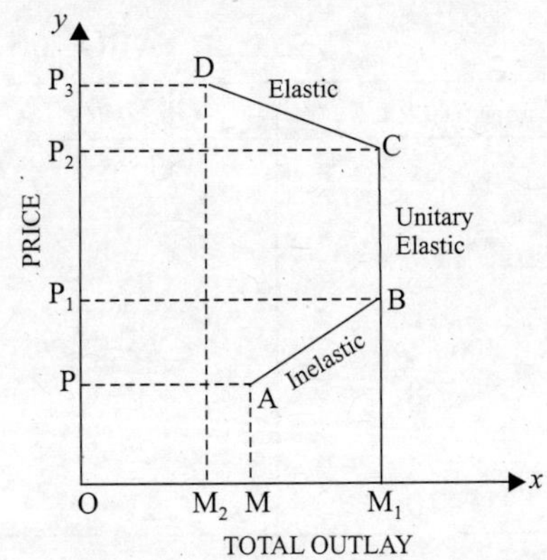

FIGURE 6.3 Slopes of the Total Outlay and the Price Elasticity

(ii) Proportional Measurement: Under this measurement we compare the rate of change in price with the rate of change in demand, where the elasticity of demand is equal to the ratio of rate of change in the quantity demanded to the rate of change in the price charged.

$$Ed = \frac{\text{Rate of change in quantity demanded}}{\text{Rate of change in price}}$$

$$= \frac{\text{Change in Demand}}{\text{Original Demand}} \div \frac{\text{Change in Price}}{\text{Original Price}}$$

In case P stands for price, Q for quantity and Δ (delta) for change, the price electricity of demand may be as follows:

$$Ed = \frac{\Delta Q}{Q} \div \frac{\Delta P}{P}$$

$$Ed = \frac{\Delta Q}{Q} \times \frac{P}{\Delta P}$$ After placing the sign of multiplication in place of sign of division

$$Ed = \frac{P}{Q} \times \frac{\Delta Q}{\Delta P}$$ After placing change (Δ) figures and original price and quantity figures separately.

This measurement will yield a negative value, therefore, in order to avoid this, a minus (–) sign is placed before this formula suggesting that it measures the electricity of demand on a price demand curve, which normally slopes negatively,

$$Ed = -\frac{P}{Q} \times \frac{\Delta Q}{\Delta P}.$$

Thus, the elasticity of demand is expressed in terms of relative numbers rather than absolute numbers. This change in demand and price may be taken into consideration on a particular point on or over certain range of the demand curve. The former type of measurement is known as 'Point Elasticity of Demand' whereas the latter is called 'Arc Elasticity of Demand'.

$$\text{Point Elasticity of Demand } (Ed) = -\frac{P}{Q} \times \frac{\partial Q}{\partial P}$$

where P stands for original price; Q for the original quantity demanded; and ∂(small delta) for small change in P and Q on a particular point of the demand curve.

This measures the elasticity of demand on a particular point of the demand curve, where the value of ∂ is to be found from the mathematical tables, which adds complications to this type of measurement. Hence it could not gain popularity despite its exactness in the measurement. It has been replaced by another formula of measurement for the elasticity between two points of the demand curve, which is known as Arc Elasticity of Demand.

$$\text{Arc Elasticity of Demand } (Ed) = -\frac{P}{Q} \times \frac{\Delta Q}{\Delta P} \quad .....(i)$$

where P stands for price, Q for quantity demanded and Δ (capital delta) for a change in P and Q between two points on the demand curve. It may be represented as follows:

This formula, however, is ambiguous, because just as we have taken the values of P and Q as given on point A in Figure 6.4, similarly we can take the values of P and Q as given on point B. We are also at liberty to take any combination of these values. Thus, there will be four possible values of price and quantity for the measurement of the Arc Elasticity of Demand.

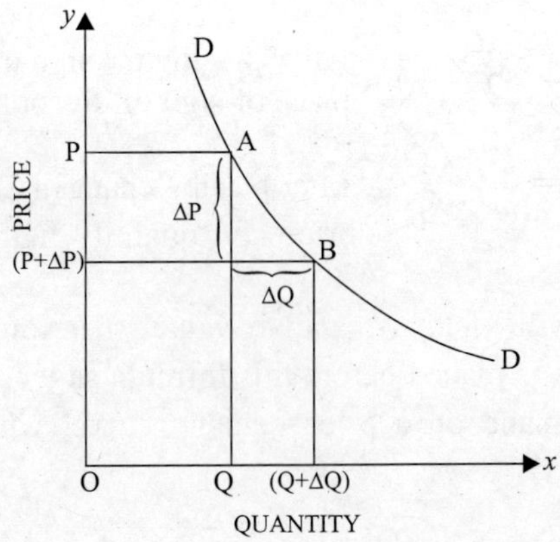

FIGURE 6.4 Measuring Arc Elasticity of Demand.

In order to avoid ambiguity, the average of the values of P and Q given at A and B points should be taken for the measurement of the Arc Elasticity of Demand as follows:

$$Ed = -\frac{[P + (P + \Delta P)] \div 2}{[Q + (Q + \Delta Q)] \div 2} \times \frac{\Delta Q}{\Delta P} \quad (ii)$$

Since both the numerator and the denominator have been divided by 2 in order to get the average value of P and Q, we can avoid this division and take the total of price and quantity as given on both points as an alternative, which is as follows:

$$Ed = -\frac{[P + (P + \Delta P)]}{[Q + (Q + \Delta Q)]} \times \frac{\Delta Q}{\Delta P} \quad (iii)$$

Another alternative is to take smaller values of P and Q, whether on point A or on point B. The price at point A is P and at point B is $(P + \Delta P)$ where the latter is lower as ΔP is negative, we will take $(P + \Delta P)$ as the original price.

Similarly, amongst Q and $(Q + \Delta Q)$, on A and B points of demand curve Q has got a lower value, hence, it will be taken into consideration in our new formula, which is as follows:

$$Ed = -\frac{(P+\Delta P)}{Q} \times \frac{\Delta Q}{\Delta P} \qquad \text{(iv)}$$

Such formulae, however, do not throw enough light on the question as to how total outlay behaves, when the price changes. Moreover, economic reasons for taking such average, total or any other value are also not clear, therefore an alternative formula, which takes into account the total change in the total amount spent on the commodity (ΔE) is taken into consideration. It is as follows:

$$Ed = 1 - \frac{\Delta E}{Q\Delta P} \qquad \text{(v)}$$

This has been derived as follows:

Change in expenditure (ΔE) = New Price $(P + \Delta P)$ multiplied by new quantity $(Q + \Delta Q)$ minus old price (P) multiplied by the old quantity (Q).

$$\Delta E = (P + \Delta P)\,(Q + \Delta Q) - PQ$$

$$\Delta E = PQ + P\Delta Q + Q\Delta P + \Delta P\Delta Q - PQ$$

$$\Delta E = Q\Delta P + P\Delta Q + \Delta P\Delta Q \text{ (after cancelling out } PQ \text{ with } -PQ)$$

Taking ΔQ as common from latter two figures.

$$\Delta E = Q\Delta P + \Delta Q\,(P + \Delta P)$$

$$-(P + \Delta P)\,\Delta Q = Q\Delta P - \Delta E \text{ (after changing the sides)}$$

By dividing both sides of this derivation by $Q\Delta P$

$$-\frac{(P+\Delta P)\Delta Q}{Q\Delta P} = \frac{Q\Delta Q}{Q\Delta P} - \frac{\Delta E}{Q\Delta P}$$

$$-\frac{(P+\Delta P).\Delta Q}{Q\Delta P} = 1 - \frac{\Delta E}{Q\Delta P}$$

Since $-\frac{(P+\Delta P)}{Q} \cdot \frac{\Delta Q}{\Delta P}$ is the measurement of the price elasticity of demand [as per formula (iv)] the other side of the equation, that is $1 - \Delta E/Q\Delta P$, will also measure the price elasticity.

Thus, in this case the price elasticity is measured taking into account the change in total outlay. All these formulae, if applied to a particular problem, may not yield same value for the price elasticity, yet there will not be wide difference in the value of the price elasticity, which will vary between zero to infinity. In between these two extremes of the price elasticity may be more or less than or equal to one depicting different degrees of the price elasticity of demand.

(iii) Geometrical Measurement: Alfred Marshall has suggested a geometrical measurement of price elasticity of demand, which is usually applied to a straight line demand curve.

AB is the linear demand curve and elasticity is to be measured at point *C*, where price is *OP* and quantity demanded is *OQ*. The price has come down to OP_0 and the quantity demanded has gone up to OQ_1.

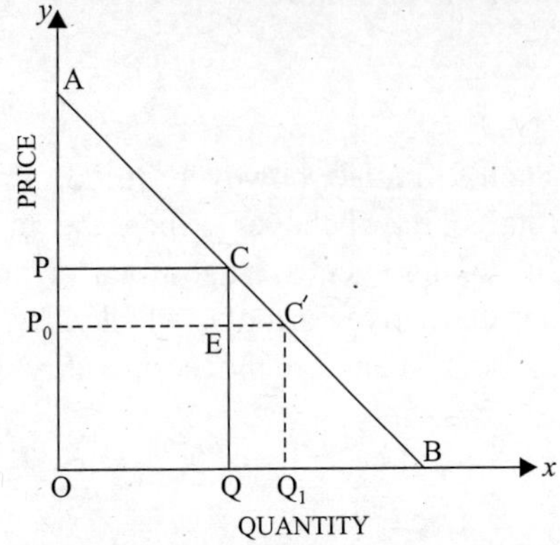

FIGURE 6.5 Geometrical Measurement of the Price Elasticity

$$Ed = -\frac{P}{Q}\times\frac{\Delta Q}{\Delta P} = \frac{OP}{OQ}\times\frac{EC'}{EC}$$

$$Ed = \frac{QC}{OQ}\times\frac{EC'}{EC} \text{ (since } OP = QC)$$

Since triangles *CEC'* and *CQB* are similar, as the three angles of smaller triangle *CEC'* are equal to the three angles of the larger triangle *CQB*, and therefore, *EC'/EC* = *QB/QC*. Thus,

$$Ed = \frac{QC}{OQ}\cdot\frac{QB}{QC}$$

Here *QC* can be cancelled out and therefore,

$$Ed = QB/OQ.$$

Again we find that the triangles *CQB* and *APC* are similar, as the three angles of triangle *CQB* and the three angles of the triangle *APC* are equal therefore, *CB/QB* = *AC/PC*, since *PC* = *OQ*, therefore.

$$\frac{CB}{QB} = \frac{AC}{OQ}$$

After a cross multiplication:

$$\frac{CB}{AC} = \frac{QB}{OQ}$$

Since, *Ed* = *QB/OQ* as proved earlier, therefore *Ed* = *CB/AC*

$$\text{Thus, } Ed = CB/AC = \frac{\text{Lower Sector of } AB}{\text{Upper Sector of } AB}$$

The ratio of the length of the aforesaid two sectors from the given point of the demand line will reveal the value of the elasticity of demand. In case, the demand curve is not linear, then we have to draw a tangent to the curve from the point on which we want to measure the elasticity of demand as per Figure 6.6(i).

In Figure 6.6(ii) exhibits different degrees of the price elasticity on different points of the demand curve *MK*. On point *M*, the value of elasticity of demand is equal to zero, as the lower sector from this point is zero, whereas upper sector is *MK*. On point *K*, the price elasticity is equal to infinity, because *KM* is the lower sector, while upper sector is nil. On point *E*, the demand is unitary elastic, as the lower sector *EM* is equal to the upper sector *EK*. On any point between *E* and *M* the demand is inelastic as the lower sector will be less than upper sector and on any point in the range between *E* and *K*, the demand is elastic, as the lower sector will be more than the upper sector. Thus, we need not search for different slopes of demand curve to exhibit different degrees of price elasticity, because a single demand curve has different degrees of elasticities at different price levels.

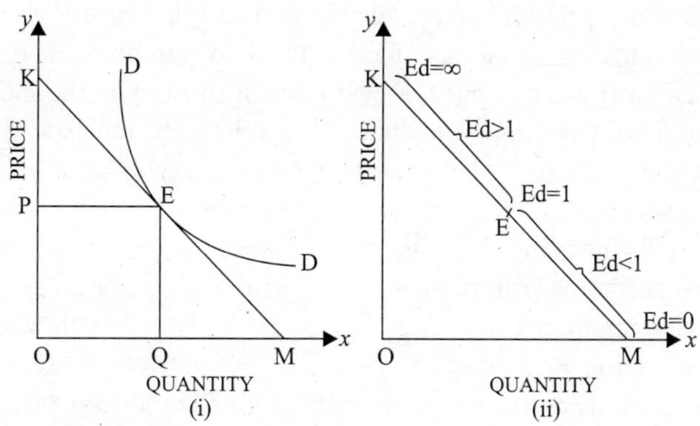

FIGURE 6.6 Five Degrees of the Price Elasticity.

These measurements reveal certain positive values ranging between zero and infinity. On the basis of these values, we can ascertain the degree of price elasticity of demand, as follows:

TABLE 6.2 Degrees of Price Elasticity

S. No.	*Types or Degrees*	*Numerical Expression*	*Description*
1.	Perfectly Elastic	$Ed = \infty$	Infinity
2.	Elastic	$Ed > 1$	More than one
3.	Unitary Elastic	$Ed = 1$	Equal to one
4.	Inelastic	$Ed < 1$	Less than one
5.	Perfectly Inelastic	$Ed = 0$	Zero

Thus, there are five degrees of the price elasticity of demand, but generally we come across only the middle three types of the elasticities.

Factors Determining the Price Elasticity

Elasticity is a relative phenomenon, because for a person at a place demand may be elastic but for another person at the same place it may be inelastic or for the same person at one place it is elastic but at the other place it is inelastic. There are several factors that affect the elasticity of demand of any product.

1. **Nature of the Commodity:** The goods may be classified as for necessities, comforts or luxuries. The demand for necessities tends to be inelastic, for comforts unitary elastic and that for luxurious goods, it is inelastic, as it is generally used by higher income group persons, who do not care for any variation in price.
2. **Range of Substitutes:** Elasticity also depends on the number of substitutes available in the market. A commodity, having a number of substitutes, has relatively elastic demand, because a rise in its price may cause tremendous reduction in its consumption, as the consumers may shift to the purchases of substitutes. On the other hand, a commodity without substitutes has relatively inelastic demand.
3. **Extent of Use:** The goods having several uses have relatively elastic demand. For example, coal, when becomes cheap, will be used for cooking, heating and industrial purposes, which will result into an increase in demand. An increase in its price may induce the consumer to put it to very urgent uses only, which will result into a reduction in its demand.
4. **Level of Income:** People with high income are less affected by changes in price than people with low incomes. A consumer with higher income will keep on purchasing the same quantity of fruits and milk, even if the price rises significantly. On the other hand, a person belonging to middle income group is bound to reduce the purchases of such commodities, when their prices rise. Thus, the demand is inelastic for rich and elastic for persons with small incomes.
5. **Part of Income Spent:** `In case a consumer spends a small part of his income on a particular commodity, the change in price does not materially affect the demand for that commodity, e.g., the demand for match boxes. Thus, a commodity claiming only a small proportion of consumer's income has inelastic demand and *vice-versa.*
6. **Durability of the Commodity:** In case the commodity is durable or reparable, a rise in price is likely to be followed by the use of same commodity already purchased after due repairs for longer period. Thus, such commodities are likely to have inelastic demand.
7. **Level of Price:** Elasticity of demand tends to be high at high prices, at least considerable for medium prices and the least at lower prices. In other words, demand is elastic at higher prices, unitary elastic at medium prices and inelastic at lower prices.

8. **Urgency of Demand:** On account of habit or social custom and non-availability of substitutes, the demand for a commodity is considered as urgent. This urgency causes the demand to be inelastic. In case the demand for a commodity is less urgent, the consumer may postpone its purchases if the price goes up and such commodities will have an elastic demand.
9. Jointly demanded goods have less elastic demand. For example, if carriages (Say Tanga) become cheap but prices of horses continue to rule high, the demand for carriage (Say Tanga) will not extend much.

Importance of the Price Elasticity

This concept contributes a lot in understanding the process of pricing and resource allocation, therefore, it is used in almost all sections of microeconomic theory. While fixing price of the commodity or planning advertisement, sellers always take the help of the concept of price elasticity of demand of their products. A monopolist trying to practice price discrimination (charging different prices for the same product from different customers) arranges his customers according to different degrees of price elasticities of demand and fixes its price accordingly. Similarly, for practicing dumping (i.e., selling the commodity at cheaper rates in foreign markets, and at higher rates in home market) this concept of price elasticity is of great help. In case of joint-product, where separate cost is not determinable (e.g., wheat and straw), the producer fixes higher price for the products, whose demand is inelastic and lower price for the product having elastic demand.

In underdeveloped countries like India, the price control policy can be pursued only after estimating the price elasticity of demand of strategic commodities. Price control is exercised-generally in case of commodities having lower degree of elasticities or inelastic demand.

Price elasticity is also influential in determining a price policy by public utility undertakings, like electric supply undertakings, railways, etc. Such undertakings determine their rates for different uses on the basis of the elasticity of demand and try to cover the losses from one group of users out of the gains reaped from the other group.

In the field of distribution, particularly for wages, the price elasticity of demand is used to demonstrate that an upward revision of wages shall succeed only when demand for the product is inelastic, otherwise, a higher wage means unemployment.

The concept is of great help in the sphere of public finance. The government can be sure of more revenues, if such commodities are taxed, whose demand is inelastic. The tax will certainly raise the price, but the demand being inelastic, people will be compelled to buy the commodity even at higher prices. Preparation of indirect tax proposals is largely an exercise in the estimation of the elasticities of demand of goods and services to be taxed.

In the field of international trade, the price elasticity of demand is helpful in ascertaining the 'terms of trade'. If exports have inelastic demand, a higher price can be charged from abroad. Similarly, if imported goods have elastic demand in the internal market, a lower price is to be fixed. Both these enable a country to have favourable 'terms of trade' in respect of international trade.

The concept of elasticity explains the paradox of poverty in the midst of plenty. A bumper crop, instead of being a cause of prosperity, may spell disaster, if the demand for the commodity is inelastic and particularly when the produce is perishable. In case the elasticity of demand for wheat is unity, the income of farmers will remain the same whatever the condition of crop may be.

INCOME ELASTICITY OF DEMAND

It shows the way in which a consumer's purchases of any commodity changes as a result of a change in his income. It measures the responsiveness of buyers to changes in their incomes, when prices and other determinants of demand remain unchanged. In other words, income elasticity of demand is equal to ratio of change in purchases of a commodity divided by a rate of change in income of the consumers.

$$\text{Income Elasticity} = \frac{\text{Rate of Change in Demand}}{\text{Rate of Change in Income}}$$

$$= \frac{\text{Change in Demand}}{\text{Original Demand}} \div \frac{\text{Change in Income}}{\text{Original Income}}$$

Taking Ei for income elasticity of demand, M for money income; Q for quantity demanded, and Δ for change, the above statement can be reduced to the following symbolical expression:

$$Ei = \frac{\Delta Q}{Q} \div \frac{\Delta M}{M}$$

$$Ei = \frac{\Delta Q}{Q} \times \frac{M}{\Delta M} \quad \text{After replacing } (\div) \text{ with } (\times)$$

$$Ei = \frac{M}{Q} \times \frac{\Delta Q}{\Delta M} \quad \text{After placing the original and change figures separately.}$$

Thus, the income elasticity of demand is the product of the reciprocal of the slope of income demand curve and the ratio of original income to quantity demanded. It is as follows:

In this diagram M/Q is the ratio of original income and original quantity demanded and $\Delta Q/\Delta M$ is the slope of the income demand curve.

The measurement on the basis of above formula may yield positive as well as negative values. Sometimes this value will also be equal to zero. In case of normal commodities, whose purchases are likely to increase along with increase in the income of the consumer, the income elasticity of demand will give a positive value of varying numerical magnitudes. The income elasticity will also have a value equal to zero, where a given increase in income fails to lead to any increase in the purchases of the commodity under consideration. Its value may also be less than zero in case of inferior goods, whose demand decreases along with increase in the income of the consumer.

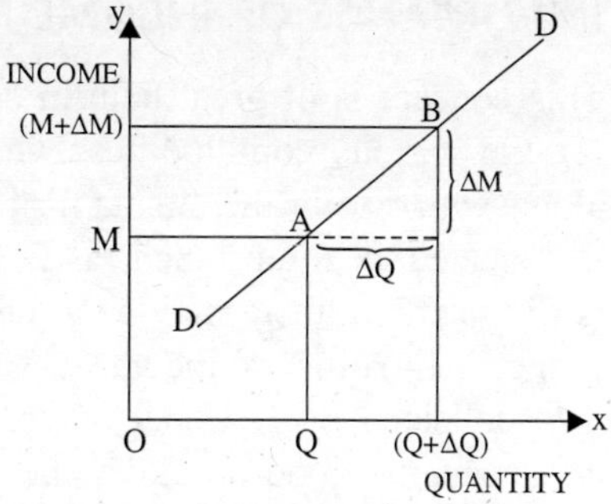

FIGURE 6.7 Measuring the Income Elasticity.

TYPES OF INCOME ELASTICITY

These are also called the degrees of income elasticity of demand, which are as under:

1. **Zero Income Elasticity:** Despite change in income, if the quantity demanded or purchased does not change, it is a case of zero income elasticity (i.e., $Ei = 0$). It serves as a dividing line, where on the one hand, there is positive income elasticity and on the other hand, there is negative income elasticity. Zero income elasticity is found in case of indifferent commodities, which are neither superior nor inferior.
2. **Negative Income Elasticity:** In case of inferior goods, the value of income elasticity is less than zero (i.e., $Ei < 0$), which indicates the extent of decrease in purchases of such commodities due to a given increase in the income of the consumer.
3. **Positive Income Elasticity:** In case increase in income leads to an increase in the quantity demanded, the value of income elasticity is positive. This positive value of income elasticity may be more or less than or equal to one. Thus, positive income elasticity is further divided into three categories.

   (a) ***Unitary Income Elasticity*:** When an increase in income leads to a proportionate increase in the quantity demanded, the value of income elasticity will be equal to one (i.e., $Ei = 1$).

   (b) ***Greater Income Elasticity*:** Income elasticity of demand may be more than unity (i.e., $Ei > 1$). In this case, an increase in income leads to a more than proportionate increase in quantity demanded.

   (c) ***Lesser Income Elasticity*:** Income elasticity of demand may be less than unity (i.e., $Ei < 1$). Here an increase in income leads to a less than proportionate increase in quantity demanded.

IMPORTANCE OF INCOME ELASTICITY

This concept is of great help in estimating the income effects on the demand for the various commodities, when income rises. In developing economies, along with rise in the standard of living, the demand for certain commodities is expected to go up much faster than that of others. If this increased demand is not satisfied, there may be a 'demand-pull-inflation'. Thus, there is need for proper estimation of income elasticities of the various commodities. As per data collected by National Sample Survey, it has been revealed that in rural areas superior food articles (wheat, rice, milk, etc.) have an income elasticity more than unity, which indicates reduced marketable surplus of these products from the rural areas. In urban areas, the demand for comforts (like auto, cycles, scooter, superior garments, etc.) have an income elasticity more than one, which will create an acute shortage of these goods and services. Therefore, a control on stepping up of their production is needed to meet the rising demand. Thus, the knowledge of income elasticity of demand in respect of goods of general use is basic to the maintenance of balance between demand and supply.

CROSS ELASTICITY OF DEMAND

The effect of change in the price of related commodity upon the demand for a particular commodity is determined by the concept of 'cross elasticity of demand'. It may be defined as, "the rate of change in the quantity demanded of a particular commodity in response to a change in the price of another related commodity". In other words, the cross elasticity of demand (Ec) is the value of the rate of change in purchases of Q_2 divided by the rate of change in the price of Q_1, where Q_1 and Q_2 are related commodities.

$$EC = \frac{\text{Rate of Change in the Purchases of } Q_2}{\text{Rate of Change in the Price of } Q_1}$$

$$EC = \frac{\text{Change in Purchases of } Q_2}{\text{Original Purchases of } Q_2} \div \frac{\text{Change in Price of } Q_1}{\text{Original Price of } Q_1}$$

Taking Ec for the cross elasticity of demand of Q_2 as the price of Q_1 (i.e., P_1) changes, where Q_1 and Q_2 are related goods; P_1 for price of Q_1 commodity; Q_2 for quantity of Q_2 commodity; and Δ for change; the above statement can be reduced to the following symbolical expression:

$$Ec = \frac{\Delta Q_2}{Q_2} \div \frac{\Delta P_1}{P_1}$$

$$Ec = \frac{\Delta Q_2}{Q_2} \times \frac{P_1}{\Delta P_1} \quad \text{After replacing } (\div) \text{ with } (\times)$$

$$Ec = \frac{P_1}{Q_2} \times \frac{\Delta Q_2}{\Delta P_1} \quad \text{After segregating the original and change } (\Delta) \text{ figures.}$$

The calculations based on the above formula may give a positive, negative or zero value, depending upon the nature of relationship of the two commodities. Where two commodities are competitive (substitute), the value of cross elasticity of demand will be positive. In case the goods are perfectly substitutable, the value will be infinity (∞), which indicates that a small fall in the price of Q_1 will cause an infinitely large reduction in the purchase of Q_2. In case the goods are complementary, the value of cross elasticity of demand will be negative, which may go up to minus infinity (–∞). This indicates that a small fall in the price of Q_1 will result into an infinitely large increase in purchase of Q_2. In real world we come across cross elasticities of varying finite magnitudes, whether positive or negative. In between the two values (positive and negative) the cross elasticity may also be equal to zero, where a small fall (or rise in price of Q_1 will have no effect on the purchases of Q_2. This happens, when commodities are independent of each other.

The concept of cross elasticity of demand is useful in handling inter-commodity relations. It serves as a basis for classification of markets. Under perfect competition, since the products of all sellers are perfect substitutes for one another, therefore, the cross elasticity of demand is infinity. The value of cross elasticity of demand lower than infinity indicates the degree of monopoly power. Thus, it is an important indicator of concentration in the industry and serves as a basis for anti-monopoly measures.

Review Questions

1. Discuss the importance of the concept of price elasticity of demand in economic analysis.
2. Explain the total outlay method of measuring price elasticity of demand.
3. Bring out the price elasticity of demand. Explain the methods for its measurement?
4. Explain the term of elasticity of demand with suitable diagrams and examples and also the effects of the price elasticity on the consumer, when (i) $Ed = 0$, (ii) $Ed = 1$, (iii) $Ed > 1$, and (iv) $Ed < 1$.
5. Explain the various degrees of price elasticity of demand and bring out the various factors influencing the elasticity of demand.
6. 'Elasticity of demand does not depend merely on the slope of demand curve, but also on the price and quantity levels.' Explain.
7. What is meant by income elasticity of demand? Elucidate the range and the various degrees of the income elasticity of demand.
8. Elucidate the cross elasticity of demand. Distinguish between substitute and complementary goods as per cross elasticity of demand.

7

Theory of Consumer's Behaviour: Cardinal Utility Analysis

The cardinal utility analysis is the original analysis of demand, which provides an explanation of consumer's demand for a product and derives the law of demand, which establishes an inverse relationship between variation in price and quantity demanded. This analysis has been subjected to severe criticisms and, as a result, there developed some alternative analyses. All these can be grouped into four categories; (i) the cardinal utility analysis; (ii) the indifference curve analysis; (iii) the revealed preference analysis; and (iv) the logical ordering analysis. In this chapter an effort is being made to discuss the cardinal utility analysis of the demand, while the remaining three analyses will be discussed in subsequent chapters. Since the cardinal utility analysis is very old and its final shape emerged at the hands of Marshall, therefore, it has also been called as Marshallian or Traditional Analysis of Consumer's Behaviour.

ASSUMPTIONS OF CARDINAL UTILITY ANALYSIS

The traditional analysis of consumer's behaviour is based on some explicit assumptions, which need be stated clearly to facilitate the exposition of this analysis. These assumptions are as follows:

1. **Utility is Measurable:** Exponents of this analysis believed that all economic goods give utility to the consumer and this utility can be expressed in terms of the cardinal numbers, like 5, 7, 21, etc. In this connection a few economists regard that utility is measurable only in principle, that is, the utility can be conceived in quantitative terms and not measured exactly in practice. On the other hand, Marshall regards that utility is measurable not only in theory but also in practice, and it is measurable in terms of money. He viewed that **the amount of money, which a person is willing to pay for a thing, instead of going without it, is the money measurement of its utility.** Some economists of the cardinal school measure the utility in terms of an imaginary unit called **'utils'**.

2. **Constancy of Marginal Utility of Money:** It is assumed that the marginal utility of money to the consumer remains constant, as he spends more and more on a commodity. Any variation in the marginal utility of money would certainly affect the measurement of the marginal utility from any commodity and that would certainly defeat the very purpose of the measurement of marginal utility. According to Professor Tapas Majumdar: **'If money is supposed to provide measuring rod of utility, evidently, as will all measuring rods, its units must be invariant; it must measure the same amount of utility in all circumstances.'** Such assumption is very meaningful, when a marginal utility curve showing the marginal utility of any commodity in terms of money, is drawn, it will be considered as the demand curve of the commodity. Marshall, however, has justified this assumption on the ground that **'his (consumer's) expenditure on any one thing is only a small part of his whole expenditure'.**
3. **Utilities of Different Goods are Independent:** It means that the utility obtained from the consumption/possession of a commodity is function of the quantity of that commodity alone. This also amounts to the fact that the total utility, which a person derives from the consumption/possession of a group of certain commodities or services is simply the sum total of separate utilities from individual units of the commodities or services. It indicates that goods bought by the consumer are neither substitutes nor complementary, but are independent. On the basis of this assumption, the utility is taken to possess additive character.
4. **Law of Diminishing Marginal Utility:** The cardinal utility analysis of the demand is built up on a fundamental premise about the applicability of the law of diminishing marginal utility. This law states that the more we have of a thing, the less is the satisfaction or utility that we derive from the additional units of it.

Thus, on the basis of these premises, the cardinal utility analysis proceeds to find out the way a consumer achieves his equilibrium. Once the consumer's equilibrium is established with given income and the marginal utility schedules of the goods the consumer wants to buy, it is possible to analyse the process of adjustment induced by rise or fall in the price of a commodity and it, in turn, derives the 'Law of Demand'.

CONSUMER'S EQUILIBRIUM

A consumer consumes a large number of goods and services in his day-to-day life. Due to a given money income and numerous wants, he fails to satisfy all his wants to the full extent, so as to get zero marginal utility (i.e., full satiety) from his consumption of all goods. He, therefore, limits the consumption of every commodity to a level lower than the full satiety level of consumption.

In fixing such limits he is being guided, knowingly or unknowingly, by the idea of getting maximum satisfaction. A consumer, getting maximum satisfaction out of his expenditure, is said to be in equilibrium. This behaviour of allocation of expenditures by consumers has been studied for the first time by a Prussian Economist **'Hermann Heinrich Gossen,** hence it has been named as **Gossen's Second Law of Consumption' (Gossen's first law being the Law of Diminishing Marginal Utility). This has also been named as the Law of Equi-Marginal Utility, which states that 'if a person has a thing, which he can put to several uses, he will distribute it among these uses in such a way that it has the same marginal utility in all**. Sometimes it is also called the Law of Substitution, as the consumer in day-to-day consumption keeps on substituting lower utility commodity with higher utility commodity.

Since all economic goods are scarce and command some price, the consumer with given money income has to make a choice between alternative satisfactions, as he is not rich enough to be able to buy everything in the desired quantity. The consumer gets maximum satisfaction from his given money income by selecting those goods, which are most desirable to him. In order to decide goods that will give the consumer the greatest possible satisfaction, goods are classified in order of preference, that is, he builds up a scale of preferences (or marginal utility schedules), which indicates that goods would be accepted as equivalent or preferred one to the other. The purchases of consumer at any time are determined by his scale of preferences and his total available resources (income), which is fixed in amount.

On the basis of such scale of preferences, the consumer decides the various commodities, which should be purchased, but the decision regarding the quantities of each such commodity is taken on the basis of their marginal significance in terms of money. A consumer will exchange money for units of any commodity up to the point, where the last (marginal) unit of the commodity, which he buys has for him a marginal significance in terms of money, just equal to its money price. Beyond this level the consumer will have no desire to buy any more of a good. This is followed in respect of each commodity, otherwise he would become only worse off, obtaining units of commodity, which as their marginal significances show, are lower on his scale of preferences than the unit of money, he would have to sacrifice in order to obtain them. When the consumer adjusts expenditure at all margins in this way, he is in equilibrium. So long as the relative importance of his different wants remains unchanged and his income and market prices remain constant, he will remain in the same equilibrium position.

Thus, in order to get maximum utility from the expenditure of his limited income, the consumer buys that quantity of each commodity, where the last unit of money spend on each of them affords him the same marginal utility. Since the consumer is faced with the problems of choice among many commodities that he would like to buy with his given income, he would allocate his given income on the purchases of different commodities in such way that it yields him the same marginal utility in all.

Assuming that the consumer has only ₹ 7 to be spent on the purchase of two commodities Q_1 and Q_1. The scale of preferences for his expenditure on the two commodities is as follows:

TABLE 7.1 Marginal Utility Per Unit of Expenditure

Unit of Expenditure	*Marginal Utility of Expenditure on Q_1*	*Marginal Utility of Expenditure on Q_2*
1	20 (i)	15 (iii)
2	17 (ii)	12 (v)
3	13 (iv)	10 (vi)
4	10 (vii)	8
5	7	4
6	3	0
7	0	–1

The first unit is spent on Q_1, as it gives the highest (i.e., 20) marginal utility to the consumer. Subsequent unit is again spent on Q_1, which again offers next higher (i.e., 17) marginal utility. Thus, the consumer will seek the highest possible marginal utility out of his expenditure and ultimately he will spend 6th unit on Q_2 and seventh unit on Q_1, where the marginal utility derived in both is equal. The consumer will, thus, plan the expenditure of 1st, 2nd, 4th and 7th units of his income on Q_1 and 3rd, 5th and 6th unit on Q_2. Such an expenditure of 4 units of expenditure on Q_1 and 3 units to expenditure on Q_2 yields him total satisfaction or utility equal to (60 + 37) 97 units. In case, the consumer decides to spend ₹ 5 (instead of ₹ 4) on Q_1, he will have only ₹ 2 left to be spent on Q_2. This expenditure will fetch him total utility of (67+27) 94 units. Similarly, if he decides to spend ₹ 4 (instead of ₹ 3) on Q_2 and the rest ₹ 3 on Q_1, his total utility will be merely (50 + 45) 95 units. Thus, the consumer will be at loss, if he decides to spend his money income in a way other than that in accordance with the principle of equi-marginal utility. This can be exhibited as per Figure 7.1 as follows.

The consumer having total money income equal to *XY* is in equilibrium, when he spends *OX* on Q_1 commodity and *OY* and Q_2 commodity, the marginal utility from *OX* expenditure on Q_1 is equal to *XX'* and from *OY* expenditure on Q_2 is equal to *YY'*. As per this pattern of expenditure on two goods, the consumer gets *x y y' x'* total utility. In case the consumer decides to spend more on Q_2, he is bound to reduce his expenditure on Q_1. In case he spends *OM* on Q_2, then he adds to his total utility equal to *YMM'Y'*, but by spending only *OC* on Q_1 his total utility from Q_1 is to be reduced by *XCC'X'*. Additional utility derived is less than utility forgone, and, thus, the total utility will be reduced ultimately. In case the consumer decides to spend more on Q_1 and as result less on Q_2, his total utility again will be reduced.

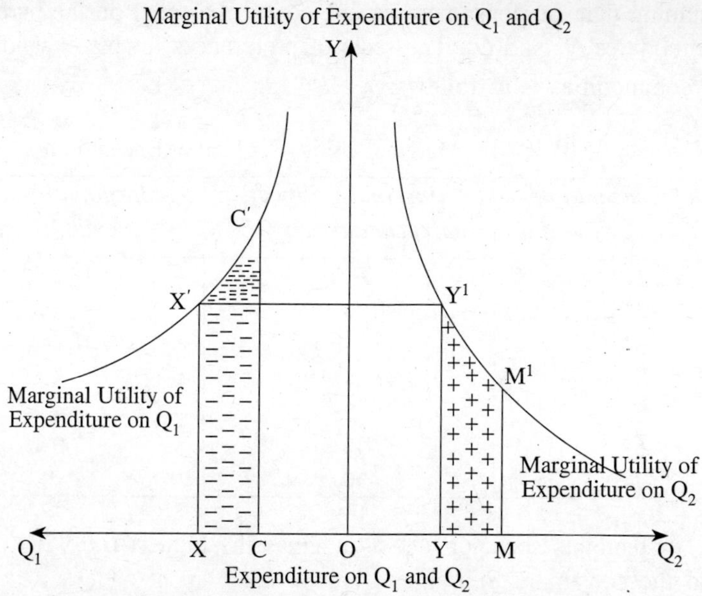

FIGURE 7.1 Equi-Marginal Utility and Consumer's Equilibrium.

Thus, the consumer with a given money income will be in equilibrium maximising his total utility, when the utility of marginal unit of purchasing power (4th rupee) devoted to any one use (Q_1) is just exactly equal to the utility of the marginal unit of purchasing power (3rd rupee) devoted to any other use (Q_2), provided that a movement in any direction will decrease his total utility. In case this was not the case, it would pay the consumer to increase his expenditure on those commodities, which yield relatively more utility to him and to reduce his expenditure on those commodities, which yield to him relatively lesser utility.

ALGEBRAIC STATEMENT OF EQUILIBRIUM

The consumer is said to be in equilibrium, where any shifting in his expenditure from one use to another can only reduce his total utility. This is possible only when the marginal unit of money devoted to any one use will add the same amount to his total utility as the marginal unit of money devoted to any other use. Algebraically:

$$\frac{U_1}{P_1} = \frac{U_2}{P_2} = \frac{dU}{dM} = U'$$

where U_1, U_2 represent marginal utilities of Q_1 and Q_2 respectively; P_1 and P_2 the respective prices; and dU/dM represents rate of change in the total utility in response to change in the money spending by the consumer, that is, marginal utility of money. U' represents the marginal utility of money devoted to any use.

On the basis of this statement, the Law of Equi-Marginal Utility has also been named as the Law of Proportionality. Now the consumer needs not spend his money income unit by unit, rather he can incur lump sum expenditures. Here the utility of marginal unit of purchasing power devoted to any commodity is nothing but the ratio of the marginal utility and price of the commodity and this should be equalised to similar ratios in respect of any other or all other commodities. Thus, it is the ratio of marginal utilities of Q_1 and Q_2 with their respective prices that need be equal and not the marginal utilities themselves. In case the consumer is in equilibrium and has no tendency to change the quantities of the commodities purchased, it must be true that all of his money income is accounted for by the uses to which it has been put. In case it is not so, the consumer may change the quantities purchased by spending those units of income that were unspent previously. Thus, all of his money income must be accounted for, and this can be stated in terms of a budget equation as follows:

$$P_1Q_1 + P_2Q_2 = M$$

Where P_1Q_1 represents the amount spent on Q_1; P_2Q_2 represents the amount spent on Q_2 and M represents the total money income of the consumer. Thus, along with the equilibrium condition, the above mentioned budget equation must also be satisfied.

DERIVATION OF DEMAND THEOREM

The demand theorem for a single consumer can be derived from his utility function (curve) assuming the utility functions of different goods to be independent of each other. It means that the utility function of each good consumed does not depend on the quantity consumed of any other good. As a result of independent utilities or additive utility functions, the relations of substitution and complementarity between goods are ruled out. Further, the marginal utility of money spending is also assumed to remain constant. We have already discussed the derivation of the demand theorem curve on the basis of the 'Law of Diminishing Marginal Utility' where we concluded that when the price of goods falls, the consumer buys more of the good, so as to equate the marginal utility to the lower price and, thus, the quantity demanded of goods varies inversely with price. Thus, the downward sloping marginal utility curve is transformed into the downward sloping demand curve.

The derivation of the demand theorem can also be analysed through the Law of Equi-Marginal Utility. This derivation again is based on the assumption that the marginal utility of money is constant. Mathematically,

$$\frac{dU}{dM} = U' = \text{a constant}$$

where dU is change in total utility; dM is change in money income and U' is the marginal utility of money income. This marginal utility of money is something as the common value of the equilibrium ratios of the marginal utilities of the commodities to their respective prices, as follows:

$$\frac{U_1}{P_1} = \frac{U_2}{P_2} = \frac{dU}{dM} = U' \text{ a constant}$$

where U_1 and U_2 represent marginal utilities and P_1 and P_2 represent prices of Q_1 and Q_2 commodities respectively; and $\frac{dU}{dM} = U'$ represents the marginal utility of money, which is a constant. This implies that

$$\frac{U_1}{P_1} = \frac{U_2}{P_2} = U' \text{ a constant}$$

In case P_1 falls, the price and the marginal utility of Q_2 remaining unchanged, the above equation is disturbed, because after a fall in the price, the ratio of marginal utility and price of Q_1 does not remain in balance with ratio of marginal utility and price of Q_2 or with the marginal utility of money. In order to restore this balance the consumer must reduce the value of U_1 and this, according to the Law of Diminishing Marginal utility is possible only when, he purchases more units of Q_1 commodity. It is, thus, obvious that other things remaining the same, the consumer will buy more of the commodity as its price falls.

The derivation of demand curve can be exhibited as per Figure 7.2 as follows:

Thus, Figure 7.2(i) reveals that U_1 remaining the same, if P_1 falls, the $\frac{U_1}{P_1}$ curve is shifted to the higher and higher levels. The ratio of marginal utility and price of Q_2 at OE level, which also represents the constant marginal utility of money spent by the consumer. With every decrease in the price of Q_1, the $\frac{U_1}{P_1}$ curve is shifted upwards in a parallel way to $\frac{U_1}{P_1'}$ and $\frac{U_1}{P_1''}$ levels. Equilibrium level straight line intersects these marginal utility/price curves at A, B and C points respectively.

Thus, the consumer, who was purchasing OQ_1 quantity at the initial equilibrium position will now purchase OQ_1' and OQ_1'' quantities of the commodity at reduced prices of Q_1 commodity. Such price-quantity relations have been shown in Figure 7.2(ii), where at OP_1 price, the quantity purchased is OQ_1. After a fall in the price to OP_1', the quantity demanded has gone up to OQ_1' and at the price to OP_1'' the quantity demanded is OQ_1''. Thus, by combining A', B', C' points, we obtain DD demand curve, which slopes downward to the right and exhibits inverse relationship of price-quantity variations.

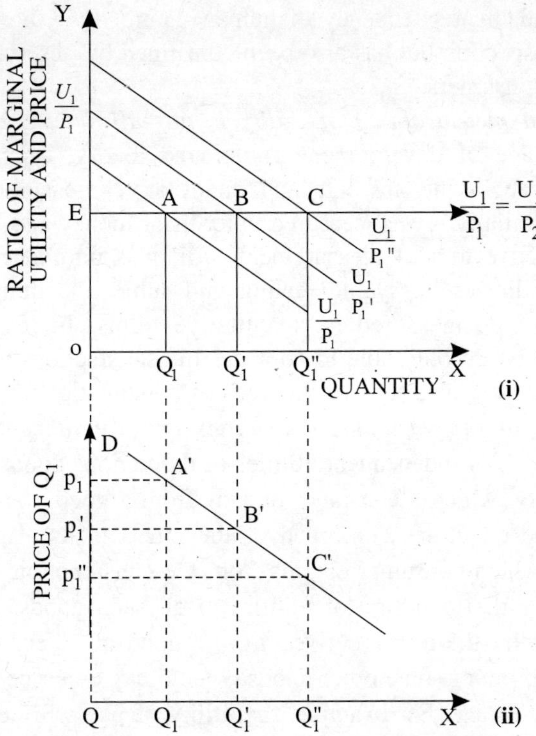

FIGURE 7.2 Derivation of Demand Theorem or Curve.

CRITICAL EVALUATION OF CARDINAL UTILITY ANALYSIS

The cardinal utility analysis has been the first to present a systematic theory of demand. Its development took over a century and a half and was perfected in its present form by Alfred Marshall. Although his successors tried to clear up the various ambiguities in the analysis, yet it could not be sustained due to the following drawbacks:

(i) ***Subjective Nature of Utility*:** It is not proper to use 'utility to explain the theory of demand, because demand is an objective phenomenon, while utility is subjective one, Utility theorists visualised a causal connection between price and utility and then between utility and desire and thus emphasised on 'desire' as originator of demand. This rendered the theory open to criticism of being based on 'individualistic' assumptions. Further, the diminishing marginal utility with successive increase in the units of commodity, which is crucial to the cardinal utility analysis of demand has been held by critics as too naive a description of human nature. However, such criticisms of the utility analysis are misplaced. The diminishing marginal utility according to even modern economists, is a familiar and fundamental tendency of human nature. It is, no doubt based on introspection but has also been confirmed by observed behaviour of the consumers.

(ii) ***Cardinal measurability of utility is unrealistic*:** Even at a very early stage of development of demand theory, economists were sceptic about the absolute and quantitative measurability of the utility. Initially it was measured in terms of money and subsequently an objective unit of measurement 'util' was introduced. However, since utility is a psychic feeling and subjective thing, therefore, it cannot be measured in quantitative terms. In real world, the consumers are only able to compare the satisfactions to be derived from the various goods or the various combinations of the goods.

(iii) ***Utilities of the various commodities are not independent*:** The assumption of independent utilities of the various goods implies that the utility, which a consumer obtains from a good does not depend upon the quantities consumed of the other goods. Thus, the total utility, which consumer obtains from the consumption of all goods, is simply the total sum of utilities of all such goods. However, in the real life the utility derived from a good also depends upon the consumption of some other goods, which may either be substitute or complementary. For example, the utility of pen will depend on the availability of ink and the utility of tea will be adversely affected by the availability of coffee. Thus, the utilities derived from the various goods are inter-dependent rather than being independent.

(iv) ***The assumption of constant marginal utility of money is unrealistic*:** In real life, as a consumer spends his money income on the goods, the money left with him diminishes and the marginal utility of money to him rises. Further, with a fall in price of goods, the real income of the consumer increases, which will change the marginal utility of money and will ultimately affect the demand for the commodity. The cardinal utility analysis ignores all these. This assumption induced Marshall to ignore the income effect of the price change and prevented him in understanding that the price effect is the sum of substitution effect and income effect.

(v) ***It is only particular theory*:** It applies to one-commodity case only and there too, the income effect is ignored. It is only a beginning of the demand theory, as according to Hicks **'the general theory of demand is a theory of the relations between the set of prices at which purchases are made and the set of quantities which are purchased'.** So, this theory, to be useful, need be generalised.

(vi) ***It fails to split up the price effect into substitution effect and income effect*:** In case the price of any commodity falls, the consumer after making usual purchases will have some money left unspent in his possession, which can be spent for purchasing additional units of the commodity, whose price has gone down. Such increase in purchase is known as income effect of fall in the price. Besides, when the price of a good falls, it becomes cheaper as compared to other goods, whose prices remained unchanged. As a result, the consumer is induced to purchase additional units of that goods, whose price has declined even by reducing the purchase of all other goods. This is substitution effect. A rise in demand due to fall in the price of any commodity is the result of both income and substitution effects, but the marginal utility analysis does not make clear distinction between the income and substitution effects of the price change. Instead, by assuming a constant marginal utility of money, the income effect has been ignored in this analysis.

(vii) ***This analysis fails to explain 'Giffen's Paradox'*:** Marshall regards it as an exception to the law of demand but failed to explain this exception. In case of Giffen goods, the negative income effect of the price change is more powerful than the positive substitution effect, therefore, when the price of Giffen goods increases, the negative income effect is overweighed the positive substitution effect and, as a result, the quantity demanded of it increases and vice versa.

(viii) ***It assumes too much and explains too little*:** It assumes that the utility is cardinally measurable, the marginal utility of money remains constant and utility of the various goods are independent and even on such assumptions it could not deduce a more general theory of demand.

(ix) ***Consumer's behaviour is not always rational*:** This law is based on the assumption that the consumer behaves in a perfectly rational manner, when he spends his money income on a number of different goods. In real life, the vast multiplicity of selections that the consumer has to make in his daily expenditure it prevents a careful weighing of utilities derived from the various goods. Moreover, the comparison of marginal utilities necessitates concentrated thinking on the part of the consumer for which he has neither time nor energy. Furthermore, he lacks necessary information for comparison and advertising often deceives him. These thing often introduce irrationality in his behaviour and, in turn, makes the analysis hypothetical.

Thus, the cardinal utility analysis has suffered from certain grave limitations, on account of which it has been discarded by modern economists, who recently introduced and perfected ordinal utility or indifference curve analysis.

Review Questions

1. What are the conditions for a consumer's equilibrium? Explain the determination of the consumer's equilibrium as per Marshallian approach.
2. Explain the concept of utility in economics and distinguish between cardinal and ordinal measurement of utility?
3. "The law of diminishing marginal utility has universal applicability and explains the method of deriving law of demand as per this law.
4. What is meant by equi-marginal utility? How can you distribute your limited resources to the various uses, so as to maximise your utility?
5. "The law of diminishing marginal utility is the basis for the law of demand". Explain this statement.
6. Examine the various ambiguities of the cardinal utility analysis.

8

Theory of Consumer's Behaviour: Indifference Curve Analysis

It has been noted that it is difficult for a consumer to weigh and express the utilities to be derived from consumption or possession of different commodities in terms of cardinal numbers, although he can very well compare the utilities of different goods under his consumption or possession. This ultimately resulted in the introduction of indifference curve analysis in the year 1934 by English Economists, J.R. Hicks and R.G.D. Allen, although this term has been discovered for the first time by an English Economist F.Y. Edgeworth. He used this term as early as 1881 to emphasise that the utility of a given commodity may be the function not only of its own quantity but also of the quantities of other commodities. This analysis has been evolved to supersede the cardinal utility analysis of demand. In this chapter an effort is being made to explain the determination of consumer's equilibrium with the help of indifference curves and price lines along with explaining the impact of change in price or income of the consumer.

ASSUMPTIONS OF INDIFFERENCE CURVE ANALYSIS

The indifference curve analysis eliminates the necessity of assuming that utility is measurable and avoids the use of the concept of 'diminishing marginal utility'. In this case, the consumer need not specify by how much does he prefer a given combination to another. Instead, he has to specify that he does or does not prefer one combination of two goods to another or he is indifferent with respect to the various combinations of the goods. Ignoring the basic assumptions of the utility analysis, it proceeds on certain assumptions as follows:

(i) The consumer has a preference criterion on the basis of which he is either indifferent to the various combinations or prefers one combination to another. In other words, if the consumer is presented with a number of the various combinations of goods, he can order or rank them in his scale of preference.

(ii) It is further assumed that more is always better than less. It means that the consumer will always prefer a combination of larger quantities of two goods than the combination of their smaller quantities. In other words, both commodities command positive marginal utility and not zero or negative marginal utility along with the various indifference curves.

(iii) Consumer's preferences are consistent with one another.

(iv) Consumer's preference and indifference relations are transitive. In case he prefers one combination to other and the other to third one, then he will certainly prefer one combination to the third one.

(v) Commodities under consideration are perfectly divisible and substitutable, which enables the derivation of a smoothly sloping indifference curves.

(vi) The consumer is assumed to possess complete information of his economic environment (goods, prices, markets, etc.) and is expected to behave rationally, that is, faced with the given prices of commodities and the sum of money income, the consumer spends his income to select that combination of goods, which is the highest attainable on his scale of preferences.

(vii) It is also assumed that the consumer formulates his scale of preferences independent of the prices of goods keeping in view only the satisfaction, which he hopes to get from the various combinations of goods.

(viii) This analysis is based on the weak ordering form of preference hypothesis, which implies the possibility of consumer being indifferent between different combinations as well.

NATURE OF INDIFFERENCE CURVE

Indifference curve, iso-utility curve or constant total utility curve, refers to a curve, the various points of which show the various combinations of two commodities, where the total utility remains constant all along as the quantities of commodities consumed or possessed by the consumer change. For example, if a consumer wants to buy Q_1 and Q_2 commodities regarding whose quantities he has no definite idea. But he knows that one combination of Q_1 and Q_2 may give him as much total utility as another combination of fewer units of Q_1 and more units of Q_2 or a combination of more units of Q_1 and fewer units of Q_2. He may not express the total sum of utility, thus derived, yet he can very well compare the utility to be derived from one combination with that of another. Thus, the various combinations of two commodities may be such that the consumer may be indifferent among them. This may be represented by a curve known as indifference curve as per Figure 8.1 as follows.

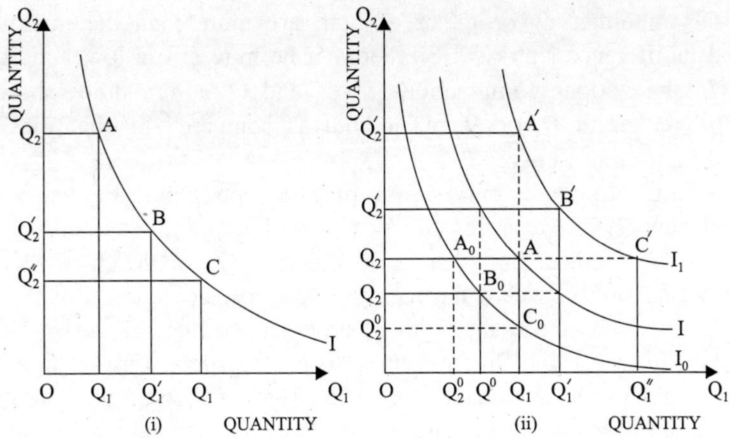

FIGURE 8.1 Slopes and Shifts of Indifference Curves.

This indifference curve is a geometrical expression of the various combinations of two goods Q_1 and Q_2 on the assumption that the goods constituting the combinations are infinitely divisible. Along with the indifference curve (*I*) in Figure 8.1(i), the various combinations at *A*, *B* and *C* points respectively may give same total utility to the consumer. In other words, the total utility remains unchanged, despite change in the quantities of goods under consideration.

Mathematically, indifference curve may be defined as curve where:

$$\Delta U = u_1 \Delta Q_1 + u_2 \Delta Q_2 = 0$$

Here Q_1 and Q_2 are quantities of two goods under consideration; u_1 and u_2 are marginal utilities of such goods and both have positive values; U is measurement of total utility and Δ (delta) represents change in respective quantities. Thus, if the marginal utilities of commodities (i.e., u_1 and u_2) are assumed to be positive, the change either in the quantity of Q_1 or Q_2 must be negative, in order to derive no (or zero) change in the total utility on an indifference curve. This explains the negative (i.e., downward to the right) slope of the indifference curve.

On a single indifference curve, the total utility remains unchanged, but the consumer gets higher utility, if he moves to a higher indifference curve, where he purchases the increased quantity of Q_1 keeping the quantity of Q_2 as constant and vice-versa or the increased quantity of both Q_1 and Q_2. Similarly, a lower in-difference curve reveals lower total utility, because on such curve, the consumer purchase lesser quantity of Q_1 keeping the quantity of Q_2 as constant and vice-versa or the lesser quantities of Q_1 and Q_2 both. In Figure 8.1(ii), if the consumer moves to a higher indifference curve, I_1, all points of this curve show the various combinations of Q_1 and Q_2 commodities, where the quantities of either Q_1 or Q_2 or of both are more than the quantities on original indifference curve (I). Similarly, if he moves to a lower indifference curve I_0, the various combinations of Q_1 and Q_2 commodities show lesser quantities either of Q_1 or Q_2 or of both as compared to quantities on the original indifference curve (I).

A set of indifference curves in a diagram representing the various levels of satisfaction is called an indifference map. The indifference curve, in fact, expresses three dimensions, that is, so much of Q_1; so much of Q_2 and the constant total utility, where the former two dimensions are variable but the third one is a constant along with a particular indifference curve. However, movement from one indifference curve to another involves variation even in the third dimension, as each curve to the right of the original indifference curve has a higher total utility and to the left of the original indifference curve a lower total utility.

PROPERTIES OF INDIFFERENCE CURVES

The indifference curves have three basic characteristics, which are as follows:

1. The indifference curve has a negative slope, which means that it slopes downwards to the right. It indicates that as the quantity of one commodity along with such curve increases, the quantity of the other commodity decreases, so as to yield the same total utility. As per the mathematical definition of indifference curve, in order to maintain the value of $u_1\,\Delta Q_1 + u_2\,\Delta Q_2 = \Delta U = 0$, where u_1 and u_2 both are assumed to be the positive marginal utilities, quantity of either Q_1 or Q_2 is bound to be negative, if we move from one point to other on any indifference curve. Other possible slopes of indifference curve may be assumed to be positive, vertical or horizontal, but on account of assuming a positive marginal utility from both commodities, none of these slopes can assure the same total utility from all combinations at the various points along with such curves.

   The slope of the indifference curve is called the marginal rate of substitution. It refers to the quantity of Q_2 the consumer stands ready to give up, in order to acquire additional quantity of Q_1. Mathematically, the slope or the marginal rate of substitution (MRS) of Q_2 for Q_1 is as follows:

$$\text{MRS} = -\ \Delta Q_2/\Delta Q_1$$

   Here, $-\ \Delta Q_2$ is the quantity of Q_2 the consumer is ready to give up, and ΔQ_1 is the additional quantity of Q_1 the consumer is ready to acquire. It can be exhibited as per Figure 8.2 as follows.

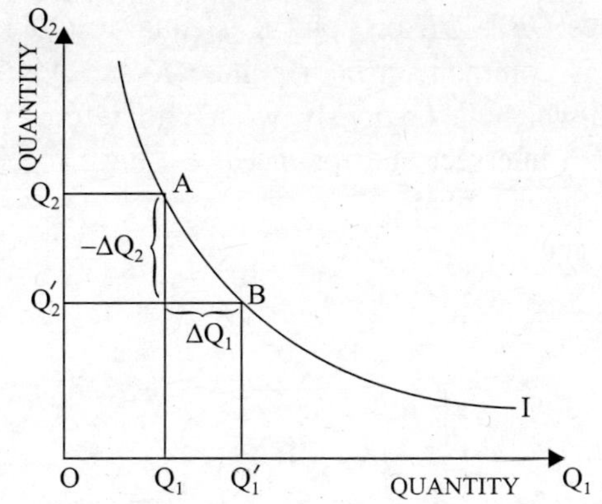

FIGURE 8.2 Slope or MRS of Indifference Curve.

In Figure 8.2, when the consumer moves from *A* to *B*, he acquires ΔQ_1, to offset the loss of ΔQ_2. The marginal rate of substitution is the same thing as the ratio of marginal utilities of the two commodities. This can be proved as follows:

$$\Delta U = u_1 \Delta Q_1 + u_2 \Delta Q_2 = 0$$

$$u_1 \Delta Q_1 + u_2 \Delta Q_2 = 0$$

$$u_1 \Delta Q_1 = -u_2 \Delta Q_2$$

By dividing both sides of this equation by $u_2 \Delta Q_1$.

$$\frac{u_1 \Delta Q_1}{u_2 \Delta Q_1} = \frac{-u_2 \Delta Q_2}{u_2 \Delta Q_1}$$

After removing the common terms in numerator and denominator on both sides of the equation, we obtain a new equation as follows:

$$\frac{u_1}{u_2} = \frac{-\Delta Q_2}{\Delta Q_1}$$

Since, $-\Delta Q_2/\Delta Q_1$ measures MRS, therefore MRS is also measured by u_1/u_2.

Thus, the marginal rate of substitution is the reciprocal of the ratio of marginal utilities of the two commodities.

2. In an indifference map the indifference curves are generally drawn parallel to each other. In case they are not parallel, the intersection between them at some points is inevitable, which will introduce inconsistency in the choice of the different combinations.

   In Figure 8.3, since all combinations of Q_1 and Q_2 on the respective indifference curves are expected to yield the same total utility, therefore, *OA* + *OF* on point *M* is equal to *OB* + *OH* on points *K*. Similarly, *OA* + *OF* on point *M* = *OB* + *OG* on point *N*.

Hence *OB* + *OH* on point *K* is equal to *OB* + *OG* on point *N*. Since OB is common on both points (*K* and *N*) *OH* should be equal to *OG*, which is obviously wrong, therefore, the indifference curves cannot intersect and for that these have to be drawn parallel in the indifference map.

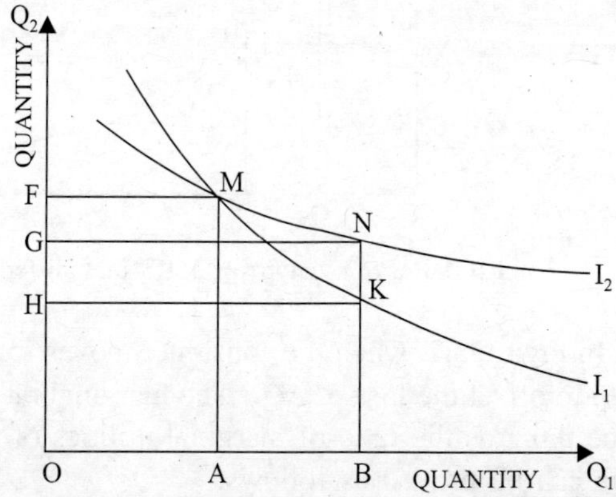

FIGURE 8.3 Intersection of Indifference Curves not Possible.

(3) Indifference curves are always drawn convex to the origin. It means that it has got a bend towards the origin. This is because of diminishing marginal rate of substitution (MRS). In case Q_2 is substituted for Q_1, then as the quantity of Q_1 is increased by equal increments, Q_2 falls by ever smaller quantities. It is because, as the quantity of Q_2 diminishes, it gains relatively more importance than the increasing quantity of Q_1 to the consumer, therefore, as the points on the *X*-axis moves to the right by equal distances along with the indifference curve, the points on *Y*-axis come down in height less and less.

Figure 8.4(i) reveals that as the quantity of Q_1 increases unit by unit, the quantity of Q_2 falls by ever decreasing number of units correspondingly. Conversely, the consumer requires increasing quantities of Q_2 to offset given decreases in the quantity of Q_1, in case we move to the left on both axes. Similarly, Figure 8.4(ii) reveals that the slope of indifference curves becomes flatter if we move towards the right and tangents drawn to successive points on the curve become progressively less steep.

The degree of convexity also reveals the nature of the relationship of the two commodities Q_1 and Q_2. The closer the indifference curve approaches to a straight line, the better substitutes the two commodities are for each other. In case the two goods are perfect substitutes, that is, for all practical purposes they are same goods

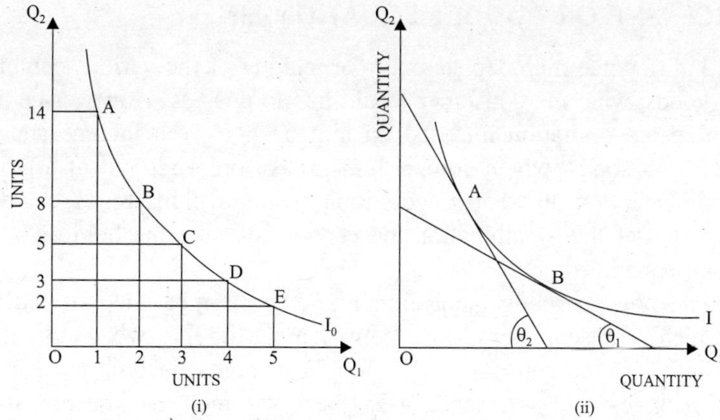

FIGURE 8.4 Changing Slopes of the Indifference Curves.

and there is no points in distinguishing them, the indifference curves are straight lines sloping negatively. This reveals that the marginal rate of substitution remains the same whatsoever combination the consumer may choose of the two commodities [Figure 8.5(i)].

On the other hand, the lesser the substitutability of the two commodities, the greater is the convexity of indifference curve towards the origin. The degree of convexity reveals the complementarity between the two commodities. Thus, it is another extreme that exists, when two goods cannot be substituted for each other, that is, the two must be used in fixed proportions only.

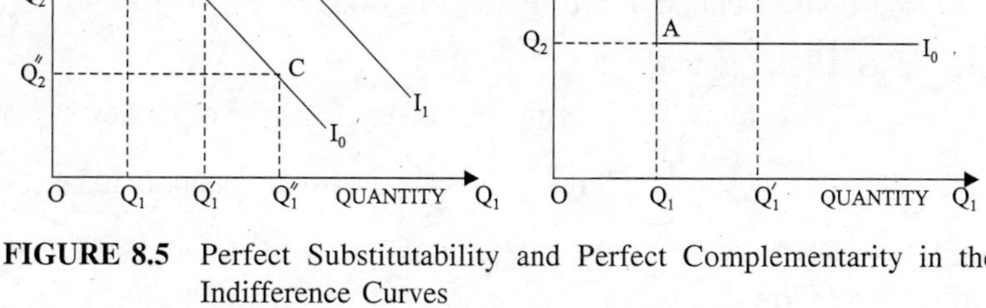

FIGURE 8.5 Perfect Substitutability and Perfect Complementarity in the Indifference Curves

In Figure 8.5(ii) the consumer is bound to take OQ_1 along with OQ_2 because even if he takes more Q_2 along with fixed quantity of Q_1, (i.e., OQ_1) the utility will remain equal to that derived from the original combination of OQ_1 and OQ_2 quantities of the two commodities.

PRICE LINE OR BUDGET EQUATION LINE

The indifference map depicts only the ranking of the various combinations of two goods, what the consumer would like to possess. However he has to bear in mind the limitation imposed on him by his given income and the prices of the two goods, which compel him to take only one out of a large number of combinations of the two goods on a single indifference curve. In order to single out that combination the economists take the help of price line or budget equation line.

The price or budget equation line is a straight line, the various points of which represent the various combinations of the two goods, that can be purchased by the consumer with the given money income at their prevailing market prices. In this respect, it has been assumed that the consumer spends on the two goods an invariable sum of money, secondly that the prices of the two goods are given and remain uninfluenced by his purchases. Thus, the price line indicates the various combinations of the two goods that the consumer can buy with his given money income at their given prices.

This line is drawn on the basis of budget equation, which relates income and prices as follows:

$$P_1Q_1 + P_2Q_2 = M$$

Here, P_1 and P_2 represent the respective prices of Q_1 and Q_2 goods and M the total money income of the consumer.

Since on the two axes of the indifference map physical quantities of the two commodities are shown, we ascertain first the maximum quantities of Q_1 and Q_2 respectively that can be acquired, if the total money income is devoted to the purchases of Q_1 maintaining the purchase of Q_2 at zero level and vice-versa. After combining the two maximum points on respective axes by a straight line, we get the price line or the budget equation line, which reveals the capacity of the consumer to have any one of a large number of combinations of the two goods along with this line with given money income at given prices of the two goods. When the quantity of Q_1 is assumed to be zero, the revised equation will be as follows:

$P_1(O) + P_2Q_2 = M$; or

$P_2Q_2 = M$; It assumes total expenditure of money income on Q_2

$Q_2 = \frac{M}{P_2}$ It represents the maximum quantity to be bought of Q_2.

Similarly, when the quantity of Q_2 is assumed to be zero, the new equation will be as follows:

$P_1Q_1 + P_2(O) = M$; or

$P_1Q_1 = M$; It assumes the total expenditure of money income on Q_1

$Q_1 = \frac{M}{P_1}$ It represents the maximum quantity to be bought of Q_1

The same can be plotted in a diagram as follows:

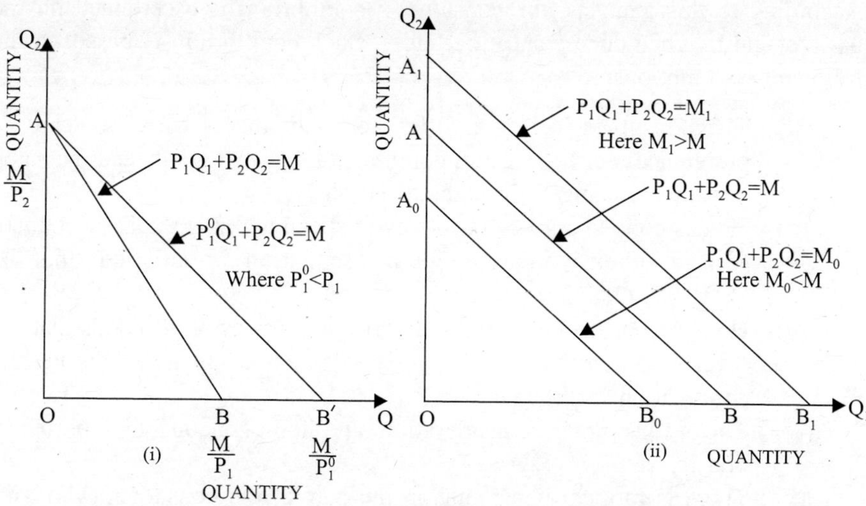

FIGURE 8.6 Budget Equation Lines or Price Lines.

The slope of the price line as given in Figure 8.6(i) is equal to

$$\frac{OA}{OB} = \frac{M}{P_2} \div \frac{M}{P_1} = \frac{M}{P_2} \times \frac{P_1}{M} = \frac{P_1}{P_2}$$

Thus, the slope of the price line is equal to the ratio of prices of the two commodities. This slope undergoes a change only when the price of either Q_1 or Q_2 changes. In Figure 8.6(i), when P_1 declines to $P_1{}^0$, while P_2 remains at the same level, the maximum quantities of Q_1 that can be acquired by devoting total money income to Q_1 goes up and this reduces the slope of the price line or budget line.

Similarly, as per Figure 8.6(ii) changes in the expenditure by the consumer shifts the position of price line upward or downward. In case expenditure increases, price of the two goods remaining the same, the price line shifts upwards to the right but this new price line is still parallel to the original price line, as the prices of the two goods remain unchanged. In case the expenditure of the consumer falls, the price line will shift downward to the left and again in a parallel way due to constant prices of the two goods.

Again, the proportionate decrease in P_1 and P_2 shifts the price line upwards to the right in a parallel way, whereas proportionate increase in the two prices shifts the price line downwards to the left in the same way. In other words, change in expenditure or proportionate change in price of the commodities shifts the price line to the right or left (upwards or downwards) but does not change the slope of such line. The slope of price line also known as Market Exchange Rate (MER), which remains constant along with such line, as it is a straight line.

CONSUMER'S EQUILIBRIUM

According to this analysis, the consumer's equilibrium is ascertained on the basis of indifference curves and price lines. Such equilibrium is based on the following assumptions:

(i) The consumer has an indifference map that shows his scale of preferences for the various combinations of two goods and the same remains unchanged throughout the analysis.
(ii) He has a given amount of money to spend and it is totally accounted for. In other words, the budget equation is satisfied, that is, $P_1Q_1 + P_2Q_2 = M$.
(iii) He is one of many buyers and knows the prices of all goods that are given and constant. Alternatively, we can say that there is perfect competition in the market.
(iv) The goods under consideration are homogeneous and perfectly divisible.
(v) There is rational behaviour on the part of the consumer, who tries to maximise his utility.

We can recall the Marshallian equi-marginal principle, which states that **'if a person has a thing which he can put to several uses, he will distribute it among these uses in such a way that it has the same marginal utility in all'.** In other words, it simply requires that the ratios of the marginal utilities to prices of the two commodities respectively must be equal at equilibrium, so that the utility of the marginal unit of income devoted to any use is just exactly equal to the utility of the marginal unit of income devoted to any other, Mathematically,

$$\frac{u_1}{P_1} = \frac{u_2}{P_2} \text{ Marshallian equilibrium condition.}$$

By multiplying both sides by P_1 and by dividing both sides by u_2,

$$= \frac{P_1}{u_2} \times \frac{u_1}{P_1} = \frac{u_2}{P_2} \times \frac{P_1}{u_2}$$

$$= \frac{u_1}{u_2} = \frac{P_1}{P_2} \text{ This derived equilibrium condition.}$$

Thus, at equilibrium the ratios of marginal utilities of the various uses of money income i.e., u_1/u_2 (which is also equal to Marginal Rate of Substitution i.e., $-\Delta Q_2/\Delta Q_1$) must be equal to the ratios of their respective prices (i.e., the Market Exchange Rate).

This may also be depicted diagrammatically with the help of the indifference map of the consumer and his price line by superimposing the price line on the indifference map. This reveals the highest combination of two goods on his scale of preference attainable with his given money income at the given prices of the two goods. Thus, the consumer would be in equilibrium only at such a point that lies on his price line and also on the highest attainable indifference curve, as follows:

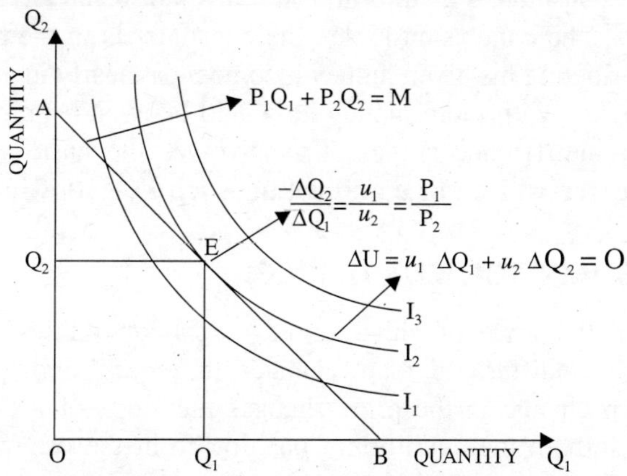

FIGURE 8.7 Consumer's Equilibrium Position.

The equilibrium position of the consumer is at point *E* on the price line, where it is tangent to the highest possible indifference curve I_2. The equilibrium quantities of the two goods are OQ_1 and OQ_2 respectively. This is the most appropriate combination of Q_1 and Q_2 goods, as any other combination of the two goods on the same indifference curve are not attainable by the price line *AB*.

In case the consumer decides to purchase more of Q_2 and consequently less of Q_1, he would move along *AB* from *E* towards *A* or if he decides to purchase more of Q_1 and consequently less of Q_2, he would move along with the *AB* price line from *E* towards *B*; both these actions would put him on a lower indifference curve. A price line can be tangent to only one convex indifference curve and no higher indifference curve can be reached with the given money income at the given prices of two goods than the one to which the budget line is tangent. At any other point the consumer cannot be in equilibrium, as these points on the price line will lie on a lower indifference curve indicating a lower level of satisfaction.

Thus, *E* is the only point of equilibrium, showing the highest level of utility, the consumer can get by allocating his income on Q_1 and Q_2 goods. Any other point even on the same indifference curve will be beyond his reach.

Moreover, at point *E* the price line (*AB*) is tangent to the indifference curve (I_2). It indicates that the slopes of the price line and of the indifference curve are equal at this point. On account of equality in the slopes of indifference curve and the price line, the marginal rate of substitution (MRS) is equal to the market exchange rate (MER), that gives the algebraic value of equilibrium as follows:

$$\text{MRS} = \frac{-\Delta Q_2}{\Delta Q_1} = \frac{u_1}{u_2} = \frac{P_1}{P_2} = \text{MER}$$

Thus, it is similar to that derived from the cardinal utility analysis, although in this analysis of consumer's equilibrium, we have not made any use of cardinal utility concepts. The conclusion is that the consumer is in the happy position, when he is distributing his given money income most nearly in accordance with his preferences and with more money he would be even happier by switching over to higher indifference curves. This involves the basic value judgment that the **'consumer will be in equilibrium when he gets what he wants'.**

PRICE CONSUMPTION CURVE (PCC)

Any change in the price of either of the two commodities, shown on the two axes of the indifference map, changes the equilibrium position of the consumer. Such change in the price changes the slope of the price line that necessitates a shift in the equilibrium position from the original indifference curve to a higher or lower indifference curve, as the case may be. Assuming that the consumer is initially in equilibrium at point A, successive decreases in the price of Q_1 places his equilibrium at A^1 and A^2, on I^1 and I^2, indifference curves respectively, where he is purchasing greater quantities of Q_1 commodity with the given amount of money income, as shown in Figure 8.8 as follows:

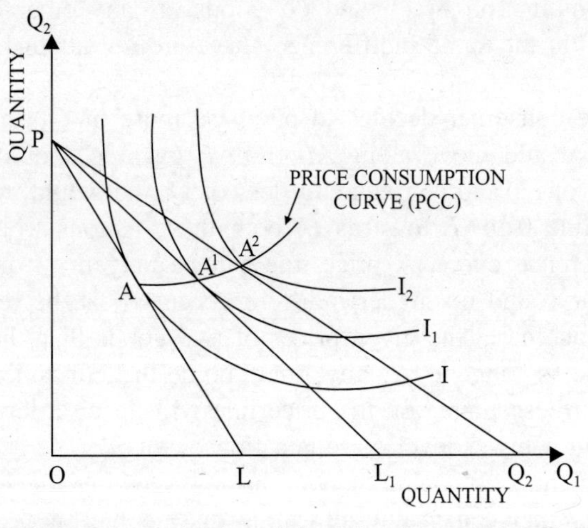

FIGURE 8.8 Derivation of the Price Consumption Curve.

Here AA^2 is the price consumption curve (PCC), which combines successive points of equilibrium, derived by the successive decreases in the price of Q_1 commodity, while the price of Q_2 and the money income of the consumer remain unchanged. At these successive points new budget lines are tangent to higher indifference curves, which indicates that the consumer's total utility has increased. Thus, price consumption curve (PCC) traces out the price effect.

There can be three possible slopes of the price consumption curve, which is based on the relationship between the goods under consideration as follows:

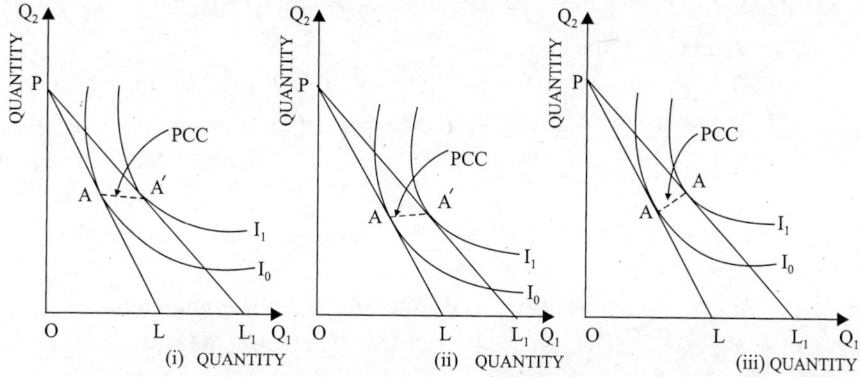

FIGURE 8.9 Possible Slopes of the Price Consumption Curves.

A negative (downward to the right) slope of the price consumption curve (PCC) as in Figure 8.9(i) shows that as the price of the commodity Q_1 falls, the more of it is purchased, even by reducing the purchases of Q_2 commodity. In other words, as Q_1 goes cheaper it substitutes Q_2 to some extent. It reveals that Q_1 is a substitute for the Q_2. On the other hand, a positive slope (upward to the right) of the price consumption curve (PCC), as in Figure 8.9(iii), reveals that with a fall in the price of Q_1, greater quantities of both goods will be purchased. It indicates that both goods are complementary. In case the price consumption curve (PCC) is parallel to the horizontal axis, as in Figure 8.9(ii), the goods under consideration are taken as independent goods.

Besides, the slope of the price consumption curve (PCC) also reveals the degree of price elasticity of demand for the commodity, whose price has declined. If PCC slopes downwards to the right, the purchase of Q_1 increases more than proportionately with the decrease in P_1 indicating an elastic demand for Q_1. Similarly, an upward slope of the PCC indicates less than proportionate increase in the purchases of Q_1 in response to a decrease in P_1, which indicates an inelastic demand for Q_1. A slope of the PCC parallel to the horizontal axis shows a proportionate increase in the purchases of Q_1 in response to a decrease in P_1, which, in turn, reveals a unitary elastic demand for Q_1. Mathematically, the value of the elasticity of demand of Q_1 in response to change in P_1 will be more than one on a negatively sloping PCC, less than one on positively sloping PCC and equal to one on PCC parallel to horizontal axis. It is as follows:

$$P_1Q_1+P_2Q_2=M \text{ (Budget Equation)}$$

$$(P_1+\Delta P_1)(Q_1+\Delta Q_1)+P_2(Q_2+\Delta Q_2)=M \qquad \text{(New Budget Equation) after change in } P_1$$

$$P_1Q_1 + P_1\Delta Q_1 + Q_1\Delta P_1 + \Delta P_1\Delta Q_1 + P_2Q_2 + P_2\,\Delta Q_2 = M$$ (On removal of brackets)

In order to derive a change by new budget equation after change in P_1 over the original budget equation, the latter is subtracted from the former, one;

$$(P_1Q_1 + P_1\Delta Q_1 + Q_1\Delta P_1 + \Delta P_1\Delta Q_1 + P_2Q_2 + P_2\Delta Q_2) - (P_1Q_1 + P_2Q_2)$$

On removal of the brackets,

$$P_1Q_1 + P_1\Delta Q_1 + Q_1\Delta P_1 + \Delta P_1\Delta Q_1 + P_2Q2 + P_2\Delta Q_2 - P_1Q_1 - P_2Q_2$$

$$P_1\Delta Q_1 + Q_1\Delta P_1 + \Delta P_1\Delta Q_1 + P_2\Delta Q_2 = 0$$ (After deduction of negative figures from the relevant positive figures)

$$P_1\Delta Q_1 + \Delta Q_1\Delta P_1 + Q_1\Delta P_1 + P_2\Delta Q_2 = 0$$ (After change in place of figures)

$$\Delta Q_1(P_1 + \Delta P_1) + Q_1\Delta P_1 + P_2\Delta Q_2 = 0.$$ (Taking common factors)

$$(P_1 + \Delta P_1)\,\Delta Q_1 = -\,Q_1\,\Delta P_1 - P_2\Delta Q_2.$$ (Changing the side)

$$= \frac{(P_1 + \Delta P_1)\Delta Q_1}{-Q_1\Delta P_1} = \frac{-Q_1\Delta P_1}{-Q_1\Delta P_1}\frac{-P_2\Delta Q_2}{-Q_1\Delta P_1}.$$ Dividing both sides by $-\,Q_1\Delta P_1$

$$= -\frac{(P_1 + \Delta P_1)}{Q_1} \times \frac{\Delta Q_1}{\Delta P_1} = 1 + \frac{P_2}{Q_1} \times \frac{\Delta Q_2}{\Delta P_1}$$

Since the first part of the above equation, i.e., $-\frac{(P_1 + \Delta P_1)}{Q_1} \times \frac{\Delta Q_1}{\Delta P_1}$ measures the price elasticity of demand, therefore, the second part will also measure the same.

Thus,

$$ED = 1 + \frac{P_2}{Q_1} \cdot \frac{\Delta Q_2}{\Delta P_1}$$

In case of negatively sloping PCC, the values of both ΔQ_2 and ΔP_1, on account of price decrease, are negative, which produces a positive value. After multiplication by P_2/Q_1 (both having positive values) we derive a positive figure which, when added to 1, produces a value of the elasticity of demand more than one. The value of the elasticity of demand more than one is indicative of an elastic demand.

On the other hand, on a positively sloping PCC, the value of ΔQ_2 is positive but the value of ΔP_1 is negative (indicating a decrease in price), which gives a negative figure and when it is multiplied by P_2/Q_1 (both positive values), it yields a negative figure though that is only a fraction of one. When this negative fraction is added to I, the resultant value of the elasticity of demand will be less than one, which indicates that demand for Q_1 is inelastic.

In case the PCC is parallel to the horizontal axis the value of $\Delta Q_2 = 0$ and, as a result, the whole division and multiplication will yield a value equal to zero, which when added to one, the value of the elasticity of demand will remain equal to one. This indicates a unitary elastic demand for Q_1.

INCOME CONSUMPTION CURVE (ICC)

The change in income of the consumer is another important factor that affects the demand for any commodity and disturbs its original equilibrium. Price remaining unchanged, as income increases the price line is shifted upwards to the right and a decrease in income shifts the price line downwards to the left, the new price lines remain parallel to the original one. As income rises and price line shifts to the right, the consumer gets the equilibrium at a higher indifference curve, which is tangent to the new price line. In case, these successive equilibrium points are combined by a curve, it is known as income consumption curve (ICC). It shows the relationship between changes in income of the consumer and the quantity of goods demanded.

Thus, the income consumption curve (ICC) combines successive points of equilibrium produced by successive increases in money income of the consumer. There are three possible slopes of this curve viz., positive, vertically parallel and negative that reveal the quality of the goods being purchased. The positive slope of the income consumption curve (ICC), as in Figure 8.10(i), reveals that the commodity purchased is of superior quality, because purchase increases, as the income increases.

In case the income consumption curve is drawn parallel to the vertical axis as in the Figure 8.10(ii) it indicates that the purchase of Q_1 does not change as money income increases. Certainly Q_1 appears to be a neutral goods. This also shows that the quantity demanded of Q_1 is independent of money income but the demand for Q_2 is a function of money income.

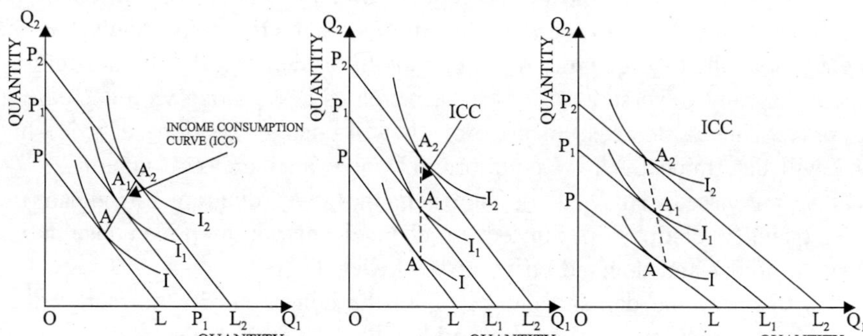

FIGURE 8.10 Possible Slopes of the Income Consumption Curves.

In case of inferior goods, the income consumption curve slopes upwards to the left as in Figure 8.10(iii). It shows that the purchase of Q_1 decreases, as money income increases with constant prices of the commodities. The slope also reveals the income elasticity of demand (*Ei*) as follows:

$$Ei = \frac{M}{Q_1} \times \frac{\Delta Q_1}{\Delta M}$$

In case of positively slopping income consumption curve, the value of $\Delta Q_1/\Delta M$ is positive, which, when multiplied by M/Q_1 (positive figures), produces a positive figure as the value of the income elasticity of demand. This positive value of the income elasticity is indicative of a normal or superior quality of goods. Similarly in case of vertically parallel income consumption curve, the value of $\Delta Q_1/\Delta M$ is equal to zero, as there is no change in the purchase of Q_1 despite positive change in the money income. This makes the value of income elasticity equal to zero. It is in case neutral goods. In case of negatively sloping income consumption curve, the value of $\Delta Q_1/\Delta M$ is negative that yields a negative value for the income elasticity of demand, which indicates inferior quality goods.

DERIVATION OF DEMAND THEOREM

The price consumption curve (PCC) of indifference curve analysis helps in deriving the individual demand curve and by combining information of these, the market demand curve can also be derived. The demand curve and the price consumption curve give almost the same information, although the former is more direct. The slope of the price consumption curves generally discloses the increase in purchases in response to decrease in the price of the goods, although this decrease in price is not directly shown on the y-axis (as is the case with the demand curve) but through changing slopes of the price line. This indirect presentation of demand curve can be shown as in Figure 8.11 as follows:

The price line PL shows the highest and PL_2 the lowest price of Q_1 commodity, which in lower diagram are OP and OP_2 respectively. At the highest price the OQ_1 quantity of Q_1 commodity is demanded in both diagrams. These diagrams have shown successive increases in Q_1 along with decrease in its price. Thus, a decrease in price of Q_1 will change the slope of price line and will determine the new equilibrium, where an increased quantity of Q_1 will be purchased. This will be shown in the lower diagram to indicate the price quantity relationship. Subsequent changes enlarge the price consumption curve in upper and demand curve in the lower diagram.

In this way the demand curves of all the consumers in the market may be derived and summing up them horizontally, the market demand curve can be derived. The usual negative slope of the individual demand curve is also found in case of market demand curve, which reveals that, as the price of the goods falls, the more of it is demanded by the buyers and vice-versa. In Marshallian utility analysis, the demand curve was derived on the assumptions that the utility was quantitatively measurable and the marginal utility of money remained constant with the change in price of goods. In the indifference curve analysis demand curve is derived even without making such assumptions.

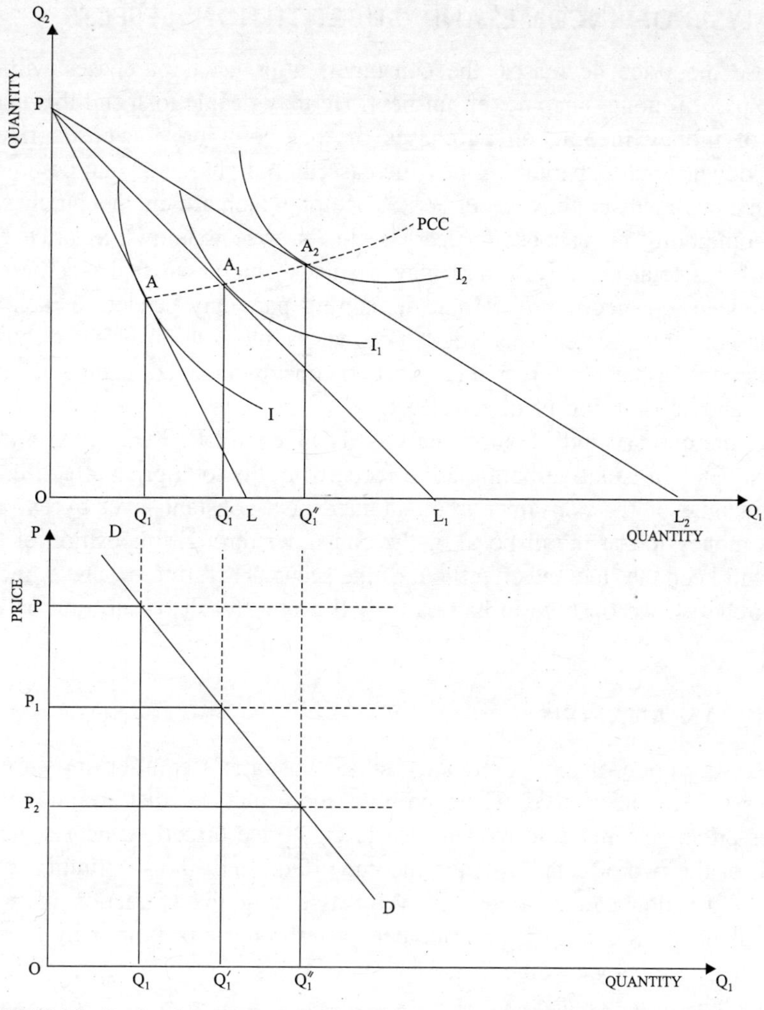

FIGURE 8.11 Derivation of Demand Theorem as per Indifference Curves and Price Lines.

Thus, when price of any commodity falls, the demand for the same extends, which is the 'price effect'. This price effect may be bifurcated into the 'income effect' and 'substitution effect' and both the substitution effect and income effect pull together in extending the demand of the goods, when price falls. Substitution effect always works in the positive direction, whereas the income effect particularly in case of inferior goods, works in negative direction. Therefore, generally we get a demand curve sloping downwards to the right but where negative income effect is powerful enough to outweigh the positive substitution effect, the demand curve will slope upwards to the right instead of sloping downwards, to the right. Thus, the indifference curve analysis can drive a positively sloping demand curve, which is generally found in case of 'Giffen Goods'.

ANALYSIS OF 'INCOME' AND 'SUBSTITUTION' EFFECTS

In case the price decreases, the consumer, after usual purchases will have some part of money income left unspent. He may decide to spend this unspent part of money income on purchases of that commodity whose price has gone down. Such expenditure may increase the purchases of that commodity, which is termed as 'income effect'. The total increase in the purchases of any commodity in response to decrease in its price is known as price effect. Out of this total increase, a part may be due to increased real income of the consumer (i.e., income effect) and remaining part may be due to inclination of the consumer for cheaper goods (known as substitution effect). Thus, the price effect has been bifurcated into its two constituents, viz, income or indirect effect and substitution or direct effect.

Contemporary indifference analysis as given by R.G.D., Allen and J.R. Hicks, helps in isolating both these effects, from the total price effect. In case, real income of the consumer is maintained at a constant level by extracting extra money left at the disposal of the consumer through imposition of taxes, this will keep the 'income effect' out of the scene. Therefore, whatever increase in purchases, we observe in that case, will be the result of substitution effect alone.

HICKSIAN ANALYSIS

In case the price of any commodity falls, consumer's equilibrium shifts to a higher indifference curve, where he buys more units of that commodity at a lower price. The increase in purchase is the 'price effect', which is the total result of the two effects, viz., 'the income effect' and 'the substitution effect.' This bifurcation can be done either by assuming the extraction of amount equivalent to the saving from price decrease through taxation or by regarding the released money income as the increase in his money income, while price has remained unchanged.

In Figure 8.12(i), the consumer is in equilibrium at *E*, where the original indifference curve *I* is tangent to the original price line *AB* and the consumer purchases *OM* quantity of Q_1 commodity. When price of Q_1 falls, the consumer gets a new price line *AB'*, which is tangent to a higher indifference curve *I'* at *E'*, where the consumer purchases *OK* quantity of Q_1 commodity at the reduced price. At reduced price, after usual purchases of Q_1 and Q_2 commodities, the consumer has some money left unspent, which may be extracted by the government through imposition of tax. This shifts the price line after tax to CD level, which is tangent to original indifference curve at *E''* point. At this new equilibrium the consumer has reduced his purchases Q_1 to *OH* quantity only. Thus, increase in purchase after price reduction by HK quantity has been due to 'income effect' because the consumer reduced his purchases by this quantity, when the increased income was extracted from his possession. The rest of the increase in purchases equal to MH is due to substitution effect.

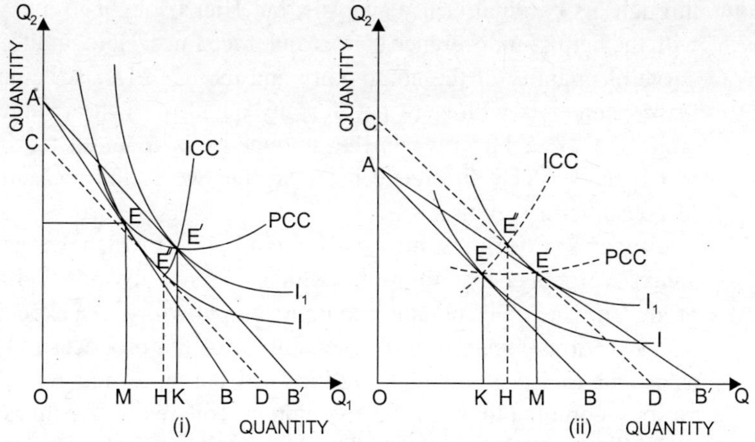

FIGURE 8.12 Hicksian Derivation of the Price and Income Consumption Curves.

Alternatively in Figure 8.12(ii), the consumer is in equilibrium at *E,* where the original price line *AB* is tangent to the original in difference curve *I.* A reduction in price of Q_1 shifts the price line to *AB′* level and the equilibrium to *E′* point, where the consumer purchases an increased quantity of Q_1 equal to MK. This fall in price of Q_1 will release some amount of money. With this increased real income the consumer will move to a higher indifference curve and will become better off than before. It is as if price has remained unchanged but his money income has increased. This fall in price of Q_1 is as beneficial to the consumer as an equivalent rise in the money income of the consumer. Thus, the consumer is imagined to be moving up to a higher indifference curve along with the income consumption curve, as if prices of Q_1 and Q_2 remaining unchanged his money income has increased, . We draw a new price line *CD* after imagined increase in income, which is tangent to a higher indifference curve I_1 at point *E″* Had there been increase in the income equivalent to money released by price reduction with no change in prices of Q_1 and Q_2, the consumer would have increased the quantity of Q_1 by *KH,* which represents the income effect. The rest of the increase equal to *MH* is the substitution effect.

APPLICATIONS OF INDIFFERENCE CURVE ANALYSIS

The indifference curve, at present, has become an important tool of economic analysis. This technique is now being increasingly used to explain the concept of consumer's surplus, substitutability and complementarity, welfare economics, taxation, subsidy, foreign trade, index numbers, exchange rate under bilateral monopoly and several other economic phenomena as follows:

(i) **Measurement of Consumer's Surplus:** The concept of consumer's surplus refers to the difference between what a consumer is willing to pay and what he actually pays. Marshall measured this surplus through his cardinal utility analysis, but Hicks sought to measure it with the help of indifference curves and price lines. Here, indifference curve of quantity of the commodity and income reveals the amount the consumer is willing to pay for any quantity of the commodity, while the price line reveals the amount he is required to pay for that quantity. The difference between the two is the measurement of consumer's surplus.

(ii) **Producer's Equilibrium:** This technique can also be used to analysis producer's equilibrium, which refers to the position of the producer, wherein he obtains maximum output with given expenditure on the various inputs. Indifference curve for the producer is known as isoquant, iso-product or productivity curve, which reveals the various combinations of the two inputs (on respective axes) that give the same total output. The budget line or the isocost line reveals the various combinations of two inputs that can be used in the production process at the given price of the two inputs with the given total expenditure. The point where the isocost line is tangent to the isoquant curve is the equilibrium point for the producer. This has been elaborated in the chapter on theory of production.

(iii) **Determination of Exchange Rate Under Bilateral Monopoly:** Under bilateral monopoly, a single buyer faces a single seller in the market. Here the exchange rate is determined on the basis of the scale of preferences or indifference curves of money and goods, the single seller stands ready to exchange with the single buyer and vice-versa. The two scales of preferences or indifference curves of the buyer and the seller in respect of money and goods are put together to determine the exchange rate, which will be of mutual advantage to both of them. This has been elaborated in the chapter on Bilateral Monopoly.

(iv) **Measurement of Effects of Price Subsidies:** The government makes certain goods available at subsidised price to certain low income group people. This requires a comparison of benefits to the consumers with the cost of subsidy to the government. Taking a case of food subsidy, where the needy families are entitled to purchase food stuffs on half the market price and the other half of the market price is paid by the government as subsidy. The effect of this subsidy on the consumer welfare and its money value to the consumers is as follows:

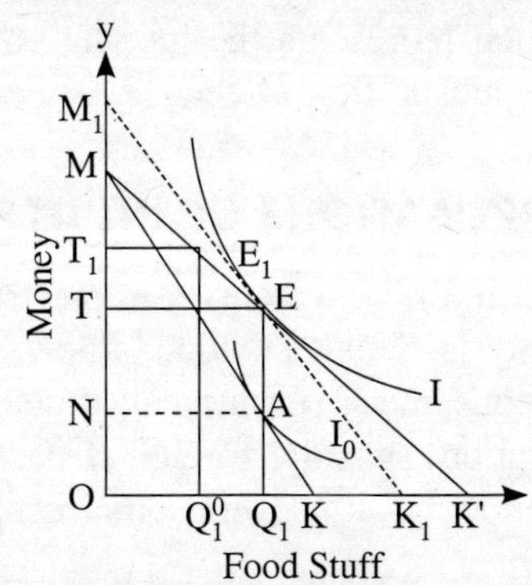

FIGURE 8.13: Impact of Subsidised Prices of Goods.

Here the consumer with *OM* money income at the given price of food stuff can purchase the various quantities of it along with *MK* price line. Since the subsidy given by the government is a half of the market price of the food stuff, the consumers will attain a new price line *MK'*. As per this new price line, the consumer finds his equilibrium at *E*, where he purchases OQ_1 quantity for *MT* amount of money. In case no food stuff subsidy was given, the price line would have been *MK*, where for OQ_1 quantity the consumer would have spent *MN* amount of money. Thus, *MN* is the market price of OQ_1 quantity of food stuff, which lies on point *A* on a lower level indifference curve I_0 exhibiting a lower level of welfare in the absence of subsidy to the needy families.

(v) **Measurement of Effects of Equivalent Income to Price Subsidies:** The subsidised price for OQ_1 quantity is *MT*, because the government gives a subsidy equal to *TN*. The money value of the subsidy can be ascertained by drawing a price line M_1K_1 parallel to the original price line before subsidy MK. This new price line is tangent to the original indifference curve at E_1, which reveals the same amount of satisfaction, as at point *E*. This means that if the consumer is paid MM_1 amount of money instead of subsidy he remains on the same indifference curve, where he has been, when the subsidy was given by the government. This MM_1 is the money value of the subsidy to the individual, as with this amount, the consumer reaches the same indifference curve (or welfare), as does with *TN* subsidy. However, here the money equivalent of subsidy to the consumer is less than the cost of the subsidy to the government. This will be true in all cases, where the indifference curves are convex and smooth. Thus, according to **D.S. Watson, 'you can make someone happier, if you give him cash instead of a commodity, even if the commodity is something he wants.'** In other words, we can make a man happier by giving him cash and allowing him to spend it as he thinks best than by forcing him take all his relief in the form of one commodity.

(vi) **Direct and Indirect Taxation:** The indifference curve analysis can also be applied to judge the welfare effects of direct and indirect taxes on individuals. Direct taxes are those taxes, whose incidence cannot be shifted to others, such as income tax, wealth tax and death duty. On the other hand, an indirect tax is one which can be passed on to others by raising the prices of goods, such as excise duty and goods and service tax. In case the government wants to raise a given amount of revenue, the question arises, whether it will be better to do so by levying a direct tax or an indirect tax from the point of view of the welfare of individuals. It can be exhibited as follows:

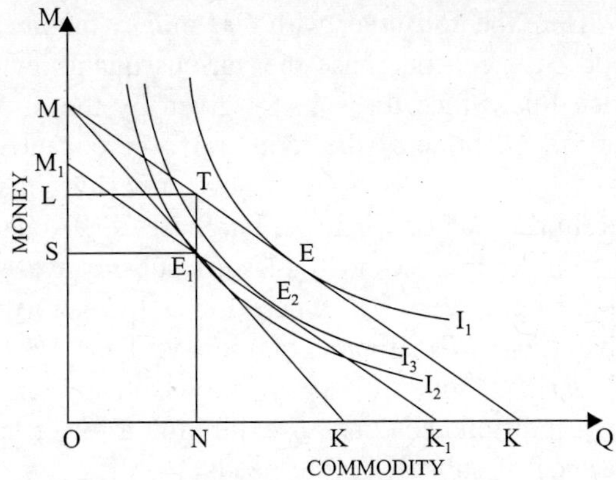

FIGURE 8.14 Welfare Effect of Taxation.

In Figure 8.14 *MK* is the original price line before taxation and is tangent to indifference curve I_1 at *E*, which is the original equilibrium position of the consumer. In case the government levies an excise duty on Q_1, the price of Q_1 will go up and, as a result, the consumer gets a new price line *MK'*, which is tangent to I_2, indifference curve at E_1 equilibrium point. Thus, it is obvious that due to imposition of excise duty the individual has shifted from higher to lower indifference curve indicating a lower level of welfare. At the new equilibrium, the consumer is purchasing *ON* quantity for *MS* amount, therefore, the difference $LS = TE_1$ is the amount of excise duty the consumer is paying.

In case, instead of excise duty **the government levies income tax** (direct tax) of equivalent amount, the price line will be shifted downwards to M_1K_1 level, which is parallel to the original price line MK. This enables the consumer to get the equilibrium at E_2 point on I_3 indifference curve. It lies at a higher level than I_2 indifference curve indicating a higher level of satisfaction or welfare. **Thus, the income tax (direct tax) reduces the individual's welfare less than that by the equivalent excise duty (indirect tax).**

(vii) **Index Number Problem:** This problem can also be explained through indifference curve analysis. It arises, when we have to compare the satisfaction of the consumer from combinations of two goods in different periods at different price levels. For example, the consumer purchases two commodities Q_1 and Q_2 in two different time periods. Assuming his money income to be ₹ 400, he purchases 15 units of Q_1 at the rate of ₹ 10 per unit and 10 units of Q_2 at the rate of ₹ 25 per unit. In case the prices of both goods undergo a change, the consumer with same amount of money income, purchases only 10 units of Q_1 at the rate of ₹ 16 per unit and 12 units of Q_2 at the rate of ₹ 20 per unit in other period.

Now the question is, whether the economic welfare has increased or decreased during subsequent time period, when the consumer has reduced the purchase of one, while he has increased the purchase of the other. To make this assessment, we assume that individual's tastes and preferences, that is, his indifference map is given and remains unchanged over the time period under consideration.

In Figure 8.15, the original price line is *MK*, which is tangent to *I* indifference curve at *E*, where the consumer takes OQ_1 quantity of Q_1 commodity and OQ_2 quantity of Q_2 commodity. After increase in the price of Q_1 and simultaneous decrease in the price of Q_2, the new price line is *M'K'*, which is tangent to I_0 indifference curve at E_1, where he purchases a reduced quantity OQ_1' of Q_1 commodity and an increased quantity OQ_2' of Q_2commodity. However, this reshuffle, after price change, places equilibrium at lower indifference curve I_0, which reveals a reduction in his welfare or satisfaction.

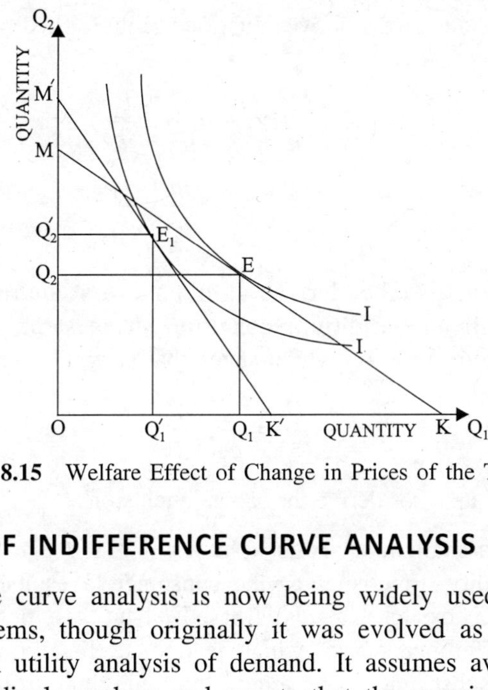

FIGURE 8.15 Welfare Effect of Change in Prices of the Two Goods.

APPRAISAL OF INDIFFERENCE CURVE ANALYSIS

The indifference curve analysis is now being widely used in the study of economic problems, though originally it was evolved as an alternative to the conventional utility analysis of demand. It assumes away measurability of utility in cardinal numbers and asserts that the marginal utility analysis assumes 'too much' but explains 'too little'. On the contrary, it proves more with fewer assumptions. Both analyses are fundamentally different from each other, but there are certain similarities between them:

(i) Both analyses are based on the assumption that the consumer behaves rationally and endeavours to maximise his utility or satisfaction.

(ii) According to the traditional or Marshallian analysis, the consumer is in equilibrium at the point, where the ratio of marginal utility and price of one commodity is equal to the ratio of marginal utility and price of another or all other commodities. On the other hand, modern analysis places the consumer in equilibrium at the point, where indifference curve is tangent to the price line and where the ratio of prices of both commodities are equal to the ratio of marginal utilities of the two commodities or the marginal rate of substitution. However, through certain divisions and multiplications to the Marshallian equilibrium conditions, we can very well deduce the Hicksian equilibrium condition as follows:

$$\frac{u_1}{P_1} = \frac{u_2}{P_2} = \frac{un}{Pn} = d$$

If we consider only two commodities, then equilibrium condition is:

$$\frac{u_1}{P_1} = \frac{u_2}{P_2}$$

If both sides of the above equation are multiplied by P_1 and divided by u_2, we get:

$$\frac{P_1}{u_2} \times \frac{u_1}{P_1} = \frac{u_2}{P_2} \times \frac{P_1}{u_2}$$

$$= \frac{u_1}{u_2} = \frac{P_1}{P_2}$$

This can also be derived through cross multiplication of the Marshallian equilibrium condition. It is same as the Hicksian equilibrium position which states that at equilibrium level–

$$\frac{-\Delta Q_2}{\Delta Q_1} = \frac{u_1}{u_2} = \frac{P_1}{P_2}$$

Thus, the two analyses derive the same conclusion.

(i) The Marshallian analysis assumes that the marginal utility of a commodity diminishes as the consumer takes its additional units, but the Hicksian analysis is based on the assumption of convexity of indifference curve, which is due to the diminishing marginal rate of substitution. The diminishing marginal utility of Marshallian analysis is the same as the diminishing marginal rate of substitution of Hicksian analysis.

(ii) Marshallian as well as Hicksian analysis employ the method of introspection for deriving the law of diminishing marginal utility and indifference map or scale of preferences respectively. In introspection, we attribute certain psychological feeling to the consumer by looking into and knowing from our own mind.

All these similarities in both approaches reveal that the indifference curve analysis has simply substituted new concept and equations in place of the old ones, but despite all these, the indifference curve analysis is considered superior to the conventional utility analysis on the following grounds:

1. This analysis is based on more realistic and valid assumptions of ordinal measurement of utility and scale of preferences. In this case the quantitative utility schedules and the concept of marginal utility have been replaced by the use of scale of preferences and the marginal rate of substitution for determining the consumer's equilibrium. Thus, it takes cross effects into account, as unlike marginal utility in Marshallian analysis, the marginal rate of substitution is not a function of the quantity of one commodity alone.
2. Assuming independent utilities, the marginal utility analysis ignores the considerations of complementary or substitute goods, but the indifference curve analysis considers the case of related goods on the basis of the very slope of the indifference curve. We know that if the indifference curve is a straight line, there is perfect substitutability and if these are drawn as right angles, there is perfect complementarity. Thus, the nearness of actual indifference curve to either of the two extremes reveals the degree of substitutability or complementarity.
3. The separation of 'income effect' and 'substitution effect' from the total 'price effect' has been made-possible through the indifference curve analysis. It has filled a genuine gap in the Marshallian 'Law of demand' and clearly tells us how much of the increase in demand is due to income effect and how much is due to substitution effect. It is no longer necessary to confine our study of demand to those cases, where only a small part of the income is spent by the consumer so that the income effect may become ignorable.
4. It enables up to enunciate a more comprehensive theory of demand than Marshallian utility analysis. The indifference curve analysis splits up the effect of the price change into (i) income effect, and (ii) substitution effect. Thus, in case of normal goods, where the income and substitution effects both are positive, the quantity demanded of a commodity increases, when its price falls. Conversely in case of inferior goods when price falls the income effect will be negative, though the substitution effect is always positive. In case, the strong negative income effect offsets the positive substitution effect, the demand may increase along with increase in price as happens in case 'Giffen Goods'.
5. This analysis enables us to evaluate the welfare consequences of a change in price of a commodity in terms of change in income. The cardinal utility analysis fails to measure an increase in the real

income of the consumer brought about by a fall in the price of the commodity. This can be easily considered by the indifference curve analysis through the indifference curves and price lines.

6. Indifference curve analysis eliminates difficulties concerning the measurement of utility, as it is based on the comparability of utilities of the two commodities and not on their measurability. It has freed, to a great extent, the theory of demand from the subjectivity of the Marshallian analysis.
7. It is not based on the unrealistic assumption of constant marginal utility of money. In Marshallian analysis this assumption was a must, as otherwise the money could no longer serve as a measuring rod of utility and, in that case, the entire analysis would break down. However, in indifference curve analysis there is no place for such assumption. This analysis based upon the ordinal utility hypothesis can validly derive the demand theorem (i.e., law of demand) without the assumption of constant marginal utility of money.

Thus, the indifference curve analysis is certainly a methodological advancement over the conventional utility analysis. It is more realistic, simpler and scientific, as it takes cross effect, minimum assumptions and ordinal utility into consideration. In spite of these merits, the indifference curve analysis suffers from certain demerits as follows:

(i) The indifference map is a highly static device, which gives no recognition to the way in which individual's preferences may be shaped by advertising, etc. and never considers the effects of habits and customs on the consumers.

(ii) On account of existence of oligopoly and monopolistic competition, the number of commodities, from which a consumer has to choose, has multiplied rapidly due to differentiation. Thus, its confinement to two goods case only reduces the applicability of the indifference curve analysis considerably.

(iii) This analysis does not explain the consumer's indifference curves rather these are taken as postulates of the system. Hence, its claim of being behaviouralistic (or objective), as opposed to the cardinal utility analysis, which is taken as subjective, is also not correct, as it does not set up functions and curves in purely objective terms. As a result, the indifference map is hypothetical in nature. Thus, its main defect is that it is neither based on observable data nor explains the consumer's behaviour like cardinal utility analysis.

(iv) The indifference curve analysis offers conclusions similar to that of the cardinal utility analysis with fewer assumptions. However, that too cannot maintain the superiority of this approach, as one cannot refuse to take into account animals with more than two feet, on the ground that only two feet are needed for walking.

(v) The indifference curve analysis requires highly introspective information from the consumer, because he is required to order all combinations according to his preference or indifference.

(vi) The analysis is based upon the weak ordering hypothesis, where the consumer is assumed to be indifferent between certain combinations of the two goods. This position of indifference is quite unrealistic, because when a consumer chooses one combination, simultaneously he considers all other combinations to be inferior to the chosen one. Thus, the ordering is usually strong and not weak, as is assumed in indifference curve analysis.

(vii) This analysis is also based on the wrong assumption that the consumer is familiar with his entire preference schedule. In other words, it assumes that every consumer is fully conscious of the various combinations of the two goods, which give him equal satisfaction.

(viii) The indifference curve analysis involves the unrealistic assumption of continuity. The indifference curves are continuous curves on which are located all conceivable combinations of the two goods, whether they are actually available in the market or not. For example, a continuous curve also involves fractions of the two goods, which may not be available in the market.

Presence of these drawbacks in the indifference curve analysis has put it in a midway between the subjective and purely objective approaches to the demand analysis. This led the economists to build up the objective theories of demand based on the observed behaviour of the consumers.

Review Questions

1. Explain the properties of the indifference curves and elucidate the concept of the marginal rate of substitution.
2. How is price line or budget equation line ascertained and how the point of consumer's equilibrium is fixed as per the price line and the indifference curve?
3. Distinguish between the price consumption curve and the income consumption curve.
4. Explain consumer's equilibrium with the help of the indifference curve and the price line.
5. Discuss the concept of diminishing marginal rate of substitution and also mention its exceptions, if any.
6. What is meant by the price line? Change in the consumer's income determines the position of the price line; whereas the change in the

prices of the two commodities determine both the position and the slope of the price line'. Discuss.

7. At what point on an indifference curve does a consumer maximise his satisfaction? Explain with the help of a diagram.
8. What is a budget line? Examine the effect on a budget line of (i) change in income and (ii) change in price of any one of the two goods.
9. What is price consumption curve? What does the slope of price consumption curve reveal?
10. Elucidate the derivation of the demand theorem as per the indifference curve analysis.
11. Distinguish between income effect and the substitution effect as given under the indifference curve analysis.
12. How is the Hicksian analysis superior to the Marshallian analysis of the consumer's behaviour?
13. Bring out the merits and dismerits of the Hicksian analysis of the consumer's behaviour.

9

Theory of Consumer's Behaviour: Revealed Preference Analysis

The revealed preference analysis has been developed by Professor Paul A. Samuelson as an alternative approach to the Hicks-Allen indifference curve analysis of the consumer's behaviour. Hicks-Allen indifference curve analysis, though logical and broad in its explanation, has been criticised for not being a behaviouristic analysis. Professor Samuelson, therefore, developed his analysis of consumer's behaviour purely on behaviouristic and psychological grounds. It seeks to explain actual demand of the consumer from his observed behaviour in the market in the various price-income situations. Thus, as against the psychological introspective analysis of consumer's behaviour through indifference curves, **this behaviourist-ordinal utility analysis is considered as the third root of the logical theory of demand'.** This theory has also been named as **'Behaviourist-Ordinalist',** because it applies behaviouristic method and also uses the concept of ordinal utility, as it still regards utility to be merely comparable and not quantifiable.

ASSUMPTIONS OF REVEALED PREFERENCES ANALYSIS

The revealed preference analysis is based on the premise that 'choice reveals preference', that is, if consumer buys a particular combination of two goods, then he is supposed to prefer this combination in relation to all other available combinations of the two goods. According to Professor Samuelson **'through any observed equilibrium point, if we draw the budget equation straight line with arithmetical slope given by the observed price ratio, then all combinations of the two goods on or within the budget line could have been bought in preference to what was actually bought. Since they weren't, they are all revealed to be inferior to that particular combination.'** Besides, this analysis is also based on the assumptions as follows:

(i) The consumer can indicate strong ordering, that is, he can single out clearly a particular combination amongst all the combinations from which he could choose. He need not reveal the indifference amongst a large number of combinations of the two goods but he has to reveal his preference by a single act of choice.

(ii) The consumer's taste is given and remains unchanged throughout the analysis, as any change in the taste would disturb the whole analysis.

(iii) The consumer is expected to behave rationally, that is, he is expected to know his interest and to try for its maximisation.

(iv) There is consistency in the behaviour of the consumer. It implies that the two observations of choice behaviour of the consumer do not provide conflicting evidence of his preference. Thus, if a consumer chooses *A* combination of the two goods over *B* then in no circumstance he will choose *B* over *A*.

(v) The choice is subject to transitivity or 'three-term consistency'. It implies that if the consumer prefers *A* to *B* and *B* to *C*, then he will prefer *A* to *C* as well.

(vi) There is the positive income elasticity of demand, as commodities under consideration are assumed to be normal one.

The concept of revealed preference states that when a consumer decides to buy a particular combination of the two goods, he does so for two simple reasons; either he likes it more as compared to other combinations of two goods that are available to him or it happens to be cheaper as compared to other combinations of two goods. For example, if a consumer is offered with two combinations *A* and *B* of two goods Q_1 and Q_2 and he chooses to buy *A* and not *B* with this much information we will not be wise to conclude that the consumer prefers *A* to *B*. It is just possible that the consumer has opted for *A* combination, because it is cheaper than *B* combination and may be even most unhappy for not buying *B*. However, on the basis of price-information, if we find that combination *A* is more expensive than combination *B* and even then the consumer purchase combination *A*, it can be concluded that the consumer prefers *A* to *B*. Thus, the consumer has revealed his preference for *A* on *B* or conversely *B* has been revealed to be inferior to *A*. This preference hypothesis is the basis of revealed preference analysis and helps in obtaining definite information about the preference of the consumer by observing his behaviour in the market. The comparison of preferences of a consumer revealed under different income-price situations helps in drawing his scale of preference. It is exhibited in Figure 9.1 as follows:

In Figure 9.1, *MN* is the price-income or budget equation line of the consumer, where the consumer's income is *ON* in terms of Q_2 goods and *OM* in terms of Q_1 goods. The triangle *OMN* is the area of choice for the consumer under the given price-income situation, where he can choose any combination lying within or on the triangle. Thus, the consumer can choose any combination between *A* and *B* on the price-income line *MN* or between *D* and *E* below this line. In case he chooses *A* combination, it is revealed to be preferred to *B*. *D* and *E* combinations are revealed to be inferior to *A*, as they are lying below the price-income line. Combination *C* is beyond the reach of the consumer, as it lies above his price-income line. Thus, *A* combination is

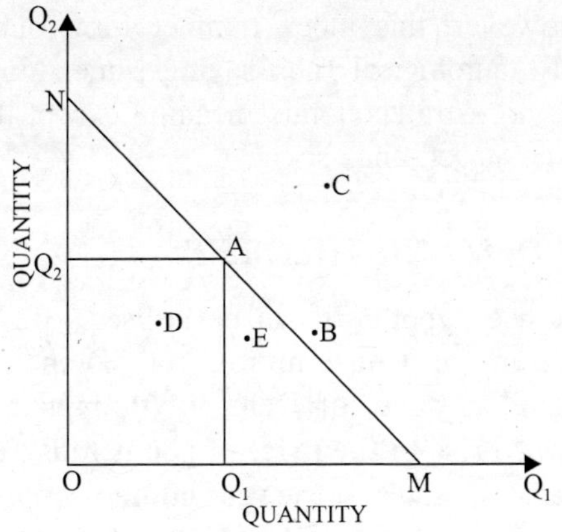

FIGURE 9.1 Revealed Preferences for Two Goods.

revealed to be preferred to all other combinations, where the consumer takes OQ_2 quantity of Q_2 goods and OQ_1 quantity of Q_1 goods.

Thus, the revealed preference analysis is based upon strong form of preference hypothesis, which implies that there is definite ordering of the various combinations in the consumer's scale of preferences and it rules out the indifference between the various alternative combinations. It is important to note that the revealed preference is not a statistical concept. **Had it been a statistical concept, the preference of the consumer for combination *A* would have been inferred from giving him opportunity to exercise his choice several times in the same circumstances.** In other words, if the consumer from among the various alternative combinations open to him chooses a particular combination more frequently than any other only then his preference for that combination would have been statistically revealed. **Samuelson's preference is revealed by a single act of choice.** It is obvious that the consumer's indifference between two or more combinations cannot be revealed by a single act of choice, therefore, it is also clear that it does not take into account the indifference relation between the various combinations of goods. Thus, the indifference relation stands rejected in revealed preference analysis and **it is not as a matter of convenience but dictated by the requirements of his (Samuelson's) methodology'.**

The revealed preference hypothesis is stated in the form of index number. In a given price-income situation '*a*', *A* and *B* are two combinations of goods at price level P_a. Under such situation, a statement that the consumer selects *A* rather than *B* can be expressed by an index number formula that $\sum P_a A \geq P_a B$. Here, $P_a A$ stands for total expenditure on A combination and $P_a B$ stands for total expenditure on *B* combination. Thus, the expenditure on *A* combination would also have sufficed to buy *B* combination. In other words, combination *B* is within the buying range of the consumer or *B* was a possibility, when *A* was chosen and, therefore, *A* is revealed to be preferable to B. However, this index number form of revealed preference hypothesis is merely tautological (i.e., saying same thing twice in different words) and contains no extra economic meaning except that it is more useful and convenient for advanced analysis.

DERIVATION OF DEMAND THEOREM

The revealed preference hypothesis can be utilised to establish Samuelson's 'Fundamental Theorem of Consumption' or 'Demand Theorem' which interprets the Marshallian 'Law of Demand' through revealed preferences. According to this law **'a rise in the price of goods must, if income and other prices are held constant, result in the reduction of quantity demanded and vice-versa'.** In other words, there exists inverse relationship between price and quantity demanded of certain goods. Samuelson's Demand Theorem states that **any good (simple or composite), that is known always to increase in demand, when money income alone rises, must definitely shrink in demand, when its price alone rises'**. It reveals that when income elasticity of demand is positive, price demand will have negative relationship between variation in price and variation in quantity demanded. In other words, the demand for the goods changes in the reverse direction of change in the price of the goods. Thus, the positive income elasticity of demand has been made a necessary qualification for the inverse price-demand relationship. The 'Fundamental Demand Theorem' can be proved by breaking the whole analysis under two situations as follows:

(i) **Price-Rise Situation:** We may consider, first, the case of a consumer, who spends his entire income on two goods Q_1 and Q_2. MN is the price income line under given situation and he chooses A combination of the two goods on that line. The triangle OMN is the consumer's area of choice for the different combinations of Q_1 and Q_2. By choosing A combination, the consumer has revealed his preference for this combination over all other combinations with in or on the triangle OMN.

In Figure 9.2, if the price of Q_1 rises, while the price of Q_2 remains unchanged, the price income line shifts to new position MN',which represents a new price-income situation. Under MN' price-income situation, A combination will not be available to the consumer. At this stage some extra money known as 'cost difference' is provided to the consumer to compensate him for rise in price of Q_1, so that he can buy A combination of the two goods even at the higher price of Q_1. This enables us to draw M_1N_1 price-income line, which is parallel to MN' and passes through point A on the original price-income line.

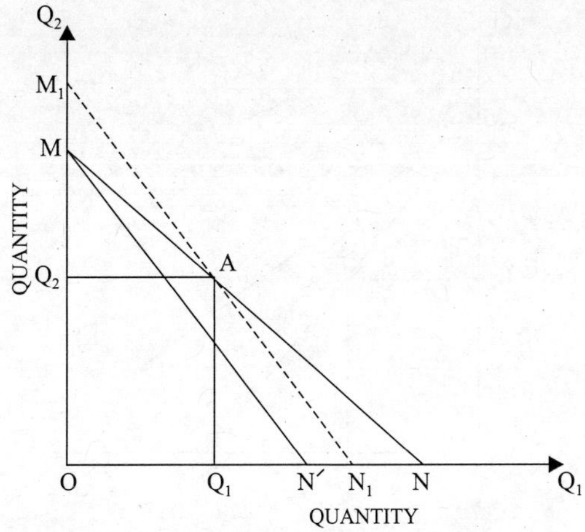

FIGURE 9.2 Derivation of Demand Theorem under Price Rise Situation.

It is obvious that the consumer will not take any combination of two goods below point *A* along *AN* or AN_1 lines, because AN_1 lies below the *AN* and he has already shown his preference to *A* over all combinations of two goods along the *AN* portion of price-income line. Thus, if we stick to our assumption of consistency of choice behaviour of the consumer, he will not choose any combination below *A* either on *MN* or on M_1N_1 price-income line. It follows, therefore, that in the price-income situation M_1N_1, the consumer will either choose the original combination lying above *A* or any other combination on AM_1 portion of M_1N_1 price-income line. It will not be inconsistent because combinations lying above *A* on AM_1 were not available to the consumer previously in price-income situation *MN*.

Thus, even after sufficient extra income has been provided to the consumer to compensate him for rise in price of Q_1, he purchases either the same or a smaller quantity of Q_1 at a higher price. In case the extra money granted to him is withdrawn, he will definitely purchase smaller quantity of Q_1 at a higher price, because the demand for Q_1 is known to fall always with a fall in income due to positive income elasticity of demand. Thus, assuming a positive income elasticity of demand, we derive an inverse price-demand relationship, if the price rises.

(ii) **Price Fall Situation:** The Fundamental Demand Theorem of inverse demand-price relationship can also be proved assuming a fall in the price of Q_1 commodity.

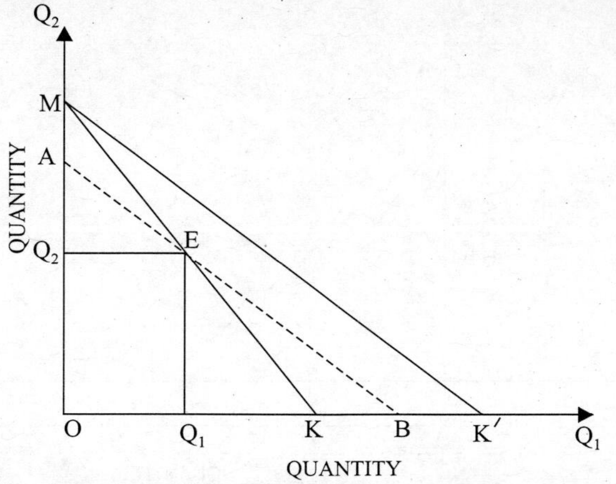

FIGURE 9.3 Derivation of Demand Theorem under Price Fall Situation.

In Figure 9.3, *MK* is the original price-income line, where the consumer reveals his preference for *E* combination of the two goods over all other combinations with in or on triangle *OMK*. In case the price of Q_1 falls, we get a new income-price situation *MK'*. This fall in price of Q_1 increases the real income of the consumer. In case such increase in real income is taken away from the consumer so that he is left with just sufficient amount of money, which enables him to purchases original combination *E* at a lower price of Q_1. As a result, *AB* becomes the new price-income line, which is parallel to *MK'* and passes through *E*.

It is obvious that the consumer with his new price-income line *AB* cannot choose any combination above *E* on *AE* portion of the new price-income line because all such combinations were available to him earlier through his original price-income line *MK* and were rejected by him in favour of *E*. The consumer, therefore, will choose either combination *E* or any other combination on *EB* portion of *AB* price income line. He will not move through *EK* portion of MK price-income line, as all combinations on this are revealed inferior to *E* combination of the two goods. His choice of E combination means that he buys the same quantity of Q_1 and Q_2 goods as in original price-income situation *MK*. The choice of any other combination on *EB* portion of *AB* price-income situation means that he buys a larger quantity of Q_1 commodity than in the original price-income situation *MK*.

Thus, even though the consumer's income has been reduced, he purchases either the same or larger quantity of Q_1 at a lower price. In case the money withheld thus for, is given back to the consumer, due to the assumption of positive income elasticity of demand, he will definitely purchase more units of Q_1 commodity at lower price on *MK'* price-income situation. The two exhibits given above together prove **Samuelson's Fundamental Demand Theorem**

according to which any good whose demand is expected to vary directly with income must definitely shrink in demand, when its price rises and expand in demand, when its price falls. This proof is based on the two implicit assumptions: (i) since the consumer chooses a combinations on the price-income line only and not within the triangle, it implicitly means that he prefers a larger combination of goods to a smaller one; and (ii) the consumer chooses only one combinations of goods in every price income situation. These two implicit assumptions along with explicit assumptions of consistency of choice and a positive income elasticity of demand, prove the inverse price-demand relationship, that is, the Demand theorem.

CRITICAL APPRAISAL OF REVEALED PREFERENCES ANALYSIS

Samuelson's revealed preference theorem definitely marks an improvement over both Marshallian as well as Indifference Curve Analysis of consumer's behaviour, as it applies the behaviouristic analysis in contrast to psychological and introspective explanations to consumer's behaviour. The revealed preference analysis is also known as 'scientific method' and regarded as the only valid method for explaining consumer's demand. According to Professor Tapas Mazumdar **'behaviourism certainly was of great advantages of treading only on observed ground; it cannot go wrong'**. It is because of the theory being based on the actual behaviour of the consumer, it has gained more popularity in recent years.

The superiority of the revealed preference theory is confirmed by its boldly abandoning the rationality assumption or utility maximisation postulate, which formed the basis for Marshallian as well as Indifference Curve Analysis. The utility maximisation postulate has been objected on the ground that it is more restrictive and therefore, difficult of realisation in actual practice. Samuelson's revealed preference analysis has replaced the utility maximisation postulate with consistency postulate to derive the demand theorem. The consistency of choice postulate is less restrictive and conforms more to the real behaviour of the consumer.

This analysis has also done away with the continuity assumption, which forms the basis of Indifference Curve Analysis. Indifference curve are continuous curves, which show innumerable combinations of two goods, whether they are actually available in the market or not. It is quite possible that equilibrium point (i.e., the point to tangency of indifference curve with price line) shows a combination of the two goods (say, in fractions), which may not be available in the market. Therefore, this continuity assumption is quite unrealistic, as it often results in absurd conclusions. It is on account of this reason that the revealed preference theory has discarded continuity assumption. No doubt, the income-price line of the revealed preference analysis is continuous and it is on or within this line the consumer has to choose any combination of the two goods. This does not imply that the continuity assumption enters into revealed preference analysis. It is well-known that this analysis is based on the actual observed choice of the consumer and he will naturally choose a combination, which is actually available in the market under given price-income situation. Thus, this analysis does not concern itself with preference relating to those combinations of goods, which the consumer does not purchase.

Although the revealed preference analysis has made certain improvements upon the earlier analysis, but it is also not free from demerits. Various criticism offered against this analysis are as follows:

The revealed preference analysis does not take into account the possibility of indifference in the consumer's behaviour. **The rejection of possibility of indifference flows from Samuelson's strong ordering hypothesis according to which the consumer is expected to reveal his preference by a single act of choice**. Economists view that if preference is to be judged from a large number of observations, the possibility of indifference cannot be ruled out. For example, a consumer reveals preference for *A* over *B*, if he chooses *A* rather than *B* more often than he chooses *B* rather than *A* from a given number of observations. The consumer will certainly be indifferent between *A* and *B* combinations, if a sufficiently large number of observations do not reveal a definite and conclusive preference for either of the two combinations. **Thus, the possibility of indifference emerges, if the preference of the consumer is to be judged from a sufficiently large number of observations.** Professor Armstrong has criticised the revealed preference analysis for its rejection of indifference relationship and has viewed that there are points of indifference on every side of chosen point because the combination of two goods actually chosen by the consumer is one of the few combinations between which he is indifferent.

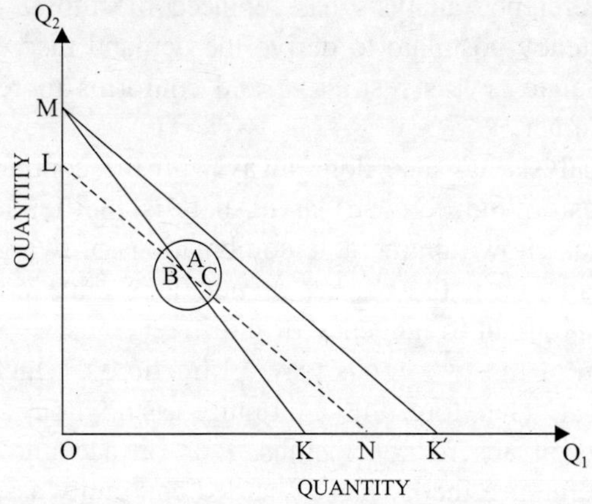

FIGURE 9.4 Possibility of Indifference in Choice under Revealed Preferences.

In Figure 9.4, *MK* is the original price-income line on which the consumer choses *A* combination of $Q_1$and Q_2. According to Armstrong's notion, points around *A* such as *B*, *C* etc. would be indifferent to *A*. Now, if the price of Q_1 falls *MK'* becomes the new price-income line, which is due to increase in real income of the consumer. In case the increased real income is extracted from the consumer, the new price income line, would be *LN*, which is parallel to *MK'* representing lower price of Q_1. On this new price line the choice of *B* instead of *A* or C (or any other point within the circle) is not inconsistent to his previous choice, because he was indifferent between points *A*, *B*, *C* etc. However, the choice of *B* in price-income situation *LN* means that the consumer buys less of Q_1 now when its price is lower and income is reduced through imposition of taxes. This is contrary to the law of demand, **thus, if Armstrong notion about points of indifference around the chosen point is accepted, then Samuelson's proof that the demand for goods increase, when its price falls break down.**

Secondly, the revealed preference theory does not attempt to separate the substitution effect from the income effect, as is done by the indifference analysis. This theory is based upon the observed behaviour of the consumer and on the plane of observation, substitution effect cannot be distinguished from income effect. This is inevitable in revealed preference analysis, which has rejected indifference relationship altogether. Since the change in demand in response to change in price comprises both income and substitution effects, this theory offers only a partial explanation of the response of demand as a result of a change in price.

Thirdly, the revealed preference theorem is conditional, Samuelson has proved his demand theorem on the assumption of positive income elasticity of demand. However, if the income elasticity of demand is negative, as generally happens in case of inferior goods, the very basis of his fundamental theorem disappears and fails him to establish his demand theorem. **It implies that the revealed preference analysis cannot explain the case of 'Giffen Goods'.** In case of 'Giffen Goods' the income effect (or income elasticity of demand) is negative and is so powerful that is outweighs the positive substitution effect. It causes the demand to vary directly with price. **The exclusion of 'Giffen Goods' is a great drawback of this new analysis. The 'Giffen Goods' is no doubt rare; nevertheless, it does exist and a realistic demand theory should provide for it. Thus, through the revealed preference he makes an improvement over earlier analyses of demand including Hicks-Allen indifference analysis, so for the methodology is concerned, but in respect of content of demand theorem, it is a few steps behind the Hicks-Allen indifference curve analysis.**

Fourthly, the revealed preference theorem deals only with individual demand curve and not with the market demand curve. This undermines the usefulness of the theory for analytical purposes.

Lastly, the assumption that 'choice' reveals 'preference' is not correct. Since the choice requires rational consumer's behaviour and a consumer does not behave rationally at all times, his choice for a particular combination may not reveal his preference for that. Thus, the chances for a difference between the ideal consumer of the preference analysis and the actual consumer of the market are always there although the theory has been based on the behaviour of actual consumer.

Thus, in view of the above limitations, there is doubt about the superiority of the revealed preference analysis of consumer's behaviour. However, the superiority of this theory lies in its applying a scientific or behaviouristic method to the consumer's behaviour and its discovery of the preference hypothesis. It may not compare well with the other demand theories, so far as its contents are concerned, but methodologically it is certainly an improvement over the Marshallian as well as Indifference Curve analyses of consumer's behaviour.

Review Questions

1. Explain the hypothesis of revealed preference analysis and make an appraisal of revealed preference theory.
2. What for the revealed preference analysis is also called the behaviourist approach? Explain the concept of revealed preference for determining the consumer's equilibrium.
3. Give reasons establishing superiority of the revealed preference theory over indifference curve analysis and bring out the demerits of the revealed preference analysis.
4. Explain the concept of revealed preference and elucidate it as a refinement over the Hicks-Allen analysis of consumer's behaviour.
5. Explain the application of the revealed preference analysis in derivation of the demand theorem.
6. 'Samuleson's revealed preference analysis is an improvement over Hicksian indifference curve analysis'. Discuss.
7. Explain consumer's equilibrium as per the revealed preference analysis.
8. Explain the derivation of the demand theorem as per revealed preference analysis.
9. Bring out the merits and demerits of revealed preference analysis.

10

Theory of Consumer's Behaviour: Logical Ordering Analysis

The emergence of the revealed preference theory, increasing use of econometrics and the appearance of mathematical analysis of strong and weak ordering prompted Professor J.R. Hicks to revise his earlier demand analysis. He was deeply influenced by Samuelson's revealed preference hypothesis and the logic of strong ordering, as he has stated that, **he owns this revision of demand theory to 'Samuelson and the Samuelsonians' though he retained 'a considerable scepticism about the revealed preference analysis'.** In this chapter, an effort is being made to explain the various aspects of this analysis, which has adopted an econometric approach to the theory of demand.

Professor J.R. Hicks is of the opinion that the demand theory, which is useful for econometric purposes is definitely superior to one that does not serve such purpose, because econometrics now is considered as a major form of economic research. In his indifference curve analysis, he made only implicit econometric reference, but in his revision of demand theory, he has made it explicit, even more than that done in the revealed preference analysis.

This analysis rejects the cardinal measurement of utility and relies on the ordinal utility. It is also strange that Hicks has given up altogether the use of indifference curves in his revised demand theory, but he has considered positions, which are equally preferred by the consumer in a different way. The indifference curves, according to him, are rejected primarily on two grounds; (i) **the indifference curves can be effectively used in those cases, where the consumer's choice relates to quantities of two commodities only, as the extension of analysis to more than two commodities causes several unavoidable complications due to recourse to elaborate mathematics, which often conceals the economic point of what is being done; and (ii) indifference curves involve the assumption of continuity, as a result, these are drawn as continuous curves on which we show all possible combinations of the two goods, whether they are available even in fractions in the market.** The continuity is such 'a property, which the geometrical field does have but which the economic does not'. Apart from these disadvantages of the indifference curve analysis, the reason which prompted Professor Hicks to offer a new method is that it is more effective in clarifying the nature of preference hypothesis.

The demand for a commodity is affected not only by the economic factors (like current prices and incomes) but also by the non-economic factors (like, population changes, social habits and customs, etc.). The task before the econometrist is to separate the effect exerted by the economic factors form that exerted by non-economic factors on the demand for a commodity. Thus, the objective of the demand theory is to help the analyst in segregating the effects of the economic and non-economic factors on demand.

ASSUMPTIONS OF LOGICAL ORDERING ANALYSIS

The revision of the demand theory is based on two basic assumptions of the presence of: **(i) an ideal consumer, who is likely to be influenced by economic factors, like current prices and incomes alone; and (ii) preference hypothesis, which implies that the consumer will behave, according to a scale of preferences. According to Professor Hicks the ideal consumer (who is not affected by anything else than current market conditions) chooses that alternative, out of the various alternatives open to him, which he prefers the most or ranks most highly**. In one set of market conditions he makes one choice, in other some other choice; but the choices he makes always express the same ordering, and must, therefore, be consistent with one another. This is the hypothesis made about the behaviour of the ideal consumer. This implies that the consumer in a given market situation chooses the most preferred combination of two goods. In indifference curve analysis the preference hypothesis is implicit in the form of a set of indifference curves but it has been made explicit in Hicks' revision of the demand analysis.

STRONG AND WEAK ORDERINGS

For elaboration of preference hypothesis, Professor Hicks has explained the logic of ordering, wherein he has distinguished strong ordering from weak ordering and then has proceeded to base his demand theory on weak ordering form of preference hypothesis. A set of items is strongly ordered, if each item has a market place of its own in the order and each item is assigned a definite number in the order of preference. Thus, against each number, there will be one and only one item to correspond. As against this, a set of items is weakly ordered, if the items are put into numbered groups, but within the group none of the items can be put ahead of the others. **According to Professor Hicks a weak ordering consists of a division into groups, in which sequence of groups is strongly ordered, but in which there is no ordering within the group.**

The indifference curves imply weak ordering, as all points on a given indifference curve are equally desirable and, therefore, occupy the same place in the order, though a higher indifference curve imply a higher order. The revealed preference theory, on the other hand, imply strong ordering, as it assumes that the choice of a combination reveals consumer's preference for it over all other alternative combinations open to him. Under weak ordering (say on a particular indifference curve), the choice of one combination and the rejection of the remaining combinations does not imply that the rejected combinations are inferior to the combination actually chosen, but it may be due to indifference towards the rejected combinations. Thus, the actual choice in this case fails to reveal definite preference.

In case we interpret a preference hypothesis to mean strong ordering, we can assume all points, which lie on or within any price-income line represent effective alternatives, as a two-dimensional continuum points cannot be strongly ordered. Moreover, if the commodities are available only in discrete units, then strong ordering is acceptable, but in case of composite commodity, like money, it is not acceptable, because money is finally divisible though not in a mathematical sense. Since the smallest monetary unit is so small in relation to the other units of goods with which we are concerned that the imperfect divisibility of money in practice is of little importance.

In case the choice is to be made between any good, which is available in discrete units and the money, which is finally divisible, the possibility of equally desired combinations must be accepted and we are bound to give up the strong ordering.

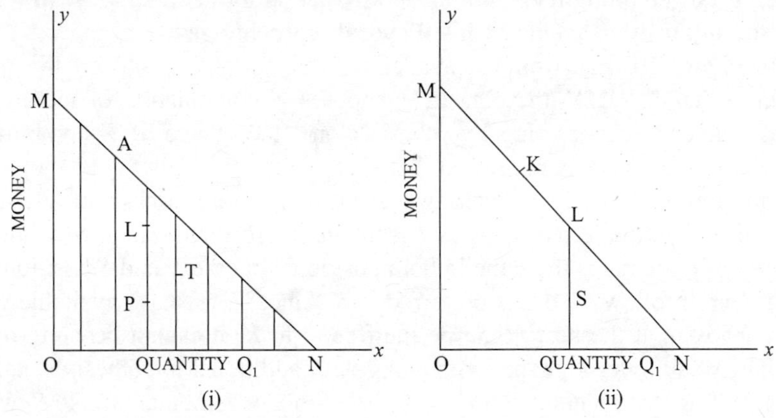

FIGURE 10.1 Possibility of Equally Desired Combinations of Money and Discrete Goods.

In Figure 10.1(i), if the consumer confronts with price-income situation *MN*, he is free to choose any combination of money and goods that lies on or within *OMN* triangle. In case the available alternative are strongly ordered then the choice of *A* will reveal that he prefers *A* over all other available alternatives.

In case we take money, which is finally divisible on *y*-axis and the commodity Q_1, which is available in integral units is shown on x-axis. These discrete units of the commodity Q_1, are shown in the diagram as the series of parallel lines. All points on the stripes will be effective alternatives, but such alternatives cannot be strongly ordered.

Further, if there are two alternative *L* and *P* on a given stripe and T another alternative on some other stripe and the relation among them is such that *L* is preferred to *T* and *T* is preferred to *P*, we can ascertain a point between *L* and *P*, which is indifferent to *T*. Thus, when the various alternatives appear as a series of stripes, there may be a relation of indifference between some of them. It is now obvious that the strong ordering is to be given up, when the various alternative combinations consist of the composite commodity money, which is finally divisible and single commodity, which is available only in discrete units. According to Hicks **'as soon as we introduce the smallest degree of continuity (such as that introduced by the 'striped' hypothesis) strong ordering has to be given up.'**

Thus, after rejecting the case of strong ordering hypothesis, **Professor Hicks has pleaded for adoption of weak ordering hypothesis. In this case, the choice of a particular combination does not indicate preference for it over all other possible combinations, but only shows that all possible combinations cannot he preferred to the chosen combination. Thus, it takes into consideration the possibility of some rejected combinations being indifferent to the chosen one. However, the weak ordering hypothesis alone will not help in derivation of demand theorem, therefore, Professor Hicks has introduced an additional hypothesis that the consumer will always prefer a larger amount of money to smaller amount of money, provided that the quantity of goods at his disposal is unchanged.**

In Figure 10.1(ii), from all available combinations in and on the price-income situation *OMN*, the consumer chooses *K* combination of money and goods. Under weak ordering hypothesis alone, the choice of *K* combination over *S* combination does not reveal that *K* is preferred to *S*, but only shows that *S* is not preferred to *K*. Considering the position *L*, on the basis of additional hypothesis, it is preferred to *S*, as *L* contains more money than *S*, while the quantity of Q_1 remains the same in both positions. In case *K* and *S* positions are indifferent, it follows that *L* is preferred to *K*. Since, *L* was also available when *K* was chosen, at the best *L* can be indifferent to *K*, it cannot be preferred to *K*. Thus, weak ordering hypothesis along with additional hypothesis is helpful in concluding that combination *K* is preferred to any combination like *S*, which lies within the *OMN* price-income situation. However, this will not help in deciding whether the chosen combination *K* is preferred to combination like *L*, which lies on the price-income line *MN*.

Thus, the difference between strong and weak ordering, according to Professor Hicks, is that under strong ordering the chosen position is shown to be preferred to all other positions within or on the price-income triangle, while under weak ordering it is preferred to all positions within the triangle, but may be indifferent to other position on the same triangle. In order to make weak ordering hypothesis more useful for demand analysis, apart from additional hypothesis, it is further assumed that the preference order is transitive, that is, if the consumer prefers *A* to *B* and *B* to *C*, then it is implied that he will prefer *A* to *C*.

DIRECT CONSISTENCY TEST

Assuming consistency in consumer's behaviour under the various price-income situations for deriving law of consumer's demand, Professor Hicks has applied a consistency test, which has been called as 'Direct Consistency Test'. It is same as the two-term consistency conditions of the logical ordering and has been considered by Professor Hicks in several alternative cases.

The commodity Q_1 is shown on *x*-axis and the composite commodity money on the *y*-axis. Under a given price-income situation, the alternative combinations available to the consumer are represented by points in or on the price-income line. In case point *K* represents the actually chosen combination, under strong ordering combination *K* is preferred to all other available combinations in or on the price-income line, while under weak ordering *K* is shown to be preferred to all combinations within the price-income line. However, it is either preferred or indifferent to all combinations on price-income line *MN*. In case the price undergoes a change with or without any change in income, it opens the various alternative combinations to the consumer under new situation, where combination at point *L* may be the actually selected combination. Since the consumer's scale of preferences is expected to remain unchanged, irrespective of change in price-income situation, the preferences must be consistent. His preferences will be inconsistent, if he reveals his preference for *K* is one price-income situation and for *L* in another situation, while both *K* and *L* combinations are available in both price-income situations. Such tests for consistency or inconsistency are as follows:

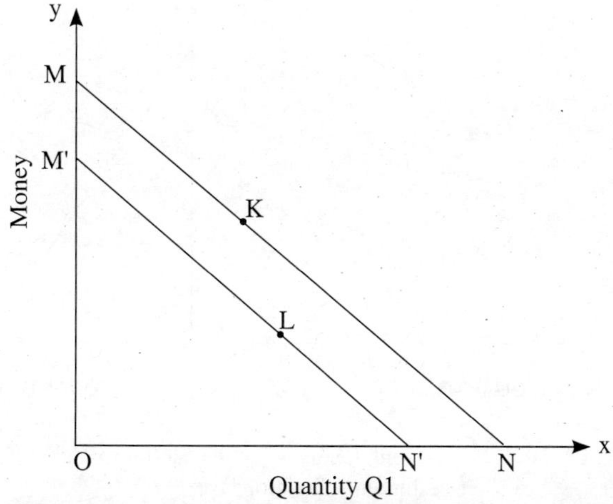

FIGURE 10.2 Consistent Choices in Two Price-Income Situations.

1. Firstly, we take a case, where commodity Q_1 is shown on x-axis and composite commodity money on y-axis. The original price-income situation is represented by *OMN* triangle. Assuming a reduction in money income, the new price-income situation will be represented by *OM'N'* triangle. Here one of the two price-income lines lies wholly outside the other.

   In Figure 10.2 *MN* price-income line lies wholly outside the *M'N'* line. The choice of *K* combination in *MN* price-income situation is preferred to *L*, both under strong and weak orderings. In other price-income situation *M'N'*, combination *K* is not available. Therefore, the choice of *K* in former situation is quite consistent with the choice of combination *L* in the latter situation.
2. In case one of the two price-income situations does not lie wholly outside the other, which is possible through a change in both the income as well as the price, then the two price-income lines will intersect each other at some point. Assuming a reduction in the income along with a fall in the price of the commodity, the portion of price-income line *MN* is outside the price-income line *M'N'* to the left of the point of intersection of the two lines and inside on the right of the cross as follows:

   In Figure 10.3(i) the chosen positions *K* and *L* lie to the left of the cross on the two price-income lines MN and *M'N'* respectively. In this case, the choice of *L* rather than *K* (as *K* is not available in the *N'M'* price-income situation) is consistent with the choice of *K* to *L* in *MN* price-income situation. Since point *L* lies within the triangle *OMN*, the choice of *K* in *MN* price-income situation reflects consumer's preference for *K* over *L* as per both strong and weak ordering.

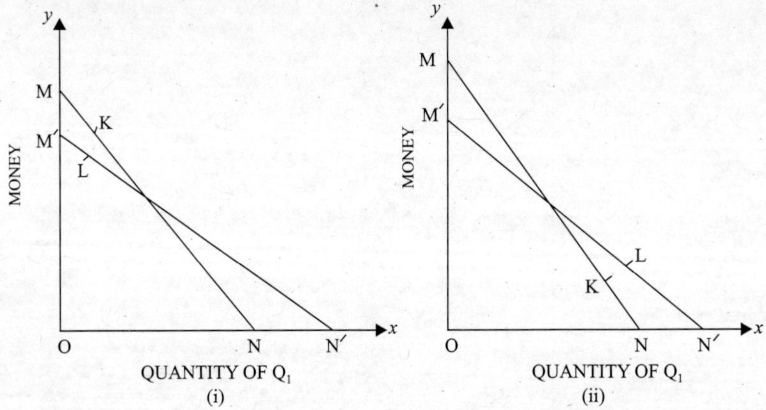

FIGURE 10.3 Consistent Choices to the Left or Right of the Cross of Price-Income Situations

Similarly, in Figure 10.3(ii) both the selected positions *K* and *L* in the two parts of price-income situations *MN* and *M'N'* lie to the left of the cross. Here, again, the choice of *L* rather than *K* in *M'N'* situation is quite consistent with the choice of *K* in *MN* situation. Since the combination *K* lies within the triangle *OM'N'*, *L* is preferred to *K* according to both strong as well as weak orderings. On the other hand, the consumer is bound to choose combination *K* in *MN* price-income situation as L is not available in this situation. Thus, in both cases the consumer's choice behaviour it quite consistent.

It is also possible that two chosen combinations *K* and *L* respectively lie outside or inside the cross as follows:

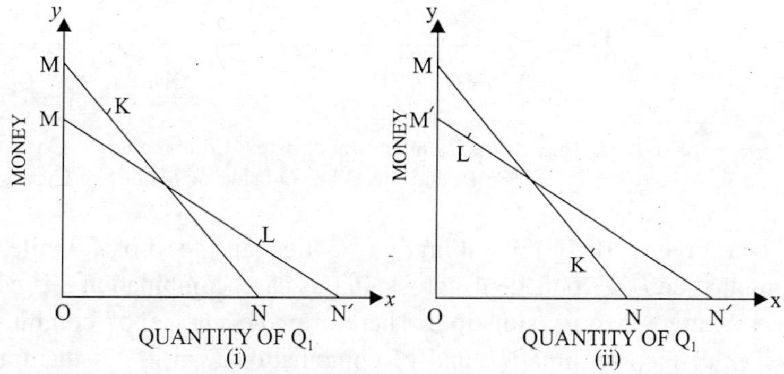

FIGURE 10.4 Consistent or Inconsistent Combinations Lying Outside or Inside the Cross.

In Figure 10.4(i), the two chosen combinations lie outside the cross, where combination *K* is to the left and combination *L* is to the right of the cross. In *MN* price-income situation, when the combination *K* is chosen the combination *L* was not available. Similarly, in *M'N'* price-income situation, when the combination *L* is chosen, the combination *K* was not available to the consumer. Therefore, the choices made under the two situations are consistent on the basis of strong as well as weak ordering.

On the other hand, in Figure 10.4(ii) the two chosen combinations *K* and *L* on the respective price-income situations lie inside the cross, where *K* lies to the right and *L* to the left of the cross. In *MN* situation, when combination *K* is chosen, the combination *L* lies within the triangle *OMN*, therefore, *K* is preferred to *L*. However, in *M'N'* price-income situation, when combination *L* is chosen combination *K* lies within the triangle *OM'N'* showing that the consumer preferred *L* to *K*. Since, in one price-income situation the consumer prefers *K* to *L*, while in the other situation he prefers *L* to *K*, the choice is inconsistent, because both combinations are available in both price-income situations.

3. There are few special cases where the two income-price lines intersect each other, but one of the two chosen combinations lies at the cross, while the other lies either outside or inside the cross as shown in Figure 10.5.

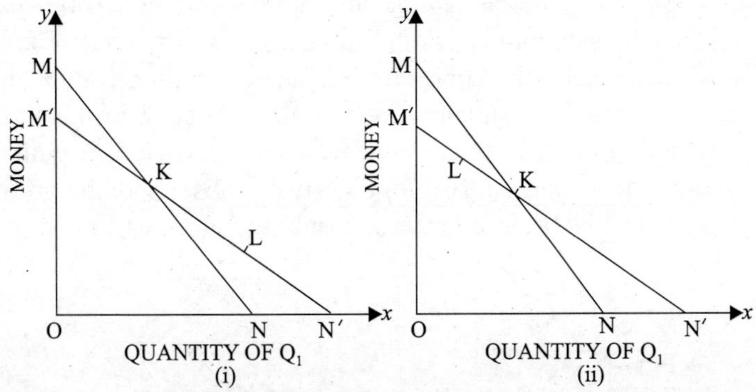

FIGURE 10.5 Consistent and Inconsistent Combinations—One Lying at the Cross and the Other Outside or Inside the Cross.

In Figure 10.5(i) combination *K* lies at the cross, while the other combination *L* lies outside the cross. In this case, combination *L* is not available in *MN* price-income situation. Therefore, the choice of combination *K* in *MN* price-income situation and of combination *L* in *M'N'* situation are quite consistent. Under *M'N'* price-income situation both K and *L* combinations are available but *L* in chosen, which means that under weak ordering combination *L* can be either preferred to or indifferent to *K*.

In Figure 10.5(ii) combination *K* lies at the cross, while the combination *L* lies inside the cross. The choice of *K* in *MN* price income situation even under weak ordering is to be preferred to *L*, because *L* lies within the triangle *OMN*. On the other hand, in *M'N'* price-income situation, the choice of *L* under weak ordering reveals that either it is preferred to *K* or is indifferent to *K* making either of the two as inconsistent with definite preference for *L* to *K*. Thus, in case one chosen point lies at the cross, while the other inside the cross, there seems to be inconsistency of choice.

Thus, we come across inconsistency on the basis of direct consistency test, when the two combinations in different price-income situations lie within the cross or when one position lies at the cross and the other within the cross, whether we apply strong or weak ordering. The weak ordering hypothesis is particularly used under the situation, where we wish to generalise, that is, we take two or more goods into consideration.

DERIVATION OF DEMAND THEOREM

The direct consistency test, based on the weak ordering hypothesis and the additional hypothesis that the consumer will always prefer a larger amount of money to smaller amount of money, provided the quantity of commodity at his disposal remain unchanged, helps in deriving all major propositions of the theory of consumer's demand. Professor Hicks has derived the law of demand for a single commodity through splitting the price effect into two parts: income effect and substitution effect. He has deduced substitution effect with the help direct consistency test, while the income effect is deduced on the basis of observation. For derivation of law of demand, substitution effect has been separated from the price effect through either the compensating variation method or the cost difference method.

Compensating Variation Method

In case the fall in the price of a single commodity Q_1 is followed by an appropriate reduction in consumer's income, then it can be shown through the direct consistency test that the quantity of the commodity demanded must rise or remain the same, it cannot fall along with fall in price. It can be exhibited with diagram having only *Y*-axis to show money leaving the *X*-axis showing quantity of the commodity to be imagined to lie somewhere near the bottom of the page. It is because the consumer is expected to incur an expenditure of small proportion of his income on the commodity Q_1 and the rest of the income to be spent on other goods.

In Figure 10.6 *MN* reveals a given price income situation, where the consumer choses *K* combination. Assuming a fall in price of commodity Q_1 while the money income of the consumer remains unchanged, we get a new price-income situation represented by *MN'*. This new price-income line lies wholly outside the original price-income situation. Here the consumer may choose some new combination say *P* on *MN'* must be preferred to combination *K* on *MN* price-income situation, whether combination *P* lies to the left or right of or exactly above combination *K*, because *K* lies within *MN'* price-income situation. Thus, it will be consistent whether there is any rise or fall or unchanged purchases of commodity Q_1 along the *MN'* price-income situation.

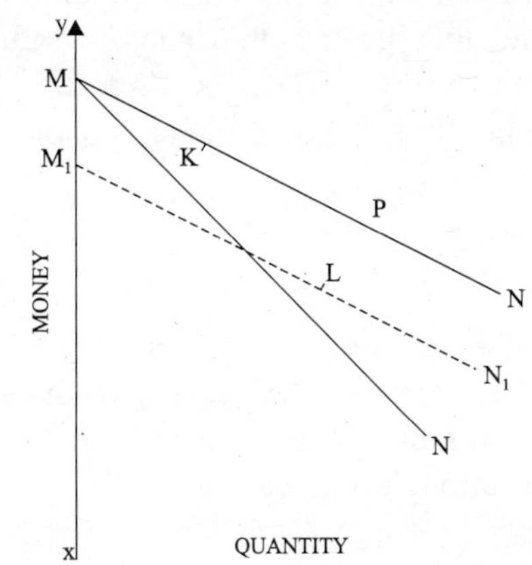

FIGURE 10.6 Derivation of Demand Theorem as per Compensating Variation.

In case P lies on MN' to the left of K, it reveals a fall in purchases of Q_1 commodity with fall in its price, and the position of P lying to the right of K means an increase in quantity demanded along with fall in its price. In case the position P lies exactly above K, it means that the quantity demanded of commodity remains constant, if its price falls. The direct consistency test is quite indifferent to all the above situations as preference of P to K will be consistent, whether it means a rise or fall or no change in the quantity demanded with fall in the price.

The direct consistency test can be helpful in this regard only when the income effect is excluded from the total price effect. We know that a fall in price results in rise in real income and if this increased real income is wiped off, then it can be proved by consistency test that the amount demanded must rise or remain the same, it cannot fall with fall in price. Such effect of change in price on the quantity demanded will be substitution effect. The rest of the effect of the change in price is called the income effect. The consistency tests fail to prove income effect, therefore, it is to be evaluated on the basis of the actual observation or empirical evidence.

Thus, we reduce the income of the consumer to such an extent that the gain in real income accruing to the consumer consequent upon the fall in the price of Q_1 is fully wiped off. Such is known as the method of compensating variation for reducing the income of the consumer. This reduction in income will construct an intermediate position L on M_1N_1 price-income situation at lower price, which will be indifferent to the original position K.

After obtaining the intermediate position with the method of compensating variation, with the help of direct consistency test it becomes possible to determine the substitution effect. Since the price after compensating variation is the same, M_1N_1 will be parallel to MN' and the consumer is indifferent between the position K and L, the price-income line M_1N_1 must intersect MN, otherwise if M_1N_1 lies wholly outside MN, L would be preferred to K and if M_1N_1 lies wholly inside MN then K would be preferred to L. Similarly, if K and L to be indifferent then both cannot lie to the left or right of the cross of respective lines on which they lie or both cannot lie within the cross or one at the cross and other within the cross. Thus, there remains only three alternatives, where K and L will be indifferent and consumer's choice would be consistent.

(i) Both K and L lie outside the cross.
(ii) One of the two lies at cross and the other outside the cross.
(iii) Both K and L lie at the cross.

In all these cases if fall in price is accompanied by reduction in income through the compensating variation, the quantity of the commodity demanded will either increase or will remain constants. In Figure 10.6 after "fall in price and reduction in income through compensating variation, the consumer chooses

L, where the movement from *K* to *L* represents substitution effect and causes an increase in quantity demanded."

In case the income taken away through the compensating variation is restored to the consumer, the exact impact of this cannot be proved with the help of consistency test, but from empirical evidence we know that in case of most of the goods the consumption increases with the rise in income. Such restoration of income will provide him an opportunity to move to *P* on *MN* price-income situation. This movement between *L* and *P* along the *x*-axis represents the income effect.

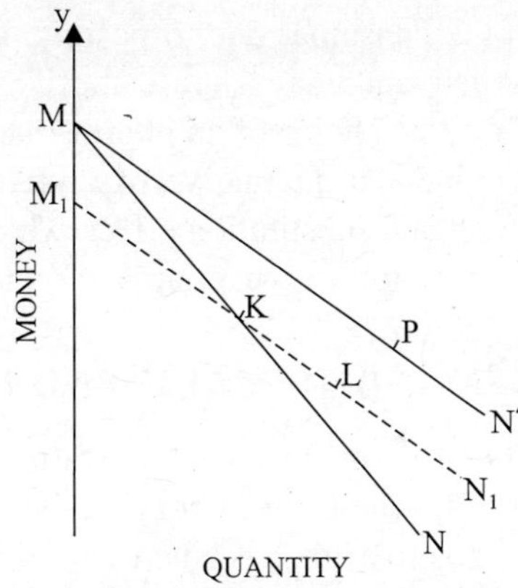

FIGURE 10.7 Derivation of Demand Theorem as per Cost Difference

Thus, it is proved that the quantity demanded increases with the fall price due to substitution effect and income effect. This proves the inverse relationship between the variation in price and quantity demanded.

Cost Difference Method

In case the fall in price of commodity Q_1 is accompanied by the reduction in income of the consumer by such an amount which will leave the consumer just able to purchase the original combination. This method is considered to be more convenient for derivation of law of demand. In Figure 10.7, the composite commodity money is shown on Y-axis and the actual commodity to be under consideration is measured on X-axis, whose location may be imagined at the bottom of the page. *MN* is the original price-income situation, where *K* is the actually chosen combination. If the price of the commodity falls *MN'* will represent the new price income situation where the consumer may choose *P* combination.

In case the fall in price is accompanied by the reduction in income of the consumer by such an appropriate amount so that he is left just able to buy the original combination *K*. Thus, the income is reduced by such an amount that the intermediate price-income situation M_1N_1 passes through *K*, where we assume an intermediate position *L*, since one of the two positions now lies at the cross of the two price-income lines. As per direct consistency tests, which are a few in this case, the intermediate position *L* on the price-income line M_1N_1 cannot lie to the left of the cross of position *K*, as that will mean inconsistency. Thus, it leaves only two alternatives: (i) intermediate position *L* lies to the right of *K* (ii) *L* and *K* coincide. It means that if the fall in price is followed by appropriate reduction in money income equal to cost difference, the demand for the commodity would either increase between *K* and *L* or the demand will remain unchanged at *K*. The movement from *K* to

L represents the substitution effect, which may either be positive or zero, but cannot be negative. Further if the part of the income taken away is restored to the consumer due to positive income effect, he may increase the purchases further and may choose the combination P on MN' price-income situation. Thus, the choice of an intermediate position through the cost difference method provides an alternative of dividing the effect of a price change into income effect and substitution effect, which ultimately explains the inverse relationship of variation in the price and quantity demanded as per the law of demand.

DEMAND THEOREM AND INFERIOR OR GIFFEN GOODS

Thus far, we discussed derivation of the demand theorem in respect of normal goods, where the income effect, on the basis of observation, was found to be positive, that is, increase in income leads to the increase in demand for goods. However, in real world, there are goods, whose consumption is likely to diminish with increase in income, that is, income effect is negative. Such goods are known as 'inferior goods' or 'Giffen goods'.

In case the price of inferior goods falls, the real income of the consumer goes up and it may cause a decrease in its consumption, because these goods are generally replaced by superior goods under such circumstances. The substitution effect of the fall in the price of the commodity always increase its quantity demanded but the income effect of a fall in price of an inferior commodity may, even reduce its quantity demanded. Thus, the substitution effect even in case of inferior commodity remains positive, while the income effect becomes negative. The price effect of a fall in price of the commodity depends on the relative strength of positive substitution effect and negative income effect. The income effect is generally quite small, because a person spends no more than small proportion of his income on a single good. As a result, even a large proportional fall in price produce cost difference of a small fraction of his income. Therefore, even though income effect works in the opposite direction, it is unlikely to outstrip the substitution effect which is usually is larger than the negative income effect.

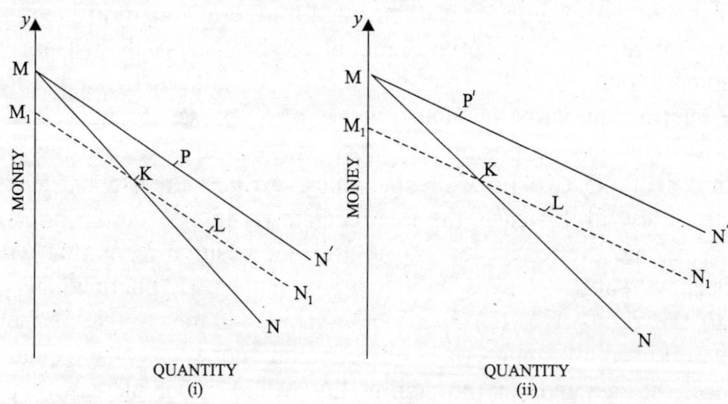

FIGURE 10.8 Derivation of Demand Theorem for Giffen Goods.

In Figure 10.8(i), the money is shown on *y*-axis, while quantity of Q_1 of inferior commodity is shown on *x*-axis, which is imagined to lie at the bottom of the page. *MN* is the original price-income situation, where the consumer chooses the combination *K*. A fall in price of the commodity shifts the price-income situation to *MN'* level. In case an appropriate amount equal to cost difference is withdrawn from the consumer, the consumer chooses combination *L* on the price-income situation M_1N_1. Thus, the substitution effect leads to the increase in the consumption of the commodity. Since, the commodity under consideration is inferior one, therefore, the income effect will tend to diminish the demand. Thus, if the amount withdrawn is restored to the consumer, he may shift to *MN'* price-income situation, where he may choose *P* combination, which means a decrease in demand from *L* to *P*. Since the income effect is smaller than substitution effect, therefore, combination *P*, though lying to the left of *L*, will lie to the right of *K*, indicating an increase in quantity demanded to the extent of *KP* as a result of working of positive substitution effect and negative income effect.

The quantity demanded of inferior good may decrease with fall in price, only when the negative income effect is so large that it outweighs the substitution effect. It is possible when the negative income elasticity is very high and the proportion of income spend on the commodity is also quite large. Such inferior goods for which there is direct price-demand relation are known as Giffen goods. Thus, Giffen goods are inferior goods, whose substitution effect is small and the proportion of income spent is quite large. In Figure 10.8(ii), the final combination *P*, after a fall in price and restoration of money income taken away, lies to the left of *K* combination. Then, the positive substitution effect is *KL* while negative income effect is *PL*, the difference between the two equal to *PK* indicates the extent of reduction in purchases in response to fall in the price of the commodity.

Thus, it can be concluded that the logical ordering theory goes deeper into the demand analysis and derives the law of demand from a few simple and self-evident propositions of preference hypothesis and logical ordering as the basic tenets of the logical ordering analysis of demand. It also corrects certain lacuna of indifference curve analysis, namely, continuity and maximising behaviour. In place of maximisation, the emphasis here is laid on consistency of behaviour. As against indifference curve analysis this can be applied to cases involving more than two goods. Hicks distinguished strong ordering from weak ordering from the preference hypothesis and by basing this analysis on weak ordering, the merits of indifference curve analysis have been retained. The logical weak ordering is also capable of bifurcating the price effect into income effect and substitution effect.

Review Questions

1. Distinguish between strong and weak ordering as per Hicksian analysis.
2. Explain Giffin's paradox as per logical ordering analysis.
3. Bring out the derivation of demand theorem as per the logical ordering analysis.
4. Explain the logic of weak ordering advanced by Hicks for rejection of strong ordering of revealed preference theory.
5. Explain the demand theorem as per the compensating variation and cost difference methods as followed by J.R. Hicks.
6. Elucidate the direct consistency tests for deciding the consistent choice of the consumers.
7. Distinguish between normal goods and Giifen goods by breaking up the price effect into income effect and substitution effect.

11

Consumer's Surplus

The concept of customer's surplus was first visualised by a French Engineer Economist Arsence Jules Dupuit in the year 1844. He sought to measure the consumer's surplus that would accrue to people from the construction of a bridge across a river through a diagram, which has also been used by Marshall afterwards. This statement of the concept was incomplete and lacked scientific character. This deficiency was removed by Marshall who, in the year 1879, gave the first version of the concept in his book titled 'Pure Theories of Domestic Values' under the chapter 'Consumer's Rent'. Later on, after improving it further, it was included in his book titled as 'Principles of Economics' under the chapter 'Consumer's Surplus'.

MEANING

The law of diminishing marginal utility reveals that through consumption or possession of successive units of a commodity or service, the consumer after a certain point, expects a decreasing satisfaction. For example, if a person buys three units of a commodity at ₹ 5 per unit, the first unit yields him more satisfaction than the second and the second unit yields him more satisfaction than the third. The person would have not purchased the third unit, had the worth of the satisfaction from this unit been less than ₹ 5. Here the first and the second units yield him more than five rupees worth of satisfaction. The excess satisfaction, the consumer gets over the price for the first two units, is known as consumer's surplus.

In real life, when a person buys a commodity his expected satisfaction is represented by the utility and the sacrifice is indicated by the price that he pays for the commodity. Since the price paid represented the sacrifice of other commodities, which otherwise would have been purchased, therefore, the price also represents the utility forgone or disutility suffered. A rational buyer always compares the utility with the disutility and makes purchases only when the former is either greater than or equal to the latter and, thus, he derives surplus satisfaction, which is called consumer's surplus.

Consumer's surplus **may be defined as the excess of utility obtained by the consumer from the purchases of a commodity over the utility forgone or disutility suffered**. It is measured by the difference between the price the consumer stands ready to pay for a commodity or service rather than go without it and the price he actually pays for it.

Marshall defined **consumer's surplus as the excess of price, which a person would be willing to pay rather than go without the thing over that he actually pays for it is the economic measure of surplus satisfaction, which may be called consumer's surplus.**

According to Marshall, 'the benefit' which a consumer derives by purchasing a commodity at a low price for which he would have paid a higher price, is a benefit derived not merely by his own actions, but in essence, it is the product of opportunities or environments or more accurately conjectures, which means the sum total of the technical, economic, social and legal conditions, which in a mode of national life resting upon division of labour and private property–especially private property in land and other material means of production that determine the demand for and supply of goods and, therefore, their exchange value; this determination being, as a rule or at least in the main, independent of the will of owner of his activity and remissness'. Food grain, salt, newspaper, electricity, cheap transport, etc. yield substantial surplus satisfaction to the consumer. Such things are available in plenty in advanced countries, therefore, there are greater opportunities in advanced countries than in underdeveloped and backward countries, which give rise to consumer's surplus. It is a product of environment also. For example, if the government stops printing of newspapers, there will be a definite loss of consumer's surplus, because the money, thus saved and spent on other commodities or service will not yield that satisfaction, which may be obtained from newspapers.

The concept of consumer's surplus is applicable to the single unit purchase as well as the multi-unit purchases. For example, **if a person, ignorant of the market price, is willing to pay more price than he is actually required to pay for, say, a radio or television set, the difference is the consumer's surplus from the single unit purchase.** On the other hand, **if a person buys a number of units of the same commodity at a certain price, the earlier (or intra-marginal) units may yield surplus satisfaction over the marginal unit. The sum of surplus, which he enjoys on all the intra-marginal units, constitutes the consumer's surplus.**

ASSUMPTIONS

Marshallian concept of consumer's surplus is based on a number of assumptions:

1. The marginal utility of money to the individual buyer remains the same throughout the process of exchange. It is because only by treating the marginal utility of one of the goods exchanged (say money) as constant, it is possible to talk of any comparison between the utility secured and the utility sacrificed in exchange. The constant marginal utility of money is possible, because a consumer's total

expenditure on any commodity or service constitutes only a small part of his total money expenditure.

2. Utility and satisfaction have a definite relationship. The utility implies expected satisfaction, whereas satisfaction refers to actual or realised utility. Often there is a difference between utility and satisfaction derived from a commodity, as the commodity may promise a high degree of utility, but on actual consumption it may yield satisfaction much less than the expectation. Marshall has assumed that there is a definite relationship between expected and realised satisfaction and these are at par. Though there is no explicit mention of this, yet it underlies in his entire theory of demand, and therefore, it also implies in his doctrine of consumer's surplus.
3. Each commodity is treated as independent, as the utility of consumption or possession of each commodity is assumed to depend on the quantity of that commodity alone.
4. Commodity under consideration does not have substitute of any kind. This assumption is essential in the construction of the demand schedule and the demand curve. The demand for any commodity will be different, if it has substitutes. In case there are substitutes, then all substitute goods are grouped together and treated as a single commodity.
5. For estimating the consumer's surplus of the entire market, differences in income, fashions, tastes, etc. amongst the purchasers are cancelled out.

MARSHALLIAN MEASUREMENTS OF THE CONSUMER'S SURPLUS

The concept of consumer's surplus is derived from the law of diminishing marginal utility and can be explained with the help of a table and diagram as follows:

TABLE 11.1 Tabular Analysis

Units of the Commodity	*Marginal Utility*	*Price*	*Consumer's Surplus*
1	20	10	20 – 10 = 10
2	18	10	18 – 10 = 8
3	15	10	15 – 10 = 5
4	10	10	10 – 10 = 0
Total	63	40	63 – 40 = 23

Assuming price to be ₹ 10 per unit, the consumer would purchase only 4 units, as the marginal utility of this unit equals the price. Beyond this level of purchase the marginal utility will be less than price, therefore, it will not be possible for the consumer to purchase any more units of the commodity. All other units preceding to the fourth unit, possess marginal utility higher than the price, leaving surplus satisfaction equal to 10, 8 and 5 respectively. The marginal (4th) unit leaves no surplus satisfaction, as in this case marginal utility equals the price. This can be exhibited in the Figure 11.1 as follows:

Thus, the consumer will purchase only *OQ* quantity of the commodity. The marginal utility is exhibited by *AEM* curve and the price is exhibited by *PE* line. For *OQ* quantity of commodity *OPAEQ* is the total utility and *OPEQ* is the total payment. The difference equal to *PAE* is the measure of consumer's surplus. The marginal utility curve also resembles the demand curve, therefore, the area under demand curve up to the price line can also be taken to be the measure of consumer's surplus [Figure 11.1(ii).]

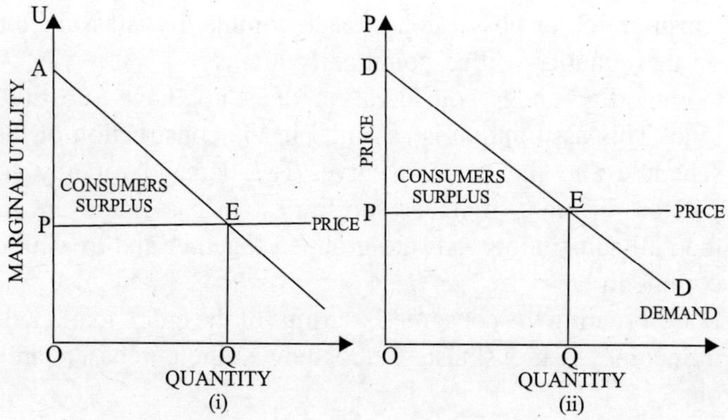

FIGURE 11.1 Measurements of the Consumer's Surplus.

This can be extended to measure the consumer's surplus for the entire market. According to Marshall, if we assume that interpersonal difference in income, tastes, fashions, etc. are cancelled out, we can measure the total surplus satisfaction enjoyed by all people from the sale of certain commodity in the market by the aggregate of the sum by which the price shown in a complete list of demand prices for the commodity exceeds its selling price.

CRITICAL EVALUATION

The concept has been criticised for the questionable assumptions and the difficulties in its measurement on the following grounds:

(i) This concept is based on the assumption that the utility and satisfaction are at par, but it is not warranted by facts of real life. The satisfaction is not necessarily the same as the utility.

(ii) The assumption of constant marginal utility of money throughout the process of exchange has been criticised on the ground that when the consumer spends money on a particular commodity, the stock of money is correspondingly reduced and, as a result, the marginal utility of money goes up. Marshall tried to answer this criticism by the statement that a consumer generally spends a very small part of his income on a commodity and, as such, the marginal utility of money may be considered as constant.

(iii) The assumption that each commodity should be considered as independent of others is also untenable. For example, the consumer's surplus from expenditure on coffee would be different if: (a) the consumer buys coffee alone; and if (b) he buys coffee after purchasing cigarettes.

(iv) The assumption concerning the absence of substitutes or complementary goods is also untenable. For complementarity and substitutability of goods, Marshall has suggested to group such commodities under one common commodity. However, it is neither proper nor possible. For such goods there can be demand, which is independent of the prices of the complementary or competing goods.

(v) The assumption that difference in incomes, tastes and sensibilities of different consumers should be cancelled out to measure the consumer's surplus of the entire market, is highly arbitrary and improper. There are a large number of buyers in the market with different incomes, fashions, tastes, temperaments, etc., therefore, they are bound to react differently to a particular economic situation.

(vi) The concept has no existence in real world. In case we take the total purchases of the consumer into account, the difference between the maximum price, which a consumer is willing to pay and what he actually does pay for a commodity is zero, because the consumer cannot think of paying more than the money income in his possession. **Professor U. Gobbi has stated that even if we take into account the purchase of a single commodity only, the total utility will be equal to the total amount paid by way of price, because the person concerned decides the price, which he is willing to pay for any quantity of a commodity after considering the utilities of all units contained in that quantity.**

(vii) The nature of the demand curve serves as the source of the consumer's surplus has also been criticised on the ground that when a person buys successive units of a commodity, the intensity of his desire for not only a succeeding units but also of proceeding units, diminishes, which makes it necessary to redraw the earlier part of the demand curve continually to represent the changed situations.

(viii) The composition and the structure of the demand schedule, which forms the basis for the measurement of consumer's surplus has also been criticised. The demand schedule contains a list of the various quantities of a commodity, which are demanded at different prices. However, while it is possible to show accurately the quantities demanded at the ruling (current) prices, it is not possible to indicate precisely the quantities which will be demanded at non-current prices. The quantities shown against the non-current prices in the demand schedule are merely conjectural or guess-work.

(ix) The consumer's surplus cannot be calculated in case of luxuries and necessaries. In case of luxury goods, generally, utility is derived from their high prices and when the price declines the utility disappears and, as a result, the consumer's surplus also vanishes. In this case, it is difficult to draw the lower portion of the demand curve. Similarly, in case of necessaries the utility is generally very high, while the price is low and, as a result, the volume of consumer's surplus is fantastically very high. Thus, for necessaries, particularly for life, the price the consumer will be willing to pay is unlimited and, therefore, it is difficult to draw the upper portion of the demand curve.

(x) There are several difficulties in measuring the consumer's surplus accurately. It is psychological and can be experienced by the consumer, when he makes a purchase, but it is not possible for him, to measure it in accurate terms. Its measurement varies from person to person, because each person depending on his wealth, status, tastes and temperaments will be willing to pay different sums of money for the same commodity. Existence of several substitutes also complicates the measurement of consumer's surplus. The difficulty may also arise if the demand schedule is indefinite and its course throughout its length is not known. Thus, to measure consumer's surplus for an individual is difficult and to measure it for the whole market is still more difficult.

Despite these deficiencies, the concept is neither entirely imaginary nor wholly impracticable. It is based on the fact that in our daily life, we express our desires and wants in money terms and despite weakness of money as a measuring rod, we are justified in expressing our subjective satisfaction in terms of money. **Professor Robertson has rightly remarked 'provided you do not expect too much from it, the concept of consumer's surplus is both intellectually respectable and useful as a guide to practical action'.**

HICKSIAN REHABILITATION OF THE CONCEPT

In the light of vehement criticisms of Marshall's concept of consumer's surplus, particularly of the assumption of cardinal measurement of utility and the constancy of marginal utility of money, Professor Hicks sought to rehabilitate the concept through the use of indifference curve analysis. In Figure 11.2 we measure quantity of the commodity along the *X*-axis and money income along the *Y*-axis.

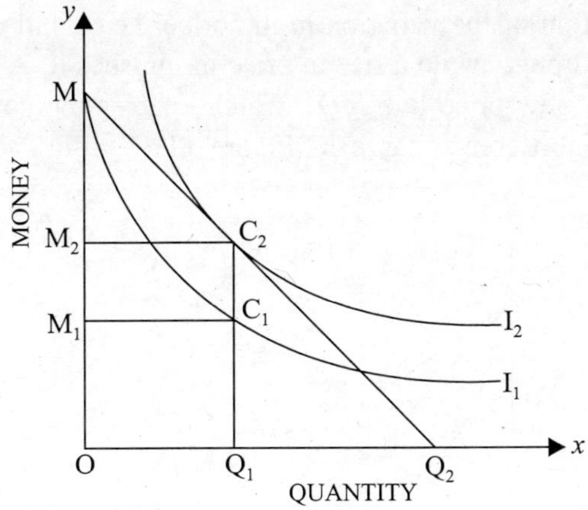

FIGURE 11.2 Hicksian Measurement of the Consumer's Surplus.

Assuming the money income to be *OM* and price of *Q* commodity not known to the consumer, he will think of the various combinations of money income and commodity *Q* shown along with MI_1 indifference curve. Assuming that the consumer selects combination of money income and quantity on C_1 point of the indifference curve, where he prefers to keep OM_1 money income along with OQ_1 quantity of the commodity. In other words, he stands ready to part with MM_1 (OM-OM_1) money income to acquire OQ_1 quantity of the commodity.

In case the consumer becomes aware of the price of the commodity *Q* and if the total money income *OM* is devoted to purchase of *Q* commodity, he can get the maximum quantity OQ_2. By combing *M* with Q_2 by a straight line, we get the price line MQ_2, which is tangent to a higher indifference curve I_2 at C_2 point. At this point, the consumer will have a combination of OQ_1 commodity with OM_2 money. The combination OQ_1+OM_2 on the new indifference curve is preferable to the combination OQ_1+OM_1 on the original indifference curve. The consumer's surplus is $(OQ_1+OM_2)–(OQ_1+OM_1)=M_1M_2$ or C_1C_2, which represents the difference between the amount (MM_1) the consumer was prepared to pay for OQ_1 quantity of *Q* commodity, when the price was not known and the amount (MM_2), he is required to pay, after the price becomes known to him through the price line. Thus, to get OQ_1 quantity of *Q* commodity, the consumer spends only MM_2 amount of money even though he was prepared to spend MM_1 amount of money. The difference equal to M_1M_2 is the measure of consumer's surplus, which **'signifies a passage from a lower to a higher indifference curve, which environment makes possible for an economic subject.'**

IMPACT OF CHANGE IN PRICE AND INCOME

In case there is change in the price of the commodity *Q*, while the income of the consumer remains unchanged, the volume of consumer's surplus varies in the inverse direction of the variation in the price, i.e., a fall in price increases the consumer's surplus, while a rise in price diminishes it. A decrease in price is represented by new price line MQ_3, which enables the consumers to reach to a still higher indifference curve I_3 (Figure 11.3).

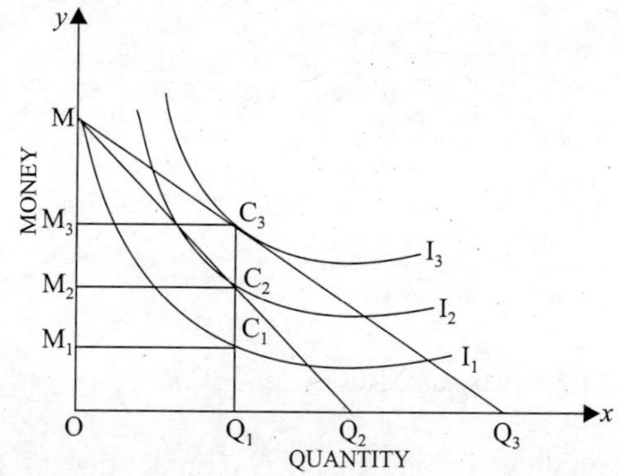

FIGURE 11.3 Change in Price of the Commodity and the Consumer's Surplus.

Thus, due to fall in price of commodity Q the equilibrium shifts to C_3 point, which lies on I_3 indifference curve, where consumer gets a combination of OQ_1+OM_3. It means that for OQ_1 quantity at lower price, the consumer is required to part with only MM_3 part of his total money income (OM), even though he was prepared to part with MM_1 part of his money income. The difference between the two is M_1M_3, which is the measure of consumer's surplus at the reduced price. Thus, due to decrease in price, the consumer's surplus has increased by M_2M_3 from M_1M_2 to M_1M_3. Similarly, if there is increase in the price, there will be reduction in consumer's surplus. This can be worked out by assuming MQ_3 as the original price line and MQ_2 as the new price line after increase in price. Due to increase in price, the consumer's surplus is likely to decrease by M_2M_3 from M_1M_3 to M_1M_2 only.

Similarly, if there is change in the money income of the consumer, while the price of the commodity Q remains unchanged. In Figure 11.4, OM is the original income and MQ_2 is the original price line. The consumer is originally in equilibrium at C_2 on I_2 indifference curve, where the consumer's surplus is equal to $M_1M_2 = C_1C_2$. In case the money income increases from OM to OM', the new price line is $M'Q_3$, which is parallel to the original price line, because price remains unchanged. Under such situation, when a person becomes richer, his preference schedules will also shift upwards. The indifference curve I_1 shows the preference schedule of the consumer, when his money income was OM. Now that the consumer's income has gone up, I_1 preference schedule has become irrelevant and a higher preference schedule I_3, based on new level of income becomes relevant to the consumer. Thus, a consumer with higher money income OM' will be prepared to part with $M'M_3$ part of his

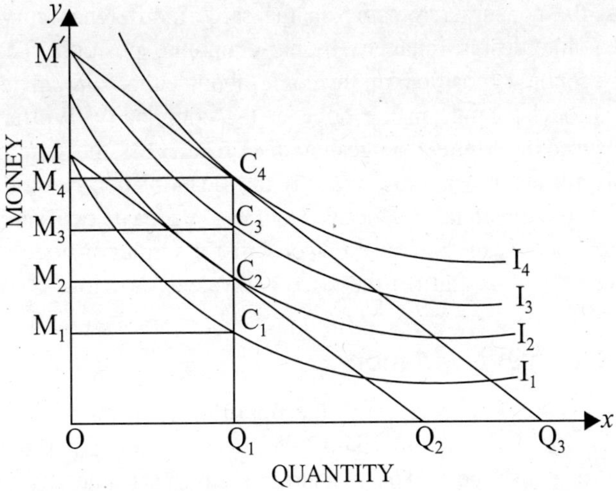

FIGURE 11.4 Change in Income and Consumer's Surplus.

money income for OQ_1 quantity of the commodity, which is available to him for $M'M_4$ amount of money only. Since the price and the quantity of the commodity remains unchanged, the amount the consumer stands ready to pay after change in income ($M'M_4$) is equal to the amount he was ready to pay at original level of income (MM_2).

The new consumer's surplus is $M_3M_4 = C_3C_4$, which may be less or more than or equal to the original consumer's surplus depending upon the slope of I_1 and I_3 indifference curves. In case both the indifference curves have the same slopes, the new consumer's surplus will be equal to the original consumer's surplus, but if the slopes of the two curves are different, the new consumer's surplus will be either less or more than the original consumer's surplus.

This measurement of the consumer's surplus is similar to that given by Marshall, because **it is measured in terms of the difference between what the consumer is willing to pay for the commodity rather than go without it and what he actually does pay for it, with the difference that Marshall measured the consumer's surplus with the utility curves, whereas Hicks has computed it with the indifference curves.** However, later on, through his well-known article 'The Four Consumer's Surpluses' published in the *Review of Economic Studies* in 1943, Hicks offered slightly different interpretation of the concept of consumer's surplus.

THE FOUR CONSUMER'S SURPLUSES

He defined consumer's surplus as that sum of money, which must either be paid to or taken away from the consumer, after some change has taken place in his economic position, in such a way as to leave his total satisfaction unaffected. In other words, the consumer remains on the same indifference curve at a raised or lowered point, despite changes in his economic position. The changes in consumer's economic position might come about either through change in the quantity or through change in the price of the commodity. We have, thus, two variations caused by finite changes in the quantity of the commodity as the measures of consumer's surplus, viz: (a) the quantity compensating variations, and (b) quantity equivalent variations. Similarly, we have two variations caused by change in price as the measure of consumer's surplus, namely: (a) the price compensative variations and (b) the price equivalent variations.

Quantity Equivalent Variation

The consumer's surplus arises from the opportunity to purchase a commodity and if that opportunity is lost or taken away from the consumer, the consumer's surplus will also disappear. The consumer's surplus is the amount of money income to be given to the consumer in lieu of the loss of the opportunity to purchase certain quantity of a commodity. It is quantity **equivalent** variation in the money income, which is a measure of consumer's surplus. For example, the government imposes rationing on *Q* commodity and stops its open market sales completely. Only those persons are allowed to purchase that commodity who possess ration cards. If a person with income of ₹ 1,000 plus the ration card for certain quantity of *Q* commodity stands ready to give up his claim for that commodity in lieu of a sum of ₹ 50, then this amount will constitute the quantity **equivalent** variation in the income and is the measure of consumer's surplus. It is because the consumer considers ₹ 1,000 plus ration card as equal to ₹ 1,050 (₹ 1,000+₹ 50). Thus, if the consumer receives ₹ 50 in lieu of forgoing his right to purchase that commodity, his total satisfaction remains the same. It is as shown in Figure 11.5.

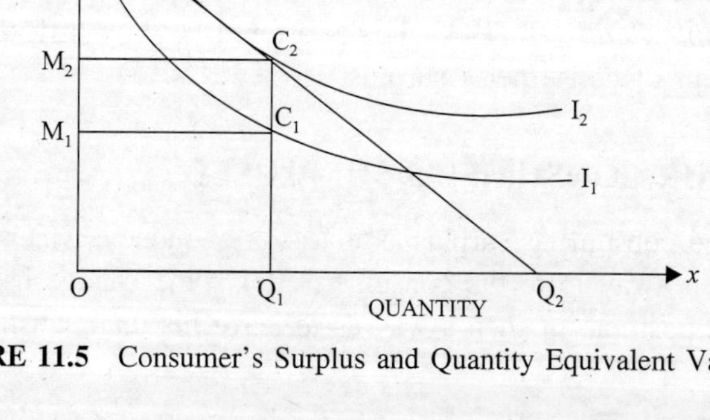

FIGURE 11.5 Consumer's Surplus and Quantity Equivalent Variation.

We measure quantity of Q commodity along the X-axis and money income along the Y-axis. The consumer's money income is OM and taking into account price of the Q commodity, MQ_2 is the price line. The consumer is in equilibrium at C_2 on I_2 indifference curve, where he is keeping OQ_1 quantity of the commodity Q and OM_2 amount of money. In case the consumer forgoes the right for OQ_1 quantity of commodity, he must get OM' amount of money to remain on the same (I_2) indifference curve. Thus, as per the diagram, if he is given MM' additional money income, his satisfaction will remain the same, because M' and C_2 points are on the same indifference curve. At M' he will combine zero unit of the commodity with OM' amount of money. Thus, the variation in money income equal to MM' is **equivalent** to OQ_1 quantity of the commodity and this quantity **equivalent** variation in the money income MM' is measure of the consumer's surplus. Initially it was measured as equal to $M_1M_2 = C_1C_2$.

Quantity Compensating Variation

It is another measurement of the consumer's surplus and is reverse to the quantity **equivalent** variation. In case initially no quantity of certain commodity is available to the consumer and later on becomes available to the consumer, what part of his money income can be taken away from him is called quantity compensating variation. In the previous example of the consumer with income of ₹ 1,000 with no ration card for Q commodity, if somebody offers that facility of ration card for the commodity, then how much of the money income the consumer will be prepared to give away, so that he is neither worse off nor better off than what he was originally. Suppose that he is prepared to part with ₹ 20 from his income for getting the facility of ration card for certain commodity. This, ₹ 980 + ration card will give him as much satisfaction as he derives from ₹ 1,000.

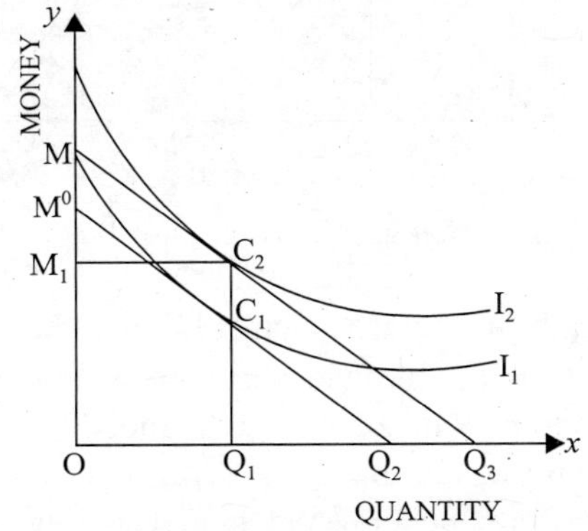

FIGURE 11.6 Consumer's Surplus and Quantity Compensating Variation.

Initially there was no Q commodity in the market, which has been introduced, later on in the market. This offers an opportunity to enjoy consumer's surplus. The consumer finds him initially at M point on the I_1 indifference curve combining zero units of Q with OM amount of money. After the commodity (Q) becomes available to him, he is enabled to buy the commodity at a price indicated by the price line MQ_3. This sets his equilibrium at C_2 point on I_2 indifference curve, where he gets the combination of OM_1 money with OQ_1 commodity. This C_2 point is obviously on a higher indifference curve I_2 showing that he is now better off than before. In case his satisfaction is to remain the same as at M point, he should be pushed back to indifference curve I_1. It is possible only when MM^0 part of money income is taken away from him, so that new price line M^0Q_2 becomes tangent to indifference curve I_1, at C_1 point. MM^0 constitute the quantity compensating variation and is a measure of the consumer's surplus.

Price Equivalent Variation

Price equivalent variation is the amount of added income that would make for the loss of opportunity due to rise in price. In Figure 11.7, when the consumer's money income is OM, taking price of Q commodity MQ_1 is the original price

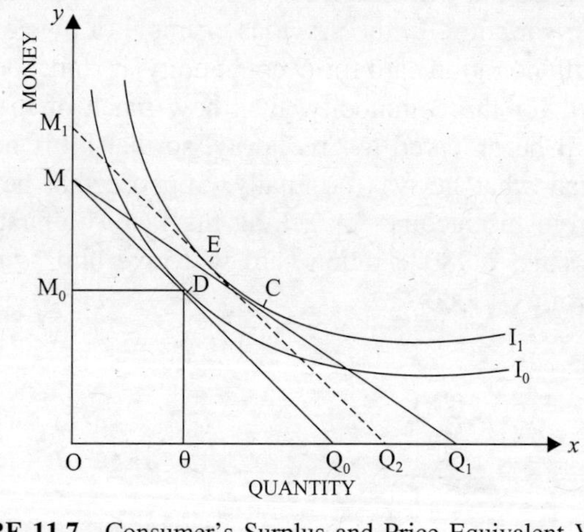

FIGURE 11.7 Consumer's Surplus and Price Equivalent Variation.

line and original equilibrium is at C point. In case the price of Q increases, MQ_0 becomes the new price line and consumer's equilibrium is at D point. The question arises as to how much should the money income of the consumer be raised to enable him to enjoy the same level of satisfaction, as he enjoyed, when he was at C before the price change. By drawing a new price line M_1Q_2, which is parallel to price line MQ_0 drawn after an increase in the price and is tangent to the original indifference curve I_1 at E point, we ascertain that increase in the money income by MM_1 will make for the loss of the opportunity of remaining on the original indifference curve (or original level of satisfaction) due to rise in price of the commodity. Thus, MM_1 is the price equivalent variation in money income, which measures the consumer's surplus.

Price Compensating Variation

It is another measurement of consumer's surplus based on the price change. By reversing the process, we adopted in measuring the consumer's surplus through the price-equivalent variation, we can ascertain the consumer's surplus through the price compensating variation as shown in Figure 11.8.

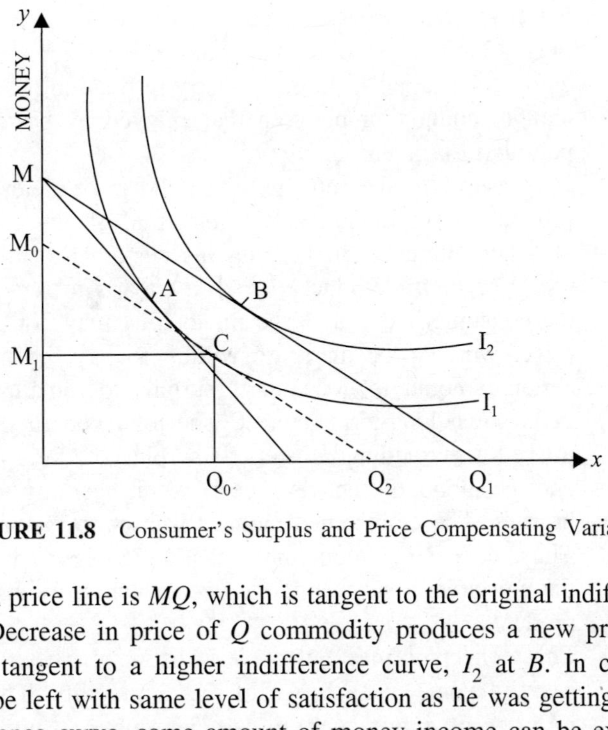

FIGURE 11.8 Consumer's Surplus and Price Compensating Variation.

The original price line is MQ, which is tangent to the original indifference curve I_1 at A. Decrease in price of Q commodity produces a new price line MQ_1, which is tangent to a higher indifference curve, I_2 at B. In case the consumer is to be left with same level of satisfaction as he was getting on the original indifference curve, some amount of money income can be extracted from him, so that the consumer is pushed back to the original indifference curve. For this, we have to draw a new price line M_0Q_2, which is tangent to the original indifference curve at C point. Here, MM_0 is the price-compensating income variation, i.e., reduction in money income to be equivalent to price reduction. Thus, the price compensating variation is the maximum deduction from the consumer's income, which will leave him in a position still to consume some quantity of the commodity without being any worse off than if the commodity were not available to him at all.

PRACTICAL APPLICATIONS OF CONSUMER'S SURPLUS

The concept of consumer's surplus has been put to a variety of uses:

(i) It helps in making economic comparison of welfare of the masses between two countries. In other words, it helps in comparing the standard of living between two areas, where money incomes may be the same, but other factors may differ. According to Marshall **the real use of the concept lies in 'comparing life in Central Africa with life in England, in saying that, though the things, which the money will buy in Central Africa may, on an average, be as cheap there as here, there are so many things, which cannot be bought there at all, that a person with a thousand a year there is not so well off as a person with three or four hundred a year here'.** Thus, it enables us to compare the amount of real income enjoyed by a person in one country in relation to a person living in another country or between that enjoyed by persons in difference periods in a given country.

(ii) It is useful to the monopolist in the price determination for his product. If the monopolist is not afraid of any competition and is also not interested in keeping his customers satisfied, he can fix the price of his product in such a way as to remove the whole of the consumer's surplus. The monopolist may not charge maximum price, which consumers are willing to pay, he may rather allow certain amount to consumer's surplus to remain with purchasers in his own long-term interest. The total benefit of a monopoly is arrived at by adding consumer's surplus accruing to the consumers and the monopoly net revenue or profit accruing to the monopolist himself. The enlightened monopolists try to maximise this benefit. Thus, a sensible monopolist cannot ignore to take into account the consumer's surplus of the people, while fixing the price of his product.

(iii) This concept brings out a clear distinction between the value in use and value in exchange of the commodity. **There are a large number of goods such as salt, newspapers, city bus transport, etc., which occupy an important place in the consumer's budget. The satisfaction derived from the consumption of such goods is considerably in excess of the disutility suffered due to payments.** Thus, the value in use of such goods is considerably greater than their value in exchange and this is of great practical use in welfare economic analysis.

(iv) It also helps in measuring the benefit from the international trade. **Imports and exports must be so arranged that the consumer's**

surplus in the country is maximised. Through international trade we import certain commodities, which happen to be cheaper than home made goods. Before their import we were paying higher prices for these goods. Such goods, therefore, yield a surplus of satisfaction, which is measured by the excess of what we would havc paid for them over what we have actually paid. The larger the surplus of satisfaction, the greater the benefit of imports.

(v) The concept of consumer's surplus originated in the pricing of such public goods as river bridge, railway connections, etc., which give a lot of consumer's surplus to their users. If their service is to be priced on the basis of their marginal cost, the price would be zero and would not cover the cost of investment. Therefore, the public utility concerns discriminate between various users of such service according to the amount of consumer's surplus they derive and fix the price accordingly.

(vi) This concept is helpful in evaluating the economic effect of a tax on a commodity. When a tax is levied on a commodity, it raises the price of the commodity and, thus reduces the demand and consequently, the consumer's surplus enjoyed by consumers. Simultaneously it brings revenue to the government. A tax will therefore be justified only if the government's gain is greater than the resulting loss of satisfaction to the consumers, who are also tax payers. This can be explained diagrammatically for industries with different costs as follows:

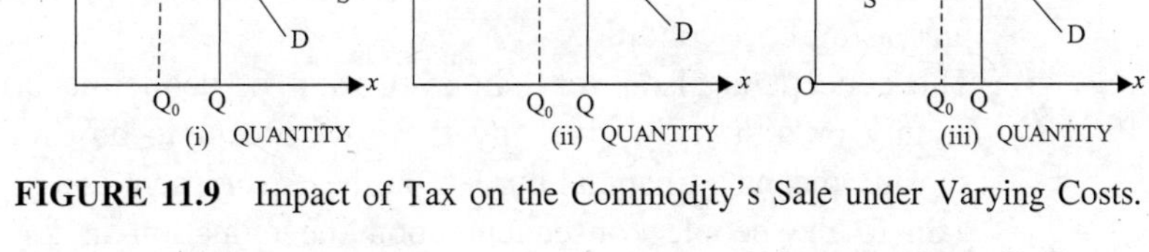

FIGURE 11.9 Impact of Tax on the Commodity's Sale under Varying Costs.

Here the quantity of a commodity demanded and supplied is shown on *x*-axis and the price on y-axis. Varying slopes of supply curves are taken into consideration depending upon the cost of production. In case the industry is experiencing a decreasing cost, its supply curve slopes negatively (i.e., downwards to the right) otherwise in case of constant cost, slope is parallel to the horizontal axis and in case of increasing cost of the supply curve slopes positively (i.e., upwards to the right). Due to imposition of tax the respective supply curves are shifted upwards in a parallel way to the *S'S'* level. Vertical difference between the two curves is equal to the amount of tax. It also shifts the equilibrium from *E* to *E'* in case of every industry, which increase the price from *OP* to *OP'* and reduce the quantity from *OQ* to OQ_0. Comparing the loss of consumer's surplus with the gain of tax revenue to the government, we can decide where the imposition of tax is justified and where it is not.

	(i)	(ii)	(iii)
Total Gain to government	*CC'E'P'*	*PCE'P'*	*CC'E'P'*.
Loss to consumer	*PEE'P'*	*PEE'P'*	*PEE'P'*
Net gain to government	Negative	Negative	Positive
Imposition of Tax	Not Justified	Not Justified	Justified

Thus, an imposition of tax is justified, if gain in terms of revenue to government is greater than the loss in terms of consumer's surplus to the people. It is true only in case of increasing cost industry, where the difference between the above two is positive. It is obvious because when price is raised by the levy of tax, people will curtail their consumption of the commodity, which will cause a reduction in production. Since the industry is an increasing cost industry, hence lower production will be at lower cost. This fall is cost of production compensates to some extent the rise in the price of the commodity as a result of the imposition of tax. Therefore, rise in price is less than the amount of tax. However, in case of constant cost industries, the imposition of tax revenue in less than the loss of consumer surplus to people. Thus, as far as possible the government should levy taxes on commodities, which are being produced under increasing cost conditions.

(vii) The concept is also useful in evaluation of economic effect of a bounty or a subsidy given by the government to any industry. A subsidy means a financial burden on the government and also means gain to the people consequent upon the reduction in the price of the subsidised commodity. It is justified only when the gain of the consumer's surplus to the people is greater than the resulting financial burden to the government. This effect of subsidy can also be evaluated in relation to decreasing, constant and increasing cost industries.

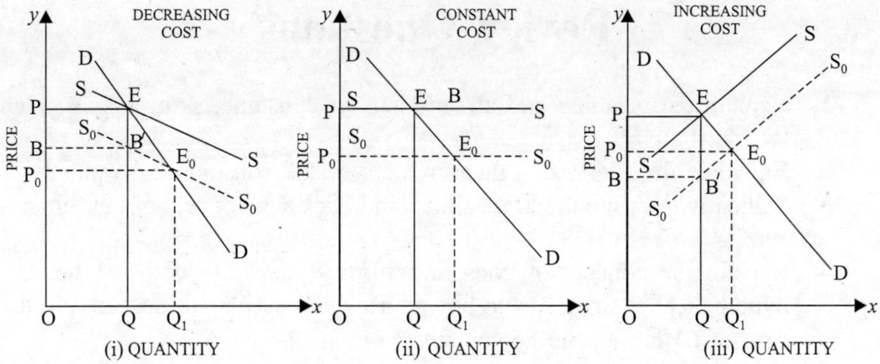

FIGURE 11.10 Impact of Subsidy under Varying Costs.

In case of decreasing cost industry, the downward sloping supply curve intersects the demand curve at E point, which is the equilibrium, where the price is OP and the quantity is OQ. In case subsidy is given, the supply curve is shifted to S_0S_0 level, which interests the demand curve at E_0 point, where the price OP_0 and quantity exchanged is OQ_1. The amount of the subsidy is measured by the vertical distance of SS and S_0S_0 supply curves. It reveals a financial burden on the government equal to $BB'EP$, but at the same time the gain to consumers is equal to P_0E_0EP. Since the gain to consumers is more than the sacrifice on the part of the government, granting of subsidy is justified.

In case of constant cost industry, the sacrifice by the government is P_0E_0BP, whereas the gain to the consumers is P_0E_0EP, which is slightly less than the sacrifice. Therefore, the granting of the subsidy may not the justified. Similarly, in case of increasing cost industry, the gain to people due to price reduction on account of granting of subsidy is P_0E_0EP, whereas financial burden on the government is $BB'EP$, which is considerably more than the benefit, therefore, granting of subsidy is not justified at all. This can also be explained as follows:

	(i)	(ii)	(iii)
Gain to the consumer	P_0E_0EP	P_0E_0EP	P_0E_0EP
Loss to the Government	$BB'EP$	P_0E_0BP	$BB'EP$
Excess of gain consumers	Positive	Slightly Negative	Considerably Negative
Subsidy	Justified	Not Justified	Not Justified at all

Thus, justification in granting subsidy is also considered on the basis of the concept of consumer's surplus.

Review Questions

1. Explain the meaning and assumptions of consumer's surplus as given by Marshall.
2. Elucidate the Marshall's measurement of the consumer's surplus?
3. Critically examine the Marshallian and Hicksian concept of consumer's surplus.
4. Explain the concept of consumer surplus. Illustrate with the help of hypothetical examples as to how consumer's surplus it measured in the case of (i) indivisible goods and (ii) divisible goods.
5. According to critics of cardinal measurement of utility, the Marshallian consumer surplus cannot be measured. Explain and state how Hicks has solved this problem.
6. Examine critically the Hicksian reformulation of the concept of consumer's surplus.
7. Distinguish between compensating variations and equivalent variations as measures of the consumer's surplus.
8. Explain consumer's surplus as per the indifference curve and examine as to how the difficulty of measuring utility is removed by this.
9. Elucidate the concepts of four consumer's surpluses as given by Hicks.

SUB PART-II
PRODUCTION

12

Production, Inputs and Production Function

Dictionary meaning of production is making, manufacturing or creating something. Adam Smith defined production as **'creation of material goods'**. However, subsequently it has been realised that man can neither create nor destroy material goods, as these are done by nature and therefore, the economist defined production as **'creation of utility'**.

Professor Sowell Thomas stated that mere creation of utility is not enough but such creation of utility should also create some value. He considered production as not only a creation of utility but also a creation of value in it. In other words, production has been regarded as 'creation of economic utility'.

Economist later on objected to the use of word 'creation' in the definition of production and stated that through human efforts the economic utility can be merely increased and not created, hence 'increase in the economic utility' has been regarded as production.

According to Professor JK Mehta **'an activity is called production, when it is looked at from the view point of that want in the process of removal of which it yields unit by unit an increasing satisfaction'.** For instance, if someone takes three hours in making a stool. Here, making a stool is want and in the process of removal of this want, as the time passes the person comes nearer to the completion of this task. This yields him increasing satisfaction and therefore, this is called production. On the other hand, if in the process of removal of a want, it yields unit by unit decreasing satisfaction or utility, it is called consumption.

METHODS OF PRODUCTION

There are several methods through which economic utility can be increased. These are as follows:

1. **Change of Form:** This is the most popular form of production. All individuals and firms engaged in agriculture, manufacturing, assembling, processing, extracting, etc. are engaged in this form of production.

2. **Change of Place:** Under this form of production, the units are engaged in transportation of goods from the places where these are less useful to the places where their usefulness is more and hence their economic utility is higher. All units engaged in road, rail, air and sea transport are engaged in this type of production.
3. **Change of Time:** The units like cold storages, warehouses, godowns, etc. are engaged in this form of production by storing goods, when these are available in plenty and releasing the same in due course of time to the market, when these can fetch a higher economic value.
4. **Change of Possession:** The units engaged in transferring goods from the possession, where these are less useful to the possession, where these become more useful and therefore, command some economic value, are also engaged in production. Thus, all wholesalers and retailers are engaged in this form of production.
5. **Performing Services:** Professionals like doctors, lawyers, teachers, actors, accountants, bankers, advisors, etc. are also engaged in production through performing services.
6. **Increasing Awareness or Knowledge:** All advertising agencies and others are engaged in this form of production, as by providing information about certain products these enhance their (products') economic value.

However, production by change of form is the most ancient and popular form of production. Agriculture has been the first to be recognised as that engaged in production by change of form. All units engaged in manufacturing, processing, mining, extracting, plantation, etc. are engaged in this form of production. This is possible through the help of certain man and material resources known as factors of production or inputs.

FACTORS OF PRODUCTION OR INPUTS

Production (or output) in any form is possible through the help of certain man and material resources known as factors of production or inputs. Alfred Marshall has identified four major factors of production (or inputs), viz. land, labour, capital and entrepreneurship and later on organisation has also been added to the list of factors of production, although for reward determination of these factors it has been included in the category of labour. All these factors of production assist in the process of production. For instance, for the production of certain goods say cloth, a piece of land is required to build the factory building. This also requires capital for purchasing machines, tools, raw cotton, fuel, power, etc. This requires labour to handle these capital goods and supervise and co-ordinate the whole process of production. Since production process is to be carried on at present to produce goods to be sold in future and if there happens to be less demand for the goods than expected, the sale of goods may not yield sufficient return. Thus, in every production, on account of this, there is risk of loss and therefore, no production may be done unless someone, either individually or in group are ready to bear this risk. The individual and the group ready to wear the loss are entrepreneurs. Thus, land, labour, capital and entrepreneurship all are important factors (inputs) of production.

The traditional four fold classification of factors of production have been modified by several economists from time to time. Some economists have added a separate factor organisation to land, labour, capital and entrepreneurship as factors of production. However, it is generally included in labour, as it involves primarily mental labour to organise co-ordinate and supervise land, labour (physical labour) and capital used in the production process. Moreover, for its rewards known as salary, there is no separate theory in distribution and it is considered under the wages in distribution. Some economists consider only two factors, viz. labour and capital, where capital includes land and labour includes organisation and entrepreneurship. Karl Marx recognised only labour as a factor of production. According to him, land is a passive factor, which cannot produce anything by itself, unless it is used by human labour. Similarly, he regarded man made capital, as the embodiment of labour and entrepreneur, as reducible to labour. However, this is an extreme consideration, which failed to gather large acceptances. Thus, the four fold classification of the factors of production, viz. land, labour, capital and entrepreneurship seems convenient and pragmatic. A brief introduction of the nature and characteristics of these four factors of production seems pertinent, before elaborating their relations with the volume of production.

Land

According to Alfred Marshall "the whole of the materials and forces, which nature gives freely for man's aid in land, water, air, light and heat are included in land." Thus the term land includes all raw materials or those, which are free gift of nature used for the satisfaction of our wants or for the production of goods and services. It does not simply refer to land as the upper surface of the earth, but also includes the resources like forests, lakes, seas, waterfalls rainfall, mountains, climate, weather, sunshine, minerals, air, etc. Land includes not only the land used for agricultural or industrial purposes, but also all the natural resources taken from above or below the upper surface of the earth. Thus, land represents the sum total of natural resources available in the country. These natural resources have value, because these are useful and scarce.

The peculiarities of land, which distinguish it from other factors of production, are as follows:

1. **Limited Supply:** A peculiar feature of land is its fixed supply. The supply of other factors of production can be increased to some extent, but it is impossible to increase land. This is because man cannot create land. He can improve the given supply of land by

draining marshy and/or irrigating deserts. Man can only clear land or change its use. He cannot increase the supply of land.

2. **Price of Land:** Land is a gift of nature given to mankind free of cost. Mankind has to spend nothing to obtain it. It has only to conserve it.
3. **Land is not Perishable:** The land is not destructible. Modern science can radically change its character, but cannot destroy it. In can go a waste or barren, but is not destructible. It shall exist in one form or the other.
4. **Heterogeneity of Land:** All land is not of the same quality. It is fertile somewhere and barren or sandy or marshy at other places. Thus, land differ in form and fertility.
5. **Land is Immobile:** Amongst all factors of production, land is totally immobile. We cannot transport land from one place to another. However, the produce of land is mobile. Besides, land is mobile from the point of view of its use. Land can be transferred from agriculture to industry. However, it is geographically immobile.

All these characteristics make certain land more valuable as compared to others and this, in turn, give rise to rent, which is the reward for using the land in the process of production.

Labour

The term labour may be defined as any action of mind or body, which is undertaken with a view to earn some monetary reward. The term labour refers to only human effort (or activity), which can be undertaken physically, mentally or in a mixture of the two. According to Alfred Marshall, 'labour is meant the economic work of a man, whether with the hand or with the head'.

Generally, labour stands for unskilled labour, but in economics, it stands for all labour, which is used in the production of goods and services. It includes skilled and unskilled labour, manual (physical) and mental labour, technical and non-technical labour, ordinary and managerial labour, and those employed in education, government, administration, justice, etc.

There are a large variety of workers, both skilled and unskilled, depending upon their health, age, intelligence, social background, education level, experience, etc. Different workers (even unskilled ones) have different productive capacities. Further each worker is not equally productive in different jobs. This difference is more among skilled workers for a specific job. Education, training, skill, health, climatic conditions, organisational set-up and personal qualities affect the efficiency of labour, which is determined by the willingness of workers to work without wasting time and effort. Willingness of worker depends, upon-several factors, like general and social atmosphere, loyalty towards job, wage rate, etc.

Labour exhibits certain peculiarities and is different from other factors. Land and capital cannot produce anything without labour. Further, since capital can be invested in labour, the latter may be called a human capital. It is mobile and can be considered not only as means, but also as an end, since production is carried on for the sake of human beings. Finally, due to the personal nature of labour, the economic considerations alone are not sufficient. The conditions and surroundings in which the worker works are also important and affect the productivity of the labour.

As a factor of production labour has the following distinuguishing characteristics:

(i) **A Human Factor:** The main peculiarity of labour is that it is a human factor. It has a will power of its own. In case the employer does not treat the workers well, they will not be loyal to the employer. A worker has humane feelings, and therefore, must be treated humanely and with dignity.

(ii) **An Active Factor:** Other factors of production depend upon labour for their productivity. It is through labour that other factors are brought into the production process. Thus, labour is an active factor of production.

(iii) **Labour Cannot be Separated from the Worker:** It is in the factor labour that the agent and the factor of production are the same. A labourer or worker has to remain present personally to put in labour. While capital can be separated from the capitalist, a labourer cannot separate his labour from his person. Therefore, labour supply is limited to the number of hours a labourer is present for work.

(iv) **Labour is a Perishable Factor:** Labour is more perishable than other factors of production In case a worker does not work for a day, then his labour hours are lost for ever. Labour cannot be stored and as such it is a perishable factor.

(v) **Weak Bargaining Power:** Workers are generally poor people. They have no savings to depend upon during periods of unemployment. Therefore, workers have to accept whatever the employer gives them. It is because of their poverty and weak bargaining power, that workers are generally exploited.

(vi) **A Mobile Factor:** Labour is mobile. It can go from one place of work to another. It is less mobile than capital, but certainly it is more mobile than land.

(vii) **Differences in Efficiency:** All workers are not equally efficient. Some workers have better training and higher efficiency. Their wages are accordingly higher, as compared to that of others.

(viii) **Labour is Both a Means and an End:** A labourer is both a means of production as well as a consumer of the production. The demand for goods is mostly linked with the level of wages.

(ix) **Capital can be Invested in Labour:** In order to increase the efficiency of labour, capital can be invested on a worker's education and training. Trained workers are also called human capital. This human capital is a very important factor in the progress of the industrial enterprises.

(x) **Indirect Nature of Demand:** Labour is not demanded directly like goods and services for consumption. The demand for labour is a derived demand. The services of a labour are demanded only when there is demand for the goods he produces.

Capital

Capital is another important factor, which plays a very significant role in the process of production. The term capital means a part of wealth, which is used for production of further wealth.

Labour and land are the two primary factors to facilitate production. Labour cannot work unless there is land to work upon. Similarly, land cannot produce anything by itself but requires labour to act on it. These two factors together produce capital. Thus, capital is produced by man (labourer) working on nature (land). It is a man-made productive resource.

According to Marshall, "capital consists of those kinds of wealth, other than free gifts of nature, which yield income". It is that part of wealth, which is used for further production of wealth. It appears in the various forms like plant and machinery, tools, buildings, roads, dams, bridges, means of transportation and communication, etc. As capital is the result of human labour diverted to the production of goods and services, meant for further production, instead of producing goods meant for consumption. Thus, capital on the one hand, makes available means of production for goods to be produced in future. On the other hand, it provides job opportunities and improves the quality of labour. Finally capital makes available resources to producers to make payments for labour, raw materials, machinery, transport and others.

Capital has certain peculiarities of its own as follows:

(i) **A Man-Made Factor:** Capital formation takes place through the savings done by human beings. Human capital is also called stored up labour. Since it takes lot of labour to create a capital asset, it is also called crystallised labour.

(ii) **A Secondary Factor of Production:** Capital is a man-made factor, whose supply is increased or the reduced through human efforts. Some economists say that capital is nothing, but transformed land and labour.

(iii) **A Depreciating Factor:** When capital is used for production, it depreciates, depending on the durability of the capital assets. Therefore, provision must be made for replacing them.

(iv) **A Mobile Factor:** Capital is the most mobile factor of production. It is easily transferable.

(v) **A Passive Factor:** Capital is unable to produce without land and labour and thus, it is a passive factor.

Entrepreneurship

The factors of production like land, labour and capital lie scattered at different places. These cannot produce economic goods and services by themselves. These have to be brought together in a coordinated manner and made to pass through a productive process to create goods and services.

Economists differ as regards the definition of entrepreneurship. This is due to the multifarious activities an entrepreneur has to his credit.

According to Frank Hyneman Knight, 'an entrepreneur is a person, who performs dual function of risk taking and control.' He considered risk taking to be the major function of the entrepreneurship. This distinguishes it from other factors, which take no risk by working on contract.

Professor Joseph Alois Schumpeter is of the view that 'entrepreneurship is associated with innovation' and innovations mean the practical application of new ideas to reduce the cost of production or to improve the quality of product.

According to Alfred North Whitehead, 'entrepreneurs are the owners of the business, who contribute the capital and bear the risk of uncertainties in business life. They may be sole traders, limited partners or shareholders.' Thus, the entre-preneurship functions may be performed by a single person or by a group of persons.

It is that factor of production, which organises, plans and brings together all the factors of production. Entrepreneur is the employer of the factors of production. It produces goods and services after supervising and coordinating the activities of the various factors of production. It also makes payments to the factors for their contribution in the production process. The entrepreneur is distinct from other factors of production in the sense that it is not employed by anyone. It gets profit (if any) for managing the business in an atmosphere of business risk and uncertainty. Its reward profit is residual, while it has to make fixed contractual payments to other factors of production. It may even suffer loss (negative profit), in case these contractual payments exceed the revenue from the sales of goods and services.

PRODUCTION FUNCTION—NORMAL AND LINEARLY HOMOGENEOUS

It reveals the various types of natural resources, labour and capital, which will have to be employed to produce one unit or a given quantity of certain commodity or service, in a given period of time. In other words, it indicates the varieties of resources (inputs) and their unique combinations, which can be transformed into desired quantities of goods and services. It reflects the state of technological possibilities of the production processes and the size of the producing units.

Thus, the normal production function is a symbolical expression of the fact that output of a product depends on the inputs employed in the production process:

$$Q = f\,(a, b \ldots\ldots, n)$$

It is read as Q (output) is function (f) of inputs (a, b......., n). In other words, it means that total output (Q), per unit of time, depends on the quantities of the inputs (a, b......., n), used in the production process. This also indicates that the total output (Q) can be varied, either by changing the quantities of all inputs proportionately or by changing the quantities of a single input only, thereby changing the proportion in which given inputs are used.

In case the proportionate change in all inputs produces a proportionate change in the total output, the production function is said to be linearly homogenous:

$$Q = A\sqrt{ab}$$

Here, Q is total output, A is a positive constant and a and b refer to the quantities of inputs used in the production process. This function suggests that both inputs are essential, as in the absence of either of the two, nothing can be produced. In case quantities of a and b are increased five times, the value of A being constant, the output Q will also show a five-folds increase.

The value of the positive constant is used to convert the units of inputs into the units of output. For example, if a represents man-hour and b machine-hour, then these units of inputs may be converted into the units (i.e., metres) of output Q (i.e., cloth). Sometimes more than one positive constants are used in the production function, where

$$Q = \sqrt{2C\,ab - D(a)^2 - E(b)^2}$$

here, C, D and E are all positive constants. According to this production function, the quantity of Q can be increased by increasing the quantity of either of the two or of both inputs simultaneously.

This property of the linearly homogeneous production function has made it very attractive both to businessmen and theorists. For the businessman it suggests that on the basis of the given input prices, he needs to decide the optimum proportion only once. After that whatever be the level of his output, he has no further input-mix problem to solve.

A specialised form of linearly homogeneous production function was given by Professors C.W. Cobb and P.H. Douglas. It assumed only two inputs labour (L) and capital (C) applied for manufacturing of the products. **This production function states that labour (L) contributes about three-fourths of increases in manufacturing of products and the remaining one-fourth is contributed by the capital (C).** In other words, one per cent increase in labour, with capital constant, will increase output by three-fourths of one percent, while one per cent increase in capital, with constant labour, will increase output by one-fourth of one per cent. The function takes the following form:

$$Q = KL^aC^{(1-a)}$$

here, Q stands for total output and K is a positive constant. The use of exponents a and $(1 - a)$ imply constant returns to scale. In case exponents of the capital (C) is independently determined, it would then be possible for the sum of the exponents to be either greater than or less than unity. In that case, it may not remain linearly homogenous production function, as the returns to scale may also be increasing or diminishing. This formula can be rewritten as

$$Q = KL^aC^b$$

The sum of exponents a and b shows the degree of 'returns to scale' in production as:

$a + b > 1$ Increasing Returns to Scale

$a + b = 1$ Constant Returns to Scale

$a + b < 1$ Decreasing Returns to Scale

This production function is very useful in research work but it assumes total output to be function of labour and capital only, ignoring all other factors of production or inputs. It regards all units of labour to be homogeneous. It is based on industry-to-industry variations, but plant-to-plant or firm-to-firm variations within an industry would seem to provide better results. However, despite these limitations 'the statistical investigation into laws of production by C.W. Cobb and P.H. Douglas is among the most celebrated in the history of econometrics.'

The production function presumes substitutability, complementary and specificity characteristics of inputs:

1. **Substitutability:** The factors of production or inputs are substitutes of one another, which makes it possible to vary the total output by changing the quantity of one input, while the quantities of all other inputs are held constant. It is the substitutability of the factors of production that gives rise to the laws of variable proportions.
2. **Complementarity:** The factors of production are also complementary to one another, that is, the two or more inputs are to be used together, as nothing will be produced, if the quantity of either of the inputs used in the production process is zero. The principles of returns to scale is another manifestation of complementarity of inputs, as it reveals that the quantity of all inputs are to be increased simultaneously in order to attain a higher scale of output.
3. **Specificity:** It reveals that the inputs are specific to the production of a particular product. Machines and equipment, specialised workers and raw materials are a few examples of the specificity of the factors of production. The specificity may not be complete, as factors may be used for production of other commodities too. This reveals that in the production process none of the factors can be ignored and in some cases ignorance to even slightest extent is not possible, if the factors are perfectly specific.

Production involves time, hence, the way the inputs are combined is determined to a large extent by the time period under consideration. The greater the time period, the greater the freedom the producer has to vary the quantities of the various inputs used in the production process. In the production function, variation in total output by varying the quantities of all inputs is possible only in the long run, whereas the variation in total output by varying the quantity of the single input may be possible even in short run. Thus, the former, known as return to scale, studies input-output relationship in the long run and the latter, known as laws of returns, analyses the same relationship in the short run. Moreover, the allocation of time period between short run and long run is also done on the basis of variability of the inputs. The period during which all inputs can be varied is called long run but if the possibility of variation is limited to one input only, while the quantities of all other inputs remain constant, it is known as short run. In both these time periods, the production theory seeks to analyse the producer's equilibrium, which deals with the optimum-mix of productive resources for a given total output.

Review Questions

1. What is meant by production? What are the various methods of production?
2. Examine the classification of factors of production or inputs, as suggested by economists.
3. 'Land is a free gift of nature', comment and elaborate the various characteristics of land.
4. 'Labour is meant the economic work of man, whether with the hand or with the head'. Examine the statement and bring out the characteristics of labour.
5. 'Capital in a produced means of production'. Elaborate this statement and state the various peculiarities of capital as a factor of production.
6. Entrepreneurship functions as a cementing force for employing the various inputs in the production process.
7. What is meant by production function? What are its various kinds?
8. Explain the Cobb-Douglas production function, as applicable in the theory of production.
9. Elaborate the various assumptions as regards the inputs underlying the production function.

13

Theory of Production Behaviour: Traditional or Marshallian Analysis

The theory of production analyses the relationship between inputs (i.e., services of land, labour, capital, organisation and entrepreneur) and the output. It states the principles according to which output is supposed to vary, as inputs vary or a single input is varied. In this chapter, we proceed to elaborate the input-output relationship, traditional or Marshallian approach to producer's equilibrium. We also examine the laws of returns and returns to scale.

This approach analyses the input-output relationship and equilibrium of the producer, as given by earlier economists including Marshall. It is also called Marshallian analysis as Marshall's contribution in this respect has excelled the contributions of all other classical economists. Basically, it centres round the law of diminishing returns and returns to scale, analysed either in average or marginal terms.

LAW OF DIMINISHING RETURNS

This principle analyses the impact of change made in the input-mix (i.e., the proportions in which inputs are used), on the output. **It states 'as equal increments of one input are added, the units of other productive services being held constant, beyond a certain point the resulting increments of product will decrease.** In case this decrease is considered in terms of the average returns, it is named as the 'Principle of Diminishing Average Returns' and if the decrease in productivity is considered in terms of the marginal returns, it is called the 'Principle of Diminishing Marginal Returns'.

'The Principle of Diminishing Average Returns has originated from the discussion of economists, like **Thomas Malthus, David Ricardo and Edward West. It states that other things being equal, if the quantity of one input is increased, while the quantities of other inputs are held fixed, eventually the total output would increase less than proportionately**. It will result in a fall in the ratio of total output and the variable input. This principle is usually applied in welfare economics, as the notion of maximum average product (i.e., the maximum ratio of total output to population) is taken as a measure of economic welfare. At a given distribution of national income, the society with high output per member is economically better off than that with low average product.

On the other hand, the 'Principle of Diminishing Marginal Return', originating from the discussions of contemporary economists, states that **other thing being equal, if the quantity of one input is increased by equal increments per unit of time, while the quantities of other inputs are held constant, eventually the total output increases at a decreasing rate.** The 'decreasing rate' points out to the marginal return, which has been preferred in place of 'average return', as the marginal return has reciprocal relationship with marginal cost, which in turn, helps in the determination of the level of output.

ASSUMPTIONS

The Law of Diminishing Return is based on certain assumptions: (i) the state of technology is given, that is, the technique of production does not change; (ii) the quantities of other productive services are held constant, as it does not apply, where the quantities of all inputs are varied harmoniously; (iii) it also assumes the possibility of varying the proportions in which the various inputs are mixed; (*iv*) the variable input is applied unit by unit; and (v) the law applies only in short run, because it is only during this period, some factors are constant and if the quantities of any input is increased, it changes the proportion of variable input with fixed inputs.

TABULAR AND GRAPHICAL PRESENTATIONS

Table 14.1 depicts the behaviour of total, marginal and average products, when the proportion of inputs changes, as the increasing amount of variable input *a* is being used with the given quantity of fixed input *b*.

It reveals that the total output (Q) increases at different rates, when an increasing quantity of variable input (a) is used along with fixed quantity of input (b). By dividing the total output (Q) with increasing quantity of variable input (a), we get the average product (Q/a) of input (a) Similarly, if the increase in total product (ΔQ) is divided by unitary increase in the quantity of variable input (Δa), the resultant is the marginal product ($\Delta Q/\Delta a$) of input (a). The average product as well as the marginal product increase initially, become constant afterwards and decrease ultimately. The marginal product of *b* input can also be calculated in the same way and will be negative in the stage I in table 14.1. It may be due to either too much use of *b* with the smaller quantity of *a* or too little use of *a* with the larger quantity of *b* in this stage. The marginal product of *b* equals zero towards the end of stage I and slopes positively throughout the stage. II, at the end of which the marginal product of *b* equals the average product of input *a*.

TABLE 14.1 Input Output Relationship

Input		*Output*		*Outputs*		*Stage*
b	*a*	*Q*	*ΔQ/Δa*	*Q/a*	*ΔQ/Δb*	
10	0	0	0	0	– ∞	
10	1	2	2	2.0	–5.6	
10	2	7	5	3.5	–3.5	
						I
10	3	16	9	5.3	–2.0	
10	4	30	14	7.5	–1.2	
10	5	40	10	8.0	–0.5	
10	6	48	8	8.0	0	
10	7	54	6	7.7	1.0	
10	8	58	4	7.2	2.6	
10	9	61	3	6.8	4.1	II
10	10	63	2	6.3	5.0	
10	11	64	1	5.8	5.8	
10	12	64	0	5.3	6.3	
10	13	63	–1	4.8	6.8	III
10	14	61	–2	4.4	7.3	

The behaviour pattern of the various product curves is as follows:

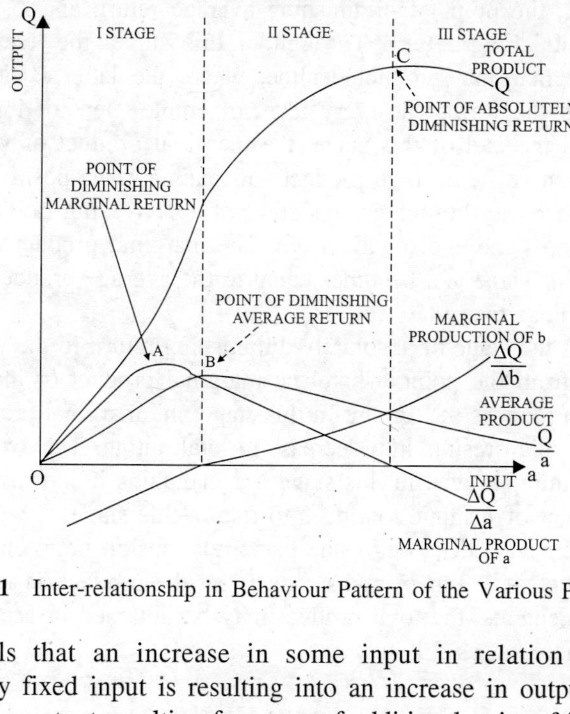

FIGURE 13.1 Inter-relationship in Behaviour Pattern of the Various Product Curves.

It reveals that an increase in some input in relation to the other comparatively fixed input is resulting into an increase in output, but after a point the extra output resulting from use of additional units of input becomes less and less, as these additional units have less and less of constant resources to work with. Thus, all types of returns are increasing in the beginning, but after certain level of employment, they start diminishing one by one. First of all the marginal productivity starts diminishing, when 4 units of input *a* along with 10 units of input *b* are employed. It is followed by the decrease in the average productivity, which starts decreasing at the employment level of 6 units of input *a*. The total productivity still continues to increase, of course, at diminishing rate, till the employment of 11 units of input *a*. Thus, as the quantity of any one input is increased, while the quantities of other inputs are held fixed, the marginal, then the average and lastly the total physical productivity of the variable input declines. The whole diagram has been divided into three stages.

Stage I is known as the stage of increasing return to variable input. The average product, which continues to rise, reaches the maximum point towards the end of this stage. The marginal product has exhibited a rising trend and reaches to the maximum level before the end of this stage, as it starts its downward journey from (*A*), the point of diminishing marginal return. The total product has been increasing at an increasing rate in the beginning, but rise at decreasing rate beyond the level of maximum marginal return up to the end of this stage. The marginal product of the fixed factor *b* is negative throughout this stage, which equals to zero by the end of this stage.

Stage II is known as the stage of diminishing average return, which lies between *B*, the point of diminishing average return and *C*, the point of absolutely diminishing return. Throughout this stage, the average product as well as the marginal product decline, where the latter is declining at a faster rate than the former at every level of employment of input *a* in this stage. Towards the end of this stage, the marginal product of variable input equals zero, though the average product still maintains its positive value. The total product increase throughout this stage at a decreasing rate and becomes maximum towards the end of this stage. The marginal product of *b* keep on increasing in this stage and becomes equal to the average product of input (a) by the end of this stage.

Stage III is the stage of absolutely diminishing return to the variable input (*a*). It begins from the point, where the marginal product of input *a* is zero and the total product is maximum. In this stage, the marginal product of input *a* is negative, which results into decrease in total output. The average product continues to diminish even in this stage but maintains its positive value. The marginal product of *b* input continues to rise in this stage.

The diagram also discloses some basic relationship between average and marginal product of *a* and *b* inputs. Assuming the production function to be linearly homogeneous, the total product may be obtained in accordance with the Euler's Theorem, as follows:

$$Q = \frac{\Delta Q}{\Delta a} a + \frac{\Delta Q}{\Delta b} b.$$

It states that the total output Q is equal to the sum of marginal products of the various inputs multiplied by their respective quantities. At the point of diminishing average return of input a, the marginal product of b input is zero, therefore:

$$Q = \frac{\Delta Q}{\Delta a} a + (0)\, b \text{ (because } \frac{\Delta Q}{\Delta b} = 0).$$

$$Q = \frac{\Delta Q}{\Delta a} a.$$

After dividing both sides by a, we get

$$\frac{Q}{a} = \frac{\Delta Q}{\Delta a}$$

Thus, the average product of input a i.e., Q/a is equal to its marginal product i.e., $\Delta Q/\Delta a$, when the marginal product of b input is zero. Similarly, when the marginal product of a is zero (i.e., $\Delta Q/\Delta a = 0$) the average and marginal product of input b will also be equal (i.e., $Q/b = \Delta Q/\Delta b$). It can be concluded that as long as the marginal product of a is greater than its average product, the marginal product of b must be negative and when the marginal product of a is less than the average product, the marginal product of b must be positive.

Secondly, the assumption of the linearly homogeneous production function renders the marginal product and the average product independent of the scale of production. Since, according to Euler's theorem.

$$Q = \frac{\Delta Q}{\Delta a} a + \frac{\Delta Q}{\Delta b} b.$$

In case the quantities of a and b inputs are increased M times, then the total output Q will also increase M times, that is,

$$MQ = \frac{\Delta Q}{\Delta a} Ma + \frac{\Delta Q}{\Delta b} Mb.$$

In case the marginal productivity of b input is taken as zero, then:

$$MQ = \frac{\Delta Q}{\Delta a} Ma + (0) Mb.$$

By dividing both sides with Ma we find that

$$\frac{MQ}{Ma} = \frac{\Delta Q}{\Delta a}$$

$$\text{Since, } \frac{\Delta Q}{\Delta a} = \frac{Q}{a}$$

$$\text{Therefore, } \frac{MQ}{Ma} = \frac{\Delta Q}{\Delta a} = \frac{Q}{a}.$$

Thus, the marginal product and average product of input *a* are the same, as they were before. This confirms that the marginal product and the average product are independent of the scale of production, if the production function is linearly homogeneous.

Thus, it is only the second stage, where the marginal products of both inputs (i.e., fixed as well as variable) are positive, therefore, the producer will seek to remain in this stage only. In case the fixed input *b* is free of cost, he will stop at the beginning of this stage, where the average productivity per unit of the variable input is the maximum. However, if the variable input *a* is free of cost, the producer will increase the employment of such factor up to the end of second stage, beyond which the additional (or the marginal) output of such factor will become negative. In practice, neither of the two inputs are available to the producer free of cost, therefore, at what point in this stage he will stop further employment of variable input depends upon the prices he has to pay for these inputs.

MARSHALL'S PRINCIPLE OF SUBSTITUTION

Marshall's principle of substitution can be of great help in this regard. Just as in the consumption theory, in order to maximise the satisfaction, the consumer equalised the ratios of the marginal utilities and respective prices of the various commodities. Similarly, in the theory of production, the total product at a given expenditure on inputs, can be maximised at the point, where the ratios of the marginal productivities and respective prices of different inputs are equal. Symbolically,

$$\frac{ma}{pa} = \frac{mb}{pb} = \ldots\ldots\ldots\ldots\ldots \frac{mn}{pn} = d.$$

where *m* represents marginal products and *p* represents prices of the respective inputs. Thus, the ratio of marginal products of *a* and *b* inputs to their respective prices must be equal and this condition must hold good in respect of all (*n*) inputs used in the production process. These, in turn, must be equal to *d*, which represents the productivity of one rupee worth of expenditure on any input.

This equilibrium condition states that the quantity of output obtained from an additional rupee worth of expenditure on any input must be exactly equal to that obtained from an additional rupee spent on any other. In case it is not met, then the total output can be increased with the given amount of total expenditure by increasing expenditure on relatively more valuable inputs and by reducing expenditure on relatively less valuable ones.

Thus, the laws of returns govern the production behaviour in short period only, where the production can be increased by increasing the quantity of one factor of production, while the quantities of all other factors remain constant. This law holds good because of the indivisibility of the fixed input, which renders it impossible to have a combination of variable input and fixed input in the best proportion. This results into increasing and decreasing returns to the variable factors of production. This principle is important not only for a firm for deciding the input-mix and the volume of output at micro-level, but also in solution of problems relating to population, low standard of living, relative prices of the various factors of production, nature of goods produced and methods of production to be employed at macro-level.

RETURNS TO SCALE

The laws of returns explain the production behaviour in short run during which the producer can change the output within the existing capacity of the plant, but cannot change the capacity. The capacity changes only when the quantities of all inputs are changed, which is possible only in long run. In long run, the producer can change the output even by changing the existing capacity, because during this period all inputs are variable. Therefore, the long run production behaviour is different from that of the short run and it is studied through scales known as 'returns to scale'.

Returns to scale refer to the behaviour of output, when the quantities of all inputs are changed simultaneously and proportionately. As against the law of variable proportions, in this case, the proportion amongst inputs do not change. The combination of fixed input with variable input is called proportion and aggregate of these proportions for the producer is a plant. Plant may be on small scale (i.e., combination of factors in smaller quantities) or on a large scale (where larger quantities of various factors are combined). When the quantities of all inputs are changed, it refers to change in the scale. Thus, the returns to scale refer to the behaviour of output of a firm in response to changes in its scale of operation.

As the quantities of all inputs are increased proportionately, the output may increase in three distinct ways. Firstly, the output may increase more than proportionately, which is called 'increasing return to scale'. Secondly, the output may increase proportionately, which is known as a 'constant return to scale'. Thirdly, the output may increase less than proportionately, which is known as 'decreasing or diminishing return to scale'.

In case of a single firm, if the scale in increased, the output may show an increasing return to scale in the beginning, constant return to scale afterwards and ultimately the diminishing return to scale. However, assuming a linearly homogeneous production function, where the average productivity is equal to the marginal productivity irrespective of the level of production, the return to scale will be constant throughout as depicted in Figure 13.2 as follows:

It reveals that as the scale is changed in normal cases, the average return to scale increases in the beginning, being constant momentarily, starts decreasing ultimately, along with increase in the scale. In case the production function is linearly homogeneous, the return to scale is constant irrespective of the number of times the scale is changed. 'Different returns to scale in normal cases,

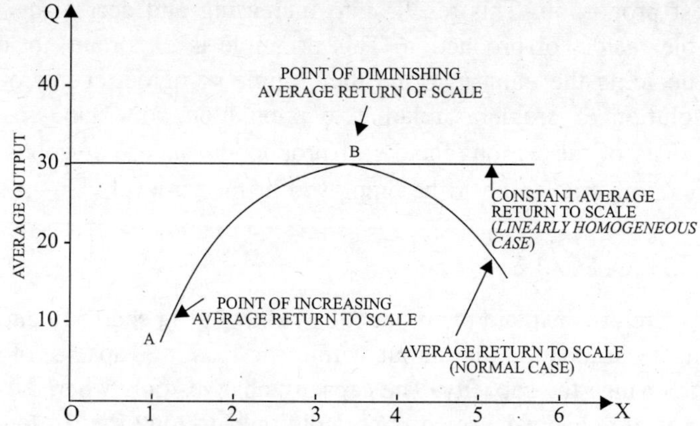

Number of Times the Scale is Changed

FIGURE 13.2 Average Return to Scale.

according to economists, is the result of internal and external economies as well as diseconomies'. They assert that increasing average return is due to increased efficiency of the various factors of production and the decreasing average return is the result of their inefficiency. Some other economists claim that the increasing and decreasing return to scale are due to indivisibility of inputs. The machines, workers, management, etc. cannot be varied perfectly, therefore, sometimes they result in an increasing return, while at other times, in a decreasing return. Greater emphasis has been placed by economists on the size of firm, as the determinant of various returns to scale. The accepted doctrine that larger firms can command superior resources and can practice greater specialisation, which ultimately leads to increasing return to scale, but beyond a point all these benefits of enlarging the scale vanish, which ultimately leads to decreasing return to scale.

Review Questions

1. Examine the law of diminishing returns and elucidate its application.
2. In what stage of products behaviour, the producer's equilibrium will be decided?
3. State Marshall's principle of substitution and examine its application in deciding producer's equilibrium.
4. State the assumptions of law of diminishing returns. How returns as per this are put in terms of average as well as marginal returns?
5. In case the production behaviour in according to Euler's Theorem, what will be the behaviour of returns to scale?
6. Elucidate the behaviours of returns to scale under normal production function and state the reasons for such behaviour.

14

Theory of Production Behaviour: Modern or Hicks-Allen's Analysis

As per this approach for analysing the producer's behaviour, we concentrate on elaboration of isoquant or iso-product curves, isocost lines, elasticity of substitution, producer's equilibrium, scale lines and expansion path.

Substitutability and complementarity of inputs, the producers' desire for attaining cost reduction through the most appropriate input-mix for a given level of total output and the ultimate tendency of returns to diminish clearly indicate the similarity of the theory of production with that of the consumption. Both the consumers as well as the producers are faced with the problem of choice from alternative combinations. For explaining choice, just as modern economists take into consideration indifference or iso-utility curves in consumption, similarly they consider isoquant or iso-product curves in the production. Thus, the modern analysis of production is based on isoquant curves and isocost lines, just as the modern analysis of consumer's behaviour is based on the indifference curves and the price lines.

ISOQUANT CURVE

Isoquant or iso-product curve is a contour line that represents the various combinations of two inputs, which produce the same quantity of the total output. Throughout this analysis, we assume that the technical conditions for production are given and constant and inputs are combined in a most efficient manner.

In Figure 14.1, the total output on I_1 isoquant curve is 25 units, which can be produced either by combining *ob* with *oa* units of *b* and *a* inputs respectively at *A* point or by combining Ob_1 with Oa_0 at *B* point or Ob_0 with Oa_1 at *C* point. Similarly, there may be a large number of combinations of the inputs to produce the same quantity of total output on a particular isoquant curve. Mathematically, an isoquant is a curve, where,

$$\Delta Q = ma \cdot \Delta a + mb \cdot \Delta b = 0$$

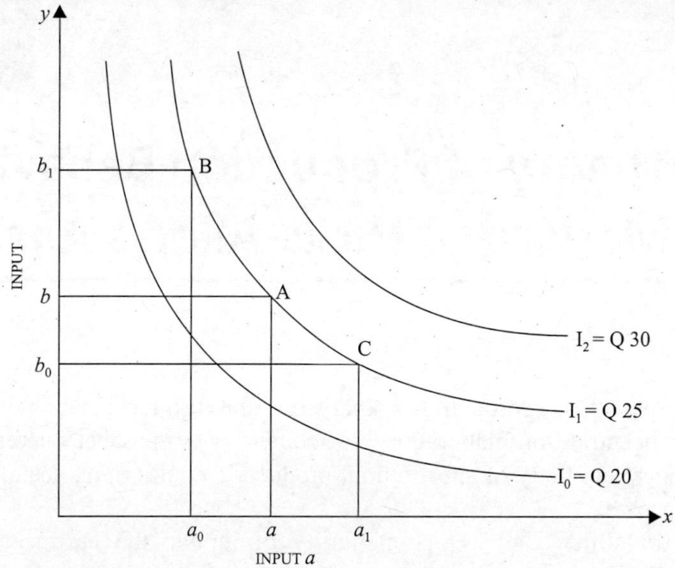

FIGURE 14.1 Slopes of the Iso-product or Isoquant Curves.

Here ΔQ represents change in the quantity of total output; *ma* and *mb* are the marginal products of *a* and *b* inputs, while Δ*a* and Δ*b* represent the change in the quantities of *a* and *b* inputs respectively.

Since the marginal products of both *a* and *b* inputs are assumed to be positive in the relevant range, if we move from one point to other alongwith the isoquant curve, the change in the quantity of either *a* or *b* input must be negative. In the diagram, if we move from *A* to *B* point, then the quantity of input *a* diminishes, while that of *b* input goes up and similarly, if we move from *A* to *C* point, then the quantity of input *b* required to maintain the output as constant diminishes, but the quantity of input a increases. The total output on a particular isoquant does not change (ΔQ=0), but if we move to a higher isoquant (I_2), the output goes up and if we move to a lower isoquant (I_0), the output declines. In case a large number of isoquant are shown in a single diagram, it is called isoquant map.

Properties of Isoquants. Isoquants have certain properties as follows:

1. **Negative Slope:** Isoquants slope downwards to the right, because if we employ less of one input, we must employ more units of the other input, to get the same volume of total output. Beyond certain ranges (i.e., beyond ridge lines) isoquants might slope positively, but such ranges could never contain equilibrium position, therefore, these can be ignored. Similarly, horizontal and vertical ranges of isoquants, through it could conceivably exist, could never include a possible equilibrium position, as we cannot diminish the quantity

of one input maintaining the quantity of the other as constant to get the same total output. Separation of such ranges is done by the ridge lines, which combine the points of zero marginal productivities of two inputs, as shown in Figure 14.2.

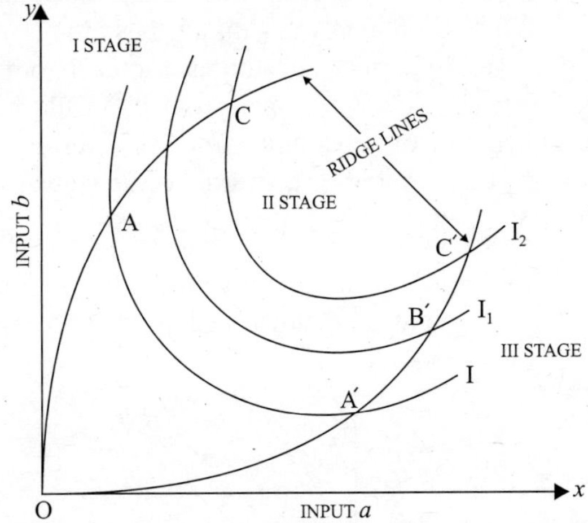

FIGURE 14.2 Roles of Ridge Lines for Isoquant Curves.

The two ridge lines combine the points of zero productivities of both inputs, which fall on *A*, *B* and *C* points for *b* input and *A*′, *B*′ and C′ points for input a on the isoquants I, I_1 and I_2 respectively. Beyond *A*, *B* and *C* points, the marginal productivity of *b* input is negative and within these points it is positive. Therefore, in between the positive and the negative productivities at these points the productivity of *b* input equals zero. It is similar to the end of first stage of the diagram representing producers' behaviour in traditional analysis. Similarly, beyond *A*′, *B*′ and *C*′ points the productivity of input *a* on respective isoquants is negative and above these points it is positive, therefore, on these points its productivity is zero. So beyond *OC*′ ridge line, there is beginning of III stage, as the productivity of input *a* is negative. Thus, the producer gets the positive productivity from both inputs within the range set by the two ridge lines, where there is negative slope for all isoquants.

2. **Parallel:** Higher isoquants indicate a higher level of output than that on lower isoquants. In order to maintain the consistency in this statement, isoquants are drawn parallel, otherwise they will intersect each other and if they do so, it will reveal that all the combinations of inputs on both isoquants result in the same total output, which is quite inconsistent.
3. **Convex to the Origin:** Just like the indifference curves, isoquants also have a bend towards origin point. This reveals the marginal

significance of one input in terms of the other. This marginal significance is measured by the amount of one input, which can be given up in exchange for one additional unit of other input without changing the quantity of the total output. This marginal significance of one input in terms of the other, technically known as the technical rate of substitution, always diminishes along with isoquants, because inputs are imperfect substitutes for each other. Had these inputs been perfect substitutes, the isoquants would have shown a constant technical rate of substitution and, as a result, it would have been a straight line sloping downwards to the right.

Technical Rate of Substitution (*TRS*) of b for a is equal to $\frac{-\Delta b}{\Delta a}$, which is equal to the reciprocal of ratio of marginal productivities of the two inputs, as shown in Figure 14.3 as follows:

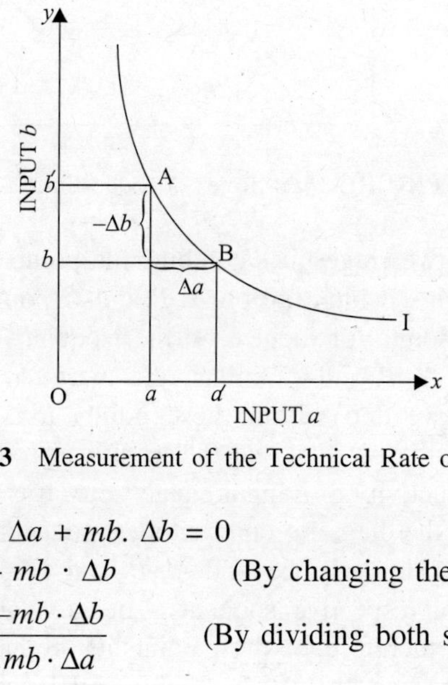

FIGURE 14.3 Measurement of the Technical Rate of Substitution.

$$\Delta Q = ma \cdot \Delta a + mb.\ \Delta b = 0$$

$$ma \cdot \Delta a = -\ mb \cdot \Delta b \qquad \text{(By changing the side of } mb \cdot \Delta b\text{)}$$

$$\frac{ma \cdot \Delta a}{mb \cdot \Delta a} = \frac{-mb \cdot \Delta b}{mb \cdot \Delta a} \qquad \text{(By dividing both sides with } mb\ \Delta a\text{)}$$

$$\frac{ma}{mb} = \frac{-\Delta b}{\Delta a} = TRS \qquad \text{(After cancelling out } \Delta a \text{ and } mb \text{ on respective sides)}$$

Thus, *TRS* is equal to the reciprocal of the ratio of the marginal productivities of the two inputs used in the production process.

ELASTICITY OF SUBSTITUTION

The convexity of isoquants is attributed to imperfect substitutability of both inputs. In the production process, the input-mix are not rigidly fixed, and simultaneously their substitutability is also not perfect. Therefore isoquants can assume neither of the following two slopes.

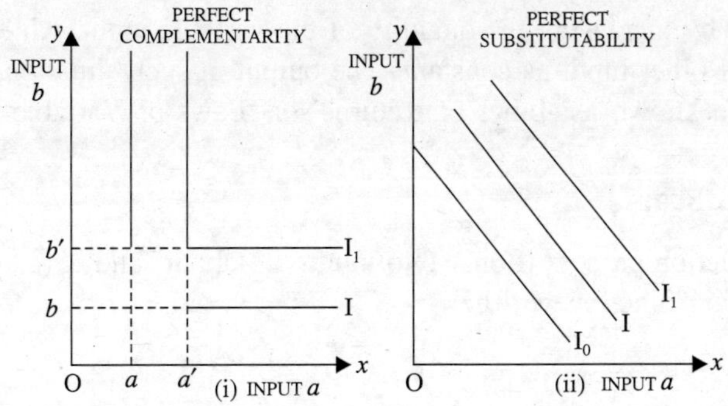

FIGURE 14.4 Slopes of Isoquants under Perfect Complementarity and Substitutability.

Thus, the isoquants have slopes in between the aforesaid two slopes depending upon the elasticity of substitution. The degree of curvature of isoquants measures the extent to which it is possible to use one input in place of the other. A higher degree of curvature of isoquants indicates that the inputs are not easily substitutable and a low degree of curvature indicates a high degree of substitutability.

The elasticity of substitution is the percentage change in the proportion of use of inputs (b/a), as the technical rate of substitution changes.

$$\text{Elasticity of Substitution} = \frac{\text{Percentage change in the proportion between inputs}}{\text{Percentage change in the technical rate of substitution}}$$

$$= \frac{\dfrac{\text{Change in proportion } \{\Delta(b/a)\}}{\text{Original proportion } (b/a)}}{\dfrac{\text{Change in technical rate of substitution } (\Delta\text{TRS})}{\text{Original technical rate of substitution (TRS)}}}$$

$$= \frac{\dfrac{\Delta(b/a)}{b/a}}{\dfrac{\Delta TRS}{TRS}}$$

$$= \frac{\Delta(b/a)/b/a}{\Delta TRS/TRS}.$$

The elasticity of substitution may have value that lies some-where between zero and minus infinity. In case value is zero it indicates that both inputs must be used in fixed proportions and are perfectly complementary, but if the value is minus infinity ($= -\infty$) it means both the inputs are perfect substitutes for one another.

Laws of Production as per Isoquants: The production function also suggests the technically feasible ways of increasing the level of output. It may be increased by increasing the quantities all inputs used in the production process. It is generally possible in long run, where the output increases as per a set pattern known as 'Returns to Scale'. The output may also be increased in short run by increasing the quantity of the variable input, while holding the quantities of other input as constant. The output in such situation, increases as per a pattern known as 'Laws of Returns' or 'Laws of Variable Proportions'.

Returns to Scale

In the production process if only two inputs L (labour) and K (capital) as used, the production function will be:

$$X_0 = f(L, K)$$

In case all factors are increased c times, the production function will be:

$$X_n = f(cL, cK)$$

Under such situation, if x_n i.e., the output at new level increases in the proportion of the increase in inputs, there will be constant return to scale and the production function is said to be linearly homogeneous. In case x_n shows an increase in output more or less than proportionately to the increase in the quantities of inputs, there will be increasing or decreasing returns to scale and the production function will non-linearly homogeneous.

Returns to scale may be graphically, shown by distance on the product line or isocline between successive 'multiple-level-of-output' isoquants, which are the isoquants that show the levels of output that are multiplies of some base level of output e.g. x, $2x$, $3x$ and so on.

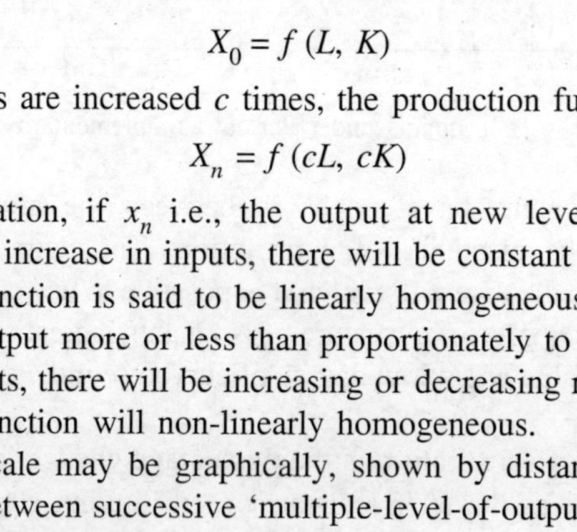

FIGURE 14.5 Slope of Product Line or Isocline.

In case the quantities of L and K are doubled and the output in just double as on $2x_c$ isoquant, it is constant return to scale. On the other hand, if the output is doubled on $2x_i$ isoquant, which is obtained with less than double of L ($< 2L$) and K ($< 2K$), it is increasing return to scale. Similarly if the output is doubled on $2xd$ isoquant, which is obtained with more than double of L ($> 2L$) and K ($> 2K$) it is decreasing return to scale. Thus, if the gap or distance between the x and $2x$ multiple level of output isoquant, is constant showing just double the quantities of the respective inputs as that on the $2x_c$ isoquant, there is a constant return to scale. In case the gap narrows down as between x and $2x_i$ isoquants, it shows an increasing return to scale and if the gap widens as between x and $2xd$ isoquants, it reveals a decreasing return scale.

Laws of Returns

These reveal the behaviour of the total output as the quantity of a single input is varied, while the quantity of the other input is held constant. The return to variation in the quantity of the single input is invariably diminishing one, in case the returns to scale is constant or decreasing, but it may be increasing if the firm is experiencing increasing return to scale. It is as follows:

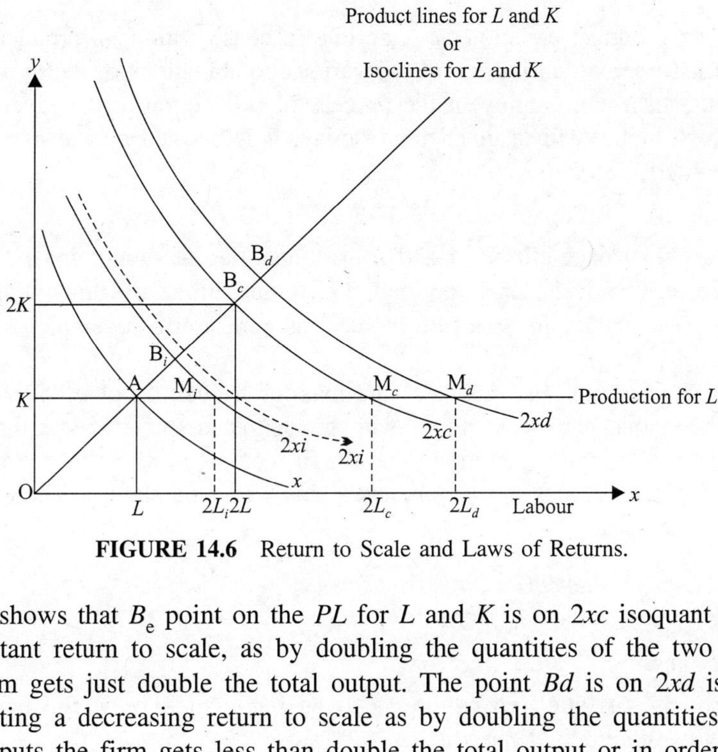

FIGURE 14.6 Return to Scale and Laws of Returns.

It shows that B_e point on the PL for L and K is on $2xc$ isoquant reveals a constant return to scale, as by doubling the quantities of the two inputs, the firm gets just double the total output. The point Bd is on $2xd$ isoquant suggesting a decreasing return to scale as by doubling the quantities of the two inputs the firm gets less than double the total output or in order to get double the total output on $2xd$ the firm has, to use the more than the double quantities of the two inputs in the production process. In both these situations, when the quantity of only L (Labour) is increased, its product line intersects $2x_c$ and $2x_d$ isoquants at M_c and M_d points, which require more than the double the quantity of labour used originally for obtaining just double the output on these isoquants. These suggest the application of the law of diminishing return in both these situations.

However, when there is increasing return to scale, by doubling the quantity of labour in the production process, the firm gets more than double the total output on > $2x_i$ isoquant or for obtaining just double the total output as at M_i point on the $2x_i$, isoquant, the firm has to employ less than double (< $2L$) labour in the production process. It reveals the application of law of increasing return to the variable input labour. Similarly, if the $2x$, is in the position of > $2x_i$ isoquant, there will be constant return to the variable input labour. Thus, the constant and increasing returns to the variable input are possible only where there is an increasing return to scale in long run, but under constant and decreasing return to scale only diminishing return to the variable input will be applicable.

ISOCOST LINE

Just like the budget equation or price line in consumption, in production we use isocost line, which represents the various combinations of the two inputs, which the firm can employ in the process of production at the given prices of the two inputs with a given total outlay. It is derived on the basis of an equation as follows:

$$ap_a + bp_b = T$$

Here T is total expenditure, a and b are quantities of inputs and p_a, p_b are their respective prices. Thus, the total expenditure equals the amount spent on input a plus the amount spent on input b, as both are to be employed in the production process.

The isocost line also indicates the maximum quantity of a and b inputs respectively that can be acquired with given total expenditure at the given price of the two inputs. Assuming that the firm employs whole of its resources on b input and decides not to take even single unit of input a. The equation may be written as:

$$\begin{aligned}(o)\,pa + bp_b &= T\\ bp_b &= T\\ b &= T/p_b\end{aligned}$$

Similarly, if the total expenditure is to be on input a only, the maximum quantity of input a is determined as follows:

$$\begin{aligned}ap_a &= T\\ a &= T/p_a\end{aligned}$$

In case both of the above maximum quantities are placed in a diagram on the respective axes, by combining the two with a straight line, we get an iso-cost line as follows:

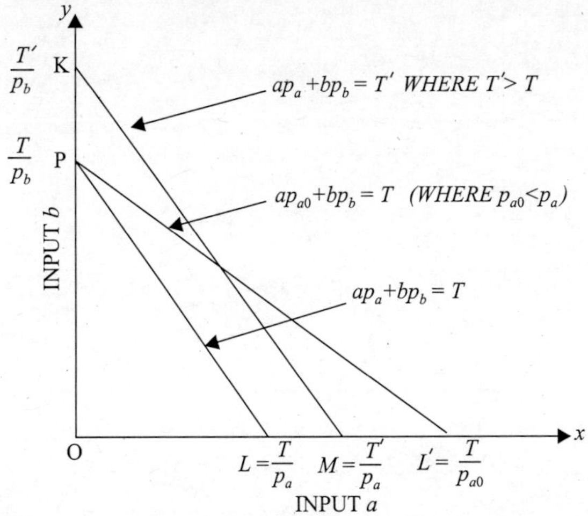

FIGURE 14.7 Slopes of Budget Euqation Line or Isocost Line.

At the original price with given total expenditure, the slope of the original isocost line *PL* is $\frac{T}{pb} \div \frac{T}{pa} = \frac{T}{pb} \cdot \frac{pa}{T} = \frac{pa}{pb}$. In case the price falls, the new isocost line has the slope, equal to $\frac{pa_0}{pb}$, which is less than the original slope. In case the producer decides to enhance the expenditure, the isocost line is shifted upwards, but it maintains the original slope equal to $\frac{pa}{pb}$.

PRODUCER'S EQUILIBRIUM

Like the consumer, who aims at getting maximum possible satisfaction out of his given income, the producer wants to get the maximum possible production out of the given total expenditure on the various inputs. Thus, both are facing the problem of optimisation, which, in case of producer, is possible through the isoquant curve and isocost line as follows:

The tangency of an isocost line with an isoquant represents the equilibrium position of the producer. At *E* point, the given isocost line is tangent to the highest possible isoquant, which reveals that the producer at given prices of inputs and with given total expenditure cannot produce more than that produced on the given isoquant *I*. At this point, the slope of isoquant (i.e., $-\Delta b/\Delta a = ma/mb$) is equal to the slope of the isocost line (i.e., pa/pb). At *E* point, whatever quantities of inputs are needed to produce the given quantity of total output that can be acquired by the producer with given total outlay at given prices of the two inputs. The producer will be in equilibrium at no point other than this, because if he moves along the isocost line, he will find

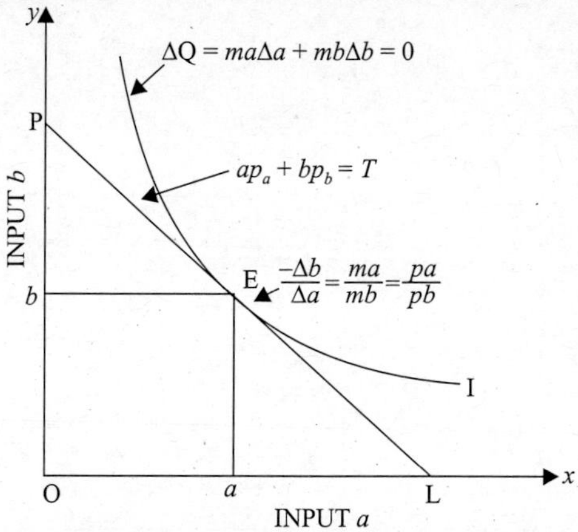

FIGURE 14.8 Producer's Equilibrium.

himself on lower isoquant representing lower total output and if he moves along the isoquant, then he fails to assemble the obtain quantities of both inputs for that level of total output.

The producer's equilibrium stated above is similar to that suggested by Marshall earlier, as by multiplying and dividing the Marshallian equation we arrive at the equilibrium equation derived by the isoquant approach as follows:

$$ma/pa = mb/pb \text{ (Marshallian Equilibrium)}$$

$$\frac{pa}{mb} \times \frac{ma}{pa} = \frac{mb}{pb} \times \frac{pa}{mb}$$ (by multiplying both sides with *pa* and dividing with *mb*)

$$\frac{ma}{mb} = \frac{pa}{pb} \text{ (Modern Equilibrium Conditions)}$$

Thus, both derive the same conclusion though these have been worded differently.

VARIATIONS IN EQUILIBRIUM POSITION

The equilibrium position of the producer changes either due to change in price of any input or due to change in the total expenditure. In case price of any input changes, the isocost line changes its slope, which brings a new equilibrium position for the producer, as follows:

The original equilibrium at *A* point is made of *PL* isocost line and I_0 isoquant, where producer employs *Oa* units of input *a* and *Ob* units of *b* input. Assuming a decrease in the price of input a, *PL'* becomes the new isocost line, which enables the producer to reach a higher isoquant I_1. After a change in price of input *a*, producer's equilibrium is established at *B* point, where he is employing Oa_2 units of input *a* and Ob_2 units of *b* input. Thus, at new equilibrium an increased quantity of inputs *a* is employed to obtain larger output on a higher isoquant I_1.

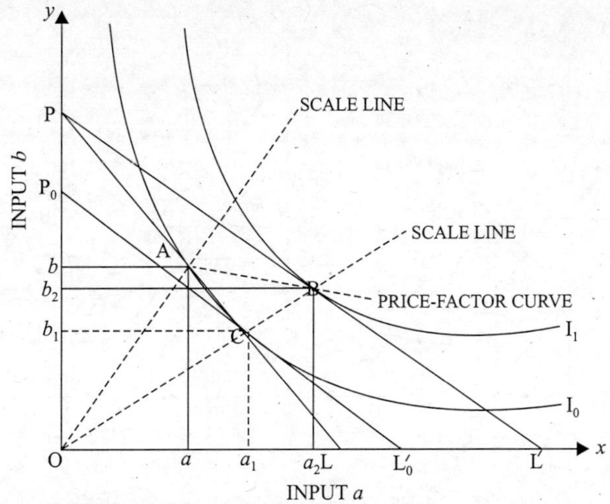

FIGURE 14.9 Slopes of the Scale Lines and Price-Factor Curve.

Thus, the change in price results in a change in the total output. It also changes the scale line. Former equilibrium is on *OA* scale line but the latter is on the *OB* scale line. It indicates that the change in price of one input not only brings a change in total output but also changes the proportion in which inputs are employed, where the former is unpredictable but the latter is certain.

It may not be advisable for a firm to enhance the output in response to decrease in the price of any input, because the firm operating under conditions of imperfect competition may find it unprofitable or undesirable to increase the output beyond the original level. Under such circumstances, the firm may like to produce the original quantity by remaining on the original isoquant. It does not mean that the producer will not take the advantage of reduced price and will come back to original equilibrium. Actually under such circumstances, he may decide to minimise the cost of total output. This shifts the isocost line to P_0L_0' level, which is tangent to the original isoquant at *C* point lying on a new scale line derived after change in price of input *a*. This implies that the producer will take the benefit of reduced price of input *a* in the form of substitution of relatively cheaper input for relatively more expensive one. Thus, the firm, which was originally in equilibrium at *A*, might get the equilibrium at *C* and continue to produce the same output at lower price of input *a*, rather than to increase its output by moving to *B*.

Similarly, if the firm increases its outlay or the price of both inputs diminishes proportionately, the isocost line is shifted upwards in a parallel way. This shifts the equilibrium position to a higher isoquant.

Such a change in outlay or proportional change in price of both inputs changes only the scale of operations and leaves proportions in which inputs are employed unchanged. On the other hand, a change in the price of one input only may change both the level of output and the proportions of the inputs employed.

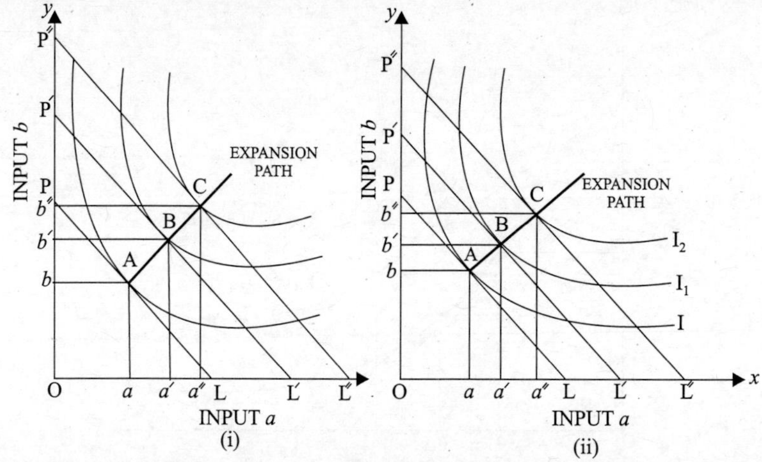

FIGURE 14.10 Slopes of the Expansion Paths.

At given input prices, the firm could expand the scale of its operations along a line from the origin formed by the points of tangency of successive parallel isocost lines with higher isoquants. It is named as expansion path. It need not be a straight line, but usually it slopes upwards to the right forming convex or a concave curve.

LIMITATIONS OF ISOQUANT ANALYSIS

The isoquant analysis of producer's equilibrium suffers from a few limitations, because of its bold assumptions. These are in particular: (a) continuity in the processes of production, which facilitates obtaining of an isoquant map; (b) perfect variability of proportions of the input-mix; and (c) no constraint on the expansion of production. These assumptions are not realised in practice. A few other limitations are as follows:

(i) **Isoquant Map is Difficult to Obtain:** There can be only a finite number of technical processes. Each process having a given input-mix. Thus, the producer has only a few alternatives from which he can choose any input-mix and not innumerable combinations, which are implied in a continuous isoquant curve. This reveals that isoquants are not smoothly sloping continuous curves, if drawn from real world situations, rather they are composed of straight lines joined by kinks, each kink showing separate process of production.

(ii) **Fixed Production Processes:** The scope for varying the proportions of inputs in the input-mix is also limited. Each process has a given input *mx*, where increasing the proportion of one factor keeping the other factors as constant would not add to production rather it will require an increase in the scale of production.

(iii) **Technical Limitation on Scale:** The scale of production can also not be changed frequently. The scale line, though drawn as continuous line, cannot be so continuous in the real world, as all inputs are not perfectly variable even in long run.

(iv) The assumption of absence of constraint on expansion of production is unrealistic and untenable. In practice a number of constraints like power, floor space, production capacity, the minimum size of plant, etc. are advanced by managers.

Thus, it reveals the nature of the problem of producer's choice, but as a realistic approach, it should take limitations of choice into consideration. According to modern economists this has been done through linear programming approach to the theory of production, which assumes linearity of the production relationship and constraints. Thus, while the isoquant approach is limited to only two inputs, the linear programming approach can consider a number of variables and take note of constraints on these variables.

Review Questions

1. Define isoquants and bring out their properties.
2. What do you mean by technical rate of substitution?
3. Explain Laws of Production as per isoquants.
4. Explain the concept of elasticity of substitution? How is it superior to the concept of marginal rate of technical substitution?
5. 'A firm buys inputs in quantities determined by the production and the prices of inputs'. Discuss.
6. Derive the optimum decision rule for attaining the least-cost-combination of inputs in a given production process.
7. Explain the various returns to scale of product.

15

Linear Programming

Linear programming is a mathematical technique for maximising or minimising a linear function of a number of variables, subject to a number of restraints stated in form of linear inequalities. This technique was developed by George B. Dantzing, a mathematician, in the year 1947. Initially this technique was applied for internal planning in U.S. Air Force, but subsequently it was used by Railways and other large organisations. Modern business executives use this technique to a number of managerial problems and particularly to the determination of: (i) optimal product lines and production processes; (ii) transportation routing; and (iii) meeting product specifications with minimum use of resources.

In this chapter, an attempt is being made to introduce the basic concepts of linear programming and to elaborate a linear programming problem, which is concerned with determining optimal allocation of limited resources to meet a given objective. It has aspects, like, 'Primal' and 'Dual' and each aspect of the problem is being solved by 'the Complete Description Method' only.

MEANING AND APPLICABILITY

Linear programming is essentially an optimisation problem, which seeks to maximise or minimise a numerical function of a number of variables, where these variables are subject to certain constraints (limitations). In a typical linear programming problem, we face: (i) some 'objective' to be attained, such as maximum profit or contribution or minimum cost; (ii) a large number of variables to be handled simultaneously, such as products, machine hours, man-hours, finance, floor space, etc.; (iii) many interactions between variables, such as in case of determining the best product-mix, we have to determine the products to be manufactured, out of potential products together with the optimal quantity of each such product; and (iv) sometimes, the objective that conflicts with the principal objective of the problem, such as in product-mix case, the producer may specify the least quantity of a product regardless of the effect on profit. Thus, linear programming tends to be associated with complex situations, many interacting variables and competing objectives along with the optimisation of some criteria of the system.

The interactions of the variables and competition of objectives are characteristics in all industrial situations in all economic systems. Therefore, many of the important problems of the industry, where the algebraic relationships between the variables are linear or can be approximated by first order equations, can be handled with this techniques, which is usually applied to the following cases:

1. **Product-Mix Problem:** In the process of production, the producer may run into a variety of capacity limitations, such as factory size, the amount of time available on different machines, warehouse space, skilled personnel, etc. of which any or all may constitute constraints. Under such situation, complete specialisation in one most profitable product may not make economical use of all capacities of the producer. One product may make good use of machine capacity, while the other product may make more effective use of limited warehouse space, leaving other capacities underutilised. Linear programming technique helps in determining the most profitable product-mix, which makes the best possible use of all resources at the disposal of the producer.
2. **Transportation Problem:** In case the producer has many plants and the production process involves transportation of items to the various stages of production, substantial savings can be expected from careful planning of commodity movements. The transportation problem is concerned with the items, which are stored in a number of origins and are needed at a number of destinations. Knowing the quantity of the item available at each origin and the quantity needed at each destination, and given the unit cost of sending the item from each origin to each destination, this technique is helpful in determining the quantity to be sent from each origin to each destination, so as to minimise the sum of the cost of transportation and ensure the availability of desired quantities of items at each destination without creating any problem of storage.
3. **Diet Problem:** This technique can be applied to determine the most economical human diet, but the same can also be extended to determine the most economical mixture of the various materials that will result in a desired product most economically. It can also be employed for determining the optimal inventory levels, the ways to minimise raw material wastes, the job assignment of specialised personnel, machines, etc.

LINEAR PROGRAMMING NOTATIONS

All these problems have one common feature, as they all search for 'best' values of variables as per some specifications known as 'side conditions'. So long as specifications are exact, the problem can be handled with marginal analysis. However, when specifications state only the minimum requirements or the maximum capacity available, they assume the form of inequalities rather than equations. The linear programming technique, under such situation, is helpful in computing such an optimum solution, which does not violate the limitations imposed by inequality side conditions. We generally use the following notations in linear programming problems:

(i) **Linear Relationship:** It implies straight line or proportional relationship among the relevant variables. In respect of each product, the total amount of each input and the associated contribution or profit are proportionate strictly to the level of output.

(ii) **Objective Function:** The objective put in a form of equation is known as objective function, which specifies relationships among the decision variables associated with each product for achieving the specified goals, which may be concerned with either maximisation or minimisation.

(iii) **Constraints:** Since resources are given, therefore their total use in the production of all the activities should not exceed the total quantity available. It is termed as constraints, which are restrictions imposed upon decision variables and are essentially inequalities. The inequalities may be strict ($X < C$ or $X > C$) or weak ($X \leq C$ or $X \geq C$). In case of linear programming, constraints are usually mentioned in the forms of weak inequalities. These constraints are resource or capacity constraints or product's non-negativity constraint.

(iv) **Feasible Region:** It is set of all values of decision variables satisfying all constraints. It reveals the various alternatives out of which only one according to the objective is to be selected. Diagrammatically, it reveals the area surrounded by segments of lines representing resources or capacity constraints and product's non-negativity constraint.

(v) **A Linear Programming Model:** Linear programming is concerned with the problem of optimising an objective function, which is linear in decision variable and is subject to linear constraints. A typical model is stated as follows:

(a) **Non-negativity Constraint:** $Qj \geq 0$ (j = 1,2, ..., n), which reveals that the quantities of all products i.e., $Q_1Q_2Q_3$, ..., Qn) will be either more than or equal to zero. None can ever be less than zero.

(b) **Objective Function:** The objective is to maximise the total profit or contribution $Z_Q = \sum_{j=1}^{n} C_jQ_j$ ...., where C represents coefficients (i.e., contribution or profit margin) of output and

Q represents respective quantities of output. $\sum_{j=1}^{n}$..... represents the total sum of the quantities (Q) multiplied by co-efficients (C) of 1 to n items of products.

(c) **Constraints:** The objective of maximisation is subject to certain resource or capacity limitations stated as:

$$\sum_{j=1}^{n} aij.\ Q\,j \leq bi \quad (i = \mathbf{1, 2, 3, ...,}\ m)$$

It means that the quantities of inputs (*ai*) employed in production of *Qj* quantities of outputs must be either less than or equal to the total quantities (*bi*) of the respective inputs.

This can be interpreted as a profit maximisation model, where *ZQ* denote the optimal value of the objective function, which is linear in decision variables *Qj*. Its co-efficients are values associated with each decision variable, which represents the various discrete alternatives called activities. The limitations or constraints for the pursuit of the objective are the systems of constraint relationships, which describe the relationship between each activity and a particular constraint. It is a typical structure of a linear programming model, which assumes prior knowledge of all the co-efficients in the model. In addition to the linearity of the objective function and the constraint equations, additivity of resources and divisibility of the decision variables are also assumed.

PRIMAL PROBLEM: COMPLETE DESCRIPTION METHOD

The primal of linear programming is concerned with maximisation of the objective function and the application of this technique through the complete description method is introductory and non-technical. Assuming that the firm produces Q_1 and Q_2 products, whose contribution (i.e., excess of price over variable cost) is ₹ 200 and ₹ 250 respectively, the input requirements and their maximum quantities are as follows:

TABLE 15.1 Quantities and Uses of Inputs

Inputs	*Per unit of Q_1*	*Per unit of Q_2*	*Maximum Quantities (Units)*
a_1	4	8	96
a_2	8	9	144
a_3	6	3	90
a_4	5	—	70
a_5	—	6	60

On the basis of this information, the linear programming problem may be stated as follows:

(i) Objective function: maximization of $ZQ = 200\ Q_1 + 250\ Q_2$

(ii) Input or capacity constraints:

$$4Q_1 + 8Q_2 \leqslant 96$$
$$8Q_1 + 9Q_2 \leqslant 144$$
$$6Q_1 + 3Q_2 \leqslant 90$$
$$5Q_1 \leqslant 70$$
$$6Q_2 \leqslant 60$$

(iii) Non-negativity constraint:

$$Q_1 \geq 0 \text{ and } Q_2 \geq 0$$

Thus, there are two unknowns (Q_1 and Q_2) and five inequalities. For the sake of computation, inequalities of capacity constraints are assumed to be equalities as follows:

$$4Q_1+8Q_2 = 96$$
$$8Q_1+9Q_2 = 144$$
$$6Q_1+3Q_2 = 90$$
$$5Q_1 = 70$$
$$6Q_2 = 60$$

This helps in ascertaining the feasible region, which contains the solution of this problem. Each equation is represented by a straight line in the following diagram:

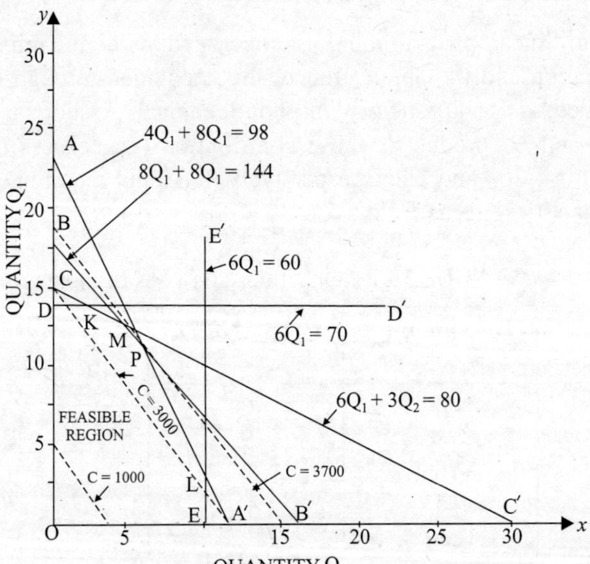

FIGURE 15.1 Determination of Feasible Region for Primal Problem.

In case of the first capacity constraint, $4Q_1 + 8Q_2 = 96$, if the firm produces only Q_1 commodity reducing the production of Q_2 to zero, the maximum quantity of Q_1 with input a_1 comes to 24 units. Similarly, if the firm decides to produce only Q_2 commodity, keeping the production of Q_1 at zero, its maximum quantity comes to 12 units. In case two maximum points on the respective axes are combined with a straight line, different points of this line will indicate various combinations of Q_1 and Q_2 that can be produced with the given quantity of input a_1. Similarly, all other constraint equations are shown with the help of various straight lines.

As per input a_1 the solution of the problem within *OAA'* region, but input a_2 has reduced this region by *BPA*. The addition to feasible region equal to *A'PB'* is ignored, as it is already out of the feasible region on the basis of input a_1. After induction of a_2 input, the feasible region is OBPA'. Introduction of input a_3 reduces this feasible region further by CMB, as the feasible region now is OCMPA'. Inputs a_4 and a_5 are single use inputs, where the former is used for production of Q_1 only and the latter is used for the production of Q_2 only. The introduction of a_4 input reduces the feasible region further by DKC. Similarly, a_5 input reduces the same by ELA'. Thus, after introduction of all inputs finally, ODKMPLE is the feasible region and the solution of the problem lies on any one of these corner points. The quantities Q_1 and Q_2 on all these points are calculated as follows:

(i) On point *D* the output is 14 units of Q_1 and zero unit of Q_2.
(ii) On point *E* the output is zero unit of Q_1 and 10 units of Q_2.
(iii) Point *K* is made of the intersection of the following two equation lines:

$$6Q_1 + 3Q_2 = 90$$
$$5Q_1 + \quad = 70$$

$$30Q_1 + 15Q_2 = 450 \text{ (multiplying the first equation by 5)}$$
$$30Q_1 = 420 \text{ (multiplying the second by 6)}$$

$$15Q_2 = 30 \text{ (Deducting the lower equation from the upper)}$$
$$Q_2 = 30/15 = 2$$
$$6Q_1 + 3Q_2 = 90 \text{ (Substituting the value of } Q_2\text{)}$$
$$6Q_1 = 90 - 6 = 84$$
$$Q_1 = 84/6 = 14$$

Thus, the output is 14 units of Q_1 and 2 units of Q_2. Similarly, values on all other corner points of the feasible region are calculated. Production and contribution on all such points are as follows:

TABLE 15.2 Total Contribution in Different Situations

Corner Points	*Output*		*Computation of Contribution*		*Total Contribution*
	Q_1	Q_2	Q_1	Q_2	
O	0	0	0 × 200 = 0	0 × 250 = 0	0
D	14	0	14 × 200 = 2,800	0 × 250 = 0	2,800
K	14	2	14 × 200 = 2,800	2 × 250 = 500	3,300
M	12.6	4.8	12.6 × 200 = 2,520	4.8 × 250 = 1,200	3,720
P	10.3	6.85	10.3 × 200 = 2,060	6.85 × 250 = 1,712.5	3,772.5
L	4	10	4 × 200 = 800	10 × 250 = 2,500	3,300
E	0	10	0 × 200 = 0	10 × 250 = 2,500	2,500

Thus, the maximum contribution is at the point *P*, where the firm produces 10.3 units of Q_1 and 6.85 units of Q_2.

There is a short-cut to arrive at this point of optimum product-mix even without the above mentioned elaborate calculations. This is done by drawing a set of iso-contribution lines as per the ratio of the contributions of Q_1 and Q_2 products, where higher lines indicate higher level of contribution. We keep on shifting the iso-contribution line till it is tangent to some point of the feasible region. The highest possible iso-contribution line is tangent to the feasible region at *P*, which provides the highest possible contribution, as any contribution beyond this line is not attainable and below this line is not desirable. This point is made of two lines representing equations $4Q_1 + 8Q_2 = 96$ and $8Q_1 + 9Q_2 = 144$ respectively. After calculating the values of Q_1 and Q_2 with these equations, we conclude that the firm will maximise the total contribution by producing 10.3 units of Q_1 and 6.85 units of Q_2. The extent of input utilisation at this level of output is as follows:

TABLE 15.3 The Extent of Employment of Inputs

Inputs	*Computation of Inputs Employed*		*Total Quantity Employed*	*Total Quantity Available*	*Surplus*
	Q_1	Q_2			
a_1	4 × 10.3 = 41.20	8 × 6.85 = 54.80	96.00	96	—
a_2	8 × 10.3 = 82.40	9 × 6.85 = 61.65	144.05	144	—
a_3	6 × 10.3 = 61.80	3 × 6.85 = 20.55	82.35	90	7.65
a_4	5 × 10.3 = 51.50	— —	51.50	70	18.50
a_5	— —	6 × 6.85 = 41.10	41.10	60	18.90

Thus, the double use inputs a_1 and a_2 are fully employed but input Q_3 is underemployed. Similarly, the single use input Q_4 and Q_5 are also underutilised. However, this remains the best product-mix, as the firm maximises the contribution at this level of output.

This method is suitable, if the firm produces only two products with given inputs, as the two output can be accommodated in a two-dimensional diagram. In case the firm produces more than two commodities, it can rely on another method (i.e., the simplex method) for solving the linear programming problem.

LINEAR PROGRAMMING: DUAL PROBLEM

For every linear programming problem, there is another intimately related problem usually termed as its dual. It states that for every maximisation problem in linear programming, there is a companion problem of minimisation and vice-versa, where the former is termed as 'primal' and the latter a 'dual'. The dual problem involves the same data, which describes the primal problem and the maximum feasible value of primal objective function equals the minimum feasible value of the dual objective function. The duality yields a number of powerful theorems, which help in finding solution of a linear programming problem and shows that old fashioned marginal analysis is always implicitly involved in the search of an optimal solution of such a problem. The transformation of a given primal problem into a dual problem involves considerations as follows:

(i) If the objective of the primal is 'maximisation', the objective of the dual is 'minimisation' and vice-versa.

(ii) The 'constraints' of primal are unknowns of the dual and vice-versa.

(iii) Co-efficients of the objective function of primal (Cj), become constant terms of the dual and the constant terms of the primal become the co-efficient terms of the objective function of the dual.

(iv) The co-efficients of the variables of the primal (aij) are allowed to remain in the same position in the dual. The only difference is that if in the primal constraint, inequalities the co-efficients were found to be going from left to right, in the dual problems they are positioned from top to bottom and vice-versa.

(v) Variables (Qj) of the primal are replaced by new variables (Yj) of its dual.

(vi) The sign of inequalities in the set of constraints of the primal ($\leqslant$) is reversed in the set of restrictions in its dual ($\geqslant$).

(vii) The non-negativity constraints in the primal ($Q\,j \geqslant 0$), is stated in respect of new variables in the dual ($Y\,j \geqslant 0$)

The primal and the dual of a linear programming problem can be stated as follows:

TABLE 15.4 Comparison of Primal and Dual Problems

Primal Problem	*Dual Problem*
Maximise:	Minimise:
$ZQ = 200Q_1, 250Q_2$	$ZY = 96Y_1 + 144Y_2 + 90Y_2 + 70Y_4 + 60Y_5$
Subject to:	Subject to:
$4Q_1 + 8Q_2 \leq 96$	$4Y_1 + 8Y_2 + 6Y_3 + 5Y_4 \geqslant 200$
$8Q_1 + 9Q_2 \leq 144$	$8Y_1 + 9Y_2 + 3Y_3 + 6Y_5 \geqslant 250$
$6Q_1 + 3Q_2 \leq 90$	$Y_1, Y_2, Y_3, Y_4, Y_5 \geqslant 0$
$5Q_1 \leq 70$	
$6Q_2 \leq 60$	
$Q_1, Q_2 \geqslant 0$	

Considering the problem of determining the profit maximising output level, subject to a number of input constraints as primal, the firm may proceed to determine the relative importance of each input as its dual. Assuming, that the producer had the option to rent out the above input capacity with per unit rental being Y_1, Y_2, Y_3, Y_4 and Y_5 respectively, he will proceed to find out these values, so that he will not be worse off in foregoing the opportunity of utilising the capacities to produce Q_1 and Q_2. It requires computation of an artificial accounting price for each of his scarce inputs, so that the sum of these computed values of inputs are high enough to account for his total profits or contributions. Although all inputs are necessary for production, yet economists impute all of the firm's profit or contribution to its scarce resources only.

Thus, the dual problem of resources allocation is simply the problem of determining the values to the firm of the inputs employed at the margin, because whether an input is scarce or not is known only at the margin. These imputed or accounting values are some-times referred as 'shadow prices' of inputs. It represents the addition to total revenue of the firm resulting from the use of an additional unit of the given input at the margin of production. For its computation, we can follow the complete description method.

DUAL PROBLEM: COMPLETE DESCRIPTION METHOD

We can rearrange the data of the primal problem on the presumption, that the value of the inputs going into the production of a unit of Q_1 or Q_2 must be greater than or equal to the contribution or profit the firm earns by producing a unit of the product. This can be rearranged in the form of inequalities as follows:

$$4Y_1 + 8Y_2 + 6Y_3 + 5Y_4 \geqslant 200 \quad \text{...(i)}$$

$$8Y_1 + 9Y_2 + 3Y_3 + 6Y_5 \geqslant 250 \quad \text{...(ii)}$$

Thus we assign each of the inputs or capacities a value, sufficiently large to impute to them all the contributions of output Q_1 and Q_2 to firm's scarce inputs.

Since inputs a_1, and a_2 are fully employed at the margin of production in our problem, the values of these inputs at the margin of production are positive. Since all other inputs (or capacities) are not fully employed, the values of additional units of these inputs to the firm will be zero. The inequalities may be stated as follows:

$$4Y_1 + 8Y_2 + 6\,(0) + 5\,(0) \geqslant 200$$

$$8Y_1 + 9Y_2 + 3\,(0) + 6\,(0) \geqslant 250$$

These inequalities are converted into equations as follows:

$$4Y_1 + 8Y_2 = 200 \quad \text{(i)}$$

$$8Y_1 + 9Y_2 = 250 \quad \text{(ii)}$$

$$8Y_1 + 16Y_2 = 400 \quad \text{(i) is multiplied by 2}$$

$$8Y_1 + 9Y_2 = 250 \quad \text{(ii) is deducted from (i) the balance}$$

$$7Y_2 = 150 \quad \text{after deducting}$$

$$Y_2 = 21.4$$

$$4Y_1 + 8 \times 21.4 = 200$$

$$4Y_1 = 200 - 171.2$$

$$4Y_1 = 28.8$$

$$Y_1 = 7.2$$

These equations are also exhibited in Figure 15.2 as follows:

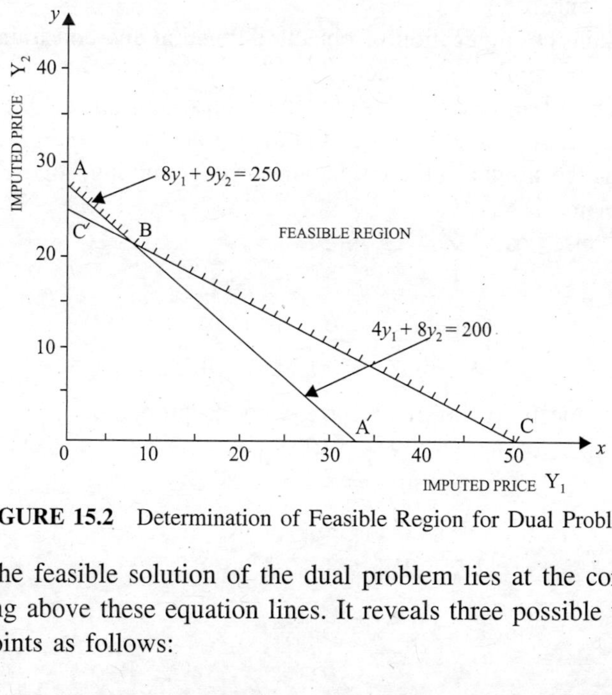

FIGURE 15.2 Determination of Feasible Region for Dual Problem

Thus, the feasible solution of the dual problem lies at the corners of the regions lying above these equation lines. It reveals three possible values at *A*, *B* and *C* points as follows:

TABLE 15.5 Cost at Different Levels of Production

Points	*Values of*			*Remarks*
	Y_1	Y_2	$Zy = 96Y_1 + 144Y_2 + 90Y_3 + 70Y_4 + 60Y_5$	— Least
A	0.00	27.78	₹ 4,000.32	—
B	7.14	21.43	₹ 3,771.36	
C	50.00	0.00	₹ 4,800.00	

Thus, our objective of minimisation of *Zy* in the dual problem is achieved at *B* point, where the total revenue has been imputed to inputs according to their values at the margin of production. Under such situation the producer would be unwilling to pay anything for Q_3, Q_4 and Q_5 inputs, as these are already lying unutilised at his disposal but would be willing to pay ₹ 7.14 for additional unit of input a and ₹ 21.4. for the additional unit of a_2 input.

Review Questions

1. What is meant by linear programming? Bring out the problem areas, where LP can be applied?
2. Explain the various ingredients of a Linear Programming Model. Distinguish between primal and dual of a LP model.
3. What is feasible region? Why is the solution available at its corner point only?
4. Explain the implication of objective function and constraints used in a linear programming model.
5. Discuss the duality in the linear programming. Bring out the characteristics and merits of the dual problem.
6. Using the simple method of the linear programming, solve the following problem.

   Minimise cost $Z = 2Y_1 + 3Y_2$

   $$Y_1 + Y_2 \geqslant 5$$

   $$Y_1 + 2Y_2 \geqslant 6$$

   Where $Y_1 \geqslant 0$ and $Y_2 \geqslant 0$
7. Solve the following linear programming problem:

   Minimise cost $C = 200Y_1 + 100Y_2$

   Subject to:

   $$3Y_1 + Y_1 \geqslant 20$$

   $$2Y_1 + 2Y_2 \geqslant 3$$

   $$Y_1, Y_1 \geqslant 0$$

8. Decide the level of output of X_1 and X_2 produced with the help of three inputs *a*, *b* and *c*, whose maximum quantities available are 60, 24 and 84 units respectively. X_1 used 5*a*, 3*b* and 12*c*, whereas X_2 used 15*a*, 4*b* and 7*c* and the two products X_1 and X_2 are sold in the market @ ₹ 20 and ₹ 15 respectively.
9. Decide the relative importance of the three inputs of the above mentioned problem as per the 'dual' of the linear programming.

16

Cost of Production

The volume of output and its selling price depend partly on demand and partly on the cost of production'. We have already examined the nature, characteristics and determinants of demand, therefore, now in this chapter an attempt is being made to explain the various cost concepts and the way these are related to the output in the various time periods. An effort is also being made to explain the various factors responsible for cost behaviour under different types of production functions. In economics we come across the various costs as follows:

Real Cost: Business units are primarily concerned with the money costs incurred to obtain the services of the various factors of production, but economists seek to go into details of the question that lies beneath these monetary payments. The reason may be the disutilities of rendering the services, which is called the 'real cost'. According to Marshall **'the exertions of all the different kinds of labour that are directly or indirectly involved in making it; together with the abstinences or rather the waiting required for saving the capital used in making it; all these efforts and sacrifices together will be called the real cost of production of the commodity'.**

It is uncomfortable or painful to work for a given number of hours a day particularly, when workers are required to work physically in unnatural environment. Similarly, it is irksome for the businessman to bear the responsibility and risk. It is unpleasant to make savings for capital, because the more is saved, the greater is the encroachment on the present consumption. In respect of the land, since neither the exertion of labour nor the abstinence from the current consumption is taken into account for either its existence or its quality, therefore, no real cost is thought to be present in this case.

However, there is no correspondence between monetary expenses and real cost. The real cost doctrine breaks down, when confronted by the fact that the salaries and wages of persons in some unattractive occupations are lower than those of persons employed in presumably more attractive occupations. Moreover, modern economists reject the notion of 'disutility' just as they have rejected the concept of utility, as these are immeasurable and are too subjective to be treated scientifically.

Opportunity Cost: The concept of opportunity cost gets its origin in choices before a worker, a producer and an investor. Choice indicates that something has been given up in favour of the thing chosen. What is given up is the cost of what has been taken up and the same is named as the opportunity cost. Thus, the opportunity cost (i.e., the cost of any particular course of action) is the amount of gain that could have been obtained by following the next most desirable alternative course of action. In case there is no real or close alternative (as in case of specialised inputs), the opportunity cost concept is inapplicable and misleading.

This concept is applicable in all economic systems, because the alternatives forgone constitute the opportunity cost, whatsoever is the nature of economy (i.e., capitalism, socialism or mixed). From the point of view of society, the opportunity cost of unemployed inputs is zero, for example in case of severe depression, the alternative to these workers would have been complete idleness or zero production and if they are placed on relief, there would be negative production.

In order to ascertain the opportunity cost of the commodities, which are close substitutes, the comparison of physical output or their money value may be taken into consideration. Thus, indirectly we take into account the value (i.e., utility) of the various activities or undertakings, which from the point of view of society is also termed as the marginal social cost. Thus, it forms the basis for evaluating the various public activities in terms of the marginal social costs and the benefits expected.

Money Cost: It refers to the money outlay of a firm on the process of production, which consists of wages and salaries paid to labour, expenditure by way of repairs and depreciation of plant and machinery and payments for materials, power, light, fuel, transportation, rent, patents, advertising, insurance, taxes, etc. and the amount of normal profit to be left for the entrepreneur. In other words, money cost means a money figure comprising of the cost of all the inputs employed to produce the given output. Such money cost may be either implicit or explicit.

Implicit cost of production refers to the money figure of payments due in respect of those factors of production, which are owned by the producer. In other words, implicit cost is the cost to the firm of using in the given way, rather than in some other, those inputs, which it owns. In case the producer finances its own inventory or expansion programmes, instead of depositing the money in the bank accounts, he is entitled to the prevalent rate of interest on this self-invested capital in addition to the normal profit he obtains as an entrepreneur.

Explicit cost, on the other hand, consists of payments made by the producer to others for the services of the various inputs owned by them. In others words, it refers to the payments made in lieu of services of the various inputs, which are not owned by the producer.

Thus, the money cost refers to the total money value of the services of the various factors of production owned by the producers or others. For money cost, it is immaterial, as to who is receiving the payment made by the producer in lieu of services of the various factors of production. In economic analysis, the money cost exhibits itself in the following forms:

1. **Total Fixed Cost (TFC):** It is the quantity of the fixed input (b) used, times the price (*pb*) of the service per unit of the fixed factor, that is, $b.pb$.
2. **Total Variable Cost (TVC):** It means the quantity of the variable input (a) used, times the per unit price (Þ*a*) of the service of such input, that is, $a.pa$.
3. **Total Cost (TC):** It is the total sum of the fixed and the variable costs of production. Symbolically,

$$TC = TFC + TVC = b.pb + a.pa.$$

4. **Marginal Cost (MC):** It refers to increase in total cost divided by the increase in the total output, that is, $\Delta TC/\Delta Q$.
5. **Average Fixed Cost (AFC):** It is the total fixed cost divided by the quantity of total output, that is, TFC/Q.
6. **Average Variable Cost (AVC):** It means the total variable cost divided by the quantity of total output, that is, TVC/Q.
7. **Average Cost (AC):** It refers to the total cost divided by the total output, which is also equal to the sum total of average fixed cost and average variable cost, that is, $TC/Q = AFC + AVC$.

TIME PERIODS FOR COST DETERMINATION

The cost of production analysis depends on the time period involved, therefore, before considering the bahaviour of the various types of the cost an introduction to the various time periods seems pertinent. There is four-fold classification of the time period, viz. very short run, short run, long run and very long run. This classification is not based on the number of hours, days, months or years involved in the analysis, but it is based on the nature of variability of the total output of the firm as per the variability of the inputs used.

Very Short Run: It refers to a period of time during which the quantity of total output cannot be changed at all. During this period the firm finds itself helpless in varying the total output by changing the quantities of even variable inputs.

Short Run: It refers to that time period during which the firm can change the quantity of total output by varying the quantities of the variable inputs only, while the quantities of fixed inputs and other conditions remain unchanged. Thus, the short run is a period of time sufficiently large to allow the producer to change, the total output from the existing capacity.

Long Run: It refers to a period of time, long enough to allow the firm to change the total output by varying the quantities of all inputs used for production. There is no fixed input in long run, therefore, the plant size is also subject to change which, in turn, changes the capacity of the firm as well.

Very Long Run: It refers to a period of time long enough to allow the economic analysis of the various factors responsible not only for changing the quantity of total output but also for rise or fall of the industries.

In cost analysis, generally, the middle two are taken into account leaving aside the first and the last. Thus, we can now proceed to study the behaviour of costs in short run as well as in long run.

COST AND OUTPUT IN THE SHORT RUN

The cost of production is closely associated with: (1) the period of time available to the firm during which it can make adjustment according to changes in the demand for its product; (2) the volume of output or the size of the firm; and (3) the price paid for the services of the production agents, not separately and independently but to all of them in interaction. Taking into consideration these variables, the behaviour of total, average and marginal costs may be explained symbolically and diagrammatically as follows:

Short Run Total Cost (STC)

It is the money figure consisting of costs of all inputs used to produce a given total output. Since, in short run, the plant size is fixed, hence the total cost of production from existing capacity is equal to the sum of expenditure on the fixed and the variable inputs. In other words, the total cost in short run is sum of the fixed cost (i.e., expenditure on fixed inputs) and the variable cost (i.e., expenditure on the variable inputs) for production of a given output. Fixed costs, also known as supplementary, secondary or indirect costs, refer to those costs, which do not vary as output varies, such as, interest on capital employed, depreciation of plant and machinery, etc. The variable costs also known as direct or prime cost, on the other hand, refer to those costs, which do vary as output varies, such as cost of labour, raw materials, etc. symbolically,

$$TC = TFC + TVC = bp_b + ap_a$$

Here TC stands for the total cost in short run, TFC for the total fixed cost and TVC for the total variable cost. The total fixed cost can also be represented by $b.p_b$, which means the quantity of fixed input (b) times the price (p_b) of such factor. Similarly, ap_a stands for the total variable cost, which indicates the quantity of variable inputs (a) times the price of such inputs (p_a).

TABLE 16.1 Short Run Total Cost of Production

Units			*Rupees*				
b	***a***	***Q***	***pb***	***bpb***	***pa***	***apa***	***TC = bpb + apa***
10	0	0	5	50	10	0	50
10	1	5	5	50	10	10	60
10	2	13	5	50	10	20	70
10	3	23	5	50	10	30	80
10	4	38	5	50	10	40	90
10	5	50	5	50	10	50	100
10	6	60	5	50	10	60	110
10	7	68	5	50	10	70	120
10	8	75	5	50	10	80	130
10	9	81	5	50	10	90	140
10	10	86	5	50	10	100	150
10	11	89	5	50	10	110	160
10	12	91	5	50	10	120	170
10	13	92	5	50	10	130	180
10	14	92	5	50	10	140	190

The quantity of fixed input (b) remains constant at all levels of total output and at a given price of fixed input (*pb*), the total fixed cost also remains constant for all levels of the total output. On the other hand, the quantity of the variable input (a) increases in order to obtain the increased total output. Assuming the price of the variable input (*pa*) to remain unchanged, the total variable cost (*apa*) increases along with increase in employment of such input for obtaining higher total output. This increasing total variable cost increases the total cost as the level of total output increases, because the total cost is the sum of constant total fixed cost (*TFC* = *bpb*) and increasing total variable cost (*TVC*=*apa*). The short run total cost curve can be drawn on basis of the slope the total fixed cost and total variable cost curves as follows:

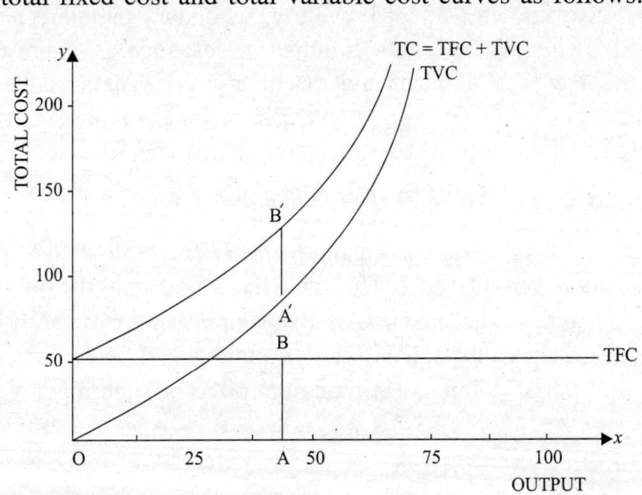

FIGURE 16.1 Behaviour of the Total Cost in Short Run.

Since the total fixed cost does not vary as output varies, the *TFC* is represented by a straight line parallel to the horizontal axis. The total variable cost does vary as output varies, hence this curve (*TVC*) slopes upward to the right. It is no more a straight line because of internal economics and dis-economies (explained later). The total cost curve have the slope similar to that of the total variable cost curve, as the total cost is the sum of the fixed cost and the variable cost. However, the former lies above the latter at all levels of output by a distance of $AB = A'B'$, which is equivalent the total fixed cost.

Short Run Average Cost (SAC)

The short run total cost divided by the number of units produced is the short run is the average cost of production. Since,

$$TC = TFC + TVC = bpb + apa$$

Therefore, the short run average cost is equal to

$$SAC = \frac{TC}{Q} = \frac{TFC}{Q} + \frac{TVC}{Q} = \frac{bpb}{Q} + \frac{apa}{Q} = AFC + AVC$$

It means the short run average cost (*SAC*) is equal to the sum of average fixed cost (*AFC*) and average variable cost (*AVC*). This relationship can be explained as follows:

TABLE 16.2 Short Run Average Cost of Production

Units	*Rupees*					
Q	$TFC = bpb$	$\frac{TFC}{Q} = AFC$	$TVC = opa$	$\frac{TVC}{Q} = AVC$	TC	$\frac{TC}{Q} = SAC$
0	50	∞	0	∞	50	∞
5	50	10.00	10	2.00	60	12.00
13	50	3.85	20	1.54	70	5.39
23	50	2.17	30	1.30	80	3.47
38	50	1.32	40	1.05	90	2.37
50	50	1.00	50	1.00	100	2.00
60	50	0.83	60	1.00	110	1.83
68	50	0.73	70	1.03	120	1.76
75	50	0.67	80	1.07	130	1.74
81	50	0.62	90	1.11	140	1.73
86	50	0.58	100	1.16	150	1.74
89	50	0.56	110	1.25	160	1.81
91	50	0.55	120	1.32	170	1.87
92	50	0.54	130	1.41	180	1.95
92	50	0.54	140	1.52	190	2.06

Since the total fixed cost is a constant figure, as the total output (Q) increases, the average fixed cost ($AFC = TFC/Q$) constantly decreases, because it has constant numerator but increasing denominator. On the other hand, the average variable cost does not decline constantly. At low level of total output, the average variable cost is fairly high but decreases as output expands. This decrease in the average variable cost stops at a higher level of total output and from this point it starts increasing along with increase in output. This produces roughly a U-shaped average variable cost curve.

The average variable cost has reciprocal relationship with the average product of the variable input:

$$AVC = \frac{apa}{Q} = \frac{a}{Q} \times pa = \frac{1}{Q/a} \times pa = \frac{1}{AP} \times pa$$

This reveals that the reciprocal of the average product (*AP*) of variable input multiplied by the price of variable input (*pa*) is equal to the average variable cost (AVC). Since the average product of variable input increases in the beginning, it becomes constant afterwards and then starts decreasing as more and more units such input are employed, or as a higher total output is obtained. The reciprocal of this behaviour of average product means that the cost (i.e., average variable cost) should decrease in the beginning, become constant afterwards and increase ultimately. It also reveals that as the average product curve has a maximum point, the average variable cost curve must have a minimum point at the same level of output.

The short run average cost (*SAC*) is the sum of average fixed cost (*AFC*) and the average variable cost (*AVC*), therefore, it assumes a slope similar to that of the average variable cost curve as follows:

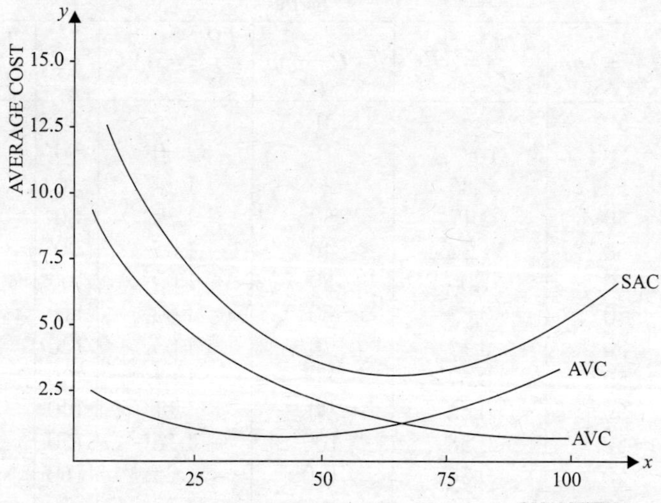

FIGURE 16.2 Behaviour of the Short Run Average Cost Curves.

The short run average cost curve is lying above the average fixed cost (*AFC*) and average variable cost (*AVC*) curves, but it is sloping downwards in the beginning, becomes constant afterwards and starts sloping upwards ultimately. Thus, the short run average cost curve is also roughly a U-shaped curve, which may also assume the slopes of a dish-shaped and V-shaped curves.

Short Run Marginal Cost (SMC)

Marginal cost refers to the additional cost incurred by the firm for the additional output. In other words, it is the ratio of increment in total cost to a small increment in output or it is the rate of change in total cost as output changes. Symbolically,

$$SMC = \frac{\Delta TC}{\Delta Q} = \frac{\Delta TFC}{\Delta Q} + \frac{\Delta TVC}{\Delta Q}$$

Since, in short run the value of ΔTFC is zero, as the fixed cost remains constant in short run therefore, the short run marginal cost (SMC) derived from change in the variable cost only. Thus,

$$SMC = \frac{\Delta TC}{\Delta Q} = \frac{\Delta TVC}{\Delta Q} + \frac{\Delta apa}{\Delta Q}$$

This reveals that in short run the marginal cost is independent of the fixed cost and is reciprocal of the marginal product of the variable input multiplied by its price. It is as follows:

$$SMC = \frac{\Delta a}{\Delta Q}.pa = \frac{1}{\Delta Q/\Delta a}.pa = \frac{1}{MPa}.pa$$

The tabular presentation of the behaviour of short run average and marginal costs of production is as follows:

TABLE 16.3 Short Run Average and Marginal Cost of Production

Units			*Rupees*		
Q	a	$\Delta Q/\Delta a$	TC	$SAC = TC/Q$	$SMC = \frac{1}{MPa} \cdot pa$
0	0	0	50	∞	∞
5	1	5	60	12.00	2.00
13	2	8	70	5.39	1.25
23	3	10	80	3.47	1.00
38	4	15	90	2.37	0.67
50	5	12	100	2.00	0.83
60	6	10	110	1.83	1.00
68	7	8	120	1.76	1.25
75	8	7	130	1.73	1.43
81	9	6	140	1.73	1.67
86	10	5	150	1.74	2.00
89	11	3	160	1.80	3.33
91	12	2	170	1.83	5.00
92	13	1	180	1.95	10.00
92	14	0	190	2.06	∞

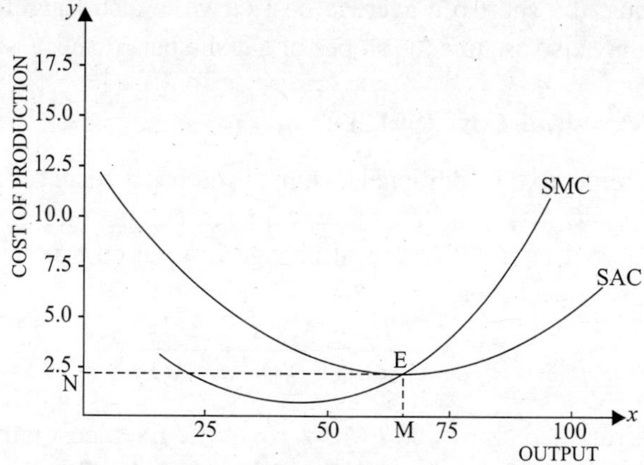

FIGURE 16.3 Behaviour Pattern of Short Run Average and Marginal Cost Curves.

Thus, there is only one marginal cost, although there are three types of total and average costs. There is no marginal fixed cost, as the increment in fixed cost accompanying an increment in output is zero. Moreover, the total costs and total variable costs are associated with the same marginal costs, as increment in total cost for an increment of output is identical with the increment in total variable cost.

The relationship between the short run average cost (*SAC*) and the short run marginal cost (*SMC*) may also be exhibited as follows:

As the total output expands, the average cost and the marginal cost declines and throughout this range the marginal costs are lower than the average costs. The marginal cost curve reaches its minimum point, while the average cost continues its journey towards the minimum point. After reaching the minimum point, the marginal cost curve starts rising at a faster rate and intersects the short run average cost curve at its minimum cost point. Beyond this point, the marginal cost curve lies above the average cost curve and shows an increasing tendency at every level of the total output.

The point on which the marginal cost curve intersects the average cost curve from below is known as the economic capacity point or the least cost point, which is at *E* in the above diagram. The economic capacity is not the same thing as the physical capacity of the plant. The latter refers to the total output that can be obtained from a given plant irrespective of the level of cost of production. However, the economic capacity refers to the level of output that can be obtained at the minimum possible average cost of production.

The level of output, where the least average cost point will be located depends on the prices of the fixed and the variable resources alike. The laws of returns state that in the first and the third stage the marginal productivity of the fixed and the variable inputs respectively is negative and both contributed positively only within the second stage. Therefore, the point of maximum efficiency (i.e., least average cost) attained by certain combination of both inputs is located somewhere within the second stage. In case the services of fixed inputs are more costly than those of variable inputs, there will be intensive use of the fixed input with the extensive use of the variable input and the more the variable input is used, the farther along in the second stage will the least cost point emerge.

COST AND OUTPUT IN THE LONG RUN

In the long run, the firm is in a position to vary the existing capacity or the size of the plant. Thus, there is no fixed input in the long run, because it is always possible for a firm to build a different size of plant by varying the quantities of even fixed inputs, which have been held constant in the short run. The behaviour of total, average and marginal costs in long run depends on the production function, which may either be linearly homogeneous or normal.

Total Cost under Linearly Homogeneous Function

The total cost of production in long run (*LTC*) is the least possible cost of producing any level of output, when all inputs are variable. Symbolically,

$$LTC = bpb + apa \text{ (when both a and b inputs are variable)}$$

Thus, the long run total cost is similar to the short run total cost as it is also equal to the total sum of amount spent on *a* and *b* inputs respectively with the difference that, in the long run, input *b* is also variable. Since all the inputs are perfectly variable, the most appropriate quantities of all inputs can be employed in the long run to obtain a given level of total output. Such combination of the various inputs is possible on every plant at certain point on the short run total cost curve, but not throughout its length. The long run total cost (*LTC*) equals the short run total costs (*TC*) on those points on the short run total cost curves.

The total cost in long run (LTC) is tangent to TC_1, TC_2 and TC_3 (all short run total cost curves on respective plants) at A', B' and C' points respectively. These points are supposed to indicate the most appropriate combination of inputs on respective plants. It is advisable to have a small plant for obtaining a lower level of total output and a bigger plant for higher level of total output, because in former case the cost of production will be higher on bigger plants, while in the latter case the higher total output will be beyond the physical capacity of the smaller plants. For example, on *B* point in the diagram, the firm will incur a cost more than BB' if it employs the third plant and cannot produce this quantity on the first plant, as its physical capacity is less than this total output.

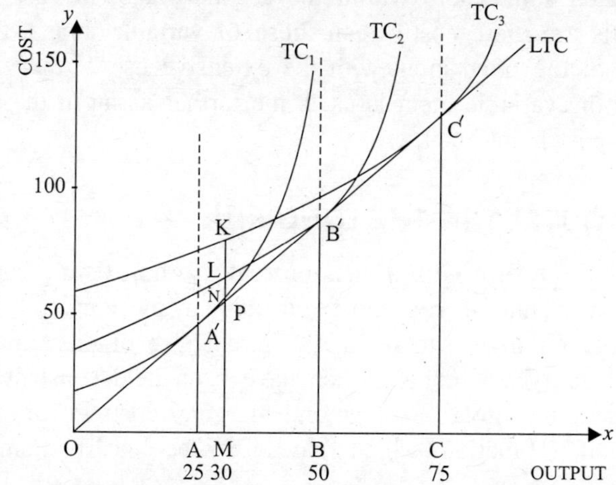

FIGURE 16.4 Long Run Total Cost under Linearly Homogeneous Production Function

Thus, the long run total cost curve combines points *A'*, *B'* and *C'* on the total cost curves of all the three plants respectively and represents the least cost of producing a given level of total output. In this case, in order to produce *OM* quantity of the total output, the firm incurs the total cost equal to *MK* on the third plant, *ML* on the second plant, *MN* on the first plant and *MP* on the long run plant. Amongst all these costs, *MP* is the least cost, which is found on the long run total cost curve.

In this diagram, the long run total cost (*LTC*) is linear through the origin. It is because the production function is linearly homogeneous and the prices of inputs are assumed to remain constant.

Long Run Average and Marginal Costs

In case the production function is linearly homogeneous and the prices of inputs are held constant, the long run average and marginal costs will also be constant, which will again be minimum possible cost of producing any level of total output. The long run average cost (*LAC*) and long run marginal cost (*LMC*) have been shown by a straight line parallel to the horizontal axis, which combines the minimum cost points on short run average cost curves of different plants. Since the short run marginal cost curves (*SMC*s) intersect the short run average cost curves (*SAC*s) at their minimum points, the long run average cost curve (*LAC*) combining these points is identical to the long run marginal cost curve (*LMC*).

The laws of returns reveal that if the production is as per Euler's Theorem, the minimum average product and the minimum marginal product of variable input will remain equal despite change in the scale of operation. Since the average and marginal costs have a reciprocal relationship with the average and

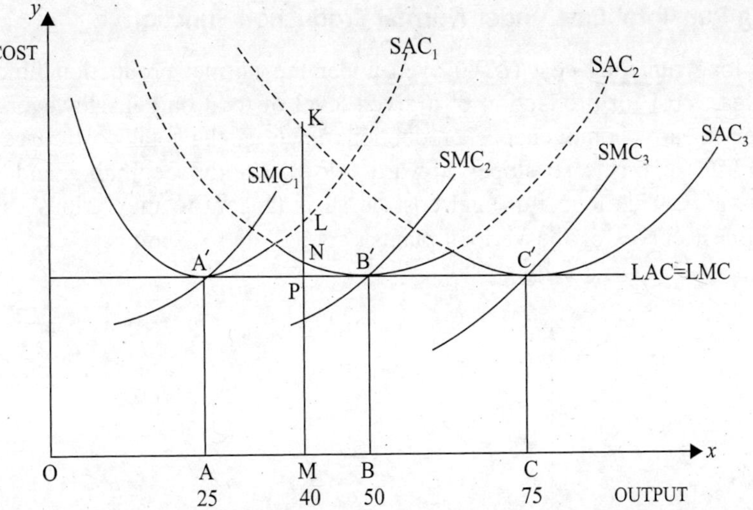

FIGURE 16.5 Long Run Average and Marginal Costs under Linearly Homogeneous Production Function

marginal productivities; the minimum average and marginal costs will remain the same at all levels of output. Thus, the minimum average cost of production on the short run average cost curves remain equal for all the plants.

Since the long run average cost curve is obtained by combining the minimum cost points of the various short run average cost curves, it represents the minimum average and marginal cost of production for a given level of total output. For *OM* total output, the average cost on SAC_3 is *MK*, on SAC_1 is *ML* and on SAC_2 is *MN* but on the *LAC* it is *MP* only, which is the least amongst all these average costs.

Since, the long run average cost (*LAC*) curve is parallel to horizontal axis and is identical with the long run marginal cost (*LMC*) curve, it represents the minimum cost point at all levels of the total output. Thus, *AA'*, *BB'*, *CC'* and *MP* all represent the average costs at different levels of output and all are equal, therefore, in the long run, if the production function is linearly homogeneous, the least cost or economic capacity point is indeterminate.

The assumption of linearly homogeneous function does not seem to be a universally valid assumption, as in the real world, because of the existence of the internal and external economies and diseconomies, the cost of production never remains constant. Just as in case of return to scale, the output increases more than proportionately up to certain level of output and then being proportionate (may be momentarily), it will be less than proportionate ultimately. As a reciprocal of the returns to scale, the cost increases less than proportionately up to certain level of total output, then it will be proportionate afterwards and more than proportionate ultimately.

Long Run Total Cost under Normal Production Function

The long run total cost (*LTC*) even under the normal production function is the least cost for production of a given level of total output. However, unlike under linearly homogeneous production function, the total cost curve in the long run in this case slopes upwards slowly in the beginning and steeply afterwards. This long run total cost curve is tangent to the various short run total cost curves of the various plants at *A'*, *B'* and *C'* points.

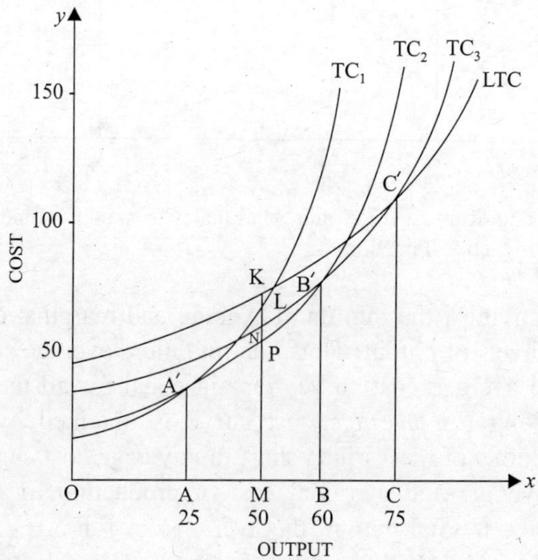

FIGURE 16.6 Long Run Total Cost under Normal Production Function.

In order to produce *OM* quantity of the total output, the firm incurs a cost equal to *MK* if it employs third plant, *ML* if it employs first and *MN* if it employs second but only *MP* on the long run plant, which is the least total cost of production for that level of total output.

Long Run Average and Marginal Costs and Economic Capacity

Long run total cost divided by the total output is the long run average cost (*LAC*) of production, which is the least average cost of production of any level of output. The real interest of the firm lies not in achieving the minimum cost output on a given plant, but in producing a given output at the minimum cost. This long run average cost (*LAC*) curve is taken into consideration in deciding the size of the plant to be employed for producing the given output. The firm in long run faces the least cost combination, when it experiences the optimum (constant) scale of production. In case the firm is operating subject to the increasing returns to scale, it is more economical to underuse a slightly smaller plant operating at less than its minimum cost output than to overuse a smaller plant. Conversely, for obtaining the output beyond the optimum level, when the firm experiences decreasing return to scale, it is more economical to overuse a slightly larger plant than to underuse a slightly larger one.

The long run average cost curve is drawn tangent to the short run average cost curves, where each such curve represents a particular scale or size of plant including the optimum scale. The long run average cost curve would be tangential to the entire family of the short run average cost curves at some points, which need not necessarily be the least cost points, as have been the case with the long run average cost curve under the linearly homogeneous production function.

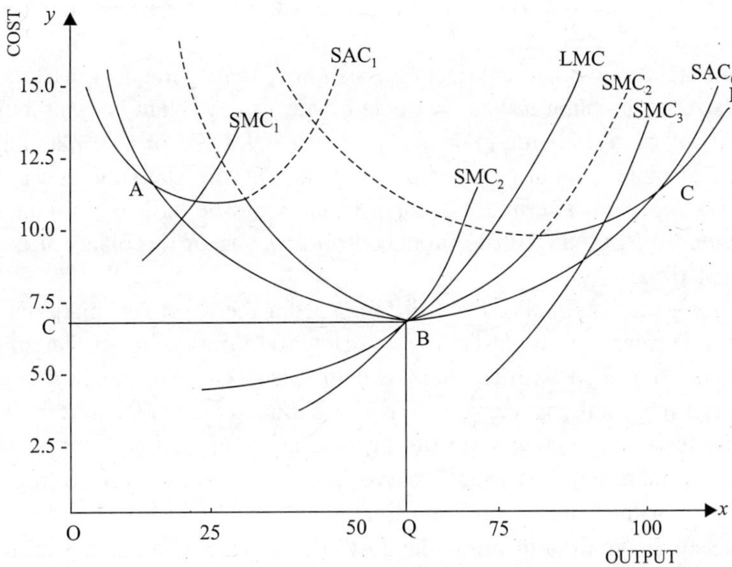

FIGURE 16.7 Long Run Average and Marginal Costs Curves under Normal Production Function

The *LAC* curve is roughly U-shaped or a dish-shaped curve, which implies a declining average cost in the beginning till the firm attains the optimum scale beyond which the average cost starts rising. Under normal production function *LAC* and *SAC* both are represented by U-shaped curves, but the *LAC* curve is flatter or less pronounced. It is because in the long run certain economies are possible, which were not available in the short run. Similarly, certain diseconomies, which are faced in the short run may not be faced in the long run. The tendency of the long run average cost to fall as the firm expands its scale of operation indicates the cost economies available with the increase in size, while the ultimate rise in the long run cost is due to the diseconomies of scale.

Since the *LAC* curve is said to envelop the various *SAC* curves, as no portion of the *SAC* curves lie beyond the *LAC* curve, it is also known as envelope curve. Thus, the *LAC* curve will never intersect a short run average cost curve, it indicates that for any given total output, the average cost cannot be higher in the long run than in the short run. This *LAC* curve will be tangent to the optimum scale curve at the least cost point, but it will touch the *SAC* curves lying to the left of the optimum scale curves at the left of their least cost point and all those *SAC* curves lying at the right of the optimum scale curve at the right of their least cost points.

The smoothly sloping long run average cost curve is drawn on the assumption that the number of possible short run curves is infinitely large. However, if we assume that a limited number of alternative size of plants are technically possible, the long run average cost curve, instead of being smooth, will be scalloped or a wavy solid line, consisting of lowest segments of all the short run average cost curves.

This long run average cost curve assists the 'management in ascertaining the best size of the plant to be constructed, when a new plant is being built up or an existing plant is being expanded. Since it helps the firm in planning the best scale of plant, it is also called a 'Planning Curve'. The short run average cost curves represent alternative plants, which could be built up, although the given amount of output will be produced on any one of the plants at a given moment of time.

The long run marginal cost is different from the short run marginal cost, because an increase in output is now associated not only with an increment in variable cost, but also with an increment in fixed cost. The relation between the long run marginal cost curve and the long run average cost curve is similar to that of the corresponding short run average and marginal cost curves. Thus, the long run marginal cost (*LMC*) curve intersects the long run average cost (*LAC*) curve at the latter's minimum point.

Since at the minimum point the *LAC* curve is tangent to the minimum point of SAC_2, the two marginal cost (i.e., SMC_2 and *LMC*) curves are equal at the minimum point B. However, both the marginal costs will not necessarily be identical because the short run marginal cost is controlled by the variable input only, but the long run marginal cost depends on both types of inputs. The short run marginal costs grow rapidly as the firm strains its fixed resources to obtain a larger output and beyond certain output marginal costs rise almost perpendicularly. On the other hand, expansion of plants avoid this over-utilisation of the smaller plants and provide the flexibility of a larger aggregate of resources, which permit lower long run extra costs with extra output.

Like the short run average cost curve, the long run average cost curve under the normal production function exhibits least cost point, where *LMC* interests *LAC*. It is named as long run economic capacity and indicates the point at which the inputs are being used in the optimum proportions, so that the average cost of production is minimum. Thus, the economic capacity in the long run refers to the level of output that can be obtained at the minimum possible average cost. Below this level of output, the average cost of production is higher though decreasing and beyond this it is again higher and increasing. This negative and positive slopes of the long run average cost curve is due to internal and external economies and diseconomies.

ECONOMIES AND DISECONOMIES OF PRODUCTION SCALE

In case all inputs are variable, the lowest cost proportion of inputs could be maintained at all levels of output. Therefore, in long run the scale of operation should have no effect on the unit costs, which will remain constant at the minimum level of any scale of operation. However, the slope of the long run average cost curve normally does not confirm this, as it slopes downwards in the beginning, becomes constant momentarily and slopes upwards ultimately, as the scale of operation expands. This has been supported by referring to certain economies and diseconomies of large scale operation, which is essentially a reflection of a technical indivisibility of inputs within given patterns of technique of production. The average cost curve slopes downwards due to internal and external economies. Similarly, the upward slope of the average cost curve can be attributed to the existence of internal and external diseconomies.

Internal Economies

It refers to economies or cost benefits, which are available to a particular firm arising from the expansion of the size of operation. It is called internal economies, as it is created within the firm itself and depends on the managerial decisions to change the size or scale. The advantages accruing to the firm can be classified into five categories.

(a) **Labour Economies:** In case the firm expands the scale of operation, it will employ more workers, which will make it possible to reduce the average labour cost (wages) by practicing the division of labour, because the division of labour increases the skill of workers and saves the time involved in changing from one operation to the other, which ultimately increase their efficiency. Such economies will be greatest in firms, where the product is complex and the manufacturing processes are capable of being sub-divided.

(b) **Technological Economies:** As the scale of operation expands, the possibility of the use of big-sized machines and scientific processes increases, as only a larger firm can afford to install modern huge machinery and to use it to the full capacity. The use of a large number of machineries by big organisations also makes possible the correct meshing of machinery and vertical or horizontal integration of the production processes. Since different machines used in the processes of production have different capacities, their correct integration to avoid idle machine time is only possible in a large firm. Again, large firm may find it profitable to utilise their bye-products and waste products. All these reduce the cost per unit, as the scale of operation expands.

(c) **Managerial Economies:** Along with increase in the size of firm, the efficiency of management usually increases, as there can be greater specialisation in the managerial staff. In larger firms, the management can delegate the various decision making responsibilities to experts, who can, in turn, use all the mechanical aid in scientific decision making. Such firms can appoint experts, to look after the various sections or divisions of business, such as purchase, sales, production, finance, personnel, etc., which is beyond the capacity of the small firm.

(d) **Marketing Economies:** A large firm can also secure economies in its purchases. It can purchase goods of its requirements in bulk and can command better terms, prompt deliveries, careful attention and special facilities from its suppliers and concessions from the transport agencies.

(e) **Financial Economies:** A large firm finds raising the fund easier and cheaper than a small firm. It is partly due to greater credit standing and attractiveness to investors and partly because the organised security market is accessible by larger firms. Thus, a larger firm is in a position to offer better security to secure better and easier credit facilities, both from its suppliers and banks and enjoys easier access to the capital market.

Internal Diseconomies

The economies of expanding scale of operation do not continue indefinitely. After the division of labour has reached a certain point, further expansion merely leads to the duplication of workers. It is also true with the use of big-sized machines, balancing of processes and utilisation of bye-products, because once the company is big enough to take the full benefit of all these factors, there cannot be further cost reduction on technological grounds, if there is further expansion in scales of operation. Similarly, the marketing economies vanish after a point, as the producer loses personal contact with the suppliers and customers and fails to pay due attention to special services, etc.

As regards management, a small enterprise has some positive advantage over the large enterprise, because in small firms major decisions can be taken more easily and quickly. The small firms are best suited to those trades, where changes are more frequent and where individuals' tastes or fashion are important. Moreover, in small firms there is personal contact with workers, hence wastes are easily detected and avoided. Such economies are not available to large firms.

Despite delegation of responsibility, there must be somebody at the top to pull the business together, but after a point the business will get so big that the managerial efficiency drops, as larger the firm the more difficult the reconciliation of conflicting views on major policy problems among the experts. There may be too much of red-tapism, large number of individuals between the management and workers and supervision may be difficult. This eventually brings diseconomies or cost disadvantages to management cost, which per unit of output tends to increase.

Thus, as the firm expands its scale of operation, it does not only find the economies being exhausted, but also experience difficulties and complexities growing to turn the economies into diseconomies after the scale of output has reached certain point.

External Economies

It refers to those economies or cost advantages that are available to all firms in an industry. For example, the construction of railway line in certain region, which reduces transport cost for all the firms, emergence of repair industries, coming up of special training schools, etc. These economies or cost advantages arise from the expansion in the size of an industry involving an increase in the number of any size of firm engaged in it.

Thus, the external economies or cost advantages are not within the control of an individual firm and depend upon increases in the output of the whole industry. These economies automatically flow to every firm in an industry, whose size increases. With the growth and localisation of industry in particular areas, all firms can enjoy the benefit of available supply of skilled labour and a well-informed and convenient labour market. Similarly, as the industry attains certain size, it becomes possible to publish technical and other information relating to industry and to make it available at cheaper rates to all the firms. All these reduce the average cost of production.

External Diseconomies

It refers to the monetary or technical diseconomies or cost disadvantages, which result from the expansion of industry as a whole. The prices of some or all inputs may rise, as a result of increased demand for inputs on the part of all firms in the industry, as it expands. Such diseconomies induce the long run average cost curve to slope upwards to the right. Thus, in case of newly started industry external economies are more powerful and easily overcome the feeble diseconomies, but there is a limit to the size of industry up to which it can enjoy external economies, as beyond this diseconomies overtake the waning economies.

COSTS AND INPUT PRICES

Cost depends not only on the length of the time period involved and the level of output but also on the input prices. The change in input prices shifts the cost curve upwards or downwards. The real impact again varies depending upon the time periods involved.

IMPACT OF INPUT PRICE CHANGE IN THE SHORT RUN

In the short run, an increase in price of a variable input will shift average and marginal cost curves upwards into a new position parallel to the old. This parallel shifting is due to the fact that the numerators in the formula for these costs change proportionately at all levels of output, while the denominators are unchanged.

In short run, since we assume that there is no change in the technique of production and that the production function remains unaltered, the average cost as well as the marginal cost will rise for each level of output as follows:

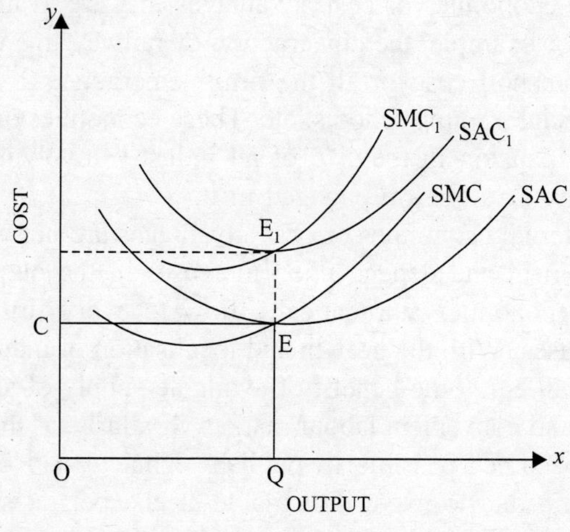

FIGURE 16.8 Impact of Change in Prices of Inputs on Short Run Average and Marginal Costs

Due to minimum wage laws or labour strikes, the wage rate per labour hour rise or due to general industrial expansion, the price of raw materials goes up, the technique of production remaining the same, the *SAC* curve is shifted upwards in a parallel way to the SAC_1 and *SMC* to the SMC_1 levels. The SAC_1 and SMC_1 cost curves trace the relation of cost to output in short run after an increase in the wage rate or the price of raw material or both.

In case after a change in the price of a variable input, the firm adopts a new technique or a new combination of productive service, the impact on the average and marginal cost curves will be different. For example, if the price of raw materials rises, while the wage rates remain unchanged, the firm may economise in the use of raw materials by employing more labour, who may take greater care of raw materials and reduce its waste. In this way, higher costs may not be avoided, but the change in technique may keep the costs from advancing as much as it would otherwise advance but again the cost curve will be shifted upwards in a parallel way.

An increase in the price of fixed input will shift the average cost curve not in a parallel way because the numerator goes up by a fixed amount (i.e., the fixed cost) while the denominator increases as usual. Hence, at low levels of output, the average cost is increased more than that at higher levels of output, because at that level the effect of price change in the fixed input is spread over more units.

IMPACT OF INPUT PRICE CHANGE IN LONG RUN

Since all inputs are variable in long run, proportional change in input prices will merely shift the *LAC* curve up or down in a parallel way. In case there is a non-proportional change in input prices, there will be substitution by relatively cheaper for the expensive ones. Thus, in long run. The effect of change in the price of inputs (treated as fixed or variable in short run) will be the same as that of change in the price of one variable input in short run.

The substitution process will operate to change the proportions among the inputs and to keep costs from rising as much as they would have in the short run, if the price of only fixed input had increased. The new long run average and marginal cost curves will not be parallel to the old, although they will be above the old cost curves as follows:

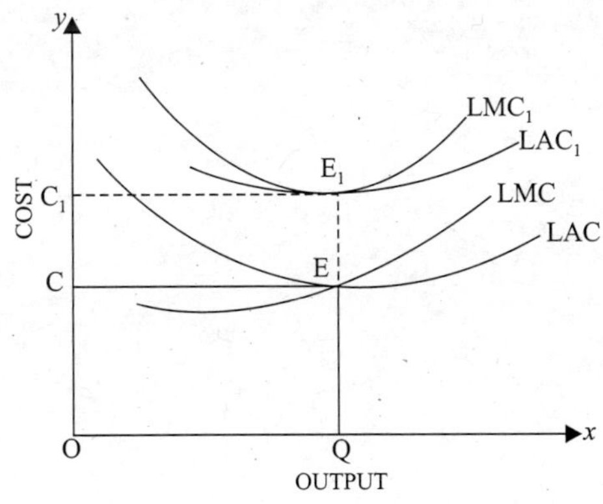

FIGURE 16.9 Impact of Changes in Prices of Inputs on Long Run Average and Marginal Costs

The figure reveals that increase in price of the various inputs shifts the long run average cost to LAC_1 and the long run marginal costs to LMC_1. These curves are not parallel to the original long run average cost and long run marginal cost curves.

Review Questions

1. Explain the concept of opportunity cost and real cost.
2. Distinguish between average cost and marginal cost and elucidate the behaviour of the cost in short run.
3. What is meant by linearly homogeneous production function? Explain the behaviour of the average cost and marginal cost under linearly homogeneous function?
4. Explain the relationship between the average cost and the marginal cost in short run.
5. What is meant by economic capacity of a plant? How is it ascertained in short run?
6. Bring out the behaviour of long run cost curve of a firm and state the various economies and diseconomies of scale.
7. Explain the salient features of *LAC* curve under the linearly homogeneous and normal production functions.
8. What do you mean by cost of production? Discuss the behaviour of average cost in the short period and long period?
9. Discuss the various internal and external economies and diseconomies of scale.

SUB PART-III
EXCHANGE

17

Supply and Price Determination

The cost analysis, particularly the marginal cost of production, determines the position of supply, which, in turn with the help of demand, determines the price of the product. In this chapter, an effort is being made to consider the concept of supply and its elasticity before passing on to the price determination in general on the basis of the Marshallian and Walrasian analyses. Lastly, the effect of time periods, imposition of taxes and granting of subsidies on price determination have also been analysed.

MEANING OF SUPPLY

It refers to the various quantities of a given commodity that a seller stands ready to sell during a given period at the various possible prices. Thus, like demand, supply also reveals a relationship between two variables, viz. the quantity of the commodity supplied and the price charged, where the price is an independent, while the quantity supplied is dependent one. **Generally this price-quantity relationship is found to be positive, that is at a lower price, the smaller quantities are supplied and as price increases, the larger quantities are offered for sale in the market.**

The supply position and the behaviour of seller can be exhibited either with a schedule of possible price-quantity combinations or with a supply curve. The supply curve may be either a curve or a straight line with the horizontal axis indicating the quantities that would be offered for sale and the vertical axis revealing the prices to the charged. The supply curve usually slopes upwards to the right, indicating that as the price rises, larger quantities are offered for sale.

The market supply or industry supply is the horizontal sum of the supply schedules of the individual sellers operating in a particular market or industry. Thus, it represents the sum of the quantities of a given commodity, which all sellers will offer for the sale in the market at all possible prices at a given moment of time. Market or industry supply also exhibits a positive relationship of the quantity supplied with the variation in the price of the commodity. Hence both types of supply curves (individual seller's supply curve and the industry supply curve) are drawn sloping upwards to the right.

The quantity supplied is generally governed by cost, which, in turn, is related to the time period, the level of output of the firm or industry and the price of the various inputs, but in short run, it is mainly affected by the changes in the price of the commodity. The very short run or the market period is a time period during which the output cannot be changed. Hence maximum supply is limited to the volume of stock or inventory in the hands of the sellers. The supply curve during this period shows the attitude of sellers towards their inventories.

The slope of the supply curve may be explained in terms of the marginal utility of the purchasing power, the seller receives and the marginal utility he forgoes along with the depleting inventory. As the seller sells more units of a given commodity, the inventory of that commodity at his disposal diminishes, which enhances the marginal utility of the commodity, at the same time the amount of purchasing power at his disposal increases along with increasing sales, which results in a decrease in the marginal utility of the purchasing power. Under such circumstances, the seller will be ready to part with additional quantities of the commodity, only when higher and higher prices are offered. This results in a positive slope of the supply curve.

There are certain exceptions to the above slope of the supply curve, where we come across backward sloping supply curve. It is generally found in case of agricultural products and labour supply. In case of agricultural products, if the farmers are interested in a given cash income to meet their fixed charges, a decline in price of agricultural products may induce the farmers to increase the acreage to produce and sell more at the lower price. Similarly, an increase in price may induce the farmers to reduce the acreage under cultivation and to use the land, thus saved, for dairy or poultry farming etc., which may reduce the output and, as a result, the quantity available for sale in the market too.

Similarly, in the case of labour supply, which is equal to the number of workers available times the number of hours they are willing to work, we come across a backward sloping supply curve. It depends on the income, the workers wish to obtain. As the wage rates increase, the labour supply increases to some extent, because workers will be willing to work even for longer periods. Where, after a point, the labour supply becomes constant and starts declining if there is further increase in the wage rate. It is as follows:

Figure 17.1(i) reveals the slope of a normal supply curve *SS*, where at *OP* price the quality supplied is *OQ*. In case the price goes up to OP_1 the quantity supplied increases to OQ_1.

Figure 17.1(ii) reveals that when price is OP_0 the quantity supplied is OQ_0. An increase in price to OP_1 increases the quantity supplied to OQ_1. However, further increase in price to OP_2 results in a decrease in the quantity supplied to OQ_2 only.

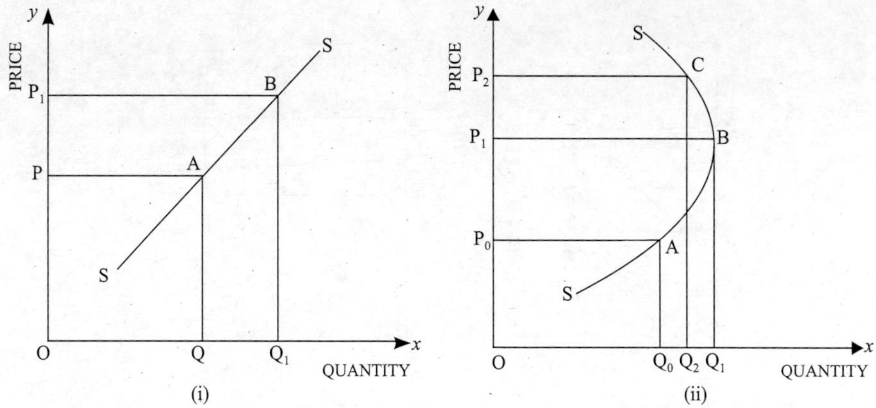

FIGURE 17.1 Slopes of Normal Supply Curve and Backward Sloping Supply Curve.

CHANGE IN SUPPLY VERSUS CHANGE IN QUANTITY SUPPLIED

The two terms are usually interchangeably used, but there is difference as **the change in supply is used for movement from one supply curve to other, while the change in quantity supplied used for movement from one point to other along with a single supply curve as follows:**

Figure 17.2(i) shows the change in supply, which involves a shift in the supply curve. An increase in supply shifts the supply curve to the right, which means that at the various prices sellers are willing to sell larger quantities of the commodity than before. In other words, the sellers are willing to sell larger quantities of the commodity (OQ_1) at the same price (OP) or the same quantity of the commodity (OQ) at the lower price (OP_0). Similarly, the decrease in supply indicates that at a given price the seller stands ready to offer for sale smaller quantities of the commodity than he was ready to sell earlier. In other words, the seller stands ready to sell lesser quantity (OQ_0) at the original price (OP) or the original quantity (OQ) at enhanced price (OP_1).

Figure 17.2(ii) exhibits change in the quantity supplied, which results in a movement along with the supply curve. As one moves from point A to B, along with increase in price from OP to OP_1, the quantity offered for sale has also gone up from OQ to OQ_1. Reversing the process we find that a reduction in price from OP_1 to OP will cause a decrease in the quantity supplied from OQ_1 to OQ.

ELASTICITY OF SUPPLY

The elasticity of supply is the measurement of the responsiveness of sellers to price changes, which is expressed in relative numbers. It refers to the ratio of relative change in the quantity offered for sale to the relative change in the price. In other words, it measures percentage change in the quantity in response to one per cent change in the price of the commodity. It is as follows:

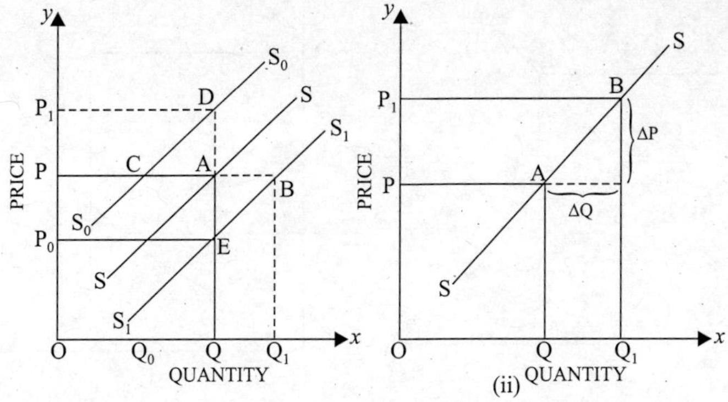

FIGURE 17.2 Change in (i) The Supply and (ii) The Quantity Supplied.

$$\text{Elasticity of Supply} = \frac{\text{Relative Change in Quantity Supplied}}{\text{Relative Change in Price}}$$

$$Es = \frac{\dfrac{\text{Change in Quantity Supplied } (\Delta Q)}{\text{Original Quantity Supplied } (Q)}}{\dfrac{\text{Change in Price } (\Delta P)}{\text{Original Price } (P)}}$$

$$Es = \frac{\Delta Q}{Q} \div \frac{\Delta P}{P}$$

$$Es = \frac{\Delta Q}{Q} \times \frac{P}{\Delta P}$$

$$Es = \frac{P}{Q} \times \frac{\Delta Q}{\Delta P}$$

The formula, thus derived, measures the elasticity of supply between two points on the supply curve. Similarly, it can also be measured on a particular point on the supply curve as follows:

$$Es = \frac{P}{Q} \times \frac{\partial Q}{\partial P}$$

Here small delta (∂) measures small finite change in price and quantity at a particular point on the supply curve. The value of ∂Q and ∂P is ascertainable as per mathematical tables.

The value of the elasticity of supply, thus, derived, varies between zero to infinity. Different degrees of elasticity of supply are as follows:

1. Perfectly Inelastic Supply $Es = 0$
2. Inelastic Supply $Es < 1$
3. Unitary Elastic Supply $Es = 1$

4. Elastic Supply $Es > 1$
5. Perfectly Elastic Supply $Es = \infty$

Since the supply curve has a positive slope, where the quantity varies directly with price, hence there is no need to put a negative sign before the formula for elasticity of supply, as was done with the formula for measuring the elasticity of demand. On account of difference in the slope of the supply curve with that of the demand curve, the graphical depiction of the elasticity of supply is also different. Unit elasticity of supply is taken as a convenient dividing line in classification of the various degrees of the elasticity of supply. Graphically, a straight line supply curve passing through the origin has unitary elastic supply as shown in Figure 17.3.

We know that $Es = \frac{P}{Q} \times \frac{\partial Q}{\partial P}$

Substituting the values from the Figure 17.3,

$$Es = \frac{OP}{OQ} \times \frac{AC}{BC} = \frac{AQ}{OQ} \times \frac{AC}{BC} \quad (\text{Since } OP = AQ)$$

Since right-angled triangles OQA and ACB are similar,

Therefore, $\frac{AQ}{OQ} = \frac{BC}{AC}$ (Ratios and not the length of respective segments are equal)

Thus, $Es = \frac{BC}{AC} \times \frac{AC}{BC} = 1$. (After replacing $\frac{AQ}{OQ}$ by $\frac{BC}{AC}$ as the ratios of respective lines of both triangles are equal.)

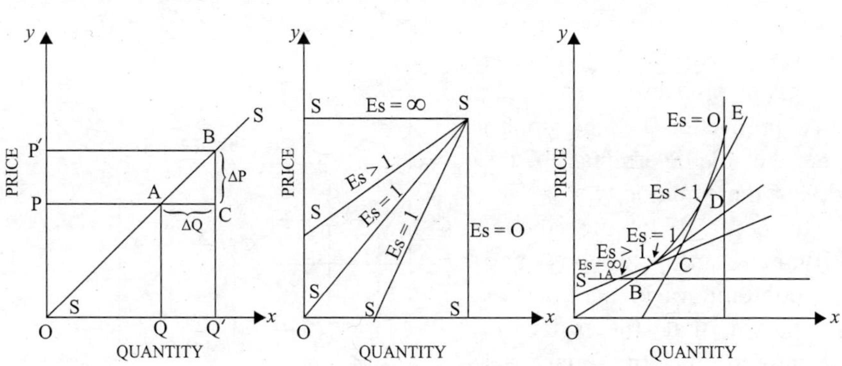

FIGURE 17.3 Elasticity of Supply on the Various Slopes of the Supply Curve.

Similarly in Figure 17.3(ii), if the straight line supply curve passes through the vertical axis, it exhibits an elastic supply and if it passes through the horizontal axis, it shows an inelastic supply. In case the straight line supply curve is parallel to the horizontal axis, it shows a perfectly elasticity supply and if it is parallel to the vertical axis, it has a perfectly inelastic supply.

In case, the position of supply is exhibited with a curve and not with a straight line, as in Figure 17.3(iii) the elasticity of supply can be shown by drawing tangents from points of the supply curve on which the measurement of the elasticity of supply is desired.

On point *A* of the supply curve, the tangent drawn is parallel to the horizontal axis, therefore, the elasticity of supply at this point is equal to infinity. The tangent on *B* point of the supply curve intersects the vertical axis of the diagram, which indicates an elastic supply. Similarly, the tangent to supply curve on the *C* point passes through the origin, which exhibits unitary elastic supply. The tangent on *D* point intersects the horizontal axis, hence there is an inelastic supply. On the other hand, the tangent at *E* point, is parallel to the vertical axis, which indicates a perfectly inelastic supply. Thus, just as different points on the demand curve exhibit different degrees of elasticity of demand, the different points on the supply curve also contain different degrees of elasticity of supply.

PRICE DETERMINATION

The classical economists, like Richard Cantillon, Nassau William Senior, John Stuart Mill and a few others were of the view that **the price (value) is dependent on the cost of production, which indirectly emphasised too much on the supply of the commodity alone in determining its price.** The cost of production merely explains the origin rather than the actual determination of the price. Moreover, the cost of production of a particular commodity differed from unit to unit depending on the level of output, but in market its price remains one. Further the price of the commodity may change after its production and very seldom we come across uniformity between the price and the cost of production. Thus, the cost of production (i.e., the supply) is not the sole determinant of the price of the commodity.

In contrast to the above, William Stanley Jevons and his contemporary economists maintained that the price is determined by the marginal utility of the commodity. **It explains that buyer will be willing to pay higher price for the commodity, which gives him greater satisfaction (utility) and**

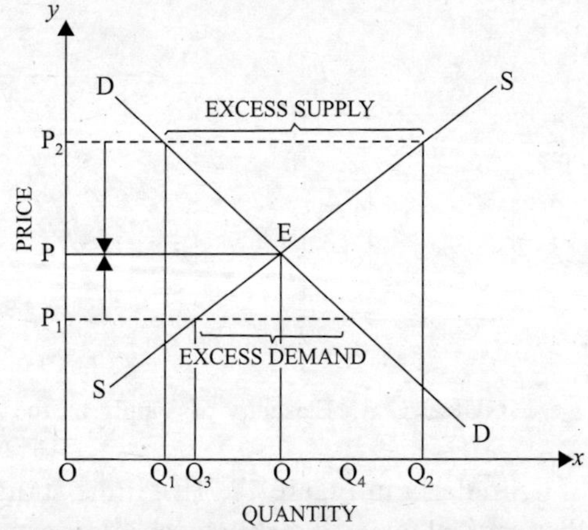

FIGURE 17.4 Determination of the Equilibrium Price.

lower price for the commodity that gives a lesser satisfaction (utility). These utility functions help in deriving the demand functions of the buyers. **Thus, these economists emphasised on the demand as the sole determinant of the price.**

Marshall synthesised the above two schools of thought and emphasised that both supply and demand, taken together, determine the price. He likened the demand and supply with the two blades of a pair of scissors that cut a piece of paper or cloth by operating together. He observed that **'we might as reasonably dispute, whether it is upper or under blade of a pair of scissors that cuts a piece of paper, as whether value is governed by utility or cost of production'.** This contention explains why air, water and sunshine, though important for human existence, command no price in the market, while diamond, being not at all necessary for human existence, command such a high price. He explained this paradox by drawing a distinction between value-in-use and value-in-exchange. Air, water and sunshine, having great value in-use, have no value-in-exchange because of their unlimited supply. On the other hand, diamond having little value-in-use (utility) have a very high value-in-exchange (price) because of its limited supply (scarcity). Thus, price is value-in-exchange, which is expressed in terms of money and is determined as shown in Figure 17.4.

The cross of demand and supply curves built up by Marshall is the widely used model for analysing the price equilibrium in the market. As the demand and supply curves have negative and positive slopes respectively, both intersect each other at certain point (*E* in Figure 17.4), which determines the equilibrium price and quantity, and this is *OP* and *OQ* respectively in this diagram. Assuming an increase in price to OP_2, the quantity demanded has come down to OQ_1, but at the same time the quantity supplied has gone up to OQ_2. Since sellers are willing to sell more at this price (OP_1) than buyers are willing to purchases, there will be competition amongst sellers, which will drive the price down until the quantity for sale is just exactly as much as buyers are willing to purchase. Therefore, the price will have a tendency to come down to *OP* level, where competition amongst sellers comes to an end, as they are getting purchasers of the quantity of the commodity, they offer for sale. Similarly, reduction in the price to OP_1 level induces the buyers to demand an increased quantity of the commodity (OQ_4) but the sellers reduce their supply to OQ_3. Under such circumstances there will be competition amongst buyers, which will drive the price up to *OP* level. Thus, *OP* is the level of price at which neither buyers nor sellers would compete among themselves, hence the price will have a tendency to get settled at this level.

Leon Walras explained the price equilibrium using the concept of excess demand and excess supply. Excess demand refers to the excess of the quantity demanded over the quantity supplied at a particular price level. At OP_1 the quantity demanded is OQ_4, whereas the quantity supplied is OQ_3, the difference (OQ_4—OQ_3) is the excess demand. So long as excess demand is present, the buyers will compete amongst themselves, which may induce the price to go up. Similarly, excess supply refers to the excess of quantity supplied over the quantity demanded. At OP_2 price the quantity demanded is only OQ_1, whereas the quantity supplied is OQ_2, the difference (OQ_2—OQ_1) is the excess supply. The presence of excess supply, results in a competition amongst sellers, which may result into price reduction. Thus, the price will have a tendency to get settled at *OP* level, as the forces of excess demand and excess supply are equal to zero.

MARSHALLIAN VS. WALRASIAN ANALYSIS

Above two views on price equilibrium differ in respect of the very assumption, where in former case, it is assumed that the quantity adjusts to price changes, whereas in the latter case, it is assumed that price adjusts to quantity changes. However, this difference in assumptions does not make any difference in the final results, which is clear from the following diagrams:

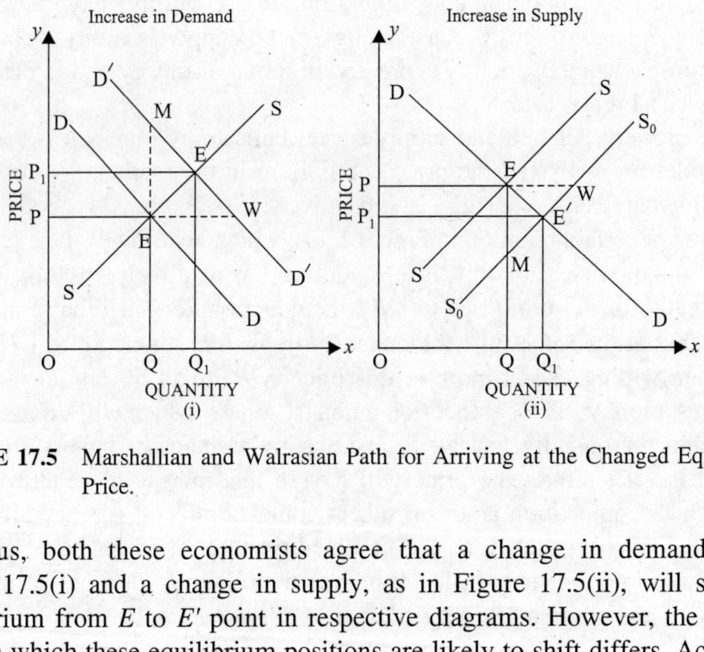

FIGURE 17.5 Marshallian and Walrasian Path for Arriving at the Changed Equilibrium Price.

Thus, both these economists agree that a change in demand, as in Figure 17.5(i) and a change in supply, as in Figure 17.5(ii), will shift the equilibrium from *E* to *E'* point in respective diagrams. However, the process through which these equilibrium positions are likely to shift differs. According to Marshall EME' (in both diagrams) is the way to reach to the new equilibrium position through an adjustment in the quantity, as price changes (i.e., rises or falls). Similarly, according to Walras *EWE'* is the way to reach to the new equilibrium position at *E'*, which shows an adjustment in the price as the quantity changes (i.e., increases or decreases).

TIME PERIODS AND EQUILIBRIUM PRICE

There has been a controversy regarding the relative importance of demand and supply in determining the price. It has been held that is depends upon the time period under consideration. The initial change in the equilibrium price is caused by the changed conditions of demand but succeeding changes in price over time depend on the supply conditions in response to the new demand situations. Thus, once the demand has changed (increased or decreased) a series of adjustments will be put into motion in every firm in the industry, which will bear the fruit one after the other as the time passes. It is the supply that adjusts according to the demand and not the demand that adjusts to the supply with the passage of time.

Thus, the time is important in determining the level of equilibrium price and its impact can be studied during three distinct time periods, namely, market period, short period and the long period. Accordingly, the price determined by the market period demand and supply is termed as market price and the price determined by the short period supply and demand is termed as short run price, sometimes also called sub-normal price. The price determined in long run, when supply is fully adjustable to changed demand is called 'long run price' or 'normal price'.

Market Price: During market period, the maximum supply of the commodity is limited to the extent of the stock, which the sellers can bring out for supply at once. The possibility for increasing the market supply does not exist, just as in the case of the supply of fish in the market on any particular day. Assuming that the fish cannot be kept overnight and the whole supply must, therefore, be sold quickly. The market price in this case will be determined solely by the demand, as the supply in the market period will play an inactive role, as follows:

In Figure 17.6 the market period supply is fixed irrespective of the levels of price. The original demand curve is *DD*, which intersects the market period supply curve at *E* point. It determines the equilibrium price at *OP* level. This fixed supply implies that the sellers are determined to sell the whole quantity at their disposal, whatsoever the price level may be. It also implies that sellers have no demand for their own product, otherwise the supply curve would have exhibited a positive slope. At this slope of the supply curve, if there is an increase in the demand, the demand curve will be shifted to *D'D'* level and the price of the product would go up to *OP'*. **It is because perfectly inelastic supply may cause scarcity that may initiate a competition amongst buyers, who would be willing to pay even higher price for the commodity.**

Short Run Price: Short run is that span of time during which producers can increase the output (hence the supply) through over-working of their plants. During this period supply would react to the change in the demand for the product. As the demand for the commodity increases, the producers vary the

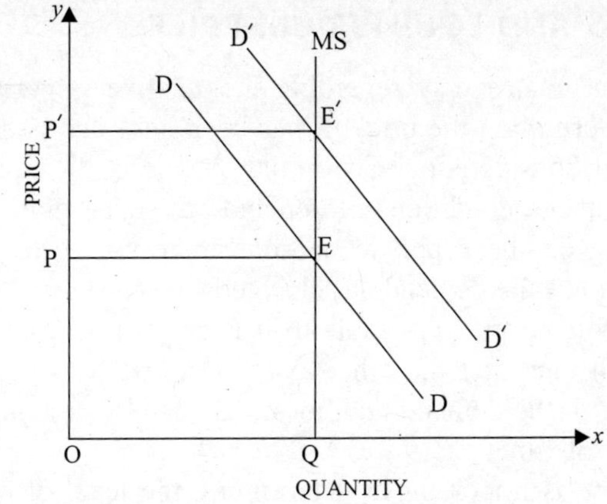

FIGURE 17.6 Determination of Market Period Price.

total output by using more of variable inputs from the existing capacity of the plant. Thus, there will be only limited increase in the output, because this period is not long enough to allow a change in the size of the plant along with change in the quantity of variable input. The price, which increased enormously during the market period, remains comparatively at a lower level in this time period. It is as follows:

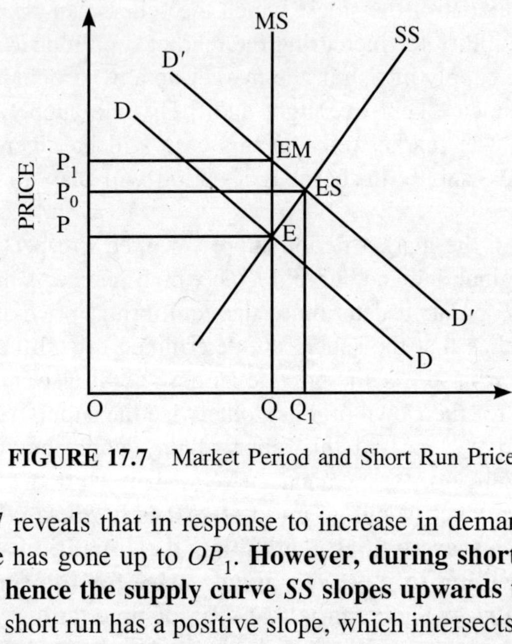

FIGURE 17.7 Market Period and Short Run Price.

Figure 17.7 reveals that in response to increase in demand during market period the price has gone up to OP_1. **However, during short run the supply is not so rigid, hence the supply curve *SS* slopes upwards to the right.** The supply curve in short run has a positive slope, which intersects the new demand curve at *ES* point, where the price has come down to OP_0 and the quantity exchanged has increased to OQ_1 as compared to the levels of price and quantity during the market period. Thus, this Op_0 price is high enough to ensure that additional variable inputs will find it worth remaining there and contribute the additional output.

Long Run Price: Long run is long enough to allow firms to make necessary adjustments in the supply to meet the increased demand. Existing firms can make adjustment with their plants for increasing the scale of operation and new firms may also enter the industry. The cumulative effect will be sufficient increase in the output and, as a result, the supply of the commodity may also increase. **The long run supply curve still slope upwards the right but the slope is very nominal.** The equilibrium price in long run is lower than the short run equilibrium price as follows:

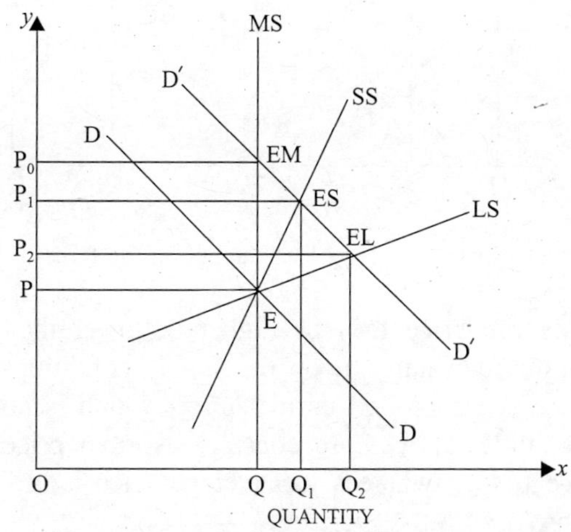

FIGURE 17.8 Price Levels in Different Time Periods.

The long run supply (*LS*) curve intersects the new demand curve *D'D'* at *EL* point, where the price is OP_2 and the quantity of the commodity exchanged is OQ_2. This price is less than the short run price, because the supply can be adjusted to the demand to a greater extent, had it been fully adjustable, the long run price would have been equal to the original price. The extent to which the long run price differs from the original price depends on the ease with which additional supplies can be acquired in the long run. It is, however, possible that the long run supply curve may be horizontal as given in Figure 17.9(i) or due to external economies it may be even falling downwards to the right as in Figure 17.9(ii). It is exhibited as follows:

Figure 17.9(i) reveals a constant cost case, where the supply is fully adjustable to demand. In this case there is no increase in the price but the quantity of the commodity exchanged has gone up to OQ_1. Thus, with constant long run costs and, as a result, with the horizontal supply curve, the long run price is the same as the original price despite increase in demand for the product. On the other hand, Figure 17.9(ii) indicates a case of decreasing cost, where the long run supply curve is sloping slightly downwards to the right. The existence of external economies has resulted into lowering the cost of production, as the output level has been enhanced to meet the increased demand. This decreasing long run supply curve intersects the new demand curve at E_L point, where the long run price is less than the original price.

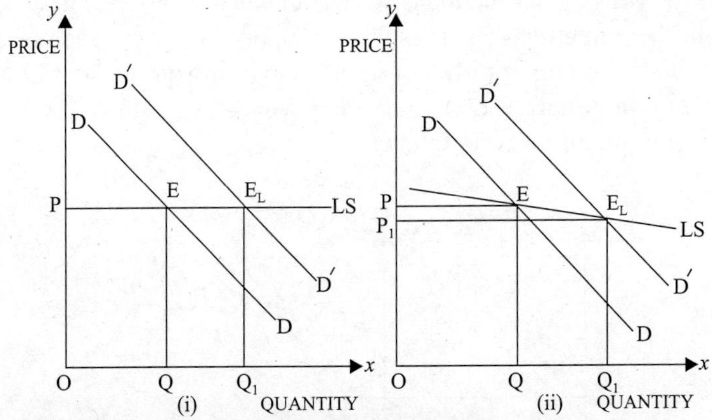

FIGURE 17.9 Impact of Long Run Supply on the Price in Long Run.

Thus, the long run price may be higher or lower than or equal to the original market price, depending upon the supply conditions of the industry. This long run price is also called normal price, which is not the same thing as 'average price' unless prices are constant. Normal price is that price to which actual price trends, whereas the average price is arithmetical average of all actual prices.

The analysis of time elements in price determination enables us to drop the assumption that demand and supply conditions are given. In technical economic language, we have proceeded from static analysis to an analysis of comparative statics, where the demand and supply conditions are allowed to change and a new equilibrium is compared with the old one.

EQUILIBRIUM PRICE AND TAX OR SUBSIDY

We have analysed the various situations under which the quantities supplied change in response to certain change in the demand. Let us also analyse situations, where supply itself changes due to imposition of tax or grant of subsidy to ascertain their impact on the equilibrium price of the commodity. It is exhibited as follows:

Figure 17.10(i) reveals that imposition of per unit tax shifts the original supply curve *SS* upwards to $S°S°$ level. The equilibrium position has also shifted from point *E* to E_0, where the price has gone up to OP_1 and the quantity exchanged has declined to OQ_0. The per unit tax imposed is equal to $KE_0 = MP_1$ or alternatively *EE'*, but the price has increased by $PP_1 = NE_0$ only.

It reveals that at new level of equilibrium price after the tax imposition, the total amount of tax realised is equal to MKE_0P_1, out of which, PNE_0P_1 is realised by the sellers from the buyers by charging higher price and the rest *MKNP* is borne by the sellers themselves.

Similarly, Figure 17.10(ii) reveals the case, where per unit subsidy is granted. It shifts the supply curve *SS* to the right to *S'S'* level, which intersects the demand curve at *E'* point, where the price has come down to *OP'* level, but the quantity demanded has gone up to *OQ'* level. The per unit subsidy is equal to *PN* = *EL* = *KM* = *E'E''*, but the price of the commodity has come down by *PP'* only. This indicates that total benefit of the subsidy will not be passed on to the purchasers, but it will be shared by sellers too. Out of the total subsidy equal to *PNMK*, the benefit of an amount equal to *PP'E'K* is derived by the buyers by way of reduction in price, but the rest equal to *NP'E'M* is going to the sellers.

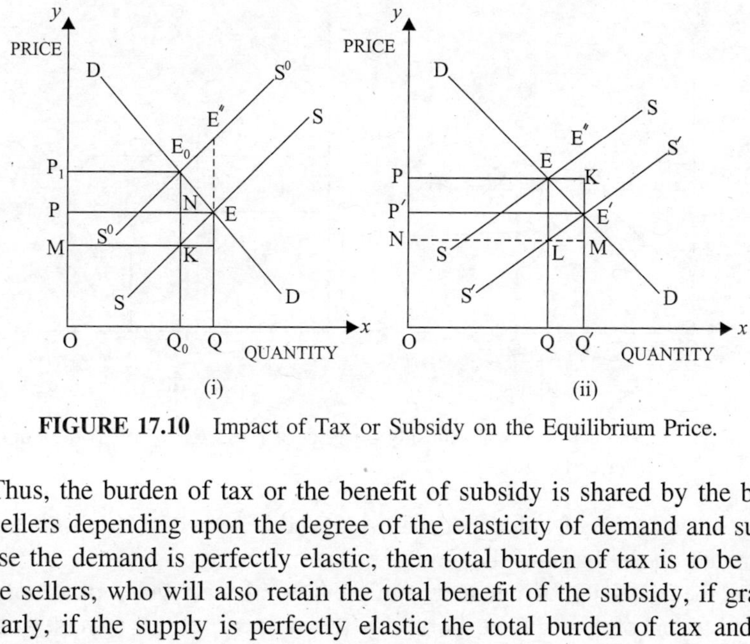

FIGURE 17.10 Impact of Tax or Subsidy on the Equilibrium Price.

Thus, the burden of tax or the benefit of subsidy is shared by the buyers and sellers depending upon the degree of the elasticity of demand and supply. In case the demand is perfectly elastic, then total burden of tax is to be borne by the sellers, who will also retain the total benefit of the subsidy, if granted. Similarly, if the supply is perfectly elastic the total burden of tax and total benefit of subsidy is to be given to the buyers. It is exhibited as shown in Figure 17.11 as follows:

Figure 17.11(i) reveals the impact of imposition of tax, when the demand for the commodity is perfectly elastic. The original equilibrium established with intersection of *SS* with *DD* at *E* has shifted to *E'* on S_0S_0. In this case the sellers will charge the same price from the buyers as before and will bear the total burden of tax. The sellers cannot increase the price, otherwise they will lose the whole of the demand for the product. Reversing the process and taking S_0S_0 as the original supply curve and *E'* as the original equilibrium position, we can analyse the impact of subsidy, which is assumed to shift the supply curve from S_0S_0 to SS level and equilibrium to E point. The sellers under such situation are not going to reduce the price and will retain the total benefit of the subsidy.

Similarly, Figure 17.11(ii) exhibits the impact of tax and subsidy, when the sellers are experiencing perfectly elastic supply. SS being the original supply curve and DD and original demand curve, the equilibrium is at point E. After the imposition of tax, the supply curve has shifted to S_0S_0 level and the new equilibrium has been established at E' point, where the price has been increased to OP' level. This increase in price is equal to the total amount of tax, which shows that the total burden will be borne by the buyers. Reversing the process, we can draw the conclusion that the buyers will be given the total benefit of the subsidy, as reduction in price will be equal to the amount of per unit subsidy. This will also happen, when the demand is perfectly inelastic. Imposition of tax or grant of subsidy is absent in case the supply is perfectly inelastic.

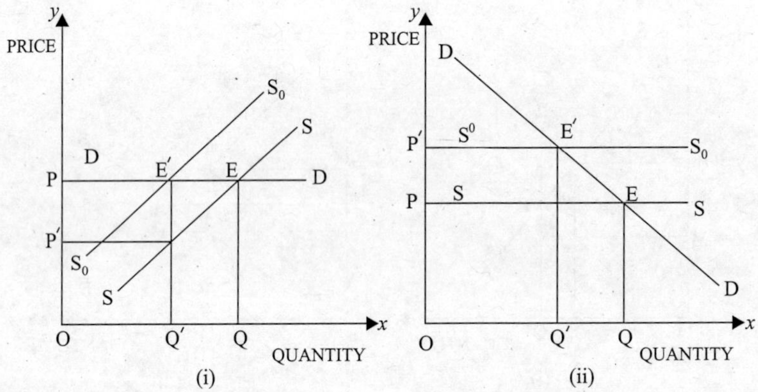

FIGURE 17.11 Impact of Tax or Subsidy on Price if (i) Demand or (ii) the Supply are Perfectly Elastic.

Thus, the share of burden of the tax or the benefit of the subsidy will be ascertained on the basis of the degree of the elasticity of demand and supply. In case the elasticity of demand is more than the elasticity of supply, the greater burden of tax will be borne by the sellers and the buyers will bear only smaller part of the burden. Similarly, if the elasticity of demand is less than the elasticity of supply, the greater share in the total burden of tax will be borne by the buyers and conversely a larger share of the subsidy will be given to the buyers. In case, the elasticity of demand and supply both are equal the burden of tax or the benefit of the subsidy will be shared equally.

MARKET MORPHOLOGY AND REVENUE CONCEPTS

The market generally refers to the physical location, where buyers and sellers settle their transactions. However, in economics it is the field of communication within which circumstances surrounding supply and demand tend to establish one price for a given commodity, except for the differences in the cost of transporting it to the buyers. The classification of market is termed as market morphology. It depends on a variety of factors, such as number of buyers and sellers, the degree of knowledge that each possess, objectives of buyers and sellers, the degree of homogeneity of the product bought and sold, the presence of legal and institutional barriers to the entry of new buyers and sellers and the mobility of buyers and sellers. The infinite number of possible market conditions, which may emerge in that way has customarily been fitted between the two extremes, namely, the monopoly and the perfect competition. Such conditions are as follows:

1. **Monopoly:** It is market structure in which there is only one seller facing a large number of buyers. The single seller enjoys the absence of competition of any kind and has complete control over supply of his single product. The seller also enjoys the control over entry into the industry and absence of mobility of buyers and factors of production. All these factors enable the monopolist to behave as a dominant price-maker. In case there is only one buyer facing a large number of sellers (e.g., sugar mill and sugar-cane growers) the market condition is termed as monopsony. This single buyer also enjoys the absence of competition and has complete control over entry into the industry.
2. **Duopoly:** It is a market condition, where there are two sellers, selling homogeneous products to a large number of buyers in the market. These sellers enjoy the control over supply of the product and also have the control over entry into the industry. In case there are two buyers facing a large number of sellers, the market condition is called as 'Duopsony'.
3. **Oligopoly:** This is a market in which there are a few (i.e., more than two but less than large number) sellers. These few sellers have control over supply of the product and each of them is expected to have some power to choose the price of his product. Thus, each oligopolist is an 'interdependent price-maker' because his power to set a price for his product is circumscribed by the decisions of his rivals. The oligopoly may be: (a) differentiated, if all oligopolists sell non-homogeneous or differentiated products; and (b) simple, if all sellers sell homogeneous products in the market. In case there are a few buyers and an infinitely large number of sellers, the market is 'oligopsony'.
4. **Monopolistic Competition:** It is a market condition advocated by Professor E.H. Chamberlin under which the elements of both competition and monopoly are intermingled. There are a large number of buyers and sellers, who have perfect knowledge of the

market and behave rationally to maximise their own interest. There is freedom of entry into or exit from the industry. Since all these competing sellers sell differentiated products, they, in a limited area, enjoy the monopolistic powers. Mrs. Joan Robinson termed this market condition as imperfect competition, because all except one condition of perfect competition, are present, which makes the competition among sellers as 'imperfect'.

5. **Perfect Competition:** It refers to the market, where there are a large number of buyers and sellers, who individually are incapable of affecting the price by their actions. The commodity, being bought and sold, is homogeneous. The spatial distribution of buyers and sellers is such that no preference arises for reasons of distance for the product of any seller. All the buyers and sellers seek to maximise their satisfaction and net revenue respectively. It is also assumed that all buyers and sellers have complete knowledge of all prices and all price offers. There exists no legal or institutional restriction on the entry of new firms into the industry.

Whatever be the market condition, the interest of buyers lies in maximisation of satisfaction (considered earlier in the chapters on consumers' equilibrium) and of sellers lies in the maximisation of net revenue and, therefore it is pertinent to consider now the various revenue concepts.

REVENUE

The sale proceeds that a firm obtains from the sale of its product in the market is termed as revenue, which may be total, average or marginal.

Total Revenue: Total revenue (*TR*) refers to the revenue from sales obtained by a sellers, which is equal to the number of units sold (*Q*) multiplied by the unit price (*P*);

$$TR = P \cdot Q$$

P being constant (as under perfect competition), $TR = PQ$ is the equation of a straight line with zero value of intercept of the vertical axis, where the total revenue is exhibited by a straight line rising upwards to the right from the point of origin. In case the competition is not perfect, the total revenue curve may rise from left to the right, but continues to go flatter, because the rate of increase in total revenue decreases as more output is sold in the market.

Figure 17.12(i) reveals the position of total revenue (R) that is represented by a straight line rising upwards to the right from the origin. In case of other market conditions, the total revenue curve is not a straight line but a concave curve although it is also rising upwards to the right [Figure 17.12(ii)].

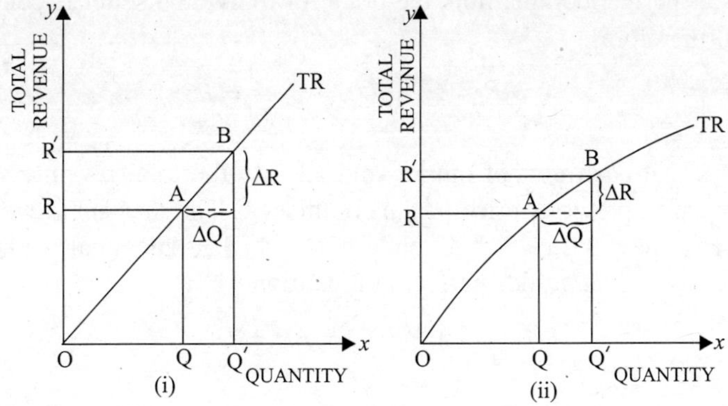

FIGURE 17.12 Pattern of Behaviour of the Total Revenue Curves.

Average Revenue: Average revenue (AR) refers to the total revenue divided by the number of units sold, therefore,

$$AR = \frac{TR}{Q} = \frac{P \cdot Q}{Q} = P$$

Thus, the average revenue is merely alternate name of the price of the product and the average revenue curve merely indicates the price curve or the demand curve of the product of an individual seller. It is different from the total market demand curve, which shows the actual amount offered for sale at the various prices by all sellers in the market. In case of perfect competition, individual seller's average revenue curve is a straight line parallel to the horizontal axis, although the market demand curve has a negative slope, but under monopoly, since there is a single seller, his average revenue or demand curve is identical to the total market demand curve.

Marginal Revenue: It refers to the exact or average rate of change in total revenue as the quantity sold changes. It is the slope of total revenue curve on a particular point (i.e., $\partial TR/\partial Q$) or between two points (i.e., $\Delta TR/\Delta Q$) on such curve. The change in total revenue (ΔTR) is the difference between the total revenue at new position *B* and at given original position *A*. Thus,

Change in Total Revenue = (New Price × New Quantity) – (Original Price × Original Quantity)

$$\Delta TR = (P + \Delta P) \times (Q + \Delta Q) - (P \cdot Q)$$

$$\Delta TR = PQ + Q\,\Delta P + P\Delta Q + \Delta P\Delta Q - PQ$$

$$\Delta TR = Q\Delta P + \Delta Q\,(P + \Delta P)$$

$$MR = \frac{\Delta TR}{\Delta Q} = \frac{Q\Delta P}{\Delta Q} + \frac{\Delta Q(P + \Delta P)}{\Delta Q}$$

$$MR = (P + \Delta P) + Q\,\frac{\Delta P}{\Delta Q}$$

Since under perfect competition, the price for individual seller is constant (i.e., $\Delta P = O$), therefore,

$$MR = (P + O) + Q\,\frac{O}{Q} = P$$

It indicates that each unit of output sold adds to the total revenue an amount exactly equal to previous price of the commodity. The marginal revenue curve is a straight line parallel to horizontal axis, which is identical to the average revenue curve. Thus, under perfect competition:

$$MR = P = AR = D$$

RELATIONSHIP BETWEEN AVERAGE AND MARGINAL REVENUES

The relationship can be examined with the help of the algebraic equation used to measure the marginal revenue, as follows:

$$MR = \frac{\Delta TR}{\Delta Q} = (P + \Delta P) + Q\frac{\Delta P}{\Delta Q}$$

This measurement of the marginal revenue $(P + \Delta P) + Q\frac{\Delta P}{\Delta Q}$ after division and multiplication by $(P + \Delta P)$, will produce a different figure but that will also measure the marginal revenue.

$$MR = (P + \Delta P) + Q\frac{\Delta P}{\Delta Q}$$ after dividing and multiplying this with $(P + \Delta P)$, we get)

$$MR = (P + \Delta P)\left(\frac{(P + \Delta P)}{(P + \Delta P)} + \frac{Q}{(P + \Delta P)} \times \frac{\Delta P}{\Delta Q}\right)$$

$$MR = (P + \Delta P)\left(1 + \frac{Q}{(P + \Delta P)} \times \frac{\Delta P}{\Delta Q}\right)$$

$$MR = (P + \Delta P)\left\{1 - \left(-\frac{Q}{(P + \Delta P)} \times \frac{\Delta P}{\Delta Q}\right)\right\}$$

Since, $Ed = -\frac{(P + \Delta P)}{Q} \times \frac{\Delta Q}{\Delta P}$, therefore, $\left(-\frac{Q}{(P + \Delta P)} \times \frac{\Delta P}{\Delta Q}\right) = \frac{1}{Ed}$

Thus, $MR = (P + \Delta P)\,(1 - 1/Ed)$

In case, we consider change in price on a particular point on the demand curve, the value of ΔP will be stated as ∂P, which will have a value tending to zero (i.e., $\partial P \to 0$), therefore,

$$MR = (P)\,(1 - 1/Ed)$$

Substituting the various values showing different degrees of the price elasticity of demand into this formula, we find certain interesting results, as follows:

1. In case the demand for a commodity is perfectly elastic (Ed = ∞)

$$MR = (P)\ (1 - 1/\text{Ed}) = (P)\ (1 - \tfrac{1}{\infty}) = (P)\ (1) = P$$

Thus, if the demand for the product of the individual seller (as under perfect competition) is perfectly elastic or that the demand is perfectly elastic in any (other market condition) at any point on the demand or price curve, the marginal revenue will be equal to the price or the average revenue.

2. In case the demand for a commodity is elastic ($Ed > 1$, say $Ed = 4$), the marginal revenue will be less than the average revenue or price but certainly more than zero.

$$MR = (P)\ (1 - 1/Ed) = (P)\ (1 - 1/4) = (P)\ (.75) = .75P$$

The marginal revenue curve under such circumstances will lie below the average revenue curve but certainly above the horizontal axis.

3. In case demand is unitary elastic ($Ed = 1$) the marginal revenue will be equal to zero:

$$MR = (P)\ (1 - 1/Ed) = (P)\ (1 - 1/1) = (P)\ (O) = 0$$

Thus, the point at which the demand is unitary elastic, the marginal revenue curve will intersect the horizontal axis.

4. In case the demand is inelastic ($Ed < 1$, say, $Ed = .2$) the marginal revenue will be negative.

$$MR = (P)\ (1 - 1/Ed) = (P)\ (1 - 1/.2) = (P)\ (-4) = -4P$$

5. Lastly, if the demand happens to be perfectly inelastic ($Ed = 0$) the marginal revenue will be infinitely negative:

$$MR = (P)\ (1 - 1/Ed) = (P)\ (1 - 1/0) = (P)\ (-\infty) = -\infty P$$

Similarly total revenue has a definite relationship with marginal revenue, as the former increases till the latter is positive and becomes constant at the point, where the latter is zero. The total revenue decreases beyond this point and becomes equal to zero at the point, where the marginal revenue is infinitely negative.

The relationship of the average, marginal and total revenues can be exhibited as follows:

Thus, at the highest level of price, the demand is perfectly elastic, hence both the average and the marginal revenues are equal. Since, the sale at this level of price is nil, therefore, the total revenue is also zero. Up to *C* point, on the average revenue curve, the demand is elastic, hence the marginal revenue is less than average revenue but more than zero. The total revenue increases in this range. At *C* point, the demand is unitary elastic where the marginal revenue is zero. The total revenue, at this level of sale, is the maximum. Beyond *C*

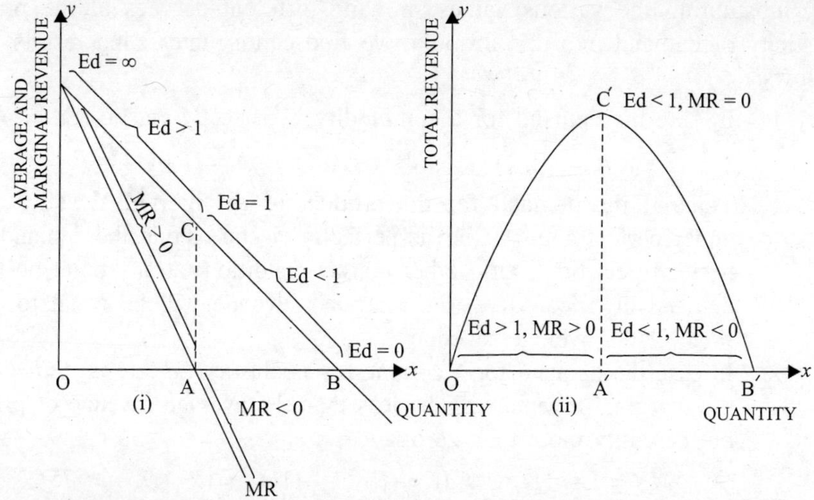

FIGURE 17.13 Inter-relationship of the Various Revenue Curves.

up to *B* point the demand is inelastic, hence the marginal revenue is negative. This negative marginal revenue reduces the total revenue. It is reduces to zero at *B'* point because at this level of sale, the elasticity of demand is zero and the marginal revenue is infinitely negative.

Review Questions

1. Explain the concept of change in supply and change in quantity supplied.
2. State the features of the long run price equilibrium.
3. Examine the role of time element in price determination.
4. Explain the law of supply. Also explain the situation under which supply curve is backwardly sloping.
5. Draw distinctions amongst market period, short-run and long-run. Does the consideration of 'period' affect the price policy?
6. Bring out the features of law of supply and explain the various degrees of elasticity of supply?

18

Pricing under Perfect Competition

Perfect competition is the most commonly analysed form of market structure in economics. It is an ideal market situation, which has a number of characteristics. Firstly, there are a large number of independent buyers and sellers in the market and each one of them is so small that his transactions have no noticeable effect on market price, no matter how much or how little he purchases or sells. Secondly, all such buyers and sellers in the market have perfect knowledge of all current opportunities. According to Marshall **'though everyone acts for himself, his knowledge of what others are doing is supposed to be generally sufficient to prevent him from taking a lower or paying a higher price than what others are doing.** Thirdly, in order to ensure that no seller has a special advantage and that no buyers has any reason to favour a particular seller, it is assumed that the product is homogeneous in every dimension. In other words, the product and its selling conditions are completely uniform, so that selling price is the only factor, which determines a buyer's purchases. It also limits the power of any supplier to sell his product at a price, which is even slightly above the market price. Fourthly, there exists rational behaviour on the part of all buyers and sellers. It means basically that buyers make decisions which will maximise their utilities (i.e., satisfactions) and sellers make decisions which will maximise their profits. Lastly, we assume freedom of entry or exit of resources including land, labour, capital and entrepreneurship. In case the owners of any productive resource perceive that a higher return is available in another industry, they will shift these resources to that industry. Similarly, the industry with higher returns will attract additional productive resources, which will quickly enter that industry because of non-existence of barriers to prevent this.

In this chapter, an effort is being made to elaborate the determination of firm's equilibrium and profit condition under perfect competition in short run as well as long run. The efforts have also been made to explain the supply conditions in short run as well as long run under such market condition.

PRICE DETERMINATION UNDER PERFECT COMPETITION

Under perfect competition, the market price for all buyers and sellers is determined on the basis of the forces of demand and supply. The individual seller takes this price as given, because due to a large number of sellers in the market, he believes that he cannot affect the price by his own action. Thus, he simply behaves as 'price taker', as is evident from the following diagram:

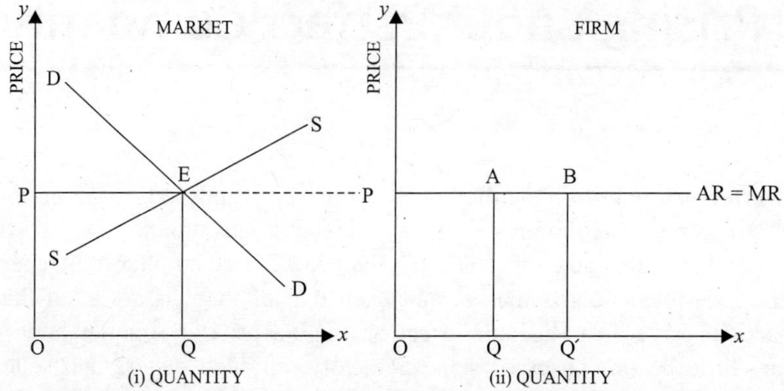

FIGURE 18.1 Market Equilibrium Price and the Price Applicable for the Firms.

The single price, thus determined, will prevail in the market and each of the buyers and sellers can purchase and sell any quantity of that product at this price. Thus, the seller is left with no option regarding the price of the commodity. He can only apply his decision regarding the quantity of the commodity to be offered for sale in the market.

FIRM'S OBJECTIVES

The quantity to be offered for sale is determined on the basis of the firm's objectives. There may be a large variety of objectives, such as, attainment of leadership, forestalling potential competition, preventing government intervention, maintaining consumers' goodwill, restraining demand, maintaining the liquidity of the firm or avoiding the risk, but in economics generally we proceed with the assumption that the firms aim at maximising the profit or net revenue ($NR > 0$). In case the firm fails to obtain profit and incurs net loss, it may seek to minimise its loss or negative net revenue ($NR < 0$). The net revenue or net loss depends upon the relationship between the price and the cost of production, usually termed as profit condition. This profit condition makes no difference in the equilibrium condition of the firm. Thus, the same equilibrium condition applies whether firm is maximising profits or minimising losses in all market conditions.

The profit may be of two types, viz. normal profit and net profit. **The normal profit refers to one, which is just sufficient to keep the right amount of entrepreneurship engaged in a particular field of economic activity.** Like the return of the various other factors of production (i.e., wages, rent, interest, etc.), normal profit is the return for entrepreneurship and it is included in the cost of production.

Net profit or net revenue, on the other hand, is the return to entrepreneur over and above the normal profit. It represents the difference between total revenue (*TR*) and total cost (*TC*) at a given level of output. Thus,

$$NR = TR - TC$$

Just as total quantity is maximum at the point, where the marginal quantity is zero, **the net revenue will be maximum at the point, where the marginal net revenue is zero. Marginal net revenue is the average (or exact) rate of change of net revenue as sales change.** Algebraically,

$$MNR = \frac{\Delta NR}{\Delta Q}$$

Again, since $NR = TR - TC$

Therefore, $\Delta NR = \Delta TR - \Delta TC$ and after dividing this equation with ΔQ, we get

$$\frac{\Delta NR}{\Delta Q} = MNR = \frac{\Delta TR}{\Delta Q} - \frac{\Delta TC}{\Delta Q} = MR - MC.$$

It measures the average rate of change between two points on the net revenue curve. The exact rate of change can be measured as follows:

$$MNR = \frac{\partial NR}{\partial Q} = \frac{\partial TR}{\partial Q} - \frac{\partial TC}{\partial Q} = MR - MC$$

Thus, **the marginal net revenue (MNR) is equal to the difference between the marginal revenue (*MR*) and the marginal cost (MC).** Since, the marginal revenue is the slope of the total revenue curve and the marginal cost refers to the slope of the total cost curve, the marginal net revenue is the difference between the slopes of the total cost and total revenue curves.

FIRM'S EQUILIBRIUM IN SHORT RUN

The equilibrium position of a single seller is ascertained at the point, where his net revenue is maximum or it is ascertained at the point, where there is minimum negative net revenue (i.e., loss), so that there exists no further incentive for the firm to vary its output. **There are two approaches to determine the equilibrium of the firm: (i) total revenue and total cost approach, and (ii) marginal revenue and marginal cost approach.**

Total Revenue and Total Cost Approach

According to this approach, the equilibrium of the firm is ascertained on the basis of the total revenue and total cost curves. In case some part of the total cost curve lies below the total revenue curve, the equilibrium is ascertained at the point, where there is maximum difference between the two curves, as it represents the maximum amount of net revenue obtained by the firm at that level of the sale.

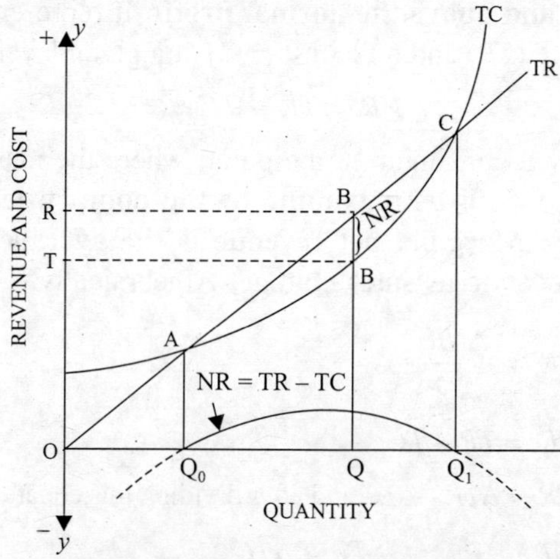

FIGURE 18.2 Patterns of Total Revenues and Total Costs for Firm's Equilibrium under Profit Condition

As is evident from the diagram, the firm will not like to produce and sell less than OQ_0, as up to this level of sale, total cost is more than total revenue. Similarly, the firm will also not like to go beyond OQ_1, as that too represents loss area, where the total cost is more than the total revenue. Points *A* and *C* are break-even points, as total cost and total revenue are equal at these points. The total area lying in between these two points is regarded as profit area, because at all levels of sales in this region, total revenue is more than total cost of production.

The equilibrium of the firm is at *OQ* level of sales, as the net profit, that is, the excess of total revenue (*TR*) over total cost (*TC*) is maximum at this level of sales. The net revenue (*NR*) curve, which starts rising above the base line from Q_0 point keeps on rising up to *OQ* level, where it is maximum. Beyond this level of sale, net revenue (*NR*) declines up to Q_1, where it again equals zero. When *NR* increases, the value of $MNR > 0$ and when it falls beyond *OQ* level, the value of $MNR < 0$. At level, where *NR* is neither increasing nor decreasing but having a constant slope, the value of $MNR = 0$. Thus at equilibrium point,

$$MNR = \frac{\Delta NR}{\Delta Q} = \frac{\Delta TR}{\Delta Q} - \frac{\Delta TC}{\Delta Q} = MR - MC = 0$$

It reveals that the firm will maximise its net revenue at the level of sales, where the marginal net revenue is zero.

In case, the total cost of the firm lies above the total revenue curve at all levels of the output, the firm will be in equilibrium at the level of sales, where the loss is minimum as depicted in Figure 18.3.

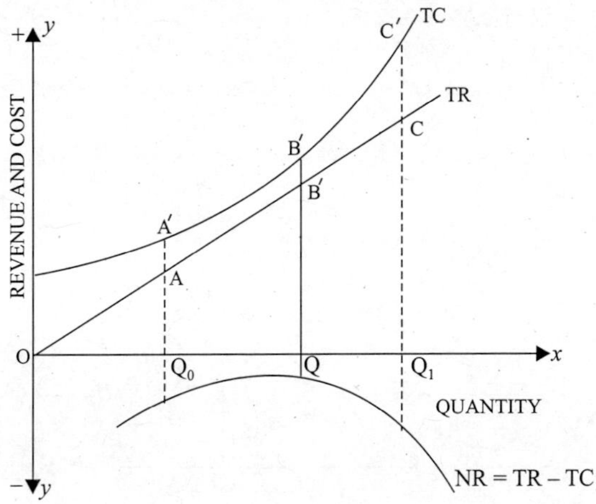

FIGURE 18.3 Firm's Equilibrium under Loss Conditions.

The very slopes of the total revenue and total cost curves show that the firm will incur a loss, whatever quantity it decides to sell in the market. In case the firm offers OQ_0 quantity for sale, the loss will be *AA′* and it is *CC′*, if the quantity offered for sale is OQ_1. Thus, both the situations exhibit higher loss as compared to the loss at *OQ* level of sale, as here the loss is only *BB′*. The net revenue curve is lying below the base line representing negative net revenue at all levels of sale. The negative net revenue curve is nearest to the base line at *OQ* level of sale, hence this will be equilibrium level of sale.

The maximum amount of loss, the firm stands ready to bear, may be equal to the amount of fixed cost. In case the minimum loss at equilibrium extends beyond the fixed cost, the firm will stop production even in short run. **Thus, if the total revenue is high enough to cover the whole of the variable cost and a part of the fixed cost, despite the loss in short run, the firm will continue its operation.**

The total revenue and total cost approach for determining the **equilibrium is defective, because the equilibrium is to be established on the basis of observation, which always leaves the room for disagreement. Thus, it is not an exact method, as there may exist controversy regarding the exact location of the equilibrium.**

Marginal Revenue and Marginal Cost Approach

The equilibrium of the firm, under perfect competition, can also be determined on the basis of the marginal revenue and marginal cost curves. The maximum revenue or loss at equilibrium level can be ascertained on the basis of the average revenue and average cost curves. **Under perfect competition, the average and marginal revenues are represented by a single straight line parallel to the horizontal axis.** Both the equilibrium and the profit conditions are exhibited in Figure 18.4.

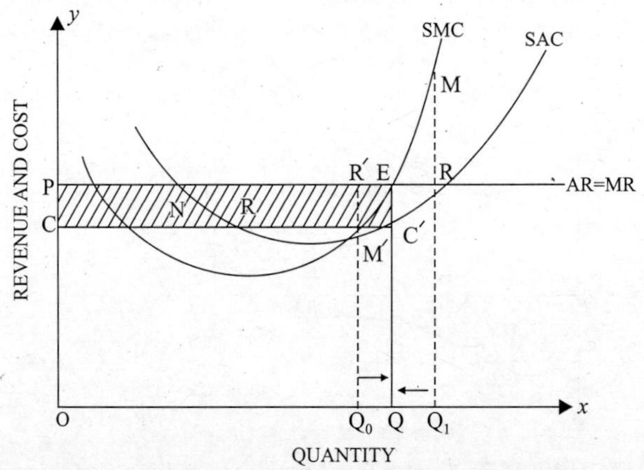

FIGURE 18.4 Firm's Net Revenue as per the Various Revenue and Cost Curves.

The rising short run marginal cost curve intersects the marginal revenue curve at *E* point, which determines the equilibrium level of output *OQ*. This quantity of the total output is sold in the market at *OP* price that earns a total revenue (*TR*) equal to *OPEQ*. The average cost of production at this level of output is $OC = QC'$, which produces the total cost $TC = OCC'Q$. The firm gets net revenue $NR = PEC'C$, which is the excess of *TR* (*OPEQ*) over *TC* (*OCC'Q*). This *PEC'C* represents the maximum net revenue (*NR*) the firm can obtain in short run. In case the firm extends the output to OQ_1, the additional cost (or the marginal cost) is MQ_1, while the additional revenue (or the marginal revenue) is RQ_1 only. Thus, due to this additional sale, the firm will incur a loss equal to *EMR*, which will reduce the value of *NR* that has already been earned up to *OQ* level of sale. Similarly, if the firm produces less than *OQ* (say, OQ_0), the marginal revenue ($R'Q_0$) is more than the marginal cost ($M'Q_0$), which provides incentive to the firm to increase the level of sales. Thus, **the firm will be in equilibrium at *E* producing *OQ* level of total output, as from this point the firm will like neither to expand nor to contract the level of sales.**

Since, $$MNR = \frac{\Delta NR}{\Delta Q} = \frac{\Delta TR}{\Delta Q} - \frac{\Delta TC}{\Delta Q} = MR - MC$$

Therefore if:

(i) $MR > MC$, then $MNR > 0$, which induces the firm for expansion;
(ii) $MR < MC$, then $MNR < 0$, which encourages the firm for contraction;

(iii) $MR = MC$, then $MNR = 0$, which induces neither expansion nor contraction. Thus, the equilibrium is established at the point, where $MNR = 0$.

Since, $MNR = MR - MC$

Therefore at the equilibrium point,

$$MR - MC = 0$$

or $MR = + MC$

or $MR = MC\uparrow$ (marginal cost rising).

This condition must be satisfied at the equilibrium point, irrespective of the profit condition (*i.e.*, whether the firms maximise net revenues or minimise their losses). The equilibrium position under loss condition is as follows:

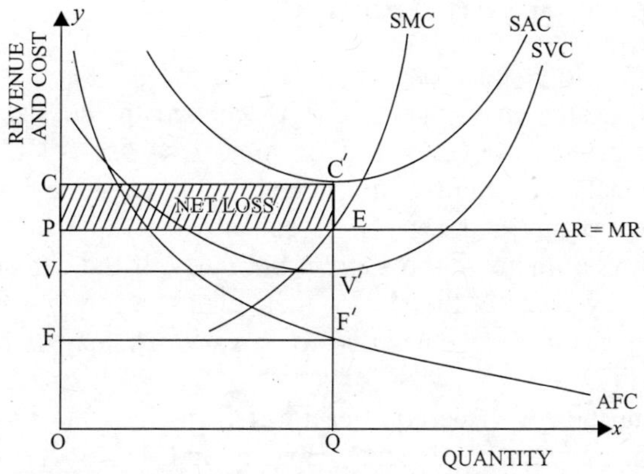

FIGURE 18.5 Firm's Net Loss as per the Various Revenue and Cost Curves.

In case the firm incurs a loss, the condition $P < SAC$ will exist, but simultaneously the condition $P > AVC$ must also exist. The equilibrium condition ($MR = SMC'$) is satisfied at E point, where the output is OQ. The firm incurs an average cost of $QC' = OC$, but the price obtainable is $EQ = OP$. It results in per unit loss equal to $EC' = PC$. The total net loss incurred at the equilibrium level of sale is $PEC'C$, which is equal to the excess of total cost $OCC'Q$ over the total revenue $OPEQ$. In case the firm expands beyond equilibrium level of the additional cost incurred will be greater than additional revenue obtained, which will add to its already accumulated net loss. Similarly, if the level of output/sale is reduced, then per unit of loss will be greater than that at equilibrium level, as the difference between the short run average cost curve and average revenue curve expands.

Thus, the firm, in short run, will continue its operation even if it is incurring a loss, provided the price is sufficient to cover at least the variable cost. The total cost incurred in short run includes fixed cost as well as variable cost. At the equilibrium level of sale, the total cost *OCC'Q*, is equal to the total variable cost *OVV'Q* plus the total fixed cost *OFF'Q*, which is also equal to *VV'C'C*. In short run, even if the firm decides to discontinue the production, it has to incur an expenditure equal to the fixed cost (*OFF'Q* = *VV'C'C*), which will represent the loss to the firm. However, in case the firm produces and sells at *OQ* level of output, the loss is only *PCC'E*, which is only a part of the total fixed cost. **Thus, if the firm continues to remain in the operation, the loss is less than that, if the firm decides to discontinue it. Even if the firm is incurring a loss equal to *VV'C'C* (i.e., total fixed cost) it may be advisable for the firm to remain in operation because of the expectation for future improvement in situation.** On the other hand, if the price level comes down below the average variable cost level, the firm must discontinue the production even in short run.

FIRM'S LONG RUN EQUILIBRIUM

Long period is a time span long enough to allow the supply to adjust fully to the demand, which may change due to change in the size of population demanding the product, development of some new uses of the product, etc. In case, the demand for commodity increases, the existing firms can enlarge the size of their plants and new firms can also set up their plants into the industry, which may increase the supply. Similarly, if the demand declines the existing firms may contract the size of their plants, a few other existing firms may close their plants altogether due to loss, which may reduce the supply of the commodity.

In long run, there will be equilibrium if firms have no incentive to build new capacity or contract the existing capacity and if there exists no incentive for new firms to enter into the industry or existing firms to leave the industry. All these conditions are satisfied only when existing firms make only normal profits. In case the firms in the industry are making net profits, the industry will attract new investments. Such an industry will expand, as new firms enter into it and existing firms grow in size. On the other hand, if the existing firms incur a loss, the industry will prove to be unattractive for investment. Under such circumstances the industry will contract, as a few firms will leave it, while remaining firms will reduce the scale of their operations. Thus, there will be equilibrium only when existing firms are getting only normal profits, because then only the industry will neither expand nor contract. It is, however, possible for an industry to be in equilibrium, while some firms are growing and others are contracting as long as, on an average, there is neither growth nor decline.

In long run the price of the product must be equal to be average cost of production as follows:

$$NR = TR - TC = 0 \text{ (No net profit)}$$

$$TR = TC$$

$$\frac{TR}{Q} = \frac{TC}{Q} \text{ or } AR = AC \text{ (i.e., } LAC\text{)}$$

However, the mere fact that the total cost is equal to the total revenue does not guarantee that a firm will be equilibrium. For both the firm and the industry to be in equilibrium, so that neither exit from nor entry into the industry occurs and no change in output from existing capacity is considered beneficial, it is necessary that the short run equilibrium condition of the firm along with zero net revenue condition is satisfied.

Thus, $MC = MR$ (short run equilibrium) and $AR = AC$ (long run equilibrium) both must be satisfied simultaneously

Since under perfect competition $AR = MR$, therefore,

$$MC = MR = AR = AC$$

There are two types of *MC* and *AC* (i.e., short run and long run marginal cost and average cost), therefore,

$$SMC = LMC = MR = AR = LAC = SAC$$

Under perfect competition in long run, when all these condition are satisfied, the firm will be operating a right size of plant and there will be right number of firms in the industry. It is as follows:

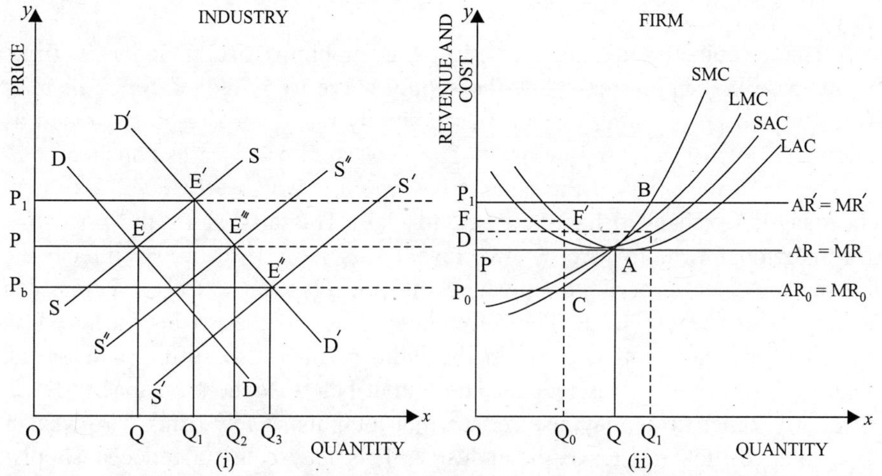

FIGURE 18.6 Long Run Equilibrium of the Industry and Firms.

In respect of the product of industry, the total demand (*DD*) curve intersects the total supply (*SS*) curve at *E* point, which determines the equilibrium price *OP* and equilibrium quantity *OQ*. The individual firm has to accept this price, where $P = AR = MR$. The minimum point of the long run average cost (*LAC*) curve is tangent to the $AR = MR$ line at *A* point. The short run average cost (*SAC*) curve is also tangent at this point. The short run marginal cost (*SMC*) curve intersects the *SAC* curve and the long run marginal cost (*LMC*) curve intersects the *LAC* curve at this point. Thus, the long run equilibrium condition ($SMC = LMC = MR = AR = LAC = SAC$) is satisfied here, as the firm gets only normal profit. Having reached this level of output, the firm will neither like to expand nor to contract the scale of production, as in both the situations the firm will incur a loss.

In case the demand of the product increases, the demand curve is shifted upwards to *D'D'* level and a new equilibrium is established at *E'* point, where increased quantity OQ_1 is sold at higher price OP_1. The individual firm accepts this price, which is shown by $MR' = AR'$ line. This line is intersected by the *SMC* curve at *B* point, which forms a new equilibrium for the firm. At this point, the firm sells an increased quantity OQ_1 at the higher price OP_1. Although this quantity is produced at an average cost $D'Q_1 = OD$, it leaves a net revenue equal to $D'DP_1B$ to the firm at the new equilibrium. **Similarly, due to increased price, other existing firms also get net revenue which, like the present firm, might increase their output even beyond the economic capacity level. This increase in output by all existing firms increases the total supply in the market. Moreover, freedom of entry coupled with the presence of net revenue of existing firms in the industry might attract new firms from outside the industry. The production by the new firms may add to the supply that has already been stepped up by the existing units.**

The combined and uncontrolled efforts of both existing and new firms to increase the supply may shift the supply curve to *S'S'* level. Since there is freedom and no planning, the increased supply may prove to be too much as compared to the increased demand. The new equilibrium is established at *E'* point, where the price in the market has come down to OP_0 level, although the quantity exchanged has increased to OQ_3. This also shifts the price line for individual firm to $MR_0 = AR_0$ level. This new MR_0 line is intersected by the *SMC* curve at *C* point, where the price is $OP_0 = CQ_0$, whereas the average cost is $F'Q_0 = OF$. The difference $P_0FF'C$ is the net loss suffered by the firm. Similarly, other firms in the industry may also suffer such losses. Due to loss, this firm has reduced the output below economic capacity level. Similarly, other firms may also reduce their outputs. A few firms with weaker financial position my leave the industry. This may cause a reduced supply, which will shift the supply curve to *S'S'* level. The new supply curve fixes the equilibrium at *E›››* point, where the original price prevails and the firms also produce at the economic capacity level and sell at a price, which is equal to the average cost of production. Thus, the output of the individual firm in the long run equilibrium position is once more the same as it was before the change in demand but the total supply in the market has increased, because all the new firms, which entered into the market later on, have not left the industry.

Thus, in long run, the firms tend to operate at the least cost point and temporary displacement of the equilibrium price results in an eventual return to the same position. The long run equilibrium possesses the following properties:

1. The price tends to be at the level of the minimum average cost of production of all firms. The firms in the industry, thus, earn no excess profit, but only normal profit, which is included in the cost of production.
2. There are no selling costs to be covered by price, because these are ruled out by the assumption of lack of product differentiation.
3. Since all the firms are operating with minimum average cost of production, the competition has forced them to operate at their lowest cost scales and at their lowest rates of utilisation.
4. The outputs of the firms are such that their long run marginal costs are equal to price.
5. Since the aggregate and average cost of every output is at the minimum and since the output is extended up to a level, where price equals average cost, the long run industry output is largest (at given factor prices, demand and technology) that can be secured subject to the condition of firms in the industry.

EQUALITY OF LEAST COST IN LONG RUN

The long run minimum average cost may not be identical for all firms in the industry. Some forms may have superior management, while some others may enjoy advantageous location, still others may have agents of unique skill in their employment. The superiority of these services expresses itself in greater output for a given aggregate outlay or in lower average cost of production. However, the agents of these special qualities will not make a gift of these qualities to the firm, but it has to bid for them, which may give rise to the opportunity cost of the favoured resources, hence their services may command a higher price in the competitive market. Thus, when these extra costs are added to the ordinary costs, the minimum long run average costs become identical for all firms in the industry. Despite homogeneity in respect of all other factors of production, there is bound to be heterogeneity in respect of entrepreneurs and their methods of production, which may bring inequality in the cost of different firms.

The economists do not seem to be in agreement regarding equal least cost of all firms in the industry, although the controversy is of only limited significance, because the long run equilibrium position is a theoretical construction and not a position attained in real world. Marshall has stated that long run equilibrium position is one towards which there is tendency to move. Thus, in long run, the cost curves of even those firms having superior factors of production will have a tendency to move upwards, as due to competition, these firms will be required to pay higher prices to retain the services of superior inputs until these are at the same level, as those of all other firms in the industry.

According to **Marshall the equality of minimum long run average cost to price is generally found in case of the marginal firm, which earns only normal profit. The marginal firm is defined as that firm, which has the**

highest average cost and which shall be the first to go out of the industry, if the price of the product falls in the long run. The supply price of the industry in the long run is determined by the minimum average cost of the marginal firms, which continue to increase their scale and expand their output at the rate the industry expands.

All those firms, whose long run average costs are less than those of the marginal firms, are known as the infra- or intra-marginal firms. Such firms enjoy net revenue even in long run, because they have a lower minimum average cost than the price at which the output is sold. Chamberlin rejected the plea and stated that intra-marginal firms will evidently have the same minimum point, if their rents are included as costs. Rents are surpluses but they are, to the individual firm, not different from any other monetary expense, although it is a cost rigidly imposed upon the firm by the competition of its rivals for the use of rent-yielding input.

Even if all the firms in the industry have the same minimum average costs, the most efficient scale of production is not necessarily uniform for all. Minimum point of the average cost curve may be at the same distance from horizontal axis for each firm, but the same may be variously distant from the vertical axis. It may be due to qualitative differences of the various factors of production employed.

SUPPLY IN SHORT RUN

Short run supply, under perfect competition, reveals the behaviour of the industry's output as price varies in short run. It is derived on the basis of the behaviour of the output of a single firm in response to variation in the market price. The firm finds its equilibrium at the point, where the marginal cost equals the marginal revenue, which, in turn, equals the market price.

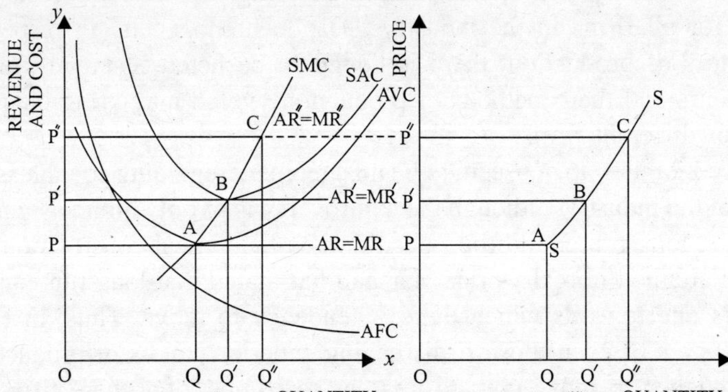

FIGURE 18.7 Derivation of Short Run Supply Position of a Product.

The firm will not supply even single unit to the market, if the price is not high enough to cover at least the average variable cost. Thus, the minimum level of supply is OQ at OP level of price, as below this price the supply will be zero. As price goes up to OP', the supply goes up to OQ', although, even at this price, the firm is getting merely normal profit as $SAC = AR$. Further increase in price results in further increase in the supply. The adjoining diagram shows the position of supply of the firm in short run. The marginal cost curve of the firm reveals the marginal cost corresponding to each level of output. This, in turn, reveals the supply curve, which indicates the prices necessary to call forth the various levels of output. For equilibrium, since the price is equated with the marginal cost, therefore, the two curves are identical.

Thus, the short run supply curve of the firm is defined as that part of the short run marginal cost curve that lies above its average variable cost curve. The supply curve represents the amount the firm would produce and sell in the alternative possible short run equilibrium position in which the firm finds itself as the price of the product changes. In other words, the short run supply curve of the firm will be a curve joining alternate possible short run equilibrium positions on successively higher short run marginal cost curves. Such supply curve rests on the assumption that the prices of the variable inputs do not change in short run, otherwise it will be shifted upwards or downwards in a parallel way.

The short run industry supply curve under perfect competition is defined as the horizontal sum of the relevant ranges of the various supply (i.e., marginal, cost) curves of the individual firms. Thus, to find the industry supply curve, we merely need to ascertain the sum of the various quantities supplied by each firm at each level of the price. This industry supply curve also slopes upwards to the right. It reflects the assumption of diminishing marginal productivity on which rests the assumption of increasing marginal cost. The steepness of the industry's short run supply curve will depend on the slope of the marginal cost curves of the individual firms. In case the cost structures of all the individual firms in the industry are identical, the elasticity of the industry's supply curve will be equal to the elasticity of the supply curves of the individual firms.

SUPPLY IN LONG RUN

The long run supply, under perfect competition, refers to the total supply, which would be available from all firms operating at successive points of the long run economic capacity, as the industry expands. Thus, the long run supply curve is a line that connects the successive points of the long run equilibrium of the industry. It rests on the assumption that all factors of production are homogenous and are also in perfectly elastic supply to the industry. We may also assume that there is perfect competition in the factor market, so that the prices of all units of each factor are the same, otherwise the long run supply curve will no more remain as infinitely elastic, but it may either be positively sloping if the costs of inputs are increasing or may be negatively sloping if the costs of inputs are decreasing.

Thus, after a change in the demand for product of the industry, the successive points of the long run equilibrium of the industry will be at the same, higher or lower levels of the prices, depending upon the type of the industry, which may be constant cost, increasing cost or decreasing cost, respectively. The position of the supply curve in all these cases may be analysed separately.

Constant Cost Industry

In this case, external economies and diseconomies present, are of equal force and prices of the inputs are assumed to remain constant, as larger quantities of them are used. Under such circumstances, an increase in the output of the constituent firms does not change the costs of firms, which remain constant.

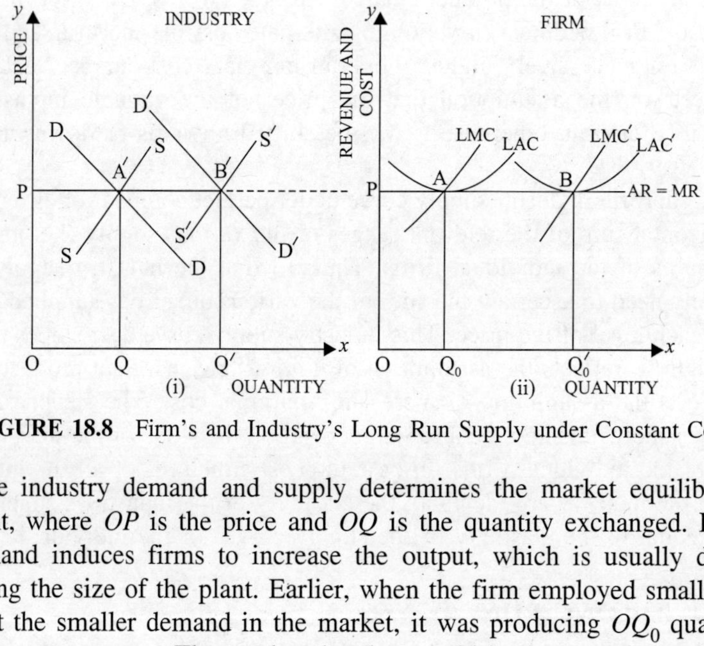

FIGURE 18.8 Firm's and Industry's Long Run Supply under Constant Cost.

The industry demand and supply determines the market equilibrium at A' point, where OP is the price and OQ is the quantity exchanged. Increase in demand induces firms to increase the output, which is usually done by enlarging the size of the plant. Earlier, when the firm employed smaller plant to meet the smaller demand in the market, it was producing OQ_0 quantity at the AQ_0 average cost. The product has been sold in the market at OP price, which earned only normal profit for the firm. The increase in demand in the market induced the firm to offer enhanced quantity of total output in the market for which it employed a large-sized plant. On this plant, the firm produced OQ_0' quantity of the total output at an average cost of BQ_0', which equals the average cost of earlier plant. New firms entering the industry would, similarly, build that size of plant on which for the output which they intend to produce, the average and marginal costs would be equal. The combined efforts of all firms in the industry shift the supply curve to $S'S'$ level, which determines the equilibrium price at B' point. New price at B' point is the same as earlier price at A' point. Combining A' with B' points, we get a line named as long run supply (*LRS*) curve, which is parallel to the horizontal axis.

Thus, in the long run, where all inputs are assumed to be variable and prices of inputs are assumed to be constant, increase in output in response to an increase in demand can eventually be met equally efficiently through (i) the action of existing firms in building new plants of larger sizes; and (ii) the entry of new firms, which build additional plants of any size. However in all cases the average cost will be equal to the price or the average revenue leaving merely normal profit to all firms.

Increasing Cost Industry

In such a case, the industry is subject to external diseconomies or where the external diseconomies are more powerful than external economies. Such industry experiences rising costs as output expands. The average and the marginal cost curves of the individual firm will shift upwards as the industry's output expands in response to increase demand for the product. The shift in the cost curves is the result of an increased price of inputs, because as additional firms enter the industry, they will bid against existing firms for the **given supply of inputs, thereby forcing the** prices of inputs to rise.

Figure 18.9 reveals that the industry price and output are *OP* and *OQ* respectively and the single firm in this case is initially in equilibrium at E point, the average cost of production and the price being *EQ* and *OP* respectively, which are equal. The increase in demand induces the industry to expand, which once more finds an equilibrium at B point, where increased demand of the product of the industry is equal to enhanced supply.

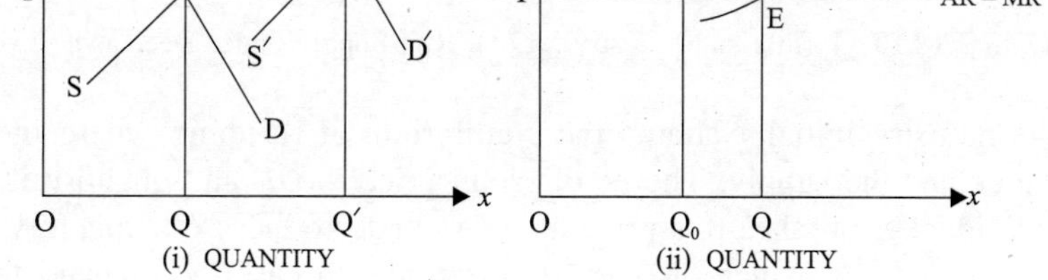

FIGURE 18.9 Firm's and Industry's Long Run Supply under Increasing Cost.

Increase in the prices of inputs shifts the marginal cost curves to the left for all firms including the one shown above. By the process of adjustment, the firm again eventually finds a new position of equilibrium at *E*′, operating smaller plant at a higher long run average cost, which is equal to enhanced price. At this new equilibrium, the output of the firm has decreased from *OQ* to OQ_0. However, since the equilibrium was initially disturbed by an increase in demand, in the final equilibrium position the total supply of the industry must be greater than what it was before the change in demand occurred. Thus, a larger quantity is being sold by the industry at a higher price than before.

The decrease in the firm's output has been the result of the disproportionate increase in the prices of all inputs resulting from the increase in the number of firms in the industry. Thus, while the individual firm's supply curve slopes upwards to the left, the industry supply curve slopes upwards to the right. Had there been proportionate increase in the prices of all inputs, the individual firms' long run supply curve would have been a straight line parallel to the vertical axis and the size of the plant would have been exactly the same as it was before. However, the industry supply curve would still have a positive slope because of increase in number of firms in the industry.

Decreasing Cost Industry

In case the industry experiences the benefits of the external economies as it expands, the set of cost curves of the firm working in such an industry shifts downwards. It is usually true with new and expanding industry.

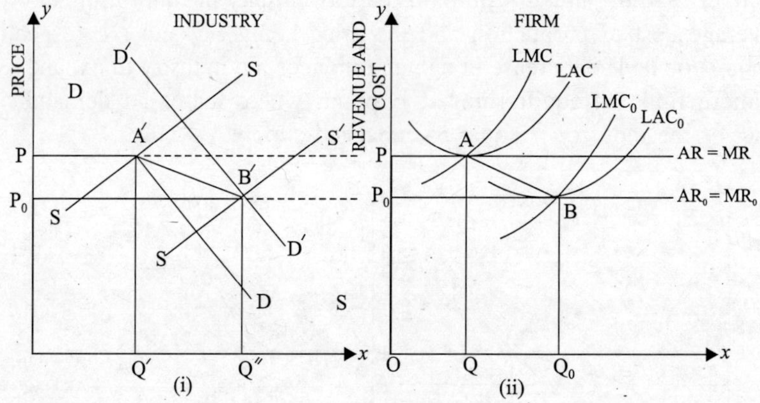

FIGURE 18.10 Firm's and Industry's Long Run Supply under Decreasing Cost.

The industry initially attains the equilibrium at *A'* point, where industry demand equals the supply. The equilibrium price is *OP* and quantity is *OQ'*. The individual firm takes this price as given and produces *OQ* quantity at an average cost of *AQ*, which also equals the price. In case the demand for the industry's output increases, it shifts the demand curve to *D'D'* level. It induces the industry to expand, which results in increased supply shifting the supply curve to *S'S'* level. It equals the new demand at *B'*, where increased quantity *OQ'* is exchanged for a lower price OP_0.

This firm also increases its output by building a bigger plant. Since the prices of the various inputs have declined, the long run average cost curve has been shifted downwards to the right from LAC to LAC_0 level, where the average cost of products at equilibrium levels has come down from AQ to BQ_0 level. The quantity produced by this single firm has increased from OQ to OQ_0. Similarly, all other firms in the industry may find it beneficial to expand the output. New firms entering into the market may also set up such plant that produces the commodity at a lower average cost.

The firm's supply curve is sloping downwards to the right from A to B indicating that the long run equilibrium output at new level is greater than the old level output. It is because of the assumption underlying a decreasing cost industry that the price of short run fixed inputs decreases relatively more than the prices of the short run variable resources. Therefore, the least-cost combination favours larger scale of plant than the old. The impact of increased output at lower average cost of all firms in the industry results in a negatively sloping long run supply curve indicating the exchange of larger quantities at lower price in long run.

Thus, the long run price is the result of the interaction of price changes in the industry and firms' responses to them in the form of their changed supplies. **The industry supply is composed of the supplies of all firms. These supply curves rest upon cost curves and, in turn, ultimately upon the theory of production is which we assume the technology to remain unchanged. This proves to be a serious limitation for the supply position of the industry in long run and renders it less useful as a basis of forecasting or policy-making as compared to the short run supply curves.**

Review Questions

1. What is meant by perfect competition? Elucidate the pricing equilibrium in short run under perfect competition.
2. Distinguish between the market price and normal price? Explain the equilibrium condition under perfect completion in long run.
3. Explain the condition for long-run equilibrium of a firm and the industry under perfect competition.
4. Why does the firm under perfect competition operate on the rising portion of its marginal cost curve? Why not on its falling portion?
5. Discuss the short-run and long-run supply curves of a firm and the industry operating in a perfectly competitive market situation.
6. Define normal profit. Why does a perfectly competitive firm normally earn normal profit in long-run?
7. Derive the long run industry supply curve with the help of cost curves of the firms under perfect competition.
8. 'Under perfect competition, a firm's average revenue and marginal revenue are equal for all levels of sales'. Discuss.

19

Pricing under Monopoly

Monopoly refers to a market situation, where a single firm controls the supply of a product without any fear of competition of very close substitutes. In other words, the term monopoly refers to the case of a single seller facing an infinitely large number of buyers and enjoying absence of competition of any kind, with complete control over supply of the product including control over entry into the market. In this chapter an effort is being made to explain the behaviour of a single seller (or the monopolist) in short run as well as long run. It is followed by the consideration of the price discrimination under monopoly.

SIMPLE OR PURE MONOPOLY

Simple or pure monopoly is that market condition, where the monopolist charges a single price for his product from all categories of buyers without any discrimination. The monopoly may arise due to: (i) grant of licence by the government to any particular firm for operating public utilities; (ii) special feature of a producer, who may possess certain scarce raw materials, patent rights, secret methods of production or specialised skill; and (iii) ignorance, laziness and prejudices of the buyers. Under such situation the single firm is considered to be an independent price-maker. However, the firm cannot charge any price it likes, because, howsoever necessary the product may be, there is a limit on its power to raise the price. It is because the consumers have only a limited income. Even if the single seller was able to force the consumers to pay as much as they could, he could never do more than take the whole of their incomes.

In case of pure monopoly, it is assumed that the monopolist is so powerful that he is always able to take the whole of incomes of all consumers, whatsoever may be the level of his output. It happens, when the demand curve or the average revenue curve of the monopolist's product is a rectangular hyperbola having unitary elastic demand throughout its length. In this sense none is full-fledged monopolist, because in the end all producers of all other goods too must be competing for the limited incomes of the consumers and as such taking the whole of the income of the consumers by a single producer (i.e., monopolist) is next to impossible. Thus, monopolist's demand curve may not be a rectangular hyperbola, but may maintain a negative slope as, in real world, the monopolist may control whole supply of only a single commodity, which has no close substitute.

Thus, a monopolist's demand curve is the demand curve for the monopolised product, which is determined by the prices of other goods, the tastes, fashion, habit and environment of buyers and incomes of the buyers.

Figure 19.1 exhibits that the monopolist cannot charge more than *OD* price, as the demand for his product at or beyond this level of price is zero, because in that case, consumers would give up consumption of the monopolist's product altogether. Thus, the monopolist can raise the price only when his product is substantially different from all other products, i.e., the value of cross elasticity of demand is zero or very nominal.

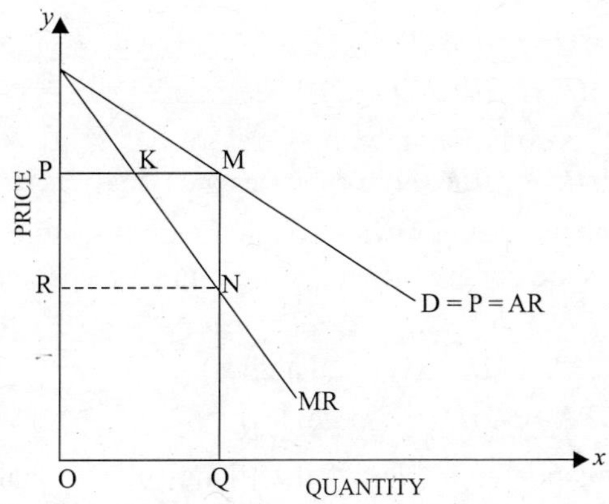

FIGURE 19.1 Relationship between Average and Marginal Revenues under Monopoly.

It also reveals that the monopolist cannot control the price of his product as well as the quantity to be sold. In case he fixes the price at *OP*, the quantity to be sold will be *OQ* and if he wants to sell a quantity more than *OQ*, he is bound to reduce the price below *OP* level. Thus, due to negative slope, the monopolist can sell only a small quantity at a high price or he can sell a larger quantity only at a lower price.

Thus, monopolist's demand curve is similar to industry demand curve under perfect competition. It is because single monopolistic firm also represents the industry. The quantity of his sale is a single valued function of price [$Q = f(P)$] and the price is single valued function of quantity [$P = f(Q)$].

Thus, while a single seller under perfect competition accepts price as a parameter and maximises the profit by varying the output, a monopolist may maximise profit varying either output or price. The monopolist cannot set both independently, since his price is determined by the level of output according to the demand for his product. Thus, the price-quantity combination, which maximises profit is invariant with respect to the choice of independent variable.

As per the relationship between average and marginal revenues (as proved earlier on pages 261–264) $MR = P(1 - 1/Ed)$.

This shows that *MR* is positive, if *Ed* > 1, zero if *Ed* = 1 and negative if *Ed* < 1. The difference between *MR* and price decreases as the elasticity of demand increases and *MR* approaches price as the elasticity of demand approaches infinity.

Thus, *MR* curve will always lie below the *AR* = *P* = *D* curve. The rate of decline of MR is twice the rate of decline of price. The Table 20.1 also explains this relationship as where the price is decreasing by ten paise the *MR* is decreasing by twenty paise for each additional unit of sale.

In Figure 19.1 the total revenue for the price–quantity combination (*OP* and *OQ*) equals the area of the rectangle *OPMQ*. It is also equal to the area covered under the *MR* curve *ODNQ*, because the sum of all the marginal revenues produced by the sale of *OQ* units is also equal to the total revenue. Thus,

$$OPMQ = ODNQ$$

$$OPKNQ + NMK = OPKNQ + DPK$$

Since *OPKNQ* is common in both, therefore,

$$MNK = DPK \text{ (both triangles are equal)}$$

Since *DKN* line has been drawn through the mid-point of *PM*, therefore, the above two triangles are congruent (i.e., similar in all respects) because:

$$PK = KM$$

$$DKP = MKN \text{ (vertical angles)}$$

$$DPK = KMN \text{ (right angles)}$$

Thus, the corresponding sides of the triangles are equal (i.e., *DP* = *MN*). The slope of price curve is *DP*/*PM* (= *RN* = *OQ*) but of the *MR* curve is *DP* + *MN* (= *DR*/*RN* (= *OQ*). Since *DP* = *MN*, therefore, the slope of *MR* curve is twice of the slope of the *AR* = *D* = *P* curve. When *AR* = *D* = *P* is linear, the *MR* curve may be drawn from the origin of the average revenue curve *D* through the mid-point of any perpendicular line drawn from average revenue curve up to the vertical axis.

Monopolist's Objectives

Monopolist, like the seller under perfect competition, is also activated by the objective of maximisation of net revenue or minimisation of net loss. This is attained at the point, where *MR* = *MC*. However, whether the firm if maximising its net revenue or minimising its net loss, depends on the relationship between the price and the average cost of production for the given output.

Thus, the equilibrium condition and profit condition under monopoly is similar to that under perfect competition. The difference lies with the degrees of control over prices under the two market situations. The firm, due to atomistic competition amongst a large number of buyers and sellers under perfect competition, accepts the price in the market as an external fact, therefore, it faces a demand curve, which is a straight line parallel to the horizontal axis. However, the single seller under monopoly can influence the price by his own actions, and therefore, the demand curve for his product slopes downwards to the right.

Monopolist's Equilibrium in Short Run

The equilibrium of the monopolist is ascertained at the point, where the equilibrium condition (i.e., $MR = MC$) is satisfied. It can be analysed assuming (a) a costless product and (b) with cost product.

Costless Product

In case, the monopolist is selling a costless commodity (e.g., water from a mineral spring or a bye product), which involves no cost of production, the total average and marginal costs will be zero and will be exhibited along with the horizontal axis. The monopolist's equilibrium will be at the point, where declining marginal revenue curve intersects the horizontal axis, because at this point it will be equal to the marginal cost which, in turn, is equal to zero.

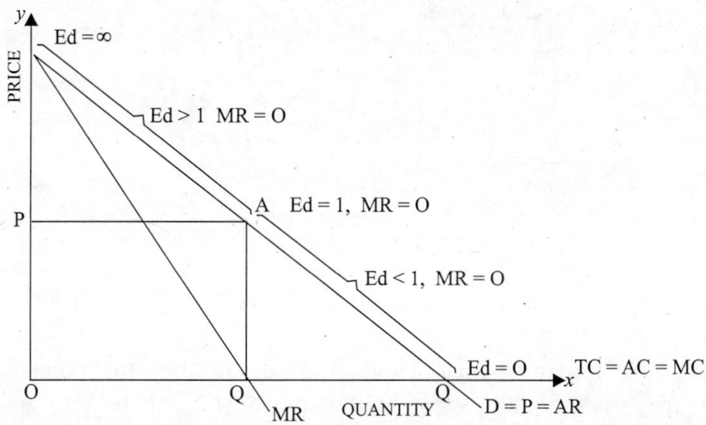

FIGURE 19.2 Costless Product to be Sold at some Price under Monopoly.

The monopolist would be maximising his net revenue (OPAQ) by selling *OQ* quantity of the commodity at *OP* price, because at this level of sale $MR = MC = 0$. In case the sale is increased beyond *OQ* level, it would reduce his net revenue, because *MR* will be < 0. On the other hand, if less than *OQ* quantity is sold, $MR > 0$ which, indicates the possibility of increasing net revenue by increasing sales. Had there been perfect competition, the condition $P = AR = MR = MC$ would have been satisfied and the equilibrium would have been at Q' point, where higher quantity would have been made available by all sellers at zero price, because there is no cost of production.

With Cost Product

In real world, generally, commodities involve some cost of production i.e., total, average and marginal costs command some positive value. Under such situation the monopolist will be in equilibrium at the point, where the marginal revenue is equal to the marginal cost of production as follows:

The short run marginal cost (*SMC*) is equal to the marginal revenue (*MR*) at point *E*, which is equilibrium point of monopolist in short run. By drawing a perpendicular from this point between price or average revenue curve and the horizontal axis, we can ascertain equilibrium quantity *OQ*, equilibrium price *QP'* = *OP* and average cost of production *QC'* = *OC*. The total revenue and total cost being *OPP'Q* and *OCC'Q* respectively, the net revenue at the equilibrium level of sale is *CPP'C'*.

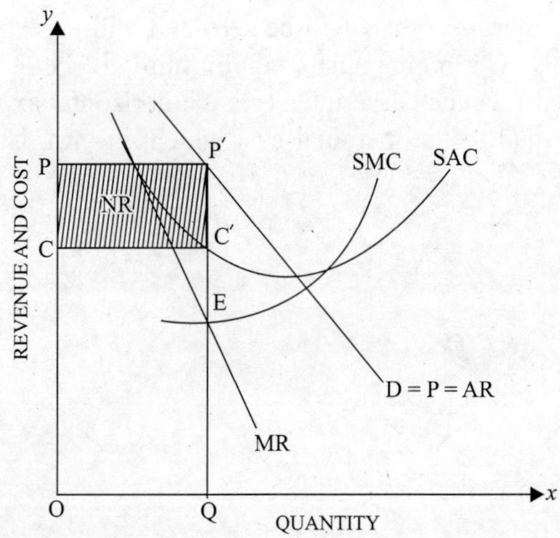

FIGURE 19.3 With Cost Product Sold at a Price Containing Net Revenue.

This is the maximum net revenue, because if the monopolist increases the output, the additional cost of production (*SMC*) will be greater than the additional revenue (*MR*), which will reduce net revenue already accumulated at *OQ* level of sale. Generally, a monopolist with no close substitutes of his product should be able to keep the price of his product equal to or more than its short run average cost, but a monopolist suffering losses in the short run is also not an impossibility and he will also minimise losses by remaining in production provided *P* > *AVC*.

It is possible for the monopolist to make a greater than normal profit at greater than, equal to or less than economic capacity output, although under perfect competition, it is possible only at greater than economic capacity output. It is because of the difference in the slope of the marginal revenue and average revenue (price) curves under both market conditions.

Under perfect competition, the marginal cost must be increasing one at or near the equilibrium level, but the firm under monopoly may be in equilibrium with rising, falling and constant marginal costs alike.

Figure 19.4(i) indicates that the equilibrium under monopoly is similar to that under perfect competition, as the rising marginal cost equals the marginal revenue at E, which determines the equilibrium price ($OP = QP'$), quantity (Q) and the maximum amount of net revenue. ($PC\ C'P'$)

Figure 19.4(ii) reveals a constant marginal cost, which equals the average cost. This condition is incompatible with equilibrium under perfect competition. In case the firm could afford to produce at such cost, there would be no limit to its size, because $AR = MR$ and $AC = MC$ will be parallel to horizontal axis. However, under monopoly, the equilibrium in such situation is established at E point, where the quantity sold is OQ, price OP and the maximum net revenue $PCEP'$.

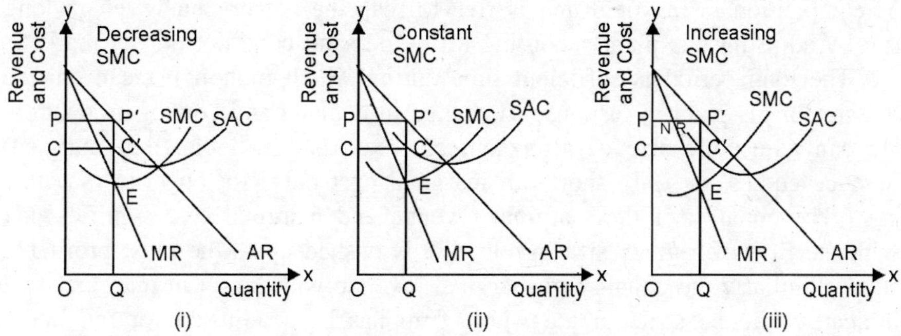

FIGURE 19.4 Monopolists Managing Net Revenue under All Cost Conditions.

Under monopoly it is also possible to attain equilibrium even though the marginal cost curve is falling provided that its decrease is less rapid than the decrease in marginal revenue, otherwise the marginal cost curve will never intersect the marginal revenue curve. Figure 19.4(i) shows that the falling marginal cost is equal to marginal revenue at E, where the firm sells OQ quantity at $OP = QP'$ price obtaining net revenue equal to $CPP'C'$.

For **an equilibrium it is necessary for the marginal cost to be greater than the marginal revenue at levels of output greater than the equilibrium level output and for the marginal cost to be less than the marginal revenue for the output less than the equilibrium level output.** In case this condition is satisfied, the marginal net revenue will be positive at output less than equilibrium level, which will induce the firm to expand the output and it will be negative at output greater than the equilibrium level, which will induce a contraction of output.

The price, determined under monopoly, is not the highest price, as all prices to the left of the equilibrium price on the average revenue (or demand) curve will be higher. Although at such prices he will sell less and will reap a smaller net profit. Secondly, monopoly price is often associated with an output, the average cost of which is still falling, as the marginal cost curve often cuts the marginal revenue curve to the left of the point of minimum average cost. Thirdly, unlike under perfect competition, the monopoly price is always more than the marginal cost. The marginal cost curve, which performs functions of supply curve (which is portion of the marginal cost curve that lies above the average variable cost) of the firm under perfect competition performs no such function for the monopolist firm.

Monopolist's Equilibrium in Long Run

The existence of monopoly in the long run requires that the entry into industry be blocked and for this the monopolist may control the sources of raw materials necessary for the production of his product or hold certain patents that prevent other firms from duplicating his product. Thus, he will be free from the threat of competition in his field and is free to reap the net revenue even in long run by adjusting his plant according to the demand condition in the market.

The long period is sufficient time during which monopolist can change the size of his plant in response to change in demand and cost of production. He can adjust the size of all resources, fixed and variable, that marginal revenue equals not only short run marginal cost but also long run marginal cost. The equality of the marginal revenue and marginal cost signifies that with the firm of a given size, production is pushed up to the most profitable stage. Similarly the equality of marginal revenue with long run marginal cost indicates that the scale of the whole firm has been adjusted for maximum profit to the monopolist.

On the basis of the demand and cost conditions in long run, the monopolist may build: (i) a less than optimum scale of plant; (ii) an optimum scale of plant; or (iii) a greater than optimum scale of plant as follows:

(i) Since, the long run marginal cost curve intersects each short run marginal cost curve at one point, but not necessarily at the minimum point of the long run average cost curve, a monopolist may produce in the long run an output less than that produced at the long run economic capacity point and may make a greater than normal profit in the process. The precise location of the monopolist's equilibrium on the long run average cost curve depends on the demand for his product.

Figure 19.5 indicates a long run equilibrium of the monopolist, when he builds a plant to use it at sub-optimum level. This happens, when the monopolist faces a very limited market so that his marginal revenue curve intersects the long run average cost curve to the left of the economic capacity point. The equilibrium is established at *E*, where the marginal revenue (*MR*) curve intersects both the long run marginal cost (*LMC*) and the short run marginal cost (*SMC*) curves.

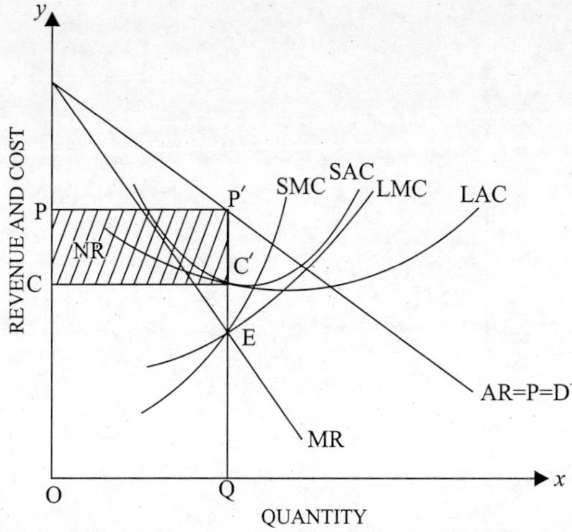

FIGURE 19.5 Long Run Equilibrium under Decreasing Cost Situation.

At the equilibrium level, the monopolist sells *OQ* quantity at *OP* (or *QP*') price, which has been produced at an average cost of *OC* (or *QC*'). This leaves the maximum amount of net profit covered by an area *CPP'C'*.

(ii) In case the monopolist's demand and cost conditions are such that allow him in long run to make greater than normal profit, while producing at the least average cost of production, the marginal revenue (*MR*) curve will intersect the long run average cost (*LAC*) at its minimum point. Thus, the monopolist will build such a plant, which will be operated at its optimum capacity. At this very point the marginal revenue curve will intersect the short run average cost (*SAC*), long run marginal cost (*LMC*), and short run marginal cost (*SMC*) curves. Thus, excepting the average revenue or price, the marginal revenue equals all other functions in the long run.

The conditions are met at point *E* (Figure 19.6) at which monopolist produces *OQ* quantity at an average cost *OC* (or *QE*) and the equilibrium price being *OP* (or *QP*') he obtains a net revenue equal to *CPP'E*.

(iii) In case the market for the product of the monopolist is very large, the marginal revenue (*MR*) curve will intersect the long run average cost (*LAC*) curve to the right of its minimum (or economic capacity) point, when he builds such a plant, which will operate at greater than optimum scale.

The monopolist's equilibrium is at point *E*, where *MR* = *LMC* = *SMC*. The equilibrium output is *OQ* obtained at an average cost of *OC* = *QC*' and sold at a price of *OP* = *QP*', which leaves *CPP'C*' as net revenue for the monopolist.

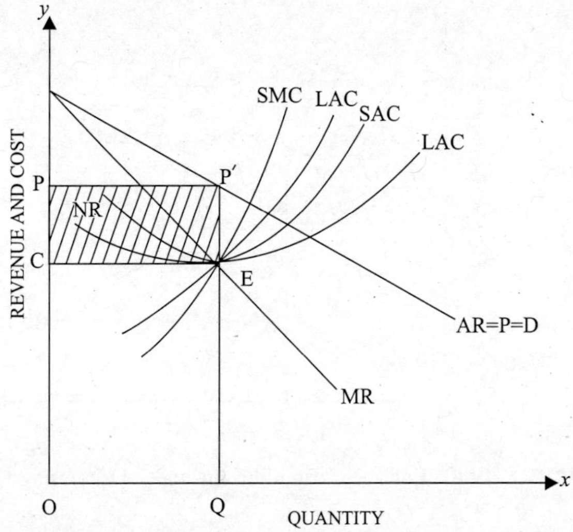

FIGURE 19.6 Long Run Equilibrium under Constant Cost Situation.

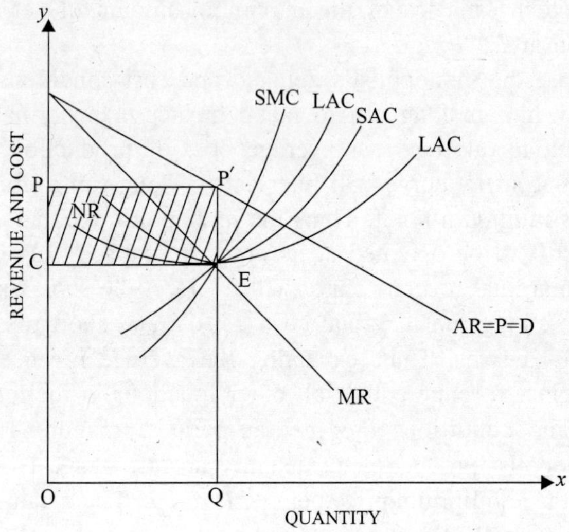

FIGURE 19.7 Long Run Equilibrium under Increasing Cost Situation.

Thus, in the long run, the monopolist will operate at the optimum or at less or greater than optimum capacity level. The most common scale of operation is optimum or greater than optimum capacity scale, yet in many under-developed countries newly started capital goods industries (i.e., machine tools, etc.) or costly consumer goods industries (i.e., cars, television sets, etc.) enjoying monopoly status, operate less than optimum capacity due to insufficient demand.

The monopolist, operating at optimum or at less or greater than optimum capacity, will obtain net revenue even in the long run. It is because of his power to restrict output and to equate marginal cost with marginal revenue and not with price. In case he produces more goods for the society, the price would come down and the net profit would disappear. Thus, the monopolist does not produce sufficient quantity of goods just for generating monopoly profits.

Social Cost of Monopoly

The monopoly involves certain cost to the society, as the monopolist's interest lies with earning the net revenue or profit and has a little care for volume of production or cost of production. The monopolist, while selling a costless commodity, restricts the output to a minimum level to charge some price from the buyers with a view to maximising net revenue, although under perfect competition such a commodity will fetch zero price with no limit to the quantity of sale. Similarly, in case of with-cost commodity, the monopolist's equilibrium will be at such a level where he commands net profit, whether he produces at optimum scale or at less or greater than optimum scale in the short run or in the long run. Thus, the monopolist is always after his monopoly profit. **Even if he stands ready to sacrifice the monopoly profit, and remains satisfied with normal profits only, the monopoly is undesirable from the point of view of the society, because the average cost will be greater than the minimum average cost of production.**

According to Figure 19.8, the equilibrium is fixed at *E* point, where he sells OQ_m quantity at OP_m price, produce at an average cost equal to $OP_m = Q_mP'$, where gets only normal profit. Since the demand curve facing the monopolist slopes downwards to the right, it reveals that when monopolist is making only normal profit, he must be producing on the declining part of the long run average cost curve. A downwards sloping average revenue curve can never be tangent to a U-shaped average cost curve at or beyond its lowest point. The monopolist's production at P' point reveals that an increase in output will be followed by a reduction in the average cost of production. Under perfect competition, production may be at *A* (i.e., minimum cost) point on the long run average cost (*LAC*) curve, where the greater quantity OQ_c will be produced at lower cost Q_cA *and made available for sale at* OP_c price. The monopolist will never produce this quantity, because at this level of output due to a lower price, he will suffer a loss equal to $KMAP_c$. Thus, in order to save himself from this loss, the monopolist will produce only OQ_m quantity at a cost of $OP_m = Q_mP'$. Thus, the society will get less quantity of commodity for consumption and that too would be produced at a higher cost or production. It indicates that under monopoly the resources of the society are wasted, therefore, it is undesirable.

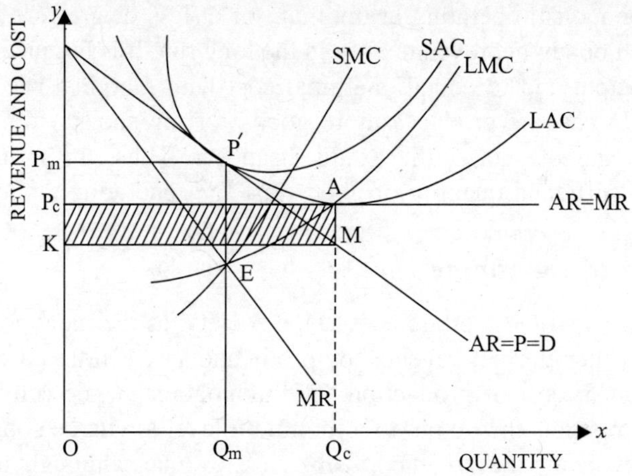

FIGURE 19.8 Cost of Monopoly to the Society.

Degrees of Monopoly Power

It refers to the amount of discretion possessed by a seller or monopolist, which governs him in formulating his policy regarding the output and price of his product and the differentiation of his product by the quantity and service. In other words, monopoly power indicates the scope of deviation from competition behaviour. Its measurement depends on the difference between the price and the marginal cost of the production of the monopolist.

Since the monopolist's marginal revenue curve will always lie below the average revenue curve and since at equilibrium the marginal revenue equals the marginal cost, it follows that in equilibrium marginal cost is less than price. The size of this difference between the marginal cost and price is generally used to measure the extent of the firm's monopoly power as follows:

$$\text{Monopoly power} = \frac{\text{Price} - \text{Marginal Cost}}{\text{Price}}$$

Under perfect competition, since at equilibrium, the marginal cost equals the price, therefore, monopoly power is zero. In case the monopolised product is a free (i.e., costless) commodity, the marginal cost equals zero and the value of monopoly power is unity (= 1). Thus, it varies between zero to unity.

This gap between marginal cost and price will depend ultimately on the elasticity of demand on the demand or average revenue or price curve of firm's product. The relationship of average revenue (or price) with marginal revenue, as stated earlier, is expressed as $MR = P\ (1 - 1/Ed)$, which can be rewritten as $MR = P\ (ED - 1/Ed)$

$$\text{Since monopoly power} = \frac{P - MR}{P}$$

$$= \frac{P - P(Ed - 1/Ed)}{P} \qquad \text{Since } MR = P\left(1 - \frac{1}{Ed}\right) = P\left(Ed - \frac{1}{Ed}\right)$$

$$= \frac{P}{P} - \frac{P}{P}\frac{(Ed-1)}{Ed}$$

$$= 1 - 1\frac{(Ed-1)}{Ed}$$

$$= 1 - \frac{(Ed-1)}{Ed} \qquad \text{(After multiplication by 1)}$$

$$= \frac{Ed - Ed + 1}{Ed} \qquad \text{(After removal of the bracket)}$$

$$= \frac{1}{Ed}$$

Thus, the monopoly power varies inversely with the elasticity of demand of the product. In other words, greater the elasticity of demand lesser is the monopoly power and vice-versa. Since the value of the monopoly power will vary between zero to one; it indicates that for inelastic demand this calculation of the value of monopoly power will not be applicable, as the value will exceed one. Moreover, a monopolist will never fix the price of his product at a level, where the elasticity of demand on the average revenue curve is less than one, because at that level, the marginal revenue of the monopolist will be negative. Thus, monopolist may go up to the level of output, where the value of elasticity of demand is equal to one to ascertain the equilibrium position, provided the product is free of cost, because at the level the marginal revenue and the marginal cost both will be zero. Since in real world, marginal cost is likely to be positive, the monopolist will have an equilibrium output, where his marginal revenue is positive (or $Ed > 1$).

A second indication of the monopoly power is the size of the net profit the monopolist is able to earn. Under perfect competition in long run, firms will not be able to earn more than normal profit, because in that case competitors will enter into the industry. In monopoly, there is normally no fear of competition, but at certain level of profit, new firms may find it worth taking the risk of trying to break the monopoly. The stronger the monopolist's position, the greater the profit he will be able to earn without attracting rivals and the greater will be his monopoly power.

DISCRIMINATING MONOPOLY

It refers to the market condition, where the monopolist practices price discrimination for selling its product. **Price discrimination refers to the practice of selling different units of certain product to different buyers at different prices. This concept may be reasonably extended to include a seller's practice of charging different prices from different buyers for**

different varieties of the same good, if the price differences are not the same as or proportional to the differences in the cost of producing these varieties of the goods. Thus, it may appear in various guises.

The price discrimination may be based on: (i) the size of purchase, such as, difference between rates for domestic and power connections for electricity or between wholesale and retail prices; (ii) the location of the buyers, e.g. rural-urban, one country and the other; (iii) the income of the consumers, e.g. lawyers use to charge a higher fee from the rich than from the poor for the same kind of service; (iv) the time, e.g. doctors may charge higher fees for visiting patients in the night than in the day; and (v) the age and the type of service, e.g. railways charge less fare for children than for adults or more fare from first/AC class passengers than from the second class passengers.

Pre-conditions for Price Discrimination

Price discrimination, which is possible only under monopoly, requires certain conditions to exist in the market. The market should be distinctly divisible into the various segments and the exchange of the products among the buyers should not be possible. A successful and profitable price discrimination also requires different degrees of the elasticity of demand in different market segments. Besides this the price discrimination may be practiced because of the following reasons:

(i) **Consumers' Peculiarities:** Some times, ignorance and irrational behaviour of the consumers make it possible for the monopolist to practice price discrimination. Thus, it is possible, where consumers in one part of the market are unaware that the prices are lower in another part of the market or it can exist, where the consumers have an irrational feeling that they are paying higher prices for a good because of its quality, although it may be of the same quality. Sometimes, the price difference may be so small that consumers do not consider it worthwhile to bother about such differences.

(ii) **Nature of the Goods:** It also makes the price discrimination possible particularly when the goods in question is a direct service, such as, that of doctors, advocates, etc. because its re-sale is not possible.

(iii) **Distances or Tariff Barriers:** The price discrimination is also practiced, where consumers are separated by distances or by national frontier, which puts tariff barriers. In case the monopolist serves a home market with a tariff and a world market without tariff, he can charge higher price in protected home market and a lower price abroad to capture greater part of the world market.

Degrees of Price Discrimination

Discrimination is designed to gain revenue by varying the price in terms of the demand prices of the customers. The extent to which a monopolist can go in charging varying prices for his product from the various customers, helps in ascertaining the following three degrees of price discrimination:

(1) First Degree Discrimination: In this case the monopolist implicitly charges each buyer the highest price each stands ready to pay for different units of any commodity. Thus, he makes the buyer pay all that he wishes under the threat of being denied the commodity altogether, for any quantity, which the seller decides to supply to him. The monopolist makes different bargain with each potential buyer specifying both the quantity the buyer can receive of the commodity and the total amount of money he must pay for it. Figure 19.9(i) explains the first degree discrimination, which is also known as perfect discrimination.

The monopolist is supposed to know the maximum amount of money the buyers of different units stand ready to pay. He, then, charges the price accordingly and thereby leaving no portion of consumers' surplus with the buyers. It is obvious that with perfect discrimination, the demand schedule of the buyer effectively becomes a marginal receipt schedule of the seller, showing the added receipts obtainable for each addition to the quantity supplied.

(2) Second Degree Discrimination: It is practiced by the monopolist, who sets different prices for different categories of customers, where those willing to pay more than the higher price are charged only that price and the customers willing to pay more than the lower price but less than the higher price will be charged only lower price. For example, a doctor may charge higher fees for examining the patient at latter's residence, while he may charge lower fees for the same work at his dispensary. Those, who call the doctor to their respective places must be willing to pay more than the higher fees but those who come to the dispensary are willing to pay less than the higher fees (otherwise they would have called the doctor to their residences) but certainly more than the lower fees (otherwise they would have gone to some other cheaper doctor).

Figure 19.9(ii) reveals that the monopolist has set two prices *OP* and OP_0 for his product. As per the demand curve, the buyers of *OQ* quantity of the commodity are willing to pay more than *OP* price but they are charged only *OP* price, which leaves the *DPA* consumer's surplus at the disposal of the buyers. Similarly, the buyers of QQ_1 quantity of the commodity are willing to pay less than *OP* price but more than OP_0 price and they are charged only OP_0 price, leaving *ABC* amount of consumer's surplus at their disposal. The schedule of rates typically charged by public utilities (i.e., Railways, Electricity Companies) may be regarded as the typical form of second degree discrimination.

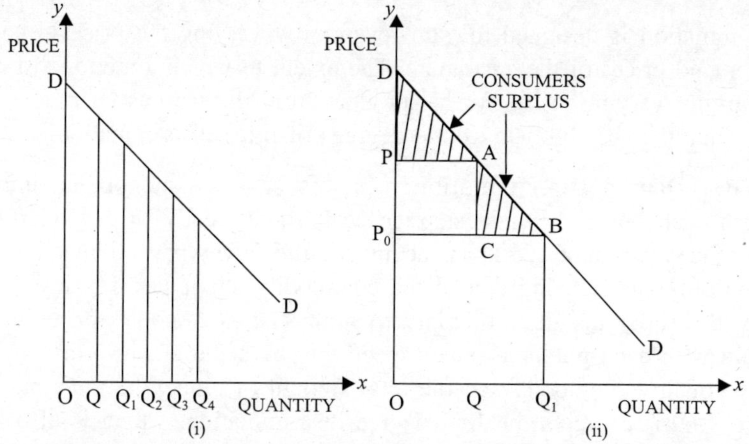

FIGURE 19.9 Degrees of Price Discrimination by the Monopolist.

(3) Third Degree Discrimination: It is the most common type of the price discrimination, where the monopolist sets two or more market prices to be charged from two or more separate groups of buyers of the same commodity. Each of the above groups represents markets and the monopolist attempts to benefit from the differences in the elasticities of demand for the product in those markets, as he charges a relatively higher price in a market with less elastic demand and a lower price in the market with an elastic demand.

In case the monopolist wants to maximise the profit or minimise the loss, it must make the marginal cost of the total output sold in both markets equal to the marginal revenue in each of the two markets. Thus,

$$MC = MR_1 = MR_2$$

Since the relationship between the marginal revenue and price is such, where $MR = P\ (1 — 1/Ed)$, therefore,

$$MC = MR_1 = P_1\ (1 — 1/Ed_1) = MR_2 = P_2\ (1 — 1/Ed_2)$$

Assuming that the elasticity of demand in the first market is 10 ($Ed = 10$) and in the second market it is 4 ($Ed_2 = 4$), if we substitute these values, we have

$$MC = MR_1 = .9P_1 = MR_2 = .75P_2$$

Thus, if the marginal cost of production is assumed to be ₹ 9 the price in the first market will be ₹ 10, but the same in the second market, will be ₹ 12. This can be exhibited as follows:

Thus, the monopolist, on the basis of the price elasticity of demand, for the product, has divided his total market into two sub-markets, where AR_1 is the average revenue curve and MR_1 is the marginal revenue curve in the first market and AR_2 and MR_2 are the average revenue and the marginal revenue

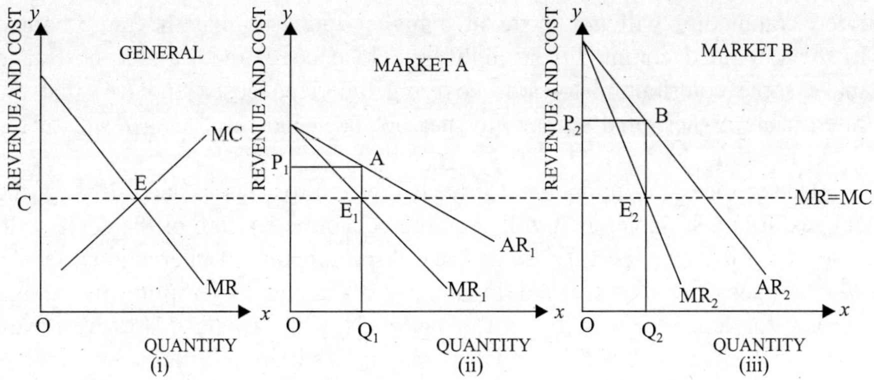

FIGURE 19.10 Multi-Market Price Discrimination by the Monopolist.

curves respectively in the second market. In general, the marginal cost curve for his total product equals his aggregate marginal revenue curve at *OC* level. The marginal cost will equal the respective marginal revenues at the same level in both markets. So the equilibrium in the first market is at E_1, where the monopolist sells OQ_1 quantity at OP_1 price. The flat slope of the average revenue curve (i.e., price or demand curve) indicates a high degree of price elasticity and consequently lower price in the first market. The equilibrium in the second market is at E_2, where the monopolist sells OQ_2 quantity at OP_2 price. A steep slope of the average revenue curve indicates low degree of elasticity and consequently a higher price in the second market.

Thus, under the third degree discrimination buyers will be charged two or more prices and any individual buyer will have no option to buy at a price lower than set for him by the discriminating monopolist. Secondly, his net revenue under price discrimination will be higher than that under simple monopoly (i.e., single price) for all sub-market, because then only he can equalise marginal receipts in the various sub-market. Thirdly, the total output supplied to the various markets may be the same as or more or less than that supplied under simple monopoly, which depends on the slopes of the various sub-market curves and also on whether the discrimination leads to supply a sub-market not supplied at all under simple monopoly pricing.

Fourthly, the prices will tend to be higher in sub-markets, where demand is less elastic and vice-versa, but its discrimination leads to an output extension with decreasing average and marginal costs, all market may have lower prices and be supplied with larger outputs than under single monopoly pricing. Finally, sometimes the practice of charging higher price to one group of buyers and lower price to another for the same goods, is viewed as unethical and unjust, but it is justifiable in case of public utilities, where large fixed facilities are already in existence and would, otherwise, go underutilised except for the practice of price discrimination. Railway freights are good example, which may prove to be beneficial to the society provided (i) that the low-rated commodity will not move at a higher rate; (ii) that the rate charged to the low-rated commodity is high enough to cover the variable costs and make some contribution towards covering the fixed costs, and (iii) that the rate on the higher-rated commodity has not been increased as a result of the discrimination.

Under price discrimination, if price is lowered for masses and raised for the classes, it is justifiable, as it will promote economic welfare of the society. In case of dumping (a special case of price discrimination at international level), where higher price is charged in home market and lower price in foreign market, foreigners gain at the cost of nationals of the country. However, even under such situation the discrimination may be justifiable, if the industry obeys the law of increasing returns, because the society will get larger output at lower cost of production. The dumping may be justified, if practiced to; (a) dispose of an over-stock casually produced due to wrong judgment about demand; (b) develop new trade connections by charging low prices; (c) drive competitors out of the foreign market; and (d) reap the benefit of a large-scale production.

Review Questions

1. What is monopoly? How does a monopoly firm attain equilibrium under different cost conditions?
2. What is meant by the concept of price discrimination under monopoly? Discuss the various types of price discrimination.
3. Suggest a measure for the 'degree of monopoly power'. What forces limit the pure monopolist's market power?
4. How price is determined under monopoly? The monopolists never determine his price-output combination in the range, where the elasticity of demand is less than one.
5. What is a discriminating monopoly? Under what conditions is price discrimination possible and profitable?
6. How is the monopolist's equilibrium determined in the long run? Elucidate the social cost of monopoly?
7. 'A monopolist is not free to determine both price and quantity to be sold according to his whims and fancy.' Explain.

20

Pricing under Duopoly and Oligopoly

In between the two extremes, viz. perfect competition and monopoly, certain real world situations also exist, where the number of sellers in a market is two or greater than two but less than their large numbers. Such situation usually involves relaxing one or the other conditions of the perfect competition or monopoly and introducing some conditions from the other extreme into the problem. Solutions of such problems are widely divergent, because competition between the two sellers (under duopoly) or amongst a few sellers (under oligopoly), may result in a monopoly price, competitive price, a determinate price in between the two or a perpetually oscillating price between the two extremes.

In this chapter, an effort is being made to analyse the case of duopoly, where there are two sellers of the identical product, facing a large number of buyers, as per the various models developed by economists. It is to be followed by the discussion of oligopoly, which is the case of a few sellers i.e., more than two but less than large number of sellers selling a single product or products that are close substitutes. We come across two types of oligopoly, viz. pure oligopoly, where all the sellers sell perfectly homogeneous products and differentiated oligopoly, where they sell non-homogeneous or differentiated products. In respect of both these types of oligopoly, there are different models for price-output determination, like cournot's independent pricing model, price leadership model, game theory model, collusive pricing model and price rigidity model.

EQUILIBRIUM UNDER DUOPOLY

It is a market situation, where there are only two firms producing and selling identical products. In this case, we assume that there is sale of perfectly homogenous products and all buyers and sellers are in full communication with each other. It is also assumed that there is complete independence of the two firms, that is, there is no actual or tacit agreement and each firm is forced by the situation to take into account the policy of its rival in determining its own policy. Since under duopoly there are only two firms producing and selling identical goods, any price or output change by one firm is bound to affect the other, whose reactions will, in turn, change the position of the first and so on.

The duopolists (the sellers or the firms under duopoly) must recognise that the rival's policy of price and output is not constant, but is determined in part by his own policy and in part by the policy followed by the rival. It means that he considers the indirect consequences of his own acts (i.e., the effect on himself of his own policy). Sometimes, the seller determines his policy under the assumption that his rival is unaffected by what he does and thus, takes into account only the direct influence, which he has upon the price. Sometimes he considers his total (i.e., direct as well as indirect) influence upon the price. Lastly, it is also assumed that the policy of the duopolist's rival may remain fixed with respect either to the quantity he offers to sell or to the price at which he offers the product.

Difference in the assumptions have given rise to different duopoly models. Some of the models assume that in deciding his price-output policy, duopolist does not take into account the possible reaction, which his rival may have to his actions. **It is termed as zero conjectural variation, which is used to designate the extent to which one seller takes into account the effect of his own actions upon his rival's actions.** Sometimes the duopolist assumes that his rival's supply will remain constant and in certain other circumstances he assumes that his rival's price will remain unchanged. Certain models are also based on the assumption of the mutual dependence. These are as follows:

Cournot's Model

The first solution to the duopoly problem has been suggested by the French Economist, Augustin Cournot in the year 1838. This oldest formal model is based on the assumptions that (i) there are only two independent firms; (ii) each firm produces and sells the products, which are perfect substitutes for each other; (iii) the product is perishable and cannot be stored; (iv) there are a large number of knowledgeable buyers of the product; (v) each duopolist knows the market demand curve for the product; (vi) the two duopolists have identical cost curves and the cost of production is assumed to be zero; (vii) the duopolist will determine the supply during a period, which will remain unchanged; (viii) neither of the two duopolists sets the price for his output, but each accepts the price at which the total planned output can be sold; (ix) each duopolist seeks to maximise his net revenue; and (x) the duopolists are aware of the mutual interdependence of their output plans, but each is quite ignorant of the direction and the magnitude of the revision in his rival's plan, that would be induced by any change in his own plan, therefore, each duopolist assumes that irrespective of the output plan that he implements in any period t_{+1} his rival will maintain his output at the same level, as in period t.

Cournot conceived of the problem, supposing each duopolist to determine the supply, which is most profitable to himself in the light of his rival's present offering and assuming it not to change. He assumed existence of two mineral springs, exploited by their two owners without incurring any cost of production and both supplying to the same market. The demand curve for the mineral water is supposed to be a straight line *DB* and that *OA* = *AB* is the daily output of each spring. In case the total possible output is supplied to the market, the price will be exactly zero and if both combine, they would supply jointly a quantity equal to *OA*, at price *AP* and will share equally joint maximum profit equal to *OAPC* = (*OCYZ* + *YPAZ*). Assuming that the first duopolist is temporarily a monopolist, who sells the entire possible output *OA* at *AP* = *OC* price, because at this level of sale $MR_1 = MC = O$ (as the total, average and marginal cost of mineral spring is zero). His total or net profit (as it is costless commodity) is equal to *OAPC*. Now the second duopolist enters the market and finds that the first duopolist is already selling *OA* units in the market. Assuming that the first one will keep on selling *OA* units, he may regard *PB* segment of the total demand curve as the demand curve for his product. On the basis of his demand curve, his marginal revenue MR_2 equals the marginal cost at point *H* (where $MR_2 = MC = 0$). He will accordingly produce AH (i.e., ½ *AB*) units, which will be sold in the market at *HQ* = *ON* price. The former monopolist and now duopolist will be bound to reduce the price to this level, otherwise he will lose the market. Thus, the total quantity offered for sale will be *OA* + *AH* (= *OH*) and total net revenue is *OHQN* shared by both duopolists, where the former will get *ONWA* and the latter duopolist will get *A HQW*.

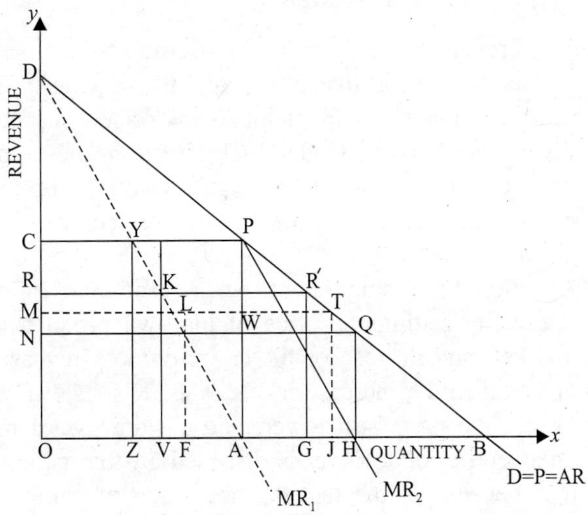

FIGURE 20.1 Cournot's Model Deciding the Share of Each Duopolist in the Market.

The entrance of the second duopolist will induce the first to re-appraise his output policy, as he is no more in a position to maximise his net revenue. Assuming that the second duopolist will keep on selling *AH* units in the market, he can increase the profit by reducing the output to ½ (*OB*—*AH*) = *OF*. This may induce the second duopolist to recast his output policy and may produce 1/2 (*OB*—*OF*) = *FJ* rendering the total supply in the market equal to *OF* + *FJ* = *OJ* which is being sold in the market at *JT* = *OM* price. This process will continue—the first duopolist being forced gradually by the moves of his rival to reduce his output and the second duopolist being enabled slowly to increase his output—until the total output by both becomes equal to *OG* shared by the two duopolists equally. In this process, each duopolist will find his maximum profit at the output equal to 1/2 (*OB* minus output of the other).

Total output under duopoly will be:

$$OB\ (1 - 1/2 + 1/4 - 1/8 + 1/16 - 1/32\ldots) = 2/3 \times OB = OG$$

The output of first duopolist will be:

$$OB\ (1 - 1/2 - 1/8 - 1/32 - 1/128 + \ldots) = 1/3 \times OB (= ½ \ . \ OG) = OV$$

The output of second duopolist will be:

$$OB(1/4 + 1/16 + 1/64\ldots) = 1/3 \times OB\ (= 1/2 \times OG)VG$$

Thus, the ultimate equilibrium position would be reached, when the amount offered by both sellers was equal to n/n_{+1} times the competitive output *OB* (here *MR* = *MC* = 0); where n is the number of sellers and the quantity offered by each seller individually would be half of this quantity.

Bertrand and Edgeworth's Model

In 1883, another French Economist Joseph Bertrand developed a different model based on the assumption that each duopolist, having unlimited output, would believe that the other would maintain his price constant, irrespective of the action taken by the rival. Under such situation, the competitive price would be charged and the competitive output would be produced, because rivals would simply engage in a price war until the competitive equilibrium position is attained.

In case each duopolist assumes that the price of his rival's product will not change, he can, by setting the price of his own product slightly lower, command the market, and dispose of his entire output, increasing his profits virtually in proportion to the increase in his sales. His rival making the same assumption, will cut the price still lower, and the downward movement will continue until their entire joint output is disposed of, that is, until the price is exactly zero. It is because of the fact that the result of competition amongst the two duopolists would be exactly the same as amongst many sellers, since either would lower his price until all his supply was sold.

F.Y. Edgeworth in 1897 made a refinement in the model suggested by Joseph Bertrand by modifying the assumption of unlimited supply of the product. He assumed that the total supply of both the duopolists is limited in such a way as to make it impossible for either duopolist to satisfy the entire demand at a lower price level.

Thus, he fixed a lower limit below which the price would not fall. He stated that there will be an indeterminate tract through which the index of the value will oscillate or rather vibrate irregularly for an indefinite length of time, between the monopoly price and the lower limit. It is because, when it reaches the lower limit, either of the two duopolists can raise it again. This model also assumes zero conjectural variation.

Edgeworth has assumed that the entire market is divided evenly between the two duopolists. Assuming the sale of a costless commodity, *RC* and *RC'* are the two demand lines for their products and *OB* and *OB'* the maximum possible output of the two duopolists, MR_1 and MR_2 are the marginal revenue curves of the two duopolists respectively and *OP* is the price, which would be set, when they combined (and behaved as monopolist) and *OQ* is the price, which will dispose of the entire output *BB'* (made of *OB* output of the first duopolist and *OB'* output of the second duopolist).

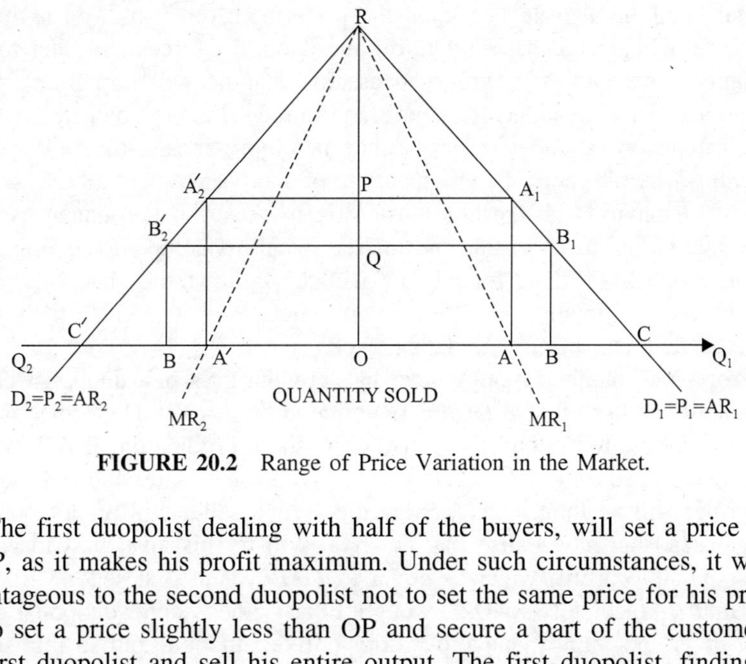

FIGURE 20.2 Range of Price Variation in the Market.

The first duopolist dealing with half of the buyers, will set a price equal to *OP*, as it makes his profit maximum. Under such circumstances, it will be advantageous to the second duopolist not to set the same price for his product but to set a price slightly less than OP and secure a part of the customers of the first duopolist and sell his entire output. The first duopolist, finding that his customers are deserting him, will lower his price and this process will continue till the price comes down to *OQ* level, where both are selling their entire output.

Realising rival's inability to raise the supply beyond *OB'* quantity that is sold at *OQ* price, the first duopolist may raise the price of his product up to *OP* and sell *OA* quantity of the commodity on the basis of his assumption that the other duopolist will not raise his price beyond *OQ*. In doing this he need not fear competition from his rival, because that rival has done worst by putting his whole supply in the market. On the other hand, the other duopolist realises that if he increases his price to a point slightly below *OP*, he can still sell OB' units and can make larger profits. This process of adjustment between the two will keep on going and the oscillation will continually take place between competitive price (OQ) and monopolistic price (OP).

The price oscillation is not because the sellers are only two but because the conditions of their competition are shifted. In order for the price to descend, their individual markets are completely merged into one, each drawing customers freely from the other by a slight reduction in the price. However in order to raise it again, their markets are completely separated, one seller supplying his customers at OQ and the other to his customers at OP.

Chamberlin's Model

According to Edward. H. Chamberlin none of the solutions given, thus far, confirms perfectly to the hypothesis that each seller acts in such a way as to render his profit maximum and for this the individual duopolist would take account of his total influence upon the price, both direct as well as indirect. It must be recognised that a move by one duopolist forces the other to make a counter-move and it is wrong to assume that he will not. Similarly, the assumption of independence does not require the sellers to compete, as though their fortunes were independent, rather it simply means the independence of action—the absence of agreement or of tacit agreement. So, a seller in seeking to maximise his profit must look to the total consequences of his move, that is, he must consider not merely what his competitor is doing now, but also what he will be forced to do in the light of the change, which he himself is contemplating. Thus, the two sellers must recognise their mutual interdependence in place of independence.

Professor Chamberlin suggested that let Cournot's first duopolist produce OA quantity and sell that at OC (= AP) price in the market. He further assumed the entrance of the second duopolist, who starts production of AH quantity, which is being sold in the market at ON (= HQ) price. After entry of the latter, the former will no longer believe that the second seller will produce only AH units, instead he may realise that the rival will try his level best to gain the largest possible profit, which is equal to $OAPC$. The first seller will reduce his output immediately to OZ level. Similarly, the second duopolist is also aware of his potentially dangerous competitive situation, and so immediately reciprocates by producing AZ units, making the total output equal to OA and price OC (= AP = ZY). The monopoly profit will become duopoly profit, which will be shared equally by the two sellers. Since both are aware of the dangerous consequence of a further move, they will decide to live together in harmony. The duopolists will set this supply because the ultimate consequences of their following through the other chain of adjustments are less advantageous than to share equally with his rival the output OA.

The result is the same, when the sellers adjust their prices instead of their supplies. Assuming the price of product of duopolists anywhere between OQ and OP, either of the two duopolists would immediately increase his price to

OP, confident in his belief that the other will follow the suit. In case each duopolist seeks his maximum profit rationally and intelligently, he will realise that when there are only two duopolists, his own move has a considerable effect on his competitor and that this makes it idle to suppose that the other will accept, without retaliation, the losses he forces upon rival. Since the result of a cut by anyone is inevitably to decrease his own profits, therefore, no one will cut and, although the two duopolists are entirely independent, the equilibrium result is the same, as if there was a monopolistic agreement between them. Thus, no one will cut from the monopoly figure, because he would force the other to follow him, and thereby work his own undoing.

Thus, his model offers a solution at monopoly equilibrium, which is based on the assumption that the response of each seller to a move by his rival is instantaneous. In case one cuts price or supply, the other is supposed to cut at once, leaving him no interval, in which to enjoy larger profit, he anticipated. Moreover, if the duopolist is in business permanently, the temporary gains of a price cut are of negligible importance. This may be a valuable contribution to the duopoly analysis, but it is not a general description of duopoly behaviour.

EQUILIBRIUM UNDER OLIGOPOLY

The term oligopoly is derived from two Greek words, namely, 'Oligoi' meaning 'a few' and 'Pollein' meaning, 'to sell'. Thus, **Oligopoly is a market situation, where there are a few firms producing and selling either homogeneous or differentiated products.** In other words, oligopoly is that situation in which a firm bases its market policy in part on the expected behaviour of a few close rivals. The number of sellers is few, which means that the number is more than two but small enough so that each seller understands that by his own actions he can influence the price at which he can sell and he may also stimulate his rivals to action. Oligopoly is mere extension of the duopoly, because from the point of view of the price theory the nature of the problem is the same, whether there are only two or a few sellers in the market.

The oligopoly situation is more common in the real world, but there is absence of an integrated general theory of oligopoly. Different models, to deal with the oligopoly problem, have been suggested by the various economists from time to time, but none of them succeeded in building up a theory. This can be attributed to the nature of this market situation, which has the following characteristics.

(i) **Mutual Interdependence:** All the sellers under oligopoly have common objective of maximisation of their net profits, but there is interdependence among them in regard to their decision marking. In case one decides to lower down the price, improve the product or enhance the advertisement, it leads to countermoves form the side of rivals. There is no single set pattern in which other oligopolists may react to any move by a single oligopolist. Hence, this kind of interdependence cannot be described by a single model of oligopoly, as a single model can explain only a single pattern of behaviour.

(ii) **Uncertainty:** It is very difficult to take account of competitor's reaction patterns, when the oligopolist thinks of any move, he considers the likely counter-moves of the competitors and simultaneously recognises that his competitors too would take into consideration this interdependence phenomenon and thus, both out-guessing each other. This ultimately leads to an interplay of anticipated strategies and counter-strategies, which complicates the solution of oligopoly problems. Economists try to simplify the analysis of oligopoly by assuming that firms ignore the interdependence for minor decisions and reserve it for rare major policy decisions. Sometimes, reactions are anticipated on the basis of guess work or past experience. A newly developed game-theory is also applied to guess the competitors' optimal moves—best possible strategies—so that he may prepare his own defences and counter-measures accordingly.

(iii) **Conflicting Attitudes:** Oligopolists have sometimes cooperating but at other times conflicting attitudes towards one another. When they realise the disadvantages of hostile competition, they combine together to maximise their joint profits. However, dissatisfaction of some oligopolists may result in price war on the question of distribution of profits and allocation of markets. Thus, the two conflicting attitudes are at work under oligopoly simultaneously, which create an atmosphere of uncertainty and make a generalised analysis very difficult.

(iv) **Non-Profit Motives:** The oligopolists may have certain objective other than usual objective of profit maximisation. These objectives may also be profit maximisation, acquisition of power and prestige, risk minimisation, etc. It becomes difficult to relate the non-profit motives with profit maximisation, in order to ascertain the price output levels under oligopoly.

(v) **Price-Rigidity and Non-Price Competition:** Oligopolists usually stick to the established price and concentrate their competitive efforts to non-price competition, such as, design, advertisement, concessions, free of cost delivery, guarantee for certain period, repair facilities, certain gifts with the product, etc. Thus, the major part of competition is in product variation and selling activity, which is hardly amenable to precise measurement and thorough analytical treatment.

(vi) **Varying Situation of Oligopoly:** Oligopoly embraces a large variety of situations, which differ among themselves with respect to the degree of sellers' concentration and size-distribution of sellers. We may come across oligopoly situation in industries, where there are (a) a few sellers each controlling a significant share of the market or industry; (b) a very few sellers controlling the great bulk of industry output and a small number of sellers dividing the remainder; (c) a moderately few sellers only; (d) a very few or a moderately few sellers controlling the bulk of industry output and a substantial number of small sellers sharing the remainder; (e) one seller supplying a large share of the industry output, the remainder being shared by a number of small firms.

The conditions of entry to the industry or the height of barriers which established firms can place in the way of potential entrants also serves as basis for classification of the various oligopoly situations. On this basis also there can be numerous conditions but for simplicity these have been grouped into two categories; (a) oligopolies of 'blockaded entry', where established sellers can jointly charge a price, which will maximise industry profit without attracting entry; and (b) oligopolies subject to threat of entry, where pursuance of such a price policy would result in the attraction of additional firms to the industry.

Thus, a large variety of situations as above and many intermediate and adjacent sub-cases render in difficult to develop any single theory of oligopoly pricing, which will apply equally to all of these sub-categories.

EMERGENCE OF OLIGOPOLY

The oligopoly refers to a situation in which a few sellers supply all or much of the total industry output. The question, therefore, arises as to how industries become oligopolistic. It may become oligopolistic when: (i) a few firms secure a dominant position in the industry from the date of origin and these protect this position against the potential competition; (ii) the industry has been initially atomistic in structure, later on, a few firms may secure and retain control of a dominant share of the market, which is possible through growth of a few firms at the expense of their many competitors; (iii) there is merger of a number of smaller firms into larger firms. Thus, the oligopoly emerges in either of the three ways, that is, with the inception of the industry, with growth to dominant size of few firms and with merger of small firms.

Again the oligopolistic firms emerge on account of a large number of factors. One important factor is the economies of a large scale production. As output expands there is scope for greater mechanisation and division of labour and, as a result, there is progressive reduction in the average cost of production. Since the larger firms are in a position to reduce costs much more than the smaller ones, as the larger firms expand, smaller ones are driven out of the market. Secondly, superior entrepreneurs have lower alternative costs than inferior rivals and the superiority may be sufficient to permit them to undersell and eliminate most of the rivals. **Thus, superior entrepreneurs are motivated by the desire for the large gains or power, prestige or leadership, usually follow aggressive policy of ruthless competition against weaker rivals to**

force them to either go out or merge with them. Thirdly, the control of the entire supply of some indispensable resource used in the manufacture of a product may also give rise to the oligopoly. Fourthly, exclusion of potential rivals by exclusive grant, patents or copyrights closely regulate the entry of new firms. Lastly, the requirement of large sums of capital, whose accumulation is very difficult, also retards the rate of entry of rivals.

Thus, the existing firms in an industry may find it to their advantage to merge or consolidate in order to eliminate competition amongst themselves, so that the competition from the side of remaining sellers may be more easily suppressed. A few firms may obtain a dominant advantage of product differentiation (where buyers prefer their product to other varieties of the same good) and thus, they are able to secure a major share of the market against all competitors. In certain cases, a few firms may secure strategic absolute advantage in cost over all others, which permits them to operate profitably at a price at which the others cannot survive. The prospective entrants to an industry are also deterred by the difficulty of marketing new product or new brand in the presence of already well established brands.

PRICE AND OUTPUT DETERMINATION

The oligopoly situations in the market are merely an extension of the duopoly situation, where the sellers may either behave independently or in collusion with others. When they behave independently, for all practical purposes, they are divided into two groups, thus, on the one hand there is single oligopolist and on the other, all his competitors combined together and presents a situation similar to that of duopoly. Sometimes, oligopoly gives rise to collusion, which bestows on the firms some monopoly power depending upon the nature and the degree of collusion. In case of the highest degree of collusion (i.e., perfect collusion), the price and output are the same as under monopoly but when this degree declines (i.e., under imperfect collusion) the output and price are nearer to that under monopoly. The collusion may vary from strict enforcement of the decisions made by a centralised cartel to a loose association of members, just meeting to arrive at an understanding on major policy issues in the industry. Moreover, the degree of collusion depends upon the number of firms in the industry, as smaller the number of firms involved, the greater will be degree of collusion.

The price-quantity combination and profit of oligopolist depends upon the actions of all members in the market. He can control his own output level (or price, if his product is differentiated) but he has no direct control over the other variables, which affect his profit. The profit of each seller is the result of the interaction of decisions of all oligopolists. There are no generally accepted behaviour assumptions for oligopolists. So, there are different solutions for oligopolistic problems, where each solution is based on a different set of behaviour assumptions. Most of the solutions are developed for a duopolistic market, but a few, such as, games-theory and collusion solutions are exclusively for oligopoly market. The Cournot's independent pricing solution and collusion solution are developed for market with homogeneous products, but the market share and kinked-demand-curve solutions are developed for markets selling differentiated products.

Cournot's Model

The classical solution of duopoly can be extended to the oligopoly situations, where all the sellers are divided into two groups; single oligopolist on the one hand and all his competitors together on the other. They are assumed to sell homogenous products, and the single oligopolists tries to maximise his profit on the assumption that the quantity produced by his rivals is invariant with respect to his own quantity decision. Under such a situation the equilibrium is reached through a sequence of instantaneous adjustments by both parties.

Both the parties are engaged in production with the objective of maximisation of the profit, taking into consideration the reaction of each other. In case the single oligopolist assumes that the rivals will always maintain their output at the level of previous period irrespective of his own level of output, then the profit maximising output will lie on a line named as oligopolist's reaction curve, which shows oligopolists reaction to any change in rivals' output. The reaction curve has been drawn as straight line, because the market demand curve is assumed as straight line and the cost of production is assumed constant at zero.

The single oligopolist may plan to produce *OM* output, if rivals' output were zero. In other words, if the single oligopolist is the sole producer, he will produce *OM*, which is monopoly output. Now due to entry of rivals in the market along with increase in their output, the oligopolist will reduce his output, which may be reduced to zero, if the rivals start producing *ON* output. Similarly, the rivals (behaving as a single producer) may produce *OK* quantity in the absence of the single oligopolist, which will decrease along with increase in single oligopolist's output and may be equal to zero, when the single oligopolist starts producing *OL* quantity. This *OL* or *ON* are the maximum quantities offered under perfect competition and *OM* or *OK* are the quantities offered for sale under monopoly.

Since both parties are interested in the maximum profits per period and assuming that the output of the other party will be maintained at its level of the previous period, irrespective of the output, which one party produces, they will ultimately come to equilibrium at point *E*, at which the two reaction curves intersect each other. Supposing single oligopolist *A* is initially a monopolist and all his rivals appear suddenly and unexpectedly in the beginning. Rivals assuming that *A* will continue to produce *OM*, plan to produce Ob_1, because that is the output that promises *A* the maximum profits, if *A* produces *OM*. Seeing that rivals, who are producing Ob_1 quantity, have established themselves

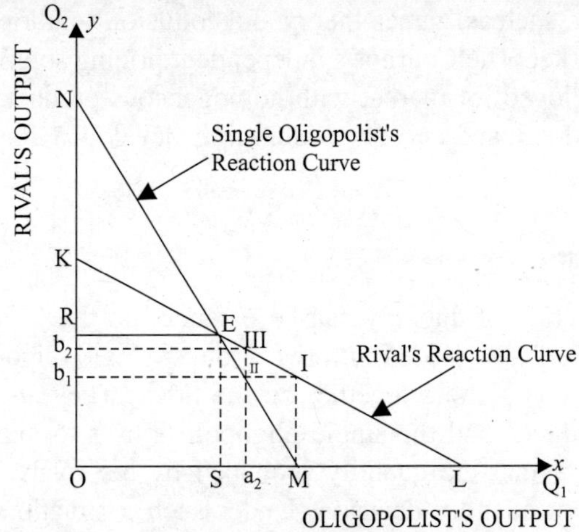

FIGURE 20.3 Oligopolist's and Rivals' Equilibrium Quantities.

in the market and assuming that they will maintain the level of output, the single oligopolist, as per his reaction curve, will start producing Oa_2. Rivals, seeing the reduced output of the single oligopolist and assuming it to remain unchanged, as per their reaction curve will start producing Ob_3 in relation to Oa_2 quantity produced by the single oligopolist. It is obvious from the diagram that these adjustments will continue until both parties come to *E* point, where they produce *OS* and *OR* quantities respectively.

Game Theory Model

Professor John Von Neumann and Oskar Morgenstern approach the problem of oligopoly from a new angle by applying the theory of games for its solution. In an oligopolistic situation, the individual seller does not control all of the variables and behave like a player, who may act to secure that result, which will be least harmful to himself, no matter what his opponents decide to do, including the possibility that his rivals may react in the most unfavourable way. Thus, the competition between firms under oligopoly is like the game of chess, where the oligopolist considers not only his own moves but also the moves, which his rivals might be expected to make. There are several courses of actions open to the oligopolist and his choice will depend on assumptions he makes about the probable reactions of other oligopolists to his own policies. It shows that there is a set of moves and counter-moves with every firm under oligopoly and the problem is to select the best (i.e., least harmful) out of them under given conditions.

Games are classified on the basis of two criteria: (a) number of participants; and (b) the net outcome. The former involves counting of number of participants with conflicting interests, whereas the latter allows a distinction between zero-sum and non-zero sum games. Zero-sum game is one in which the algebraic sum of net outcome for all the participants equals zero for every possible combination of strategies. In case the net outcome undergoes a change, it is classified as non zero-sum game. Usually we restrict our analysis to two parties and zero-sum game, where one party's gain always equals the absolute value of the other's loss.

Assuming that there is a given demand for the product of a group of oligopolists and that profits are proportional to sales, if the oligopolist's sales increases, the sale of his competitors will decrease in an off-setting way to keep the group's total sales constant. Since the profits are proportional to sales, so the total profit is also constant, which is assumed to be 100 units for all the oligopolists. The distribution of profit for the various strategies of both parties is as follows:

TABLE 20.1 Game Theory and Oligopolists' Behaviour

Oligopolist's Alternative Strategies	*Competitors' Alternative Strategies*			
	Raise Price	*Price Unchanged*	*Lower Price*	*Increase Advertisement*
Raise Price	55	46	44	50
Price Unchanged	56	54	47	48
Lower Price	58	55	50	51
Increase Advertisement	54	52	48	49

It shows the amount of profit the single oligopolist expects to make as a result of the various alternative strategies, which he may adopt, when his competitors are also adopting the various strategies. The oligopolist's alternative strategies include: (a) raising the price; (b) keeping the price unchanged; (c) lowering the price; and (d) increasing advertisement. The competitors of the oligopolist are expected to react as a group and this single-minded group of competitors may adopt strategies similar to those adopted by the single oligopolist. The profit as a result of oligopolist's strategies are shown in the rows (which are read horizontally) and that of competitors' strategies are shown in the columns (which are read vertically)

In case oligopolist raises the price and the competitors also follow the suit, the profit of the oligopolist is 55. However, when in response to price rise by the oligopolist, the competitors decide to maintain the price unchanged, lower the price or increase advertisement, the share of profit of the single oligopolist stands at 46, 44 and 50 units respectively. Similarly, if the oligopolist decides to keep the price unchanged but the competitors follow the various alternative strategies, his profit will be 56, 54, 47 and 48 respectively. In case the single oligopolist lowers the price, his profit is 58, 55, 50 and 51 respectively for the various alternative strategies adopted by the competitors. In case the single oligopolist decides to increase the advertisement for increasing his profit for the various strategies adopted by the rivals his share of profit will be 54, 52, 48 and 49 only. Thus, given the knowledge of the various possibilities open to him, as well as those open to his competitors and given the ability to quantify the effects of the combinations of their various policies in terms of profits, the oligopolist must, then, decide which of the available policies to follow.

One policy may be to 'play it safe', assuming that his opponents will follow that strategy, which produces the worst possible result from the single oligopolist's point of view. Thus, pessimistically, he may believe that his opponents will always adopt the strategy, which produces the worst possible result for him. This happens when the competitors lower their prices, in response to all types of strategies adopted by the oligopolist. Under such circumstances the oligopolist will adopt that strategy, from amongst those that provide him with the maximum of the various minimum gains. Thus, assuming that the worst will happen, the best strategy would be to lower the price, because his gain in that situation will be maximum out of the various minimum gains against the various strategies followed by the rivals.

On the other hand, the competitors adopt the strategy of maximising their own profits and for this, they will seek to minimise the profits earned by the oligopolist, because whatever is the profit of single oligopolist, the same is the loss of competitors and *vice-versa*. In the effort of seeking the maximum profit, the single oligopolist may lower down the price, because this strategy provides him the maximum profit, but simultaneously the competitors will respond to his policy of lowering price by lowering their own prices. For, if they respond by raising their prices, keeping their prices unchanged or increasing advertising, their loss will be 58, 55 and 51 respectively, but when they respond by lowering their own prices, their loss will be only 50. Thus, the competitors follow the strategy of selecting the policy that will produce the minimum-maximum (Mini-Max) loss.

The strategies followed by both parties are mutually consistent in the establishment of a stable equilibrium position, known as saddle point, where the maximum-minimum (Maxi-Min) profit of the oligopiolist (50) is equal to the minimum-maximum (Mini-Max) loss of his competitors.

Collusion Model

The oligopolists may recognise their mutual inter-dependence and agree to act in unison in order to maximise the total profit of the industry. They may form cartel by transferring certain management decisions and functions of individual firms to a central association. Under cartel agreement, the price and output of the industry and that of the separate member firms, are decided solely by a central administrative agency in such a way as to maximise the joint profit of the member firms, which is then divided among the participating members. It is complete form of cartel known as profit-sharing cartel, but there can be another type of cartel called the market sharing cartel.

(i) Profit Sharing Cartel: In this cartel there is complete collusion among members, where the central administrative agency decides the price and output in such a way as to: (i) minimise the aggregate cost of any industry output produced; and (ii) produce just that industry output, which maximises the joint profit of the member firms. Thus, the central administration will determine separate output of member firms and the price they will charge in the way a single monopolist operating several plants would do. Thus, it is essentially a monopoly problem, where the profit will be maximised at such a level, where the industry marginal revenue equals the industry marginal cost.

Firstly, the cartel will estimate the industry demand curve, showing the aggregate quantity, which the several oligopolists may sell at each alternative prices and from this, a marginal receipt curve may be derived, which shows the additions to industry aggregate receipts for successive additions to industry output. Secondly, the industry marginal cost curve is obtained from the short run marginal cost curve of individual firms of the industry, which must be at the minimum level. The cartel administration must allocate the quotas for production in such a way that the marginal cost of each firm, when producing its quota is equal to the marginal cost of producing respective quotas of every other firm.

The industry marginal cost of producing each successive industry output is obtained by horizontally adding the several marginal cost curves of the operating firms. Assuming the existence of only three firms in the industry, the separate marginal cost curves of the firms are respectively mc_1, mc_2 and mc_3. The industry marginal cost curve is obtained by adding these curves together, which is designated as *MC*. This industry *MC* is equal to the industry *MR* at point *E*.

Here total quantity *OQ* will be produced, which will be sold in the market at OP price. This results in the largest attainable industry profit that will be divided among member firms according to some agreed plan. The distribution of profit may be according to production quotas assigned to individual firms or may be on 'as earned' basis, which is usually ascertained as per the negotiation or compromise among the members.

Such type of 'perfect collusion in oligopoly' is rarely found in real world. It is because of mutual distrust among the members and their unwillingness to surrender too much of their sovereignty to a central cartel administration.

(ii) Market Sharing Cartel Is another type of collusion, where the members of the cartel share the market either in agreed proportions or in proportions determined by buyers' preferences for their products and each receives that part of market, which he can make as per his own sales. Such a collusion may arise from the express agreement or simply from the tacit agreement implied by a consistently observed system of price leadership.

In case there is market sharing with effective collusion on price alone, each seller receives a given fraction of the industry demand, charging certain price identical to that of his rivals. The oligopolist's demand curve might appear as *DD* in Figure 20.5 and each of the several oligopolists may envisage identical

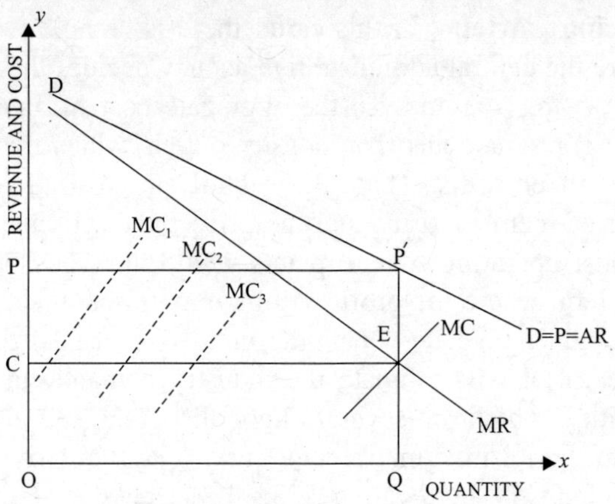

FIGURE 20.4 Price and Total Volume of Output, if the Oligopolists Collude.

curves, if there are equal market shares or different demand curves, if there are different market shares, but each will face the same elasticity of demand as the industry demand curve. Each oligopolist may derive the marginal revenue curve from their respective demand curve. For the sake of price agreement each seller will wish to have his rivals agree with him on that price (*OP*) at which his marginal cost equals the marginal revenue. In case all sellers charge this price, this seller will make the largest possible profit from his designated market share. However if the average and marginal costs or market share of the sellers are different, the *OP* price, thus determined by all the oligopolists, will not be identical. Thus, there will be a range of alternative maximising prices from which the oligopolists must choose. Price agreement will require some compromise on a price not too far from the optimal price of anyone.

The results, thus obtained, may deviate in three ways from those of a perfect cartel. Firstly, since market shares are not determined so as to minimise costs, the cost of production is likely to be higher than that under perfect cartel.

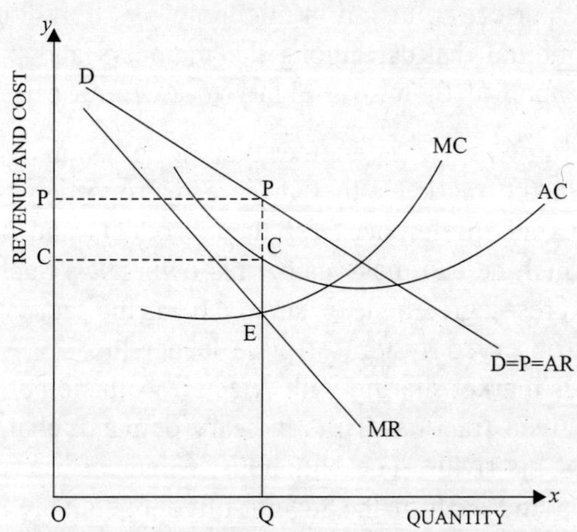

FIGURE 20.5 Pricing under Market Sharing Cartel.

Secondly, the price and output derived will generally not be exactly the same as under perfect cartel. Lastly, the joint profit realised by the oligopolists will be smaller than the monopoly or perfect cartel profit.

Price Leadership Model

The collusion may exhibit itself in two ways: formal agreement (or cartel) and tacit agreement, where without face-to-face contact and without correspondence there develops among the member firms a unity of behaviour with regards to price and output policy. It is usually exhibited in price leadership, where there is no formal agreement or organisation and is also not open to the charge of conspiracy to restrain trade.

Price leadership varies in character. Firstly, **there may be price leadership of the dominant firm**, which produces a sizeable proportion of the total output and dominates the market almost with the power of a monopolist. The small producers ignore their own impact upon the market and do not wish to combine to challenge that large producer. The dominant firm knows the industry demand for the product and the marginal costs of small firms. From the total industry demand at the various prices, the dominant firm sets aside the quantity of output the small firms stand ready to sell in view of their marginal costs and decides to offer the rest for sale in the market. Thus, the dominant firm derives its own demand schedule and will set a price at a level, which equals the marginal revenue with the marginal cost. The small firms will not charge more than this price, otherwise they will lose the trade and will also not cut the price, because they can sell the total quantity they produce at that price. The small firms are, thus, more or less price takers having a horizontal demand curve at the price fixed by the dominant firm.

Secondly, there may be **barometric price leadership**. In this case, one firm—old, experienced and respected — assumes the task of evaluating the changing market conditions with regard to demand, cost, competition with related products and the phase of the business cycle and sets the price of the product accordingly, which is adopted by other firms in the market. Such firm plays the role of price leader, not because of its dominant position in the market, but because other firms regard its actions as a suitable barometer of changing market conditions. The powers of a barometric price leader are restricted by its realisation that other firms will follow only within reasonable limits, therefore, the firm has to consider the reactions of other firms to its actions.

Thirdly, there may be **exploitative or aggressive price leadership,** where the powerful firm may decide to crowd out some of its rivals or it may desire to force the other firms into acquiescence in its price leadership.

The price leadership models are built on the various assumptions regarding size, cost and share of market of the various firms, possibility of entry of new firms and outlook of leader firm towards its own as well as smaller firm's profits. Taking a simple case of two firms, producing a homogeneous product, where the cost of production of one firm is lower than that of the other, we find a difference between the price and output policies of the two firms. Each of the two firms has a demand curve $D = P = AR$ and MR is their marginal revenue curve. MC_1 and MC_2 are the marginal cost curves of the higher and lower cost firms respectively. The two firms are in equilibrium at such level, where price and quantity of the former is OP_1 and OQ_1 and that of the latter is OP_2 and OQ_2 respectively. Since, the higher-cost firm is to compete with the lower cost firm in the market, where the latter has an advantage over the former, the lower-cost firm automatically becomes a price leader. The higher-cost firm will like to follow the lower-cost firm in order to remain in existence.

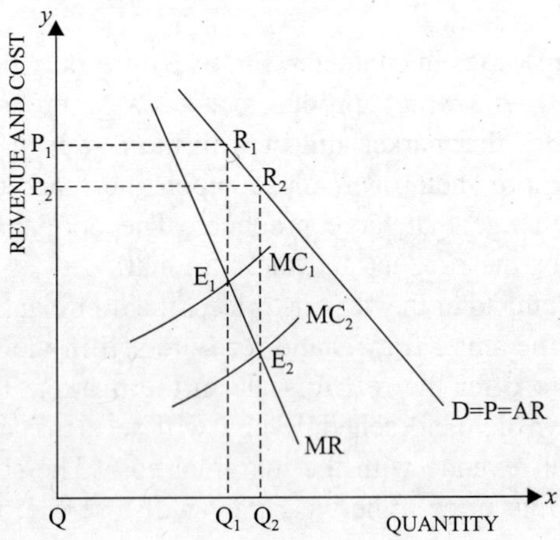

FIGURE 20.6 Price Leadership between Two Firms.

In case of price leadership by the dominant firm, the oligopolists, for avoiding large scale price cutting, may reach a tacit agreement to follow price leadership of one large firm. The process of the price determination may be explained, assuming the existence of a single dominant firm and a large number of small firms. The dominant firm, taking into consideration the industry demand of the product and share of the small firms in the market, sets such price on which small firms can sell as much as they desire, i.e., for the small firms, there is perfectly elastic demand curve at the level of established price and the average and marginal revenue curves, which coincide and will be parallel to the horizontal axis. The small firms will produce at the level, where the marginal cost equals the marginal revenue, which, in turn, equals the price set by the established firm. Supply of the small firms is represented by their respective marginal costs and by summing them up horizontally we can deduce the supply curve for all small firms. It is represented by ΣMC curve, which shows how much the small firms together will sell at each possible price.

The market demand curve is $DD = P = AR$, where the demand left after that met by the small firms. The demand curve of the dominant firm is represented by $dd = Pd = ARd$, which is obtained by subtracting horizontally ΣMC curve from DD curve. In case the dominant firms sets the price at OP_2, the total market demand is met by the small firms and if the price comes down to OP_0, the small firms supply very nominal part of the market demand and major part is supplied by the dominant firm, because this is equal to average variable cost (*AVC*) of the small firms. In case the price happens to fall below this level, the small firms will drop out of the market leaving the entire market to the dominant firm.

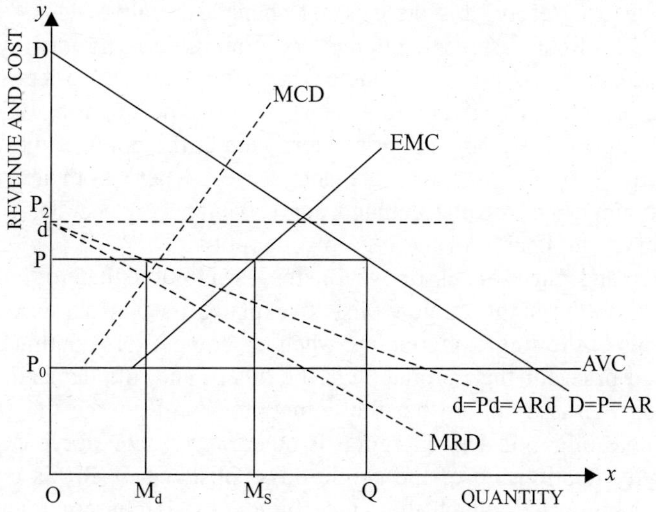

FIGURE 20.7 Price Leadership of the Dominant Firm.

Having traced the demand or average revenue, and marginal revenue curves of the dominant firm along with its marginal cost curve, we can ascertain the equilibrium of the dominant firm at *Ed* where $MC_d = MR_d$. The price (or average revenue) of the dominant firm is *OP* and the same price will be charged by the small firms, which may sell as much as they desire. The small firms adjust their output to this price simply by equating their marginal cost with this price, which is their average as well as marginal revenue. Their equilibrium is at E_s, where the total output is OM_s the total demand for the product in the market at this price is OQ out of which OM_s quantity is met by the small firms and the rest M_sQ = (= OM_d) is met by the dominant firm.

Price Rigidity or Kinked Demand Model

Oligopolistic market is also characterised by the price rigidity, even despite changes in market demand and costs. The oligopolist may not like to vary the price due to several reasons. Firstly, in the absence of collusive agreements, there is good deal of uncertainty regarding the demand for firms' products, which discourages the firm from lowering the price, as it may provoke rivals to unpredictable reactions and also from enhancing the price because of apprehension of losing its customers. Secondly, the oligopolistic firms do not deem it proper to change the price because of certain inconveniences and irritation of the customers. Thirdly, the present price might have been established after prolonged price war. Fourthly, when oligopolistic firms are confronted with falling demand, instead of reducing the price to maintain demand, they may intensify the sales promotion activities. Lastly, the oligopolists are often content to leave well enough alone, and with a view of forestalling the entry of new firms, they may deliberately fix the lower price, which gives good long run profit and, therefore, this price is not changed usually.

Thus, the oligopolists will attempt to minimise uncertainty by refusing to change the price, once a reasonable satisfactory level of price is reached, because it is better to adhere to it, instead of experimenting with rivals' reactions to new prices. This price is determined at the point of the Kink (i.e., point of intersection of the two demand curves, where both are drawn on different assumptions) on the demand curve, which is a peculiar type of the demand curve, applicable in the case of oligopoly.

The demand curve *dd* is drawn on the assumption that the competitors will not follow the single oligopoplist. It explains the various price–quantity combinations of the single oligopolist, when his competitors continue to charge certain fixed price for their product. On the other hand, the demand curve *DD* is drawn on the assumption that the competitors will charge the same price that the single oligopolist is charging. It other words, *DD* curve explains the price-quantity relationship of the single oligopolist, when all his competitors charge the same price, which the single oligopolist is charging. The Point *E* on the two demand curves reveals that the single oligopolist can charge *OP* price and sell *OQ* quantity of the commodity, whether the competitors follow or do not follow the single oligopolist.

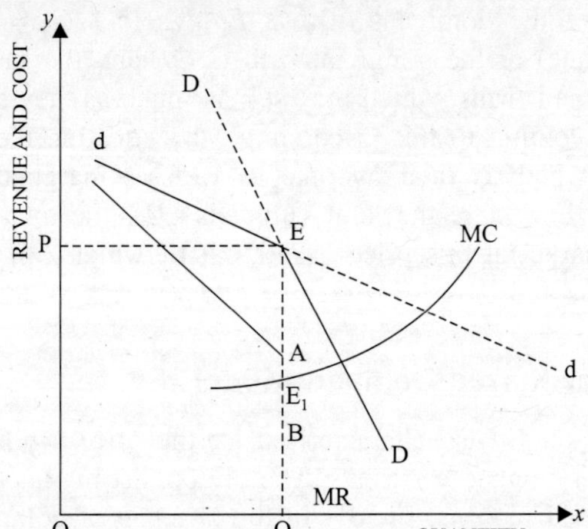

FIGURE 20.8 Slopes of a Kinked Demand Curve.

Assuming that the industry is a matured one and a price is fairly acceptable to all the firms has been established, if the oligopolist lowers the price, the competitors will follow him by under-cutting the price to retain their share of the market. Similarly, if the oligopolist increases the price, the other oligopolists will not follow the price increase.

Thus, the oligopolist will face a demand curve consisting of upper part of the *dd* curve and lower part of the *DD* curve from the point of kink at *E*. The darkened parts of both these curves represented by the *dED* is the kinked demand curve, where the oligopolist fixes the price and quantity at the point of kink. In case the oligopolist lowers the price, despite drastic cut in price, he will be able to capture a very insignificant part of the market, because all other oligopolists will start under cutting the price and, on the other hand, even if he increases the price only slightly, his share of the market decreases very significantly, as no other oligopolists would follow him by increasing the price. Moreover, at this point the segmented marginal revenue curve equals the rising marginal cost curve. In case he decides to sell more than OQ_1 the marginal revenue is less than the marginal cost, which lowers the net revenue earned up to the sale of *OQ* quantity of the commodity. Similarly, if he sells less than *OQ* quantity the marginal revenue will be more than the marginal cost, which reveals the chances for increasing the net revenue by enhancing the sales.

On account of sudden change in the slope of the demand curve under oligopoly at point *E*, there is break in the marginal revenue curve. For the demand curve (or the average revenue curve) *dED*, the marginal revenue curve is *MR*, which has a break between *A* and *B*. Since the average and marginal revenues are related on the basis of the elasticity of demand [i.e., $MR = AR(1 - 1/Ed)$] in response to sudden fall in the degree of the elasticity of demand at *E*, there if sudden fall in the marginal revenue at this level of sale from point *A* to *B*. Upper part is the marginal revenue for *dE* portion of the average revenue curve and for *ED* portion of the demand curve lower part is the marginal curve.

This peculiar shape of the demand (or average revenue) curve and the marginal revenue curve under oligopoly explains clearly the price-rigidity, as it will remain constant, even if there is change in the cost of production as follows:

The oligopolist's kinked demand curve or average revenue curve is *dED* and *MR* represents his marginal revenue curve. Originally $SMC_1 = MR$ at E_1 point, where $OP = QE$ is price and OQ is quantity of the commodity sold in the market. This quantity is produced on an average cost of $OC_1 = QC_1'$ and leaves a net profit represented by $PC_1C_1'E$ area to the oligopolist. In case, the cost of production increases, the short run average cost and marginal cost curves are shifted upwards to the level of SAC_2 and SMC_2 respectively. Again $SMC_2 = MR$ at E_2, where $OP = QE$ is the price and OQ is the quantity,

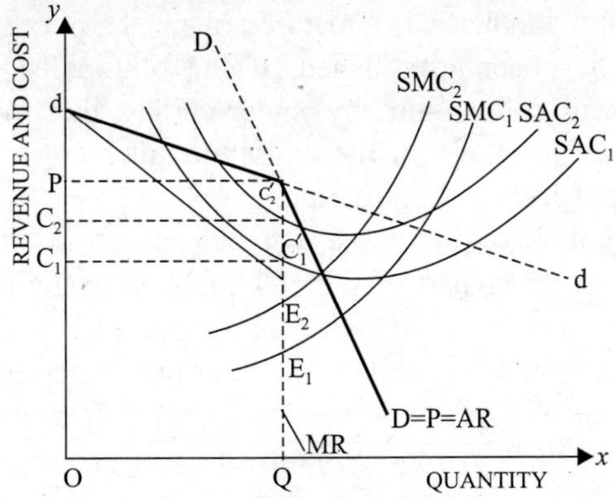

FIGURE 20.9 Price Unchanged Despite Change in the Costs.

which is produced at an average cost of $OC_2 = QC'_2$. It leaves the oligopolist a reduced net profit represented by $PC_2C'_2E$. Thus, despite increase in the cost of production, the equilibrium price and quantity sold remain unchanged. On the other hand, if there is a reduction in the cost of production, occasioned by a reduction in the wage rate or in the excise duty or price of raw materials, the average and marginal cost curves will alike shift downwards from SAC_2 and SMC_2 to SAC_1 and SMC_1 respectively. The equilibrium remains at the same level of price and output it will bring an increased net revenue to the oligopolist.

Similarly, if there is a change in the demand for the product, the quantity exchanged by the oligopolist may undergo a change, but the price of the product is likely to remain unchanged.

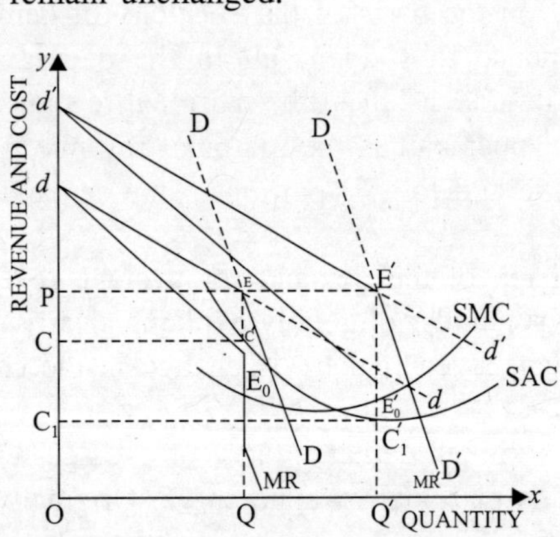

FIGURE 20.10 Price Unchanged Despite Change in Demand of the Goods

It reveals that oligopolist's demand curve is *dED*, where his equilibrium price is fixed at point *E*, as the marginal revenue (*MR*) equals the short run marginal cost (*SMC*) at point E_0. The firm produces *OQ* quantity at an average cost of $OC = QC'$ and this quantity is being sold in the market at $OP = QE$ price.

This enables the oligopolist to obtain a net revenue equal to *PCC'E*. Assuming an increase in the demand, the oligopolist's demand curve is shifted to *d'E'D'* level. Since, there is no change in the cost of production, the short run average cost and marginal cost curves remain unchanged and the short-run marginal cost (*SMC*) curve intersects the new marginal revenue curve (*MR'*) at E'_0 point. At this equilibrium level, the oligopolist produces and sells *OQ'* quantity at $OP = Q'E'$ price. The average cost of production (*SAC*) being $OC_1 = Q'C'_1$, the oligopolist obtains a net revenue equal to $PC_1C'_1E'$. Thus, the oligopolist reaps the benefit of increased demand in the form of an enlarged net revenue. By reversing the whole of the above process, we can understand the impact of decrease in demand on the oligopolist. Thus, whether there is increase or decrease in the demand for the product, the oligopolist will simply vary the quantity produced and sold but will maintain the price unchanged.

In the long run, if there is freedom of entry, the market of each oligopolist is of same size, the elasticity of demand in each market is the same and cost conditions are the same, only normal profits will be earned by the oligopolists. In case they obtain net profit, on account of freedom of entry, new firms may inter into the industry. As a result, the share of the oligopolists in the market, along with the price, declines because their demand curves are shifted downwards. On the other hand, if the oligopolists incur losses, in long run a few oligopolists with weak financial standing may leave the industry. This may reduce the number of oligopolists in that industry and consequently the share of remaining oligopolist in the market, along with the price, may go up, because the demand curves of the remaining oligopolists are shifted upwards. This increased price may equal the average cost production, leaving only normal profits to the oligopolists.

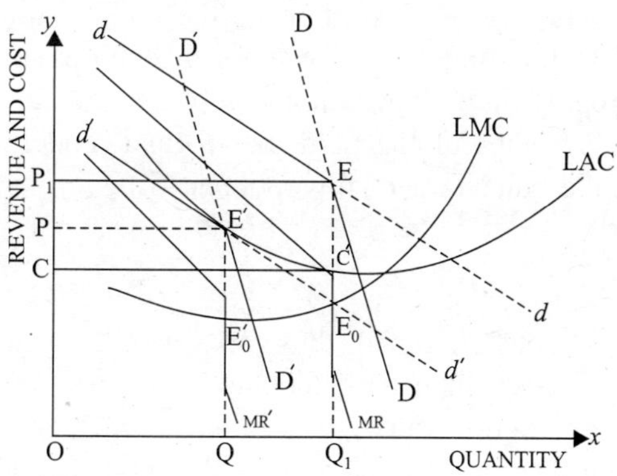

FIGURE 20.11 Long Run Equilibrium under Oligopoly

The *dED* represents oligopolist's original demand curve, which is forming the kink at *E* point, where he is in equilibrium getting CP_1EC' amount of net profit on the sale of OQ_1 quantity at OP_1 price. This induces new firms to enter into the industry which, in turn, reduces the oligopolist's share in the market by shifting the *dED* the demand curve to level *d'E'd' level,* which forms a kink at *E'* point. The long-run average cost (*LAC*) curve is tangent to this kinked average revenue curve at *E'* point. The long run marginal cost (*LMC*) curve intersects the segmented marginal revenue curve at E_0' point. At this equilibrium level, the oligopolist charges *OP* price and sells *OQ* quantity of the commodity, which is being produced at an average cost equal to *QE'*. At this equilibrium level of sale, the oligopolist is getting only normal profit.

Kinked demand analysis has been criticised on the ground that it is neither theoretically very sound nor empirically supported and is of limited application in explaining price inflexibility. Kinked demand curve is subjective and exists in the minds of decision makers. The belief, that price increases of one firm will not be followed by rivals but price reductions are to be followed, has no statistical backing.

In real world under oligopoly, the price may be determined at such a level, which may avoid the potential competition, unfavourable public opinion and legislative reaction. This may also be due to desire for security, as the oligopolist seeks a continued existence and wants to maintain the position in terms of the volume of output, financial strength and customers' goodwill. In case the number of sellers is small, they may develop a sense of group loyalty and a spirit of live and let live, which may lead to collusive pricing.

OLIGOPOLY AND RESOURCE ALLOCATION

The analysis of many alternative oligopoly models reveals that there is no general agreement regarding appropriateness of any existing oligopoly model for analysing the behaviour in any industry, which renders it difficult to predict the equilibrium solution for a particular oligopolistic market. We, therefore, cannot state with any degree of confidence the equilibrium levels of market price, output and factor usage. Despite these difficulties, in order to indicate the effects of oligopoly on the allocation of resources in an economy, we have to go beyond the confines of the particular formal model and use empirical knowledge about the bahaviour of oligopolistic firms.

Prices

The oligopolistic models examined, thus far, generally lead to prices that are above the levels that would usually prevail under perfect competition. The amount, by which an oligopoly price exceed the competitive price, is a function of the number of firms in the market and the degree of freedom of entry. Thus, the greater the number of firms in the market, the higher the probability that the price will move towards the competitive level. However, at the same time, size distribution of firms must be considered because, if there are only one or two large firms and a group of small firms, then the dominant firm model is likely to apply and the price will be nearer to the monopoly price. Similarly, if the entry is easy (i.e., if new firms face no barriers, such as, patents, lack of raw materials, shortage of technical knowledge or high capital requirements) the price will tend towards the competitive level, as the possible entry of new firms is a constraint on the price policies of existing firms in the industry. Free entry exposes the industry to increased competition, if profits become larger and the rate of return on capital is higher than normal.

In oligopoly market usually prices are most likely to remain above the competitive level, where there are small number of firms, a relatively small market and great economies of scale. Under such circumstances, a new firm must build a relatively large plant to compete effectively and this may mean potential excess capacity in the market at any given price level. Along with this, huge capital requirement for a large plant may present barrier to entry, which will generate protected oligopolistic market. This leads the price nearer to the monopoly price level rather than competitive price level.

However, prices in oligopolistic industries are more stable than prices would be under perfect competition, as they are more likely to keep prices constant despite great shifts in demand and to adjust t these demand changes by varying the quantities supplied than by altering prices.

Output

As long as the oligopolists price is higher than the competitive price for any given market demand curve, the total output in the industry will be less under oligopoly than under perfect competition. However, it may not be reasonable to compare oligopolistic and competitive market structures using the same market demand curve. The extensive expenditures for advertising and new product development, common to oligopolistic industry may shift the market demand curve to the right. Therefore, both output and price may be higher in an oligopolistic market than if the same industry had perfectly competitive market. On account of price rigidity under oligopoly, over a course of business cycle, total output may vary more in oligopoly than in perfect competition. This means that fluctuations in employment and the utilisation of other productive factors may be more extreme with the existence of oligopoly.

Non-Price Competition

Although the formal models of oligopoly have not explicitly dealt with the various forms of non-price competition but empirically it is more important for oligopolies than for perfectly competitive markets. It primarily involves attempts to differentiate the oligopolist's product from its rivals' products by establishing in the consumers' minds, through advertising, real or imaginary differences in quality and style. From the point of view of the consumers, the effects of using advertising to sell the products, rather than price reductions, may be undesirable. Assuming no economies of scale in production, it is clear that some consumers would be better off, if they buy the products alone rather than the products plus bundles of additional services, which are in fact provided by the advertising expenditures of the producers. The aim of product differentiation is to establish a segment of the consumers with whom the firm has a monopoly position, which may be accomplished by the development of nationally advertised brand names. Once the monopoly position is established, the producer can gain large profits by exploiting the market through a variety of means, including price discrimination.

Profit

The rates of return earned by oligopolists should be higher than the rates of return earned by perfectly competitive firms, as long as there are some barriers to entry into the oligopolistic market. There is considerable amount of empirical evidence to indicate that in fact the average profit rate earned by firms is an increasing function of the degree of concentration in industry.

Review Questions

1. What is meant by duopoly and examine the various duopoly models?
2. Explain the price rigidity and non-price competition under oligopoly.
3. "Duopoly model suggested by Edgeworth is based on disequilibrium analysis". Explain
4. Distinguish between 'barometric and dominant price leadership. How oligopolistic price is determined under dominant price leadership?
5. Discuss the kinked demand model of oligopoly. How far this offers a satisfactory explanation to the behaviour of oligopolist firms.
6. Discuss the unique characteristics of oligopoly. How does interdependence lead to indeterminateness under oligopoly?
7. 'Reorganisation of interdependence of firms in an oligopolistic market in Chamberlin's model give a result quite different from that of Cournot's model.' Explain.
8. What is oligopoly? What will happen if the firms under oligopoly (i) collude and (ii) collide?
9. Elucidate equilibrium determination under collusive oligopoly.
10. Explain price and output determination under the price leadership models in an oligopolistic market. Bring out the weaknesses of this model.

21

Pricing under Monopolistic Competition

Monopolistic competition is a real world situation in between the two extreme market situations of prefect competition and monopoly. It is nearer to the perfect competition but the elements of monopoly are also found present in this market situation. In this chapter, an effort is being made the elaborate the pricing decisions in short run as well as in long run under the monopolistic competition. Selling cost and product variation constitute an important variable under monopolistic competition, therefore, these have also been analysed. It also seeks to discuss the excess capacity, inferior commodity and wasteful advertising expenditure as important wastes under the monopolistic competition situation in the market.

CHARACTERISTICS OF MONOPOLISTIC COMPETITION

Monopolistic competition refers to a market situation, where there are a large number of firms selling differentiated products. It contains elements of both monopoly and perfect competition. It is akin to the perfect competition, because there are a large number of buyers and sellers, who are supposed to have rational behaviour and perfect knowledge of the market along with the freedom of entry and exit. It is akin to the monopoly, because each seller sells differentiated product and faces a negatively sloping demand curve for his distinct product. On account of differentiated sales, despite a large number of sellers in the market, each seller, to a limited extent, enjoys monopolistic power, therefore this situation has been aptly termed as monopolistic competition by American economist, Professor E.H. Chamberlin. British Economist Mrs. Joan Violet Robinson has almost at the same time named it as 'imperfect competition', because under such market situation all conditions of the perfect competition are satisfied excepting the condition of the homogenous sale, indicating an imperfection of the competition. Thus, monopolistic competition is a market structure in which there are many firms selling, products, which are close, but not perfect substitute for each other. Such markets have the following characteristics:

1. **Atomistic Competition:** There are a large number of buyers and sellers, so that no one controls a significant portion of the total demand and supply for the product in the market. The control of each seller is little enough so that by substantially extending or restricting his own sales, he does not perceptibly affect the sales of any other individual seller. Similarly, each buyer must be so small that any variation in his purchases has no noticeable effect on the market price. Moreover, due to a large number, there cannot be collusive agreements among the buyers or the sellers.
2. **Perfect Knowledge:** All sellers and buyers are aware of all current opportunities. One's knowledge of what others are doing is sufficient to prevent him from taking a lower or paying a higher price than what others are doing.
3. **Rational Behaviour:** All buyers behave in the manner that maximises their utilities (i.e., satisfactions) and all sellers behave to maximise their profits. In other words, both the parties are aware of their own interests and try to maximise them.
4. **Freedom of Entry and Exit of Resources:** The productive resources, like, land, labour, capital and entrepreneurship, can enter or leave any industry, whenever their owners wish. In case the owners perceive that a higher return is available in another industry, they will shift some of their resources to the industry with higher returns. Thus, it is assumed that no barriers exist to prevent entry and exist of the resources.
5. **Differentiated Sale:** It is in important characteristics of the monopolistic competition that alone distinguishes, it from the perfect competition. Products are differentiated by brands, trademarks, distinctive designs, packaging, colour, style, etc. Product differentiation is practiced, where any of the above significant basis exists for distinguishing the product of one seller from that of another. Such basis may be real or fancied, but it must lead to a preference for one variety of the product over another. When products are differentiated, that is, buyers are given a basis for preference, they will be paired with sellers not on random basis (as under perfect competition) but according to their preferences. Under imperfect competition, the market of each seller is not perfectly merged with those of his rivals, so that the whole is not a single large market of many sellers, but a network of related markets one for each seller.

Thus, the industry under monopolistic competition has many sellers, where each seller supplies insignificant portion of the total demand. It indicates that each seller will pursue independent policies with respect to pricing, advertising and product variation without any explicit regard for the behaviour of his competitors and without any concern for retaliatory measures from his competitors. Secondly, monopolistic competition concerns itself not only with the problem of an individual equilibrium (the ordinary theory of monopoly), but also with that of a group equilibrium (the adjustment of economic forces within a group of competitors).

Since the market of single seller under monopolistic competition is separate to a degree from those of his rivals, his sales are limited and depend upon three different types of action, which he may take to influence his volume of sales. Firstly, he may change his selling price. Secondly, he may vary the nature of his product. Thirdly, he may alter his expenditures on advertising and other methods of sales promotion. The former one represents a movement along with the demand curve, whereas the latter two represent shifts of his demand curve.

The demand for the product of a single firm is highly elastic, which also varies from firm to firm. In case one of the sellers have succeeded in creating stronger preferences among the buyers for one's product, the demand is likely to be less elastic, as compared to that of the products of his rivals. This high degree of elasticity reveals that the demand curve is not horizontal straight line as under perfect competition. Under such situation, each seller is somewhat a monopolist, as he can raise the price without losing all his customers. It is because some will still prefer his product to those of his competitors. Simultaneously, he faces a hard competition, as the price reduction will not bring him an infinite volume of business. It is because the other buyers will still be attached to the products of the competing sellers. Thus, at each level of price the seller can sell only a limited quantity and, as a result, the demand curve has slightly negative slope.

PRICING DECISIONS UNDER MONOPOLISTIC COMPETITION

Sellers under monopolistic competition are also guided by the objective of maximisation of profits or minimisation of losses. It is achieved by variation in the price, the product or the advertising outlays, the latter two being the peculiar features of the monopolistic competition. In case we assume away the product variation and advertising outlays, the pricing by a firm under monopolistic competition is reduced to pricing under monopoly. On account of differentiated sale, it is difficult to identify the industry, hence Professor E.H. Chamberlin has introduced the concept of the 'group' in place of an 'industry'. The group or cluster of firms, producing goods, which are very near substitutes having a high degree of cross elasticity of demand. Therefore, along with the equilibrium of the firm, he has considered the group equilibrium in place of the industry equilibrium. Here we consider the determination of equilibrium price assuming that the firms have already determined their most profitable varieties of the product and volume of advertisement outlays.

Firm's Equilibrium

Assuming given conditions with respect to nature and prices of substances, firm will try to adjust the price in such a way as to earn the maximum net revenue. The firm faces a negatively sloping demand curve, whose elasticity depends upon the distinction its product has over that of rivals. The different varieties of the products of the various firms will also cause the cost conditions to differ. Accordingly the equilibrium levels of the various firms will be different. A few firms working with excess capacity will be getting only normal profits, while others may be getting net profits and still other firms may be getting net profits, whether working at the optimum capacity level or beyond such level.

Figure 21.1 reveals the short run equilibrium position of a firm under monopolistic competition, where AR represents the average revenue or demand curve of the firm assuming the given varieties of all products and of all other prices and *SAC* represents the short run average cost of production. *MR* and *SMC* represent the marginal revenue and the short run marginal cost of production respectively. The short run marginal cost curve intersects the marginal revenue curve at point *E*, which represents the equilibrium level, where the price is $OP = QP'$ and the average cost of production is $OC = QC'$. The difference between the price (OP) and the average cost of production (OC) happens to be maximum, which is equal to $PC = P'C'$. The firm obtains the maximum net revenue (NR) equal to $CPP'C'$ by selling OQ quantity at this equilibrium level.

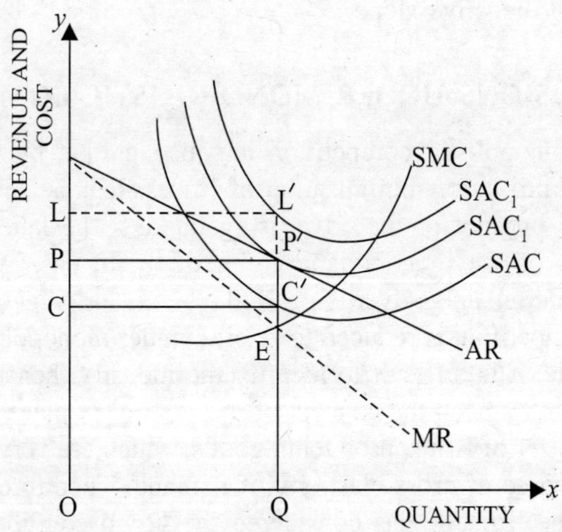

FIGURE 21.1 Short Run Equilibrium under Monopolistic Competition.

Similarly, the case of a firm, whose cost of production is higher (represented by SAC_1) and, as a result, getting only a normal profit under monopolistic competition, is also exhibited in the above diagram. The firm's equilibrium is at point E, where the marginal cost equals the marginal revenue. At this equilibrium level, firm's sale remains at OQ level, where the price and the average cost of production is $OP = QP'$. In case the cost of production of a firm is still higher, the firm may even incur a loss but will keep on producing and selling OQ quantity at $OP = QP'$ price, provided $OP > AVC$ (the average variable cost). The average cost of production being $OL = QL'$, the firm will incur a net loss (NL) equal to $PLL'P'$.

The firm's equilibrium is at E point, because as production increases up to this point of intersection of the marginal revenue to the marginal cost at E, the profits are continually increased, since each additional unit adds more to the revenue than to the cost. Beyond this, the reverse is true, therefore, the net profits will accordingly be maximum, when output is OQ.

In the long-run, since there is freedom of entry, profits greater than normal cannot exist. Being allured by the net profits of the existing firms, new firms may enter into the market shifting the demand curve of the firm to the left, which indicates a reduced share of the total market at all levels of prices. This new demand (or average revenue) curve will be tangent to the long run average cost curve leaving only normal profit to the firm.

In Figure 21.2, $D = AR$ represents the original demand or average revenue curve of the firm, whose long run marginal cost (LMC) and short run marginal cost (SMC) curves intersect the marginal revenue (MR) curve at E point, which reveals the equilibrium of the firm. At this equilibrium level, the price is $OP - QP_2$ and the average cost of production is $OC = QC_2$. It leaves PCC_2P_2 as net profit to the firm. This net profit of the firm may attract new entrants in the industry, each producing a different make from the varieties already present in the market.

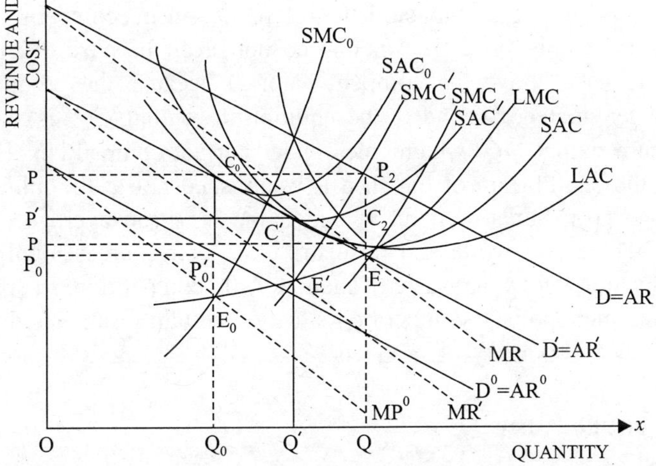

FIGURE 21.2 Long Run Equilibrium under Monopolistic Competition.

The customary notion of entry, which means the reproduction of the commodity, has undergone a change under monopolistic competition, where entry designates the appearance of a new firm with an article different from the variants already in existence in the market segment. As new firms invade the field, the existing customers are divided among more sellers, so that at the various prices each firm would sell smaller quantities of its particular make. The demand curve shifts down to the left, sometimes even below the average cost curve, if the new firms keep on entering. This would mean that the market is so over-crowded with firms that sales are insufficient to cover the average cost.

Thus, the demand curve has been shifted to $D^0 = AR^0$ level, where the marginal revenue (MR^0) intersects the long run marginal cost (*LMC*) as well as short run marginal cost (SMC^0) curve at E^0 point, which is the new equilibrium after unrestricted entry into the market. At this position the firm may sell OQ_0 quantity at OP_0 price, although the same is produced at an average cost of $Q_0C_0 = OP$. the firm incurs a loss equal to $P_0PC_0P'_0$. Similarly, other firms may also incur losses. On account of this a few firms may leave the market, which will shift the demand curve to the right.

Thus, $D' = AR'$ is the new demand or average revenue curve of the firm, where MR', being the new marginal revenue curve, intersects the original long run marginal cost and a new short-run marginal cost (SMC') curve at E' point, which is new equilibrium for the firm. At this point, the firm's output is OQ', which is being sold in the market at $OP' = Q'C'$ price. Since the average revenue curve is tangent to the long-run average cost (*LAC*) and short run average cost (SAC'), it leaves only normal profit (i.e., zero net profit) to the firm.

This long run equilibrium price (OP') is higher than the competitive price and like monopoly price, it is above the marginal cost. This unique long run equilibrium price is the characteristics of monopolistic competition. Despite it being a monopoly price, it contains no net profit because of the freedom of entry. It stays above the competitive price because the product of each firm is differentiated. Secondly, the equilibrium output OQ' is smaller than the optimum output OQ, which rules under perfect competition. Under such situation, the equilibrium of the firm is established not at the minimum long run average cost, but at a point at which the long run average cost is still declining. There is a waste and misdistribution of resources involved in this under-utilisation known as waste of monopolistic competition. In spite of such a waste, the monopolistic competition situation certainly satisfies the desire to the buyers for the variety of products.

Group's Equilibrium

The group ordinarily refers to a number of producers, whose goods are fairly close substitutes. Under such a situation, each producer within the group, is a monopolist, yet his market is interwoven with those of his competitors. There is widest variation in the quality of products, which leads to wide divergences in the curves of cost of production. Similarly, differences in the buyers' preference may account for a corresponding variety of demand curves in respect of shape (elasticity) as well as the position (distance form horizontal and vertical axes). All these result in heterogeneity of prices and variation in scales of production and profits.

This analysis is based on the assumption that both demand and cost curves for all the products are uniform throughout the group, which means that consumer's preference be evenly distributed among different varieties and that differences between them be not such as to give rise to differences in cost. Secondly, any adjustment in price by a single producer spreads its influence over so many of his competitors that the impact felt by anyone is negligible and does not lead him to any readjustment of his own price. Thirdly, it is also assumed that the number of firms in the group will remain unchanged.

A given seller in this group may feel that he can vary the price of his product without provoking the other firms into reacting with a price change of their own. The curve *dd'* in Figure 21.3 describes the market for the product of any seller, when all products and all other prices are given. In other words, it reveals the position of demand for his product at the various prices, when all his competitors continue to charge the fixed sum for their products. Similarly, *DD'* curve reveals the demand for the product of any one seller at the various prices on the assumption that his competitors' prices are always identical with his. This latter curve will be less elastic than the former, as the concurrent movement of all prices eliminates incursions by one seller, through a price cut upon the market of others.

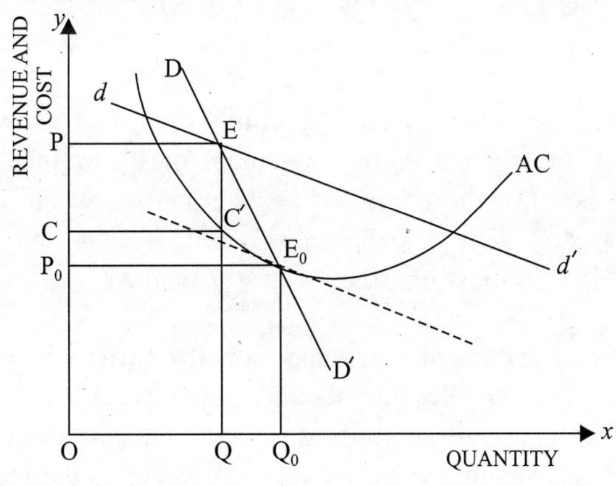

FIGURE 21.3 Group Equilibrium of Firms.

The diagram reveals that the seller is in equilibrium at *E* point, where he is getting the maximum profit equal to *PEC'C*. The *dd'* is drawn through *E*, which indicates the increased sales the seller may enjoy by lowering his price, provided the competitors continue to charge *OP* = *QE* price. Thus, the seller will get increased profit by moving to the right along with *dd'*. The incentive of larger profit, which prompts one seller to reduce his price, leads others to do likewise. When every seller starts lowering the price *DD'* curve shows his actual sales as the general downward movement takes place. The *dd'* curve slides downwards along with the *DD'* curve as the prices are lowered and such movement comes to a stop at the price Q_0E_0. No one will cut the price beyond this level, as the cost of producing larger output would exceed the price at which it could be sold.

The position of *DD'* in Figure 21.4 depends upon the number of sellers in the market. It lies nearer to the vertical axis, if there are more of them, as the share of each in the total market is then smaller and farther from the vertical axis, if there are fewer of them, as the share of each in the total is then larger. Assuming that, at prices in the neighbourhood of *EQ*, additional sellers are attracted and entrench themselves in the field before the price cutting starts. The entrance of new firms in the market will push *DD'* leftwards to a position of tangency with *AC* curve, where the price is *OP* = *QE* and the quantity sold is *OQ*. The cost of production of this quantity is also equal to the price. This equilibrium is unstable due to the possibility of increased profits represented for any producer by the demand curve *dd'*. Since each and, therefore, all are engaged in price cutting, they are involved in ever increasing losses, which is evident form *DD'* that reveals the sales of each firm as the prices of all are lowered. In case the price comes down, each firm is expected to sell *OA* quantity, where these incur losses. Any seller by cutting price to *Q'E'* level may avoid losses and exactly cover his costs. *E'* appears to be the equilibrium as new d_0d_0 is tangent to *AC*. However, the number of sellers is so great that when all cut their prices to *Q'E'*, the sales of each are not *OQ'* but *OM* as indicated by *DD'* and losses are larger than before. So the equilibrium can be achieved only by diminution of firms, which may shift the *DD'* curve to the right and the movement must continue until it passes through *E'*, that is, until the output of each producer, when all are charging the *Q'E'* price, is *OQ'*. Thus, at the equilibrium: (i) d_0d_0 must be tangent to *AC* curve; and (ii) *DD'* must intersect both d_0d_0 and *AC* curves at the point of tangency.

On account of freedom of entry and exit, the firms will get only normal profit, but there will be smaller outputs and higher average costs of production than under perfect competition. It is due to downward slope of *dd'* curve, which is necessarily tangent to the average cost curve to the left of the latter's minimum point. Under such a situation, the firms are operating at less than the optimum scale of plant and hence there exists excess capacity in the industry.

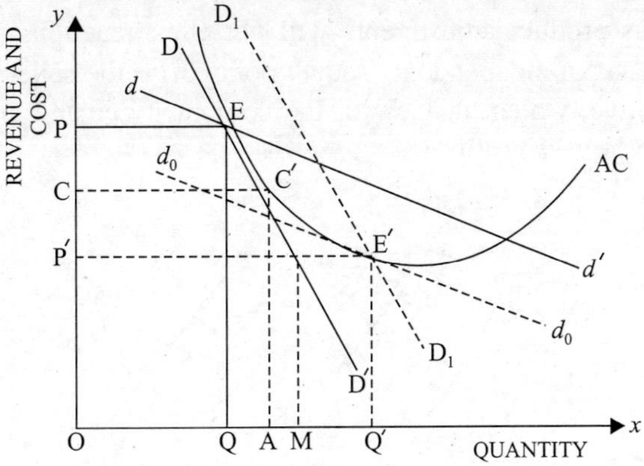

FIGURE 21.4 Group's Long Run Equilibrium.

Product Variations

Since the sellers, under monopolistic competition, offer non-homogeneous products for sale, apart from the competition in respect of the price, there will also be competition in respect of the quality of the product. The entrepreneurs may accept a price generally prevalent (i.e., the price established by tradition or trade practice) and for which the customers are habituated. Under such situation the efforts are made to modify the product to suit the tastes of the buyers, so that they develop a strong preference for that product and confer on the seller a degree of monopoly power over the price to be charged.

This leads to product variation, which refers primarily to the physical aspects of the product, that is, changes in the materials, workmanship, durability, style shape, colour, packaging and attractiveness and separate usefulness of container. It may also refer to the differences in the services associated with the sale, for example, the convenience of the location of the store, its furnishing and general atmosphere, the personality of persons attending to the customers, terms and conditions of sale, promptness of delivery, readiness to accept returned goods, willingness to make alternations, the guarantee for free service and repair for a certain length of time, the trade-in allowance for credit facilities. A variation in any one of these will make a difference between two otherwise identical goods.

Unlike variation in price, the product variation does involve changes in the cost of production alongwith the changes in the demand for the product. So, we are faced with the problem of selecting the product, whose cost and demand allow the largest total profit, price being given. Since the product variation is qualitative rather than quantitative, it cannot be measured along with an axis and displayed in a diagram. In this case, we usually resort to imagination of a series of diagrams, one for each variety of the product. Thus, the fundamental considerations are such that: (i) each seller is able to select from a range of alternative products; (ii) as he shifts one product to another, the level of demand curve for his product shifts and his production costs also change; (iii) his product adjustments will not elicit reactions from his rivals and he can pursue an independent product policy; (iv) the seller will select that product alternative, which, in view of the combined demand and cost effects, allows him the largest profits.

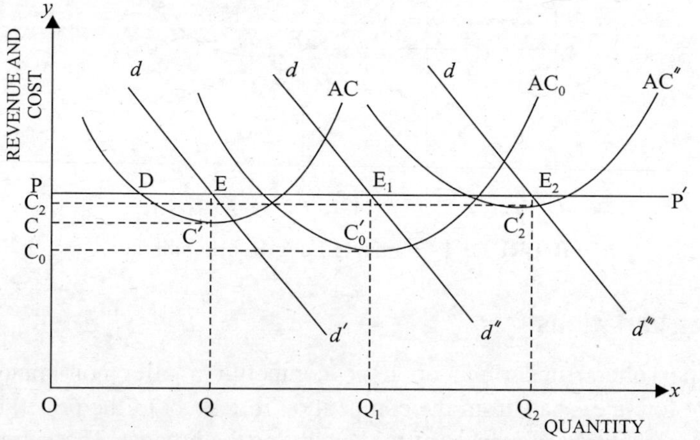

FIGURE 21.5 Group's Equilibrium under Product Variation.

In Figure 21.5, let *OP* be the fixed price and the *dd'* the demand curve of the firm for the former product, whose average cost of production curve is *AC*. The equilibrium is at *E* point, where the firm sells *OQ* quantity at $OP = QE$ price, though the same is produced at average cost of $OC = QC'$. It leaves a net profit equal to *PEC'C*, which is the largest profit, the firm obtains. In case the firm decides to produce and sell another (i.e., superior) variety of the product, it can rightly expect a higher demand, which involves a shift in the demand curve to *dd"* level. Such change in the variety of product also changes the cost of production, which involves a movement from one curve to another that has been represented by AC_0. Under such a situation, the equilibrium is at E_1 point, where the firm sells OQ_1quantity at $OP = Q_1E_1$ (i.e., the old) price. As this quantity is produced at an average cost $OC_0 = Q_1C_0'$, it leaves net profit equal to $PC_0C_0'E_1$, which is larger than the profit before the product variation. In this way, the seller can plan trials with many varieties of the product and calculate the anticipated amounts of the profits resulting from them and choose that variety from the sale of which the highest amount of profit is forthcoming.

It must be noted that the product selected is not necessarily that whose cost of production is the lowest, nor it is necessarily the one, the demand for which is the greatest. For example, the firm will not produce that variety, whose demand is *dd'''*, as the cost of production of that variety is fairly high and leaves very nominal amount of profit. Moreover, the output bears no relation to the most efficient scale of production, revealed by the lowest point on the average cost of production curve. The possibilities of the extra profit are more and more restricted, as the competitive pressure increases. Better and cheaper substitutes mean perhaps a lower price line and perhaps a higher cost curve through the necessity for improving the product and ultimately perhaps a recession in demand. In case the demand is only *PD* for the original product and if no better product choice were possible, minimum costs would only just be covered and if the demand is less than this, the production would have to be ceased. Similarly, if the cost curves were higher or the price line lower, profit opportunities would be more restricted and if the former lies above the latter, for every possible variety, production at a point would be impossible.

We can consider the product equilibrium of the group, where we assume that the markets of all competing sellers are alike and despite the differences between the products of all sellers, possibilities of product variation open to firms are uniform for all of them, so that the adjustments of each may be represented by a single diagram as in the price equilibrium.

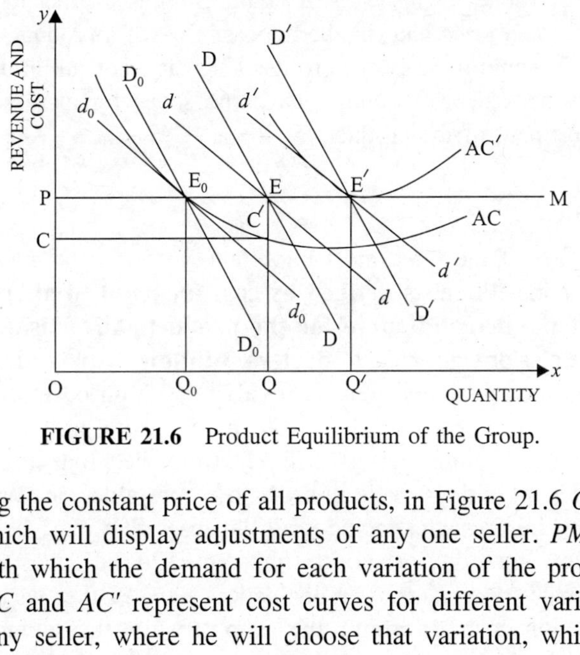

FIGURE 21.6 Product Equilibrium of the Group.

Assuming the constant price of all products, in Figure 21.6 *OP* represents the price, which will display adjustments of any one seller. *PM* serves as a line along with which the demand for each variation of the product may be measured. *AC* and *AC'* represent cost curves for different variations in the product of any seller, where he will choose that variation, which offers the largest total profit. *AC* is the cost curve for the optimum variation of the product. The demand for the product is *OQ*, which is produced at an average cost equal to $OC = QC'$ and sold for a price equal to $OP = QE$. Thus, he obtains a net profit equal to *CPEC'*, which is the largest.

This, being the optimum variation of the product, involves no further product adjustment but this extra profit will however attract new competitors to the field and reduce the sales of each until they reach OQ_0. At this level of sale, the cost of production equals the price prevailing in the market, hence there will be no further movement of *DD* to the left. In case number of competitors were so great that the market of each was reduced below OQ_0, the losses would drive some of them out from the market until those remaining had markets equal to OQ_0 and were again meeting their costs.

Even this equilibrium at E_0 is not going to be stable one, as any seller can think of increasing the profit by improving his product, while the product of his competitors is assumed to remain unaltered. Such an improvement would increase demand along with *PM* and increase costs, shifting *DD* upwards and to the right. A new and larger profit area would result for the new product. However, when the competitors, with same objective make a similar move, the increases in sales enjoyed by each would be only his proportionate share of the total increase for the general class of product on account of its general improvement. This general movement of all sellers will reduce the profit of each, as the cost of production will also be higher. This process will be repeated and will continue so long as it is possible for any seller to increase his gains in this way. Ultimately the equilibrium will be at *E'*, where *OQ'* quantity will be sold by each seller. This level of equilibrium is characterised by (i) the equality of cost and price and (ii) the impossibility of a product adjustment by any one, which would increase his profits. Thus, at this equilibrium point, each firm gets only normal profits and it leaves no scope for increasing profits by further improvement of the product.

Selling Costs

Selling cost, one of the three most important factors to be considered under monopolistic competition, is **defined as cost incurred to alter the position and shape of the demand curve for the product. Advertising, salesman's salaries, commissions granted to dealers, window display, demonstrations of new goods etc., are regarded as involving selling costs.** Such costs are incurred by a firm to persuade buyers to purchase its product in preference to those of others. Selling cost is different from the production cost, as the former includes all outlays made in order to secure a demand or a market for the product, while the latter includes all expenses that must be met in order to produce the commodity or service, transport it to the buyer and put it into his hand to satisfy his wants. The distinction between the two is significant, as the production costs determine the supply, while the selling costs affect the demand. The two extreme market situations of perfect competition and monopoly, the selling cost has no place, as in the former case it is wasteful and in the latter case it is unnecessary.

The firms, under monopolistic competition, are tempted to incur selling costs due to: (i) imperfect knowledge of buyers, and (ii) possibility of altering peoples wants by advertising or selling appeal. Buyers are generally ignorant of the existence of sellers other than those from whom they are accustomed to buy or of goods other than those they usually consume. They are also not aware of prices charged or quality of product offered by different sellers. Advertising is helpful to the seller in strengthening the preferences of those, who are already buying and winning over those, who are buying from others or not buying at all. Thus, it increases the seller's market and changes the location and shape of the demand curve of the sellers' product. Advertisement may be either (i) informative, which is meant for spreading of information about the lower price offer, or (ii) manipulative, which is for promotion of knowledge about the quality of the product. The former affects the shape of the demand curve, while the latter affects its location.

Selling costs are incurred to secure an increase in the demand for the product, which involves a shift in the demand curve upwards to the right. The response of increase in sales to a given increase in selling costs varies, as more and more is spent, which is termed as varying returns to the selling cost. At first, the selling costs yield an increasing return, because of the easiness to attract more customers, and improvement in the organisation of advertising expenditure. However, such return is available only to a certain extent till the more easily accessible buyers are already won over beyond which, if selling cost is increased, the more resistant buyers have to be approached, which yields ever smaller results. Thus, the forces working for increasing returns get weaker and for diminishing returns stronger. The point, where increasing return to selling cost ends and decreasing return starts, we experience a constant return. In case we draw a curve of average selling costs showing output sold on horizontal axis and average selling cost on the vertical axis, it will fall at first, reach a minimum and then start rising. This average selling cost curve can be added to the average production cost curve and a combined average cost may be obtained.

The product variation and selling cost both will shift the demand curve upwards and will make it comparatively less elastic, the two will also shift the average and marginal cost curve upwards suitably. This will set the firm's equilibrium at a new level, which may be as follows:

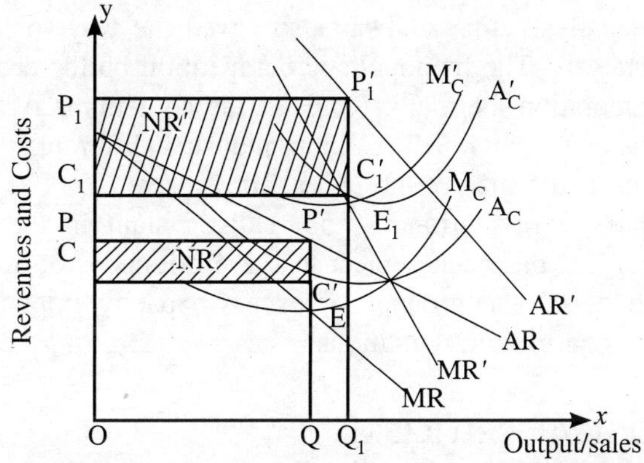

FIGURE 21.7 Firm's Equilibrium Involving Selling Costs.

The firm's original equilibrium is set at *E* point, when the original marginal cost (*MC*) curve, intersects the original marginal revenue (*MR*) curve. Here the output/sales in *OQ*, price is $OP = QP'$ and the original average cost is $OC = QC'$ providing $CPP'C'$ maximum net revenue to the firm.

The product variation and/or selling cost have shifted the demand and cost curves upwards to *AR'* and *AC'* levels and the marginal revenue and marginal cost curves to *MR'* and *MC'* levels. The new equilibrium is set at *E'*, where the new marginal cost (*MC'*) intersects the new marginal revenue (*MR'*) curve. At this new equilibrium level the new output/sales is OQ_1 price is $OP_1 = QP'$ and the new average cost in $OC_1 = Q_1C_1'$ providing $C_1P_1P_1'C_1'$ maximum net revenue to the form.

Thus, after product variation or advertising selling expenses, the firm's output, product's price and cost have gone up and the firm is also able to manage an increased net revenue from the market.

EVALUATION OF MONOPOLISTIC COMPETITION

Prior to the development of the theory of monopolistic competition, economists concentrated on perfect competition and monopoly, the extremes not ordinarily found in the real world. Most market situations constitute a blend of some competition and some monopoly, these may be safely categorised as monopolistic competition. It is more general and allows us to introduce in our analysis, the heterogeneity of the product in all degrees, which has got the existence in real world and affects the functioning of the market. Secondly, it is assumed to embrace all types of product markets having two, a few or a large number of producers. Thirdly, it considers selling activity as an integral part of the firm's behaviour and recognises that the firm can compete not only with price changes but also with product variations. Moreover, the product refers not only to the physical product or service, but also to all circumstances (e.g., location of store) associated with its sale. Lastly, it allows the firm to have motives other than the profit maximisation and by making the minimum use of marginal analysis, this analysis also paved the way for the 'full cost' or 'cost plus' analysis. The monopolistic competition builds economic theory taking into consideration the major forces in the contemporary world, that is, the imperfections or fewness of firms in an industry, differentiation of product and manipulation of the market through selling costs.

Despite all these revolutionary and realistic slant in the monopolistic competition theory, it has been subject to serve criticisms on methodological grounds as well as on the grounds of excess capacity implications, which follows from the equilibrium conditions.

METHODOLOGICAL CRITICISMS

The economists have criticised the three assumptions underlying monopolistic situation regarding group, uniformity and symmetry. Since under monopolistic competition, there is difficulty in determining the precise boundaries of an industry due to lack of homogeneity in the product, Professor E.H. Chamberlin used the term 'group' as an approximate equivalent to an industry. The group is ordinarily regarded as composing one imperfectly competitive market, where each producer is a monopolist yet his market is interwoven with those of his competitors and he is no longer to be isolated from them. However, delineation of a group of firms in the economy is purely arbitrary, as a seller under monopolistic competition competes in varying degrees with all other firms in the market.

G.J. Stigler, the most severe critic of E.H. Chamberlin's methodology stated that the definition of the group is ambiguous, as it may contain only one firm or all the firms in the economy. The diversity and unsystematism may make products of the various firms heterogeneous from the technological view point. Usually a large or dominant role is played by firms outside the group in determining prices and profits within the group. Moreover, on the one hand, Chamberlin assumes that each firm is a monopolist, which implies that there is a low cross-elasticity of demand for the products of the group, on the other hand, he assumes that the group is closely interdependent, which implies that there is a high cross-elasticity of demand among the products of the group.

Professor E.H. Chamberlin attempts to simplify the analysis by the uniformity assumption, where both demand and cost curves for all the firms are uniform for the group. However, for the uniformity assumption to make sense, the firms in the group must be selling physically homogeneous products, and if it is so, then it is not clear why each firm should have a negatively sloping demand curve. Similarly, another simplifying assumption (known as symmetry assumption) that the changes by one firm regarding price, quality of the product and/or selling cost affect such a large number of firms that these do not evoke retaliation by any other firms. Now, with the introduction of the symmetry assumption, G.J. Stigler has argued that we have utterly abandoned the picture with which our analytical technique was designed to deal with: there is no variety and there is only one possible type of inter-relationship (substitution) between products.

EXCESS CAPACITY CRITICISMS

The excess capacity refers to the equilibrium condition under the monopolistic competition to an output which is less than the output for which long run average costs are minimum. It deals with firms having excess productive capacity as compared to that under perfect competition, where in long run equilibrium the firm is operating at the minimum point on the long run average cost curve. So long as the demand curve has a negative slope, the excess capacity is bound to exist, because the point of the tangency between any downward sloping demand curve and a U-shaped long run average cost curve must be above and to the left of the minimum point of the average cost curve. Since the long run demand curve is assumed to have a flatter slope than the short run cost curve, the amount of excess capacity is less in long run that in short run.

Thus, firms working under monopolistic competition would tend to operate with excess capacity, price would be higher and output made available to consumers lower than that under perfect competition. Just as for a given variety of a product, price is inevitably higher under monopolistic competition than under perfect competition, so far a given price the quality of the product is invariably somewhat inferior. In other words, if a seller under perfect competition can give to the consumers the same quality of the product at a lesser price than under monopolistic competition, he could similarly give a better quality of the product for the same price.

In Figure 21.8 the demand curve dd is tangent to the average cost curve at point *R*, where the price charged is *OP* = *AR* and the quantity offered for sale is *OA*. Had there been perfect competition the demand curve P_0Q would have been tangent to the average cost curve at the minimum average cost point Q, where the seller would have offered *OB* quantity for sale at $OP_0 = BQ$ price. Assuming the price to be constant at *AR* and if any seller could dispose of any quantity he pleased at that price (as under perfect competition) each would expand the output to approximately *OB*. Each seller will then realise a per unit extra profit equal to *QO'*, which will be reduced by general improvement in the quality of the product with consequent rise in the cost curves to the *AC'* level, whose minimum point gives only normal profit. Thus, due to monopolistic competition the firms operate at excess capacity, which results in a higher price or inferior quality and lower quantity of the product as compared to that under perfect competition. These are the wastes of monopolistic competition.

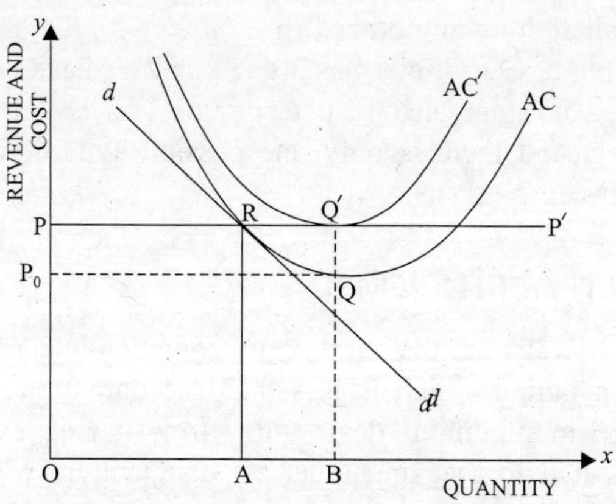

FIGURE 21.8 Excess Capacity of Firms under Monopolistic Competition.

Some economists are inclined to think that the wastes due to monopolistic competition are small as compared to the satisfaction that consumers get in the form of variety and breadth of choice. However, again it is a controversial issue, whether consumer would prefer products with lower cost but with no variety (as under perfect competition) or products with higher costs but with some choice in varieties.

Thus, the monopolistic competition model is not very useful addition to economic theory, as it does not describe any real world market situation. The market with large number of relatively small firms in which there are no barriers to entry, are generally markets in which firms sell a standardised product. This condition brings it nearer to the perfect competition situation. Even if there is slight product differentiation, the individual seller would possess only a limited power to set their own prices. In other words, their demand curves would be so nearly horizontal that the market wide implication derived on the basis of the perfectly competitive model would be reasonable approximation to reality.

Markets in which brand preferences among consumers are strong, usually have a relatively small number of firms, which can be most appropriately analysed under oligopoly. Similarly, market in which a firm sells a product for which there is no close substitute is most appropriately analysed using the monopoly model. The most frequently cited class of markets for which monopolistic competition is supposed to be appropriate is the retail sector in any large city, such as retail groceries, shoe or medical stores, etc. Considering Chamberlin's symmetry assumption, such market situation is inapplicable, even in these cases, because the impact of a price change by any one retailer will be greatest on those retailers in his immediate marketing area.

The monopolistic competition, thus, is merely a transitory phenomenon, as it leads the firms eventually to learn that their actions, in fact, induce reactions from competitors and that the recognition of these interdependencies can lead to greater profits for all firms, which can be appropriately analysed by oligopoly. Secondly, if the firms in the market do not recognise their interdependence and continue to compete as though they were independent, then he would expect the number of firms to decrease, as the more successful firms 'win out', which again leads market towards oligopolistic situation. Thus, the monopolistic competition model seems to be only an empirically empty economic model.

Review Questions

1. What is meant by monopolistic competition? State the features of Champerlin's monopolistic competition.
2. Elucidate the reasons for product variation under monopolistic competition.
3. Why does there exist excess capacity under monopolistic competition? Why does Chamberlin consider group in place of industry under this market situation?

4. 'In long run perfectly competitive firm makes its production at optimum level of plant but under monopolistic competition a firm works below its optimum capacity'. Explain.
5. Bring out the features of monopolistic competition given by Chamberlin and elucidate the equilibrium determination under monopolistic competition in short run as well as long run.
6. Explain why a firm under monopolistic competition earns only normal profit in the long run. How does the long run equilibrium of a firm under monopolistic competition differ from that of a purely competitive firm?
7. Why is advertising expenditure peculiar to monopolistic competition and incompatible with perfect competition?
8. Explain the concept of selling costs. How do these costs influence the equilibrium of a firm under monopolistic competition?
9. What is meant by excess capacity? Why does it exist under monopolistic competition?
10. Discuss the meaning and main features of monopolistic market situation. Draw a diagram to show equilibrium of the firm with excess capacity.

SUB PART-IV
DISTRIBUTION

22

Income Distribution: General Principles

The theory of distribution concerns with the sharing of the wealth produced by the firms among the agents of production (i.e., the owners of the various factors of production) It may be named differently, such as, pricing of the productive resources, deciding compensation for the factors of production, factor pricing or resources allocation. It is concerned with the evaluation of the services of factors of production, the study of conditions of demand and supply of inputs and the influences bringing about changes in their market price. The distribution may be personal or functional. The former refers to the distribution of income among individuals, whereas the latter refers to the distribution among the agents of production for the functions, which their services or the services of their properties perform in the process of production. In case a single individual represents in his person all the agents of production, e.g., a peasant proprietor, who is entrepreneur, manager, labourer, capitalist and landlord, the total amount he obtains will be studied under personal distribution, but the reward he gets for supplying each of the above factors of production constitutes the functional distribution.

In this chapter an effort is being made to explain the general principles governing the functional distribution of the total income at micro level among the various agents of production. The theories of distribution have been classified in three categories, viz. (i) the classical theory, (ii) the marginal productivity theory and (iii) the modern theory.

CLASSICAL THEORY OF DISTRIBUTION

Classical economists, like David Ricardo, Adam Smith and a few others considered the rewards for the various factors of production, but they have not propounded any general theory of distribution. They were more concerned with **'what determines the respective shares of the various agents of production in national income' rather than 'with the prices of the services of the various factors of production'.** They paid more attention to the allocation of national income between the land, on the one hand, and labour and capital on the other. Taking rent as an economic surplus, these economists faced the problem of ascertaining the reward for labour and capital. The reward for labour (i.e., wages) has been determined independently and by deducting the amount of wages, they regard the residual amount as share of the capitalist, who has been considered as a residual claimant. Thus, they could not distinguish between interest and profit.

For functional distribution, the classical economists contributed principles in respect of rent, wages and interest. The rent has been considered as surplus over the output of the marginal land. It is a differential surplus, which superior land commands over the marginal (i.e., the least fertile) land. Similarly, in respect of wages, they attempted to decide the share of labour in the total income and named it as 'wage fund'. It had been determined arbitrarily and dividing this 'wage fund' by the number of workers in the economy, they decided the wage rate that was expected to be sufficient for subsistence and regarded it as the 'iron law of wages'. Residual share of the total output, after deciding the rent and wages, represented the amount of interest and profit, which went to the capitalists.

Thus, the classical theory did not provide a general principle for distribution, but advocated separate principles for different types of distribution. It also ignored the functional theory of distribution, as instead of ascertaining the reward for individual units of the various factors of production and by summing up these the reward for class of the factor as a whole, it ascertained the share of a class of the factor and by dividing this share with the number of units of the factor, the reward of the individual unit of the factor of production.

MARGINAL PRODUCTIVITY THEORY OF DISTRIBUTION

The principle of marginal productivity, propounded by John Bates Clark, Philip Henry Wicksteed, Leon Walras and a few others and elaborated by John Robinson and Sir John Richard Hicks, throws light on some important ground common to almost all kinds of distribution. This principle states that in order to maximise its profit, firm will hire units of a productive service up to the point at which the marginal outlay on the service equals the marginal revenue product or the marginal value product of the services, which, in turn, depends on the marginal productivity of the productive services. Marginal productivity refers to the addition that is likely to be made to the total production, if the firm employs one more unit of a particular factor of production.

Since the producer always desires to produce a given output at the minimum cost, therefore, he considers the contribution of every factor of production in his total product before employing it. The factors of production are both complementary and competitive, therefore, the producing unit for its equilibrium, employs the various factors of production in such a way that the ratios of the marginal physical productivity to price of every factor of production is the same for a given total output. Alternatively, the ratios of the marginal physical productivities of any two factors must be the same as the ratio between their prices:

$$\frac{ma}{pa} = \frac{mb}{pb} = \dots\dots\dots\dots\dots\dots\dots\dots \frac{mn}{pn} = d$$

Alternatively, if only a and b inputs are employed:

$$\frac{ma}{mb} = \frac{pa}{pb}$$

Here m represents the marginal physical productivity of a, b or n inputs and p represents the prices of the respective inputs. This ratio is equal to d, which is the productivity of one rupee worth of expenditure on any input. This equation clearly states that the prices of the factors of production depend on their marginal productivities, as factors having higher marginal productivity will command a higher price and *vice-versa.*

ASSUMPTIONS OF THE MARGINAL PRODUCTIVITY THEORY

The theory is based on the assumption of the perfect competition in the factor as well as the product market. Secondly, factors of production are homogeneous and perfectly mobile. Thirdly, units of the inputs are assumed to be variable and substitutable. Fourthly, it is possible to vary the quantity of any input without disrupting the organisation and working of the production unit. Fifthly, the technique of production, despite change in the scale and proportion of the inputs, is assumed to remain unchanged. Sixthly, the firm is assumed to have an objective of maximisation of profit. Lastly, we assume full-employment in the economy and applicability of the law of variable proportions or law of diminishing returns to the production.

IMPLICATIONS OF THE MARGINAL PRODUCTIVITY

Marginal productivity is a key word, which refers to the addition to total output by the use of an additional unit of an input, while all other inputs are held constant. However, in the marginal productivity theory, it has the following implications:

(i) **Marginal Physical Productivity (*m*):** The additions to the total output on account of use of additional unit of any input ($\Delta Q/\Delta a$) is usually expressed in terms of physical units and is termed as the marginal physical productivity. This productivity varies according to the law of variable proportions, where the productivity increases at the initial stages of employment of any input and reaches to a maximum before it starts declining.

(ii) **Marginal Revenue Productivity (*mr*):** The interest of producer lies with the marginal revenue productivity rather than with the marginal physical productivity. It is the value to the firm of the marginal unit of an input employed in the production process and refers to the addition to the total revenue on account of the use of an additional unit of any input in the production process. It is as follows:

$$mr_a = \frac{\Delta TR}{\Delta a} = \frac{\Delta TR}{\Delta Q} \cdot \frac{\Delta Q}{\Delta a} = MR \, . \, ma$$

Here TR is the total revenue, Q is total output, a is the quantity of input a and Δ(delta) refers to change in the respective quantities. The marginal revenue productivity also shows demand of the firm for that input at a given price of the product, when the quantities and prices of all other inputs are given.

(iii) **Value of Marginal Product (*vm*):** It is the value to the society and refers to the money value of the addition to the physical product by the use of one more unit of an input.

Thus, $vm_a = ma.p$

Since under perfect competition in the product market, the marginal revenue equals the price, the value of marginal product (*vm*) will also be equal to the marginal revenue product (*mr*) of the input:

$Vm_a = ma.p$ (P is the price of product)]

$mr_a = ma.MR$ (MR represents the marginal revenue)

Since, under perfect compitition $MR = P$, therefore, $vm_a = mr_a$

$$\text{Alternatively, } mr_a = P\left(1-\frac{1}{Ed}\right)ma. \text{ because } MR = P\left(1-\frac{1}{Ed}\right)$$

Now since the value of $Ed = \infty$ (infinity) under perfect competition, therefore,

$mr_a = P \times 1 \times MPP_a$ (MPP_a = Marginal Physical Product of Input a)

$mr_a = P \times m_a = vm_a$

Thus, under perfect competition in the product market $vm_a = mr_a$, but in all other market conditions, vm_a will be more than mr_a ($vm_a > mr_a$).

Average Gross Revenue Productivity (AGRP): It is the total revenue divided by the number of units of any input employed in the production process. Thus,

$$AGRP = \frac{TR}{a} = \frac{QP}{a} = \frac{Q}{a} \times P = APP \times P.$$

In other words, average gross revenue productivity is equal to average physical productivity (APP) of the input multiplied by the price of the product.

The marginal physical productivity, the marginal revenue productivity, the value of marginal product and the average gross revenue product under the perfect competition as well as under imperfect competition are shown in Table 22.1.

Table 22.1 reveals that under perfect competition the value of marginal product and marginal revenue product are equal, because the price of the product remains unchanged. Since both vm_a and mr_a are dependent on the marginal physical productivity, these increase initially and start decreasing afterwards. Both values can be placed on one another as both have the same values.

TABLE 22.1 Determinants and Positions of Value of Marginal Product (vma) and Average Revenue Product (ARP) under Perfect as well as Imperfect Competitions

Inputs	*Outputs*	*Perfect Competition*							*Imperfect Competition*				
b	*a*	*Q*	m_a	*P*	*TR* = *P* . *Q*	*vma* = *P* . *ma*	*mra* = *MR* . *ma*	*ARP* = *TR* ÷ *a*	*P*	*TR* = *P.Q*	*vma* = *P.ma*	mr_a = *MR.ma*	*ARP* = *TR* ÷ *a*
1	**2**	**3**	**4**	**5**	**6 = 5×3**	**7 = 5×4**	**8* = 5 × 4**	**9 = 6 ÷ 2**	**10**	**11= 10×3**	**12=10×4**	**13***	**14 = 11 ÷ 2**
10	0	0	0	2	0	0	0	0	3	0	0	0	0
10	1	2	2	2	4	4	4	4	2.9	5.8	5.8	5.8	5.8
10	2	7	5	2	14	10	10	7	2.8	19.6	14.0	13.8	9.8
10	3	16	9	2	32	18	18	11	2.7	43.2	24.3	23.6	14.4
10	4	30	14	2	60	28	28	15	2.6	78.0	36.4	34.8	19.5
10	5	40	10	2	80	20	20	16	2.5	100.0	25.0	22.0	20.0
10	6	48	8	2	96	16	16	16	2.4	115.2	19.2	15.2	19.2
10	7	54	6	2	108	12	12	15	2.3	124.2	13.8	9.0	17.7
10	8	58	4	2	116	8	8	14	2.25	130.5	9.0	6.3	16.3
10	9	61	3	2	122	6	6	13	2.20	134.2	6.6	3.7	15.0
10	10	63	2	2	126	4	4	12	2.15	135.5	4.3	1.25	13.5

*Under perfect competition *P* = *MR* hence *vma* = *mra*, but under imperfect competition it has been taken as equal to the difference made to total revenue by employment of successive units of input *a*.

In case of imperfect competition, the price undergoes a change along with increase in total output, because in order to sell greater quantities, price reduction is a must under such market situation. It results in a difference between vm_a and mr_a both increase initially, become constant afterwards and decrease ultimately, but at every level vm_a values lie at a level higher than the level of mr_a values. The table also reveals the position of the average gross revenue product under both market conditions. It rises at initial stages of employment of input, then it becomes constant later on and finally, it starts decreasing.

The position of vm_a and mr_a under perfect competition as well as under imperfect competition may be shown diagrammatically as follows:

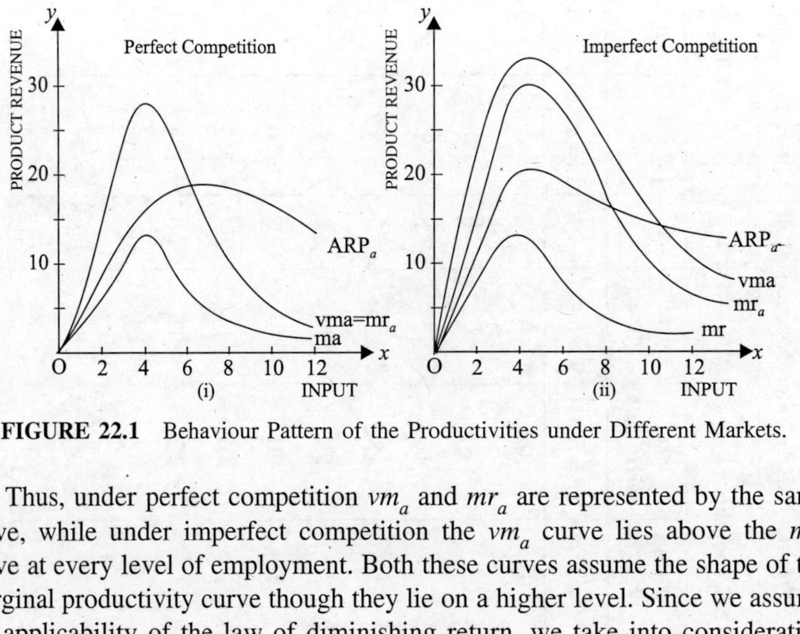

FIGURE 22.1 Behaviour Pattern of the Productivities under Different Markets.

Thus, under perfect competition vm_a and mr_a are represented by the same curve, while under imperfect competition the vm_a curve lies above the mr_a curve at every level of employment. Both these curves assume the shape of the marginal productivity curve though they lie on a higher level. Since we assume the applicability of the law of diminishing return, we take into consideration the declining part of *ma*, vm_a, and mr_a and *ARP* in our subsequent analysis of the marginal productivity theory.

The marginal revenue productivity discussed, thus far, reveals the level of demand for input and now we pass on to consider the position of supply of inputs with the help of marginal and average costs of an input. Marginal cost of input may be defined as the rate of change in total cost along with change in the quantity of any input.

$$MC_a = \frac{\Delta TC}{\Delta a}$$ where, *TC* is the total cost and *a* is quantity of input *a*.

Similarly, average cost of any input is defined as the total cost of the input divided by the number of units employed in the production process.

$$AC_a = \frac{TC_a}{a} = \frac{ap_a}{a} = pa$$

Here a is an input and pa is price of that input, which is the same as its Ac_a.

Assuming perfect competition in factor market, the firm believes that it is so small a purchaser of an input in relation to total supply of the input that it cannot influence the price of the input by the quantity purchased. So, the supply curve of the input for the firm will be perfectly elastic. Imperfection in the market makes the supply (i.e., marginal cost) curve of input slope positively. It also induces the average cost curve to slope upwards to the right.

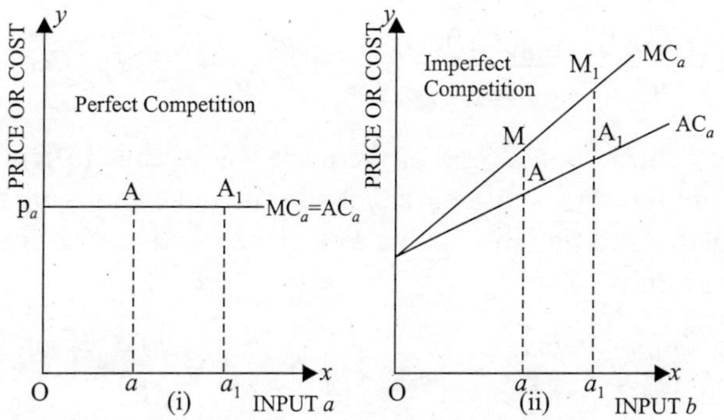

FIGURE 22.2 Costs Behaviour under Different Markets.

Thus, under perfect competition, whatever quantity of input a, the firm purchases from the market, it has to pay the same price making $MC_a = AC_0 = pa$. On the other hand, under imperfect competition, if the firm desires to purchase a larger quantity of input a, it has to pay a higher price (AC_a), which makes MC_a still higher.

GENERAL INPUT EQUILIBRIUM

Under the perfect competition, in short run the firm will employ that quantity of any input, where the marginal cost of the input is equal to its marginal revenue product. This condition must be satisfied in respect of all inputs:

$MC_a = mr_a$, $MC_b = mr_b$, $MC_n = mr_n$, where a, b, …….. n are the various inputs. In long run, apart from making the marginal cost and marginal revenue products of respective inputs equal, the firm also tries to equalise their ratio with that of the other inputs including those that have been held fixed in short run.

Input equilibrium is based on the output equilibrium and shows that the equilibrium in the factor market is similar to that in the product market. Marshall's principle of substitution states that in equilibrium, input will be employed in such a way that the output obtained from an additional rupee's worth of expenditure on any input is just exactly equal to that obtained from the expenditure on any other input:

$$\frac{ma}{pa} = \frac{mb}{pb} = \ldots\ldots\ldots\ldots\ldots \frac{mn}{pn} = d$$

This reveals that inputs are being used in the most efficient proportions and this condition must be met for all variable inputs in the short run and for all inputs in the long run. We may, now, monetise the principles by multiplying all the numerators by the marginal revenue (*MR*). Since, there is perfect competition in the factor market P_a, P_b and P_n, the denominators of the ratios, will also be equal to the marginal cost of the respective inputs. Thus,

$$\frac{m_a(MR)}{MC_a} = \frac{m_b(MR)}{MC_b} = \ldots\ldots\ldots\ldots \frac{m_n(MR)}{MC_n} = (d)(MR)$$

Since for the equilibrium, the ratio of the marginal revenue (*MR*) and marginal cost (*MC*) of the product must be equal to unity, the ratios of the marginal revenue products of all variable inputs to their respective marginal costs must also be equal to unity. Thus,

$$\frac{mr_a}{MC_a} = \frac{mr_b}{MC_b} = \ldots\ldots\ldots\ldots\ldots\ldots \frac{mr_n}{MC_n} = \frac{MR}{MC} = 1$$

Thus, for equilibrium position in the product market, the condition MR/MC = 1 or $MR = MC$ must be satisfied. Similarly, in the factor market $mr_a/MC_a = 1$ or $mr_a = MC_a$ and $mr_b/MC_b = 1$ or $mr_b = MC_b$ and $mr_n/MC_n = 1$ or $mr_n = MC_n$. Since we assume perfect competition in the factor as well as the product markets, therefore,

$$\frac{mr_a = vm_a}{MC_a = p_a} = \frac{mr_b = vm_b}{MC_b = p_b} = \ldots\ldots\ldots\ldots\ldots \frac{mr_n = vm_n}{MC_n = p_n} = 1$$

It reveals that on account of the assumption of perfect competition $MC_a = p_a$, $MC_b = p_b$, $MC_n = P_n$ and $mr_a = vm_a$, $mr_b = vm_b$, $mr_n = vm_n$ in the factor market, because $MR = P$ in the product market. Similarly, for the long run equilibrium under perfect competition, since $SMC_a = LMC = MR = P = SAC_a = LAC_a$, it follows that:

$$\frac{mr_a = vm_a}{MC_a = p_a} = \frac{mr_b = vm_b}{MC_b = p_b} = \frac{mr_n = vm_n}{MC_n = p_n} = \frac{MR = P}{SMC_a = LMC_a = LAC_a}$$

Thus, in the long-run under perfect competition, all inputs are used both in the correct proportions and in the 'correct' quantities. The position of the input equilibrium, under perfect competition may be exhibited as follows:

Figure 22.3(i) reveals that the firm is in equilibrium at *E*, where it employs *Oa* quantity of in *a*, whose marginal revenue product (mr_a) and marginal cost (MC_a) are equal. In case it employs Oa_1 quantity of input *a*, the marginal cost (MC_a) is Aa_1, whereas the marginal revenue product (mr_a) is Ba_1. The firm will suffer a loss equal to *AB* and this will induce it to reduce the employment of input *a* to *Oa*. Similarly, if the firm employs Oa_0, units of *a* input, the mr_a is equal to Ca_0, but the *MCa* is only Da_a, the difference between the two equal to *CD* represents gain to the producer. This will induce the firm to increase the employment of input *a* up to *Oa* level.

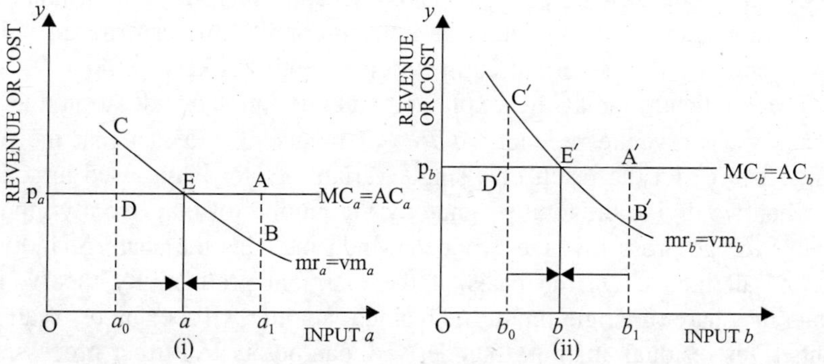

FIGURE 22.3 Determination of Employment Equilibrium for Different Inputs.

This can also be applied in respect of *b* input, if it is assumed to be a variable one. Firm will be in equilibrium by employing *Ob* quantity of *b* input, because at the level of employment $mr_b = MC_b$. At lower than this level of employment, the firm will be deprived of some grain and if it employs more than *Ob*, it will suffer a loss. Thus, the firm will neither like to employ less or more than *Ob* quantity of *b* input. Similarly, for all variable inputs, the marginal costs of the inputs must be equal to their respective marginal revenue products at their respective equilibrium levels.

APPLICATIONS OF THE MP THEORY IN DISTRIBUTION

According to J.B. Clark in long run under perfect competition inputs would tend to receive a real rate of return, which was just exactly equal to their marginal physical productivity. Since *ma.P* = *vma* and *vma* = *pa*, at equilibrium level of input *a*.

$$\text{Therefore, } ma = \frac{vma}{P} = \frac{pa}{P}.a$$

This price of input (*pa*) divided by price of the produce (*P*) (i.e., *pa*/*P*) represents the amount of the product, which the price of input will purchase is termed as real rate of return to that input. The total return received by any one input could be computed by multiplying this rate of return by the quantity of the input employed (i.e., ap_a or bp_b). Thus in the long run, under perfect competition, if each input receives a return just equal to its 'value to the firm' (i.e., *vm*) the total product would be exactly exhausted, because then the producers will receive only normal profits, which will be equal to their marginal physical productivities of the inputs.

This can be applied to a firm, an industry or the economy. When applied to a firm, this is usually named as the theory of employment, as the firm takes the price of the input, as given under perfect competition and when applied to the industry as a whole, it is termed as theory of returns to inputs, as the quantity of input is assumed to be given. Despite this distinction, this theory is a mere statement of long run equilibrium condition of a firm, an industry or the economy under perfect competition in both markets.

The application may be explained, taking into consideration the term average gross revenue product (*AGRP*) of inputs. It is a fact that the output of any firm is not the result of a single variable factor being used in solution. So, when we divide the total revenue by the number of units of any input, we obtain average gross revenue product, which includes the share of individual units of all inputs. On the basis of the marginal productivity theory, if we isolate the share of single input, the residual amount will be shares of all other inputs. This residual amount, thus derived, can be put to further processing on the basis of the marginal productivity theory to ascertain the share of some other input. This will continue till the final residual amount is left, which is taken as entrepreneur's gain. This distribution in respect of a and b inputs may be exhibited in Figure 22.4.

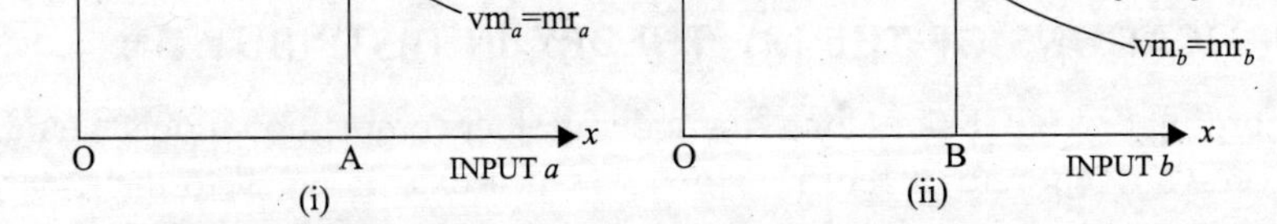

FIGURE 22.4 Determination of Rewards for Different Inputs.

Figure 22.4(i) reveals that the firm will employ *OA* units of *a* input, because at this level of employment *pa* ($MC_a = AC_a$) is equal to $vm_a = mr_a$. The average gross revenue product of *OA* units of input *a* is *AA'* = *OC'*, out of which *AE* = *Opa* is the share of input a and the rest *EA'* (= *Cpa*) is the share of all other factors of production. Thus, out of the total revenue (= *OAA'C*) the total reward for input *a* is represented by *OAEpa* and residual of *CA'Epa* is the total reward for all other factors of production.

Similarly, in Figure 22.4(ii), we ascertain the reward for *b* input on the basis of the marginal productivity theory. The firm, at equilibrium level, employs *OB* units of *b* input and 'pays $BE' = Op_b$ to every unit. The average gross revenue product for *OB* units of *b* input is $BB' = OD$ representing a total revenue product of *OBB'D*. The total reward for *b* input is *OBE'Pb* and the residual *E'B'Dpb* is the reward for all other inputs including *a*.

Thus, the total product (or total revenue product would be just exactly exhausted, if inputs were paid at a rate equal to their marginal productivities. On account of perfect competition among employers price of the inputs would be equal to the $vm = mr$ of that input. On the other hand, the competition among suppliers of inputs would keep the price from rising above the level.

The problem of product exhaustion attracted the attention of a large number of economists, who used a mathematical principle named as 'Euler's Theorem' to show that the sum of the marginal products adds up exactly to the total output that there was neither surplus nor deficit left at the end, provided there is constant return to scale in production. In other words, assuming a linearly homogeneous production function, the total product will be just exactly equal to the sum of the respective marginal productivities of the inputs multiplied by the respective amounts of the inputs used,

Euler's Theorem states that

$$Q = \frac{\partial Q}{\partial a}a + \frac{\partial Q}{\partial b}b + \ldots\ldots\ldots\ldots\ldots \frac{\partial Q}{\partial n}n$$

The equation states that the marginal product of input *a* ($= \partial Q/\partial a$) multiplied by its quantity (a) plus the marginal product of *b* input ($= \partial Q/\partial b$) multiplied by its quantity (b) plus marginal product of any number of inputs ($\partial Q/\partial n$) multiplied by their respective quantities (*n*) is equal to total product *Q*. Multiplying the whole equation by *P*,

$$QP = R = \frac{\partial Q}{\partial a}aP + \frac{\partial Q}{\partial b}bP + \ldots\ldots\ldots \frac{\partial Q}{\partial n}nP$$

$$QP = R = \left(\frac{\partial Q}{\partial a}P\right)a + \left(\frac{\partial Q}{\partial b}P\right)b + \ldots\ldots. \left(\frac{\partial Q}{\partial n}P\right)n$$

$$QP = R = (m_a \,.\, P)\,a + (m_b \,.\, P)\,b + \ldots\ldots\ldots\ldots (m_a \,.\, P)n$$

$$QP = R = (vm_a)\,a + (vm_b)\,b + \ldots\ldots\ldots\ldots (vm_n)n$$

$$QP = R = (vm_a = mr_a)\,a + (vm_b = mr_b)\,b + \ldots\ldots\ldots\ldots (vmn = mr_n)n$$

Thus, if individual units of inputs are paid equal to their marginal revenue productivities or value of marginal products, the total payment will be equal to the total revenue. In other words, if the prices of the inputs are equal to the money values of their respective marginal products, the total revenue will be just exactly exhausted by total payments to inputs.

The only objection to this statement is that the Euler's theorem assumes a linearly homogeneous production function or constant returns to scale. This does not apply in normal cases throughout the length of U-shaped long run average cost curve, but applies at the long run least cost point or the point of long run economic capacity, because at this point returns to scale are momentarily constant.

INTERRELATIONSHIP BETWEEN PRODUCT AND FACTOR MARKETS

This analysis, thus far, reveals that both product and factor markets are interdependent. This can be analysed under three assumptions. Firstly, we assume that the price of inputs in factor market remains constant although the price of the product in the product market changes. Secondly, we assume a change in the price of both input and output in respective markets. Lastly, there may not be any change in the price of the product but the price of input may undergo a change.

(i) Constant Input Cost but Changing Product Price: Under perfect competition in product market in long run initially the firm will be in equilibrium at the least cost point of long run average cost (*LAC*) curve. In the factor market, the price of the input a will remain unchanged, hence $MC_a = AC_a$ will be a straight line parallel to the horizontal axis. This line will remain unaffected by changes in the price of the product in the product market.

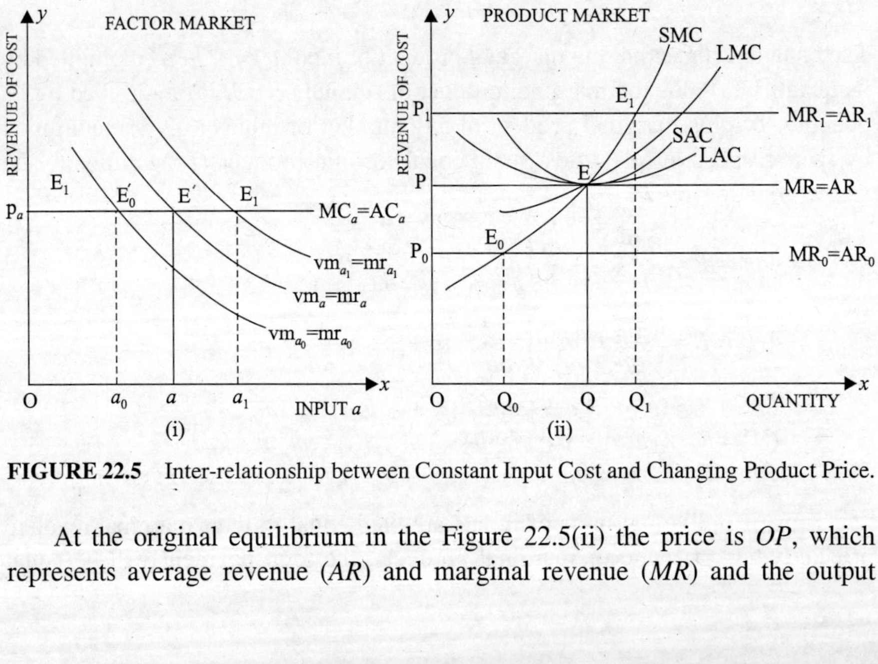

FIGURE 22.5 Inter-relationship between Constant Input Cost and Changing Product Price.

At the original equilibrium in the Figure 22.5(ii) the price is *OP*, which represents average revenue (*AR*) and marginal revenue (*MR*) and the output is OQ. In the factor market at this level of average and marginal revenue, the $vma = mra$ slopes negatively and intersects the constant $MC_a = AC_a$ at E' point, where the firm employs Oa units of input a.

Assuming an increase in the demand for the product, $AR = MR$ may be shifted to the $AR_1 = MR_1$ level, which intersects the short run marginal cost (SMC) curve at E_1 point, where price is OP_1 and quantity of product sold OQ_1. Such a price enables the firm to earn net revenue, which induces the existing firms to increase the output and new firms to enter into the industry. This price increase will shift the $vm_a = mr_a$ curve to the level of $vm_{a1} = mr_{a1}$ which intersects the $MC_a = AC_a$ curve at E_1' point, resulting into an increase in the employment of input a. This increased employment of input a is consistent with the increased output in the product market. This increased use of input a may reduce its marginal productivity but the increased price of the product will affect it, leaving the price of input a to remain unchanged.

This increased output may reduce the price of the product later on, which may shift the $MR = AR$ to $MR_0 = AR_0$ level. This may shift the $vm_a = mr_a$ curve to $vma_0 = mra_0$ level, which intersects the $MC_a = AC_a$ curve at E_0' point, where the firm has reduced the use of input a. On account of decrease in price of the product, the firm has to reduce the employment of input a, so that increased marginal productivity (due to reduced use of it) multiplied by a reduced price of the product, led the price of input a to remain at the original cost level. Moreover, on account of reduced price, the firm will suffer a loss, as a result, in the long run a few firms may leave the industry and existing firms may reduce the output. For this remaining firms may need reduced quantities of the various inputs including a. Thus, the conditions of factor market are dependent upon the conditions of the product market.

(ii) Changing Product Cost and Input Price Both: There may be a change in the price of inputs in the factor market and output in the product market. On account of changes in both markets the actual position cannot be accurately forecasted, because it depends on the relative changes in both. If the relative increase in the price of output in product market is higher than the relative increase in the price of the input in the factor market, the employment of the input may increase and vice versa. Similarly if changes in both markets are in the inverse direction, the employment position may behave similar to that when the cost remains constant but the volume of change may be greater. In other words, there will be greater increase or decrease in the employment as compared with the position, where the cost remains constant.

Figure 22.6(ii) reveals that the firm is originally in equilibrium at E in the product market, where it sells OQ quantity at OP price. The long run average cost is equal to the average or marginal revenue, therefore, the firm obtains only normal profit.

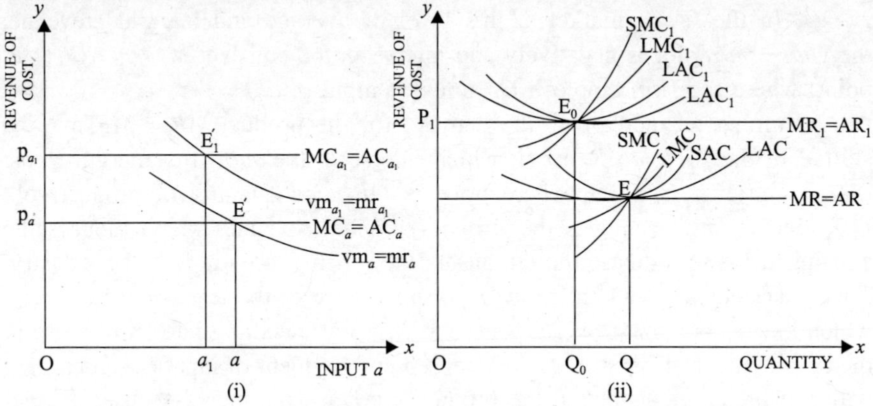

FIGURE 22.6 Inter-relationship between changing both the Product Cost as well as the Input Price.

In order to produce this quantity of output, the firm employs O_a units of input *a*, as at this level of employment $vm_a = mr_a = MC_a = AC_a$. Further we assume an increase in the demand for the product, which, in turn, increases the price. Simultaneously, due to external diseconomies, the prices of all inputs including that of an increase, which shifts the marginal or average cost of the input a to $MC_{a1} = AC_{a1}$ level. On account of increase in both the price and the cost, firm's new equilibrium is at E_0 point in the product market, where it is producing OQ_0 (lesser) quantity of Q commodity and selling the same at OP_1 (higher) price. In the factor market, its new equilibrium is at E_1' point, where the price is opa_1 and employment is oa_0 units of *a* input. Had there been no change in the price of input *a*, its employment would have gone up. This reduction in the employment is quite consistent, because the firm has also reduced its output. By reversing the process we can analyse the case of decreasing price of input and cost of the product.

Thus, the factor price depends upon the supply of and demand for the inputs, which is derived from the demand for the products. In case input prices increase, costs will increase, and product prices will also rise in the long run; and if input prices decrease, costs will decrease and product prices will also fall in the long run.

(iii) Changing Input Price and Constant Product Cost: In case the input prices change, while demand for products and prices do not, the use of the inputs changes in its reverse direction. It is very likely that other industries experience a greater demand, which, in turn, has increased the price of the input. An increase in the price of an input without an increase in the price of the product must result in a decrease in the quantity of input employed. Similarly, a decrease in the price of an input without a decrease in the price of the product will ultimately increase the employment of that input.

Figure 22.7(i) reveals that an increase in the price of the input is followed by a decrease in its employment, because in order to maintain the price of the product constant, input a will be substituted by other inputs. When lesser quantity of input a is employed, its marginal productivity will be higher. So despite higher price of this input its contribution to the cost of production will remain unchanged. So when price of input a goes up to $Op_{a1} = MC_{a1} = AC_{a1}$, the $vm_a = mr_a$ intersects it at E_1' point, where it employs O_{a0} units. Similarly when price of input a decline to $OPa_0 = MCa_0 = ACa_0$, the $vm_a = mr_a$ intersects it at E_0' point, where the firm employs Oa_1' units. Again this greater use of a input will reduce the marginal productivity. This reduced productivity coupled with reduced price will have same contribution to the cost of production. At the reduced price, the firm will like to use more units of input a, because it will be beneficial to substitute other inputs with a.

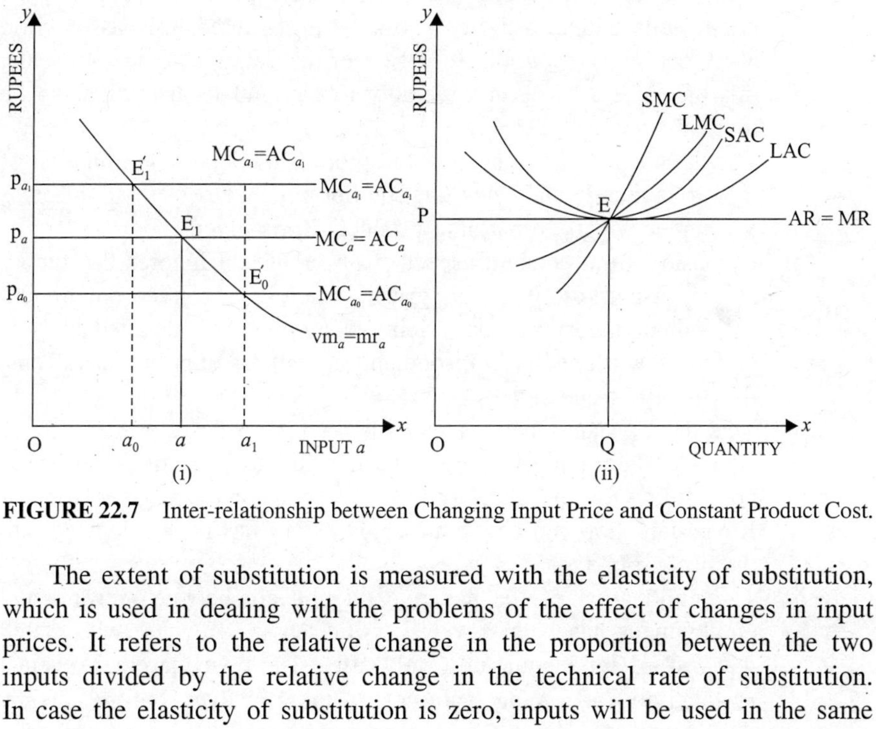

FIGURE 22.7 Inter-relationship between Changing Input Price and Constant Product Cost.

The extent of substitution is measured with the elasticity of substitution, which is used in dealing with the problems of the effect of changes in input prices. It refers to the relative change in the proportion between the two inputs divided by the relative change in the technical rate of substitution. In case the elasticity of substitution is zero, inputs will be used in the same proportion irrespective of changes in their relative prices. However, if, due to small increase in price of input a, the entire output was to be produced with b alone, the elasticity of substitution would be infinity.

CRITICAL EVALUATION OF THE MP THEORY

This theory has been recently subjected to serve criticisms due to its unrealistic assumptions and socially unpalatable conclusions. The main criticisms are as follow:

(i) It is based on the assumption that all units of a single input are perfectly homogeneous. However, in reality, land, labour and entrepreneurial talents are heterogeneous, as they differ widely in their productivity and efficiency. The difference in the productivity gives rise to differential rents, which has been ignored by the marginal productivity theory.

(ii) It also assumes that inputs are perfectly divisible, which enable to make infinitesimally small changes in the amount of factors employed. However, beyond a limit factors are not divisible, which restricts the free choice of input proportions and if such types of substitutions is not possible marginal productivity of the various factors may remain unequal.

(iii) On the basis of perfect divisibility and variability assumptions, this theory assumes constant returns to scale. Since the variability of proportions and divisibility of inputs are limited, this assumption also does not hold good. In case there is variable returns to scale, this theory has to be considerably rebuilt and its use will also be much reduced.

(iv) The theory does not elaborate the process of price determination of inputs; it merely indicates the equilibrium level of employment of any input, when its marginal productivity is given.

(v) It considers the demand aspect of an input and ignores the supply aspect, assuming it to be given, whereas for a complete and determinate theory of input pricing, there must be a detailed analysis of forces working on both demand as well as supply sides. Thus, this theory is one-sided.

(vi) This theory states that the rewards for different factors tend to be equal to their marginal productivities in the long run. So, it has no validity for the short run. With the advent and popularity of Keynesian short run economics, this theory has been relegated into the background.

(vii) The implication of the negative relationship between reward and employment has been severely criticised by Keynes, who stated that reward for labour ultimately affects its own marginal revenue productivity (*mr*). Wages are cost to the employer, but are income to the labour, which forms a major part of the source of total expenditure in the economy. The expenditure is the source of demand for the products, which, in turn, increases the price, the marginal revenue productivity and ultimately the employment in the economy. Thus, the total employment in the economy depends upon the effective or aggregate demand and not on the level of wages.

(viii) According to this theory, the reward is determined by the marginal productivity, which is misleading because the two are interdependent. Higher wages to workers mean higher standard of living and satisfaction, which leads to the higher productivity. Thus, the theory unnecessarily makes employers conservative towards the demand for labour.

(ix) John V. Robinson pointed out that in case there are economies of large scale production, the marginal productivity of a unit of an input to a particular firm will be considerably less than that to the industry as a whole. This may be due to the practice of division of labour in the industry. Similarly, when industry has adjusted itself to the new supply, it is possible that the marginal productivity of an input to an individual firm is less than that to the industry, because its withdrawal will mean greater loss to the industry than to an individual firm. In such industries, therefore, the marginal productivity of a factor is indeterminate.

(x) It is based on the assumption of perfect competition. In real life, since there is no perfect competition, therefore, the rewards paid to inputs do not conform to their relative marginal productivities. Joan V. Robinson extended its application even to the monopolistic world, but that too is not much useful practically. E.H. Chamberlin argued that this theory must take into consideration advertising (selling) cost, since they influence the marginal revenue productivities of all factors. Thus, the simplified form to the theory is neither theoretically complete nor practically helpful.

(xi) The contention that the total product is equal to the marginal productivities of all inputs and payment to every input equal to its marginal revenue productivity must exhaust the whole product, is true only when the firms operate under constant returns to scale and do not face any uncertainty. Even under complete certainty usually a surplus is left after the inputs are paid according to their marginal revenue products. This surplus depends upon the extent of co-operation among the inputs in the production process.

Thus, the marginal productivity theory is essentially a positive and not a normative principle, as it never states that the reward of an input according to this theory is a just reward. According to Samuelson. **'It is not a theory that explains wages, rents, and interest, but it simply explains how factors of production (inputs) are hired by the firm, once their prices are known'. Similarly, Fraser has observed, the economists would claim that the theory is yet incomplete even as a purely academic structure or framework. It has defects of its qualities. Being simple and self-consistent, it is abstract and impersonal. It is guilty of sins both of omission and commission, its postulates are unnecessarily rigid and narrow.** The generalisation of principles of distribution is to be achieved only at the cost of practical utility.

Thus, in spite of all these drawbacks, to brand this theory as useless will be unwise. The theory, however, simplified and abstract in nature, does underline a major force operating on the demand side of all inputs. Modern economists have tried to adjust the theory by supplementing the consideration of supply side and influence of monetary factors, in order to have a satisfactory theory of input pricing.

MODERN THEORY OF DISTRIBUTION

Modern economists are of the view that the theory of product pricing and the theory of input pricing are parts of one whole. The structure of the modern theory of distribution assumes that: (a) each firm has a demand curve for inputs and this curve has negative slope because of the diminishing marginal physical productivity; (b) supplies of inputs at the various prices are determined by decisions of their owners to offer the various quantities of inputs; and (c) the input prices are determined by demand and supply of the various inputs. Thus, the principles that govern product pricing also govern the input pricing.

Demand for Inputs

The demand for inputs is not a direct demand, instead it is a derived demand. It depends on the demand for the product, it helps to produce. It follows, therefore, that if the demand for the product increases, the demand for the input also increases and if the demand for the product is elastic or inelastic, the demand for inputs will behave accordingly. The demand for the input is also dependent upon the quantity of other inputs required in the process of production and the elasticity of substitution between them. The value of the finished product in the production of which input is used and the productivity of input also affect the demand for any input.

The demand for input of a firm is ascertained on the basis of marginal revenue productivity, which combines the influence of both the nature of the product market and the technological conditions of production (i.e., production function). The marginal revenue productivity (*mr*) is the marginal physical productivity (*m*) multiplied by the marginal revenue (*MR*). The nature of the production function determines slope and shape of marginal productivity curve and the nature of product market (i.e., perfect competition, monopoly, monopolistic competition, etc.) ascertains the slope of *MR* curve and both will determine the shape of *mr* curve at every level of employment. Thus, the demand of the firm for any input depends on the *mr* and the amount of an input to be employed depends on its prevailing price level. In case the price level is higher, the employment will be lower and vice versa. The demand curve of a firm is derived as follows:

The Figure 22.8(i) reveals the employment position of input a in the firm. At *pa* price, the firm is in equilibrium at *E* point, where $mra = MC_a$ and it demands *Oa* quantity of *a* input. Similarly, at *p'a* price the demand for input is *Oa'* and at *p›'a* price the demand is of *Oa'* units of the input a. Thus, mr_a is the demand curve of input a for the individual firm.

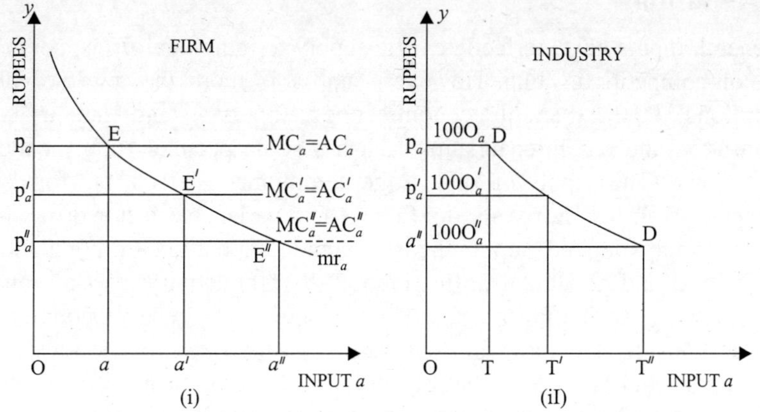

FIGURE 22.8 Demand for Inputs by Firms and Industry.

For price determination of input, the demand of the individual firm has little influence. Actually more importance is attached to the sum total of the demand of all firms in the industry. Assuming that the industry is composed of one hundred identical firms, therefore, for a given price p_a the total demand will be 100 times of the demand by the individual firm at this price. The total demand curve is derived by the lateral summation of the marginal revenue productivity curves of all firms. At p_a price the demand of input *a* by a firm is *Oa*, but the demand of the whole industry at the same price is *OT′* which is equal to 100 *Oa*. Similarly at *pa′* the demand of the firm is *Oa′* but the whole industry *OT′*, which is equal to 100 *Oa′*. Thus, the industry demand curve of the input DD slopes downwards to the right, which is similar to the slope of the marginal revenue productivity (mr_a) curve.

The extent to which demand for input rises, in response to a given fall in the price, it is measured by the elasticity of demand for the input. It is equal to proportionate change in demand for input divided by the proportionate change in its price. Since, the firm's demand is represented by $mr = m.MR$, therefore, its slope will reveal the elasticity of demand for inputs. The slope of *mr* depends on the marginal physical productivity (*m*), which, in turn, depends upon the technical conditions of production and the *MR* is affected by change in the price of product that the input helps to produce. In other words, the elasticity of input demand depends upon the technical rate of substitution and the nature of the demand for the product that the input helps to produce. The substitutability is more in the long run than in the short run, therefore, the demand for input is likely to be more elastic in long run.

Thus, the demand for an input is likely to depend upon: (i) the nature of production function, which determines the slope of the marginal physical productivity (ii); the elasticity of demand of the product, which determines the slope of the marginal revenue (*MR*); (iii) the share of input cost in the total cost of production; and (iv) the time period, that is, short run or long run.

Supply of Inputs

In general, inputs have perfectly elastic supply to individual firms, competitive and non-competitive, alike. However, supply is more the result of physio-institutional factor than of economic ones. Inputs— land, labour, capital, organisation and entrepreneurship- each has some peculiar supply conditions of their own. The supply of land to the community is fixed, but for any one industry or firm it is fairly elastic. Labour is a perishable factor of production and its supply depends upon the size and composition of population, its occupational and geographical distribution, its productivity, cost of education and training, cost of movement, expected income and relative preference for work and leisure. It is now an established fact the rise in wage level beyond a particular level leads to a contraction in the hours of work offered, because workers then prefer leisure to work. This results into a backward sloping supply curve. In case of capital, supply depends on the level of incomes, expenditures, savings and interest, rates, etc. but usually supply of capital exhibits a positive relationship with interest rate. The supply of entrepreneurs also depends upon the rate of return of the industry.

Modern economists also make use of the concept of transfer earning (or opportunity cost) to explain the supply and remuneration of input. Transfer earning is the minimum price, which must be paid to an input to induce it to stay in the industry. In case this price is not forthcoming the input will transfer itself to next best alternative employment. Joan V. Robinson observed that "each individual unit of each factor will be fitted into a place, where its earnings will be greater. When the earnings in that use fall, it will retreat to its next most profitable use". In spite of different peculiarities of each input, generally if the price of a factor increases its supply will also increase and vice-versa. Different supply curves are as follows:

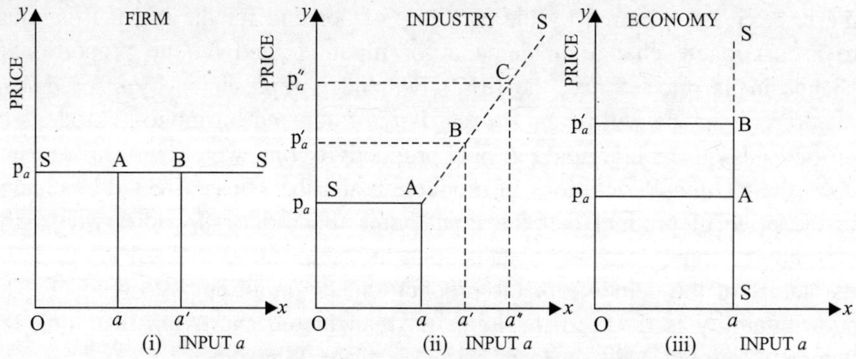

FIGURE 22.9 Supply of Inputs for Firm, Industry and Economy.

Thus, an individual firm may employ any amount of input *a*, but it has to pay the same price. A group of firms, namely, the industry may have a horizontal supply curve up to *A* point, but beyond this level of employment, a rise in employment may necessitate an increase in its price. For all industries (i.e., economy) the supply is perfectly inelastic, as despite rise in price, the supply of a input remains the same. Despite perfectly elastic and inelastic supply curves, in general, we come across a positively sloping supply curve.

Input Employment Equilibrium

On the basis of negatively sloping demand curve and positively sloping supply curve, we can ascertain the equilibrium price of the input as follows:

Figure 22.10 reveals that the demand and supply forces are equal at *E*, where equilibrium price is *pa* and employment is *Oa*. This price of input is ascertained in the perfectly competitive markets. In case there is monopsony or imperfect competition in the factor market, it may not be possible to derive demand and supply curves for the industry, therefore, we may have firm by firm analysis.

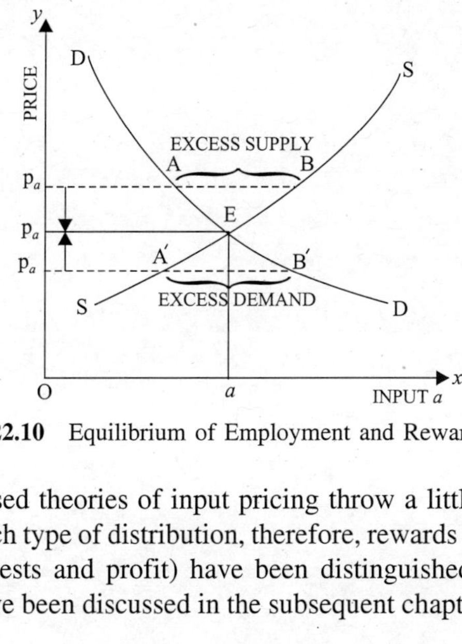

FIGURE 22.10 Equilibrium of Employment and Reward for Inputs.

Such generalised theories of input pricing throw a little light on problems associated with each type of distribution, therefore, rewards of the various inputs (rent, wages, interests and profit) have been distinguished and their separate determinations have been discussed in the subsequent chapters.

Review Questions

1. Explain the concept of derived demand and explain the need for separate theory of price determination for factors of production.
2. Distinguish between marginal revenue productivity and marginal physical productivity?
3. How does the marginal productivity theory distributes the total production amongst the factor-owners?

4. What is the difference between factor pricing and product pricing? Discuss the need for a separate theory of distribution.
5. "If all the factors of the production are remunerated according to their marginal productivity, total product will be exhausted". Examine the statement.
6. Explain the concept and interrelationship of marginal physical product, marginal revenue product and value of marginal product of a factor of production.
7. Examine the determinants of supply of factor of production from the point of view of: (i) the whole economy, and (ii) a particular firm.

23

Theories of Rent

The reward for contribution of land in the process of production is termed as rent. The general theories of distribution failed to throw enough light on the determination of rewards of the various factors of production including land, because of their differing peculiarities. The conditions of demand and supply of land, are affected by a variety of factors, therefore, the determination of reward of this input requires a separate and detailed analysis. This chapter seeks to explain the concept of rent elaborated by classical as well as modern economists. It is to be followed by the consideration of the Ricardian Theory of Rent at both the intensive and extensive margins of production. A deviation from this principle as suggested by Marshall in the form of quasi rent is also discussed here. We also discuss the Modern Theory of Rent as given by Joan Violet Robinson as well as a few allied topics, like rent of situation, rent of ability, etc.

MEANING OF RENT

The term 'rent' refers to a hiring charge, such as, rent of a house, a farm, a machine or an automobile. In economics, it is known as economic rent, which refers to **'that portion of produce of earth, which is paid to the landlord for the use of original and indestructible power of soil.'** Total payment by tenant to the landlord may be termed as gross rent or contractual rent and it may include payment for interest on capital invested by the landlord in reclaiming, fertilizing and/or providing fences, drainage, wells, etc. to the land to make it suitable for cultivation. Economic rent is merely a part of the gross or contractual rent and according to Marshall **it is 'the income derived from the ownership of the land and other free gifts of nature'.** These definitions emphasise the fact that rent is the price paid for the use of land. By land, initially they meant the upper surface of the earth but, later on, they included all free gifts of nature in form of air or sunshine, forests or minerals, soil and water. David Ricardo and his contemporaries associated rent with land and the other free gifts of nature, because of peculiar characteristics of the land that its supply will remain fixed irrespective of the level of rent.

Marshall, later on, introduced the concept of Quasi Rent, which serves as a deviation from the Ricardian concept and emphasised that man-made equipments and appliances can also acquire qualities similar to that of nature made land, at least in short run. So, these can also obtain rent in short run called a quasi rent. It is quasi rent because it exists in short run and will vanish in the long run.

Modern economists have started referring land as a quality and not as a thing, and, therefore, they extended the concept of rent to all factors of production, because all inputs can acquire land quality or land element in varying degrees. On account of this land element all inputs have less than perfectly elastic supply. Payment to land is rent, because its supply is perfectly inelastic. Thus, the extent to which supply of an input is less than perfectly elastic, its reward includes rent. According to Kenneth Ewart Boulding **'any payment to a unit of factor of production in an industry in equilibrium is rent, which is in excess of the minimum amount necessary to keep that factor in its present occupation.'** The credit for elaboration of the modern concept of rent goes to Joan Robinson, who has observed that **'the essence of the conception of rent is the conception of surplus earned by a particular part of a factor of production over and above the minimum earnings necessary to induce it to work.'** Thus, every factor, in real world, is getting surplus over minimum earnings. In case of land, the total payment is surplus, because the supply of land in general, though not for a particular use, is absolutely inelastic. Higher rent cannot attract more of it and lower rent cannot drive it out. This makes the minimum necessary earnings (i.e., the transfer earnings) zero and whole of its earnings, is branded as economic rent. Thus, on account of zero transfer earnings and scarcity in relation to demand, land commands economic rent. Other inputs differ from land, because their minimum necessary (or transfer) earnings are positive and their supply is also not absolutely inelastic.

Thus, the modern economists have widened the scope of rent, which is inherent in rewards for all inputs, although it's content in the various rewards differ from input to input, depending upon their transfer earnings and the degree of elasticity of their supply.

RICARDIAN THEORY OF RENT

This theory has been propounded by David Ricardo during the course of his debate with Thomas Robert Malthus on 'English Corn Laws' during 1813-15. **He opposed 'Corn Laws' and stated and rent was a 'price determined cost' rather than a 'cost determining price'.** High price of food grains means high rent cost and *vice-versa.* His statement in British Parliament **'corn is high not because rent is high but rent is high because corn is high'** is often quoted for expressing the nature of rent.

His main contentions were: (a) rent is the return for the use of the 'original and indestructible power of soil and (b) high rents are not the sign of bounty of nature but they are an indicator of niggardliness of the nature. Earlier economists including Adam Smith laid great stress on the bounty of nature as the cause of rent and stated that after payment to labour, capital and enterprise, the residual of the total produce is rent. It is regarded as the share of land's contribution, which is due to the bounty of nature. Ricardo maintained that while land is clearly useful, it is also scarce and while the usefulness or the productivity of land may be sign of the bounty of nature, more or less fixed total supply is clearly a sign of niggardliness of nature. He was confident that high rent was there on account of scarcity of agricultural land and not due to their abundance.

The contention that rent is a payment for the **'original and indestructible power of the soil'** hints at the fertility of land, which helps in isolating the produce due to original fertility with that due to acquired fertility on the basis of improvement in land and use of manures, fertilizers, etc., because portion of produce due to acquired fertility may be of interest and the produce attributable to the original fertility is rent.

The rent owes its origin to increase in demand for food grains and the process of meeting that through the extension of cultivation to even inferior land or the intensive use of land already under cultivation. There are two ways of increasing production to meet the rising demand due to increasing population: (i) intensive cultivation; and (ii) extensive cultivation. In both cases, more units of labour and capital are employed, but the output increases less than proportionately.

Intensive Cultivation

Under this method, the area of the land remains fixed, but the increasing output is obtained to meet the rising demand by employing more units of labour and capital. It is held that the scarcity of land in relation to the demand is not the only reason for rent but the responsibility is shared by the law of variable proportions or diminishing returns. The tract of land remaining constant, if successive applications of the variable factors to it yield consistently proportional output, no rent will emerge. However, in reality diminishing returns do set in, after a certain point and rent makes an appearance.

Rent appears when the average product for per unit of variable input happens to be above their marginal product. In that case the yield per unit of variable input exceeds the reward going to these inputs, a surplus appears on each plot of land and this surplus multiplied by the number of variable factors is claimed by the owner of land as rent. Since land is free, this total is economic rent.

This reveals that rent is a residual share left after deducting the returns to the factors working on land, but it can be worked out even under the conditions, where other factors are held constant and only land is allowed to vary. It is because rent is just the marginal product of land, which may be either fixed or variable.

In Figure 23.1(i), we assume a farm of one acre as the fixed quantity of land and apply to it successive units of variable factors (i.e., labour and capital), where the variable inputs are measured on the horizontal axis and the output on the vertical axis. The average physical productivity (*AP*) and the marginal physical productivity (*m*) of the variable inputs have negative slopes. At *OA* level of employment of the variable input a marginal product is *AR*, which is reward for each unit of the variable input. However, the average productivity of the variable input is *EA*, which leaves a surplus of *RE* = *TN* per unit of the variable input. Thus, for all units of variable input, the total rent is RENT.

In Figure 23.1(ii) we assume that the composite units of labour and capital are fixed and apply successive fractions of one acre of land until we have put to use the whole of one acre of land. Again *AP* and *mb* curves indicate the average physical product and the marginal physical product of the successive fractions of one acre of land. When the full acre has been placed in collaboration with given amount of composite inputs, the marginal product of land is *RE*. The total rent is *RENO*. All other inputs are getting residual reward equal to *ETLN*.

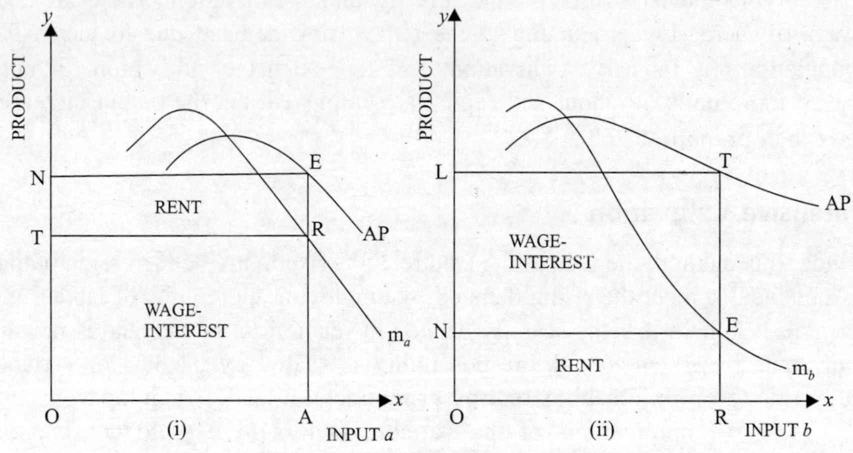

FIGURE 23.1 Determination of Rent and Wage-Interest.

The economic rent on the farm having intensive cultivation can also be analysed in terms of the average and marginal costs, in place of the average and marginal productivity. Here, again, we assume the tract of land as given, where the output can be increased by increasing the variable inputs. *AC* and *MC* curves represent the average and the marginal cost curves, when the varying quantities of combined input of labour and capital (*a*, the variable input) are employed to a given tract of land *b* (the fixed input). In the market, on the basis of forces of demand and supply, the equilibrium price is *OP*, which has been considered as given for the single firm, which assumes $AR = MR$ curve, as parallel to horizontal axis. The average cost (AC) curve is minimum at E_0, where the marginal cost (MC) intersecting the AC also intersects $AR = MR$. At this equilibrium point, the price is $OP = AC$, hence no surplus and no rent. Upto this level of output, the land is a free good. As long as it remains a free good and all plots of land are of equal grade and quality, farmers will not produce beyond OQ on each plot of land, as this is the point of diminishing returns to variable input. In other words, at this point we get the optimum combination of variable and fixed inputs and beyond this the productivity of the variable input begins to fall.

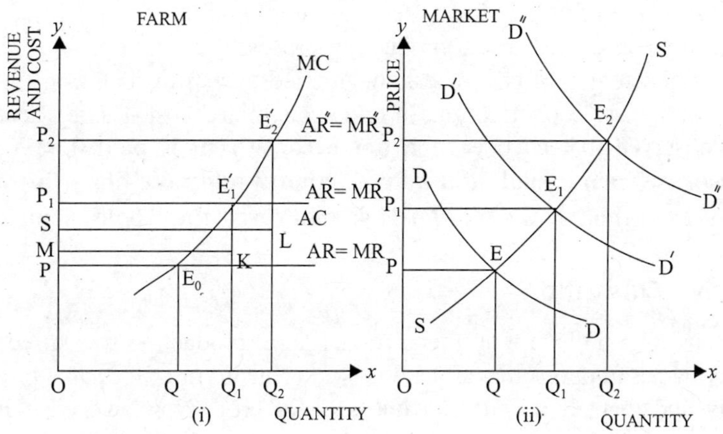

FIGURE 23.2 Rent of Farms under Intensive Cultivation.

In case, there is an increase in the demand, the market demand curve shifts to $D'D'$ level. This increases the price of the product and puts pressure on the farmers to increase the production. However, for this more land is not available, hence the farmers are forced to increase production by making fuller use of their existing physical capacity, because now that capacity cannot be increased. This increased demand fixes the equilibrium price at OP_1 and $AR = MR$ of the firm to the level of $AR' = MR'$. The production will be increased by increasing the variable input a with the given quantity of b, up to that level, where the marginal cost of output equals the new higher price. The equilibrium of the firm at higher price will be E_1', where price is OP_1 and the quantity is OQ_1. This leaves surplus over the cost of the combined input a and the fixed input b, equal to $P_1E_1'KM$, which is the economic rent. Since the supply of land is limited, other farmers cannot undertake to produce the product without purchasing land from the existing owners or without offering to pay them a sum for its use. Thus, the land, which was a free input at lower level of the demand for the product, has acquired an economic value with increase in demand for the product.

Further increase in demand will shift the demand curve to $D'D'$ level, which will raise the price to OP_2 demand and cause even more intensive use of the land by the individual farmer so that the output will be increased to OQ_2. The area $SP_2E_2'L$ represents the rent. Thus, due to increase in demand for the product, the production occurs in the stage of diminishing return to the variable input, which causes a rent to be paid to the landlord. Under such conditions, if the farmer does not pay the rent, other farmers may offer a part of this economic rent to the landlord for getting the permission to use that land. A few others may offer still higher amounts out of this unearned surplus. Thus, a process of competitive bidding will take place and will continue until the entire sum equal to economic rent is being paid to the landlord. This enables the best possible use of the land, because only highest bidders will be able to get land for being used in the production process.

Thus, the rent is a cost-determining price to a firm, but from the point of view of society economic rent is price-determined cost. David Ricardo has rightly observed that **corn is high not because rent is paid, but a rent is paid because corn is high and no reduction would take place in the price of corn, even though the landlords should forgo the whole of their rent.**

Extensive Cultivation

The discussion on the rent at intensive margin of production was based on two simplifying assumptions that all land is homogeneous or of the same productive capacity and that all raised only one kind of crop. Now, we may drop the first assumption, because tracts of land vary in quality and the variation is reflected in the difference in the average costs of production excluding rent. The physical qualities of the soil, the rainfall, temperature, humidity, drainage and topography render one plot of land superior to another, so that it costs less to produce a given output on one plot than on another.

The assumption is not going to introduce new angles into the theory of rent. It simply explains the reasons for the higher rents on superior lands and lower on the inferior lands. A few economists preferred to term it as the **'differential rent',** because the rent is different on each grade of land. The grade of land, which is now only just worth cultivating is said to be on the extensive margin of cultivation, therefore, a few economists also termed the rent ascertained on this basis as the **rent at the extensive margin of cultivation.** David Ricardo considered this kind of situation and observed that land, which for the whole farming industry, is on or beyond the extensive margin of cultivation, will have to pay no rent and may be termed as **marginal or no-rent land.**

Assuming three grades of land, where *A* grade land is the best in regard to productivity, grade *B* is of lower productivity and grade *C* is the least productive land. The analysis has been carried on in terms of the monetary

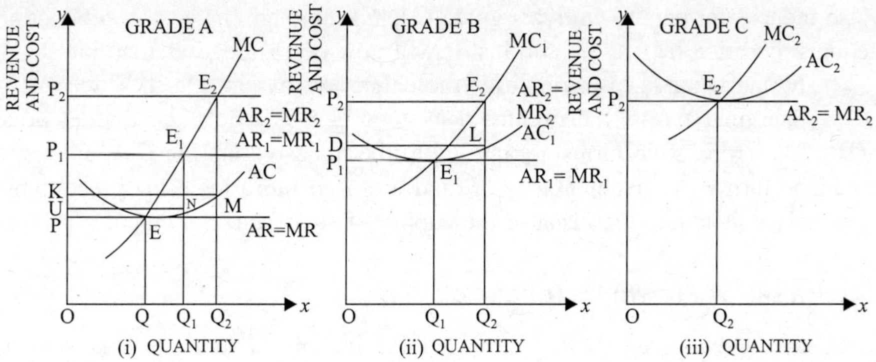

FIGURE 23.3 Rent of Different Farms under Extensive Cultivation.

cost and price instead of output. In case the population of the country is small, the forces of demand and supply determine the price of farm product at *OP* level. In that case, only *A* grade lands will be taken under cultivation, which will not leave any economic surplus, because the cost of production will be equal to the price. Each farm will operate at optimum level, where the marginal and the average costs coincide and both are equal to the price or the marginal revenue. There is no rent at this stage. Farms of poorer grades producing at a minimum average cost in excess of the price in the market will stay idle and will be branded as sub-marginal farms.

In case the demand for agricultural product goes up due to increase in population and/or its purchasing power, this may push the price up to OP_1 level, where $MR_1 = AR_1$. Under such circumstances, the farms of grade *A* will be cultivated more intensively and the new equilibrium will be at E_1, where increased marginal cost equals the increased $MR_1 = AR_1$. The farm will produce OQ_1 output on an average cost excluding rent equal to $Q_1N = OU$. The price being $OP_1 = Q_1E_1$ leaves an economic surplus equal to UNE_1P_1, which may be termed as economic rent. On account of increased price, it may also pay to put B grade lands under cultivation, where each will give an output equal to OQ_1 at $Q_1E_1 = OP_1$ cost, which is also the price of the product. Since it leaves no economic surplus, it is termed as marginal land. Grade *C* farms are still sub-marginal farms and remain idle. Grade *A* lands are super-marginal, therefore, they bring an economic rent.

Further increase in population pushes up the demand for the product further, so that the equilibrium price goes up to OP_2 level, where $AR_2 = MR_2$ for the products of all grades of farms. The farms of *A* grade will now produce OQ_2 at E_2Q_2 marginal cost, which equals the $P_2 = AR_2 = MR_2$, although the average cost is $Q_2M = OK$ only. This leaves an economic surplus equal to KME_2P_2. On account of such a rise in price, rent makes an appearance on the *B* grade lands, which are now cultivated more intensively to produce OQ_2 quantity at $Q_2L = OD$ average cost. It leaves an economic surplus equal to DLE_2P_2. This also induces farmers to cultivate grade *C* lands although the cost of production equals the price leaving no surplus. It will now be regarded as marginal land.

The marginal farm exemplifies the extensive margin. On the superior or super-marginal farms, the minimum average cost is below the market price OP_2. Therefore, such farms are pushed to the intensive margin OQ_2 on *A* and *B* grade farms. As better grades of land are used more intensively economic rent arises as a surplus, because the supply of such land is limited.

Appraisal of Ricardian Theory of Rent

This theory has been widely criticised for both its assumptions as well as conclusions. Firstly, the Ricardian belief that rent is paid for the use of original and indestructible power of soil has been questioned. It is very difficult to identify and trace out the extent of originality of these powers. In reality no land, in its natural form, is cultivable, as it has to be reclaimed through investment of capital and labour. Moreover, there are no powers of soil, which are indestructible. Howsoever, fertile a farm may be, its fertility is much reduced by over-cropping without maturing. Besides, the climate, sunshine, air, situation, etc., which contribute to the fertility of a piece of land, are all fixed by nature and are all 'original and indestructible'.

Secondly, Ricardian theory has used the concept of fertility of land in a very vague term. Apart from the situation of land, the fertility also depends on the ability of the farmers, methods of cultivation and the order and pattern of the crops grown. Thus, the degree of fertility of land, as the measure of rent earning capacity, does not seem very sound.

Thirdly, Ricardian theory assumes the existence of a marginal or no-rent land, which only repays the cost of cultivation. It can be used as a datum to measure the differential rent from the super-marginal lands. However, for substance of the theory, its existence is not necessary. Thus, the concept of no-rent land is imaginary and theoretical and is not realistic.

Fourthly, Ricardian theory has attributed the origin of rent to the natural differential advantages of superior land over inferior land. However, despite all lands being superior, the rent may still arise. So the rent owes its origin to the operation of law of diminishing returns, when the land is intensively cultivated. The fact is that rent arises not on account of superiority or inferiority of land, but because land is scarce and on this scarce land, when more units of labour and capital are applied, their marginal units must be compensated by the product. The earlier units will earn surplus over costs, which will constitute rent. Thus, the Ricardian theory explains that superior lands will fetch higher rents, but fails to explain why rent arises at all.

Fifthly, the Ricardian assumption that best lands are cultivated first is not borne out by the historical sequence of the extension of cultivation in newly discovered areas. The first cultivated lands are not usually the best but are the most easily accessible. Actually, by the best land Ricardo never meant the most fertile land but that land which was the best from the point of view of both fertility and accessibility.

Sixthly, modern economists viewed that the inelasticity of supply of land is not a sound basis to separate rent from the rewards of other inputs. Supply of land may be extremely inelastic and the demand may be determining the rent entirely, but the other inputs like specialised machinery, technical labour and entrepreneurship usually have an inelastic supply at least in short run. Thus, the rent is related not only to the land alone but we may have element of rent in the rewards of all other factors as well.

Seventhly, it is fallacious to consider the earnings of even purely natural land as unearned surplus. Behind such surplus there always lies human efforts, because it is made cultivable through reclamation, etc. Thus, if rent is taxed assuming it to be unearned surplus, it will affect adversely the land reclamation, improvement and maintenance.

Finally, Ricardo's contention that rent is price-determined is also erroneous, as it is because of his assumption of zero transfer earning of land. In other words, he considered only one use of land and that is cultivation. However, in reality land can be put to a variety of uses and minimum rent has to be paid to retain it in the existing use. Thus, the rent also emerges as price determining rather than being price-determined only.

Despite these criticisms, the Ricardian theory has sufficiently explained the nature and origin of rent. Much of what has been done in regard to the theory of rent, later on, is by way of an extension and modification of ideas of this theory.

QUASI-RENT THEORY

The concept of 'quasi-rent', introduced by Alfred Marshall, refers to the surplus earned by inputs other than land, particularly man-made machines and other appliances. He observed that inflexible supply also exits in case of inputs other than land, but ordinarily only for short periods. Since the supply of land and other natural gifts are fixed for all times to come, their earning is termed as rent. The supply of 'man-made machines and appliances' is likely to remain fixed at least in short run, therefore, earnings of such inputs during that time period can also be described as rent. However, it remains a quasi (i.e., temporary or half) rent, as it accrues to 'man-made machines and other appliances' in short run only. Thus, quasi-rent is only a temporary surplus, which vanishes with increase in the supply of such inputs in the long run.

According to Marshall **'quasi-rent is a surplus of total receipts over prime (money) costs governed by more or less accidental relation of demand and supply for that time.** He also observed that the **'additional payment for these agents of production, the supply of which, though alterable in a long period, is fixed in a short period, is technically known as quasi-rent.'**

In case the demand for a commodity rises in short run, it is usually met by more intensive use of fixed inputs (i.e., machines) by dosing them with more units of the variable inputs up to the scale at which the marginal revenue equals the marginal cost. The surplus return measured by the difference between price and average variable cost is 'quasi-rent'. Sometimes quasi-rent refers to the difference between total revenue and total variable cost. It is, thus, short run price-determined cost. Since all costs are variable in the long run and for equilibrium, under perfect competition such cost are equal to the total revenue, therefore, this 'quasi-rent' will disappear.

This can be explained on the basis of the process of short run price determination under perfect competition. The demand and supply forces for the product *Q* in the market determine the price, which is represented by *AR* = *MR* curves of the firm. In short run, the firm uses two types of inputs—fixed and variable and, as a result, faces two types of costs, viz., the fixed cost and the variable cost. The average variable cost is represented by *AVC* curve and the short run average cost is represented by *SAC* curve. The difference between the two is equal to the average fixed cost, which is also represented by *AFC* curve.

The minimum price, which is a must for the firm to continue the production of *Q*, must be equal to the variable cost. In case the price is less than this, the firm will discontinue the production and if the price of the product rises to more than this minimum, there will arise a surplus over and above the variable cost, which is termed as quasi-rent. The firm's equilibrium is at *E* point, where the output is *OQ* and the price *OP*. The average variable cost at *OQ* level of output is *QV'* = *OV* and the price for the same is *OP* = *QE*. It leaves surplus equal to *V'E* = *VP* per unit, where the total surplus *VV' EP* and this may be termed as 'quasi-rent'. Out of the above total quasi-rent *VSS 'V'* covers the fixed cost and remaining area equal to *SPES'* represents the pure or net profits.

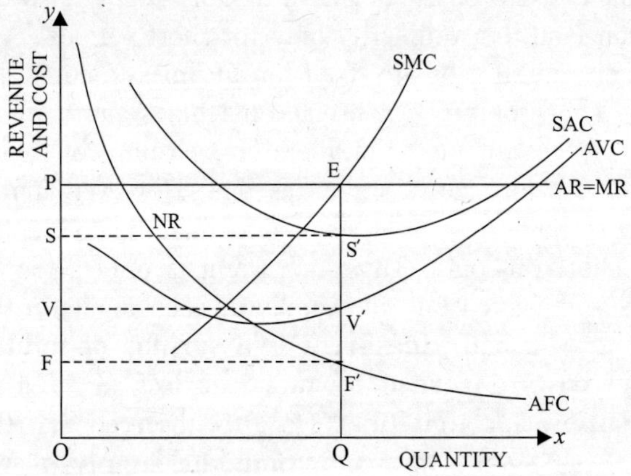

FIGURE 23.4 Determination of Quasi Rent.

The quasi-rent may be greater than, less than or equal to the fixed costs. In case the investment yields a higher rate of return than the investment on an average elsewhere in the economy, the quasi-rent is greater than total fixed costs and the firm makes a pure profit. If the quasi-rent is less than fixed costs, the firm incurs a loss, as it obtains less than average return on investment, but if it equals the fixed cost, the firm makes a normal return on investment.

Thus, the quasi-rent is the difference between total revenue and total variable cost and can exist in the short run only. Under perfect competition, in the long run, quasi-rent must disappear, because all costs are variable and the firm gets the equilibrium at a level of production, where total revenue and total variable costs, i.e., long run total costs are equal. Quasi-rent should not be confused with economic rent, as the former is a short run concept. Moreover, economic rent is a surplus above and beyond the full cost of production, while the quasi-rent represents a surplus over the variable cost of production.

Marshall has taken the parable of meteoric stones to explain the concept of quasi-rent. Assuming that there is a single shower of meteoric stones in a particular area within a very small radius. In case these stones are found to be useful for industrial production, the owner may charge scarcity rent, as they own a free gift of nature, whose supply is perfectly inelastic.

In Figure 23.5 *IS* represents the fixed supply of meteoric stones and the DD represents the demand curve for the same. The demand and supply forces are in equilibrium at K, where the price *OE* and the fixed quantity supplied is *OS*. The total revenue *OEKS* is economic rent to the owner, as they are getting this revenue for the commodity, whose cost of production is zero. In case the demand rises to *D'D'*, but in the short run the supply remains at the same level, because it takes time to react to a changed demand and, therefore, it gives rise to quasi-rent represented by *EKCN*.

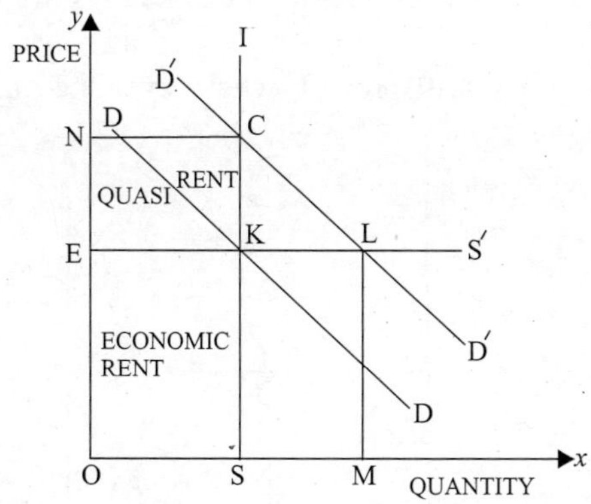

FIGURE 23.5 Determination of Economic Rent and Quasi Rent.

Similarly, in the long run meteoric stones may fall in such a way that they become available in unlimited quantities, provided that the buyer pays the cost of finding the stones. Assuming that the stones are equally easy to collect, the cost of production will remain constant and the supply curves *ES'* is perfectly elastic. The original demand *DD* fixed the equilibrium at *K*, where the price is *OE* and the quantity is *OS*. Since the total revenue equals total cost at this level of equilibrium, the rent is zero. A rise in demand may push the demand curve to *D'D'* level and the supply curve, being perfectly elastic, fixes the equilibrium at *L*, where the price and the cost remain at the same level, although the quantity increases to *OM*. Again there is no rent.

Thus, in short run, on account of perfectly inelastic supply, the higher price obtained *EKCN* is the quasi-rent. Since in the long run, the supply curve *EKLS'* is horizontal, the price of meteoric stones falls to *OE* again. This price is equal to the cost of production (collection), hence, despite increase in supply to *OM*, the rent remains zero. In the short run, whatever was termed as quasi rent, the same forms a part of the cost of production in the long run.

MODERN THEORY OF RENT

Modern economists, particularly Mrs. Joan V. Robinson and Kenneth *E.* Boulding have gone further in determination of rent, which according to them is inherent in payments of all factors of production. The rent is not the price for use of land but the price for use of land element inherent in almost all inputs. It is based on the classification of factors of production given by Austrian Professor Von Weiser, who classified them into two categories, namely, specific and non-specific. Specific inputs may be put to only one use, as they lack mobility, while non-specific inputs can be shifted to several uses, as they are perfectly mobile. On account of specificity, the input may have completely inelastic supply, which reveals that the same quantity will be supplied even if the price is zero as shown in Figure 23.6(i). On the other hand, if inputs are perfectly non-specific, they can be shifted to other uses very easily. On account of this the supply curve is drawn perfectly elastic, which means that the same price will prevail, whatsoever the quantity is supplied.

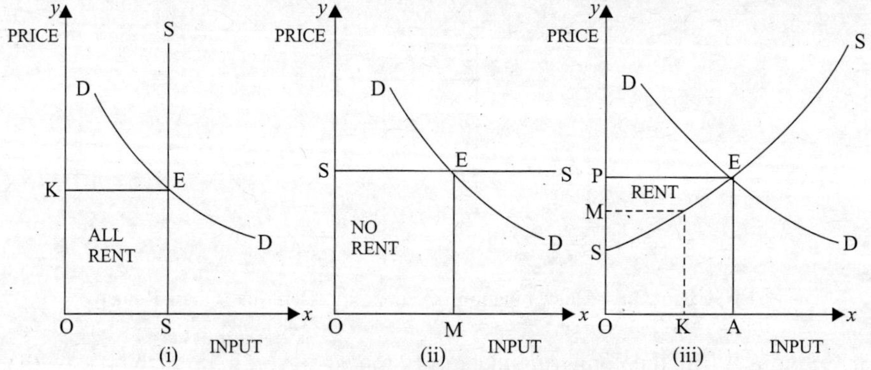

FIGURE 23.6 Determination of Economic Surplus or Rent.

Perfect specificity and non-specificity are extremes. In reality, even land may to some extent be non-specific. In case industry offers higher return than others more land can be shifted to this industry. For example, if sugarcane cultivation offers higher return than the cotton cultivation, more land may be shifted to the cultivation of former, where the sugarcane growers have to pay a rent to the landlord higher than what he was getting from the cotton growers. Thus, the supply of land to particular industry starts at a minimum positive (i.e., > 0) rent and then becomes rent elastic that is the higher the rent, the greater will be supply of land. It is evident from the Figure 23.6(iii), where the minimum supply price is *OS*. In case employer wants to pay a price less than this, he will get no supply of this input. Similarly, in Figure 23.6(iii), the minimum supply price is *OS* and if the employer wants to pay less than or equal to this price, he will get no supply of this input. A higher price *OM* may fetch *OK* quantity of this input. Further rise in price may increase the quantity of input supplied further.

The demand for inputs is a derived demand. A higher demand of the product may produce a higher demand for inputs. It usually depends on the marginal revenue productivity and slopes downwards to the right. The total demand for an input is the sum of demand of all individuals and this demand curve too has a negative slope. This reveals the demand price of the input. Here the level of employment and the price of input is determined by the interaction of the demand and supply curves of inputs. At the equilibrium level of employment, the excess of equilibrium price over the minimum supply price is termed as rent.

Figure 23.6(iii) reveals the equilibrium at *E*, where demand and supply forces of inputs come to equality. At this equilibrium, *OA* is the level of employment and *OP* is the price of that input, indicating total price payable to the owner equal to *OPEA*. The minimum total supply price up to the equilibrium level of employment is *OSEA*. Therefore, the difference between the two (i.e., *OPEA* — *OSEA*) is equal to *SPE*, which reveals a surplus earning of the input on account of its less than perfectly elastic supply. Had there been perfectly inelastic supply, the minimum supply price would have been zero and total payment at the equilibrium level of employment would have been rent. Similarly, had the supply been perfectly elastic, the minimum supply price and equilibrium price at equilibrium level of employment would be equal, which would leave no surplus, and therefore, no rent.

Thus, any factor (land, labour, capital, or entrepreneur), whose supply is inelastic, can earn rent, which is included in their respective prices. Marshall has rightly observed that in passing from the free gifts of nature through the more permanent improvement, to farm and factory building, to steam engines and finally to less durable and less slowly make implements, we find a continuous series of rents. In other words, it is no more in respect of land alone. Mrs. Joan V. Robinson has also claimed that if the supply of any factor of production is limited and incapable of much increase by human efforts in any given period of time, then the income to be derived from it is to be regarded as of the nature of rent rather than profit. She also opined that the surplus earnings of a factor of production over and above what is the minimum necessary to attract it to particular employment is the rent. It depends on the inelasticity of supply—greater the inelasticity of supply, greater is the rent.

Thus, the modern economists indirectly rely on the 'transfer earnings' for the measurement of rent. Transfer earnings refer to the earnings of a factor, which it can get in its next best use. In other words, it is the price, which is necessary to retain a given unit of an input in a certain industry. An input, having perfectly inelastic supply has zero transfer earnings. Therefore, the total payment is in excess over transfer earnings and this can be termed as rent. In case, the input has perfectly elastic supply, the price and transfer earnings are the same, which leave no surplus earnings and, therefore, there is no rent. But whenever the actual supply of an input is in between the perfectly elastic and perfectly inelastic supply situations, part of its earnings is a surplus, which can be called rent.

In real world, we come across such type of elasticity of supply in case of all inputs. Efficiency of workers vary and all cannot perform all tasks, so that a specialised labour may get more wages than minimum needed to retain him in the industry. This excess is the amount of rent included in the wages. Similarly, the extra gains, which a producer or dealer obtains through superior talents for business or superior business arrangements are very much similar to rent. In case of capital, the prevailing rate of interest is such that compensates the marginal investor but the intra-marginal investors, who were prepared to save at a lower rate of interest, now enjoy a surplus or rent.

URBAN RENT

It refers to the economic rent accruing to city sites on which buildings to be used for different purposes are built. The rental on the building may include, in addition to the pure rent, interest on and amortisation of the investment in structure, payment for the public utilities provided, a salary and profit to the landlord. Just as the differences in the fertility of agricultural land give rise to the economic rent, similarly differences in the location of the sites give rise to the urban rent. The appropriateness of the site depends on the purposes of the buildings erected on the sites. The buildings may be used for stores, offices, hotels and theatres, apartment houses, warehouses, material yards, light and heavy manufacturing. A good location for retail store in an area, where people with money in their pockets have a tendency to concentrate. A desirable location for factory site is marked by the availability of power, efficient means of transportation, etc. A good residential site is away from the noise of business sections and near enough to schools hospitals, railway and bus stations, shopping centres and must have respectable or fashionable neighbourhood.

In case the desirable sites were plentiful in relation to the demand for them, there would be no rent on them, but good sites like fertile lands, are scarce. Like agricultural land, urban sites may also be intensively used by substituting labour and capital for land in order to economise land space. The law of diminishing returns to variable inputs also applies in this case, as more stores are built on a given site the cost rises progressively. Thus, a point comes, where the marginal revenue product of the building facilities equals the marginal cost of producing the facilities. It is a mathematical relationship that where marginal cost is rising, the average cost is less than this, therefore, the gap between the two costs is a surplus, which is also known as rent. It is similar to rent at intensive margin of land. Apart from this, the advantageous site may also bring more revenue than the same building in a poor location, the difference may be urban rent. It is similar to rent from extensive cultivation. The productivity of good location can also be measured by the volume of business at such places, as compared to the same at poor location, when the business employs the same amount of labour and capital. Thus, the rent is paid to secure a larger volume of sales.

RENT OF ABILITY

Economic rent is the reward for scarcity and inelasticity of supply. Similarly rent of ability refers to that part of the income of an individual, who possesses special talent not possessed by mankind in general and which, therefore, are scarce. Natural ability, which cannot be reproduced even if earnings rise, is frequently present in some units of labour. The genius clearly possesses scarce and non-reproducible ability, which is undoubtedly born and not made even by the best education. The supply of genius over period of time may be variable, but it does not vary in response to changes in its price. In case such talents are valuable, the individual will receive an income, because he possesses something, which is wanted and of which the supply is limited. High incomes of artists or athletes are mostly in the nature of rent for ability.

Review Questions

1. What is economic rent? Distinguish between differential rent and scarcity rent.
2. Explain the modern theory of rent and bring out the concept of transfer earnings.
3. Discuss the modern theory of rent, in what respect if differs from the Ricardian theory of rent?

4. Why do land values and rentals increase in urban areas?
5. "Rent is price-determined and not price-determining." Explain.
6. "Rent arises, when factor possesses less than perfectly elastic supply". Comment.
7. 'Rent is a differential surplus'. Critically examine this statement.
8. "Rent is the surplus earned by a factor over the above the minimum earnings necessary to induce it to work". Discuss.
9. What is quasi-rent? How does it differ from economic rent?

24

Theories of Wages

The term 'wages' refers to the reward for labour—mental or physical—that assists in the production process. In a wider sense, wages forms that part of national income, which goes to those, who work with their hands or brains, whether independently or for an employer. **Wages is, thus, the price of the services of labour, which also includes salaries, fees, commissions, etc.** It is the single expression of payments for personal services, embracing alike salaries and bonuses of those employed in fixed scales, fees of surgeons, advocates, commissions of selling agents, dealers and brokers and the earnings of the unskilled manual workers. In a narrow sense, according to Benham, **'Wages refers to a sum of money paid under a contract by an employer to workers for services rendered'.**

It may be either piece wages, where payment to the worker is made per unit of the goods produced or time wages, which is paid according to hours of work performed. The wage payments may be measured in terms of either money or goods and services, where the former is termed as the money wages, while the latter is known as the real wages. Classical economists did not make any distinction between the two, but modern economists emphasised the 'money illusion' of workers and considered wages in terms of money wage rate per hour of work. It measures the compensation for a unit of effort and constitutes the basis of the firm's calculation of the labour cost of production.

Labour is a human factor of production, where the agent (the worker) and input (the labour) cannot be separated. The demand for labour depends on the efficiency of the worker, which depends on regular payment of reasonable wages. The worker cannot wait for reward till the product is sold. The supply of labour does not always exhibit a positive relationship with the wage rates, because when the wages increases beyond a certain level, the supply of labour may decrease instead of increasing. Peculiar institutional and behavioural factors also affect bargains in the labour market and social and political conditions are also to be considered in the determination of wages. All these peculiarities of labour necessitate separate theories of wages, which are expected to describe the forces causing different levels of wages.

In this chapter an effort is being made to examine the determination of general wage level and its limitations, because classical as well as neo-classical economists were interested in ascertaining the share of labour in the total product of the economy. The application of the marginal productivity theory to wage determination under the various market situations has been elaborated and the extent of exploitation and effectiveness of trade unions and minimum wage laws as remedial measures have been examined. The modern theory of the collective bargaining in wage determination has been discussed and finally the recent thinking on the problem of wage determination has also been added. Consideration of the various classical theories (like, Subsistence Theory, Wage Fund Theory, Residual Claimant Theory, etc.) and neo-classical theories have been deliberately avoided as these are concerned with the determination of total share of labour in the national income.

GENERAL WAGE LEVEL THEORY

It is a general concept compounded of the wage rates of many kinds of labour in the numerous trades and pursuits and, thus, symbolising a heterogeneous mass of items. It is a vague, yet useful and even indispensable concept, on occasions, when we compare wages of one country with that of another or the wages of a given country at two different times. The general wage level can be determined on the basis of forces of demand and supply of labour in the economy. Since the labour does not present itself as one large mass of identical units, therefore, to start with, we consider the position of demand and supply of labour to a firm, then to an industry and ultimately to the economy, as a whole.

Demand for Labour

It refers to the various amounts of labour that will be hired by firms at corresponding wage rates. The schedule of wage rates offered by a firm depends on the marginal revenue product ($mr = m.MR$) which is the additional revenue the additional employment may generate. The marginal revenue productivity is the foundation element in wage determination, although the actualities of social life force departures from this principle. The demand for labour depends on a number of determinants. One such determinant is technology or the production function (i.e., input-output relationship) employed by a firm. In case the technology is such, where proportions of the fixed inputs and the labour are so inflexible that the additional labour will contribute little to the total product. It will induce the marginal revenue productivity to decline very sharply, which will result into a sharp fall in wages, if the firm employs additional units of it. However, when the technology employed is such that additional employment of labour contributes a gradually diminishing marginal product, a slight drop in wages may induce the firm to employ more labour. Since the demand for labour is a derived demand, it is determined by the nature of the demand for the commodity produced. The greater the consumer's demand for the product, the larger will be the demand for labour, because the firms are engaged in translating the demand for output into its own demand for inputs including labour. Similarly, the prices of other inputs on the basis of substitution effect also affect the demand for labour.

The elasticity of demand for labour depends on its marginal physical product (*m*). A sharp decrease in marginal physical product will make the demand inelastic and a gradual decrease may cause greater employment of labour along with decrease in wages. It also depends on the elasticity of demand of the product, the labour helps to produce. In case demand for product is elastic, the marginal revenue product declines less gradually and makes the demand for labour more elastic. The firm's demand for labour is more elastic, when it sells its product in a competitive market than when the market is monopolistic one, as in the former case the firm enjoys a perfectly elastic demand, while in the latter the demand is less than perfectly elastic. The elasticity of demand for labour also depends on the availability of substitutes. In case the substitutes are readily available, a small increase in wages may reduce the employment of labour considerably and a small drop in wages may encourage the use of labour as a substitute for other inputs.

Thus, the demand for labour by a firm is the function of wage rates, technology, price of product and price of other inputs. The horizontal addition of the demand curves of the individual firms—the addition of the quantities of the services of worker hired by each firm at each price—will give us the demand curve for the industry as a whole. However, the fallacy of composition may be involved, because what applies to parts does not apply to the whole. The difficulty arises from the difference in the impact upon the commodity price between the firm and the industry. The demand curve of each competitive firm's product being horizontal, if on account of drop in wage rate of labour, only one firm reacts by hiring more of this labour and by increasing its output, the price of the article will not be affected. However, when all firms in the industry hire more units of the labour and expand production, the combined increase in sales will depress the price. This lower price of output may cause a reduction in the marginal revenue productivity, whose curve may be shifted downwards, meaning thereby a lower demand for labour. It reveals the hiring by each firm of less additional labour at lower wage rate than was anticipated by each firm in expectation of a constant selling price of the product. This makes the horizontal summation of unadjusted demand curves for the labour by the firms in the industry inadequate.

Thus, the firm's demand curve for labour needs preliminary modification to render it suitable for horizontal addition. Assuming that the wage rate of a given type of labour has declined, the modification process has a few steps. Firstly, the product supply curve of industry is shifted to right and downward, which exhibits an increased supply due to induced lower cost of production. Secondly, the interaction of the consumer demand with this new supply curve will give lower equilibrium price for the product and larger sales, which also indicates larger employment of this labour. Thirdly, this lower commodity price will shift the marginal revenue product curve of the firm to the left and downwards, which suggests a decline in the firm's demand for this labour. Fourthly, the supply curve of the labour to the firm intersects the new demand curve for labour, which gives another point to the revised demand curve, the first one being the price-quantity data before the change in the wage rate. Fifthly, we can obtain more such points by assuming successive drops in the wages, then we can draw a revised demand curve for labour. Sixthly, such modified demand curves are then obtained for each firm. The horizontal addition of the revised demand curves of all firms will give us the industry demand curve for that type of labour. The industry demand curve, thus derived, will also slope downwards to the right.

Similarly, it is equally inadequate to obtain the demand for labour for the whole economy by horizontal addition of the demand curves of all the industries. The interactions among industries producing mutually cancelling effects must be taken into account. For example, if the price of cotton textile declines, its use may increase at the cost of the use of woollen goods. So, there may be a decrease in the demand for labour in the woollen industry. Moreover, increase or decrease in the wages rates, instead of reacting negatively, increases or decreases the total employment in the economy. An increase in wage rates of workers, due to high propensity to consume increase their expenditure, which, in turn, increases the aggregate demands. As a result, the volume of employment, far from falling on account of the higher wage rates, may experience an upswing. On the other hand, a falling wage rate may result into less employment instead of more. Thus, the wage rate is not only a cost to the firm, but also an income to the recipient. Therefore, as an income it reacts favourably on the demand for labour. Trade unions are inclined to resist the decline of the demand for labour by preventing substitutes for labour and attempt to raise the demand, when the demand would otherwise decline. Thus, on account of a variety of reasons, the demand for labour has a tendency to increase over a period of years.

Supply of Labour

It refers to the various amounts of the labour hours offered for hire at the various wage rates. It is function of the number of workers presenting themselves for work and the number of hours they are willing to work per day. It depends upon (1) the size of the population; (2) the sex composition of the population; (3) the age distribution within the population; and (4) the attitude of the population towards work. In the short run, the first three are held constant, while the last one is assumed to be a function of wage rate. The supply of labour is determined by balancing the opposite forces of wage rate and of disutility of working or the desire for leisure. The supply position of labour can be explained by taking workers to be making a choice of a combination of income and leisure, just as a consumer would choose combinations of two commodities. He has twenty-four hours a day at his disposal, but he cannot work all the time, like a machine. He sets aside some hours for rest and the remaining period is utilised either for work or for enjoyment of leisure. For making a choice between work and leisure, he has to bear in mind that if he chooses to have more leisure, he can work for lesser number of hours and thus he can earn lesser income. Conversely, if he works more, he can earn larger income, but the leisure time will be reduced. Thus, the income and leisure between which a worker has to choose, are highly competitive. Every worker has his own taste about this choice, which can be depicted with the help of an income-leisure indifference curve, which slopes negatively, but it becomes steeper as it approaches the two axes, because the worker will like to have some minimum leisure and income, whatsoever may be the wages rate and period of work out of twenty four hours a day.

In Figure 24.1(i) the total income is measured on vertical axis and the hours of leisure time per day, are measured on the horizontal axis. *OR* (24 hours) is the maximum leisure per day, when the worker will get zero wage (or income) and *OM* is the maximum wage (or income), which may be obtained by working for all the twenty-four hours or when he gets zero leisure period. The I_0 is the income –leisure indifference curve, the various points of which indicate the various combinations of income and leisure, which worker will have, while *RM* line shows the combination of income and leisure, which he can have. Both are tangent at *E*, which is the equilibrium of worker, where he will have *OW* wage with *OL* leisure. In other words, he is prepared to work for *RL* hours to get *OW* wage or he is prepared to sacrifice *MW* wages in order to have *OL* leisure.

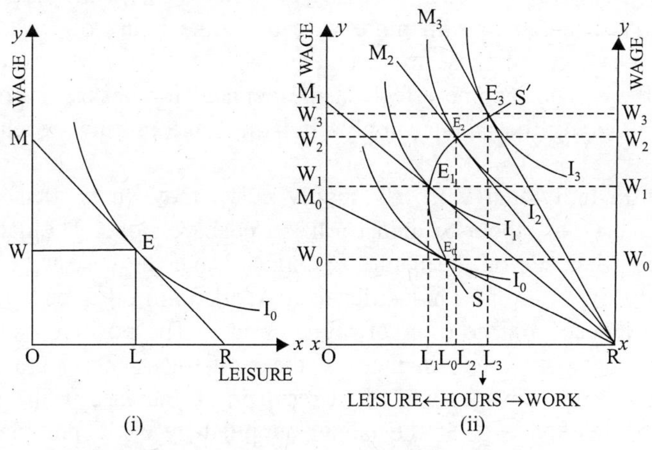

FIGURE 24.1 Determination of the Supply of Labour.

In Figure 24.1(ii), by superimposing the various wage lines, showing wage rates, on the indifference map for income and leisure, we get the various equilibrium at E_0, E_1, E_2, and E_3 respectively. The M_0R wage line is tangent to I_0 indifference curve at E_0 point, which fixes the wages at OW_0 level and individual worker's labour supply at RL_0 level. Since the worker has a maximum of OR hours of leisure time and if he is prepared to work for RL_0 hours, he will get OL_0 hours leisure time. Subsequently, the wage rates increase, which are shown by RM_1, RM_2 and RM_3, which enables the worker to go to I_1, I_2 and I_3 leisure-income indifference curves, where the subsequent equilibrium are at E_1 E_2 and E_3 respectively. At E_1 equilibrium the wages is RW_1 (= OW_1) and the labour supply is RL_1 but at E_2, when wages increased up to RW_2 (= OW_2) the labour supply declined to RL_2. Similarly, further rise in wage rate fixes the equilibrium at E_3, where labour supply has declined to RL_3. In case we combine successive points of equilibrium, then we derive an individual's labour supply curve, which is also known as regressive or backward sloping supply curve. This curve depicts the one possible attitude towards work by the working population and explains that after the income has reached some given level, the desire for leisure overrides the desire for income, so that at very high levels of wages, less efforts will be forthcoming than at lower wage levels.

Labour is such a service for which the worker has also a demand, as he wants more leisure and, therefore, less work. The behaviour of labour supply by an individual worker is similar to the behaviour of demand for leisure by him. Thus, the worker is simply a buyer of leisure, while wage rate per hour is the price he pays for its purchase. The behaviour of worker's demand for leisure can be analysed in terms of substitution effect and income effect. At a higher wage rate leisure becomes dearer, as a result, the worker wants to purchase less of it. Thus it has negative effect on the demand for leisure and works, as labour supply slopes positively. Similarly, when the wage rate rise, the worker is enabled to earn more with the same hours of work. He feels richer and wants to purchase more of enjoyable things of life, where leisure is one of them. The income effect on the demand for leisure is positive and works for reducing the labour supply after the wage rate has reached certain level.

While an individual worker's supply curve may be backward sloping, the supply curve of labour to industry has a positive slope. The nature of the supply curve depends on the nature of industry and the ease with which the worker can shift from other industries to it. Workers in other occupations will have to be induced by the offer of higher wages. The positive slope implies that the number of workers in most of the industries can change easily and quickly and a rise in wages will often result in an increase in the volume of total labour supplied even if the labour supplied by each individual worker declines. It is because of (i) increased hours of work by some workers and (ii) greater number of workers offering to work in the industry.

Equilibrium of Wage and Employment

The forces of demand and supply which are opposed to each other will determine the equilibrium or general level of wages. The demand or the marginal revenue productivity curve of labour slopes negatively indicating that a decrease in wages is followed by an increase in demand for the labour and vice-versa. On the other hand, the supply is sloping positively indicating an increase in labour supply along with the increase in wages and vice-versa. Both these curves intersect each other at *E*, where *OL* units of labour are employed at *OW* wages. The treatment of wages, in any economy at any time, as a comprehensive entity standing for the general level of returns to labour is inadequate. Labour does not present itself as one large mass of identical units. Therefore, the wages of individuals differ and it exhibits mainly three types of differences amongst; (i) non-competing groups; (ii) jobs within a non-competing group; and (iii) geographical areas.

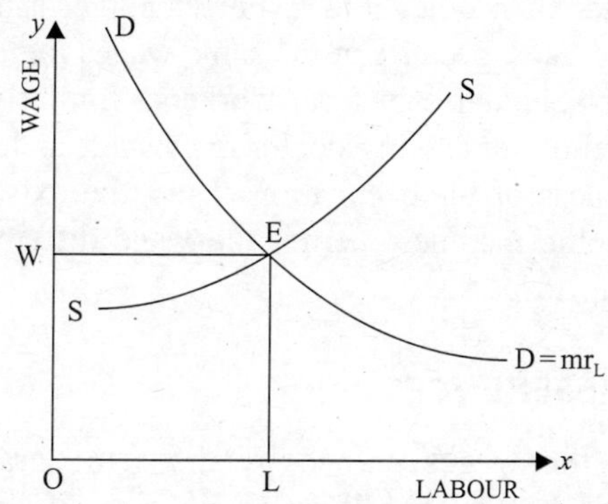

FIGURE 24.2 Wage and Employment Equilibrium.

NON-COMPETING GROUPS

The labouring population may be classified into separate large divisions and crossing of the boundary of one division to another by workers is not an ordinary occurrence. For example, unskilled and skilled workers, professional peoples, like doctors, lawyers, actors, businessmen, teachers, etc., who usually do not compete with the members of other groups at least in short run. Existence of such non-competing groups means that a single wage level is inadequate to explain the wage levels of these various groups and we need a large number of such diagrams, one for each non-competing group, to explain wage differentials, which may arise from the lack of mobility among such groups.

EQUALISING DIFFERENCES

Within a single non-competing group, there are differences in money wages. It may be on account of racial or sex prejudices, as workers belonging to the different racial or sex groups may be hired for different emoluments. The difference in wages may also be attributed to the difference in the natural endowments of workers, as all individuals do not possess the same ambition, the patience and the ability to master a calling, which requires long training and mental alertness. Similarly, the difference in environment—the home atmosphere, the neighbourhood associations and educational opportunities also play a vital role in this regard, as it exerts an over-shadowing influence in shaping the inclinations of a young person.

The differences in wages within a non-competing group may be explained in terms of equalising differences or psychic incomes. Within the given group, some trades are more pleasant, less dangerous, offer better opportunities for advancement, more regular employment and a longer working life than other trades. At the same wage rates their favoured callings would be crowded, while the less advantageous pursuits would be sought by small numbers. This, in turn, makes the marginal productivity of labour in the less desirable trades higher and wage rate greater than other trades. For example, a miner will get more wages than a farm worker, because at the same wages there would be shortage of miners and super-abundance of farm workers. Similarly, a professor earns less than his class fellow practicing doctor or lawyer, as he is required to pay dearly for attractiveness of his occupation. Thus, the existence of 'equalising differences' or 'psychic incomes' permit the wage differences even within a non-competing group to persist.

GEOGRAPHIC DIFFERENCES

In different areas, the wages earned by the same grade of labour vary considerably. It may be due to difference in cost of living at the various places. It also lies in the immobility of labour, which is due to lack of knowledge regarding better wages in other places or reluctance to move to new surroundings. Thus, the possibility of prevalence of single wage in the whole economy is rare.

All the three types of differences work for barriers to a worker's movement from a low paid to a highly paid position. Had there been no barrier, that is, all people have equal endowment and opportunity, all tasks are equally pleasant or unpleasant and the distance presents no impediment, the wage rates of all people would have been identical. However, in the world of reality, with all these barriers in existence, a single wage rate can hardly explain different wage rates of different people.

MARGINAL PRODUCTIVITY THEORY OF WAGES

The theory states that under conditions of perfect competition, every labour of same skill and efficiency in a given industry receives a wages equal to the value of the marginal product of that type of labour. As detailed earlier, the value of marginal product (*Vm*) is derived by multiplying the marginal physical product (*m*) with the price (*p*) of the product prevailing in the market. The marginal physical product (*m*) refers to the addition made to the total product of the firm by the employment of one additional, worker. Since, the firm is to face the 'Law of Diminishing Return' the marginal product must start declining sooner or later, therefore, the value of marginal physical product curve is drawn sloping downwards to the right, as the decrease in quantity multiplied by a constant price, as under perfect competition, produces a decreasing value. Thus, the value of marginal product of labour is the price at which the marginal product can be sold in the product market.

Under conditions of perfect competition, an employer will go on employing workers until the value of the marginal physical product (*Vm*) of the marginal worker, he employs, is equal to the marginal or additional cost of employing that worker. Further, the conditions of perfect competition in the factor market implies that the marginal cost of labour is always equal to the wage rate, irrespective of the level of employment and the curve showing this will be a straight line parallel to the horizontal axis.

Figure 24.3(i) reveals the general wage level of a particular industry, where demand and supply forces fix the wages at *OW* level, which is taken by the firm as given, hence the *AW* = *MW* line represents the wage rate or average wages, which is also equal to the minimum wages. In the product market, the price of the product is determined by the forces of demand and supply for the product at *OP* level, which represents the average as well as the marginal revenue for the product of the firm. On account of equality of average and marginal revenues, Vm_L (= $m \cdot AR$) is equal to mr_L, (= $m . MR$). The two are represented by a single curve which, on account of diminishing marginal physical product, slopes negatively.

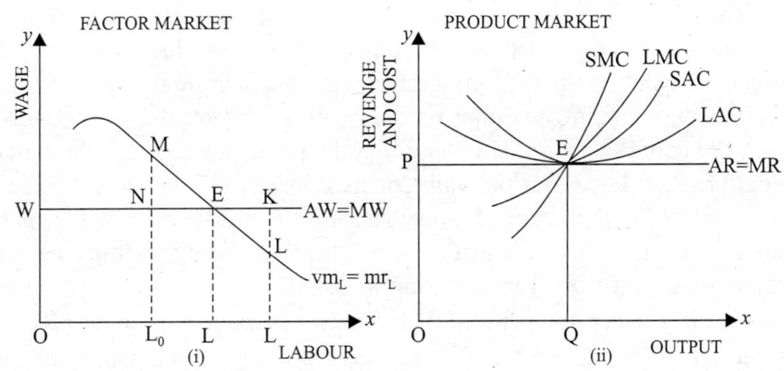

FIGURE 24.3 Wages and Employment of Labour as per its Marginal Productivity.

Since the firm's objective is maximisation of net revenue, it will hire units of labour up to the point at which the marginal cost of labour or marginal wage equals the marginal revenue product of the labour. The condition of equality of the marginal cost of labour with its marginal revenue product is satisfied at E, where OL is employment of labour and $OWEL$ is the total wage payment by the firm. In case the firm employs OL_0 (less than OL) labour, the mr_L, is greater than MW, which enables the firm to earn net revenue and, in turn, induces it to increase the employment till net revenue attached to the subsequent unit of labour is exhausted completely. Similarly, employment beyond OL units will make the marginal wage greater than the marginal revenue product, where the firm will incur a loss on account of excess employment of labour. Thus, according to the marginal productivity theory, under perfect competition in the long run, average wage can neither be more nor less than marginal revenue product or the value of marginal product (i.e., $AW = MW = mr_L = Vm_L$) of labour.

Market Imperfections and Exploitation of Labour

The marginal productivity theory was built on the assumption of perfect competition in the factor as well as product market. Joan V. Robinson and E.H. Chamberlin introduced this concept even under imperfect or monopolistic competition situations in the market. They brought out the implications of this on wage determination and measured the extent of 'exploitation of labour under imperfect competition and that under perfect competition.

Under perfect competition in both markets, wage rate of the labour is determined by equating the value of marginal product with the marginal cost of labour. This was considered to be an ideal wage rate and departure from it was taken by A.C. Pigou to be a sign of exploitation. He viewed that the labour is exploited, when it is paid a remuneration less than the value of its marginal physical product. This idea has been discounted by Mrs. Joan V. Robinson, who pointed out that payment of wages equal to the value of marginal product is possible only under perfect competition in the product market. Under imperfect competition in the product market, the marginal revenue product is less than the value of marginal product and, therefore, the workers can be paid a wage equal to marginal revenue product and not equal to the value of marginal product. Excess of the value of marginal product over the wage rate is not the sign of exploitation of labour, because this difference will remain in existence under imperfect competition, whether the firm is getting net profit or only normal profit or even incurring a loss.

Assuming perfect competition in the factor market, the $AW = MW$ curve is drawn parallel to the horizontal axis at OW wage level, which has been ascertained on the basis of demand and supply forces of labour for the industry. Further assuming imperfect or monopolistic competition in the product market the average revenue (AR) curve slopes downwards to the right and the marginal revenue (MR) curve also lies below the AR curve. Since $AR > MR$, therefore, Vm_L $(= m \cdot AR) > mr_L$ $(= m. MR)$. On account of this, the Vm_L curve, while

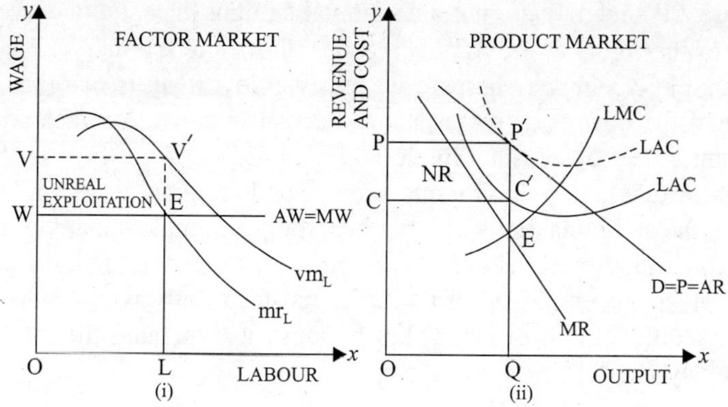

FIGURE 24.4 Interdependence of Factor and Product Markets.

sloping downwards to the right lies above the mr_L curve in determining the employment level in the factor market. In the product market originally the firm is getting net profit at the equilibrium *E*, where $MR = LMC$. At this point, the firm's output is *OQ* and price is $OP = QP'$. Since the long run average cost (LAC) at this level of output is $OC = QC'$, the firm obtains the net profit equal to *PCC'P'*. Assuming an increase in the average cost, the *LAC* curve has been shifted to *LAC'* level, where the equilibrium remaining at *E*, the firm obtains only normal profit as $AR = LAC'$.

This increase in the long run average cost has no effect on any curve in the factor market, therefore, the equilibrium in the factor market will not be disturbed due to shifting of *LAC* curve. Thus, whether the firm earns a profit or gets only normal profit the equilibrium will remain at *E* in the factor market and the difference between vm_L, and mr_L will always appear, which does not represent a real exploitation. Mrs. Joan V. Robinson has observed that the wages of labour may be equal to its vm_L only, when there is perfect competition in the product market. Under imperfect or monopolistic competition in the product market, the marginal revenue product (mr_L) will always be less than the value of marginal product (vm_L), hence the labour can be paid wages according to its mr_L and not vm_L. Professor E.H. Chamberlin has also noted that the existence of imperfections in the product market ensures that mr_L curve of all inputs will lie below their respective vm_L curve, therefore, it is improper to assert that any single input (or labour), if given reward (i.e., wages) equal to mr_L only, is being exploited.

Professor E.H. Chamberlin observed that the 'exploitation of labour may be attributed to: (a) monopolistic conditions in the product market and (b) monopsonistic conditions in the labour market. The former one is beyond the control of even the employers, as if the employer is made to pay wages according to the value of marginal product, he himself will be exploited. Therefore, the latter one is usually responsible for the exploitation of labour, as in this case *AW* and *MW* are not a horizontal straight lines, but a curve sloping upwards to the right, where *MW* curve lies above the *AW* curve. Under such conditions, the labour may be paid wages even less than its marginal revenue product and the difference represents the actual 'exploitation of labour.'

Assuming monopsonistic (single buyer) position of the firm in the factor market, these diagrams exhibit rising average and marginal wage curves, which reveal that the additional units of labour can only be employed at higher prices. In order to employ more labour, the employer must pay a higher price for all the units of labour employed. That is, he must not only pay a higher rate to obtain an additional unit of labour but he must also increase the rate at which all previously employed units are paid.

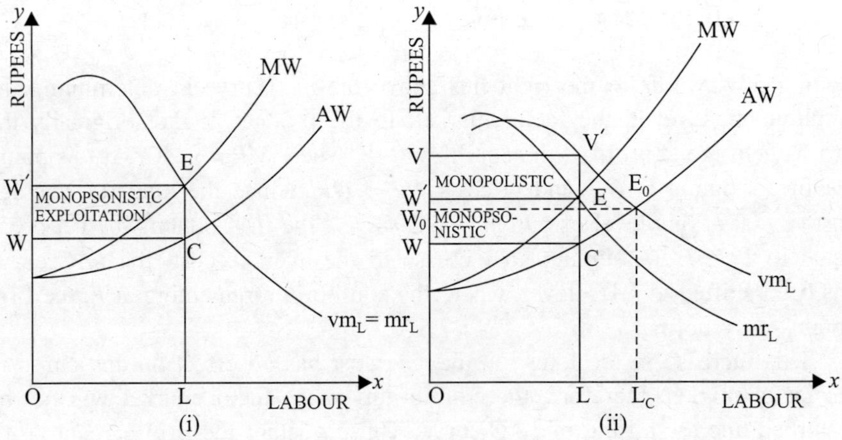

FIGURE 24.5 Wage and Employment of Labour and Its Exploitation.

Figure 24.5(i) assumes perfect competition in the product market, therefore, the negatively sloping vm_L and mr_L curves are identical. The rising *MW* curve intersects mr_L curve at *E*, which is the equilibrium position of the firm in the factor market. The firm, at equilibrium level, employs *OL* labour and pays *OW* wages, which is equal to the average wages (*AW*). The labour's marginal revenue product is *EL* = *OW′* but the payment of wages is *CL* = *OW*, which shows that the labour is being exploited to the extent of *WW′* = *EC*, as this represents the part of revenue due to the labour, but pocketed by the employer. In such a situation the labour is being exploited due to monopsonistic conditions in the factor market and may be termed as 'monopsonistic exploitation'.

Figure 24.5(ii) reveals the monopolistic as well as monopsonistic exploitation on the basis of the assumption of monopolistic competition in the product market and monopsonistic situation in the factor market. The firm selling the product in the monopolistic market has a declining vm_L and mr_L curves, where the latter lies below the former. On the other hand, due to the monopsonistic position of the firm in the labour market, the average wage (*AW*) and the marginal wage (*MW*) curves slope positively, where the former lies below the latter. The *MW* curve intersects the mr_L curve at *E* point, which is the equilibrium of the firm, where it employs *OL* labour and pays *OW* wages. Since the marginal revenue product of labour is *OW'* = *EL*, it shows that labour is being exploited to the extent of *WW'* = *EC*. Now, since the value of the marginal product of labour at this level of employment is *OV*=*LV'*, it leaves an excess over the marginal revenue product equal to *W'V* = *EV*, which may be termed as the monopolistic exploitation, because it arises on account of existence of monopolistic competition in the product market. Under perfect competition, the equilibrium would be at E_0, where the employment would be OL_0 and wages OW_0, but under monopolistic competition the employment is *OL* and the wage rate is *OW*. Thus, the labour faces exploitation in respect of both rate as well as employment.

Under the monopolistic position the total exploitation equals to *VWCV'*, where *VW'EV'* is the monopolistic exploitation, as it arises on account of monopolistic competition in the product market and *WCEW'* monopsonistic exploitation, as it arises on account of monopsony in the factor market. The former is an unreal exploitation, as this difference between vm_L and mr_L will always remain so long as there is less than perfect competition in the product market, but the latter one is the real exploitation, which represents the part of labourer's earnings pocketed by the employer. This is also known as 'Bargaining Area'. Other things being equal, adoption of a minimum wage laws or action by a labour unions can be effective within this area in raising wage level without reducing the employment.

Trade Unions and Marginal Productivity Theory

This theory states that wages is ascertained on the basis of the marginal productivity of labour, therefore, unions can do no more than forcing the employers to pay a wages no less than the marginal productivity. In case the unions compel the employers to pay a wages more than the marginal productivity, the employers will contract the employment in order to equalise the higher marginal cost of labour with the productivity. The unions argue that it rests on the assumption that the marginal revenue product curve is given and rules out an upward shift in the same due to a higher wages. In reality, if workers are paid higher wages, it increases their efficiency which, in turn, shifts the marginal revenue product curve to the right. Increase in wages may also force the employers to improve the efficiency of their production process, which also increases the marginal productivity of labour. Due to upward shifts in the marginal revenue product curve, despite higher wage rate the employment may remain at the original level. Even if there is no shift in the marginal revenue productivity, the trade union activities may help removing the exploitation of labour under monopsonistic factor market.

Figure 24.6(i) reveals that the firm is in equilibrium at *E*, where negatively sloping $mr_L = vm_L$ curve intersect the horizontal $MW = AW$ line. It is based on the assumption of perfect competition in the factor as well as the product market. At the equilibrium level, the firm employs *OL* labour and pays OW wages. In case on account of trade union activities or minimum wage law, the wages is enhanced to *Tw* = *Mw* level, the equilibrium is shifted to E_T, where the firm employs only OL_0 labour and pays *OTw* wages. Thus, when firms are compelled to pay more than equilibrium level of wages, the employment is bound to diminish, because the firm will try to equate the higher wage with the marginal revenue productivity, which is possible only at lower level of employment. It may also be argued that the payment of higher wages, may increase the efficiency of labour, which may shift the marginal revenue productivity curve to $mr'_L = vm'_L$ level. The new marginal revenue productivity $mr'_L = vm'_L$ curve may allow the employment to remain at the original (*OL*) level.

The Figure 24.6(ii) reveals a case of imperfect competition in the product as well as the factor market. On account of monopsony in the factor market both the average (*AW*) and the marginal wages (*WM*) curves slope upwards to the right, where the former lies below the latter. Similarly, due to imperfect competition in the product market, the marginal revenue product curve of labour (mr_L) will be different from the value of marginal product of labour (vm_L) curve. Since vm_L curve is of a little use for the fixation of wages, therefore, it has been exhibited by $mr_L < vm_L$ curve. The mr_L curve intersects the *MW* at *E*, which is the equilibrium of the firm, where it employs *OL* labour and pays *OW* = *LW'* wages. The marginal revenue productivity at this level of employment being *EL*, while the wage payment *LW'* reveals that the labour is being exploited to the extent of *EW'* = *WTw*. On account of trade union activities or minimum wage laws if the wage rate increases to *OTw*, it will remove the exploitation along with maintaining the employment at the (*OL*) level.

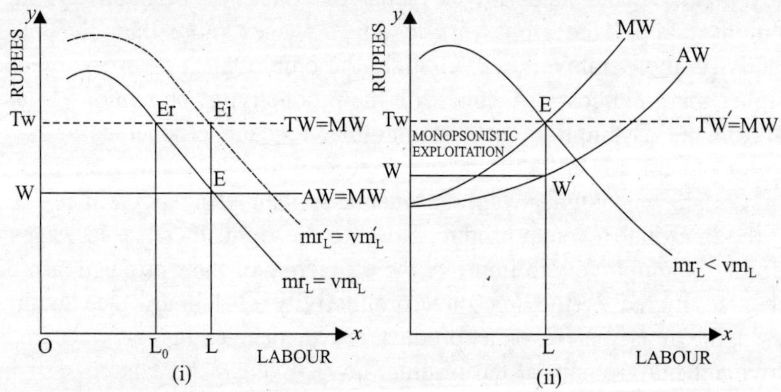

FIGURE 24.6 Trade Unions for Removing Monopsonistic Exploitation.

Trade unions can also help to remove exploitation of labour under monopsonistic discrimination, where the monopsonist pays different wages to different workers. Thus far, it has been assumed that the additional supply of labour to the firm is available only at a higher wage rate, which must be paid not only to the new workers, but also to workers already employed. However, the monopsonist may try a separate wage bargain with each worker and pay different wages to the various workers along with *MW* curve. The trade unions may force the employer to end this practice and raise the wages of the exploited workers. Thus, under monopsonistic discrimination the labour has been generally exploited, which can be avoided by the trade union activities.

MODERN APPROACH: COLLECTIVE BARGAINING

The wage theories based on the assumption of perfect competition discussed earlier have outlived their utility with the advent of trade unionism in the recent decades. In respect of employment of labour, we usually find bilateral monopoly, where the association of employers (i.e., a monopsonist purchaser of labour) negotiate wages with labour unions (i.e., a monopolist seller of labour). The wage rates, in modern world, reflect internal political necessities rather than sound economic principles. Under such situation it is difficult to find out determinate solution in the absence of definite assumptions about the behaviour of trade unions and employers' associations. The varying assumptions of the various economists have resulted into a large number of models of collective bargaining for the wage determination. We shall, now, examine the three important models, namely, maximisation model under collective bargaining, optimum combination of wage and employment and bilateral monopoly.

Maximisation Model

It has been developed by John T. Dunlop, who asserted that trade unions try to maximise their ends, which may be: (i) to keep all of its members employed; (ii) to maximise the total income of its members; (iii) to maximise hourly wage rate along with keeping at least the core group of its members employed. The unions may or may not achieve these ends simultaneously. In Figure 24.7, *DD'* represents the industry demand curve for the labour, which is the horizontal sum of individual firm's demand curves. It is sloping negatively, because industry is not monopsonist. The demand curve for labour *DD'* also represents the price (P_L) and the average wage (*AW*) curve of the labour and *DMW* represents the marginal wage for the labour. In case the union has *OL'* units of labour, which it wants to be in employment, it will result into wage level equal to OW_0. In case unions fight for higher than this level of wages, some units of labour are bound to be thrown out of employment.

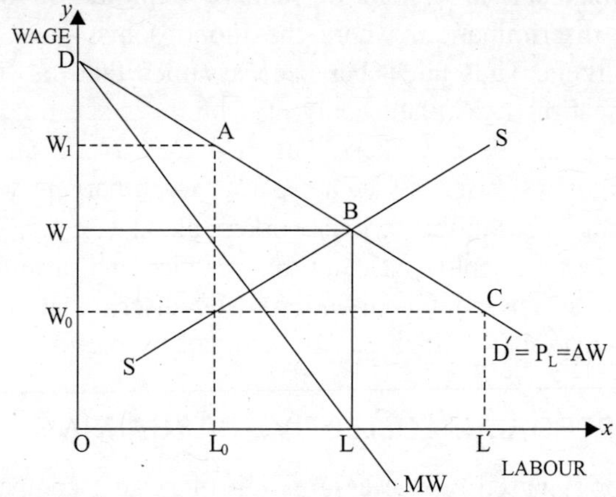

FIGURE 24.7 Maximisation of Labour Employment and Wages under Collective Bargaining.

Similarly, if the union wants to maximise the total wage earnings of its members, then it would like *OW* wages and *OL* employment, as *OWBL* is the maximum area lying within the base line and the negatively sloping demand line. At this level of employment, the marginal wages is zero, which makes the total wages maximum. In case the wage rate is more than *OW* the employment will be less than *OL* units, where the marginal wages (*MW*) will be positive, which reveals that some part of the total wage remains unrealised. On the other hand, if the wage rate is less than *OW*, the marginal wage will be negative, which will reduce the maximum wages already attained. Therefore, for maximisation of total wages of its members, the unions will strive for *OW* wages, which ensures employment of *OL* units of labour.

In case the unions are interested in maximising the wage rates of its core members and has OL_0 units of such members, it may demand a wage rate equal to OW_1. Similarly, if the union is interested in maximising the total wage payments to its members, it may demand OW wages and may sacrifice the employment of *LL'* units of labour. It may reconcile the first and third goals by demanding *OW* wage rate and somehow redividing that amongst all members, where *LL'* may be thrown out of employment, as after redivision, the wage rate will be higher than it would be, if all members were employed. The labour unions may have the goal of maximisation of wage rates of core members, where the industry usually hires a number of temporary workers, who are given membership in the union, but whose welfare is not of much importance to the union, as they are not accepted as belonging to the union by its permanent members.

Similarly, there may be a large number of goals and the wage levels the union seeks, would depend upon the circumstances in which the union is set up. Considering the union similar to the business monopoly, if the demand for labour is inelastic, it may strive for higher wage to increase the total income of its members, but where the demand is elastic (due to higher proportion of labour cost, substitutability of labour with capital or elastic demand of the product) the union will have a modest desire for a higher wage level. Unions may also try to maximise the number of its members. At each wage rate the union can negotiate, there is a particular number of members, who actively support it and this number increases along with increases in the wage-level negotiated. Thus, the supply curve (*SS*) of labour is the function of membership, which slopes positively. Assuming that the union is aware of the demand curve for services of its members, the wages demanded will be fixed at the level, where the supply is equal to the demand.

Optimum Combination Model

This model has been suggested by William Fellner, who stated that in the process of collective bargaining unions are guided by the desire to have an optimum combination of wages and employment. This analysis makes the use of indifference function of the trade unions between more wage and more employment, which, in turn, describes the supply function of labour. The shape of these indifference functions depends on the views of unions regarding wage rate and employment. In extreme cases, if unions are interested in achieving the maximum possible wage rates without considering the level of employment, the indifference functions are represented by the various horizontal straight lines showing higher and higher wage levels. The employer's demand for labour is represented by the marginal revenue productivity curve of labour (mr_L). In case the union knows the value of marginal productivity of labour (vm_L) and the marginal revenue productivity of labour (mr_L), it can easily ascertain the wage rate it should demand.

Figure 24.8(i) reveals the horizontal straight line indifference curve of the trade unions which is interested in higher wage rates without any regard to the level of employment. By superimposing the vm_L and mr_L curves, we come to the conclusion that the wage can never go up to OW_2 as it is more than the vm_L. At OW wage rate, the OL_1 units of labour will be employed, as the union's indifference function is equal to mr_L at this level. Since the value of the marginal productivity of labour is more than this wage rate, the union having a strong bargaining power will demand a higher wage rate up to OW_1, which is the highest possible wage rate obtainable, where the vm_L is tangent to the indifference function.

At this level of wage, the employment will be at *OL* level. However, this highest wage attitude of the union may prevail, when it bargains with a single firm. While negotiating with the industry, the union cannot overlook the employment aspect, while stressing for higher wages in the process of collective bargaining. The cost conditions may differ and if the union insists on a higher wages, the high cost firms may be forced to close down resulting in the unemployment.

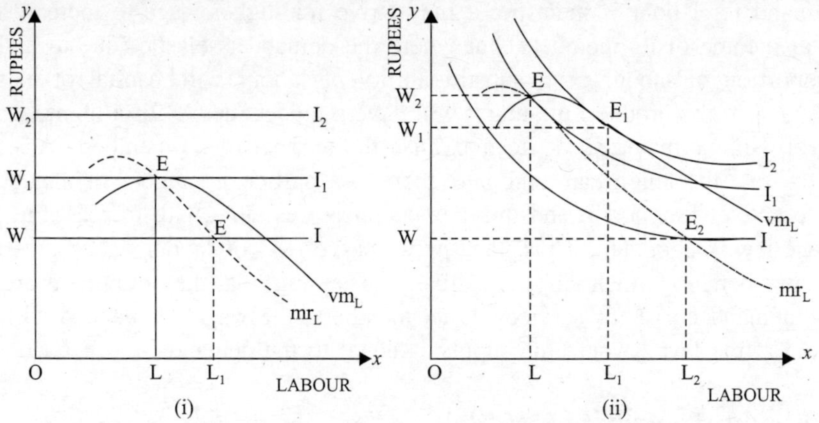

FIGURE 24.8 Optimum Combination of Wages and Employment.

The unemployed labour may threaten to form a breakaway union and negotiate separately for a lower wage rate. In order to avoid this, the union will seek an optimum combination of wage and employment. Thus, the wage and employment being the competitive and complementary ends of the union, represent the indifference functions by downwards sloping curves. Such curves will be convex to the origin, as the wage and employment are imperfect substitutes.

Figure 24.8(ii) exhibits a set of indifference functions of the union, where the vm_L and mr_L curves have been super-imposed, which enable to identify a range of wage levels within which the wage rate may be fixed on the basis of negotiation with the employer, who is left free to offer the level of employment at the settled wage rate. At the given wage rate, the employer will like to offer that level of employment at which the wage rate equals the mr_L, which means that from his point of view, the equilibrium wage rate must lie on mr_L curve. On the other hand, union will like the equilibrium wage to lie on the highest reachable indifference curve. Thus, the wage equilibrium is to be fixed at *E* point, where the marginal revenue productivity curve of labour is tangent to the highest indifference curve. The wages OW_2 should be acceptable to both the employer and the union.

The OW_2 wages assumes the existence of a strong union, which can force the employer to pay that wage rate, which it demands. In case the employer happens to be powerful, he may drag the equilibrium down along with the mr_L curve to E_2 point, where the wage rate is *OW*. In case the union can gain sufficient power and fight the cause of labour on 'all or nothing' basis, it can force the equilibrium to be at *E*, where the vm_L curve is tangent to the union's indifference curve I_2. Usually the collective bargaining is done on the give and take basis, therefore, the parties will settle the wages at a level between *E* and E_2 points, the exact location depending on the relative bargaining power of the both parties viz. the trade union and the employer. The labour union may sacrifice some employment for the trade sake of a higher wage rate or it may sacrifice some portion of wage rates for the sake of higher employment in order to reach to settlement with the employer. Thus, E to E_2 is the area of indeterminacy, where the bargains may be settled at any point.

The main drawback of this model lies with the fact that it judges the employer's behaviour by the marginal revenue productivity curve. It also assumes that the wage and employment are substitutes to some extent irrespective of the level of the wage and employment, whereas in the real world, labour resists vehemently a wage cut whatsoever the employment is offered. This model concentrates much on the supply side and lays less emphasis on the demand side.

Bilateral Monopoly Model

This model has been suggested by Professor A.M. Carter, who has also introduced the employers' preference (or indifference) functions indicating the various levels of profit at different levels of wage and employment along with union's preference functions. While considering the unions' preference (or indifference) functions, he also emphasised that the degree of substitution between wages and employment depends on the prevailing wage level in the employment. The employer's and trade union's bargaining behaviour is represented by their preference functions respectively, where by superimposing one on the other, one can identify the bargaining area.

The substitutability of wages and employment depends on the wage employment level and for deviation from such level it would take a considerable increase in the wages to compensate for a reduction in employment and it would cause a considerable increase in employment to compensate for a wage reduction. Thus, according to trade unions, wages and employment are imperfect substitutes and it considers reduction in one only with a large increase in the other. Due to this, the trade union's indifference functions have been exhibited with highly convex curves.

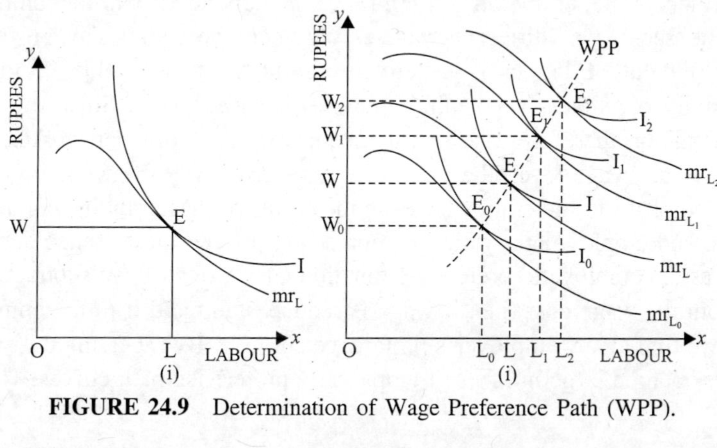

FIGURE 24.9 Determination of Wage Preference Path (WPP).

Figure 24.9(i) reveals that the indifference curve of the union is tangent to the mr_L curve at E. The indifference curve has some curvature around E and is nearly vertical and horizontal on the two sides, which indicates that the union is prepared to forgo some employment only for a large increase in wages or it may forego some wages for a large increase in employment. Here mr_L curve represents the demand curve of labour for an employer. At E point, unions are prepared to accept OW wages and OL level of employment and the employer is prepared to give OW wage and employ OL units of labour. Thus, it is the equilibrium level of wages and employment.

Figure 24.9(ii) with the help of a set of mr_L and indifference curves, reveals the trade unions' reactions to increase and decrease in the demand for labour. The original equilibrium lies at E, where mr_L is tangent to the I indifference function. In case, the demand for labour rises, the mr_L curve is shifted to the right at mr_{L1} and mr_{L2} levels, which are tangent to higher and higher indifference curves at E_1 and E_2 points respectively. Similarly, a decrease in demand for labour shifts the mr_L curve to the mr_{L0} level, which is tangent to the indifference function I_0 at E_0 point. By combining these points of equilibrium, we get a curve, which is known as wage preference path. It reveals that if the demand for labour increases, trade unions lay more emphasis on enhanced wages, rather than on enhanced employment. Similarly, in case of decrease in the demand for labour, the unions resist the wage reduction more than the employment reduction.

Thus, the trade union will prefer to use an increase in demand primarily for a wage increase and will prefer an increase in employment only when the increase in demand for labour is quite substantial. Similarly, with a decrease in demand, a wage cut will be resisted unless the decline is quite substantial. The wage preference path, thus, reveals the trade union's wage-employment policy in response to changes in demand from the prevailing level.

Employer's Preference Functions

It reveals the behaviour of the employer at the various levels of wages and employment. The employer's preference is dependent on the amount of profit, he secures at different wage-employment bargains. The profitability of employment of labour is usually represented by the value of marginal productivity of labour (vm_L) minus the average wage cost. Since the vm_L (= $m_L.P$) is given, therefore, rise in wage squeezes the profit per worker.

At certain wage level, the wage cost may take away the whole of the vm_L leaving no profit to the employer. Here the employer has a unique combination of wage and employment, which is represented by the indifference curve also known as the employers' preference function curve. In case we subtract a fixed sum from the wage cost (i.e., if wage is reduced) and add it to the employers' profit, we find a new employer's preference curve I_1. By repeating this process, we may obtain a large number of employers' preference path curves. Thus, the set of employers' preference path curves, on the one hand reveal higher and higher profits to the employers and a lower wage for the union of workers. As we move from the highest preference function curve to the next, we find that maximum point is also shifting to the right. It reveals that the employer is prepared to employ additional labour as wage rate is reduced.

Figure 24.10 reveals that the employers' preference curve rises initially, reaches maximum and them starts decreasing. This is the shape of the all subsequent profitability curves. By combining the maximum points *A*, *B* and *C* on these curves, we can derive mr_L curve. Thus, at *OW* wages, the employer will prefer to employ *OL* labour and at lower the wage rate the higher will be the desired level of employment.

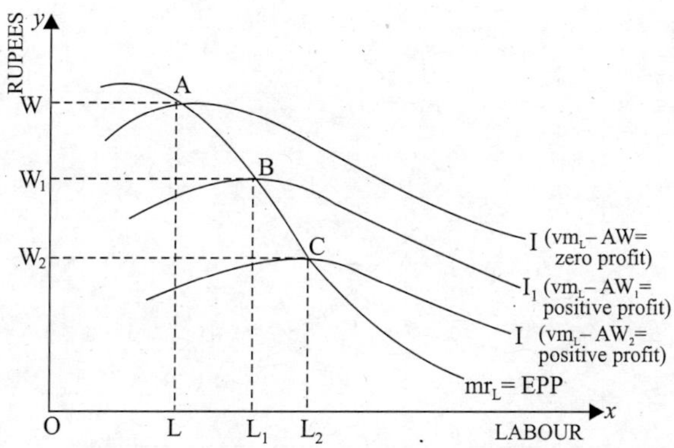

FIGURE 24.10 Determination of Employers' Preference Path (EPP).

In order to determine the wages and employment, we superimpose the employer's preference map on the union's preference map, where we assume perfect bargaining conditions i.e., each party knows the preference map of the other party in full and each party wants to reach a compromise settlement. The mr_L curve represents the prevailing level of demand as well as the employer's preference path along with changes in wage rates. Similarly, wage preference path of the union is sloping upwards, which intersects the employer's preference path at *E*, which is the equilibrium point for wage and employment under collective bargaining. The union's preference function curve *U* is also tangent to the employer's preference function curve *F* at this point, which reveals the satisfaction of both parties at the level of wages and employment. The deviation from *E* point will be of no benefit to both parties. In case employer tries to fix a lower wage along with the $mr_L = EPP$ curve, he will put the union on lower indifference curve, which will be vehemently opposed by the unions until the employer comes back to *E* point. Similarly, if the unions fix more than *OW* wages, again it will place itself on a lower indifference curve. Thus, it will not be in the interest of the union to move upwards and downwards from E along with the labour demand curve mr_L = EPP. The union should move to a higher point on the union preference path, but that too is not possible because the employer is free to fix the lower level of employment at the higher wage level. In case the union plans to demand OW' wages at point C on the union preference path, the employer will move to a higher preference function curve $F'I'$, which determines the employment at OL' for this level of wages, because the maximum point of employer's indifference curve intersects mr_L curve at D point. Point D lies on the lower preference curve of the union, therefore the move of the union to raise the wages will make it worse off. In the absence of changes in demand conditions, it is better to maintain the status quo.

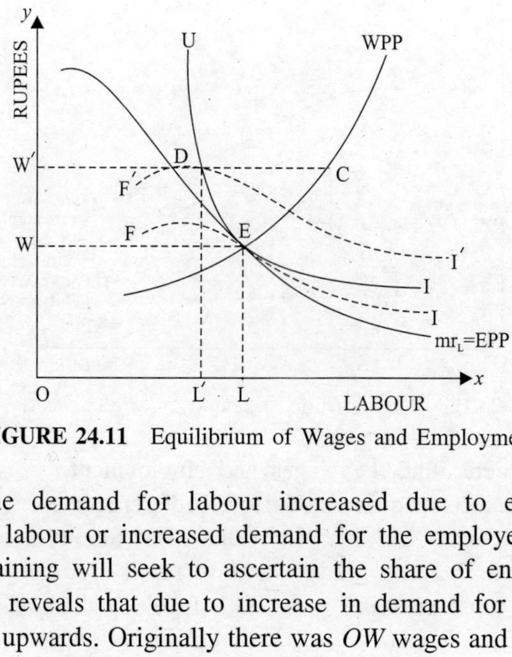

FIGURE 24.11 Equilibrium of Wages and Employment.

In case the demand for labour increased due to either increased productivity of labour or increased demand for the employers' product, the collective bargaining will seek to ascertain the share of enhanced revenue. Figure 24.12(i) reveals that due to increase in demand for labour, the mr_L curve is shifted upwards. Originally there was OW wages and OL employment at the equilibrium point E, where employer's and union's preference paths (UPPs) intersect each other and the union's preference curve is tangent to the employer's preference curve (F. I). In case the demand for labour increases, the mr_L is shifted to mr'_L level and will disturb the original equilibrium position at E. The union will strive for a new wage-employment settlement, which may lie between A and D points, as these points are lying on the unions original preference curve as well as the new mr'_L curve, because by being within this limit the labour will be at least as well off as at point E. However the union will strive for wage-employment settlement at C, as it lies on union's wage preference path (UPP) as well as the employer's new preference path mr'_L = EPP.

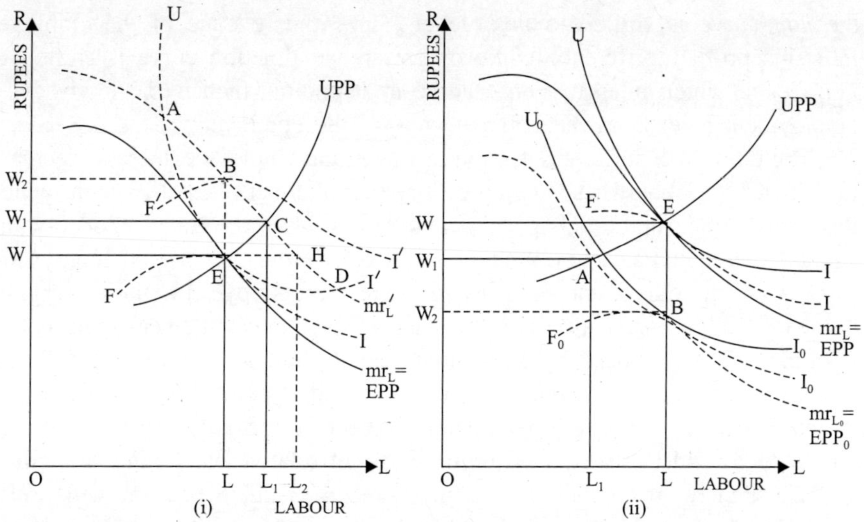

FIGURE 24.12 Wage and Employment Equilibrium under Changes in Demand for Labour.

The employer, on the other hand, will experience a sudden increase in his profits on account of the upwards shift in the mr_L curve. It will shift, the employer's indifference function curve to $F'I'$ level, which intersects mr'_L curve at B point. The employer will like to have wage and employment settlement at B point or at any point below B along with the mr'_L curve, because lower the point the lower will be the profit of the employer. The employer can move along with the mr_L curve up to H point only, because reduction of wages below the previous level is not possible for the employer. Thus, the employer may either like to employ OL labour and pay OW_2 wages or employ OL_2 labour and pay OW wages or employ labour less than OL_2 and pay wages less than OW_2. The interest of the employer and the union coincides if the wage-employment settlement moves from B up to C, but beyond C up to the maximum of H, the employer's interest comes in conflict with that of the union.

Thus, the wage between OW_1 and OW_2 and any employment between OL and OL_1 is acceptable to the union but the employer will try to force the wage level below OW_1 up to OW and will like to employ more than OL_1 up to OL_2, therefore, the exact wage-employment settlement will lie within CH range of the mr_L curve, where the trade unions would like to be nearer to C, but the employer would like to be nearer to H. The exact settlement will depend on the relative bargaining strengths of the two parties which, in turn, will depend on a number of psychological, sociological and institutional factors. The exact determination by economic theory is not possible and wage employment under bilateral monopoly is indeterminate.

Figure 24.12(ii) reveals collective settlement of wages and employment under the conditions of decreased demand. If the demand for labour decreases, the mr_L curve is shifted to mr_{L0} level. Since the revenue of the employer falls, his profit indifference curve or preference function curve is shifted to F_0I_0, level, which intersects mr_{L0} curve at *B* point, which is the likely wage employment level from the point of view of the employer.

The union will suffer a reduction in wages and employment due to decrease in demand for labour. It's solution of wage-employment lies at *A* point, which lies on the trade union's wage preference path. Here the trade union favours slight decrease in wages to OW_1 although slightly more decrease in employment to OL_1. On the other hand, it is beneficial to the employer to employ original number of labour and pay a reduced wages OW_2. Any settlement lying below *A* point will be opposed by the unions and the employer will never like to move upwards alongwith the mr_{L0} curve beyond *B* point. The range between *A* and *B* will be the range of bargaining, where the exact level of wage and employment will be ascertained on the basis of relative bargaining strength.

Thus, under the conditions of increased demand, the union will prefer higher wages to more employment and under the conditions of decreased demand the trade union would resist a fall in wages even if it means laying off some labour. On the other hand, the employer under the former condition would like to employ more labour and pay slightly higher wages and under the latter condition, he will like to employ same labour, but will like to pay sufficiently low wage. The conflicting attitudes leave no room for exact solution, but provide a range within which the exact level of wages and employment may be ascertained on the basis of the relative bargaining strength of both parties.

Review Questions

1. Bring out the concept of wages and distinguish between nominal wages and real wages.
2. What are the factors determining the demand for and supply of labour.
3. Explain the determination of wage rate under conditions of perfect competition in the product market as well as the labour market.
4. Discuss the role of trade unions in wage determination for labour.
5. Why does wage rate become indeterminate under the conditions of bilateral monopoly?
6. How does collective bargaining of trade unions affect wage determination?
7. Critically examine the marginal productivity theory of wage determination?

25

Theories of Interest

Interest is the reward for capital used in the production process. Historical evolution of the economic thoughts reveal more controversy and debate on the role and determination of the interest than on any other factor reward. It is due to the peculiar nature of the capital, which is a non-human input, but comes into being through human decisions and is the result of non-consumption of past income. It refers to those instruments of production, which are deliberately made by man to be used for carrying on future production. A major difficulty in building up the general theory of interest is due to lack of all acceptable definition of capital. However, economists have tried to resolve this difficulty through the various means. Up to a few decades ago, the time preference theory or the real theory had been the ruling theory of interest. At that time money and monetary policy were usually not projected into the analysis of interest, but subsequently there developed the liquidity preference theory and the loanable fund theory, which are at least partly monetary theories of interest.

In this chapter an effort is being made to elaborate the classical (or time preference) theory, the neo-classical (or loanable fund) theory, the Keynesian liquidity preference theory and the modern theory of interest. However, before considering these theories along with their merits and demerits respectively, a few words regarding the nature of interest seem to be pertinent.

NATURE OF INTEREST

It depends on the theory of interest one accepts. The followers of the time preference (or real) theory, regarded interest as the payment for use of capital goods. They also regarded interest as payment necessary to induce people to save. The upholders of the liquidity preference theory treat interest as the reward for parting with the liquidity of the fund saved. Those accepting the loanable fund theory hold that interest is the price paid by borrowers to the lenders for the use of money (i.e., the loanable fund).

Usually the term rate of interest denotes the contractual or gross interest, which is the total payment by the debtor to the creditor. This, besides the pure or net interest, also includes insurance against risk, cost of management of lending business and payment for inconvenience involved in savings for making funds available for lending. Thus, the gross interest consists of four components.

1. **Pure or Net Interest:** It is payment for completely risk-less loan or only for services of capital. It is charged on loans, which are totally riskless and have no administrative costs. Government securities bear lowest rate of interest, as the loan given to the government is riskless. Since the securities are subscribed by general public, the cost of administration of lending is virtually nil, it represents the net interest.
2. **Insurance Against Risk:** The lender is exposed to the risk while lending the money. Therefore, he expects some payment to cover the risk. The risk may be (a) personal risk, which owes its origin to unreliable character of the borrower; and (b) trade risk, which is due to the varying fortunes of the business in which money is invested. Thus, the lender may fear either the borrower may refuse to pay back his money or he may lose the money in his trade. The greater the risk, the higher the interest, the lender will expect before showing willingness to lend. The risk also depends on the time period for which loan is given and the nature of security offered for the loan. Therefore, the long period loans with the security of fixed assets command higher rate of interest as compared to short period loans with the security of liquid assets.
3. **Administrative Cost:** A part of the payment of interest may be due to the cost of administering the loan. The lender is expected to have some organisation for collecting and making the money available as capital. It requires maintenance of office, account books, staff, etc., the cost of which is to be met out of the interest realised on lending.
4. **Payment for Inconvenience:** In case one lends money, he loses command over it for certain period, as he will not be able to use when he wishes to and, as a result, favourable opportunities of its employment may slip away. Thus, the lender may not get back the money when he needs and may have to borrow from others on interest or he may get the money when he is not getting some safe and lucrative investment for it, so that the money lies idle and he loses interest. He, therefore, tries to compensate himself for such losses by charging something extra over and above pure or net interest.

These elements of gross interest result into a family of different rates determined in a number of dependent but connected loan markets. There are different interest rates for government bonds, real-estate mortgage bonds, industrial debentures, bank loans, call loans, etc. These rates vary over time, not necessarily in identical proportions, but often in the same direction. There are the differences in gross interest. The pure or net interest tend to be the same, if calculated over the same period of time in the same money market.

In real world even net interest may be different in different investments because of the differences of:

(a) **Place:** Usually people prefer to invest their capital near their homes. This may create imbalance between demand and supply of capital on account of its comparative immobility.
(b) **Time:** In case people have to part with their money for a long period, they expect higher rates than when they lend money for a short period but gross interest of short term loans may be higher, because relending of the amount realised increases the inconvenience of management.
(c) **Amount:** Generally the rate of interest varies inversely with the amount of the loan that is the rate decreases as the amount of the loan increases and vice-versa.
(d) **Liquidity:** It refers to the ease with which loan given can be called back or the ease with which an asset (like securities) can be encashed without monetary loss. The more liquid the securities, the lower the rate of interest.
(e) **Market Imperfection:** This enables charging different rates from different borrowers. A bank in small town with monopoly power in local money market may charge higher rate from local people, as they consider it inconvenient to 'shop around' at banks in distant cities. Their rates may also vary from customer to customer.

In addition to the above, difference in gross interest may also be due to differences in social esteem, as a person with better reputation or integrity can borrow at lower rates. It also owes its origin to the differences in productivity, because where capital can earn greater reward for the producer, he will be willing to pay higher interest.

The interest rates charged from individual business is usually determined in personal negotiation between the bank and the borrower. It reflects such attributes as the borrower's size and general credit standing, his access to alternative credit sources, the size and the maturity of loan, the character of the borrower's business, the value to the bank of his deposit account and the nature of the security, etc. Similarly factors related to the lender, such as size of the lender, the size of the centre in which the bank is located and the area of the country, where the loan was made, also affect the rates of interest to be charged.

Thus, there are a number of complex interest rates, each depending on the marginal lending and marginal borrowing rates in their respective markets. The markets have common frontiers and there will be crossing of borders, if the differential between two neighbouring rates departs from the usual magnitude. Talking about the interest rate, we do not refer to the whole list of rates in the various markets, but to one particular rate with other rates standing above it or below it with more or less consistent gradations.

THEORIES OF INTEREST

The theories can be classified into two categories, viz: (a) those concerned with reasons that give rise to the payment of interest; and (b) those concerned with determination of the rate of interest. Productivity Theory, Waiting or Abstinence Theory, Agio Theory and Time Preference Theory are in the former category, while Classical or Real Theory, Neo-Classical or Loanable Fund Theory and Liquidity Preference Theory belong to the latter category.

A-1: Productivity Theory

Classical economists held rate of interest to be the reward for productive nature of capital. It is productive in the sense that land and labour, assisted by capital, produce more than that without capital. Use of capital increases the productivity of land as well as labour considerably. It is due to the helping nature of capital that the interest is paid to its owner. Thus, these economists tried to explain the payment of interest on capital from the demand side.

The inadequacy of this theory becomes obvious from the fact that it neglected completely the supply side of the capital. In case supply of capital is plentiful, the interest would be zero. So, it is the relative scarcity rather than productivity of capital—excess of demand over supply—that explains the interest. Moreover if interest depends merely on productivity, the interest rates should vary in proportion to the productivity of capital, but in reality net interest tends to be the same in the same market. Further, the capital, being passive factor, itself can produce nothing. It simply helps the labour to produce more but it is difficult to find out how much of the extra production is due to labour and how much is due to capital. Further-more, the interest is paid even on consumption loans, although they are unproductive. Therefore, the productivity theory of interest seems to be inadequate.

A-2: Waiting or Abstinence Theory

Unlike the productivity theory, it seeks to explain the interest from the supply side of capital. According to this theory, capital is built out of savings. The savings are possible only when people abstain from consumption of their total income. Since abstinence from consumption is painful and involves sacrifice, it is necessary to reward the people for this act. The interest is, thus, considered as the necessary compensation to the saver—the supplier of capital for his abstinence.

This theory emphasised the supply side of capital, but the idea that capital comes from savings and interest is payment for inconvenience caused by savings has been subject to criticisms. It is rich people, who supply major part of the savings and they do it without any inconvenience. Marshall substituted the term waiting for abstinence. According to him savings implies waiting. When a person saves he does not refrain from consumption, but he merely postpones present consumption to a future date. Since most people do not like to wait, an inducement in the form of the interest is necessary to encourage this postponement of consumption.

Some waiting may be forthcoming without any inducement, as in the case of rich persons and other people may wait even with negative inducement, but the aggregate savings, thus made, will not be adequate to meet the total demand for capital. Interest must be paid to induce many more people to save to whom waiting does involve any inconvenience. The higher the rate of interest, the greater will be savings of the people.

This 'abstinence or waiting' theory offers good explanation of the supply side of capital, but it remains just a partial explanation of the payment of interest and overlooks the forces working on the demand side of capital.

A-3: Agio Theory

It is a psychological theory, initially propounded by Joan Rae, but given its final shape by Austrian economist Bohm Bawerk. According to him people prefer present goods to future goods, so there is an 'agio' or 'premium' for the present goods. The present gratification is attached greater importance than the future satisfaction. Thus, the future satisfaction, when viewed from the present, undergo a discount. Interest is a payment to compensate this discount and must be paid to induce people to lend money by postponing present satisfaction. Interest is intended to equate future satisfaction with the present satisfaction.

People prefer present satisfaction, because the future is uncertain, intensity of present wants is more than that of the future wants and present goods possess a technical superiority over future goods. Like 'abstinence or waiting theory' it analyses in greater detail the supply of capital, but it seems to be an abstract and complicated attempt.

A-4: Time Preference Theory

It has been propounded by Professor Irving Fisher and is based on the fundamental assumption that people prefer present consumption to future consumption, even though the future consumption is equally certain. This theory seeks to explain why there is interest and how it is determined. People in receipt of income try to change the successive amounts of income available for consumption at the various times by means of savings and borrowings. The price, people stand ready to pay for income now rather than for income later is the rate of interest. The intensity of preference of the people for future consumption is determined by forces classified as willingness or impatience and opportunity forces. The degree of willingness or impatience depends upon the size of the income, its distribution over time, the degree of certainty regarding enjoyment in the future and the temperament and characteristics of the individual.

People with larger incomes are in a position to satisfy present wants more fully and may discount the future at a lower rate than poorer people. As regards distribution over time, the income may be evenly distributed, or it may increase or decrease with time. In case the income is uniform, the degree of impatience to spend depends on the size of income and temperament of the individual. In case the income is rising one, it means the future is well protected and people will tend to discount the future at a higher rate and *vice-versa.* As regards the degree of certainty, the greater the certainty of future enjoyment of income, the smaller the degree of impatience and lower the rate of discounting for the future. The temperament and characteristics of the individual also influence the degree of impatience. A man for foresight will discount the future at a lower rate, as compared to a man with spend-thrift. Thus, there are factors that work to induce people to redistribute their consumption as between present and future.

Similarly, the investment opportunity principles also give rise to interest by inducing people to redistribute their investment. An individual may have many investment options and he can withdraw from one and invest in another. Withdrawal from one investment means withdrawing one income stream, which is the cost, while the gain that results from investing in a new income stream is the return. The rate of return over cost is that discount rate, which is compared with the market rate of interest in order to take the investment decision.

The rates of individual time preference, thus determined, tend to become equal to market rate of interest. An individual with higher rate of time preference compared with market rate of interest tends to borrow money in order to satisfy his more pressing wants. In a reverse situation, he will lend to the market and make a gain thereby. Thus, the individual will vary his income stream by borrowing and lending and this process will tend to equalise the rate of interest with the rate of time preference.

A-5: Liquidity Preference Theory

It has been propounded by Professor John Maynard Keynes, who discounted the idea that interest is a reward for waiting or a payment for time preference and stated that people wish to keep their saving in liquid form. They would like to part with liquidity only, when they are given some reward, which is known as interest.

B-1: Classical or Real Theory of Interest

This theory is a contribution of Austrian economist Eugen von-Bohm Bawerk, who substituted it for earlier theories of other classical economists. It is called the real theory of interest, because it is not monetary in character and has in its frame of reference real factors like productivity and thrift, (i.e., the productivity of capital goods and the savings). This theory argues that the reason, why interest can be paid, lies in the net marginal productivity of capital and that the reason why it must be paid, lies in the fact that people prefer current consumption and to make available savings for investment, only if they receive a premium in the form of an interest payment. It is a demand and supply theory, as the interest, according to it, is determined by the demand for savings to invest in capital goods and the supply of savings. The interest is considered as the price, which equalises the demand for and supply of the savings. J.B. Clark identified capital as a certain amount of money permanently invested in succession of perishable things and distinguished it with capital goods, which he defined as perishable things in which capital was invested. For the sake of our analysis, capital goods have been regarded as produced means of production. In other words, it stands for objects, which man produces for the purpose of using them as an aid in making goods and are in the form of machines, factory buildings, raw materials, inventories, etc. This theory regards capital as a distinct factor of production, the services of which can be paid for, if its marginal (net) productivity is positive, which explains the demand aspect, but fails to explain why interest must be paid (i.e., the supply aspect).

Demand for Capital

The demand for capital sometimes known as an investment demand, prospective or anticipated marginal net revenue productivity, marginal efficiency of capital (MEC) or the marginal efficiency of investment (MEI), comes from producers, who desire to invest in the purchase of capital goods, which could be used to produce other goods further. These capital goods have capacity for the revenue productivity and for every type of capital goods, it is possible to draw a marginal revenue productivity curve, which shows the addition made to the total revenue by the additional units of such goods.

The marginal revenue productivity of capital is more complex concept, as capital goods are expected to last for long, which continues to yield returns for many years. Therefore, the entrepreneurs have to judge the uncertainties for the future and estimate the return from capital after making allowances for maintenance and operating costs, which is termed as net expected marginal return. It is also subject to diminishing return, because as entrepreneurs demand more units of capital goods, their net expected marginal returns diminish. Thus, the marginal revenue productivity curve of capital slopes negatively (i.e., downwards to the right).

Under the assumption of perfect competition in the factor market, it is profitable for entrepreneurs to employ that amount of capital up to a point at which the price of capital (i.e., the interest) equals the marginal revenue productivity. Thus, the entrepreneur will demand capital to purchase capital goods up to the point at which the net expected marginal return (i.e., the marginal revenue productivity) of the capital goods equals the rate of interest. The negative slope of the marginal revenue productivity curve reveals that as the rate of interest falls more capital goods will be demanded and *vice-versa*. The marginal revenue productivity (*mr*) curve of capital goods slopes downwards to the right. It is true for individual firms, industries and the economy as a whole. Thus, the demand for individual capital goods and for capital goods in general will increase as the rate of interest declines.

Supply of Capital

The money used for purchasing capital goods is made available by persons, who save by curtailing consumption from their current income. Since people prefer current consumption to future consumption, which the savings involve. If people are persuaded to save money and to lend it to entrepreneurs, they must be offered a premium in the form of interest. This is termed as time preference, which owes its origin to the fact that people are not certain that they will remain alive, the price level may rise and people are generally so constituted that prospective enjoyment is generally not valued as highly as the present enjoyment. Thus, the interest is offered to them as an inducement to overcome their time preference. In case the person is to save more and more, the premium must rise to overcome his increased marginal time preference. The higher the rate of interest, the greater is the number of persons, whose rates of time preference are covered. As he saves more the marginal utility of what he has left for consumption grows, whereas the present marginal utility of the cumulating funds for the future declines. To induce him to save more, a higher rate of interest must be offered.

Accordingly, the horizontal addition of the individual savings curves give us a supply schedule of savings, which slopes positively, that is, upwards to the right, because as the rate of interest rises, the savers are induced to save more, while the abstinence or time preference of more people is covered, the number of people making savings also rises. This theory assumes that, by and large, the prime incentive at the back of savings is the receipt of interest and that savings are not hoarded, that is, savers invariably become lenders.

Equilibrium Rate of Interest

The rate of interest is determined by the interaction of the demand for investment and the supply of savings or by the expected productivity of capital and time preference. Since the saving's supply curve is thought to have a positive slope, while the curve of the demand for capital, which is based on the net marginal productivity of capital is believed to have a negative slope because of the principle of diminishing marginal returns to capital. The equilibrium rate of interest is ascertained at the point, where the volume of savings demanded for investment equals the savings coming forth from people.

The equilibrium rate of interest is that which equates the cost of borrowings with the marginal productivity of capital on the one hand and on the other, induces the marginal saver to save, whose savings is the addition to the volume of savings, which makes it equal to the volume of demand for them. In Figure 25.1 positively sloping *SS* curve represents the supply curve of savings and the negatively sloping *II* = *mr* curve represents the demand curve for capital (i.e., the demand for savings to invest in capital goods). Both intersect each other at *E*, which determines the equilibrium rate of interest at *OR* and the equilibrium amount of capital demanded and supplied at *OC*. At any other rate of interest, the volume of savings introduced will be less or more than the amount of investment the entrepreneurs wish to make. In case of change in the demand for investment and supply of savings, both the curves will shift and accordingly the equilibrium rate of interest and/or volume of investment will also change.

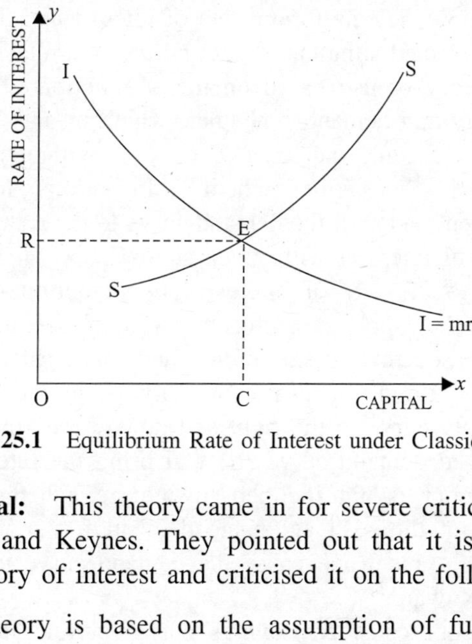

FIGURE 25.1 Equilibrium Rate of Interest under Classical Theory.

Critical Appraisal: This theory came in for severe criticisms at the hands of neo-classicals and Keynes. They pointed out that it is an inadequate or indeterminate theory of interest and criticised it on the following grounds:

(i) This theory is based on the assumption of full employment of resources, which means that an increase in the production of one thing must mean the withdrawal of some resources form the production of other things. According to Dillard, D. **"within the framework of a system of theory built on the assumption of full employment, the notion of interest as a reward for waiting or abstinence is highly plausible. It is the premise that resources are typically fully employed that lacks plausibility in the contemporary world."** In a world with large scale employment of resources, there is no need to pay a higher rate of interest to induce people to postpone or to abstain from consumption, so that more resources should be devoted to the production of capital goods.

(ii) It ignores the influence of changes in the income level on the savings and investment. It is based on the assumption of given level of income coming out of the full employment of resources, which is rare and changes in employment hence in income, takes place so quite often that a theory based on a given level of employment is quite inadequate and indeterminate. By neglecting the changes in the income level, this theory viewed that the rate of interest is the factor, which brings equality of savings and investment. However, Keynes has rightly pointed out a sequence, where change in rate of interest changes the investment, which, in turn, changes the income and, as a result, savings out of it also change, which will ultimately affect the rate of interest. So we cannot assume the savings and investment schedules to be invariant to changes in income. He further asserts that equality between savings and investment is brought about not by changes in the rate of interest, but by changes in the level of income. So the equilibrium rate of interest and the level of income are determined simultaneously and are interrelated.

(iii) This theory is also based on the assumption of the independence of supply and demand schedules, which means that the investment demand schedule can change or shift without causing a change or shift in the savings schedule. In case an invention increases investment and shift the demand curve to the right, this new demand curve will intersect with given supply curve at a higher point and will raise the rate of interest. The invention is not assumed to increase the supply of savings by virtue of increased income induced by increased investment activity and, thus, shifts the supply curve to the right and downward. Similarly, if increased thriftiness bring the supply curve to the right and downwards, the intersection with unchanged demand curve (*II*) will bring the rate of interest down. This theory is not inclined to enquire, whether increased thrift would not diminish aggregate demand for goods, reduce income and employment and cause the demand curve to move to the left and downwards.

(iv) This theory considers savings out of current income as the only source of investible funds. However, in real world, savings out of current income must be supplemented with past hoarded savings to get at the current supply of funds for investment. In case there are unemployed resources, then even bank credit may serve as source of investible fund. Thus, the classical theory failed to imagine these two additional sources of funds for investment.

(v) It takes into consideration real factors, like the time preference and the marginal productivity of capital and neglects altogether the monetary influences. The classical economists considered money merely as medium of exchange—a veil over real goods and services. However rate of interest is only a monetary phenomenon and, therefore, the classical theory offers only a partial explanation of the rate of interest.

Thus, the classical theory was built on the unrealistic assumption of full employment and given level of income, which is the fundamental flaw with the theory. The other theories developed subsequently, viz., the liquidity preference theory and loanable fund theory were improvements over the classical theory, as they deal with unemployed resources taking the monetary influences into account.

B-2: Keynesian Liquidity Preference Theory

J.M. Keynes in his famous book 'The General Theory of Employment, Interest and Money' advocated that the interest is the reward for parting with liquidity for some period. Though his liquidity preference theory has not resulted in a determinate rate of interest, yet the concept of liquidity preference has become a standard part of all contemporary theories of interest in one form or the other. **His theory deals with stocks of money and attitude of people towards these stocks and the demand for money by the people (*i.e.*, their liquidity preference level) and the supply of money together determine the rate of interest.** In other words, given the supply of money at a particular time, it is the liquidity preference of the people, which determines the rate of interest.

Individual income receiver has to decide how much to consume, which depends on the marginal propensity to consume and how much the save, which depends on the marginal propensity to save. Given the savings, he has to make another decision regarding the way he should hold it that is how much in the forms of cash, fixed deposits, loans and advances and the various securities. The decision depends upon his **'liquidity preference', which means the desire of the individual to hold the wealth in the form of money rather than in the form of assets like, deposits, loans and advances, securities, etc.** According to the A.L. Meyer, **'liquidity preference is the preference to have an equal amount of cash rather than that of claims against others'.**

Demand for Liquid Funds

The liquidity preference of individual depends upon several considerations, but Keynes observed three motives behind the desire for holding the wealth (savings) in perfectly liquid form:

(a) **Transaction Motive:** It relates to the demand of money for the current transactions by households and firms. They hold cash to be able to make the ordinary purchases in the periods of time between receipts and payments are not synchronised. Incomes are received periodically, while the expenditures are incurred day by day, therefore, certain amount of ready money is kept in hand to make current payments. This amount will depend upon the size of the individual's income, the interval at which the income is received and the prevalent methods of payments in the locality. Similarly, the business units too must keep cash balance with them to meet expenses, as the inflow of revenue from the sale of the product does not coincide with the stream of disbursements. The demand of liquid funds (cash) by households and firms for transaction motives depends upon number of transactions, as the larger the number, the larger will be the amount needed to cover current expenses and it is completely interest inelastic.

(b) **Precautionary Motive:** It refers to the desire of people to hold cash balance for unforeseen contingencies like sickness, accidents, fire, theft and unemployment. In business, it is necessary to retain funds to cope up with an unfavourable volume of turn-over. The cash balance held for these two motives is usually a stable amount. Households and business alike are accustomed to an even flow of expenditures on transactions. On the basis of their experience, they also set aside definite sums for contingencies. The amount needed for these purposes is governed chiefly by the level of one's income and is almost completely interest inelastic.

(c) **Speculative Motive:** It refers to the desire to hold resources in perfectly liquid form, so that it may be converted into earning assets. **It represents the demand for money to be used for making more money by means of speculation in fixed income securities.** The speculative propensity of the people can be satisfied only with cash and depends on the changes in the prices of fixed income securities (i.e., bonds, etc.). The changes in the prices of fixed income securities are inversely related with the change in the rate of interest. That is, at high rates of interest speculators will prefer to hold bonds rather than money, both because such securities have high rate of return and also because of expectations that the bond prices will rise further or at least will not decline. Similarly, they prefer to hold money rather than bonds at low interest rates, because in future the possibility for earning more revenue is expected.

Thus, the demand for money under speculative motive is the negative function of the rate of interest, which decreases as the rate of interest rises and increases as the rate of interest falls. It makes the speculative demand curve to slope negatively. The liquidity preference curve, which also represents the total demand of liquid funds, is parallel to the vertical axis to the extent it represents the transaction and precautionary demand but beyond that it starts sloping negatively.

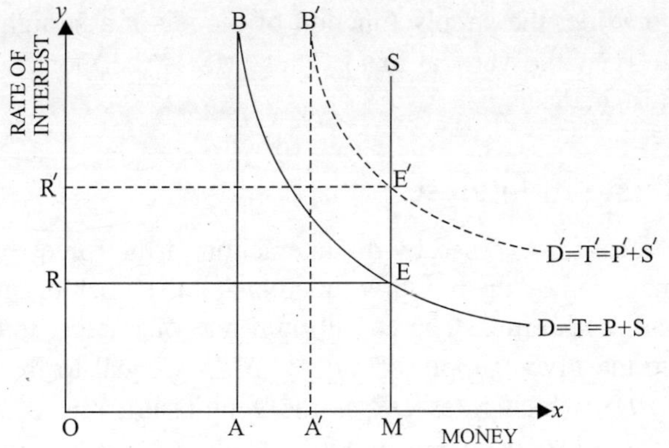

FIGURE 25.2 Equilibrium Rate of Interest under Keynesian Theory.

In Figure 25.2, *AB* represents the transaction and precautionary demand curve that is parallel to the vertical axis, showing that such demand is independent of the rate of interest, but *BD* portion of the total demand curve exhibits the behaviour of the speculative demand, which is interest elastic. Thus, *ABD* represents the total demand for money, which shows that *OA* money will always be demanded irrespective of the rate of interest, but the demand for money beyond *OA* (i.e., the speculative demand) is dependent upon the rate of interest. When the rate of interest is high, people expect it to fall in future and the prices of the fixed income securities to increase, making these securities more attractive on account of expected capital gains. Under such a situation, the cash is less attractive, therefore, the demand for cash for speculative purposes is either nil or very low.

On the other hand, when the rate of interest is low, people expect it to rise in future, and as a result, the prices of fixed income securities are expected to fall, which may cause a capital loss. Under such a situation, people are more attracted to cash, hence they demand more cash. At extremely low rates of interest, the liquidity function becomes perfectly elastic, which is called 'liquidity trap', as at such a low rate of interest people possess an insatiable demand for money.

Supply of Liquid Funds

The amount of money in the economy is the other determinant of the rate of interest. It depends on the central bank and the treasury. The central bank by its credit policy can regulate the reserves of the commercial banks and thereby their lending power and the volume of bank deposits. Such regulations may be imposed on the basis of the discount rate, open market operations, changes in the reserve requirements. Keynes maintained that the volume of money supplied to the economy is, at least over a short period, a given stock independent of the interest rate in the loan market. Since the money is a stock at a moment of time, the supply function of money is a straight line parallel to the ordinate (i.e., the vertical axis). Thus, MS is the money supply curve, which is interest inelastic.

Equilibrium Rate of Interest

The rate of interest is governed by the interaction of the forces of demand and supply of money, i.e., by the liquidity function and the stock of money supplied by the monetary authorities. The equilibrium rate of interest is determined at *E* point, where the given supply of money (*MS*) is equal to the total demand for money (*ABD*), which fixes *OR* as the equilibrium rate of interest. At a higher rate of interest, people would like to hold less than *OM* amount of money, that is, they would prefer to hold fixed income securities rather than cash. The quantity of money in the economy remaining at *OM*, the outcome of the attempt to get rid of cash in favour of bonds is to raise the price of bonds, which will ultimately lower the rate of interest until it is again equal to *OR*. On the other hand, if the rate of interest falls below the equilibrium rate, people will strive to have more money. For this, they will exchange bonds for cash, which may result in a decrease in the price of bonds that will keep on dropping until the rate of interest is pushed up to *OR*. Thus, *OR* is the rate of interest, where the volume of money in the economy equals the volume, which the public is content to hold without any incentive to sell bonds or to shift to bonds.

The money supply and the liquidity preference are entirely independent and are brought together only by changes in the rate of interest. The monetary authorities may increase money supply to lower the rate of interest, which may be effective only, when the level of liquidity preference remains unchanged. In case, the rate of interest is already very low and the liquidity preference curve is infinitely interest elastic, increased money supply may go to meet the insatiable demand for cash balances and it may not lower the rate of interest any further.

In determining the rate of interest, the interest-inelastic liquidity preference for transactions and precautionary motives both exert an influence, but only indirectly. In case income rises, the demand for cash for the two purposes will be increased and the vertical line will move to right to *A′B′*, which shifts the entire demand curve to A′B′D′ level. In case monetary authorities do not inject more money into the economy (i.e., money supply remaining at OM level) the rate of interest rises. Conversely, when income falls, the interest rate will decline, because *AB* vertical line may be shifted leftwards, which will shift the entire liquidity preference curve to the left. Money in circulation remaining at the same level, it will fix a lower rate of interest.

The liquidity preference theory considers rate of interest as a monetary phenomenon and suggests the process of adjustment in the money and capital market for bringing about changes in the interest rate. Secondly, it is more general than the classical theory, in the sense that it is applicable not only to the full employment economy but also to the economy with less than full employment. Thirdly, it helps to integrate the theory of money to the general theory of output and employment and to this extent it is more dynamic and realistic. Fourthly, on the basis of 'liquidity trap' this theory has proved the ineffectiveness of monetary and banking policies during depression. Lastly, this theory has made it clear that it is the income and not the interest that can be considered to be the equilibrating mechanism, between savings and investment. Thus, the theory presented a comprehensive analysis of the monetary factors and their link with the real factors, which has paved the way for an integrated determinate theory of the rate of interest.

Critical Evaluation

This theory marked the beginning of a revolution in the field of money, interest and output and provided a systematic treatment of the role of money in determining the rate of interest, but it has been criticised widely **Firstly,** the liquidity preference curve is drawn on the assumption of a given level of income and there may be as many liquidity preference curves as the levels of income. Considering income changes, the rate of interest according to this theory becomes indeterminate. **Secondly,** it ignores real factors like thrift, marginal productivity of capital and abstinence needed for savings and considers rate of interest as purely a monetary phenomenon. Though it cannot be denied that money supply and demand exert a lot of influence on the determination of the rate of interest, yet for a complete and determinate theory of interest, real factors like the supply of real savings and the marginal efficiency of investment cannot be ignored. **Thirdly,** this theory assumes that the choice is always between liquid cash and illiquid bonds, but in real world there are the various types of investible assets of varying degrees of liquidity. People do not want their savings to be either wholly cash or illiquid bonds, but want to keep some cash, some liquid assets and some illiquid assets. This aspect has been ignored by the liquidity preference theory for determining the rate of interest.

In short, although Keynes' contribution was great, as he analysed both the conditions of monetary equilibrium and income equilibrium, he failed to relate the two equilibrium conditions in developing his liquidity preference theory of interest. He also failed to emphasise the mutual interdependence of savings, investment, income and the interest rates.

B-3: Loanable Funds Theory

The economists of Neo-Classical school consisting of Swedish economists, like Knut Wicksell, Bertil Gotthard Ohlin, Erik Lindahl and Gunnar Mrydal and English economists Sir Dennis Holme Robertson and Jacob Viner developed this theory to improve upon the classical theory of interest by incorporating the influence of the monetary factors, which were ignored, hence it is also called 'Neo-Classical Theory'. These economists were of the view that in addition to such real factors as thriftiness, waiting, productivity of capital, the monetary factors, like hoarding and dishoarding of savings, making current expenditure more than their income of the preceding period, creation of credit by banks, consumption credit, etc., should be taken into consideration. **According to this theory, interest is payment for the use of loanable funds and the rate is determined by the equilibrium of the demand and supply of loanable funds in the credit market.** The supply of loanable funds comes from the savings supplemented by dishoardings and bank credits and such funds have four-fold demand, viz. business or investment demand, government demand, consumption demand and speculative demand.

Supply of Loanable Funds

The supply of loanable funds is derived from four sources, viz: (a) savings (b) dishoardings (c) bank credit, and (d) disinvestment.

(a) **Savings(S):** The savings of households constitute a prime source of loanable funds. Usually by savings, we mean the difference between income and consumption, but propounders of this theory considered savings in a different way. Swedish economists view savings as *ex-ante*, which refers to the savings planned by the individuals at the beginning of a period in the perspective of expected income and anticipated expenditure on consumption. It is different from *ex*-post savings, which refers to the actual amount of savings from the actual income. English economists considered time lag in respect of savings, as the income earned today is not disposed of today. They viewed savings (S) as the income of the previous period (Y_{t-1}) minus the expenditures on the consumption in the current period (C_t) (i.e., $S = Y_{t-1} - C_t$).

Savings may be done by individuals either voluntarily for rainy days or compulsorily by means of social security instalment payments or semi-voluntarily by means of paying insurance premiums or automatically by persons with high incomes. Some individuals may even dissave, as their current expenditure may be more than their income of the preceding period. For the nation as a whole, net savings is equal to total savings minus total dissavings (i.e., consumption loans). The dissavings have negative functional relationship with the rate of interest, that is, at lower rate of interest, the opportunity cost of dissavings is small, therefore, more dissavings and vice-versa. This makes the net savings curve to slope positively.

In addition to the personal savings of individuals, loanable funds are also derived from depreciation reserves and retained earnings, set aside by businesses from their earnings. These are also more closely related to corporate policies and to the nature of business enterprise than to the rate of interest. However, a high market rate of interest means a high cost of borrowings and this encourages business savings as a substitute for the borrowings from the market. Like individuals, businesses can also dis-save, as they can declare dividends out of the savings of the past. The net business savings curve is also drawn sloping positively.

(b) **Dishoarding (–H):** Apart from business and personal savings from current income, account must be taken of the fact that at any given time the amount of money, which economic entities desire to hold as cash balances may not be equal to the total amount of money held. The difference is hoarding (*H*), which, when positive reveals that the amount people want to hold is greater than the amount they do hold and if negative, it reveals that the amount held exceeds the desired balance and there occurs dishoarding. Hoardings are more sensitive to the interest rate and they are interest elastic. At a low rate of interest more idle cash will be kept, while at a high rate of interest less or no idle cash will be kept. In case of interest continues to rise, then beyond certain level of interest, the idle balances of the previous period become active balance of the present period and are available as loanable fund. Thus, to the current saving we can add dishoarding or deduct hoarding as a component of the supply of fund on the loan market.

(c) **Bank Credit (ΔM):** Banking system serves as another source of loanable funds. Banks create credit money and by granting new loans, or making investments out of the deposits credited to the depositors, they increase the stock of money in the given period. Banks can reduce the volume of money by contracting their lending or by selling securities to individuals and deducting the price from the deposit balances of the buyers. This component of the supply of loanable funds bears direct relation to the rate of interest. Although, the pattern of rates does not sensitively move up and down as the volume of bank credit grows or shrinks, but generally rates are high in prosperity, as loans expand and low in times of slow business, when loans reach smaller aggregates. Thus, the supply curve of funds from this source is positively interest-elastic.

(d) **Disinvestment:** It is opposite of investment and is known, as consumption of capital goods and inventories. In such a case, the existing stock of machines and other equipment is allowed to wear out without being replaced. Inventories are drawn below the level of previous period. This may happen due to structural changes in the industry, which may require less capital or the investment may prove to be unwise venture. Under such circumstances capital is allowed to depreciate and part of the revenue from sale of the product, instead of going into capital replacement, flows into loan market. Dis-investment

(ΔM) is encouraged by high rate of interest on loanable funds. When the rate is high, some of the capital may not produce a marginal revenue product to match the rate, therefore, the firm may decide to let this capital run down and to put the depreciation funds in the loan market. This constitutes a deduction from the demand for funds for investment, therefore, it is taken into consideration, while drawing the investment demand curve.

By the lateral summation of the curves of the savings, dishoarding and bank credit, we may obtain total supply curve of the loanable fund or $SL = S - H + \Delta M$. Since the various components of the supply of loanable funds have positive relationship of varying degrees with the rate of interest, the total supply curve slopes positively, indicating greater supply of loanable funds at higher rate of interest and vice-versa.

Demand for Loanable Funds

Like the total supply, the total demand for loanable fund is made up of different demands. Firstly, there is investment or business demand of loanable funds for the purchase or manufacture of new capital goods, including the building up of inventory. The expectation of rising cost of supplies or of higher selling prices of the output or of a general inflation may induce business firms to enlarge their inventories. The investment in plant and equipment is due to the advantage of the roundabout process of production and the negatively sloping marginal revenue productivity curve of capital. The interest charged for the borrowed funds is generally a prominent cost to sway the firm in considering a marginal investment. This indicates that investment demand is somewhat interest-elastic and has negative relationship with the rate of interest. At lower interest rates marginal ventures can be undertaken, but at higher rates they would seem prohibitive.

Secondly, governments (national, state and local) also demand loanable funds. Such demand is motivated less by interest rate consideration than by other considerations, therefore, it is relatively interest inelastic. Thirdly, there is consumption demand of loanable funds, which ranges from the demand for funds for vacations to the demand for mortgage loans for housing. The consumption demand has already been taken into consideration, while ascertaining the net saving or supply curve, therefore, we need not consider it again. Lastly, there may be speculative demand for loanable funds. This too has already been considered, while determining $S - H$ curve. Thus, the sum of the business demand (I) and the government demand (L_g) constitutes the net demand for loanable funds (DL), or

$$DL = I + L_g$$

Since the investment demand for loanable funds (I) is negatively related with the rate of interest and the government demand is also slightly interest elastic, therefore, the total demand curve for loanable funds (*DL*) slopes negatively showing that the demand for loanable funds increases as the rate of interest falls.

Equilibrium Rate of Interest

Usually the equilibrium rate of interest is ascertained at E_2 point, where the total supply (*SL*) equals the total demand for loanable funds (*DL*), but according to some other economists E_0 and E_1 may also represent equilibrium positions.

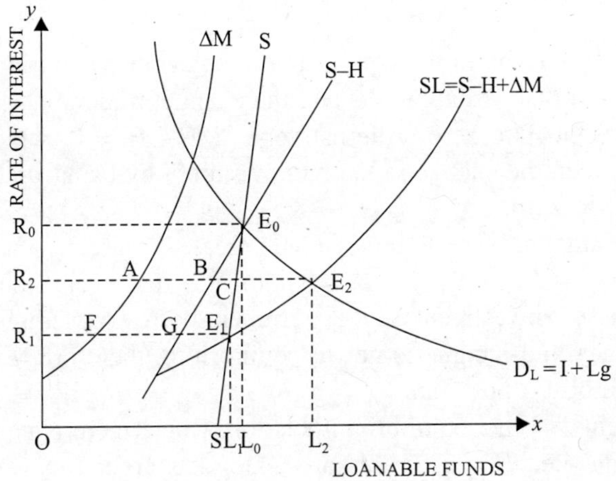

FIGURE 25.3 Determination of Rate Interest for Loanable Funds.

E_2 represents equilibrium, where the supply of loanable fund is equal to its demand, that is,

$$SL = DL$$
$$S - H + \Delta M = I + L_g$$

This represents monetary equilibrium, but fails to represent income equilibrium, which is a must for such equilibrium. Considering income (*Y*) from the expenditure point of view:

$$Y = C + I + G$$

Here *C* is consumption; *I* is investment; and *G* is government expenditure.

Similarly, considering income from disposal point of view,

$$Y = C + S + T$$

Here *C* is consumption, *S* is savings and *T* is taxes.

By setting these two equations equal to each other and eliminating *C*, which is common on both sides, the income equilibrium condition is reduced to,

$$S + T = I + G$$

Since $G - T = L_g$ which means that the government expenditure minus taxes is equal to government borrowings.

$$S = I + (G - T) = I + L_g$$

This means that the income is in equilibrium, when saving is equal to investment and government loans (i.e., the net demand for loanable funds). Subtracting income equilibrium equation from the loanable fund equilibrium equation, we have

$$\begin{array}{r} S - H + \Delta M = I + L_g \\ -S = -(I + L_g) \\ \hline -H + \Delta M = 0 \end{array}$$

Thus, if income is to be in the equilibrium along with equilibrium of loanable funds, the sum of dishoarding ($-H$) and the change in money supply by banks (ΔM) must be equal to zero. Alternatively, $\Delta M - H = 0$, which means the difference between the change in the money supply by banks and the hoarding must be equal to zero.

At E_2 the amount of new money (ΔM) created is greater than the amount of hoarding, i.e., AR_2 ($= BE_2$) $> BC$. It indicates that even though $SL = DL$, some of the private investments and government borrowings are being financed with new money and income is not in equilibrium, therefore, E_2 cannot be a complete equilibrium position.

E_0 represents another equilibrium position, where there is neither hoarding nor dishoarding (i.e., $H = 0$) Professor Ackley has argued that in equilibrium not only their sum, but both H and ΔM must be zero. He defined hoarding as the difference between the amount of money people want to hold and the amount they do hold. People or firms desire to hold funds with transaction (D_T), precautionary (D_P) and speculative (D_S) motives and actual money (M) held by them must be equal as follows:

$$H = (D_S + D_T + D_P) - M = 0$$

We know that the static monetary equilibrium is attained at the point, where

$$D_S + D_T + D_P = M$$

It means that the amount of money held in balance must be equal to the amount economic entities desire to hold in their balances, which gives a conclusion that in the static monetary equilibrium, H must be equal to zero. Since, the condition $\Delta M - H = 0$, must be met, if the static income and static monetary equilibrium conditions are to be met simultaneously, it follows that $\Delta M = H = 0$. Thus, at E_0, where both monetary equilibrium and income equilibrium conditions are satisfied, there is desired equilibrium.

At E_1, S curve intersects SL curve, which reveals that at this point, savings and the supply of loanable funds are equal and all the new money created is being hoarded, that is ($\Delta M = FR_1$) $=$ ($H = GE_1$), or $\Delta M - H = 0$. Thus, it may be possible for planned savings and planned investment plus government borrowings to be equal at E_1 and for some kind of monetary equilibrium to exist there, but it is not possible for a static monetary equilibrium to exist at E_1, because $H > 0$.

Thus, there are three possible equilibrium at E_2, E_0 and E_1 respectively, where E_2 can be regarded as partial equilibrium, E_1 may be more than partial but less than full equilibrium. It is only at E_0 where we come across a full equilibrium, because at this point both monetary and income equilibrium conditions are met simultaneously.

Critical Evaluation

It has been pointed out that the loanable funds theory is just an extension of the classical theory, therefore, it is open to the criticisms similar to that of the classical theory. In classical theory savings comes out of the current income, while in loanable funds theory it comes from the income of the previous period. The loanable funds theory includes bank credit and dishoarding in addition to real savings as source of fund but the classical theory considering the savings out of the current income takes bank credit and dishoarding into account indirectly, because it increases the current income, which, in turn, increases the current savings. Thus, for practical purposes there is not much difference between the two theories except the fact that the term loanable funds has been substituted for current savings.

Secondly, loanable funds theory like the classical theory is indeterminate. Loanable funds are compounded of savings plus bank money and dishoarding. Since the savings vary with the level of disposable income, it follows that the total supply of loanable funds will vary with income making the rate of interest indeterminate. However, the supply of savings is taken to be determined by the income of the preceding period, which including other components of the loanable funds, determines the rate of interest in the current period and that, in turn, affects the determination of income of the succeeding period through investment.

Thirdly, it compounds together the monetary factors and real factors influencing the rate of interest. Since the two are different in their origin and impact, therefore, they must be separately accounted for, to get a complete, determinate theory of interest and income determination.

Fourthly, Professor G. Ackley has argued that loanable funds theory contains much confusion, since savings, investment and income are all flow concepts, while hoardings and dishoardings refer to a difference between two stocks. These magnitudes cannot be defined without reference to some time period and require that the time period applicable to the analysis should be specified. Accordingly, he remarks that the loanable funds theory should be treated as a disequilibrium theory, concerned with a dynamic analysis, not as a static theory.

B-4: Modern Theory of Interest: J.R. Hicks-Alvin Harvey Hansen Analysis

Both the classical or neo-classical theories and the liquidity preference theory, taken separately were indeterminate, as both determine the rate of interest at a given level of income, but, in real world, the rate of interest and the level of income both are inter-dependent. This analysis took important elements of all other theories of interest and synthesised them into a new theory also known as the **Determinate Theory of Interest.** The classical theory considered only real factors—real savings and real investments—but Keynesian theory took into account only the monetary factors—liquidity preference and money supply—for determination of the rate of interest. Hicks-Hansen analysis has successfully combined the four variable—savings, investments, liquidity preference and money supply—into a well integrated theory. It has combined together the monetary and non-monetary factors together for the determination of the rate of interest.

In every economy there are two sectors—monetary sector and goods or real sector—and two sectors are interrelated. For equilibrium in monetary sector, the rate of interest and the level of income must be such that the supply of money equals the demand (liquidity preference) for it. Similarly, the real sector will experience equilibrium, when the savings equals the investment. Thus, an equilibrium or determinate rate of interest is one which brings about equilibrium in monetary as well as in real sectors. Thus, money supply affects both the income level and the rate of interest but it is only one determinant, the other determinants are the investment function, the savings function and the liquidity preference or demand function. J.R. Hicks-Alvin Hansen analysis or modern theory of interest has evolved two curves—IS function curve and LM function curves—where all points of the IS function curve show the equilibrium in the real sector, while all points of LM function curve represent the equilibrium in the monetary sector. The point of intersection of the two exhibits such equilibrium rate of interest, where both real as well as monetary sectors are in equilibrium. In other words, at this equilibrium rate of interest, total savings will be equal to total investment and the total demand for money will equal to the total supply of money.

The IS Function

In real world, income, investment and rate of interest are all inter-dependent. Investment is an 'income generating' expenditure. Every level of investment has a corresponding level of income assuming that the multiplier process has fully worked itself out. This investment is a decreasing or negative function of the rate of interest. At a high rate of interest, the investment demand is low and vice versa. As a result the investment demand function will be negatively sloping in relation to the rate of interest. On the other hand, the saving is an increasing or positive function of the level of income, therefore, the savings function will be sloping upwards in relation to the level of income. Our task is to find out those pairs of the rate of interest and income corresponding to which the total investment equals the total savings.

Figure 25.4(i) reveals that as the income rises, the savings curve shifts to the right and the rate of interest, which equalises the savings and investment, falls. In the Figure 25.4(ii), we measure the income on the horizontal axis and plot the corresponding rates of interest determined by the equality of savings and investment. By combining A′B′C′D′ points, where the equality of savings and investment is established as per Figure 25.4(i), we derive IS (investment-savings) function curve sloping downwards to the right. It is because, as the level of income rises, the volume of savings increases, which, in turn, reduces the rate of interest.

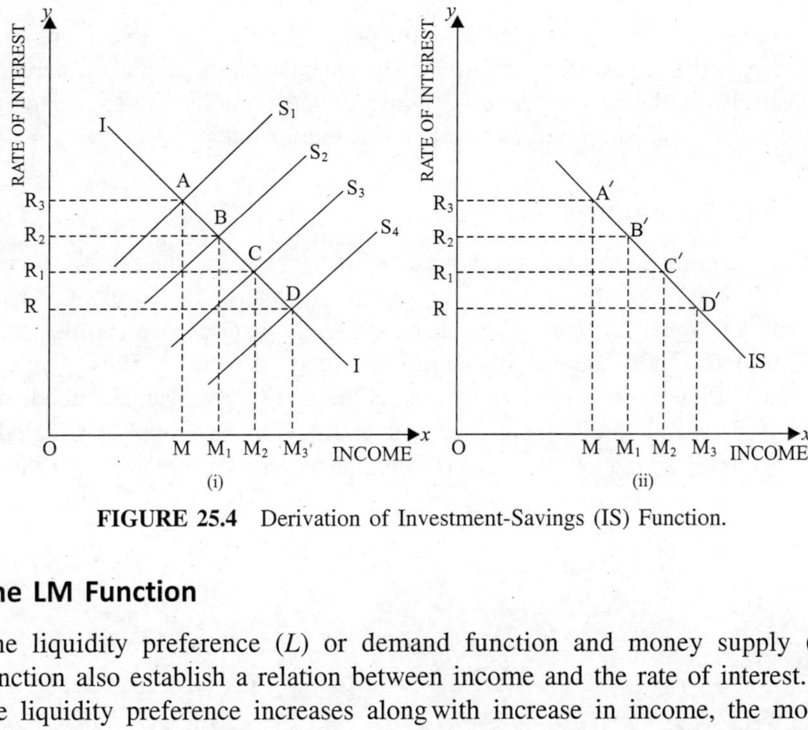

FIGURE 25.4 Derivation of Investment-Savings (IS) Function.

The LM Function

The liquidity preference (*L*) or demand function and money supply (*M*) function also establish a relation between income and the rate of interest. As the liquidity preference increases along with increase in income, the money supply remaining unchanged, the rate of interest will be low, when income is low and it is high, when income is high. This helps in derivation of liquidity preference and money supply (*LM*) functions curve.

Figure 25.5(i) reveals that as the liquidity preference rises, the money supply remaining at *OM* level, the Keynesian equilibrium shifts from *A* to *B* and *C* points respectively, showing a higher and higher rate of interest. Increase in liquidity preference follows the increase in income. The adjoining diagram 26.5 (ii) shows the various rates of interest that equalise the demand for cash (the liquidity preference) of the people with the supply of cash at the various levels of income. Here the *LM* curve slopes positively showing that as

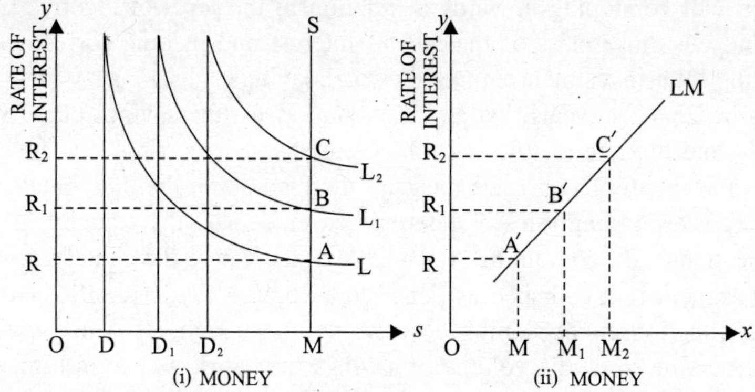

FIGURE 25.5 Derivation of Liquidity Preference and Money Supply (LM) Function.

the income level increases, the liquidity preference (or the demand for cash) of the people increases and consequently the rate of interest also increases. Conversely as the income level diminishes, the liquidity preference of the people also diminishes and, as a result, the rate of interest declines.

Equilibrium Rate of Interest

The two curves *IS* and *LM* relate the level of income and the rate of interest, but none alone can reveal either the rate of interest or the level of income. By putting *IS* and *LM* curves together in a single diagram, we can determine simultaneously both the rate of interest and level of income. Thus, given the marginal efficiency of capital and marginal propensity to consume embodied in the *IS* curve and liquidity preference (demand) and money supply embodied in the *LM* curve, the rate of interest is *OR* and the income level *OM* are as follows:

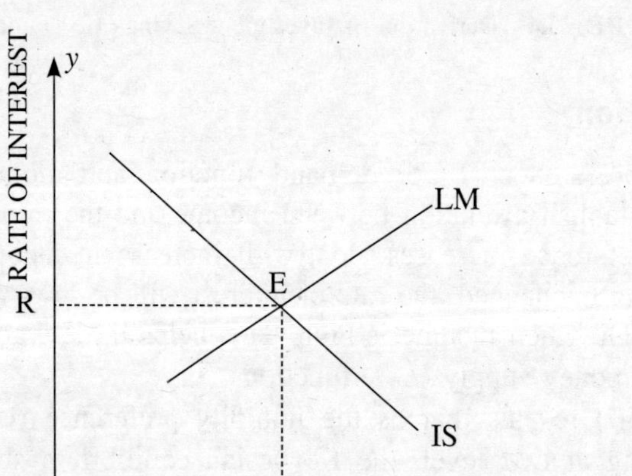

FIGURE 25.6 Equilibrium Rate of Interest as per Modern Theory.

Thus, real factors, viz. productivity and thrift and monetary factors, viz. the demand for money (liquidity preference) and supply of money play vital roles in the determination of rate of interest. Any change in these factors will cause shift in *IS* or *LM* curve and will, therefore, change the equilibrium level of the rate of interest and income. Thus, it also explains better the effect of changes in certain economic variables, such as desire to save, the supply of money, investment and liquidity preference on the rate of interest, which can be analysed as the follows:

(a) **Change in the Money Supply:** Assuming liquidity preference function to be given, if there is increase in the supply of money, more money is likely to be held for speculative purposes at each level of income, the interest rate, as a result, will fall. This will shift the *LM* curve, to the right to *LM'* Figure 25.7(i), which sets a new equilibrium position *E'*, where the rate of interest will be lower and the level of income greater than before. On the other hand, if there is a decrease in the supply of money, less money will be available for speculative purposes at each level of income. This will shift the *LM* to LM_0 level, which will set a new equilibrium with *IS* curve at E_0 point, where the rate of interest will be higher and the level of income smaller than before.

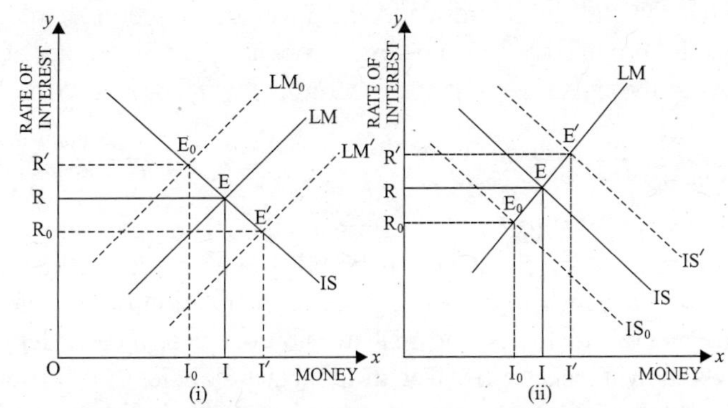

FIGURE 25.7 Impact of Change in LM and IS Function.

(b) **Change in the Propensity of Consume or Save:** In case the desire (propensity) for consumption rises or conversely the propensity to save decreases, the level of income will rise at each rate of interest. This will shift the *IS* curve to the right to *IS'* level, as in Figure 25.7(ii). The *LM* curve remaining unchanged, the new equilibrium position is set at *E'* point, where the rate of interest as well as the level of income will be greater than before. On the other hand, if the propensity to consumer falls or conversely the propensity to save rises, the level of income falls for each rate of interest. This shifts the *IS* curve to the left to IS_0 level. The LM curve remaining unchanged, as in Figure 25.7(ii), the new equilibrium is set at E_0 point, where both the rate of interest and the level of income will be smaller than before.

(c) **Change in Investment and Government Expenditure:** Such changes shift the *IS* curve upwards or downwards as the case may be. In case the private investment or government expenditure goes up, the level of income also increases, which shifts the *IS* curve to the right to *IS'* level, as in the Figure 25.7(ii) and the sets the equilibrium at *E'*, where the rate of interest as well as level of income is higher than before. A decrease in investment and government expenditure shifts *IS* curve downward to the left to IS_0 level and sets the equilibrium at E_0 point, as in Figure 25.7(ii), where the rate of interest as well as the level of income is lower than before.

(d) **Change in Liquidity Preference:** In case liquidity preference decreases, it shifts the *LM* curve to the left to LM_0, as in Figure 25.7(i), which sets the equilibrium at E_0, where the rate of interest will be higher, but the level of income will be lower. On the other hand, if the liquidity preference increases, the *LM* curve shifts down wards to *LM'* level, as in Figure 25.7(i), which sets the equilibrium at *E'* point, where the rate interest will be lower, but the level of income will be higher than before.

Thus, the rate of interest and the level of income can be influenced by changes in propensity to consume, propensity to save, private investment, money supply and government expenditure, which shifts *IS* or *LM* curves.

Critical Appraisal

J.R. Hicks-Alvin Hansen's determinate theory of the rate of interest is a useful integration of classical and liquidity preference theories and has made a significant advance in explaining the determination of the rate of interest. It is more general, inclusive and realistic approach to interest determination and succeeds in synthesising fiscal with monetary policies and income theory with monetary theory. Moreover, this can explain many policy riddles, which could be explained neither by classical economists nor by Keynesian Theory. For example, in underdeveloped countries the rate of interest is found to be low despite the demand for capital being very high. This could not be explained either by classical or by Keynesian theory of interest. Modern theory reveals that the rate of interest and the level of income are simultaneously determined. Since in underdeveloped countries the level of income determined by the real and monetary factors is low, therefore, the rate of interest is bound to be low.

In spite of these merits, the modern (Hicks-Hansen) theory is not without limitations. **Firstly,** this analysis is significant only if the rate of interest is free to move rather than being maintained at a certain level by central bank of the country. **Secondly,** it also assumes that the investment is interest-elastic, that is, the interest rate does exercise some influence on the volume of investment. Besides it has been criticised for being too artificial and over-simplified, as the division of economy into monetary sector and real sector is unrealistic, because the two are interwoven and act and react on each other. Further, it has ignored the influence or changes in the various determinants of rate of interest, such as money supply, liquidity preference, propensity to consume or save and investment.

Review Questions

1. Explain the nature of interest and distinguish between money rate of interest and natural rate of interest?
2. What are IS function and LM function curves and explain the assumptions of modern theory of interest?
3. Explain the motives of demand for money in the economy.
4. 'Interest is the reward for parting with liquidity'. Explain.
5. "At the equilibrium rate of interest, there must be equality not only between the supply and demand of money, but also between savings and investment". Discuss.
6. Hicksian interest theory incorporates both the ideas given by Keynes as well as classical economists regarding interest'. Discuss.
7. Explain the concept of interest and bring out the classical savings and investment approach to the determination of interest.
8. "The liquidity preference theory provides only the LM curve, it fails to explain the determination of rate interest." Comment.
9. How do you determine the interest rate as per the classical theory? If the people want to spend less and the firms want to invest more, how would we use the classical theory to study the effect on the rate of interest?
10. What do you mean by "the demand for loanable funds"? Elucidate the application of the loanable funds theory to determine the interest rate.

26

Theories of Profit

Profit refers to the surplus that goes to the entrepreneurs after deducting all expenses from the sales revenue. The prospect of the profit is the moving force for the economic activities and economic progress. The profit motive sets in motion policies for setting up and expansion of firms and industries, providing increased employment and income; launches the testing of new ideas, which raise the efficiency of production; stimulates improvements in old varieties of goods and the introduction of new varieties; and induces efforts for expansion of demand and widening of markets. The prospects of low or non-existent profits will slow down economic activity and, if dismal prospect is widespread, the economy is paralysed and the productive activities will come to a standstill.

In this chapter, an effort is being made to examine the nature of profit, to look into the causes or sources of profit, and to enquire as to who precisely does the job for which profit is a return.

MEANING OF PROFIT

The term 'profit' is used in two distinct senses: (a) in the sense of business or accounting profit; (b) in the sense of economic profit, **where the former refers to the amount left to the entrepreneur from the sales revenue after he has paid all the expenses of production and sales to the various factors, whose services were hired, borrowed or leased.** According to this view profit includes the implicit or imputed interest on capital, which he owns in the business, rent on own land used in the business and the wage or salary earned for the work done by him, which would commonly be done by hired managers. On the other hand, the latter seeks to exclude the aforesaid wage, interest and rent elements included in the business profit to arrive at the economic profit. In economists' views cost includes both implicit (i.e., cost of services of factors owned and supplied by the entrepreneur himself) and explicit (i.e., cost of services of factors hired by the entrepreneur) costs.

Thus, the economists' profit—true profit, or pure profit—stands for the return to the entrepreneur, exclusive of the implicit returns, i.e., the income he could earn, if the money or land, which he owns and uses in the business were lent or leased to another business and exclusive of such wage of management, as he could earn, if he hired out his services to another firm. In other words, profit is the residue left from the sale of goods after the deduction of all (implicit as well as explicit) wage, interest and rent. It is the revenue obtained from the output (or product) market minus the cost incurred in the factor market and can be positive as well as negative.

NATURE OF PROFIT

There is no unanimity of opinion regarding the nature of profit. **American Economist Frank William Taussig regarded it as mixed and vexed income. Classical economists considered profit as reward to the capitalist, who supplied capital to the business. Marshall regarded profit as an average remuneration, which is necessary to bring and maintain sufficient supply of entrepreneurship and is akin to wages. An American Professor Walker considered profit as a determinate return for a production activity performed by an entrepreneur with a superior ability. According to Professor F.B. Hawley profit is a reward for the risk to be borne by the entrepreneur.** Modern economists **regard profit as an income which arises out** of change, uncertainty and friction inherent in a dynamic world and which the belated operations of competitive forces tend to eliminate.

The survey of the various situations in which profit exists reveal that the underlying causes of profit cannot be easily reduced to one significant common denominator. The prime source or cause of profit is uncertainty. The entrepreneur cannot predict the outcome of his decisions. Circumstances beyond his control may change the conditions of demand and supply by the time his product is sold. This may cause a deviation in the revenue left after the payment of wages, interest and rent from the anticipated amount. The primary reason for uncertainty lies with the dynamic situations in the economy. Which may be induced either by the entrepreneur himself through innovations or external changes force risk-laden choices on the entrepreneur. A second source or cause of profit can be traced to the position of advantage, which some firms enjoy in the market over other firms.

THEORIES OF PROFIT

Profit theory has a chequered career of development and is regarded as a by-product of development of the theories of value. Classical economists considered labour as the only productive input to which, later on, they added capital as another explicit input and realised that land is also an important input. Therefore, in their writings, profit could not get specific mention as a return to an input separate from land, labour and capital, but simply attempted to liken profit to other factor income, like rent and wages. Neo-classical economists considered entrepreneurship as a separate input and profit as a return to such input. They built up marginal productivity theory, which was followed by the various other theories of profit propounded by modern economists.

Rent Theory of Profit

Professor Francis Amasa Walker, an American Economist, considered profit to be the rent of ability of the entrepreneur. Entrepreneurs differ in ability, just as land differs in fertility and may be graded as marginal and super marginal. The marginal entrepreneurs earn only enough to cover their wages of management, to keep him engaged in the field of economic activity. Super marginal entrepreneurs earn a surplus over their cost of production, including wage of management, which is profit. This theory is subject to weaknesses similar to that of the 'Ricardian Theory of Rent'. Moreover, it regards entrepreneur to be a manager only and ascribed profits to a differential reward to the talent of management, but this idea of profit is suitable only to a static world, where due to perfect competition price is given and management try to reduce costs to earn a surplus. Nevertheless, it could explain neither the origin nor the nature of profit.

Wage Theory of Profit

Professor Taussig considered profit as a special type of wages earned by a class of workers called entrepreneurs. The entrepreneurship has been considered as a profession and profit as a reward for this. However considering entrepreneurship as similar to the labour, it has ignored the fact that wages is a contractual reward, while profit is essentially a residual income. Profit may be negative, but the wages can never be negative. Unlike rewards for other inputs, profit is a dynamic income.

Marginal Productivity Theory of Profit

This theory was propounded by German economist T.H. Von Thunen in 1826 and further developed by J.B. Clark, M.E. Leon Walras, Robert Barone, David Recardo and Alfred Marshall later on. According to this theory, reward for each input depends on its marginal revenue productivity. The number of entrepreneurs in any industry will depend on how much they earn (i.e., marginal revenue productivity). For land, labour and capital, it is possible to calculate the marginal revenue productivity of the factor to an individual firm, but the same of entrepreneurship for a single firm is unrealistic. Therefore, we calculate the marginal revenue productivity of entrepreneurship for the whole industry, because in industry the number of entrepreneurs can be altered and the results of such alternations can be studied.

Assuming homogeneous units of entrepreneurs, the marginal revenue productivity declines as the number of entrepreneurs in any industry increases. Thus, the more the entrepreneurs in an industry, the smaller will be their marginal revenue productivity. On the other hand, due to homogeneous units of entrepreneurs, their supply curve is straight line parallel to horizontal axis, which reveals that all must earn the same (certain minimum) amount of profit, if they are to remain in the industry. The point, where declining marginal revenue productivity curve intersects the constant profit line of entrepreneurs in any industry, is the equilibrium, where all are earning just their transfer earnings (i.e., normal profits).

It is a long run situation, as entrepreneurs will enter or leave the industry until all are earning normal profits. However, in short run, the industry might have lesser number of entrepreneurs, which may enable them to earn supernormal profit, as their marginal revenue productivity will be higher than their transfer earnings.

This attempt of explaining rewards of all in terms of the marginal productivity failed miserably in determining profits. In terms of the marginal productivity theory uncertainty bearing or decision-making is considered as a separate input like land, labour and capital, because as per Euler's Theorem nothing should be left over for profit, if the production function is linearly homogeneous. Moreover, it is misleading to apply the marginal productivity theory to profit, because the entrepreneur performs a variety of functions and the element of uncertainty defies standardisation. Nevertheless, the entrepreneurial talent is so scarce and heterogeneous that its marginal productivity cannot be guessed or calculated. In fact, the entrepreneurship does not have a distinguishable marginal product, as such its reward depends on the productivity of other inputs, whose risk it bears.

Dynamic Theory of Profit

Professor J.B. Clark pointed out that profit owes its origin to the dynamic nature of economy and has no existence in a static economy in which future changes are known, risk and uncertainty are completely non-existent and production process is routine that can be carried on by paid managers. He defined profit as the difference between selling price and cost. Since, in static economy, the amount of capital, the methods of production, managerial and technical organisation and the demand structure all remain the same, profit tends to vanish under the forces of competition. He observed that we are living in a dynamic world, where five 'generic' changes are constantly in progress; viz. population, wants, capital, methods of production and forms of industrial establishment. These changes generate a surplus over cost for entrepreneurs, who undertakes the risk of production in such dynamic situation. In case these changes are eliminated by assumption, the price of goods and the cost of production there of coincides and the entrepreneur is left with no real profit but he will get merely the wages of management. The difference, if any, will wipe away by the competition, but due to frictions in the process of economic adjustment, in short run, frictional profits may be earned by the entrepreneurs.

This theory has touched the fundamental characteristics of profit, viz., its dynamic nature, yet economists consider it as hazy and imprecise. Not all but only those changes, which cannot be foreseen and provided for in advance, give rise to profit.

Innovation Theory of Profit

Professor J.A. Schumpter attributed profit to the introduction of innovation in the process of production or sale of the product. Entrepreneurs are induced to introduce innovation in the expectation of reaping the windfall or profit. Innovation consists of all changes in the process of production or sale of the product, which aims at either reducing cost of production and sale or raising the revenue, so that the gap between cost and revenue is widened. **Innovation may involve introduction of a new and improved technique of production, a change in managerial set up, use of new type of materials or fuel, change in the shape and quality of the product, a search of new source of raw materials or new market for the product.** Mere conception of new ideas or methods cannot constitute innovation, unless it is put to commercial use. The person, who puts new ideas in commercial use is the entrepreneur and he obtains profit for it.

Innovation puts the entrepreneur in advantageous position in the industry and gives him a surplus, called the profit. Such profit is of temporary nature, because soon the competitors emulate it out. This process may continue for ever. Thus, the profit is the result of a constant striving on the part of the entrepreneur for newer methods of production, organisation or sale. **According to this theory profit is a dynamic income, which exists in dynamic economy to entrepreneurs, who can introduce innovations, otherwise, he is merely an imitator, who uses widely known process or technology and gets the wage of management and not the profit.** His profit has the hall-mark of being innovational in origin and temporary in nature.

This theory does not offer full explanation of profit. In all innovation, risk and uncertainty is inherent and profit is really reward for bearing the risk involved in innovations.

Risk Theory of Profit

Professor F. B. Hawley considered risk-bearing as the main function of the entrepreneur and profit as a reward for it. An entrepreneur is faced with four types of risks, namely (i) risk of replacement and obsolescence; (ii) risk of marketability of product; (iii) risk proper; and (iv) uncertainty. Risk of replacement is calculable and is provided for by way of depreciation, as an item of cost. Similarly, the risk of obsolescence although less calculable due to difficulty in imagining the technological progress, is usually provided for and counted as cost. Risk of marketability and other uncertainties may upset the plan of entrepreneurs and no provision is made for such risks in costs of production. Such risks are borne by entrepreneurs in anticipation of profit. The profit is simply the reward for staying in business. **'The greater the amount of risk involved in a business, higher is the expected profit necessary to induce entrepreneurs to bear the risk.**

This theory points out the strategic factor, which gives rise to profit. Even modern economists regard that the profit contains some element of remuneration for risk taking. However, it would be incorrect to attribute profit entirely to risk taking. Windfalls or profits obtained by entrepreneurs, are usually out of proportion to the risk involved. Highly risky enterprises are not necessarily the highly profitable enterprises. Truly speaking, **profits are made not because risks are borne, but because efficient entrepreneurs are able to reduce them. Entrepreneurs partly reduce the risks and partly bear the unavoidable risks.**

Uncertainty Bearing Theory of Profit

Professor F. H. Knight, after surveying the then existing theories of profit, propounded this theory as a refinement of the risk bearing theory. **He classified risks in two categories, viz. insurable and non-insurable.** Risks of fire, theft, accident, etc. are statistically measureable and insurance companies undertake such risks in return for a premium, which can be included in the cost of production. Certain risks, like that of change in the production process, development of new substitutes and varieties of products and change in demand are unforeseen and uninsurable, which is also called uncertainty. **It is the uninsurable risk or uncertainty, which is to be borne by the entrepreneurs in expectation of a reward called profit.**

This uncertainty bearing is the main function of the entrepreneur and has been raised to the status of a separate factor, whose supply price depends on the degree of uncertainty involved in a venture. The conception of the marginal productivity theory regarding production exhaustion, if physical inputs are paid according to their marginal productivity, can be explained even after taking non-physical inputs like entrepreneurship into consideration. Goods are produced for future consumption, which depends on the price of the product and determines the demand for inputs. The product price cannot be determined unless the reward for input is determined and the latter cannot be determined unless the former is fixed. The entrepreneur resolves this by guessing the price of the product and, on this basis, converts the marginal physical product into marginal value product, which determines the demand of inputs. Inputs, hired on contractual basis, are rewarded their anticipated marginal value product and the entrepreneur as a residual claimant may make greater profit, if actual sales revenue exceeds the anticipated sales revenue.

This theory has been criticised on the ground that it has raised the uncertainty bearing to the status of a full-fledged cause for profit. Taking profit as a reward for bearing the real cost of uncertainty or an inducement to bear uncertainty, it implies that there is a connection between the level of profit and the degree of uncertainty, but in real world no such connection exists.

J.F. Weston, a follower of Professor F.H. Knight, has further clarified the concept of uncertainty and the nature of profit. **He considered profit as the**

difference between *ex* post and *ex ante returns*. He viewed profit not as a distinct distributive share, but as an element found in the payments to all types of productive agents. It may be positive, if the entrepreneurs take a bearish view of the future, because in that case, the contractually hired agents will receive less than the realised value of their marginal product. Thus, the profit is really drawn from production inputs themselves, but it cannot be considered as exploitation, because in the absence of entrepreneur, the factors themselves would have to gamble on the future. In case the entrepreneurs are bullish in their outlook, there are losses (or negative profits), because the hired inputs are rewarded on the basis of their anticipated marginal product, which exceeds the value of the marginal products that are ultimately raised when the products are sold in the market. Thus, the profit, in a sense, is a tax on the productivity of the hired agents.

This rejects the classical conception of profit as an income accruing to a socio-economic class enjoying the status of employer and combining the functions of both the capitalist and the manager and considers the conception of profit as a non-contractual windfall-gain, accruing to a disembodied entrepreneur.

Knightian theory includes no unequivocal notion of entrepreneurship. Uncertainty-bearing, decision-making, organisation of inputs and combination of a number of activities, have been considered by some economists as entrepreneurship. However, none of these could identify the entrepreneur in a joint stock company, where the ultimate decision-making in the organisation rests mainly on salaried managers with little or no ownership interest and ultimate uncertainty bearing dissolves upon the absentee stockholders. To resolve this controversy, the entrepreneurial functions are attributed to an artificial personage, namely the firm itself, which too fails to provide a clue to the allocation or distribution of profit among the natural persons of the firm's ownership and control groups. Secondly, the Knightian theory is incompatible with facts, because in the real world businessmen or promoters estimate profits *ex ante* and the public thinks of profit as income of a special class of society. Thirdly, the Knightian theory is heavily insulated from empirical testing. Economists have given empirical meaning to uncertainty and apply two techniques, where either they express expected net returns as a probability distribution or they determine the policy on the basis of the expectations, as to receipts less a risk premium, against which they balance the cost of investment.

The entrepreneurs may be grouped according to the size of risk premium they would feel it necessary to deduct from anticipated receipt in determining, whether a particular venture would be worth undertaking. Entrepreneurs can also be grouped according to their ability to bear uncertainty, which depends upon the amount of their capital and their ability to raise additional funds in an imperfect capital market. When an entrepreneur conceives the idea of entry, the expected rate of profit must be sufficient to cover not only the risk premium with respect to uncertainty regarding future receipts and costs, but must also be enough to cover a risk premium against the possibility of competition with other new firms entering simultaneously in the industry. In theory it is all right, but in practice, it is very difficult to give an empirical shape to such ideas.

PRESENT STATE OF PROFIT THEORY

After studying the various theories, we conclude that the profit theory is in the most unsatisfactory state at present. These theories can be grouped into two categories; viz.,: (a) those, which regard profit as a residual income or the excess of price over cost; and (b) those, which regard profit as a reward for an input called entrepreneurship. Both types of theories continue to exist together with a loose link in between.

Theories considering profit as a residual surplus have been closely associated with Chamberlin's theory of monopolistic competition. These theories attribute the existence of profit to monopolistic restriction on output or successful innovation. Profit may be the outcome of uncertainty, which has the effect of making entrepreneurs plan for wide safety margins, so that, many firms are discouraged from entering the industry, while more enterprising ones, who do enter, are rewarded with a profit. It may also arise from the indivisibility of important resources, which may restrict entry into the industry. Thus, in all such situations persistence of profit depends on lack of freedom of entry.

On the other hand, propounders of the functional theory of profit have stressed the relation between profits and dynamic changes in the economy. They attribute profit to some function or functions performed by the entrepreneurs. The major difficulty in such situation lies in defining the entrepreneurial function and its location in the corporate form of enterprise. Empirical researches reveal that profits get widely diffused and are appropriated institutionally. Profits are not entirely related to some functions and the relevance of change and uncertainty in the theory of profit lies in loosening the link between productivity and remuneration.

Thus, we need an effective theory, which integrates the basic elements of different theories into a consistent and coherent theory applicable to the modern form of business organisations.

MONOPOLY PROFIT

Uncertainty and dynamic forces, which foster profit do not account for all situations in which profit exists. Profit exists even in static conditions and owes its origin to peculiar advantage with respect to demand or cost enjoyed by the firm, which may be in a position to charge a price higher than the marginal cost or has the benefit of a cost below the market price. It usually happens in monopoly, wherein firm hinders the entry of new firms and tries to maintain such favourable position. Monopoly and oligopoly are formed by the various conditions and devices, which give the firm the leverage to regulate the supply of the article and to bring profits into being. It is monopoly profit, which is derived from the power possessed by the firm to command a profit-bearing price.

Sometimes monopoly profit is attributable to certain property rights. In case entry is restricted, because the existing firms possess patent rights, it may continue to earn excess profit, although it may be in the nature of rent, so long as the patent right is non-reproducible. The restricted entry may also be due to a larger scale of the plant and heavy initial investment requirements, which may earn monopoly profit to firms already in the industry. In case the excess profit rate is expected to continue, it will be capitalised, which will raise the sale value of the enterprise, and if the firm is sold, the new owner would receive only a normal return on their investment. Thus, it is similar to rent.

MONOPSONY PROFIT

Profit also arises due to monopsonistic influences in factor markets. Due to the lack of the knowledge, immobility, etc. of inputs, competition is often not perfect in factor markets. In such circumstances, some firms are able to pay less than the competitive rates of rewards. Such firms will earn higher profit for themselves by paying the input less than their due under perfectly competitive conditions. However, if all the firms are able to obtain similar monopsonistic benefits, the excess of profit will tend to disappear. Significant source of monopsony profit for a firm is its failure to pay top management personnel a reward to the full extent of their contribution to the enterprise. Since the market for management personnel is highly imperfect, the firms often succeed for a considerable period in paying efficient managers less than what they would earn in the employment of other firms, if their abilities were known well.

WINDFALL PROFIT

In addition to the existence of monopoly and monopsony, there is a large family of circumstances, accidental and short lived, which place some firms in a favourable situation to make money. Such extra return is called windfall profits. A strike, a fire or a shift in population may bring loss to some firms, but may also bring benefit to some other firms. Many such accidental occurrences are also marked by the uncertainty attending dynamic changes. In some instances the accident, chance or luck brings the mixture of uncertainty and the position of exclusive advantage to some concern. In other instances it brings windfall profit to some and only risk of loss to others. The essence of windfall profit dwells in the circumstances that the favoured position is not removed by the instantaneous entry of new firms and accidental losses are not asserted by the immediate exit of firms. Thus, it is the inflexibility of supply that accounts for windfall profit.

PROFIT IN A CAPITALISTIC ECONOMY

Profit is more a residual than a functional return, even then it has important function in a capitalist economy. Firstly, the anticipation of making profits by some firm induces other firms to reformulate their policies. Existence of such profit induces the competitive firms to adopt of policies of successful firm or to find out new ideas to earn a higher profit. In a competitive industry failure to keep pace with new development means losses and earning of profits by a new firms is a signal to other firms to change their policies suitably, if they are to avoid future losses. Secondly, the expectation of profit is an important incentive for innovations in their field, which, in turn, maintains economic progress and investment necessary for full employment in the economy. Thirdly, firms revise their behaviour in the hope of making pure profits. Lastly, if existing firms in an industry earn high profit, it induces additional firms to enter the industry, which results in reallocation of resources, so as to conform more closely to changes in consumers' demand.

Besides, profit has some social function in such economy. The preservation of national resources entrusted to any economic enterprise is its foremost duty. In case the firm fails in this regard, it not only weakens its own power to survive, but impoverishes the whole society. Secondly, it has to perform the function of social insurance, that is, it has to fill 'dry holes'. In other words, successful enterprises, which earn profit must cover the loss of unsuccessful ones. Further, profit earning successful ventures must bear the cost of social services, like, education, health services, unemployment relief, old age pensions, defence and civil administration. Profit earning institutions may themselves or government from profit taxation may finance researches for innovations, which is carried on by the research institutions. Thus, bringing about the technical progress is the most important function of profit in a capitalist economy.

PROFIT IN A SOCIALIST ECONOMY

Socialist thinkers have always questioned the desirability of profit and were convinced that profit would not arise, if government were to own all the means of production. In a free economy, profit operates as an allocator of resources and directs them into channels of production most desired by consumers. The existence of profit is a signal to entrepreneurs outside the industry to enter into it and devote more resources to the industry.

In a socialist economy an efficient allocation of resources is achieved by fixing such a price, which prevails, if demand and supply forces reflecting consumer's preferences and technological restraints, were allowed to play their role freely. The allocation of resources is usually in accordance with the social benefit conceived by the Central Planning Authority. Such profit is distributed as national dividend.

The invention-innovation, induced by profit in a free economy is induced by salary differentials of top managers in a socialist economy. Sometimes, a successful innovation is also shared with concerned manager.

Thus, even a socialist economy could not dispense with profit as functional return. Since the risk and uncertainty attached to production, organisation and distribution are undertaken by the state, which also owns all the means of production, therefore, profit as uncertain and residual income goes. There is no profit as a special income of a special class, but it does exist as a reward for entrepreneurial functions performed by mangers of state enterprises.

RENT AND PROFIT

In the process of distribution, both rent and profit are price determined surpluses, but they are quite different in nature. Rent is payment over the above the minimum needed to bring forth the desired supply of any input. This minimum amount is the transfer earnings of the input and excess over it is called rent. This surplus depends upon the nature of supply of inputs. In case the input has a perfectly elastic supply, its actual earnings and transfer earnings will be the same, leaving no rent element in such earning. On the other hand, if the supply is perfectly inelastic, the transfer earning is zero and total amount of actual earning is rent. Thus, the greater the inelasticity of supply of input, the greater is the element of rent in its earnings.

Profit, on the other hand, is also a surplus left to the entrepreneur over and above his cost of production. Partly it is taken as return for the input called entrepreneurship and partly it is a chance income unrelated to the supply of entrepreneurship. Superior entrepreneurs, by their ability, produce wider profit margin and to that extent it is in the nature of differential surplus, which is just like rent.

Thus, part of the profit is rent and both are surpluses determined by price. A clear cut distinction between the two is difficult, yet economists regard rent as a non-functional payment, whereas profit is a necessary payment for the services of entrepreneurs to the society. Secondly, rent is only a surplus payment, for an input, whose supply is inelastic. It may appear in short run, but may vanish in long run (i.e., quasi rent). In respect of profit, in short run, it may be positive, zero a negative, but in long run profit cannot be zero, because the entrepreneurship must get at least normal profit. Thirdly, rent is a contractual income, while profit is a residual one. Rent is determined before the production starts but profit in determined after the sale of the product. Thus, rent can at the most be zero, while profit can be negative also. Fourthly, rent is essentially a static surplus, while profit is a dynamic surplus. Rent, as a contractual payment, will remain fixed till the expiry of the contract, while entrepreneurial service is supplied on the basis of an expected income likely to fluctuate widely over time. Lastly, since rent is a scarcity-determined differential surplus, it is likely to go up, as more and more uses of the fixed resources are devised, but profit is very likely to fall along with development of the economy.

Review Questions

1. Discuss the meaning and nature of profit and differentiate between rent and profit, as both are considered as differential surplus.
2. How does the innovation theory of profit differ from dynamic theory of profit?
3. "The source of profit is the monopoly power exercised by the producer". Examine this statement.
4. "Theory of profit regards the entrepreneur's contribution to the process of production as that of bearing non-insurable risks and uncertainties". Discuss.
5. Discuss the nature of profit. In what respects profit resembles rent?
6. Discuss the role of risk and uncertainty in the emergence of profits. In what respect does the profit differ from the rewards to other factors of production?
7. Discuss the modern theory of profit. Critically examine the theory of profit you appreciate most giving reasons for your choice.
8. Bring out the role of profit in a capitalistic and socialistic economies.

PART-III

MACROECONOMICS

27

National Income—Concepts and Measurements

DEFINITIONS

National income refers to the total value of goods and services produced annually in a country. It is also referred to as national dividend, national output or national expenditure and, as a result, the national income may be defined in the different ways. However, it is commonly referred to as the total amount of income accruing to a country from its various economic activities annually. It may also sum up the payments made in forms of rent, wages, interest and profits to all the respective resources like land, labour, capital and entrepreneurship used up in the production process.

Definition of the national income can be grouped into two categories, viz. traditional and modern. Amongst traditional definitions, according to Alfred Marshall 'labour and capital of a country acting on its natural resources produce annually certain net aggregate of commodities-material and non-material, including services of all kinds, this is called National Income or National Dividend'. The word 'net' in this definition indicates for deductions made from the gross national income regarding depreciation for wear and tear of the capital goods used in the production process. This definition gives no indication for avoiding double counting of the numerous goods and services produced in the country and fails to include goods produced for self-consumption.

Another definition in this category is of Arthur Cecil Pigou and according to him 'national income is that part of objective income of the community including, of course, income derived from abroad, which can be measured in terms of money.' Taking only those goods and services for deciding the national income, whose value can be measured in terms of money, it avoids double counting of goods and services and it also takes the income received from abroad for deciding the national income. However, it avoids taking goods not exchanged for money from being included in national income. Similarly it includes the services of domestic help, which is exchanged for money is deciding the national income but avoids including similar services rendered by housewives, as that is not exchanged for money.

In this category Irving Fisher has decided the national income as per the consumption of goods and services and not as per production, as has been done by Marshall and Pigou. According to Fisher 'the national dividend or income consists solely of goods and services as received by ultimate consumers; whether from their natural or from their human environments' It is considered as a better definition, as it is the consumption and not production on which our standard of living or our economic welfare is based. However, it is more difficult to estimate money value of net consumption than that of net production in deciding the national income.

Amongst modern definitions according to Paul A Samuelson 'national income is the sum total of all labour and property incomes earned in producing the national product.' It is, thus, obvious that sums provided as wages, salary and profit to labour, organisation personnel and persons providing entrepreneurship respectively and rent and interest for land and capital used in the production of different goods and services will decide the national income. However, it makes, no mention of income from abroad for deciding the national income.

National Income Committee, 1948 defined the national income 'that measures the volume of commodities and services turned out during a given period counted without duplication'. It has taken the value of all goods and services produced in a year avoiding double counting, that is, same goods are not counted two or more times for deciding the national income of the year.

According to Simon Kuznets, 'national income is the net output of the commodities and services flowing during the year from the country's productive system in the hands of the ultimate consumers or into the net addition to the country's capital goods'. This has emphasised on production of goods and services, whether used for ultimate consumption or for addition to capital goods of the country. It takes net production, which indicates that from the total production, the depreciation is set off for wear and tear, due to use of capital goods in the production process. However, as per this definition, double counting of goods produced could not be avoided for deciding the national income accurately.

NATIONAL INCOME CONCEPTS

Several concepts are used in national income analysis. These are Gross Domestic Product, Gross National Product, Net National Product, Personal Income and Disposable Income. These concepts are explained as follows:

Gross Domestic Product (GDP)

GDP came to light in 1937 in a report to US Congress. This concept was conceived and presented by Simon Kuznets, when the pre-eminent system of measurement of the national output was Gross National Product (GNP). After Bretton Woods Conference in 1944, GDP has been widely adopted as standard measurement of the national economic health. USA also switched over to this measurement of economic welfare in 1991.

Gross Domestic Product (GDP) is the money value of all finished goods and services produced with in a country during a specified period (generally a year). It provides an economic snapshot of a country, used to estimate the size of an economy and its growth rate. GDP can be calculated in three ways, using expenditures, productions or incomes and can be adjusted for inflation and population to provide for deeper insights. Despite certain limitations, GDP is a key tool to guide the policymakers, investors and businesses in strategic decision making.

As per expenditure or spending approach, GDP is decided as equal to consumption spending (C) plus government spending (G) plus investment expenditure (I) plus net exports (Nx). Thus,

$$GDP = C + G + I + Nx$$

Here 'C' represents consumption spending to buy consumption goods and services, which is the biggest component of GDP, 'G' represents government's consumption expenditure and its gross investment on equipments, infrastructure and payroll, 'I' represents private business investment on machineries and plants, which increases the productive capacity and employment, and 'Nx' is the net exports, which is calculated by deducting the value of imports from the value of exports, where a positive Nx will boost up nation's GDP, while a deficit will drag on GDP.

Production approach estimates the total value of economic output from which the costs of intermediate goods are deducted that are consumed in the process of production like materials and services.

The income approach for determination of GDP takes into consideration total sum of income earned by all the factors of production including wages paid to the labour, rent earned by land, return on capital in form of interest and corporate profits.

Besides GDP there is another measure called gross national product (GNP), which measures overall production of native persons/corporations including those based abroad, while excluding domestic production by foreigners. Gross National Income is another measure, which is the sum of all income earned by the nationals of a country regardless of whether underlying economic activity takes place domestically or abroad. GNI is computed as domestic income plus indirect taxes and depreciation as well as its net foreign factor income, which is equal to payments received from abroad minus payments made to the foreigners. In an increasingly globalised economy, GNI is considered as a better measurement for overall economic health than GDP.

Gross National Product (GNP)

It represents the total value of all final goods and services produced in the country in a year. GNP is the current market value of all goods and services produced in the economy in the income period. It is decided in either of the following two ways:

1. Counting only final goods and services meant for direct satisfaction of consumption needs, ignoring the intermediate goods, which have been used in the production process.
2. Counting only value added in each production sector in the economy. The value added represents the difference between the values of the product in each production sector minus the value of the materials used by the production sector.

The total sum of the values added by all production sectors would provide the value the Gross National Product.

Thus, GNP is the total measure of the flow of goods and services at market value resulting from the current production in a year including income from abroad. There are three approaches for measurement of GNP as follows:

1. **Income Approach:** Under this approach the total sum of wages, rent, interest, dividend, reserves, mixed incomes, taxes, depreciation and net income from abroad (i.e., exports-imports) in the income period will represent the gross national product (GNP).
2. **Expenditure Approach:** Under this the total expenditures of consumption, investments and government expenditure represent the gross national product. Thus, GNP = C + I + G

   Where 'C' is consumption spending, 'I' is investment expenditure and 'G' is government expenditure.
3. **Value Added Approach:** As per this approach the GNP represents the money value of the products of the various production sectors of the economy minus the value of the materials from other production sectors used in the production process of each production sector. For this the economy is usually divided into several production sectors, which are interdependent, as the output of one production sector may be used as raw materials in another production sector. Thus, the value added will be equal to the value of total output of all production sectors minus the value of materials used from other production sectors.

Net National Product (NNP)

In producing the total output of consumption goods and investment goods, certain portion of fixed capital is used up, as the fixed equipments wear out due to use in the production process. This is called depreciation and it is deducted from the gross national product to derive net national product. Thus, NNP is equal to GNP minus depreciation (i.e., NNP = GNP – Dep.). This depreciation represents the loss of value suffered by nation through wear and tear of stock of fixed capital. Thus, the NNP means the market value of all final goods and services after providing for depreciation on the fixed capital used in the production process.

There are two approaches for measurements of the net national product as follows:

(i) **Flow of Product Approach:** As per this the net value of final goods and services produced in a year is decided for NNP. Since it is evaluated at the market price of products, it is also called NNP at market price.

(ii) **Earnings or Income Approach:** Under this the total market price of the product is allocated amongst the various stakeholders in forms of wages, rent, interest and profit. These are factor earnings of labour, land, capital and entrepreneurship. This is also called NNP at factor cost for which the chief constituents are:

(i) all wages, salaries and supplementary incomes,
(ii) interests paid to private individuals,
(iii) net rents paid to all individuals,
(iv) net profits of all kinds of businesses.

From this total sum, the amount of transfer payments is deducted. Transfer payments represent the sum for which no productive service is rendered in return, such as social security payments like pension and others and interest paid on national debt. The chart given below reveals the two approaches for determination of the net national product or national income as follows:

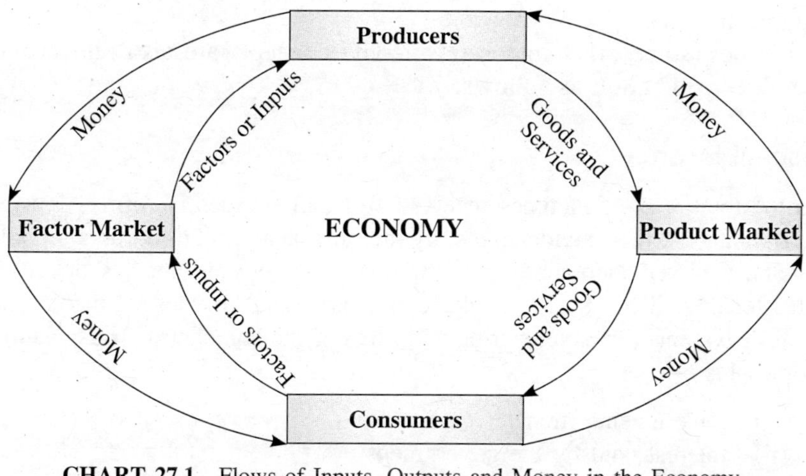

CHART 27.1 Flows of Inputs, Outputs and Money in the Economy.

In the real world economies, goods and services flow from producers to the consumers via product market. Factors or inputs flow from consumers to producers via factor market. In the opposite direction there is continuous flow of money from consumers to producers via product market and from producers to consumers via factor market. The NNP can be measured either as per market price of the flow of goods and services from producers to consumers via product market or as payments flowing from producers to consumers for the flow of factors or inputs via factor market. The former is called NNP at market price and the latter is called NNP at factor cost, which also represents the National Income.

The money values of the NNP, as per flow of products approach, also includes indirect taxes and subsidies. Similarly the government may also set up its own industries and may earn profit not allowing it to go to individuals. As a result, the NNP at the market price of the product flows will not be the same as the NNP at factor cost. Adjustments are needed in NNP at market price as per product flows in regard to subsidies granted, indirect taxes imposed and profits from public enterprises retained by the government to equalise it with the NNP at factor cost or National Income.

Thus, NNP at factor cost = NNP at market price + Subsidies
– (Indirect Taxes + Govt. Profit) OR

NNP at factor cost = GNP – Depreciation – (Indirect Taxes and Govt. Profits)
+ Subsidies = National Income.

It is, thus, obvious that the subsidies given by the government is added to the NNP at market price and the indirect taxes and profits obtained by the government from its public enterprises are deducted from it to derive the NNP at factor cost, which is also known as National Income. By making the aforesaid adjustments along with deducting depreciation from the Gross National Product (GNP), we derive the NNP at factor cost or National Income.

Besides, some other important income concepts are also relevant and deserve consideration as follows:

Personal Income

It is the total sum of incomes received from all sources in forms of wages, salaries, interest, rent, dividend, etc. by individuals as well as corporate bodies. It includes mixed incomes of self-employed persons, farmers, shopkeepers, professionals and others. Personal incomes are equal to national income plus transfer payments minus undistributed profits of the companies. Thus, National Income plus (+)

(i) governments' transfer payments;
(ii) interest paid by the government;
(iii) interest paid by consumers; and
(iv) dividends;

(v) minus (–)
(vi) corporate profits;
(vii) employers' contribution for social insurance; and
(viii) employees' contribution for social insurance; is equal to personal income of individuals.

Disposable Income

The total sum of personal income is not available to the individuals for discretionary spendings. The demand for the various goods and services can be estimated as per the disposable income. The disposable income (DI) represents the personal income minus the income tax payable and the social insurance contributions to be made by the individuals. There is another way for considering the disposable income, which is equal to personal consumption plus personal savings.

Real National Income

It is also called the National Income at constant price. For this we adjust the NNP at factor cost or national Income for the current year with the ratio of the base year's index with current year's index.

$$\text{Thus, Real National Income} = \text{NI for the Current Year} \times \frac{\text{Base Year's Index}}{\text{Current Year's Index}}$$

Such estimation of the real national income brings the current year's national income comparable to the national income of some base year of the past and may, thus, reveal the growth in national income is real terms. It is needed because national income of different years at respective current year prices are not rendered comparable on account of rising prices of goods and services in the economy.

Per Capita Income

It represents the average income of the total population of the country. It is derived by dividing the national income with the population of the country. It assists in studying the inequality of income distribution by comparing average income of individuals in different sections of the population with the per capita income of the population.

MEASUREMENTS OF THE NATIONAL INCOME

According to the British Economist Alexander Cairncross, the national income can be looked upon in any of the three ways as: (i) the national income measured by adding everybody's income, (ii) the national product measured by adding up everybody's output; and (iii) the national outlay measured by adding up the values of all the things that people buy and adding the sum of their savings too.

Since the volume of flows during a particular time period must be equal, that is, income = product = expenditure on product, which makes NI = NNP = Expenditure on NNP.

It reveals that the measurements of the national income will yield the same result whatsoever method is followed for its measurement. It is because when production takes place, inputs or factors of production are paid their rewards, which result into income flows as well as product flows. The outputs from product flows are purchased by the people through spendings on the products. Thus, there are three methods for measurement of the national income, which are as follows:

1. **Product Method:** It is also called Inventory Method or Commodity Service Method. It takes the market value of all final goods and services produced in the economy in a given period. However, by taking the production of only final goods meant for direct and final consumption, the productions of intermediate goods are ignored in computation of the national income. For this the concept of 'Value Added' has been relied upon, where current values of all goods minus the value of the materials used in the respective production processes are taken into account in place of current value of final products for deciding the national income.
2. **Income Method:** Producers of all goods and services pay to the owners of the various factors of production in forms of rent to landlords, wages to the labour, interest to the capitalists and profit to the entrepreneurs. The total sum of the rewards to owners of the various factors of production represents the aggregate income of all persons, which is called the national income.
3. **Expenditure Method:** It involves the addition of the personal consumption spendings, gross private domestic investments, state purchases of the goods and services and the net foreign investments in a given period. Such an aggregate provides the GNP at market price and by deducting the depreciation for wear and tear in the value of capital goods used in the production process, we derive the NNP at market price and by deducting the indirect taxes from it, the NNP at factor cost or National Income is derived.

The aforesaid three methods for measurement of the national income require different types of the statistics. Thus, the product method for measurement of the national income requires census of manufacturing of goods and of agricultural output. The income method requires the data of personal taxes and the financial statements of the various industrial and service enterprises. The expenditure method requires extensive family budget data. In developed countries such statistics are easily available, therefore these obtain the national income estimates consistent with one another.

However, on account of non-availability of relevant statistics for the measurement of the national income in our country, reliance is being placed on the national income estimates. For pre-Independence India the estimates of national income had been done by Dada Bhai Noroji, Lord Curzon, Findley Shirras and Simon Commission, but there was no uniformity in such estimates for the national income. In post-Independence period as per recommendations of the National Income Committee (1948-54) the National Income unit of the Central Statistical Organisation (CSO) started preparing national income estimates as per the product method and income method. It has divided the whole economy into thirteen sectors, viz. agriculture, livestock, forest, fisheries, mines, factory establishments, small units, organised banking and insurance, commerce and transportation, professions, fine arts, domestic service, public utilities, housing and transfer payments. Here for the first seven sectors, the national income estimates are based on 'Product Method' and for the rest of sectors, it is based on 'Income Method'.

PROBLEMS IN MEASUREMENT OF NATIONAL INCOME

In measurement of the national income there are certain problems as follows:

1. **Identifying the Nation for NI:** It includes not only the income generated within the boundaries of the nation but also the income generated for the nation beyond the territories of the country. Thus, for NI the nation is confined not only within the boundaries of the country but also extends to all other countries from where the income is earned by the country.
2. **Non-Marketed Services:** It does not take money value of the services that are performed not for making money but for love and affection kindness, mercy, patriotism, etc. As per this the services rendered by housewives will not be given any value, although the similar service by the domestic help will commend some value to be considered for deciding the national income.
3. **Selection of the Stage for Compilation of National Income:** There exists a problem in selection of the stage for deciding the national income, as to whether the national income be counted at the stage of production, consumption or distribution. In case the nation is concerned with economic growth, the national income is to be counted at the production stage of the various goods and services. Similarly, if the nation is concerned with economic welfare, then the national income will be counted at the consumption stage and if the nation is concerned with the distributive justice, the national income will be counted at the distribution stage.
4. **Pancity of Relevant Data:** The national income measurement also suffers from the lack of accurate statistics on production in different

sectors in the economy or on consumption of the various goods and services by different sections of the society. In most of the cases its computation is based on the estimates.

5. **Possibility of Double Counting:** In case the national income is decided as per product flows in the economy, there exists the possibility of the same materials being counted twice or thrice in the process, unless the reliance is placed on 'Value Added' method for national income determination.
6. **Identification of Transfer Payments:** Transfer payments refer to payments generally by the governments in forms of pensions, social security payments, interest on public debts, etc. for which there is no productive activity in return. A large number of things are also provided by governments to certain sections of the society, whose value may add to the income of individuals but that will not be taken into consideration for deciding the national income.
7. **Production for Self-Consumption:** Such production is ignored in deciding the national income, as there is no marketing for such goods. These goods command no price, hence ignored in computation of national income although these also represent the production in the economy.
8. **National Income Measures Exclude Certain Goods and Services:** The national income measures take value of goods and services generated in the economy in terms of money, ignoring those goods and services for which no money value can be assigned like that for a good painting, a hobby or bringing up children by mothers, etc.
9. **Income from Illegal Activities:** Such income is not included in the national income, though generated within the economy e.g. income from smuggling income from illicit activities, etc.
10. **Capital Gains:** The gains emerging from increase in market value of capital assets are also ignored from being counted for deciding the national income on the plea that these are not the result of current economic activities, although these also add to the wealth of the nation similar to the income generated by current economic activities.

IMPORTANCE OF NATIONAL INCOME

National income of any country forms the basis for several types of economic policies, as follows:

1. National income forms the basis for national policies, like employment policies, savings and investment policies, etc.
2. Relevant information on national income, national output, national consumption and national savings is helpful for economic planning for the sake of economic development of the nation.

3. National income is significant for country's per capita income, whose comparison with per-capita income of the earlier years will reveal the economic progress as well as economic welfare.
4. The volume of income received in forms of the various constituents of the national income like wages, rent, interest and profit, the disparities or inequalities in income distribution may be ascertained, whose minimisation or eradication may promote economic welfare of masses.
5. It assists in identifying and removing the inflationary or deflationary gaps from the economy, which results in inflation or deflation situations in the country.
6. Budgetary policies are also designed as per the level and components of the national become. Taxes should be imposed on what sections of the society and financial assistance should be given to what sections of the society are decided as per the income levels of the various sections of the society.
7. The national income generated in public and private sectors helps in deciding the economic structure of the country.

Review Questions

1. How are the traditional definitions of the national income different from its modern definitions?
2. What is meant by GDP? How is it computed?
3. What methods may be followed for computation of GNP of any nation?
4. Discuss different approaches for measurements of NNP.
5. How is the NNP at market price different from the NNP at factor cost? Which one is considered to represent the national income?
6. What adjustments are done in national income to derive the personal income?
7. Distinguish personal income from disposable income and per capita income.
8. Why and how is the real national income computed?
9. Bring out the various methods for computation of the national income.
10. Examine the various problems faced in computation of the national income.
11. How is the national income important for a nation?

28

National Income Equilibrium

The equilibrium level of national income is decided as per the equality of income and expenditure in the economy. Whatever income is earned by the individuals, the total sum of that is not normally spent on consumption. Certain part of the income is devoted to savings. This reduction in spending on consumption generates inequality between income and expenditure, which may be compensated by expenditure on investment. Certain portion of expenditure may also be from the government's side. Thus, the national income attains the equilibrium at the level, where consumption (C) plus investment (I) plus government expenditure (G) all are found to be equal to national income. The consumption behaviour is decided as per the propensity to consume, which refers to the desire of individuals to devote their income to consumption that has a tendency to increase along with increase in the total income. However, it is generally less than the increase in income, which is due to declining marginal propensity to consume (MPC). On the other hand, amount devoted to savings increases at increasing rate along with increase in income of the individuals. It is due to increasing marginal propensity to save (MPS).

MARGINAL PROPENSITY TO CONSUME (MPC) AND SAVE (MPS)

Households or individuals spend their money income on food, clothing, housing transport, education, medical care, recreation, etc., the total spending on these items is consumption. It generally depends upon the level of income at the disposal of individuals or households. It is called consumption function expressed as $C = f(Y)$, where C is consumption, Y is income and f is read as 'function of' which means 'depends on'. Poor families generally have lower levels of income, which these spend on C, sometimes even more than their income on the necessities. However, as the income rises their consumption also shifts to items of comforts and luxuries. As a result, the consumption increases less than proportionately to income. Similarly in regard to savings, it is generally negative at very low level of income, may become zero at the moderate level of income and may become increasingly positive along with increase in income. This savings (S) is also a function of income (Y) i.e., $S = f(Y)$. The tabular and diagrammatic behaviours of the marginal propensity to consume and the marginal propensity to save are as follows:

TABLE 28.1 Behaviours of Marginal Propensity to Consume (MPC) and Save (MPS)

Y	*C*	ΔC	*S*	ΔS	*MPC* = $\Delta C/\Delta Y$	*MPS* = $\Delta S/\Delta Y$
7000	7110	–	–110	–	–	–
8000	8000	890	0	110	0.89	0.11
9000	8850	850	150	150	0.85	0.15
10000	9600	750	400	250	0.75	0.25
11000	10240	640	760	360	0.64	0.36
12000	10830	590	1170	410	0.59	0.41
13000	11360	530	1640	470	0.53	0.47

It reveals that for every increase in income (Y) by ₹ 1000, the increase in consumption (ΔC) is showing a decreasing trend from ₹ 890 to ₹ 530 and for every increase in income the marginal propensity to consume per rupee of increase in income (MPC = $\Delta C/\Delta Y$) is decreasing from .89 to .53. On the other hand, for every increase in income (ΔY) by ₹ 1000, the increase in savings (ΔS) is increasing from ₹ 110 to ₹ 470 and thus for every increase in income the marginal propensity to save per rupee of increase in income (MPS = $\Delta S/\Delta Y$) has increased from .11 to .47 making MPC + MPS = 1.

The patterns of behaviour of the consumption and saving as well as of the marginal propensity to consume and marginal propensity to save can be exhibited through curves as follows.

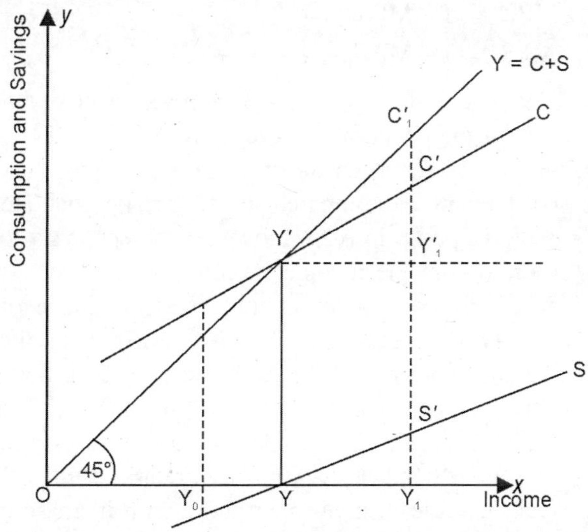

FIGURE 28.1 Behaviour Pattern of Consumption and Savings with Increase in Income.

It is obvious that at *OY* level of income, consumption is equal to income, as the consumption curve intersects the 45° line (on every point of which consumption plus savings will be equal to income) and savings will be equal to zero, as the savings curve interests the base line. Below OY level of income, the consumption curve lies above the 45° line showing that consumption is more than income, which may be managed through borrowings and savings curve lies below the base line showing the negative savings. Similarly beyond OY level of income, the consumption curve lies below the 45° line showing that the consumption is less than income and remaining part of the income is devoted to savings. The MPC and MPS are represented by the slopes of the consumption and saving curves respectively. Thus, MPC = $\Delta C/\Delta Y = Y_1' C'/Y'Y_1'$ and MPS = $\Delta S/\Delta Y = Y_1'S'/YY_1$ and MPC and MPS both together will be equal to one.

It suggests that MPC represents the extra consumption generated by an extra unit of income. The slope of consumption curve reveals the level of MPC, which means a steep slope of consumption curve indicates a high MPC and a flat slope of the consumptions curve is indicative of low MPC. Similarly, MPS represents the extra savings generated by an extra unit of increase in income. Since the savings represents something that is not consumed, therefore,

$$C + S = Y$$

$$\Delta C + \Delta S = \Delta Y$$

$$\frac{\Delta C}{\Delta Y} + \frac{\Delta S}{\Delta Y} = \frac{\Delta Y}{\Delta Y}$$

$$\text{MPC} + \text{MPS} = 1 \text{ (as } \Delta C/\Delta Y = \text{MPC and } \Delta S/\Delta Y = \text{MPS)}$$

In other words.

$$\text{MPC} = 1 - \text{MPS}$$

$$\text{MPS} = 1 - \text{MPC}$$

Since MPC < 1, it reveals the importance of investment out of savings for generating demands in the economy, as the individuals and households fail to spend on consumption as much as the increase in income. In order to cope up with decreased demand, as compared to the income generated, reliance is placed on investment to pump in extra money in the economy to generate the demand commensurate with the income level.

Investment refers to creation of capital assets in the economy, as the financial investments are regarded as mere transfer payments and not investments. There are two types of investments: (i) autonomous investments, and (ii) induced investments. Autonomous investments reveal the given level of investments, which are quite independent of the level of income. Induced investments, on the other hand, have a positive relationship with the level of income, showing an increase in investment along with increase in the level of income. In order to determine the level of national income, the investment schedule in superimposed on the consumption schedule. In case of autonomous investment the C + I schedule in parallel to the consumption schedule (C) and in case of induced investment, the C + I schedule is shown slightly rising upwards along with increase in the level of income. The consumption plus investment, autonomous as well as induced, decide the total expenditure coming back to the economy from the given income level.

METHODS FOR NI EQUILIBRIUM DETERMINATION

There are two methods, viz. (i) income and expenditure method and (ii) savings and investment method, for deciding the equilibrium level of the national income (NI).

Income and Expenditure Method

The national income equilibrium is determined as per the income and expenditure method taking total expenditure on consumption as well as on investment, whether autonomous or induced. It is as follows:

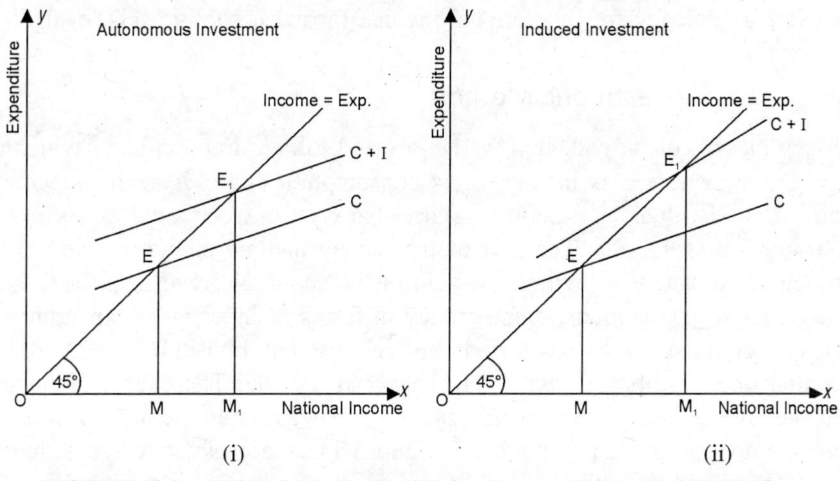

FIGURE 28.2 National Income Equilibriums as per Income and Expenditure.

Figure 28.2(i) and (ii) both reveal that consumption schedule is intersecting the income = expenditure line or 45° degree line (on all points of which the income is equal to expenditure) at E point. Since the consumption is not the only item on which the expenditure is incurred, the investment schedule, which represents another item of expenditure, is superimposed on the consumption schedule to derive the $C + I$ schedule in both diagrams. In case the investment is autonomous as in Figure 28.2(i) the $C + I$ schedule is drawn parallel to the consumption schedule. On the other hand, if there is induced investment, as in Figure 28.2 the $C + I$ function will not be parallel to the consumption function C but $C + I$ function will have increasing gap with C function with increase in the income level. This $C + I$ schedule in both diagrams intersects the 45° line representing the equality of income and expenditure at E_1 points, which set the equilibrium level of the national income at OM_1 levels. These income levels in both diagrams reveal that whatever income is received by the individuals or households from the economy, similar amount comes back to the economy in forms of consumption and investment expenditures. In case the income level goes beyond OM_1, the income received by individuals or households will be more than consumption and investment expenditures in the economy and as a result, the stock of goods and services will pile up, which will induce reduction in production reducing the national income till it gets settled at OM_1 level again. Similarly, if the income level remains below OM_1 level, the consumption and investment expenditures will be more than the income received by individuals or households. This will reduce for more output by increasing employment of resources in the economy. This, in turn, will result into an increase in the income till it gets settled at OM_1 levels in both diagrams.

Thus, OM_1 is the equilibrium level of the national income, as any other level of national income below or beyond this level will not sustain and will generate a tendency for the national income to return back to this level.

Savings and Investment Method

Money income of individuals may be devoted to consumption and savings as $Y = C + S$, where Y is income, C is consumption and S is savings. Money going to individuals as income returns back to the economy is forms of consumption spendings. The part of the money income of the individuals or households devoted to savings goes out of the economy. Investment activities bring back to the economy some money in forms of investment expenditures. Thus, economists have suggested the savings and investment method for deciding the equilibrium level of the national income. The excess of money income over consumption spendings in known as savings and investments refers to the net capital formation for improving the productive capacities of the economy. In primitive societies savings and investments are done by the same set of individuals or households. However, in modern societies separate set of individuals, households or institutions are involved in savings and investment activities.

Savings in modern societies is done by individuals or households for a variety of reasons, such as providing for the old age, future expenses, rainy days i.e., sudden mishaps in the family, education of the children, power and prestige in the society or for internal satisfaction like that of misers. Thus, savings has nothing to do with the investment opportunities in the economy. Such savings depends upon the level of income, which may be even negative at a very low level of income but it will have a positive relation with increase in the level of income.

Investment, on the other hand, is the capital formation, which refers to the net increase in the community's real capital like, equipments, factories, inventories, etc. Individuals or households consider it as investment, when a piece of land, an old security or any title to property is bought, but these are only 'transfer payments' where one buys and the other sells. The investment takes place only when additional real capital is created. It depends on new discoveries, new products, new territories, new sources of resources, new population, need for larger production and need for generation of larger income. The investment for the aforesaid depends on development of technology, optimistic expectations, government tax and expenditure, legislative policies, etc. This investment may be of two types; one the autonomous and other the induced. Autonomous investment maintains the level despite change in the level of national income. The induced investment maintains an increasing trend along with increase in the level of national income.

The equilibrium of national income is decided at the level, where a positively sloping saving curve interests the investment curve. The equilibrium position of the national income as per autonomous as well as the induced investments are as follows:

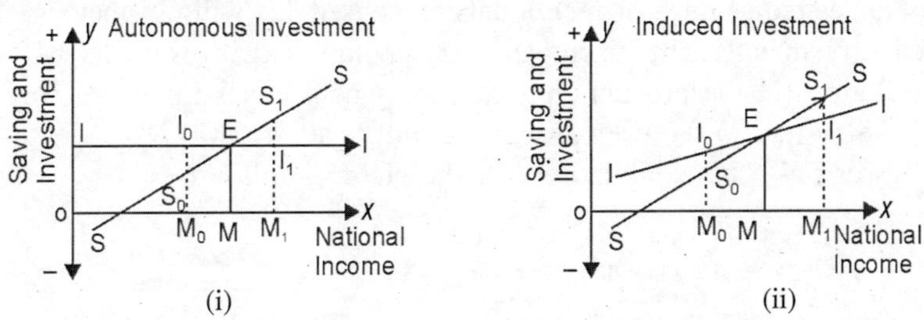

FIGURE 28.3 National Income Equilibrium as per Savings and Investment.

The savings function has a positive relation with the level of income and therefore it is sloping upwards alongwith increase in the income under autonomous as well as under induced investments. The investment function is constant for autonomous investment as in Figure 28.3(i) and it is positive for induced investment as in Figure 28.3(ii), where it is sloping upwards along with increase in the income. The equilibrium in both cases is set at E, which is the point of intersection of investment function with savings function, where OM is the equilibrium level of national income.

At the equilibrium level **E**, the investment function and savings function both are in equality, which indicates that the amount individuals or households are taking away from the economy in forms of savings is being brought back to the economy in forms of investments–autonomous as well as induced. At this equilibrium level, what the economy wants to invest is equal to what the individuals or households want to save and as a result, savers and investors will keep on doing the same what they have been doing earlier. Investors (businesses) will neither find inventories piling up nor will they find sales so brisk as to force them to produce more goods and services and, therefore, the production, employment and income spending will remain the same.

In case, the national income is higher than OM, say OM_1, the national income cannot remain stable at OM_1, because at such level of income individuals or households savings i.e., refraining from spending on consumption, will be more than what investors will be willing to keep on investing. In such a situation, the investors (businesses) will find that they have too few customers and that their inventories are piling up and therefore, they cut back production and lay off workers, which will reduce the national income from OM_1 to OM level. Similarly, in case the national income is less than its equilibrium level OM, say OM_0, individuals or households' intended savings falls short of investors' intended investments. This reveals the consumption of more goods and services than these are being currently produced. This will induce investors (businesses) to expand production and hire more workers, which will keep on raising the national income till it again attains its national income equilibrium at OM level.

Thus, the only level of national income equilibrium is OM at E point, where the savings and investment schedules intersect each other. At any other point the desired savings of individuals or households will not match with the desired investments. The discrepancy in savings and investments will result into variations in the production and employment levels in such a way as to return the system to the original equilibrium level at OM.

This can also be exhibited as per the chart as follows:

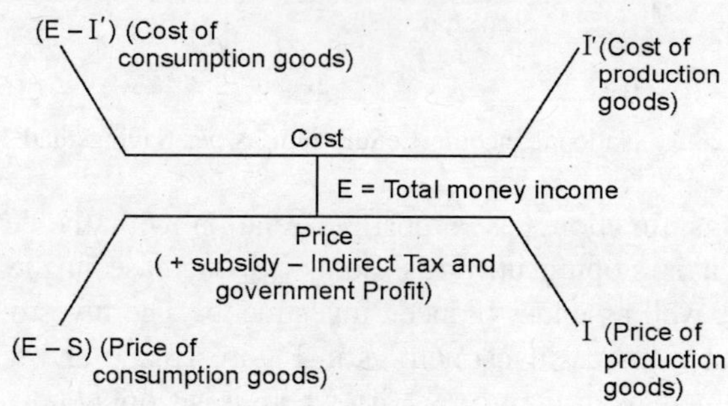

CHART 28.1 Equilibrium Level of National Income.

The difference between the price and the cost of production as well as consumption goods represents the profit, which may be:

(i) Normal, which is included in the cost of production of consumption and production goods, hence it does not create any imbalance in the balance shown in the above chart.

(ii) Net profit or windfall profit, which may create imbalance in the above chart.

This net or windfall profit may be from production goods as well as from consumption goods.

Thus, the total windfall profit (W) = windfall profit from production goods (W_1) plus the windfall profit from consumption goods (W_2)

Here, $W = W_1 + W_2$, where $W_1 = (1 - 1')$ and $W_2 = (E - S) - (E - 1')$

Thus, $W = (1 - 1') + (E - S) - (E - 1')$

$W = 1 - 1' + E - S - E + 1'$ After removal of brackets

$W = 1 - S$. [After setting off $(+ 1' - 1')$ and $(+ E - E)$]. Since the total wind fall profit is supposed to be equal to zero, so that the balance is maintained in the aforesaid chart, the equation derived may be reproduced as follows:

$$W = 1 - S = 0$$

or

$$1 - S = 0$$

or

$$1 = S$$

Thus maintaining the balance or equilibrium the 1 (i.e., price of production goods or investments) is equal to S (savings), as by deducting this from the money income, the price of consumption goods is derived.

Integration of the Two Methods

The national income determination as per the money income and expenditure (ME) method as well as the savings and investment (SI) method derive the same level of national income. This may be examined as per the table as well as the diagram as follows:

TABLE 28.2 National Income Equilibrium as per ME and SI Approaches

(₹ in Crore)

NI	*Consumption (C)*		*Savings (S)*		*Investment (I)*	*NI*		*Spendings (C + I)*	*Travel for (NI)*
(1)	(2)	–	(3)		(4)	(5)		(6)	(7)
700	710	–	– 10	–	50	700	<	760	
800	800	.9	0	.1	50	800	<	850	Expansion
900	880	.8	+ 20	.2	50	900	<	930	
1000	950	.7	+ 50	.3	50	1000	=	1000	Equilibrium
1100	1010	.6	+ 90	.4	50	1100	>	1060	Contraction
1200	1060	.5	+ 140	.5	50	1200	>	1110	

Assuming the various levels of the national income (NI) in column (1), consumption (C) in column (2), savings (S) in column (3), and autonomous investments (1) in column (4) and showing levels of NI again in column (5) for comparison with the total of spendings on consumption and investment in column 6, it reveals that NI at the levels of 700, 800 and 900 is less than the total spending on consumption and investment of 760, 850 and 930 respectively. Till the total spending on consumption and investment is more than the expenses incurable by businesses to generate NI, it will encourage the producing units to expand the output and employment, which will result into expansion of the national income.

It also reveals that the expenditure incurred for generating NIs at the levels of 1100 and 1200 are more than total spendings of 1060 and 1110 on consumption and investment and as a result, the NI generating units will incur losses and will be discouraged from maintaining the production at the given levels. These will be induced to reduce production and employment, which will, in turn, result into contraction of national income.

The national income will be in equilibrium at the level of 1000, where there is no tendency for expansion or contraction. Here the expenditures incurred for generation of NI in equal to total spendings on consumption and investment, which is coming back to NI generating units in the economy.

At this equilibrium level of national income savings and investments both are equal at the level of 50. Thus, the same equilibrium level is attained through income and expenditure method as well as savings and investment method. This can also be exhibited through the diagram as follows:

The Figure 28.4 reveals that at OA level of national income, the income in equal to consumption and therefore, savings is zero. Below this level of income the consumption is more than income and therefore, the savings is negative. Beyond OA level of income consumption is increasing less than proportionately, while the savings is increasing more than proportionately to income.

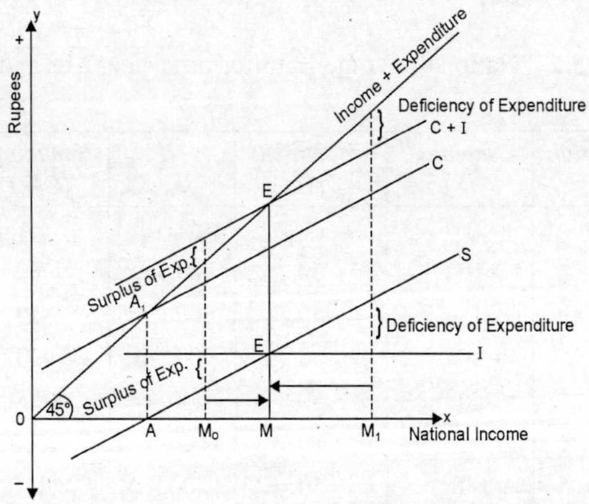

FIGURE 28.4 Equilibrium Level of National Income.

The I curve indicates the level of investment and when it is superimposed on consumption curve, it reveals the C + 1 curve, showing the behaviour pattern of total expenditure on consumption and investment. The C + 1 curve intersects the 45° line on E point, which shows the equality of income and expenditure. On the other hand, rising savings savings curve also intersects the autonomous investment line, which is parallel to the horizontal axis, on E point. Both these E points decide the equilibrium level of the national income at OM level. National income beyond this level, say OM_1 cannot sustain due to deficiency of expenditure in the economy commensurate to the expenditure incurred by producing units for generating the national income. This will induce for reduction in production and employment, which will result into reduction in the national income till it reaches again at OM level. Similarly, if the national income is below the OM equilibrium level say OM_0 level, on account of surplus of spendings over the expenditure incurred for generating the national income, there will be excess demand for goods and services, which will provide inducement for expanding production and employment. This will cause an increase in the national income till it gets settled at OM level. Thus, both approaches for deciding equilibrium of the national income derive the same conclusion in this regard.

INFLATIONARY AND DEFLATIONARY GAPS

The national income equilibrium at the level of equality of savings and investment functions or of the consumption and investment functions with income functions tends to stay, but may not be necessarily the optimum national income equilibrium level. In fact the optimum level of national income is one, where there is full employment of the resources of the economy and this optimum level may be at a higher or lower level, as compared to the equilibrium level of the national income. During depression period the national income equilibrium is likely to be below full employment level, while during boom period the national income equilibrium level may be beyond the full employment level.

Full employment in the economy refers to the situation, where every input or factor of production remains fully employed in the production process and all enterprises produce at their practical capacity levels.

Inflationary gaps in the national income equilibrium at full employment level exist, if the total expenditure on consumption and investment in the economy tends to be more than income as per 45° line at the full employment level, where the business enterprises will not be able to produce more to cope up with the larger demand of goods for consumption and investment. This gap will only increase the prices of goods and services for establishing the national income equilibrium at a level beyond the full employment level.

Similarly, if the scheduled investment in the economy tends to be more than scheduled savings at the full employment level, the gap between the investment and savings at this level will be called inflationary gap, as the national income equilibrium beyond full employment level will be attained not by increase in production and employment but by increase in prices of the various goods and services only. These can be exhibited as follows:

In Figure 28.5(i) the national income equilibrium is set at E_1 point as per the equality of consumption and investment with income shown on 45° line

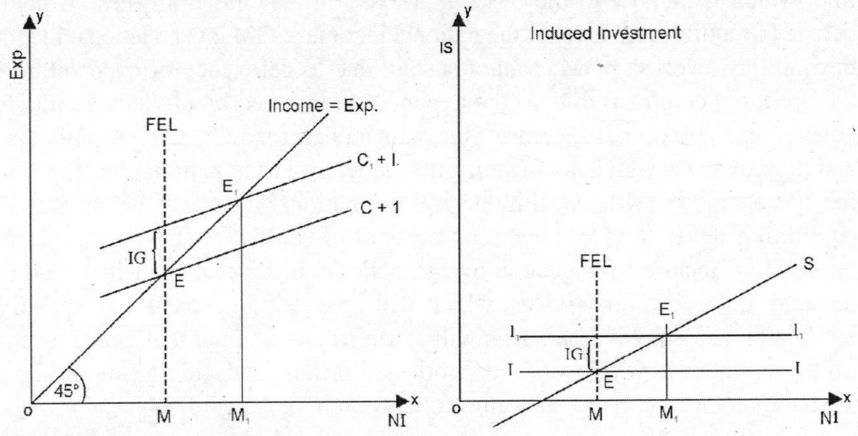

Note: FEL = Full Employment Level and IG = Inflationary Gap

FIGURE 28.5 National Income Equilibrium and Inflationary Gaps.

or as per the equality of investment with savings on investment and saving functions as in Figure 28.5(ii), where the full employment national income happens to be at OM level in both diagrams. In case the consumption and investment rises, C+1 (consumption and investment) curve is shifted to C_1I_1 level in Figure 28.5(i) and in case the investment rises, the investment curve is shifted to I_1I_1 level in Figure 28.5(ii). These set the new equilibrium at E_1 points in both diagrams, where the new equilibrium level of national income is OM_1 in both cases. At these new equilibrium levels, there exists some excess of consumption and investment expenditures over income as shown on 45° line or that of investments over savings at full employment level in Figure 28.5(ii). This excess in both cases is known as inflationary gap, because increase in national income from OM to OM_1 is on account of increase in prices of goods and services produced at full employment level and not due to increase in production and employment in the economy.

The deflationary gap in the national income equilibrium at full employment level may come into existence if the consumption and investment expenditures under income-expenditure method or investment expenditure under savings and investment method are lowered. These are as follows:

In Figure 28.6(i) the original equilibrium of the national income is at *E*, where expenditures on consumption and investment are equal to the income shown on 45° line. It sets the national income equilibrium at OM level. In case the expenditures on consumption and investment decline, it shifts the consumption and investment function to C_0I_0 level. This new C_0I_0 curve interests the 45° line setting a new equilibrium on E_0 point, which decides the new equilibrium of national income at OM_0 level. Since the national income was earlier in equilibrium a OM level, a reduction in national income up to

OM_0 may not be through reduction in production and employment, at least in short run, but only through lowering of the prices of goods and services. Thus, the excess of income over consumption plus investment expenditure at full employment level is called deflationary gap, which results into lowering of prices of goods and services till the new equilibrium level of national income is attained at OM_0 level.

In Figure 28.6(ii) the original equilibrium level of national income was OM at E point made of intersection of original savings and investment functions. This happens to be the full employment level national income. In case the investment level in the economy declines, the savings function intersects the new investment function at E_0, when OM_0 is the new level of national income. Since the economy was at full employment equilibrium level before reduction in investment function, it decides to continue with the original level of production and employment and may decide to sell of the total products by lowering the price instead of allowing the stock of goods produced to pile up in the store, at least in short run. Thus, the deflationary gap between savings and investment at full employment level, on account of a decline in investment, may induce for reduction in prices of goods and services resulting into lowering of the equilibrium level of national income from OM to OM_0.

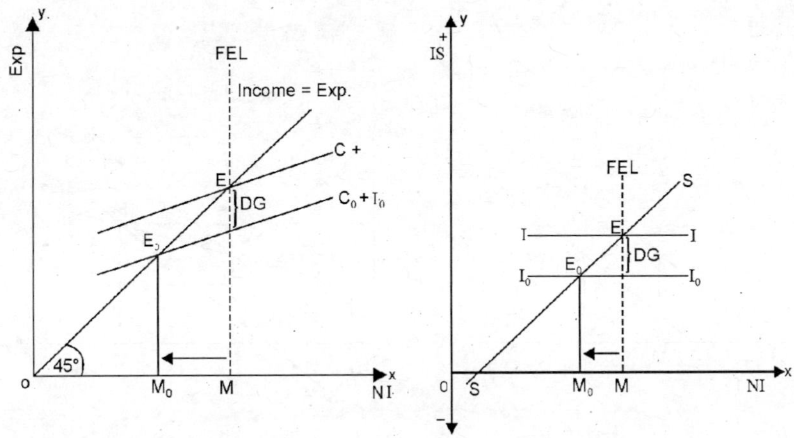

(i) (ii)

Note: FEL = Full Employment Level and DG = Deflationary Gap

FIGURE 28.6 National Income Equilibrium and Deflationary Gap.

However, these inflationary and deflationary gaps are only temporary phenomena. These exist only in short run and in long run on account of state's intervention, the necessary corrections may be introduced to remove such gaps. Full employment in the economy is also an imaginary situation, because in real world economies, dynamic changes take place continuously in regard to (1) population, (2) wants, (3) capital resources (4) methods of production, and (5) forms of industrial organisations. Besides, the various types of innovations, like (1) introduction of a new and improved technique of production, (2) changes in managerial setups, (3) discovery of new types of materials or fuels (4) changes in shape and quality of products (5) search of new sources of raw materials and (6) finding new markets for products are continuously taking place in the real world economies, due to changes in population and other resources, there will hardly be full employment in the economies at any time. These changes render the inflationary and deflationary gaps to gain existence for the time being only.

PARADOX OF THRIFT

Thrift refers to the quality spending of one's money very carefully, so that it is not wasted. In other words, it refers to the desire for savings more and more money from the current income of individuals. It is considered good for individuals to save larger sums for old age, future expenses, rainy days (or sudden mishaps in the family), education and establishment of children. There are persons, who save money by nature and at times people save for power and prestige in the society. For whatsoever reason savings is done by individuals, it is considered good for them but too much emphasis on savings by individuals collectively may not be in the interest of the economy. It is as follows:

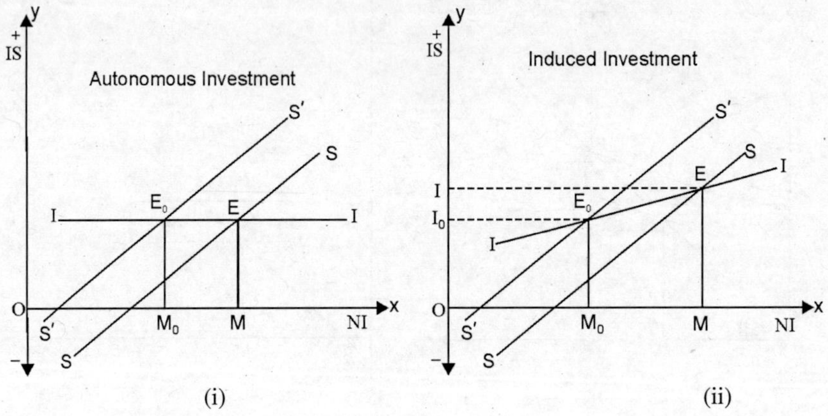

FIGURE 28.7 Impact of Increase in Savings on National Income.

Figure 28.7(i) reveals the case of autonomous investment, where savings and investment are in equilibrium at E. Here the equilibrium level of national income is OM. In case, there is an increase in savings it shifts the savings function to S′S′ level, which shifts the equilibrium to E_0, where OM_0 is the new equilibrium level of national income. It shows that on account of increase in savings the national income has declined from OM to OM_0.

Figure 28.7(ii) considers the case of induced investment, which increases with increase in level of the national income. The original savings function intersects the investment function at E, where equilibrium level of national income is OM. The increase in savings shifts the savings function to S′S′ level, which intersects the investment function at E_0, where the equilibrium level of national income is OM_0. At this new equilibrium level, the investment in the economy has also declined from OI to OI_0. Thus, increase in savings will not only reduce the national income but also the investment as well as the savings in the economy.

Thus, savings may be good for a single individual, but what is good for individuals separately is not found good for the whole community, as it reduces the national income as well as the investment and the savings, which may throw out many people out of jobs. This shows the paradoxical situation, as normally it is believed that the savings is good for people but it is not good for the society or nation.

FISCAL POLICY MEASURES AND NI DETERMINATION

In case there exists deflationary gap or the government is keen for the income acceleration, it may come forward with government expenditure for removing the deflationary gap to ensure increase in national income. Similarly, if there exists inflationary gap, the government may come forward with imposition of tax for reducing the disposable income, which, in turn, may shift the consumption and investment schedules downwards and thus, it may remove the inflationary gap for the determination of national income. Thus, imposition of tax and government expenditures on infrastructural facilities are two important fiscal measures that assist in the national income determination suitably.

The government through its expenditures plays a vital role in deciding the national income level beyond the levels set by consumption and investment expenditures or that set by savings and investments. The government expenditure (G) is super imposed on $C + I$ functions taking $C + I + G$ to a higher level as compared to the level set by $C + 1$ only as per the income and expenditure method or this G is super imposed on investment function taking $I + G$ functions to a higher level as per the savings and investment method for deciding the equilibrium level of the national income. The may be exhibited as follows:

Figure 28.8(i) reveals that $C + I$ schedule intersects the 45° line at E_0, which decides the national income equilibrium at OM_0 level. On account of the government expenditure, the C + I + G schedule is drawn at a higher level, which intersects the 45° line at E point. This decides the national income equilibrium at OM_1 level, which is higher than the earlier national income equilibrium level at OM_0. This has been made possible through the governmental expenditure on developmental activities in the economy.

Figure 28.8(ii) indicates that the investment function schedule intersects the savings function schedule at E_0 point, which determines the equilibrium of the national income at M_0 level. Again through the governmental expenditure on developmental activities in the economy, the $I + G$ function schedule is shifted to a higher level, where it intersects savings functions schedule at E

deciding a higher equilibrium at OM level of the national income. Thus, the government expenditure helps in enhancing the level of the national income, which was earlier at lower level due to lower level of investment expenditure.

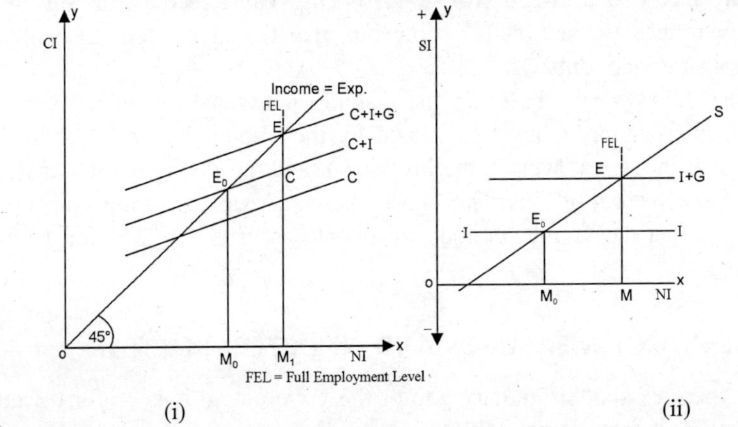

FIGURE 28.8 Impact of Government Expenditure on National Income Equilibrium.

In case, there is inflationary pressure in the economy, where the national income increases due to increase in prices of goods and services only and not due to increase in production and employment, the government may remove such inflationary pressure from the economy through imposition of tax, which is another fiscal measure to be adopted by the government. The imposition of tax may reduce expenditure and consumption and it may reduce the savings as well. These are shown as follows:

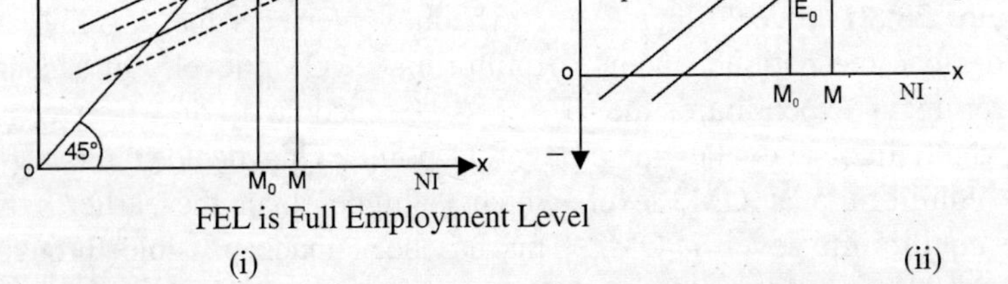

FIGURE 28.9 Impact of Imposition of Tax on National Income Equilibrium.

Figure 28.9(i) reveals that $C + I + G$ schedule intersects the 45° line at E point, which decides the equilibrium of the national income at OM level. In case, there is, inflationary pressure in the economy, where the national income has increased due to increase in prices of goods and services only and not due to increase in production and employment, the government may decide to impose some tax, which may reduce the consumption expenditure from C to C_0 level. This, in turn, will shift C + I to C_0 + I level and C + I + G to C_0 + I + G level, which intersects the 45° line at E_0 deciding the new equilibrium of national income at OM_0 level which happens to be the FEL (i.e., full employment level).

Figure 28.9(ii) reveals that imposition of tax may remove some part of savings shifting the savings function schedule from S to S_0 level. The original equilibrium OM of the national income is set at the point of intersection of I with S at E point. On account of imposition of tax, the new lower level S_0 function schedule intersects the I at E_0 point, where national income equilibrium in set at OM_0 level, which is the real national income at full employment level (FEL) as per the production and employment and not as per the higher prices of products in the economy. Thus, the imposition of tax removes the inflationary pressure from the economic system.

Review Questions

1. What is meant by the marginal propensity to consume (MPC) and how is it related with the marginal propensity to save (MPS)?
2. Distinguish between the national income equilibrium under autonomous and induced investments.
3. Prove that the national income will be in equilibrium, when the savings are equal to the investments.
4. Prove that the national income will be in equilibrium at the same level, whether we follow income—expenditure method or investment-savings method for its determination.
5. How do the inflationary gaps come into existence in determination of the national income equilibrium? What are the effects of such gaps?
6. Deflationary gap at the equilibrium level of the national income will result in reduction of its level further.
7. What is meant by paradox of thrift? How does it affect the level of income and investments?
8. How do the fiscal policy measures affect the national income equilibrium level in the economy?
9. Fiscal policy measures will also help in containing the inflationary and deflationary gaps in national income equilibrium determination.

29

Multiplier and Accelerator—Concepts and Measurements

Consumption, investment and savings are three interrelated important terms used in national income analysis. In case, there is an increase in the investment it will, in due course, increase the income comprising consumption as well as savings, certain number of times, which is known as the multiplier. It depends upon the marginal propensity to consume as well as the marginal propensity to save. Similarly, in case there is an increase in expenditure on consumption, it will result into an increase in the investment certain number of times, which is known as the accelerator. These two concepts, their measurements and other related matters are being considered separately in this chapter.

THE CONCEPT OF MULTIPLIER

It was discovered by Kahn R.F. for the first time in twentieth century, but it was Employment Multiplier. The concept of multiplier used in national income analysis is the investment multiplier, which was discovered by J.M. Keynes approximately at the same time in twentieth century.

According to Keynes 'In case there is an increment in investment, the income will increase by an amount, which is K times the increment of investment.' Thus, $\Delta Y = K.\Delta I$, where ΔY is change in income, ΔI is change in investment and K is the multiplier.

According to Lars Peter (L.P.) Hansen 'Multiplier is a coefficient relating the increment of investment to the resulting increment of income. Thus $K = \Delta Y/\Delta I$, which is read as K (multiplier) is equal to the change in income (ΔY) divided by the change in investment ΔI.

According to Paul A. Samuelson 'the multiplier is the number by which the change in investment must be multiplied in order to present us with the resulting change in income.

Thus, the multiplier is the numerical coefficient showing how much above unity is the increase in the national income resulting from an increase in the investment.

Since, $\Delta Y = K.\Delta I$ therefore, $\frac{\Delta Y}{\Delta I} = K$

Where, Y denotes national income

I indicates the investment

Δ (Delta) refers to the change

K is the multiplier

The value of the multiplier may be decided as per the values of the marginal propensity to consume (MPC) as well as that of the marginal propensity to save (MPS) as follows:

Since $\Delta Y = K . \Delta I$

So $\frac{\Delta Y}{K} = \Delta I$

$$\frac{\Delta Y}{K} = \Delta Y - \Delta C \text{ (since } \Delta Y = \Delta C + \Delta I\text{, so } \Delta I = \Delta Y - \Delta C)$$

By dividing both sides of the equation by ΔY, we derive

$$\left(\frac{\Delta Y}{K}\right) \div \Delta Y = (\Delta Y - \Delta C) \div \Delta Y$$

By changing the sign of division into sign of multiplication, we derive

$$\left(\frac{\Delta Y}{K}\right) . \frac{1}{\Delta Y} = (\Delta Y - \Delta C) . \frac{1}{\Delta Y}$$

By removing the brackets, we derive

$$\frac{\Delta Y}{K} . \frac{1}{\Delta Y} = \frac{\Delta Y}{\Delta Y} - \frac{\Delta C}{\Delta Y}$$

It can be put as $\frac{1}{K} = 1 - \frac{\Delta C}{\Delta Y}$

$$\frac{1}{K} = (1 - MPC) \text{ (because } \Delta C/\Delta Y = \text{MPC)}$$

By changing the sides for K and (1 – MPC) we get

$$\frac{1}{(1 - MPC)} = K$$

or

$$\frac{1}{MPS} = K \text{ (Because MPC + MPS = 1, therefore MPS = (1 – MPC)}$$

It is, thus, obvious that $\frac{1}{(1 - \text{MPC})} = \frac{1}{\text{MPS}} = K$

As per this derivation, if the assumed MPC = .8, the value of *K* (multiplier) will be 5 (i.e.$^{1}/_{.2}$), which means that if the investment is raised by certain amount, the national income is likely to rise five times of the amount of increase in the investment.

Working of the Multiplier

In case the investment is increased, the additional investment in the economy becomes the incomes of certain sections of the society resulting into the primary increase in the national income. Such additional primary income of the members of the society may be devoted to consumption as per their marginal propensity to consume. Such amount devoted to consumption again becomes the incomes of certain others members of the society in the next period. This will develop a chain of secondary consumptions and incomes in the periods to follow. Although the chain of secondary consumptions and incomes is endless, yet it is dwindling chain and ultimately it adds up to a finite amount. Its working can be analysed through the 'sequence analysis' as follows:

TABLE 29.1 Tabular Presentation of Changes in Investment, Income and Consumption in Successive Periods

Periods	*Increase in Investment* (ΔI)	*Increase in Income* (Δy)	*MPC*	*Increase in Consumption*	*MPS*	*Increase in Savings*
I	1000	1000	.8	800	.2	200
II	–	800	.8	640	.2	160
III	–	640	.8	512	.2	128
IV	–	512	.8	410	.2	102
V	–	410	.8	328	.2	82
VI	–	328	.8	262	.2	66
	⋮	⋮	⋮	⋮	⋮	⋮
Total	–	5,000	.8	4,000	.2	1,000

It reveals that including the initial investment of ₹ 1000 and the aggregate amount devoted to consumption of ₹ 4000 and that devoted to savings is ₹ 1000 over different periods, it has generated an increase in income (ΔY) equal to ₹ 5000, which is five times of the increase in investment initially. It indicates that the value of multiplier is 5, derived as per the given formula for the multiplier i.e., 1/(1 – MPC) or 1/MPS. Since MPC = .8 and MPS = .2, as assumed, the value of K = 1/1 – .8 = 5 or 1/.2 = 5. Since the increase in savings represents the sums retained by the individuals, it is not returning back to the economy but results into an increase in income. The total savings sum up to ₹ 1000 at the end of all multiplier periods. It is derived by multiplying the total sum of the increase in income by the marginal property to save (i.e., 5000 × .2 = 1,000).

It can also be exhibited as per change in equilibrium positions due to change in investments, as per (i) income and expenditure method as well as (ii) savings and investment method as follows:

Figure 29.1(i) reveals the original equilibrium at E point, where $C + I$ functions curve intersects the 45° line. At this point, the equilibrium level of income is OM. Increase in investment by ΔI shifts the $C + I$ function curve to $C + I'$ level, which intersects the 45° line at E' point, where the new equilibrium level of income is OM_1. Thus, it is obvious that the increase in investment by ΔI has increased the national income by ΔM, which is a few times of the increase in investment.

Figure 29.1(ii) shows the original equilibrium at E, where investment function curve (II) intersects the savings function curve deciding the original equilibrium income level at OM. An increase in the investment by ΔI shifts the investment function curve to 1′1′ level, which intersects the savings function curve (SS) at E' point, deciding the new equilibrium income level at OM_1. This again shows an increase in the income level (ΔM), which is a few times of the increase in investment (ΔI) due to multiplier operations.

It is, thus, obvious that the income increases by a multiplied amount of investment, the value of multiplier depends on the marginal propensity to consume, as the higher the MPC the larger the value of multiplier and vice-versa.

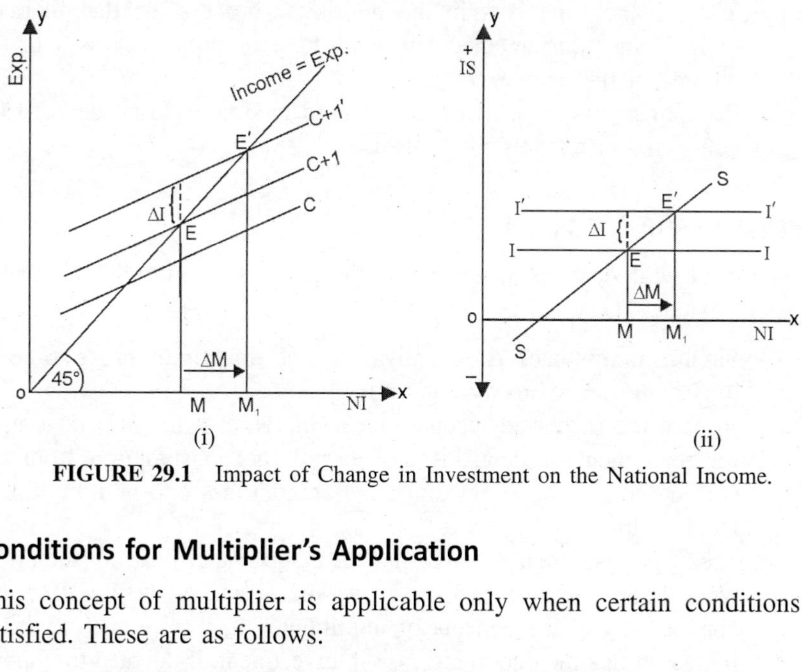

FIGURE 29.1 Impact of Change in Investment on the National Income.

Conditions for Multiplier's Application

This concept of multiplier is applicable only when certain conditions are satisfied. These are as follows:

1. Multiplier is found applicable only in industrial economies, where people, by and large, are accustomed to consume industrial products to be produced through investments.

2. The concept is applicable in those economies, where there exists some involuntary unemployment of resources, so that the resources get employed through increase in the investment.
3. It is applicable, when there exists excess capacity in consumption goods industries, so that production of consumption goods are increased immediately after the income increases due to increased investment.
4. It also assumes existence of the closed economy, because in open economy the increased income due to increase in investment may also be spent on imports. In this, way the increased income will get transferred to other countries and, thus, hampering the application of the multiplier.
5. The marginal propensity to consume is also assumed to be constant for the application of the multiplier.
6. It is also assumed that the additional investment is sufficiently large, so as to generate effective increase in the income of people. Insufficient increase in investment will not produce multiplier effect on the income generation.
7. Imposition of taxes on incomes of people will take away some part of increase in income derived due to increase in investment, which will hamper the application of multiplier.
8. There is no time lags in the multiplier process, so that increase in investment instantaneously leads to a multiple increases in the income of the people.
9. Price of goods on which the increased income is to be devoted for consumption remains unchanged.

Leakages of the Multiplier

There exists several leakages, which render the concept of multiplier applicable to a lesser extent. These are as follows:

1. Savings unless backed by equivalent investment may prove to be an important leakage to the multiplier.
2. In case the increased income due to increase in investment is used for repayment of debts, it will curtail the consumption from the current income and, as a result, it will render the concept of multiplier inapplicable.
3. In case goods were hoarded earlier and made available for consumption, when desired due to increase in income, it will adversely affect the applicability of the concept of multiplier.
4. Increased income due to increase in investment, if devoted to imports of the goods from abroad, it will divert the increased income to other countries and thus containing the application of the multiplier.

5. Price inflation also renders the concept of multiplier less effective.
6. In case, there is very strong liquidity preference, people may not devote their increased income to consumption rather they may save a large share of it, this may hinder the application of multiplier.
7. Progressive taxation on income in the country will also weaken the multiplier's application.
8. Existence of excess stock of consumption goods does not induce for further production and, as a result, the applicability of the multiplier remains subdued.

Importance of the Multiplier

It is considered to be an important contribution by J.M. Keynes to the development of income and employment theories. Its importance can be indicated as follows:

1. The national income will attain the equilibrium at a level, where the investment is equal to the savings. In case there is an increase in the investment, it leads to an increase in the income through application of the multiplier.
2. It highlights the importance of investment in income and employment generation in the economy.
3. The multiplier with accelerator offers a convincing explanation of the various phases of the business or trade cycles and may also assist in controlling the trade cycles.
4. The multiplier is also helpful in formulation of economic policies to achieve the level of full employment in the economy.
5. It may also assist in formulating suitable policies for deficit financing and of public investments, that is, expenditure on public works.

Critical Evaluation of the Multiplier

This concept has been criticised on several grounds as follows:

1. It is based on extremely simplified assumption of increase in consumption as a result of increase in income.
2. It is a mechanical concept, which is made applicable to the real world economics quite mechanically.
3. It has used arithmetical multiplier as the investment multiplier and it seems to be a mere tautological concept.
4. It ignores the acceleration effect i.e., the effect of consumption on investment and concentrates on the effect of investment on consumption.
5. It is timeless concept, as there seems to be no end of dwindling chain of consumption and savings due to increase in income resulting from an increase in investment. Its end is simply assumed but in reality it is not so.

6. It is static in nature, as it assumes the MPC as given but in reality it may also change.
7. It ignores the impact of induced consumption on induced investment, although there exists a positive relationship between the demand for capital goods and the demand for consumption goods.

Applicability of Multiplier in Developing Economies (DEs)

In developing or underdeveloped economies, there exists low level of income for individuals generally and therefore, the MPC is very high, which generates a very high value of the multiplier. Increase in income as per this high value of multiplier for an increase in investment is rendered difficult to achieve. Moreover, there are certain lacuna with these economies causing inapplicability of the concept of multiplier as follows:

1. There exists disguised unemployment in place of involuntary unemployment is underdeveloped economies. Under disguised unemployment people feel that they are employed but in reality they are not gainfully employed. As a result, they are not readily available for employment for increasing production, as may be the case when there is some involuntary unemployment.
2. Existence of excess capacity in industries is a pre-requisite for applicability of the multiplier, but in underdeveloped economies there exists no excess capacity for increasing the production immediately to meet the increased demand for consumption goods, as a result of increased income due to increased investment.
3. There does not exist the elastic supply of the desired labour force though that is a pre-requisite for increasing production to meet the increased demand for consumption goods.
4. The supply of the desired capital in under-developed countries is also not elastic one, as whatever types of capital goods are needed for increasing the supply of consumption goods, when needed due to increased income, these are not readily available.

On account of the aforesaid, the multiplier may not achieve the high value as per the high level of the marginal propensity to consume in underdeveloped economies.

THE CONCEPT OF ACCELERATOR

The investment depends on the level of consumption in the economy. Just as a change in investment changes the level of income certain number of times as per the concept of multiplier (K), change in consumption also changes the level of investment certain number of times, which is called accelerator (a). Multiplier (K) and accelerator (a) are parallel concepts, where 'K' shows the effect of changes in investment on income in the economy, 'a' shows the effect of change in consumption on investment.

According to Friedrich August Von (FAV) Hayek, 'Since the production of any given amount of final output usually requires an amount of capital goods several times larger than the output to be produced with it during a given period, any increase in the final demand will give rise to an additional demand for capital goods several times larger than the new final demand of consumption goods.

Thus, accelerator (a) = $\Delta I/\Delta C$ where ΔI is the change in investment and ΔC is the change in consumption of final goods.

Comparison of Accelerator and Multiplier

The concept of accelerator, in fact, helps in understanding the process of income generation. Certain level of income could be attained as per the concept of multiplier alone, but when the concept of accelerator joins hands with the multiplier, the process of income generation in the economy is speeded up. There are several grounds as per which the distinction can be drawn between the multiplier and accelerator as follows:

(i) The multiplier shows the effect of change in investment on income through a chain of increase in consumption, while the accelerator shows the effect of change in consumption on the investment in capital goods in the economy.

(ii) The multiplier depends on the given level of the marginal propensity to consume, while the accelerator depends on the durability of the capital goods.

(iii) The multiplier is a psychological concept, while the accelerator is a technological concept.

(iv) The multiplier functions in both directions with equal force, which means that increase in investment will result into an increase in income through a chain of increase in consumption, while a decrease in investment will reduce the income with the same force through a reduced consumption. On the other hand, while the accelerator increase the investment in capital goods with increase in consumption but it will remain restricted in downward direction to the rate of replacement of the capital goods only.

Assumptions

The concept of accelerator is based on certain assumptions as follows:

1. There exists no excess capacity in consumer goods industry, so that whenever there is an increase in consumption, a new capacity is to be developed by using additional capital goods.

2. There exists surplus capacity in capital goods industries, so that the additional capital goods are made readily available immediately after their requirements are placed by consumption goods industries on increase in demand for consumption goods.
3. The increase in demand for consumption goods must be sustainable and not of temporary nature.
4. Capital-output ratio should remain constant, which requires that there is no technological improvement so as to change the capital–output ratio.
5. Capital, raw materials and other resources must be easily available so that the supply of capital goods can be increased immediately after receiving the orders for such goods.
6. There exists fluidity in the economy, which means that finished stock of capital goods are turned out as fast as these are demanded. Similarly, man and material factors of production are made available for being used in the production process as fast as the process of producing capital goods requires them.

Working of the Accelerator

The effectiveness of the concept of accelerator depends on the durability of capital goods and the rate of change in consumption. Assuming capital–output ratio to be 1: 10 and 10% rise in demand for consumption, the working of the accelerator for different life-times of capital goods may be analysed as follows:

TABLE 29.2 Working of the Accelerator

Percentage Increase in Consumption (C)	*Period*	*Consumption (C)*	*Capital Equipments Needed*	*Additional Capital Goods Needed*			*% Change in Gross Investment*
				Gross Additions	*Replacement*	*Total*	
Assuming Life of Capital Goods to be 10 Years							
10% increase in (C)	0	1000	100	Nil	10	10	
	1	1100	110	10	10	20	100%
Assuming Life of Capital Goods to be 20 Years							
10% increase in (C)	0	1000	100	Nil	5	5	
	1	1100	110	10	5	15	200%
Assuming Life of Capital Goods to be 5 Years							
10% increase in (C)	0	1000	100	Nil	20	20	
	1	1100	110	10	20	30	50%

The level of demand for consumption goods in zero period in all the aforesaid three cases is 1000 units. The capital-output ratio is assumed to be

1: 10, hence the capital goods needed for being used in the production process of consumption goods are 100 units in all these cases. With 10% increase in demand for consumption goods in period 1 in all cases, the demand for consumption goods has gone up to 1100 units and the capital goods needed for producing this level of consumption goods is 110 in all the three cases. Additional capital goods needed due to increase in consumption goods is 10 in all cases, but the capital goods needed for replacement is 10, when life of capital goods is assumed to be 10 years, as one-tenth of 100 capital goods are to be replaced in every period. Similarly when life of capital goods is assumed to be 20 years. One-twentieth of 100 capital goods are to be replaced in every period and when the life of the capital goods is assumed to be five years, one –fifth of 100 capital goods are to be replaced in every period.

In case, the life of capital goods is assumed to be 10 years for 10% increase in demand for consumption goods, there will be 100% increase in total capital goods needed for additions as well as replacement from 10 in zero period to 20 in *I* period. Similarly when the life of the capital goods is assumed to be 20 years in response to 10%. Increase in demand for consumption goods, there will be 200% increase in demand for capital goods from 5 to 15 between 0 and 1 periods. Assuming the life of capital goods to be 5 years, in response to 10% increase in demand for consumption goods, there is 50% increase in capital goods from 20 to 30 over 0 to 1 period.

It is, thus, obvious that the value of accelerator i.e., relative increase in need for capital goods in response to increase in demand for consumption goods depends on the percentage increase in demand for consumption goods and the life duration of the capital goods, but the accelerator like multiplier has some positive value. Both these concepts are complementary to each other and work to speed up generation of national income of the country.

Applicability of Accelerator in DCs

The applicability of the accelerator is underdeveloped countries is also constrained like that of the multipliers. It is due to the reasons as follows:

1. Most of the consumer goods industries in underdeveloped countries generally do not rely on capital intensive techniques for production and whatever modern industries exist there, these usually have excess capacities.
2. Most of the investment in capital goods industries are of autonomous type, which are generally guided by non-economic considerations, like those in defence, public utilities, social overheads, etc.
3. Money and capital markets in underdeveloped countries are ill organized and, as a result, these do not suitably respond to the impulses generated in any part of the economy.

4. Industrial and technological bases in the underdeveloped countries are very narrow and, as a result, even if there is a rise in demand for consumption goods, it does not invoke much investment spending on capital goods.
5. There exists a wide spread uncertainty about the future of large scale production and, as a result, the industrialisation remains hampered.

Review Questions

1. Define the concept of investment multiplier. How is its value ascertained?
2. Elucidate the working of the investment multiplier and bring out its importance for any economy.
3. Discuss the conditions for application of multiplier. Also examine the leakages of the multiplier.
4. Evaluate the concept of multiplier and examine its applicability in the underdeveloped countries.
5. What is meant by the concept of accelerator? Compare this with the concept of multiplier.
6. Bring out the assumptions of the concept of accelerator. How is the value of accelerator ascertained?
7. Explain the working of the accelerator in any economy.
8. How does the concept of multiplier and accelerator work together for speeding up income generation? Examine the applicability of accelerator in the developing economies.

30

Macro Income Distribution—Theories and Inequalities

The distribution part of microeconomics comprising the theories of rent, wages, interest and profits concerns mainly with the functional or factorial distribution of income (i.e., distribution of income amongst the factors of production as rewards for their contribution in the process of production). However, macroeconomics concerns with personal distribution of income amongst the various individuals in the society. Individual members of the society may own just one factor (or input) or two or more factors (inputs) and therefore some members of the society may get the reward for the single input they own and other members of the society may get rewards for two or more inputs they own. As per the ownership of the non-human resources like land, factory buildings, capital equipments, as determined by the society's structure for property rights, the personal distribution of income depends on the prices of the various factors and also on the ownership pattern of the various human and non-human resources owned by individual members of the society. Thus, macro distribution concerns with the determination of the aggregative shares of the various categories of the factors of production in the total national income and from this the personal income may be derived by the members of the respective groups and also as per the non-human resources they may own.

These aroused the interest in macro theory of distribution and as per the past empirical findings, the share of wages to national income remained almost constant over the last 100 years, despite the fact that there had been changes in techniques of production and a rapid progress in terms of per capita income and capital accumulation relative to labour. However David Recardo was of the view that as the economy develops, the relative shares of rent, wages and profits would vary. Besides Recardian or classical theory of income distribution, many other endeavours were made for developing the macro theory of income distribution.

MACRO INCOME DISTRIBUTION THEORIES

The various theories concerned with distributive shares or aggregative shares of rent, wages, profit, etc. in the national income are as follows:

1. Recardian or Classical Theory.
2. Marxian Theory
3. Kalecki's Degree of Monopoly Power Theory
4. Marginalists' or Neo-Classical Theory
5. Kaldar's Keynesian Theory

Recardian or Classical Theory of Income Distribution

The Recardian or Classical Theory of income distribution has divided the economy in two broad sectors, viz. agricultural and industrial, where the agricultural sector is considered crucial, as the forces working in this sector decide the distributive shares in industry. This theory is based on the following three assumptions.

1. The Law of Diminishing Returns applies to agriculture, where if more labour is employed to agricultural land, the marginal and average production of labour diminishes.
2. The Malthusian Theory of Population is applicable, as per which the population is expected to increase with increase in wage rates beyond the minimum subsistence level and is likely to decrease with decrease in wage rate below the minimum subsistence level requiring the wage rate to remain equal to the subsistence level of wage rate in long run.
3. The profit is to be the necessary incentive for capital accumulation, which is essential for economic growth.

As per these assumptions, this theory distributes the national output into rents, wages and profits based on two separate principles, viz. (i) the Marginal Principles and (ii) the Surplus Principles. As per the marginal principles, it decides the share of rent in national output and on the basis of surplus principles, it decides the share of national output minus rent as wages and profits. Rent is the difference between the product of labour on the marginal land and the product on the above marginal land or the difference between the average and marginal product of labour. It may be exhibited as follows:

Here *X*-axis reveals the labour employed in agricultural sector and Y-axis reveals the average and marginal productivities of such labour. On account of application of law of diminishing returns, both the average product (AP) and the marginal product (MP) curves are sloping downwards. In case *OL* labour is employed in agriculture, the marginal products of labour is *CL* and average product of labour is *BL*. The excess of *BL* over *CL* (i.e., *BC*) represents the rent earned on land per unit of labour employed and the total rent earned by land is equal to MABC i.e., *BC* = *MA* multiplied by *OL* = *MC*.

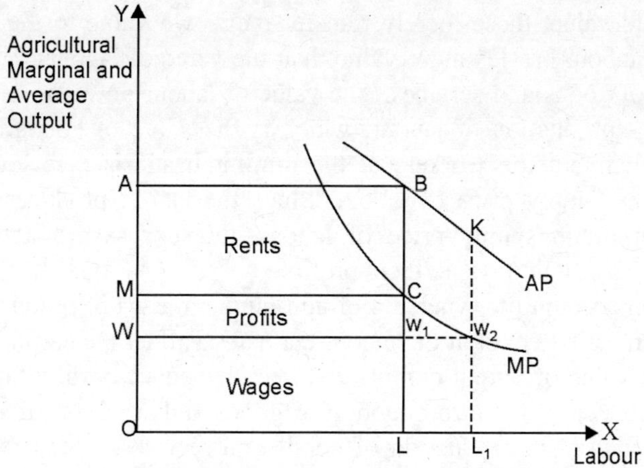

FIGURE 30.1 Distribution of National Output.

Subsistence wage level is decided as per biological and cultural needs of labour force out of the surplus remaining after paying for the rent, which is equal to OW = LW_1. This leaves a portion of surplus after paying the rent and wages out of the national output as profits, which may provide incentive for capital accumulation and that, in turn, may increase the employment of labour to OL_1 = WW_2. Since the average and marginal productivities have decreased at a higher level of employment of labour, which will continue to be at OW = LW_1 = L_1W_2 increasing the subsistence level of wage share to OW W_2L_1, which is there at the expense of the profits that shrinks continuously with increase in output and employment.

However, actual events in the course of development have been quite contrary to what Recardo has provided through this macro distribution theory. Empirical studies revealed that the relative share of labour (i.e., wages) in the national output had remained almost constant over a long period of time. Moreover, the share of profits in the national output has also not found declining in reality along with increase in the employment of labour. This theory of distribution has been found lacking on account of its assumption about the application of 'Law of Diminishing Returns' and also about the application of 'Malthusian Theory of Population'.

Marxian Labour Theory of Income Distribution

The Marxian theory is essentially an adaptation of Recardian surplus theory and rests on the labour theory of value, which Karl Marx adopted from the ideas developed by Adam Smith and David Recardo. This labour theory contends that the value of a commodity is determined by the labour necessary for its production. Karl Marx opined that it is the labour alone that is the ultimate source of all value. According to Marx, equipment and raw materials do not create value, these merely transfer their own value to the product. As against this labour creates more value than the value of labour power spent on production of goods and services. The value of labour power is determined by the cost of reproduction of labour, which is the value of goods and services needed to maintain the workers at the minimum subsistence level that also represents the supply price of labour. Since the labour produces more value than the minimum supply price of labour, this excess production may be appropriated by capitalists as their profits.

Thus, on account of ownership of non-human means of production that the capitalists are able to exploit the labour class and extract the surplus value from it. The total value of output comprises three elements: (i) value of capital and raw materials consumed in production of goods and services; (ii) the value of labour power used in production of goods and services, which represents the minimum subsistence wages also, and (iii) the value of output that contains the surplus value created by workers over and above the value of their labour power, which is appropriated by the capitalist class as profit. Thus,

Total Value Output = (i) Constant Capital (C) + (ii) Variable Capital (V) + (iii) Surplus (S) = C + V + S

In case, the value of *C* is deducted from the total value output, we derive net output.

Net output = V + S = Wage Share + Profit Share

The ratio between the profit share and wage share i.e., S/V has been called the rate of exploitation by Karl Marx.

An increase in the ratio is indicative of increase in profit relative to wages. This ratio can be increased in three ways: (i) by lengthening the working hours per day; (ii) by increasing to intensity of labour, that is, inducing the workers to do greater amount of work per day (iii) by increasing the physical productivity of workers through use of advanced technology. This use of technology requires accumulation of capital, so the rate of profit will be:

$$P = S/(C + V) \text{ or } P = S/V \cdot V/(C + V)$$

Here V/(C + V) is the ratio of variable capital to total capital and S/V shows the ratio of surplus to variable capital. In case, both are multiplied with each other we get the ratio of surplus to total capital employed i.e., S/(C + V).

In case S/V (i.e., rate of exploitation) remains constant, the rate of profit (i.e., S/(C + V) is likely to decline as a result of capital accumulations and consequent increase in the composition of capital. Thus, when more capital is accumulated the capital-output ratio rises, but as more capital intensive production techniques are employed, the rate of profit has a tendency to fall.

However, this theory of income distribution has been found lacking in several respects as follows:

1. It divides the national income in two parts, viz. wages to workers and surplus appropriated by capitalists as profits, ignoring the claims of other industrial groups in the economy.

2. The contention that the wages of labour will remain at subsistence level despite technological advancement and larger capital accumulation is also not found correct in real world situations.
3. Its contention that with increase in capital accumulation and technical progress, there will be a decline in profit rate is also not found correct in real world situations.
4. This theory of income distribution is based upon the labour theory of value is also not acceptable, as capital adds greatly to the productivity of labour and creation of good deal of value.

Michal Kalecki's Monopoly Power Theory of Income Distribution

It explains the distribution of national income into profits and wages depending upon the degree of monopoly power in the economy. It applies the microeconomic formula for the degree of monopoly power (i.e., (P – M)/P, where P stands for price and M for marginal cost) to the national income distribution between the capitalists and the labour class. In this theory the marginal cost includes cost of labour and raw materials and cost of labour includes wages of manual labour only. Salaries, which represent wages of white collar employees, are lumped-up with the income of the capitalist class. Thus, (P–M) indicates income of capitalist class including entrepreneurs' profits and aggregate overhead costs viz. interest, depreciation and salaries.

This theory of income distribution is based on two assumptions:

(i) equality of short run marginal and average costs
(ii) output of the firms is below their maximum capacity output, which means that there exists excess capacity in the economy. This indicates a general market imperfection and widespread monopolies or oligopolies.

As per A.P. Lerner's measure of the degree of monopoly power (D) of a single firm, it is the ratio of the difference between the price (P) and the marginal cost (M) to the Price (P) as follows:

$$D = (P - M)/P$$

Since a constant cost is assumed, the marginal cost will be equal to the average cost, and the above formula may be put as

$$D = (P - A)/P \text{ or } DP = (P - A)$$

Here, (P – A) reveals the difference between the price (P) and the average cost (A) per unit of output, it represents entrepreneurial profits, interest, depreciation and salaries and thus represents capitalists' income (inclusive of salaries) per unit of output. In case this per unit income is multiplied by the total output, it generates gross income of the capitalist class and when the output by all employers are added up (Σx (P–A), it generates the gross capitalists' income of all firms in the economy. As per this, the macro degree of monopoly power can be obtained by dividing gross capitalists' income (Σx (P – A) with aggregate turnover (T) in the economy (i.e., D = Σx (P – A)/T).

Labour's share in national income can also be derived as per degree of monopoly power. In case *Y* stands for national income and W for total wage bill in the economy, the *Y* – W will also represent the gross capitalist class income and W/Y will represent the relative share of wages in national income, which will decline if *Y* rises due to increase in prices of final goods as well as intermediate goods.

However, by attributing profits to the degree of monopoly power alone has glossed over other factors in causing profits and affecting distributive shares using the microeconomic concept of the degree of monopoly power macro-economically is difficult and not free from pit falls. The marginal costs lie at different levels for different firms and bringing them to a single level through averaging is an incorrect approach.

Secondly this theory ignores the power of labour altogether and concentrates on the power of capitalists alone. Labour unions exercise a countervailing power to the power of capitalists owning the manufacturing industries, and thus, raising the labour's share in the national income. Moreover, labour unions through collective bargaining have succeeded in wresting the monetary advantages for labour, which are passed on to the general consuming public in forms of higher prices.

Thus, it is true that the firms with price-setting power will certainly affect the distribution of income but the importance of other factors involved in process should not be ignored.

Marginalists' or Neo-Classical Theory of Income Distribution

Just as in micro distribution this theory is applied to determine the rewards of the individual factors as per their marginal productivities, the same marginal principles can be applied in macro distribution to all factors. Taking all factors to be variable, their rewards are determined equal to their marginal products. Thus, the labour gets wages equal to its marginal product, capital gets interest as per its marginal product and land gets rent equal to its marginal product. The total share of the various factors is determined by the respective marginal products multiplied by their respective quantities used in the production process. Similarly, the relative share of a factor in national income is the aggregate share of all units of that factor divided by the total national product.

Assuming the supply of all factors as given and fixed independently of price and all factors are substitutes for each other to some extent, as per the aforesaid the marginal products of the various factors are known from the production function. Taking rewards as equal to the marginal products of the factors, the absolute rewards and relative share of the factors can be decided. Representing labour by (L) and total output (Q) by employing (L) labour in the production process, the marginal product may be represented by $\Delta Q/\Delta L$, which shows a change in total output (ΔQ) when there is a change in the employment of labour (ΔL). The absolute share of labour is marginal product of labour multiplied by total units of labour employed in the production process is ($\Delta Q/\Delta L$) × L. By dividing the absolute share of labour by the total national product (Q), we may derive the relative share of labour in the total product as follows:

$$\text{Relative share of labour in National Product} = \left(\frac{\Delta Q}{\Delta L}.L\right) \div Q$$

$$= \frac{\Delta Q}{\Delta L}.\frac{L}{Q}$$

It represents the marginal product of labour (ΔQ/ΔL) multiplied by the reciprocal of the average product of labour. By interchanging the places of denominators Q and ΔL, we derive,

$$\frac{\Delta Q}{Q}.\frac{L}{\Delta L}$$

By changing the sign of multiplication into the sign of division, we derive that the relative share of labour in national product, which is equal to–

$$\frac{\Delta Q}{Q} \div \frac{\Delta L}{L}$$

This shows that the relative share of labour in national product is equal to the relative change in production divided by the relative change in employment of the labour. This also represents the elasticity of production is respect of labour, which in turn, shows that the relative share of labour in national income is equal to the elasticity of production with regard to labour.

Similarly, the relative share of capital can also be ascertained taking K as capital and Q as total output as follows:

$$\text{Relative share of Capital in national product} = \left(\frac{\Delta Q}{\Delta K}.K\right) \div Q$$

$$= \frac{\Delta Q}{\Delta K}.\frac{K}{Q}$$

After interchanging the places of ΔK and Q, we derive that

$$\frac{\Delta Q}{Q}.\frac{K}{\Delta K}$$

After changing the sign of multiplication into the sign of division, we derive that.

$$\frac{\Delta Q}{Q} \div \frac{\Delta K}{K}$$

This measures the elasticity of production with regard to capital.

Thus, the relative share of capital in national income is equal to the elasticity of production with regard to capital. In the same way the relative shares in national income of all factors can be decided as per the elasticity of production with regard to all respective factors of production. In regard to labour it may be exhibited as follows:

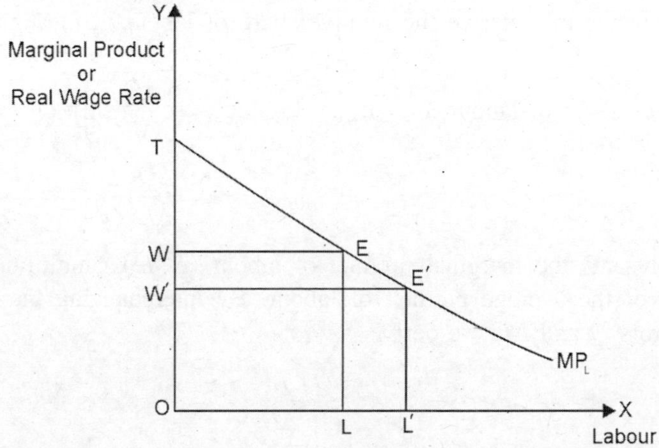

FIGURE 30.2 Share of Labour in National Income and Impact of Change in Employment.

The absolute share of labour in national product or income and change in it, as a result of change in the employment of labour, reveals that at OL level of employment of labour, the marginal product of labour is OW and the absolute share of labour comes to OLEW. An increase in employment of labour to OL′ reduces the marginal product of labour to OW′ and the new absolute share of labour OL′E′W′, which may be larger, smaller or equal to the earlier absolute share, depending upon the elasticity of the production of labour exhibited by the slope of the marginal product of labour (MP_L) curve.

Since this marginal principle for rewarding factors is according to their respective marginal products and the reward for OL labour is decided at OWEL, the remaining product as per MP_L i.e., WET will become reward for all others factors to be processed in the similar way. Thus, when all factors of production are paid rewards as per their respective marginal products, the total product may be just exhausted with neither any surplus left nor any deficit faced.

However, rewards for all but last remaining factor can only be processed through the marginal productivity. Amongst five factors, viz. land, labour, capital, organisation and entrepreneurship, the reward is processed for labour including organisation and for capital including land may be processed through their marginal productivities and the residual of the total national product may become the reward for entrepreneurs, who may get profit, if some surplus is left or may incur loss if some deficit remains after rewards for labour and capital as per this theory. Moreover, by combining organisation with labour and land with capital, it becomes difficult to compute their productivities, as their uniformity is affected and determining the absolute or relative shares of these factors in national product is rendered difficult.

Kaldor's Keynesian Theory of Distribution

Professor N. Kaldor has given a theory of distribution of the national product between profits and wages and has called his theory as Keynesian theory of distribution, because he has employed the Keynesian theoretical framework or Keynesian apparatus of thought to explain the factors, which form the basis for distribution of income between profits and wages. The wages represent the share of labour class that includes rewards for manual labour, salaries and the profit that indicates the share of property owning class that includes ordinary profits, rents and interest.

This theory of income distribution is based on three assumptions; (i) there is full employment in the economy and, as a result, there is a given total output or income; (ii) the marginal propensities to consume (or save) are constant for wage earners as well as property owners; and (iii) the marginal propensity to save of wage earners is smaller than that of property owners.

As per this theory Y = W + P, where Y stands for the national income, W for wages and P for profits. Thus, the total national income is composed of the sum of aggregate wages and aggregate profits. The equilibrium of national income (Y) is attained at the level, where I = S i.e., aggregate investment (I) is equal to the aggregate savings (S).

The ratio of aggregate profits (P) to national income (Y) (i.e., P/Y) depends upon the ratio of investment (I) to the national income (Y) (i.e., I/Y). An increase in investment to income (i.e., I/Y) ratio will bring about an increase in share of profits in national income (i.e., P/Y) and a corresponding decrease in the share of wages in the national income (i.e., W/Y). As per Kalder's Model, the ratio of investment to total income (as in Keynesian theory) is treated as independent variable, which is unresponsive to the changes in saving propensities of the property owners (SP) and the same of the wage earners (SW). The model holds good, when the saving propensity of the property owners is greater than the saving propensity of wage earners (i.e., SP > SW).

The share of profit in the national income is a function of investment to income (i.e., 1/Y) ratio and the greater the investment to income ratio, the larger is the share of profits in the income and vice-versa. A shift in the distribution of income in favour of the property owning class is essential for continued full employment equilibrium with the higher level of real investment in the economy. This, in turn, through rise in general price level increases the profit margins of the property owning class, as the wage rates lag behind the rise in prices. It increases the share of profits in the national income and correspondingly decreases the wage shares in the national income. This model may yield meaningful result in regard to income distribution, provided (i) the wage level is more than minimum or subsistence wage level (i.e., $W > W_{min}$) and (ii) profit margins i.e., profit to income ratio is more than the minimum price level below which the entrepreneurs will not reduce the prices (i.e., $P/Y > P_{min}$). Here (i) may permit a decline in wage share due to rise in the price level so as to bring about a redistribution of income in favour of profits, and (ii) implies that the entrepreneurs would be willing to accept lower profit margins that are associated with price reductions in the periods of deficient demand. In the absence of this (ii) constraint an excess of savings over investment at the full employment level, instead of being rectified through a fall in prices and the profit margins would be eliminated by a fall in income and employment. This re-distributive mechanism is the crux of this theory of income distribution.

This model highlights the fact that the savings and investment determine the distribution as well as the ultimate size of the national income and reveals that it is the changes in distribution rather than the changes in the level of income that suggests the adjustment mechanism between the savings and investments. In fact, the savings decisions are sub-sequential rather than being consequential to the investment decisions and this provides a more realistic explanation of the macro income distribution.

However, the first constraint related to excess of wages over subsistence wages permitting reduction in wage share due to rise in price level resulting from increase in investment as frictionless, takes this model away from the reality. This theory ignores the relationship between the share of profits and marginal products, substitutability of factors and life of capital goods, considering this income distribution model to work, when there exists a strong complementarity of the factors. Moreover, it ignores the impact of technical progress on the income distribution as between property owners' share and labour's share in total national income.

Similarly the second constraint that the entrepreneurs would accept a reduction in their profit margins up to certain minimum, so as to wipe out the excess of full employment savings over investment, but in real world situation, the prices are rigid in downward direction. In reality, in place of adjusting prices, the producers generally prefer to make adjustments in output levels in face of periods of deficient demands. Besides, all price reductions need not be accompanied by reduction in profits' share, as in view of the adoption of advanced technology, the cost reduction may be more than the price reduction and, as a result, the price reduction and increase in profits' share may move hand in hand.

Besides, this theory of distribution proves the relative share of profits in the national income at the full employment level, when the investment is undertaken to increase the capacity, but it does not provide an explanation as to how the distributive shares will be affected by increase in investment and resultant expansion in output and real income below the level of full employment.

This theory of income distribution has failed to incorporate human capital and has concentrated on physical capital i.e., material instruments of production. A rise in investment to income ratio resulting into an increase in profits' share in national income and consequently a decreasing share of wage earners, which include highly skilled workers, engineers, managers and scientists. This will adversely affect the human capital bringing a reduction in real income and output. This has left the theory to be considered as too simple to explain the complexities of the real world situations.

INEQUALITIES OF MACRO INCOME DISTRIBUTION

All macro income distribution theories from Classical or Recardian to Neo-Classical and Kaldar's Keynesian theories endeavour to decide the share of labour class and the share of property owning class from the total national product or income. Labour class including manual workers, technicians, experts, professionals, engineers, managers, scientists, etc. constitute a vast majority in every economy as compared to the number of the property owning class including landlords, business owners and fund providers. As a result, the average income of the labour class has been always and everywhere lower, as compared to that of the capitalists' class. Moreover, this average income of the labour class as well as of the capitalists' class is of little significance to the individuals of both the labour as well as capitalist classes, as they always compare their share in the national income with such shares of others. Truly speaking the share of an individual in the national income is his personal income, which is also an index of the level of his economic welfare or standard of living. The per capita income, derived by dividing the national income with the size of population, simply represents the average figure for individuals' income. However, individuals in reality do not get the income equal to per-capita income, as there has always been unequal distribution of income in almost all countries and majority of mankind have always remained poor.

The Italian economist of French origin Vilfredo Pederieo Domaso Pareto during 19th century studied the pattern of income distribution of the various countries and, as per the findings, a law has been propounded, which is called 'Pareto's Law of Distribution'. As per this law, in case X signifies a given income and N signifies the number of persons with income exceeding X and if a distribution curve in drawn of which the ordinate (i.e., the vertical axis) denotes the logarithms of X and the abscissa (i.e., horizontal axis) denotes the logarithms of N, the income distribution curve is approximately a straight line inclined to vertical axis at an angle, which is no country will vary by more than 3° or 4° from 56° (i.e., tan 56° = 1.5). It is as follows:

In Figure 30.3 the horizontal axis shows the logarithms of number of persons (N) having income exceeding X, which is the logarithms of income shown on

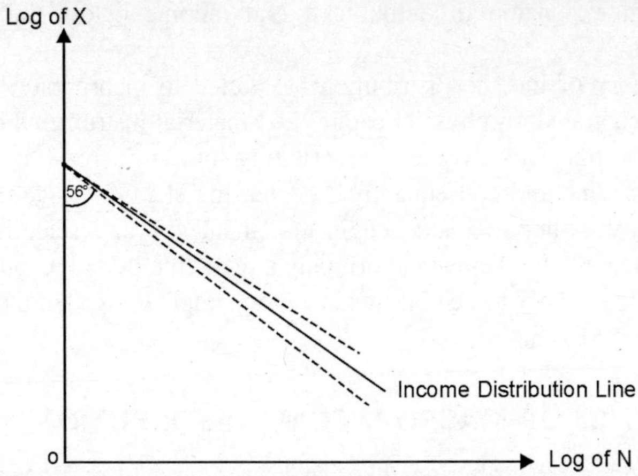

FIGURE 30.3 Pattern of Pareto's Law of Income Distribution.

the vertical axis. The income distribution is represented by a straight line sloping downwards having a slope equal to 1.5 that forms a 56° angle from the vertical axis. This angle of the line showing income distribution may vary ± 3° to 4° from the 56°. In other words, the income distribution line may form an angle from 53° to 59° or from 52° to 60° in the various countries and at different times in the same country. This indicates that there is an inevitable tendency for the income to be distributed in the same way regardless of the social and political institutions and also regardless of the taxation. However, later studies have revealed that the inequality of income distribution is everywhere, though the magnitude may differ slightly.

MEASUREMENTS OF INEQUALITY OF INCOME DISTRIBUTION

The measurements of the inequality of the income distribution reveal how great is the spread of income distribution. In case the income or wealth is equally distributed, the lower 10% of income or wealth will go to the poorest 10% of the population and the highest 10% of the income or wealth will go to the wealthiest 10% of the population. Thus, in case there is perfectly equal income distribution, every person in the population would have the same or equal income. In such a case N% of the population would always have N% of the income. In contrast, a perfectly unequal distribution of income or wealth would be one in which only one person would have all the income and everyone else have none. The actual distribution of income would be in between the aforesaid two extremes. The difference between the absolute equality of the income distribution and actual distribution of the income is the measure of the inequality of the income distribution. Economists have suggested three measurements of inequality of income distribution, as follows:

Lorenz Curve

It has been developed by Max O Lorenz in 1905. It is a graphic presentation of the distribution of income or wealth. It is often used to represent income distribution, where it shows for bottom $x\%$ of population what percentage of the total income (Y) they have, when the percentage of population are plotted on X-axis and the percentage of income is plotted on Y-axis. A perfectly equal distribution is generally depicted by a straight line, where the percentage of population (X) is equal to percentage of total income (Y). It is as follows:

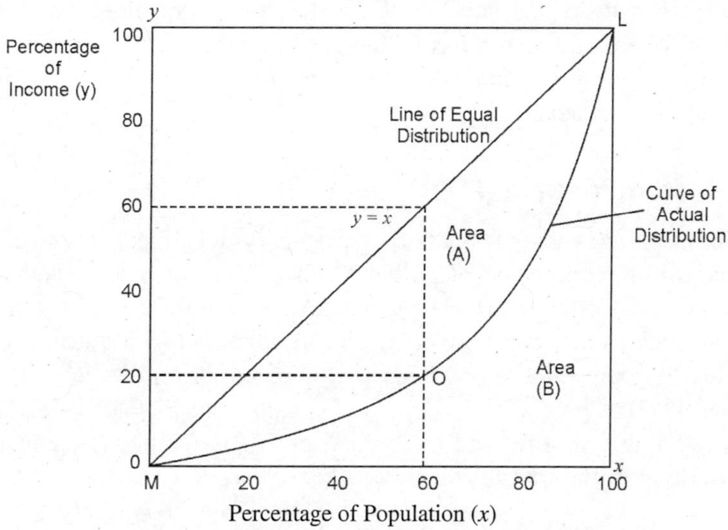

FIGURE 30.4 Derivation of the Area of Unequal Distribution.

It is obvious that ML the straight line represents equal distribution as on all points of this percentage of population (X) is equal to the percentage of income (Y) indicating 0% income for 0% population, 60% income for 60% population, 100% income for 100% population. The actual distribution of income is exhibited on MOL curve, which reveals 0% income for 0% population, 20% income for 60% population and 100% income for 100% population. This MOL curve for actual distribution of income is called Lorenz Curve developed by Max O. Lorenz.

Here, areas $A+B$ are under the line of equal distribution of income, while area B is under the curve for actual distribution. The area A bounded by the line of equal distribution and the curve of actual distribution of income represents area of inequality of distribution. The larger the area A, the greater is the inequality of income distribution and vice-versa.

Gini's Coefficient

It is also called 'Gini's Index' or 'Gini's Concentration Ratio', which is a measure of dispersion intended to represent the income or wealth distribution of a nation's residents and is most commonly used measure of inequality of income distribution. This measurement has been developed by Italian Statistician Corrodo Gini in 1912.

It represents the ratio of the area between the line of perfectly equal distribution and the observed Lorenz Curve (i.e., area A) to the area between the line of perfect equality and the area of perfect inequality (i.e., area A+B). The higher the coefficient, the more is unequal distribution and vice-versa.

Gini's coefficient with the value zero expresses perfect equality, where all values are the same (i.e., everyone has the same income). In case Gini's coefficient has the value equal to 1 (or 100%), it expresses the maximum inequality, where one person has all income and others have none. The nearer the value of Gini's coefficient to zero, the more the equal distribution of income and vice-versa.

Pigou-Dalton Principle (PDP)

It is a principle in welfare economics, particularly in cardinal welfarism. It has been named after the name of Arthur Cecil (A.C.) Pigou and Hugh Dalton. It states that all other things being equal, a social welfare function should prefer allocations that are more equitable. In other words, a transfer of utility from rich to poor is desired as long as it does not bring the rich to a poorer situation than the poor. Let $U = (u_1, u_2, ...u_n)$ and $U' = (u'_1 + u'_2 .... u'_n)$ be the two utility profiles and the second profile is found to be equal to the first profile after the transfer of utility like,

$U' = (u'_1 + u'_2 + ... u'_n) = \text{U} = (u_1, u_2 + u_n)$, it is likely to promote economic welfare.

In such a situation, the social welfare ordering should prefer the second utility profile U', as it reduces the inequality through a transfer from rich to poor, while keeping sum of their utilities as unchanged. Thus, as per this principle, the inequality can be measured as per the formula as follows:

$$\text{IID} = \frac{\text{AEWA}}{\text{EWAPE}}$$

Where IID stands for inequality of income distribution, AEWA for actual economic welfare attained and EWAPE for economic welfare attainable under perfect equality of income distribution. Obviously this formula underlines the case for transference of income from rich to poor, so that the sum of total utility after transfers equals the sum of total utility before transfers through adjustments in their utility functions.

CAUSES OF INEQUALITY OF INCOME DISTRIBUTION

Inequality of income distribution generally owes its origin to the following reasons:

1. **Differences in the Endowment of Talents and Capabilities of Individuals:** The earning capacities of individuals differ on account of differences in their mental and physical capabilities. Thus, the equality of the income distribution is ruled out by the nature itself, as the more talented and capable persons will be able to get a higher income than the income earned by less talented and less capable persons.
2. **Existence of the Private Property:** In fact it reinforces the differing capabilities to earn income by different individuals in the economy. It enables the individuals holding the various production resources, to get enhanced their incomes significantly. Thus, while there is some limit on earnings by one's labour, there exists no limit to the earnings from the ownership of the various productive properties.
3. **Institution of Inheritance:** On account of this institution, the various properties and wealth of individuals get transferred to their heirs on their demise. As a result, the heirs get an edge over others, who may get lesser or no property as per inheritance. This perpetuates inequality in earnings through properties from generation to generation.
4. **Inequality of Opportunity:** There may be a large variety of social, cultural and religious factors responsible for inequality of opportunity, which give rise to inequality in earnings of the individuals. As a result, the children of rich persons even with lesser mental capabilities due to better education and training, get a better start in life and continue to earn more, as compared to others, who are not that fortunate.
5. **Differences in Bargaining Power:** Rich persons can withdraw their productive resources from the market, if it does earn satisfactory returns, whereas the poor persons, who generally belong to labour class cannot withdraw their resources (i.e., labour), even if it gets lower wages, so as to remain in existence. They have poor bargaining power, because if they lose the employment of their labour on any day that cannot be retained for future period.
6. **Inequality a Natural Phenomenon in Capitalist System:** Rich persons in the economy are generally employers, who earn profits, while poor persons are generally workers, who earn wages in return for their labour. Profit is generally residual income, while wages in normally a contractual income. Rich persons, who are generally employers, after making contractual payments to the various factors employed in the production process, normally retain a larger share of total revenue as their profits.

MEASURES TO CONTROL INEQUALITY OF INCOME DISTRIBUTION

The governments in modern times generally maintain a system of checks and balances to promote equitable distribution of incomes in the country. Certain measures are as follows:

1. **Encouraging Trade Union Movements:** A single labour will have a weak bargaining capability against the employer, but if they are encouraged to form trade unions to enter into bargaining with the employers on behalf of labour force for securing better emoluments, facilities, working conditions, etc., the trade unions will have a larger possibility to succeed and this may go a long way in ensuring somewhat equitability in income distribution.
2. **Assistance to Unemployed:** In case the able bodied persons willing for some gainful work remain unemployed due non-availability of the opportunities, provisions for some assistance should be made for them till they get some gainful employment. This will also lead to somewhat equitable income distribution.
3. **Provision for Adequate Educational and Training Facilities:** Sufficient number of educational and training institutions should be made available for imparting education and training to individuals for this development and employment. This may enable them for a better start in life, which will contribute for equitable distribution of income.
4. **Relative Expansion of Public Sector:** The government should also endeavour to establish and develop public sector enterprises to provide larger and better employment opportunities for the individuals. This will also go in favour of equitable income distribution to a certain extent.
5. **Provision of Negative Income Tax or Family Allowances:** The government, by making provisions for negative income tax, where individuals with lower income are given some family allowances, while individuals with comparatively higher income are required to pay income tax, may reduce the spread of income distribution, which may lead to more equitable income distribution. It is as follows:

TABLE 30.1 Tax or Aid on Personal Earnings

Personal Earnings	*Tax (–) or Aid (+)*	*Personal Income after Tax or Aid*
1,000	+ 8,000	9,000
3,000	+ 7,000	10,000
8,000	+ 3,000	11,000
15,000	0	15,000
25,000	– 3,000	22,000
50,000	– 15,000	35,000

Thus, the spread of personal earnings before imposition of tax or provision of aid was from 1,000 to 50,000, but after tax or aid it is from 9,000 to 35,000, which shows a comparatively more equitable income distribution.

6. **Transference of Income from Rich to Poor:** The transference of income from relatively rich to relatively poor persons, either directly or indirectly by the government, will also play an important role in ensuring equitable income distribution. Some economists are of the view that some voluntary transference of income is possible, but it is too little to be effective and compulsory transference may not be possible, as all money taken by government from rich to be given to poor is in fact taken from poor, who will give it back to rich in form of lower wages or reduced employment. The compulsory transference through progressive taxation on rich persons may have some adverse effect on national income, as it may (i) drive men capable of earning large incomes by their work to live and work abroad, (ii) induce rich persons to make investments abroad, or (iii) induce rich persons to work less than what they would have done had there been no taxes.

Similarly the expectation of assistance by poor persons from public funds may tempt them into idleness and thriftlessness. Thus, the proposals for housing accommodation, insurance premium and free provisions for education of children are denounced on this ground, as it may result into reduction in national income. However, the transferences to poor persons through government, which are (i) conditional upon the recipients for making provisions for themselves like, provident fund contribution, (ii) dependent upon performances of standard work, like certain period of service for pension, or (iii) dependent upon the attainment of certain conditions not variable through voluntary action, like old age pension, universal endowment of motherhood, etc. may result in an increase in the national income.

The national income may be used for (i) provision of goods consumable by rich, (ii) provision of machines for assisting in future production, or (iii) provision of goods consumable by poor, where a transfer for (iii) at the cost of (i) and (ii) may increase the national income provided return yielded by investment in poor through increase in efficiency is more than the return on investment in material capital goods. However, even if the aforesaid transferences fail to make poor persons efficient even then the transference is desirable for other considerations. Thus, the transference of income from relatively rich to relatively poor persons is always considered desirable, if it is in the forms of:

(i) industrial trainings to poor persons.
(ii) medical attendance and treatment of poor persons free of cost or on subsidised rates.
(iii) free education, training and nurture of children of poor persons.

The transferences for all the aforesaid must be made reasonably effective taking all aspects of recipients into consideration.

Review Questions

1. How is the macro distribution different from the micro distribution of income?
2. Elucidate the Recardian theory of macro distribution of income.
3. Examine the improvements brought about by the marginalists or neo-classicals over the classical theory of macro distribution of income.
4. State the Marxian theory of macro distribution of income and compare it with Kalacki's degree of monopoly power theory.
5. Bring out the salient features of Kaldar's Keynesian Theory of macro distribution of income.
6. Bring out the Pareto's Law of income distribution.
7. How is the inequality of income distribution measured through the Lorenz Curve?
8. Examine the Gini's coefficient and Pigou-Daltan principles for measuring the inequality of income distribution.
9. What are the various causes of inequality of income distribution?
10. Discuss the measures to be taken for containing the inequality of income distribution.
11. Bring out the effectiveness of transference of income from rich to poor on the national income of the country.

31

Business Cycles

Capitalistic economies are normally characterised with occasional fluctuations in economic variables marked in investments, output, price, income and employment. Such changes at times are abrupt and isolated, but at other times these may continue for a long time. All such changes in the economic variables are as follows:

(i) **Secular Trends:** It refers to the persistent movement in economic variables in upward or downward directions over a long period. It is exhibited in the physical volume of industrial production, in the level of price, in trade and in any other economic variable.

(ii) **Seasonal Fluctuations:** It refers to the periodic movements in the various economic variables within the period of a calendar year. Thus the industrial production, agricultural output, interest rates, demand for certain goods, etc. may witness upward or downward movements in certain specific months of the calendar year.

(iii) **Cyclical Fluctuations:** It indicates continuous movement of economic variables, like investment, production, price, wages, interest rate, profit, etc. through alterations of rise and fall, It contains oscillating movements in economic variables form peak to trough and again from trough to peak continuously. Such up and down movements in economic variables are similar to that of seasonal fluctuations, but it differs in rhythms and periodicity, which are set and known in seasonal fluctuations but these are free and indefinite in cyclical fluctuations.

(iv) **Random Fluctuations:** These bring about sporadic changes in economic variables, which are caused by events of non-recurring and irregular nature, like earthquakes, fire, storms, floods, famines, strikes, etc. These events bring random fluctuations in economic variables, which are unpredictable and non-measurable and their impact remains localised and confined to certain period.

Amongst all these four types of fluctuations in economic variables in a country, the cyclical fluctuations have attracted the major attention of economists, because these bring about huge changes in the economy and their causations are also not easily perceivable.

DEFINITIONS OF BUSINESS CYCLES

Business or trade cycles generally refer to the wave like fluctuations in the economic variables particularly in employment, output and income.

According to American Economist Wesley Clair Mitchell, 'business cycles refer to fluctuations in aggregate economic activities'. Thus, the aggregate of production, employment, income, etc. keep on fluctuating in real world economies through alterations of rise and fall, which has been designated as business or trade cycles.

Austria born American Economist Gottfried Herberler has opined that 'business cycle, in the general sense, may be defined as the alternation of the periods of prosperity and depression; of good and bad trade'.

Another American Economist Robert James Gordan has defined it as 'business cycles consist of recurring alternations of expansion and contraction in aggregate economic activities; the alternating movements in each direction being self-reinforcing and pervading virtually all parts of the economy'.

CHARACTERISTICS OF BUSINESS CYCLES

The business cycles are recurrent fluctuations of the economic variables observable in statistics of output, income and employment. It moves from prosperity to depression and swings back again without any uniformity in the time span or in the degree of intensity. All the aforesaid definitions reveal certain characteristics of business cycles as follows:

(i) Business cycles represent a wave like fluctuations in economic activities.

(ii) Business cycles are recurrent in nature, as they move from prosperity to depression and again from depression to prosperity and thus again and again.

(iii) Business cycles have cumulative self-reinforcing nature of movements in both expansion and contraction phases. Once started it persists in the given direction of expansion or contraction till the forces accumulate to reverse the direction of movement in economic variables.

(iv) Business cycles contain self-generating forces, which tend to ensure the progress of the phase of prosperity or depression

(v) Business cycles are all pervasive in their effects, as the expansion or contraction phases of the business cycles affect virtually all segments of the economy in due course.

(vi) There in the presence of crisis in the business cycles. Peak and trough of the business cycles are not symmetrical, as the movement from peak to trough is more sudden and violent, but the movement from trough to peak remains slow and low.

(vii) Business cycles are recurrent in nature but these are not periodical. It means the extension and contraction phases will recur alternatively, but there is no definite periodicity for these phases of the business cycles.

PHASES OF BUSINESS CYCLES

Business cycles vary greatly in timings and amplitudes, yet these follow a set pattern of development, which carries them through different phases in the same sequence, cycle after cycle. Peaks and troughs are the mark off points in the business cycle. The cycle can be explained either from peak the peak or from trough to trough, where each oscillation completes a cycle. There are four well defined and interrelated recurring phases of the business cycle, titled as: (i) Prosperity phase and the highest level of prosperity is called Peak phase; (ii) Recession phase; (iii) Depression phase and lowest level of depression is called Trough phase; and (iv) Recovery phase. These phases of the business cycle are exhibited as follows:

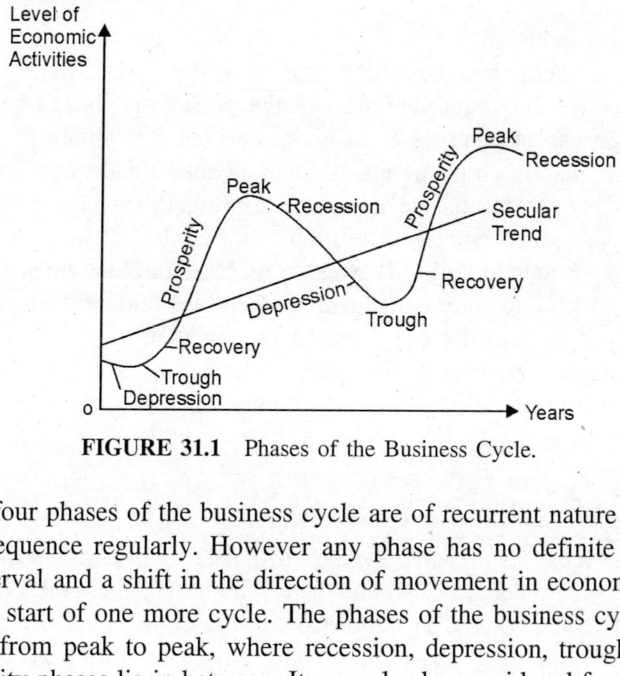

FIGURE 31.1 Phases of the Business Cycle.

These four phases of the business cycle are of recurrent nature and follow the same sequence regularly. However any phase has no definite periodicity or time interval and a shift in the direction of movement in economic activity induces the start of one more cycle. The phases of the business cycle may be considered from peak to peak, where recession, depression, trough, recovery and prosperity phases lie in between. It may also be considered from trough to trough with recovery, prosperity, peak, recession and depression phases lying in between. The characteristics of these phases are as follows:

Prosperity Phase

This phase is characterised to have a large and rising volume of production and trade, a high level of employment of human and material resources overall rising prices, rising interest rates, larger expansion of credit and borrowings, a higher and rising level of real investment and a rising level of wages. During this phase the dynamic forces will operate in such a way that the expansion in economic activities becomes all cumulative, where a rise in prices will lead to a larger profit that will induce for a larger investment leading to a larger employment of resources and to more output and income. These, in turn, will give rise to demand for more goods and services and thus leading the economic activities to reach its peak (i.e., the highest level).

However, the forces leading to expansion in the economy may get weakened with passage of time. In fact, the profit inflation and over optimism that increased the tempo of economic activities carry with them the seeds of self-destruction. In view of the high profit, the entrepreneurs go for larger investment leading to tremendous increase in productive activities, but paucity of demand for certain product may render the business calculation wrong, heralding start of the recession phase of the business cycle.

Recession Phase

It is a turning point in the business cycle, where the forces responsible for contraction in economic activities win over the forces that resulted into expansion of the economic activities in the prosperity phase of the business cycle. The recession phase is characterised with the beginning of liquidation in the stock market, repayments of bank loans and decline in prices are the outward symptoms of the recession. During this phase businesses start holding pessimistic view about the future profitability of investments. People start to have greater liquidity, expansion of economic activities stops, orders for supply of products are cancelled, workers are laid off, employment and income of people start declining, and demand for products also start falling, This recession in like a forest fire, once underway it creates its own draft and give internal impetus to its destructive ability leading to the depression phase of the business cycle.

Depression Phase

In case the recession remains unchecked, it leads to the depression phase of the business or trade cycle, where there will be considerable contraction of the economic activities. The depression phase of the business cycle is just reverse to its prosperity phase. It is characterised by shrinkage in volume of production and trade, increase in unemployment, overall fall in prices of the goods and services, fall in wages, profit and aggregate expenses leading to prevalence of the overall pessimism in the field of economic activities. On account of contraction of credit, banks accumulate excess resources, as these get little opportunity for investment of funds. Prices of all shares and securities come down to a very low level in the stock market. Interest rates decline and people have a strong desire for liquidity. Construction works for plants and buildings come to complete stand still.

However this depression phase in the economy is also not permanent, as business units which have been postponing the replacement of their old plant and machineries and the consumers, who have been postponing the purchases of consumer durables, accumulate huge funds, which they try to use for the aforesaid. Thus, the consumers start purchasing consumer durables, which induce businesses to produce more consumer durables by expanding and replacing their old plants and machineries and this, in turn, may increase employment allowing the depression phase in economy to enter into the recovery phase of the business cycle.

Recovery Phase

It refers to the lower turning point at which the economy undergoes changes from depression/trough towards the prosperity. It begins with revival for the demand of capital goods, which increases the investment and employment in capital goods industries. This increase in income through increased employment in capital goods industries, push-up the general demand for goods and services, which in turn, leads to rise in prices and profits, This may induce for investment and employment in other industries, which increases the income and demand for the various other goods and services.

Thus, once it starts, it also gathers momentum, which slowly and steadily increase the level of employment, output, income, prices of goods and services and profit of the business enterprises, stock market become more sensitive, where bullish atmosphere starts prevailing. This revival or recovery phase slowly merges with the prosperity phase of the business cycle in the economy.

The aforesaid four phases of the business cycles appear in the same sequence starting from any phase but there is no definite periodicity or duration of the different phases. Economists have tried to find out the seasons that give rise to the cyclical fluctuations in the economy and for this several business cycle theories have been propounded by them.

THEORIES OF BUSINESS CYCLES

Economists have searched out a large variety of causes responsible for the cyclical changes in economy, known as theories of the business cycles, which are as follows:

Sunspot or Climatic Theory

This theory has been propounded by British Economist William Stanley Jevons, but later on it has been developed by H.C. Moore. As per this theory, the business cycles have been related with the climatic variations on account of sunspots, as when these come in front of the country on the earth, these affect the rainfall, which, in turn, affects the agricultural crop production and ultimately that affects all segments of economy. Thus, when the sun spot comes in front of the nation on the earth, the rainfall is adversely affected, which will result in reduced agricultural crop production that reduces the raw materials supply, which, in turn, may reduce industrial production in the economy leading to depression phase of the business cycle. In case the country on the earth does not face the sun spot, it may get good rainfall, which may increase agricultural crop production and that, in turn, may increase the industrial production in the economy leading to prosperity phase of the business cycle.

However, much reliance cannot be placed on this theory, as there is no basis to establish correlation between appearance of sun spot before a nation on the earth and the amount of rainfall it gets and alterations in the level of economic activities it experiences. In case this theory is to be correct, then business cycles should not be applicable in non-agricultural or highly industrialised countries, but in reality, this is not the case, as highly advanced countries suffer the most from the business or trade cycles.

Psychological Theory

This theory has been contributed by British Economists John Stuart Mill, William Henry Beveridge and Arther Cecil Pigou. It states that there are moods of optimism and pessimism amongst businessmen and banke₹ Optimism and pessimism both are catching phenomena by nature, as when one businessman is pessimistic, he passes it on to others and in similar way optimism spreads from one to others. The business cycles owe their origin to the waves of optimism, which results in recovery and prosperity phases and of the pessimism, which results in recession and depression phases. Many modern economists have relied upon 'expectations' for explaining upward and downward movements in the economic activities. This expectation is also a psychological factor but it has been given secondary importance only in explaining the cyclical fluctuations.

Thus, there appears some element of truth in psychological theory in the sense that psychological waves of optimism and pessimism do play an important role in business cycles. However, the existence of business confidence or absence of it is often the result rather than being the cause of business fluctuations. Further, the theory does not satisfactorily explain the start of depression (i.e., recession) or start of prosperity (i.e., recovery), as there exists no tangible basis for change of mood (i.e., optimism or pessimism) of the businessmen.

Over-Savings or Under-Consumption Theory

This is one of the earliest business cycle theories contributed by the economists like John Atkinson Hobson, Cecil North Douglas, Thomas Robert Malthus and Karl Marx. According to these economists, the root cause of business cycle in over-saving or under-consumption, which occurs on account of the existing pattern of distribution of income and wealth amongst the members of the society in the capitalistic economies. There is a lot of concentration of income and wealth in a few hands, while the majority of population remains poor getting meagre income and wealth. Since the marginal propensity to consume is lower amongst rich persons, they devote comparatively smaller part of their income to consumption, while a larger part of their incomes goes to savings. Poor persons, who are in majority in every economy, have lower income and, as a result, have a higher marginal propensity to consume and therefore, they devote larger part of their smaller incomes to consumption and only a smaller part of the their income goes to savings. The overall position in the economy remains that people make substantial savings by under cutting their consumption spending. In fact the savings have double effects, because, on the one hand, it reduces the consumption and, on the other hand, it increases the production through investments from savings. As a result, the market is glutted with unsold goods, which initiates the recession culminating in to depression.

However, this fails to explain the revival and prosperity phases of the business cycles. Moreover, it envisages that savings automatically get invested for production of more goods, though it is not true in real world situations. Entrepreneurs decide upon the investment not as per the availability of savings but as per the prospects of profitability of such investments.

Monetary Theory

This theory has been propounded by Sir Ralph George Hawtrey, who has given purely monetary explanation of business cycles. According to this theory non-monetary factors, like wars, earthquakes, strikes, crop failures, etc. may cause a partial and temporary depression in certain sectors of the economy. On the other hand, changes in the flow of money are exclusive and sufficient cause of the changes in economic activities, of the alternative phrases of prosperity and depression and of good and bad trade. He opines that the basic cause of business cycles is the expansion and contraction of money in the country, which is decided as per the volume of money in circulation and its velocity.

The changes in the volume of money are brought about by the changes in the rate of interest. In case, the banks reduce the rate of interest due to reduction in Repo (Bank) Rate by the Central Bank of the country, the producers and traders will be induced to borrow more from the banks at a lower rate of interest, so as to expand their production and trade, which will lead to larger employment, increase in income and rise in prices of goods and services leading to expansion in business activities. In case the banks raise their interest rates on lending on account of increase in Repo (Bank) Rate, the business, enterprises will reduce their borrowings from banks as that will be available at a higher interest and this will reduce volume of money in circulation reducing the demand for goods and services, which, in turn, will lead to the curtailed business activities.

Thus, depressions is directly induced by a decline in volume of money in circulation and its velocity causing a fall in consumption spending, while propensity is characterised by an increase in the volume of money in circulation and its velocity, resulting in an increase in consumers' spending. It is, thus, obvious that the business cycles are nothing but a small scale replica of outright money inflation and deflation.

However, expansion and contraction of bank credit is the result of prosperity or depression phases of the business cycles, rather than being their causes. Business enterprises plan their investments not merely on the basis of the availability of bank credit, but, in reality, on the basis of prospects of demand for their products in the market. In modern times business units generally rely on ploughed back profits for investments, instead of relying solely on the bank credit. Thus, the bank credit, at the best can accentuate a boom or a depression rather than originating it and as such the expansion or contraction of bank credit can be a supplementary cause and not the main cause of the business cycles.

Over-Investment Theory

This theory has been propounded by Anglo Austrian Economist Friedrick August van Hayek. It states that business cycles are due to monetary over-investment and consequent over-production. Hayek opines that there are two types of rate of interest: (i) natural or equilibrium rate of interest, where the demand for funds in equal to the supply of funds from savings; (ii) market rate of interest decided as per the demand for and the supply of loanable funds in the market. As long as the market rate of interest is the same as the natural or equilibrium rate of interest, there will be stability in business activities and any disparity between the two will lead to cyclical fluctuations.

In case, there is a fall in market rate of interest below the natural or equilibrium rate of interest, it will lead to more investment resulting in an upward swing in the business activities. On the other hand, a rise in the market rate of interest over the natural or equilibrium rate of interest will lead to a fall in investment, resulting into a downward swing in the business activities. It is based on certain assumptions as follows:

(i) Utilisation of investments in capital goods industries would encroach upon the resources used in production of consumption goods, as the resources are being fully employed.

(ii) Investments normally have a tendency to be equal to the savings (i.e., I = S) but this equation is generally upset by the banking policies.

(iii) It is not possible to transfer resources from consumption goods industries to the capital goods industries and vice-versa.

(iv) Increase in demand for products causes shortening of the production process and vice-versa.

As per this theory the alternating phases of prosperity and depression are due to lengthening and shortening the processes of production, which is the same as increase and decrease in demand for the products. This is brought about by changes in money supply, which causes a change in the market rate of interest away from the natural or equilibrium rate of interest. The lengthening of the process of production (i.e., using round about methods of production) in brought about by increase in money supply, which is the result of market rate falling below the natural or equilibrium rate of interest. Shortening of the process of production is brought about by a decline in money supply, which is the result of an increase in the market rate of interest beyond the natural or equilibrium rate of interest. Thus it is the level of money supply that causes the cyclical fluctuations in economic activities. In other words, a low market rate of interest and a large bank lending to business enterprises bring about expansion of investment and production and high rate of interest puts a stop to this expansion and starts recession leading to depression.

However, the theory places too much emphasis on the rate of interest neglecting the real factors, such as technological changes and innovations influencing the volume of investment. As per this theory, a lower market rate of interest induces entrepreneurs to adopt more capital-intensive methods of production, but it does not mention as to how investment is related to consumers' demand.

Moreover, it has been observed by the economists (particularly J.M. Keynes) later on that neither savings nor investment are affected by the rate of interest prevailing in the economy. Besides, the remedy suggested by him for containing the business cycles through controlling the money supply by banks seems to be based on the old quantity theory of money, which could not command general acceptance.

Keynesian Theory

From Keynes' General Theory of Income and Employment this theory on business cycles has been deduced. As per British Economist John Maynard Keynes the level of income and employment in a capitalist economy depends on the effective demand comprising total consumption expenditure and investment expenditure. Thus, changes in total expenditure are responsible for fluctuations in business activities. Since, normally the consumption expenditure is relatively stable, it is the fluctuations in investment expenditures that are responsible for changes in the levels of employment, output and income. The investment in the economy depends on (a) the marginal efficiency of capital and (b) the rate of interest. The marginal efficiency of capital (MEC) also represents the profitability of capital and the rate of interest represents the cost of borrowing capital from banks.

The rate of interest, as per J.M. Keynes, depends upon the liquidity preference of the people for transaction, precautionary and speculative motives (purposes) and the volume of money available, which is constant in short run and therefore, the rate of interest being stable will not result in any cyclical fluctuations in the business activities. Thus, the fluctuations in business activities are accentuated by variations in the marginal efficiency of capital (MEC).

The marginal efficiency of capital (MEC) is the real strategic variable determining the investment function in the economy, which, in turn, determines the level of employment and thus, playing a significant role in the business cycles. The MEC depends on (a) prospective yield and (b) supply price of capital assets or rate of interest. The latter remains constant in short run and, therefore, it is the variation in the prospective yield that ultimately determines the new investment, employment and income. This reveals that the business cycles are the results of variations in prospective yield or expectations.

The expansion phase of the business cycle is occasioned by the high value of the marginal efficiency of capital relative to the rate of interest. Thus, if the marginal efficiency of capital is more than the rate of interest (i.e., MEC > RI), there will be more investment in the economy resulting in higher level of employment, production and income to bring the prosperity phase in the economy. In case there is a decline in the marginal efficiency of capital due to more investment in capital goods and high supply price of capital assets, the prospective yields decline to a lower level below the rate of interest (i.e., MEC < RI). This will result is decline in investment resulting into a decline in employment, production and income leading to the depression phase of the business cycle in the economy.

Keynesian analysis of the business cycles has been regarded as quite convincing in its explanation of the cumulative processes both in the upswing as well as in the downswing and its advocacy for fiscal policy to bring about stability has been widely used. The real contribution of Keynesian theory lies with the explanation of turning points of the business cycles. This, he has done by introducing the concept of consumption function, which states that the marginal propensity to consume is normally less than one (i.e., MPC < 1). This indicates that consumption spending do not increase in proportion to increase in income. This automatically sets a limit to expansion of output, which may lead to over production during the prosperity or boom. The fact may react upon the marginal efficiency of capital, which may tend to decline. In the same way the contraction or depression also cannot be prolonged for indefinite period for the simple reason that a given reduction in income is associated with a relatively smaller reduction in demand for consumption goods.

However, the Keynesian theory is a general theory, which lacks factual proof about the operations of the business cycles. Keynes has relied much on the marginal efficiency of capital, which is very vague and ambiguous concept. As per Keynes' own standards, the business cycle theory should be capable of revealing the periodicity of such cycles, but he himself has failed in this respect. As per Keynesian theory the rate of interest plays a minor role in deciding the level of investment in the economy. This rate of interest is decided as per the liquidity preference and the supply of money in the economy. However, the concept does not tally with actual market conditions, as despite high liquidity preferences during depression period, the rate of interest in the market is low and despite low liquidity preference during boom period the rate of interest remains high.

Innovations Theory

This theory has been propounded by Austrian Economist Joseph Aloi Schumpeter. It states that innovations are the originating cause for business cycles. Innovation refers to commercially applied inventions, like new techniques of production, new methods of organisation of factors of production, searching out of new markets for the product or new source of raw materials or change in the business organisation. These innovations may change the supply and/or demand conditions for the firm or the industry. The changes may render the cost of production to change rapidly and continuously and may shift the demand curve continuously in such a way that the final position of the change becomes indeterminate.

Cyclical upswing starts, when the entrepreneurs start investing in commercial applications of such new ideas. This will develop a chain of investments assisted by the banking system's readiness to provide credit facilities. This will raise investments in the economy, which, in turn, will raise the employment, output and income leading to the prosperity phase of the business cycle. Thus, when a new product introduced in the market becomes commercially successful, bringing sufficient profit for promoters, similar products and imitations are introduced by competito₹ This may set in motion the expansion of many other related industries, resulting into a period of cumulative prosperity.

In case the novelty of innovation is lost with the production of many competing varieties of the products, the abnormal profits vanish for the firms. Some firms may incur losses and get out of business laying off workers and employees, and others facto₹ This will reduce the demand and firms will have lesser liquidity leading to recession and further to depression.

The innovation theory is based on two assumptions: (i) full employment of the resources in the economy; (ii) financing of the innovation by means of bank loans. However, these assumptions do not hold good in a real world situation. In case the economy functions below full employment level, there will not be any diversion of the factors from the older industries. Besides innovations are normally financed by promoters from their own resources and not by bank loans. Moreover, innovation is just one and not the only cause for the operation of business cycles.

Multiplier-Accelerator Interaction Theory

This theory has been developed by Sir John Richard Hicks to which Paul Anthony Samuelson, Sir Henry Roy Forbes Harrod and Lars Peter Hansen have also contributed. It is based on the analysis of combined leverage effects of the multiplier and the accelerator on the national income propagation.

According to Hicks 'the theory of multiplier and the theory of accelerator are the two sides of the theory of fluctuations, just as the theory of demand and the theory of supply are the two sides of the theory of value'. There are three important concepts which play their roles in this theory. These are: (i) Warranted Rate of Growth; (ii) Induced and Autonomous Investment; and (iii) Multiplier and Accelerator.

The warranted rate of growth is the rate, which is capable of sustaining itself. It is the rate of growth consistent with the equilibrium of saving and investment. The multiplier and accelerator are expected to weave their path of economic fluctuation around the warranted rate of growth.

This theory considers two types of investment - autonomous and induced, where the former is not the function of the level of the national income, while the latter has a tendency to increase with increase in the level of the national income.

The multiplier mechanism shapes the movement of consumption in view of the variations in income, while the accelerator shapes the movement of investments in view of the variations in consumption spendings. Both these concepts are supposed be applicable with a time lag. Thus, the consumption spending in period 't' is regarded as the function of income of the previous period (i.e., $t - 1$) and not the income of the current period (t). Thus, consumption of current period (c_t) is function of the income of the previous period (y_{t-1}) or $ct = f(y_{t-1})$. Accelerator is also used with a time lag. Thus, the induced investment in the current period also responds to changes in the consumption of the previous period (i.e., $\Delta 1 = f(c_{t-1})$ There is a fixed ratio between the changes in output and the changes in the induced investment as well as in the changes between income and consumption.

This theory is based on certain assumptions as follows:

(i) There are fixed values of multiplier and accelerator throughout all phases of the business cycles.

(ii) There is a direct restraint on the upward expansion of the economy on the basis of full employment ceiling. However there is no such limit on the contraction of the economy.

(iii) Consumption and investment coefficients are moderate, that is, neither too high nor too low.

(iv) The economy is a progressive one in which the autonomous investment increases at a regular rate.

Assuming the marginal propensity to consume to be equal to .5 (i.e., MPC = $\Delta C/\Delta Y = .5$) and the accelerator to be equal to 2 (i.e., $\Delta I/\Delta C = 2$), the variations in the national income is exhibited as follows:

TABLE 31.1 Variations in National Income as per Multiplier and Accelerator Interactions

Multiplier Period	*Investment Outlay*	*Induced Consumption (MPC = .5)*	*Induced Investment (a = 2)*	*Increase in National Income*
0	10	0	0	10
1	10	5	10	25
2	10	12.5	15	37.5
3	10	18.75	12.5	41.25
4	10	20.62	3.74	34.36
5	10	17.18	– 6.88	20.30
6	10	10.15	– 14.06	6.09
7	10	3.04	– 14.22	– 1.18
8	10	–0.59	– 7.26	2.15
9	10	1.08	3.34	14.42
10	10	7.21	12.26	29.47

Note: MPC = Marginal Propensity to Consume and *a* = Accelerator

Initial outlay in ₹ 10 crore, which also represents the increase in national income, as there is no increase in consumption as well as induced investment in this period, because both these increase with a time lag in the next period. The induced consumption in the first period is ₹ 5 crore (as MPC = .5), which lead to an increase in induced investment (as *a* = 2) to ₹ 10 crore. This increases the national income by ₹ 25 crore. In this way, if the calculations are done for increase in consumption due to increase in income as per MPC and increase in investment due to increase in consumption as per the accelerator for different time periods, we find that the result in quite a moderate type of recurring cycle, which repeats itself indefinitely. This also shows that the rise in income is progressively slowed down due to the fact that some part of increase in income in each successive period is not spent on consumption.

However this theory of business cycle has also been criticised on several grounds as follows:

(i) It is based on the assumption of a fixed value of the marginal propensity to consume but that may change with variation in the level of income.

(ii) It relies much on crude and misleading acceleration principles.

(iii) It is highly mechanical and the behaviour pattern of the national income in real world may not be exhibited so mechanically.

(iv) Ceiling on expansion of national income as per the full employment level for explaining the business cycles is unnecessary and its existence in real world is also doubtful.

Thus, the basic concept of multiplier-accelerator interaction is, no doubt, very important, yet these are not really expected to explain the observed business cycle by a mechanical application of these concepts.

It is obvious that the opinions of the economists differ widely about the causes responsible for operations of the business cycles. A large number of economists believe in credit expansion or contraction in the economy, as the root cause of cyclical fluctuations. Few economists have also emphasised upon non-monetary factors to be the root cause of business cycles and modern economists decide the business cycles as per the cycle of investments in the economy. However, it is commonly agreed that the expansion and contraction phases of business cycles are cumulative processes that move the economy in the respective directions with cumulative forces, but regarding turning points (i.e., recession and recovery or revival) no satisfactory explanation in available. All these contradictions simply indicate the differences in emphasis among the numerous factors at work to generate the cyclical variations.

MEASURES FOR STABILISING THE BUSINESS CYCLES

Business cycles causing fluctuations in economic activities may have favourable effects on certain sections of the society, but their overall impact on all sections of the society is definitely not favourable. The period of expansion or prosperity is accompanied by large profits to producers but on account of overall rising prices in this period the fixed income group persons suffer a lot. The period of depression witnesses a declining prices but it is also followed by acute unemployment, poverty and miseries to poor as well as distress to business classes due to decline in prices and business failures. Thus, it is always in the interest of all sections of the society to have stabilisation in business activities and therefore it is considered as the main objective of economic policies of the government. The government for elimination of the cyclical fluctuations may adopt measures as per the (1) monetary policies (2) fiscal policies, (3) functional finances, and (4) direct control.

1. **Monetary Policies:** For curtailing or increasing money supply to the economy such policies are followed. These consist of:

   (i) Bank Rate or Repo Rate Policy: As per this during boom periods by increasing the Bank Rate or Repo Rate, the money supply to the economy is reduced through curtailing bank loans, which may result into the deflation, causing a general reduction in the prices of the goods and services. Similarly, by reducing Bank Rate or Repo Rate the money supply to the economy is enhanced during depression periods through expanding bank loans, which may result into the inflation, causing a general increase in the prices of the goods and services.

(ii) **Open market Operations:** The government by selling securities may withdraw money from the economy during boom periods and by repaying or buying back securities, it may pump more money into the economy during depression period.

(iii) **Changes in Reserve Ratio:** The central bank of the country requires the commercial banks to keep certain portion of the deposits accepted by them (as statutory reserve) with the central bank and certain portion in cash (as cash reserve) with them and only thus, remaining portion of deposits may be given by the banks by way of loans. By increasing the reserve requirements, the funds available with banks for lending is reduced during boom periods and by lowering reserve ratios, the funds available with banks for lending will be increased during depression period.

(iv) **Selective Credit Control:** This is adopted for affecting specified type of credit for a particular purpose and usually it is done through margin requirements. Banks usually need some collateral security for granting loans to intending borrowers. By raising the margin requirements for banks loans to the enterprises of a particular sector, the bank loans to enterprises of such sector are reduced and by lowering the margin requirements to the enterprises of specific sectors, the bank loans to such enterprises are increased.

For effective control of business cycles, these measures are to be adopted simultaneously. These measures have been found very effective in controlling the inflation during boom periods but the monetary policy measures have not been found that effective in containing the depression, because of three time lags as follows:

(i) Recognition Time Lag: Sufficient time elapses before recognising the need for action.

(ii) Administration Time Lag: There exists some gap between recognising the need for action and actual action.

(iii) Operational Time Lag: There exists some time lag between the time when action is taken and the time when impact of action is realised.

Thus, for making the monetary policy measures effective, proper attention must be paid to curtail the aforesaid three time lags as much as possible.

2. **Fiscal Policies:** It refers to the government actions affecting its receipts and expenditures through which undesirable variations in private consumptions and investments are offset. It involves management of government expenditures and taxes and handling of public debts in such a way as to accomplish the stabilising of the

business cycles. There may be two constituents of fiscal policies, viz. (i) budgetary policies, and (ii) compensating fiscal policies.

Government may prepare a deficit budget, where the expenditures will be more than the receipts. Such budgets put more money in the economy by the government than the money it withdraws through imposition of the various types of taxes. It helps in ensuring growth in the economy and containing the depression. It may prepare a surplus budget, where the receipts will be more than the expenditures, thereby withdrawing some surplus money from the economy, which will help in containing the boom periods.

The government may also follow a compensating fiscal policy, which refers to manipulations in public expenditures and taxes for compensating the economy against chronic tendencies towards inflation and deflation for containing booms and depressions.

3. **Functional Finance:** Professor A.P. Lerner has suggested six effective instruments to control cyclical fluctuations. These are (i) taxing, (ii) spending, (iii) borrowing, (iv) repaying of public debts, (v) issuing of new money, and (vi) withdrawal of money. For checking inflation (or boom) the government may ensure that tax yields exceed its spendings (i.e., public expenditure) and the surplus, thus derived, to be used for repaying public debts or for accumulating cash. Similarly for controlling deflation (or depression) the government should ensure that the public expenditures exceed the tax yields and the deficit, thus emerged, and could be met by credit creation or public borrowings.
4. **Direct Control:** It aims at proper allocation of scarce resources for the purpose of price stabilisation. Such controls may be implemented in forms of licensing, rationing, price and wage controls, export duties, exchange controls, anti-hoarding controls, monopoly controls, etc. These are effective in removing inflationary pressures from the economy. However, it pre-supposes existence of an efficient and honest administration in the country, otherwise it will lead to black marketing corruption, speculation, etc.

Since all cyclical fluctuations bring miseries to one or other sections of the society, all out efforts are needed for containing such fluctuations. This may effectively contain fluctuations within limits through its monetary policy and fiscal policy measures and also through direct controls as well as through its price support measures and unemployment insurance schemes.

Review Questions

1. Bring-out the different types of fluctuations in economic activities of a country. What for cyclical fluctuations have drawn the major attention?
2. Define business cycles and state the characteristics of business cycles.
3. What are the characteristics of the different phases of a business cycle?
4. Bring out the sunspot or climatic theory and psychological theory of business cycles.
5. Examine the over-saving or under-consumption theory of business cycles.
6. Discuss the monetary theory of business cycles and examine its applicability.
7. 'Over-investment theory of business cycles is caused by divergence of market rate of interest with that of equilibrium or natural rate of interest.' Comment.
8. 'Marginal Efficiency of Capital (MEC) is the real strategic variable causing business cycles'. Examine the statement.
9. 'Innovations are the originating cause for business cycles'. Explain.
10. Critically examine the multiplier-accelerator interaction theory of business cycles.
11. Examine the monetary policy measures for stabilising the business cycles.
12. Bring out the fiscal policy measures and direct controls for containing the cyclical fluctuations.

32

Theories of Employment

Governments in all countries aim at having all persons in the working age group (i.e., from 15 to 60 years of age) to remain gainfully engaged in the productive activities. Since the employment of all other resources is associated with the employment of the labour force, it refers to the employment of labour force only. The goal of public policy has always been the removal of unemployment and the achievement of full employment in the economy. It is imperative to understand the meaning and kinds of unemployment for comprehending the term full employment.

TYPES OF UNEMPLOYMENT

The unemployment refers to 'involuntary idleness of persons, who are otherwise willing to work at the prevailing wage rate, but are unable to get the work. Thus, the voluntarily unemployed persons, who do not want to work for economic gains, like idle rich persons will not be considered as unemployed persons. There are several kinds of unemployment as follows:

1. **Frictional Unemployment:** It exists, when there is lack of adjustment between the demand and supply of labour force. It may be on account of lack of knowledge on the part of the employers about the availability of the desired type of workers. It may also be due to lack of the necessary skills for a particular job, immobility of labour, break-downs of the machinery, non-availability of the raw materials, etc. The period of unemployment between the date of losing one job and the date of finding another is included under frictional unemployment.
2. **Seasonal Unemployment:** It results from seasonal fluctuations in demand for labour. Workers in ice factories or sugar factories get employment in summer or in sugarcane crushing season only and they remain unemployed in off season. Similar is the ease with agricultural labour, who get employment during sowing and harvesting seasons, but remain idle for rest of the year.
3. **Cyclical Unemployment:** It arises due to cyclical fluctuations (i.e., alternating periods of booms and depressions) in the economy.

During the period of downswing of the business cycle, the productive activities are curtailed, leading to decrease in production and income, which, in turn, leads to a widespread unemployment.

4. **Structural Unemployment:** It arises due to structural (i.e., long-term) changes in the economy, which implies massive, extensive, deep-seated changes amounting to transformation of the economic structure of the country. It may be on account of lack of co-operant factors of production.
5. **Technological Unemployment:** Modern production process is essentially dynamic in nature, where innovations lead to adoption of new techniques of production and, thereby, displacing the existing labour force. In case the old technology in replaced by a new one requiring lesser labour force than before, there will be technological unemployment.

MEANING OF THE FULL EMPLOYMENT

As against the aforesaid kinds of unemployment, the full employment implies that every individual in the country, who is fit and willing to work is employed productively on every day of his working age. Such a full employment may go side by side with the aforesaid certain kinds of unemployment.

According to classical economists, full employment refers to the absence of involuntary unemployment as voluntary unemployment may remain in existence even when there is full employment in the economy. These economists believed that the economic system automatically provides full employment for the labour force and unemployment, if any, was due to rigidity of the wage structure, as the trade union activities or minimum wage laws interfere in the working of the free market system.

According to Arthur Cecil (A.C.) Pigou 'with perfectly free competition, there will always be at work a strong tendency for wage rates to be so related to demand for labour that everybody remains employed.' The full employment of this type is quite consistent with some amount of frictional, voluntary, seasonal or structural unemployment.

According to John Maynard (J.M.) Keynes 'with a given organisation, equipment and technique of production, the real wages and the volume of output are uniquely correlated, so that, in general, an increase in employment can only occur to the accompaniment of a decline in the rate of wages.' Thus, full employment is a situation in which everybody, who wants to work, gets the work and is quite consistent with the frictional and the voluntary unemployment. He has opined that deficiency in effective demand results into underemployment of labour in the sense that there are men unemployed, who are otherwise willing to work at less than existing real wages. The test of the full employment suggests that when any further increase in effective demand is not accompanied by any increase in output, there is full employment in the economy. Since the output is at its maximum at full employment level, any increase in effective demand further will lead only to inflation in the economy.

According to Lord William Henry (L.W.H.) Beveridge 'full employment is a situation, where there are more vacant jobs than unemployed men, so that normal (time) lag between losing one job and finding another will be very short. Thus, he rules out the possibility of frictional unemployment to stay for a long period.

According to American Economic Association 'full employment means that the qualified persons, who seek jobs at the prevailing rates can find them in productive activities without considerable delay.' Thus, people may remain unemployed for some time before getting a suitable job as per their qualifications.

According to U.N. Report on National and International Measures for Full Employment 'the full employment may be considered as a situation in which the employment cannot be increased by an increase in effective demand and the unemployment does not exceed the minimum allowances that must be made for the effects of frictional and seasonal factors. This suggests that along with full employment, there may remain some frictional and seasonal unemployment, but that must not exceed the reasonable limit. Thus, all these definitions suggest that full employment exists, when all capable and willing persons of the working age remain engaged in some productive activities in the country.

THEORIES FOR ATTAINING FULL EMPLOYMENT

Economists have tried to propound certain theories for attaining the full employment level of which the Classical Theory and the Keynerian Theory are being considered here.

CLASSICAL THEORY OF EMPLOYMENT

This theory considers long-run equilibrium in a laissez faire (i.e., free) capitalist economy at full employment as normal and any deviation from it, as abnormal. In case, there is less than full employment at any time, it tends towards full employment through variations in wage rates. In fact, there is no specific classical theory of employment, as it has been analysed as per A.C. Pigou's demand and supply of labour, J.B. Say's Law of Markets, Marshall, Fisher, Taussig and other's theory of interest and Copernicus and Miltan Friedman's Quantity Theory of Money.

This theory is based on certain assumptions as follows:

(i) There exists the closed economy, where there is neither export nor import of goods.
(ii) There exists the free economy, where there is no interference from the side of the government.

(iii) Labour and capital are mobile freely without any restriction.
(iv) There exists perfect competition, where all features of perfect competition are present.
(v) Savings are available from individuals and not from firms or companies.
(vi) Absence of monetary illusion, which means that people are affected not by money value of goods and services but by their real values.
(vii) Interest rates, wage rates and prices all are variable.

As per these assumptions the classical economists like A.C. Pigou, J.B. Say and others stated that there would never be unemployment in the economy, as the forces will set in the economy to lead it to always remain in equilibrium at the full employment level. A.C. Pigou has applied the demand and supply of labour for the determination of the equilibrium of wages and employment in the economy. The demand for labour is negative function of the wage rates, while the supply of labour is a positive function of the wage rates. The demand and supply cross determines the equilibrium level of wage and employment in the economy. This rules out the possibility of involuntary unemployment in the economy.

Pigou has opined that unemployment is caused by high wage rate at which supply of labour will be in excess of demand for labour and this situation can be removed only through lowering of the wage rates. Similarly, at a lower wage rate, the demand for labour will be higher than the supply of labour, which depends on the number of persons available for work and the number of hours they are ready to work. This will result into scarcity of labour, which can be removed only through an increase in the wage rate.

A.C. Pigou has suggested the Pigovian Equation for deciding the level of employment as per which N = aY/W. Here, N is the number of labour force in employment, a is the portion of Y (National Income) going to labour force, Y is the national income and W is the wage rate. In case the labour force is given a lower wages, on account of the given portion of national income going to labour force it will result into a larger employment and vice-versa.

According to Pigou a lower wage rate would mean a lower price of the product produced with the help of that labour force. This is likely to result in larger sales of the product, which will induce for a larger scale of production resulting into a larger demand for the labour force. Pigou's demand and supply cross for deciding the wage rate and the level of employment of labour force is shown in Figure 32.1(i) as follows:

The supply of labour is equal to the number workers willing to work multiplied by the number of hours they are ready to work. It is normally represented by a backward sloping supply curve (SL) for the labour force. The demand curve (DL) for labour force slopes negatively showing a smaller demand for labour, when the wage rate is higher and a larger demand for it, when the wage rate is lower. As per Figure 32.1(i), the employment and

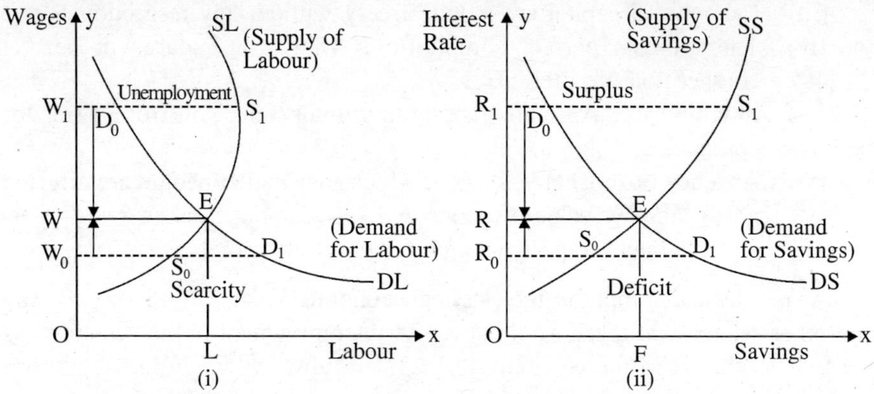

FIGURE 32.1 Determination to Wage Rate and Interest Rate.

wage rate equilibrium is at E, where the demand for labour (DL) is equal to the supply of labour (SL). In case the wage rate is high, say OW_1 the supply of labour (W_1S_1) is more than demand for labour (W_1D_0) resulting into unemployment of labour force, which may be corrected only through the wage reduction up to OW level. In case the wage rate is low, say OW_0, the demand for labour (W_0D_1) is more than the supply of labour (W_0S_0) resulting into scarcity of labour, as people do not show any willingness to work on such a low wage rate. This can be corrected only through an increase in the wage rate to OW.

Thus, through a variation in the wage rate only, there can be equilibrium level of employment for ensuring all persons willing to work to remain engaged in productive activities. This rules out the possibility of involuntary unemployment, though there can still exist some voluntary and frictional unemployment in the economy.

However, even if the economy is in full employment as per the equality of demand and supply of labour, on account of deficiency in aggregate demand due to marginal prosperity to consume generally being less than one (i.e., MPC < 1), there exists the possibility of surplus production, which may induce for lowering the production resulting into some involuntary unemployment in the economy.

For such a situation, the economists have resorted to 'Say's Law of Markets' which states that 'supply always creates its own demand.' This law rules out the possibility of surplus production and, therefore, also of general unemployment. It is based on the logic that along with production, the necessary purchasing power is also generated at the same time to absorb the output or supply. In fact the production has been considered as coextensive with consumption, which is the sole cause of demand. It never furnishes the supply without furnishing the demand both at the same time and also to an equal extent. The main source of demand is the flow of factor income generated from the process of production, which has been assumed to be spent on consumption. Even if certain part of the income is not spent on consumption but devoted to savings, it has been assumed that the flexible rate of interest will bring equality between the savings and investment as in Figure 32.1(ii). It suggests that whatever income is obtained that will be spent on consumption and investment and thus, it rules out the diminution in the flow of income into the economy.

Implications of Say's Law of Markets: Jean Baptiste (J.B.) Say has pro pounded the law known as Say's Law of Markets, which considers that all income earned by the owners of the factors of production will be spent on consumption and the savings, if any, will be spent on investment. The implications of the 'Say's Law of Markets' are as follows:

(i) It indicates the automatic adjustment in the demand for funds for consumption (C) and investment (I) and the supply of funds through payments of rewards for factors of production and thus, rules out over-production. It obviates the necessity of the government intervention in business matters, as that will come in conflict with the automatic adjustment mechanism of the markets.

(ii) Since the supply of goods is expected to create its own demand, the over-production is generally ruled out and possibility of reduction in employment resulting in involuntary unemployment is also ruled out.

(iii) As long as there are unemployed resources in the economy, it will always be possible to employ them, as these can pay for their own employment. In other words, when unemployed resources are employed, these lead to more production, so as to cover their own costs.

(iv) It assumes the existence of flexible rate of interest, which is likely to bring equality between savings and investment. Thus, whatever is saved the whole of that is invested and therefore it rules out the possibility of deficiency in aggregate demand.

(v) Pigovian formulation that flexibility of wage rate is enough to bring about full employment in the economy also emerges from this law. It leads to policy implications of non-interference of the government in regulating the wage rates, interest rates and prices.

(vi) Since goods are exchanged for goods, money acts as a veil and has no independent active role to play in it. Money is just a medium of exchange to facilitate the transactions.

Critical Evaluation of the Say's Law of Markets

The classical theory reigned supreme for quite long time before the Great Depression of 1929, which was widespread and persisted for several years without any sign of recovery. It has been realised that classical conclusions that supply creates its own demand failed to conform to real world facts. Say's Law of Markets has been supposed to suffer from the following deficiencies:

(i) It ignored the possibility of deficiency in effective demand, which is based on aggregate demand for consumption as well as investment. Consumption depends on the current income, which may not increase as much as income, because marginal prosperity to consume in less than one (i.e., MPC < 1). Similarly the investment in the economy depends up marginal efficiency of capital and the rate of interest. Both are not so interrelated as to assure the aggregate consumption and investment to be equal to aggregate income, which indicates that total demand would not always be such as to guarantee adequate market for the total output in the economy.

(ii) Prolonged depression starting in 1929 proved that supply alone was incapable of creating its own demand, otherwise there had been no reason for the stocks to pile up in the factories and a general slump for setting in the economy.

(iii) It is based on the assumption of investment in the economy being interest elastic. It has been observed later on that it is the variation in income and not the variation in rate of interest that brings the equality between savings and investment.

(iv) Say's Law of Markets has been formulated on the assumption of perfect competition in the economy. In reality, however, imperfect competition is the rule and perfect competition is only an exception.

(v) Say's Law of Markets is defended in terms of being a long run equilibrium but there has been no mention of length of long run.

Critical Evaluation of the Classical Theory of Employment

John Maynard (J.M.) Keynes, while propounding his theory of employment through his book titled 'General Theory of Employment, Interest and Money' published in 1936 vehemently criticised the classical theory of employment on several grounds as follows:

1. He rejected fundamental classical assumption of full employment equilibrium in the economy. He was of the view that full employment is not warranted by the facts, as there always exists some unemployment in the free economies. Booms and depressions are common in free economies and investments are not only inadequate but also fluctuating. As a result, less than full employment is a rule and full employment in the economies is only an exception.
2. He was of the view that supply creates its own demand is not correct as proved by the advent of the Great Depression in 1929. All incomes received by people is not spent on buying of the products for consumption, as marginal propensity to consume is not equal to one rather it is normally less than one (i.e., MPC < 1). Similarly, savings are also not equal to investments (i.e., $S \neq 1$), as the saving is a function of current income, while investment is a function of

its productivity (or the marginal efficiency). In case saving is more than investment, there will be a deficiency in aggregate demand, which will lead to over-production and, as a result, in general unemployment.

3. Keynes did not agree with 'laissez faire' (free economy) policy of the classical economists advocating for automatic and self-adjusting process for full employment. He advocated for state intervention for adjusting the supply and demand within the economy through fiscal and monetary policy measures.
4. For classical economists the savings was to be equal to investments at full employment level and divergence, if any, to be adjusted through the variations in the rate of interest. However, Keynes has opined that savings depends upon income, while investment depends upon the marginal efficiency of capital. In case savings is more than investment, there will be less demand for the products leading to over production, which will lead to a fall in investment, income, employment and output and this will result in less savings, so as to make it equal to investment. Thus, equality between savings and investment is brought about by variation in income and not by variation in, the rate of interest.
5. Keynes refuted the Pigovian formulation that a cut in wage rate will result into an increase in employment to achieve the full employment level in the economy. The wage cut may increase the employment in one industry but it will reduce the employment in the economy. It is really not a remedy for full employment, as wage cut will reduce the income of the labour force, which will demand a lesser quantity of the products resulting in lesser production and that will ultimately lead to lesser employment.
6. Classical economists have propounded the theory for long run full employment equilibrium through the self-adjusting processes. However, Keynes had no patience to wait for long period, as according to him 'in long run we are all dead." Therefore, his analysis of employment is confined to short run phenomenon only.

KEYNESIAN THEORY OF EMPLOYMENT

Prior to Keynes, economists generally believed in full employment in the economy. Thomas Malthus for the first time pointed out about the deficiency of the aggregate demand resulting into surplus production and general unemployment.

According to John Maynard Keynes, the total employment in any economy depends on the aggregate demand for consumption and investment and the deficiency in the aggregate demand results into unemployment.

The fundamental principle is that as income increases, the consumption also increases but such increase in consumption is always less than increase in the income, as the marginal propensity to consume (MPC) is normally less than one (i.e., MPC < 1) and, therefore, for sustaining employment, the real investment must increase to fill up the gap between the income and consumption demand out of that income. The total demand in equal to the demand for consumption and investment goods, but when it is fully met by forthcoming supply, it is called effective demand. Keynes termed the intended spending on consumption and investment as the aggregate demand (AD) and if it falls below what the businesses expect to receive for supply of goods, there will be cutbacks resulting into unemployment. Similarly, if the aggregate demand (AD) exceeds the aggregate supply (AS), the expectations will increase, which will stimulate the production and employment in the economy.

Thus, AD represents the amount expected to be spent by the people on consumption goods as well as on investment goods. The money to be received by businesses through their supply of consumption goods as well as investment goods is to be paid to the owners of the various factors of production in forms of wages, interests, rents and profits at the various levels of employment, which is also called aggregate supply. It is, thus, obvious that the effective demand represents the national expenditure on consumption and investment goods. It is also equal to the national income, which in turn, is equal to the national output.

Determinants of Effective Demand

There are two determinants of effective demand viz. (i) the aggregate demand function (ADF) and (ii) the aggregate supply function (ASF). These are as follows:

Aggregate Demand Function (ADF)

It represents the expected proceeds from sale of goods produced at the given level of employment, which, in turn, depends upon the expected expenditure of people on consumption goods as well as on investment goods. All producers in a free economy make an estimate of the demands for their products and also estimate the anticipated profit from their sale proceeds. The total sum of payments made for the various factors of production plus entrepreneurs' profits reveal the total income or proceeds resulting at a given level of employment. This aggregate income is also called the 'aggregate demand price' of the output at a given level of employment. The sales proceeds, which they expect to receive is nothing but what they expect people to spend on their products.

A schedule of proceeds expected from the sale of output resulting from the varying level of employment is called aggregate demand schedule or the aggregate demand function. Symbolically,

$$\text{ADF} = f(\text{N})$$

Here D is the aggregate demand function, N is the level of employment and *f* is read as function of which also means depends on. It shows that the aggregate demand price increases as the level of employment increases revealing that D is an increasing function of employment. This relation of expected sales proceeds with employment and with output of the Keynesian theory has been attributed to:

(i) his main involvement with determining the employment rather than output,
(ii) his idea about movement of employment and output in the same direction; and
(iii) total production in the economy being consisting of a large variety of goods and there being no better measurement than the labour employed in production.

The aggregate demand function increases initially very steeply and goes flatter and flatter with increase in the level of employment. This is due to the nature of consumption function, which is high at lower level of income and declines at the level of income rises.

Aggregate Supply Function (ASF)

It refers to the proceeds of output that entrepreneurs think will just make it worthwhile to provide a certain level of employment. Thus, minimum expected proceeds arising from the sale of output resulting from given level of employment are called aggregate supply function of that output. In other words, these are the minimum expected proceeds, which are considered just necessary to induce entrepreneurs to provide a certain level of employment.

It is also an increasing function of the level of employment, that is, the minimum sales proceeds necessary to go on increasing, as the level of employment and output are raised. This happens due to rise in the cost of production with increasing output with the given capital stock, the technique of production and organisation in short run.

The ASF rises slowly initially due to easy availability of unemployed resources, but as the bottlenecks in production are faced, the diminishing returns or increasing costs become more prominent.

Equilibrium of ADF and ASF

Aggregate demand function is the expected sale proceeds, while the aggregate supply function is the minimum sales proceeds necessary at the various levels of employment. As a result, there will be difference between the two, because at certain levels of employment, the producers may expect more sales proceeds than the minimum sales proceeds necessary, while at certain other levels of employment, the sales proceeds expected may be less than the sales proceeds necessary. It is as follows:

In Figure 32.2 the original ADF intersects the ASF at E, which decides the level of effective demand. It indicates that there are innumerable points on

ADF, the effective demand is indicated only at E, where ADF and ASF both are equal. Before E level the ASF lies below ADF and beyond E level the ASF lies above the ADF. The effective demand at E decides the equilibrium level of employment, which is ON. In case the level of employment is below the equilibrium level of employment, the expected sales proceeds ADF is larger than the minimum sales proceeds (ASF) (i.e., NoDo > NoSo). This will induce the producers to increase the employment for producing more goods than before.

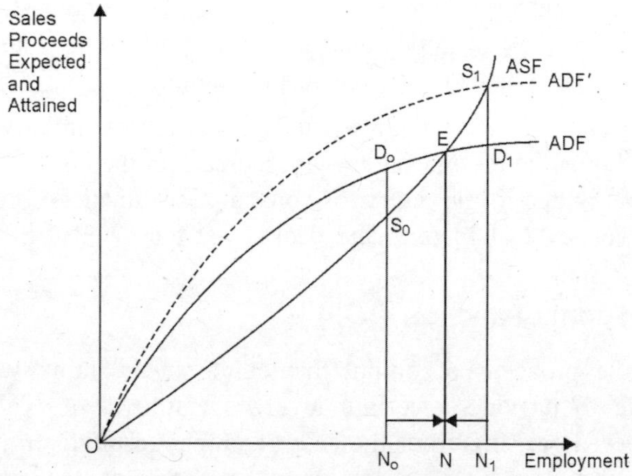

FIGURE 32.2 Determination of Employment Equilibrium at Effective Demand Level.

Similarly, at ON_1 level of employment, the sales proceeds expected (i.e., N_1D_1) are less than the sales proceeds necessary (i.e., N_1S_1). This may discourage the producers, who may reduce the employment to ON level. Thus, ON is the equilibrium level of employment, as deviation from it in any direction will bring back the employment to this ON level again. It is simply because the sales proceeds what entrepreneurs expect to receive is equal to what they must receive, if their cost of production at that level of employment is to be just recovered.

However, this ON level of employment decided as per effective demand may not be the full employment level. In case some portion of labour force remains unemployed involuntarily at the level of effective demand, it is called under-employment equilibrium, which is very common in real world economies. The effective demand (i.e., equality of ADF with ASF) at the full employment level is possible, provided the new investment happens to be equal to the gap between the aggregate supply price corresponding to the full employment level and the amount that consumers and producers choose to spend on consumption and investment out of full employment income. Since the private investment is less likely to be equal to the gap between income and consumption, there exists the possibility that effective demand (i.e., equality of ADF and ASF) at a point below full employment level, which will result into under-employment equilibrium.

This theory has concluded that the effective demand in attained at the level, where Y = C + 1 + G. Here 'Y' is total income, 'C' is the consumption, which depends on the consumption function and the marginal propensity to consume, 'l' is the investment that depends on the marginal efficiency of capital and the rate of interest and increases as per the multiplier effect and G is the government expenditure.. The effective demand is affected by C + l + G, where increase in any or any combination or all will increase the employment. However, Keynes did not consider G (i.e., government expenditure) as it depends on the political decisions, hence economic analysis is not warranted in this regard. As per Keynesian theory, employment in any country is positively related to the effective demand till it attains the full employment level.

Critical Evaluation of the Keynesian Theory

Despite theoretical and practical significance of the Keynesian theory of employment, it suffers from certain failure and weaknesses as follows:

(i) Aggregate demand combines the inactive consumption demand and active investment demand together and ignores the possible effects of relative prices prevailing in different sectors.

(ii) Keynesian treatment of aggregate supply function is inadequate and it is considered to be stable in short run. The intersection of 45° line by C + l curve for determining the national income equilibrium suggests the Keynesian belief that 'demand creates its own supply' which indicates passive role of aggregate supply.

(iii) Effective demand has been criticised for taking aggregate supply to be stable and assuming a direct functional relationship between the effective demand as determined by aggregate demand and the volume of employment.

(iv) In consumption function also, the relationship does not simply run from 'current income to current consumption' but in a real world situation, consumption is also affected by wealth effect (i.e., past income), technological changes, education, expectation, attitude towards assets, etc.

(v) Keynesian theory has related investment with the marginal efficiency of capital and ratc of interest, where the former is mainly based on expectations, which introduces uncertainly in the analysis.

(vi) Rate of interest as per Keynesian theory is based on demand for and supply of money only, ignoring all other factors like hoarding, dishoarding, bank money, etc. for determining the rate of interest.

(vii) The national income equilibrium is attained at the level, where savings and investments are in equality. However, in Keynesian theory greater emphasis has been placed on analysis of investments than on the analysis of savings.

(viii) Keynesian under-employment equilibrium is based on the wage rigidity and has suggested increase in money wages or reduction in real wages to remove unemployment from the economy.

(ix) Keynesian equilibrium is applicable in short run and not in long run.

(x) Keynesian theory of employment is too aggregative, as the consumption demand for durable and non-durable goods and the demand for investment in plants, equipments and stocks have been clubbed together to derive the aggregate demand function, though there exists wide differences in the nature of all such demands.

(xi) It is based on the assumption of a closed economy, which has no interaction with other world economies, but in modern times, there is hardly any economy in the world that can be branded as a closed economy.

(xii) This theory is regarded as a general theory applicable in all situations, but in reality it is not so, as the situations in different countries are different and unique.

POST-KEYNESIAN VIEWS ON EMPLOYMENT

Modern economists have not given any complete theory of employment after the Keynesian theory of employment. Modern developments in the theories of employment are generally in form of some improvements in the Keynesian, theory of employment. These are as follows:

(i) **Pigou's Effect:** This has been suggested by Arther Cecil Pigou through an article published in 1943. As per this, in case due to decrease in money wages, the price level declines, which, in turn, increases the real value of the money balances and assets and also increases the purchasing power of persons having such balances and assets. This is likely to increase consumption which, in turn, may increase employment.

(ii) **Reid's Indebtedness Effect:** According to Michael Reid on account of decrease in price level, the real value of loans of borrowers increases, which, in turn, increases their real liabilities. In case the marginal propensity to consume of the lender is more than that of the borrower, repayments of loans will increase the propensity to consume. This may increase consumption, which will, in turn, increase the employment.

(iii) **Income Re-distribution Effect:** According to American Economist Gary Sheldon Fields, the decrease in price level will benefit the fixed income group persons but harm the interests of the variable income group persons. In case the marginal propensity to consume of the fixed income group persons is more than that of variable income group persons, the total consumption in the economy is likely to increase, which will ultimately increase the employment for increasing production to cope up with the increased consumption.

(iv) **Haavelmo's Effect:** It is generally considered that the government expenditure through taxation will not affect the employment. However, according to Trygve Magnus Haavelmo the government expenditure even though derived through taxation will increase income, consumption, production and employment.

(v) **Hicks-Hansen Coordination:** It is also known as 'General Equilibrium Analysis' in which the interdependence of the rate of interest, investment, income, consumption, savings, demand for money, etc. are considered simultaneously. This interdependence is as follows:

(a) Wage reduction may result into interest reduction, which may, in turn, increase the investment and employment.

(b) Wage reduction affects business expectations adversely, but it depends upon the elasticity of demand for the product, whose production is likely to be increased through increased investment and employment.

(c) Wage reduction may cause substitution of other inputs by labour, which may increase the employment.

(d) Wage reduction may cause reduction in price level, which may increase the real burden of loans. As a result, it may affect the investment and employment adversely.

(e) Wage reduction may cause reduction in price level, which may increase the consumption resulting into an increase in employment.

MEASURES FOR FULL EMPLOYMENT

Full employment in the economy is an ideal situation and for its attainment (1) monetary policy measures, (2) fiscal policy measures and (3) certain other measures have been suggested by the economists.

Monetary Policy Measures

It refers to the central bank's policy measures with regard to regulating the currency and credit flows in the economy. It concerns with lowering the rate of interest for increasing the investment and consumption expenditures and for strengthening the cash positions of banks and offsetting the decline in velocity of money in circulation. For this the measures may include:

(i) **Lowering the Re-Discount Rate or Bank Rate or Repo Rate:** A decline in it is followed by decline in interest rates on loans by banks leading to increased borrowings for consumption and investments. Member banks may discount their commercial papers for increasing their liquid resources, which may be utilised for lending purposes.

(ii) **Purchase of Securities:** The government or the central bank of the country may buy the securities of the banks and other institutions to increase the volume of liquid funds with banks and other institutions for being utilised for lending for consumptions and investments.

(iii) **Lowering of Reserve Requirement:** Banks are required to keep certain percentage of deposits as statutory reserves with the central bank of the country. A lower reserve requirement would increase the liquid resources with the banks, which may be given as loans for promoting consumption and private investments.

All the aforesaid measures will make easy and cheap credit available to the businessmen or entrepreneurs, who may resort to new investment and thereby increase the employment. However, monetary policy measures may not prove very effective, if the depression is very intense and prolonged, when the marginal efficiency of capital is very low because of wide spread pessimism. It should therefore, be followed by fiscal and other measures simultaneously.

Fiscal Policy Measures

These are implemented through the various ingredients of the public finance, like taxation, public expenditure and public borrowings. The fiscal policy measures may aim at increasing both consumption and investment expenditures, so as to stepping up the effective demand, which may, in turn, step up income and employment. These measures are as follows:

(a) **Budgetary Policy Measures:** The government may adopt a deficit budgeting in which more money is pumped in the economy through public expenditures in comparison to the revenue raised from public through imposition of the various types of taxes. This increased public expenditure along with expenditure on consumption (C) and investments (I) will raise the national income and output and will result into an increase in employment.

(b) **Public Expenditures:** It may take the form of–

   (i) *Pump Priming*: This refers to the volume of initial public expenditure, which helps to initiate and revive economic activities in the economy.

   (ii) *Compensatory Spending*: It refers to the expenditures on public works like, roads, buildings, parks, schools, canals, hospitals, sports complexes, etc.

   (iii) Social security spendings, like that on pensions, unemployment benefits, etc.

   (iv) Repayments of public debts, which may raise the volume of money in circulation in the economy. Such repayments may be managed-through public revenues or public debts.

Other Measures

In order to ensure a rise in employment, government may adopt certain other measures as follows:

(a) *Wage Reduction Policy Measures*: Under this minimum money wages may be cut down to provide incentives to the businessmen to expand employment.
(b) *Price Support Policy Measures*: Under this the government makes bulk purchases of commodities (e.g., agricultural goods) and store them with a view to arresting a further fall in their prices. This may restore the producer's confidence with regards to their investment in production of goods.
(c) *Removal of Labour Market Imperfections*: Imperfections in labour market may exist on account of workers' ignorance of the job opportunities. Such labour market imperfections may be removed through establishment of employment exchanges. In case unemployment is due to lack of skill or training, it may be removed through launching the training and skill development programmes.
(d) *International Cooperation*: Under this for increasing employment international monetary, commercial and political cooperations of the developed countries may also be sought.

Review Questions

1. Why is the employment of labour only considered under employment? What are the various forms of unemployment of the labour force?
2. Define full employment that may be attained in the economy.
3. State the various assumptions of the classical theory of employment.
4. How are the variations in wages and interest rates are expected to bring about full employment as per classical economists?
5. Discuss the implications of the Say's Law of Markets for ensuring full employment in the economy.
6. Bring out the various deficiencies in the classical theory of employment and also the deficiencies observed by John Maynard Keynes.
7. Examine the determinants of effective demand as per Keynesian theory of employment.
8. Bring out the critical evaluation of the Keynesian theory of employment.
9. Elucidate the post-Keynesian development in theories of employment.
10. Discuss the measures suggested for attaining full employment in the economy.

Index